FIFTH EDITION

INFORMATION SYSTEMS

Theory and Practice

Wiley Series in Computing and Information Processing

Hugh J. Watson, University of Georgia-Athens, Series Editor

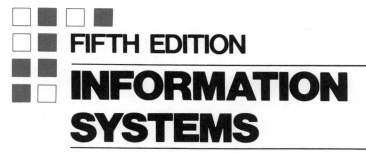

FIFTH EDITION

INFORMATION SYSTEMS

Theory and Practice

John Burch
University of Nevada at Reno

Gary Grudnitski
San Diego State University

WILEY

JOHN WILEY & SONS
New York   Chichester
Brisbane   Toronto   Singapore

Cover illustration: Roy Wieman
Cover and interior design: Dawn L. Stanley
Production supervisor: Suzanne Hendrickson
Production manager: Martin Bentz
Copy editor: Gilda Stahl
Managing editor: Joseph Dougherty

Library of Congress Cataloging in Publication Data:

Burch, John G.
  Information systems : theory and practice / John Burch, Gary
  Grudnitski.

      p.   cm.
  Includes bibliographies and index.
  ISBN 0-471-61293-6
  1. Management Information systems.   I. Grudnitski, Gary.
  II. Title.

  T58.6.B87   1989
  658.4′038--dc19

Printed in Singapore

10 9 8 7 6 5 4 3 2

88-31935
CIP

To our wives Glenda and Mary

PREFACE

The fifth edition of *Information Systems: Theory and Practice* represents a major revision of the book as well as its related teaching aids. The book is designed for both accounting and information systems majors and those who need to understand how information systems are built.

When students complete a course using this book, they will know how to build information systems for any kind of organization. Specifically, they will be able to:

- Discuss information systems as strategic resources.
- Describe the trend toward information systems integration.
- Demonstrate how building blocks and design forces combine to form viable, user-oriented information systems.
- Apply the strategic planning process and systems development methodology to analyze, design, and implement information systems that are congruent with companies' business goals.

ORGANIZATION OF THIS BOOK

This book is organized into four parts. Parts 1 and 2 build a conceptual foundation. Part 3 provides a detailed treatment of input, models, output, technology, data base, and controls—the six information systems building blocks. Part 4 demonstrates how information systems are planned, built, and managed.

TEACHING METHODS

Each part opener of the text contains a window that provides a broad visualization of that part's contents. A brief narrative gives an additional description of each part.

Each chapter includes an introduction and chapter objectives. In addition to the text material, all chapters contain multiple vignettes, examples, figures, key terms, and summaries that offer further explanation and insights.

Plentiful review questions, questions for discussion, and exercises and problems are presented at the end of each chapter. The review questions focus on major concepts and definitions. Questions for discussion provoke broader perspectives and thought. Exercises and problems require additional analysis and, on occasion, a dose of creativity. An instructor's manual available from the publisher contains our answers and solutions to the exercises and problems.

A comprehensive case, the NSU Tigers Event Center, evolves from strategic information systems planning, to systems analysis, to general systems design, to systems evaluation, to detailed systems design, and finally, to systems implementation. The case serves two main purposes. First, it reinforces, in everyday terms, chapter content. Second, the case provides a model for building information systems, which we believe serves as an ideal vehicle to guide students in a project-based course.

SUPPLEMENTS

Several useful supplements are available from the publisher:

An *Instructor's Manual* containing detailed solutions to end of chapter problems and exercises in the text as well as an invaluable set of objective test questions.

A complete set of *transparency masters* from the text. These figures have been specially drawn to assure the highest projection quality.

The test questions are also available on *Microtest* in both PC-DOS and Macintosh formats. This tool allows you to generate exams or quizzes for your students from the printed bank of questions. The program allows a wealth of features like random question generation, multiple versions of the same test, and customization abilities that enable you to integrate your own questions or modify existing files.

Last, we would like to especially thank our wives, Glenda Burch and Mary Pilney, for their tireless and unswerving commitment to this project. Without their devotion, tolerance, and hard work, this edition would not be a reality.

JOHN BURCH
Reno, Nevada
GARY GRUDNITSKI
San Diego, California

ACKNOWLEDGMENTS

We wish to acknowledge the substantial assistance of several individuals in preparing this edition of *Information Systems: Theory and Practice*. First, we want to thank the following individuals who reviewed this edition for their valuable suggestions: Professor Gary Baram, Temple University, Professor Ahmed Zaki, College of William and Mary, Professor Larry Cornwell, Bradley University, Professor Karen Forcht, James Madison University, Professor Alan Chmura, Portland State University, and Professor Robert T. Kein, Arizona State University.

Next, we would like to extend our thanks to key individuals at John Wiley. Joe Dougherty, our editor, contributed significantly to this book by being able to take our ideas and translate them into the contents of the printed page. Suzanne Hendrickson, our production supervisor, did a superb job of guiding the book (and us) through the long and sometimes stressful production process. Dawn Stanley, our designer, whose efforts added materially to the attractiveness of the book, and finally, to Gilda Stahl, our copy editing supervisor, who smoothly coordinated the editing and crucial design phases.

We also wish to thank Martin Kyte and Ellen Jacobson for their work on the NSU Tigers Event Center Case, Dana Edberg for her work on the data base chapters, Jeanette Livingston-Divine, Theresa Gartner, and Pat Doty for their word processing skills, and Shannon Easton for her CAD/CAM expertise.

CONTENTS

8
OUTPUT 260

9
TECHNOLOGY: THE COMPUTER AND AUXILIARY STORAGE 301

10
TECHNOLOGY: TELECOMMUNICATIONS AND NETWORKING 326

11
TECHNOLOGY: SOFTWARE APPLICATION AND DEVELOPMENT 367

12
DATA BASE: DATA MANAGEMENT AND ORGANIZATION CONCEPTS 396

FIFTH EDITION

INFORMATION SYSTEMS

Theory and Practice

PART 1

DESIGN FORCES

SYSTEMS DEVELOPMENT

ORGANIZATION

SYSTEMS DEVELOPMENT

STAKEHOLDERS

SYSTEMS DEVELOPMENT

INPUT   OUTPUT

MODELS

DATA BASE

TECHNOLOGY   CONTROLS

SYSTEMS DEVELOPMENT

INNOVATION

INFORMATION SYSTEMS

FUNDAMENTALS

In a world that focuses on achievement and advantage, information can be the critical factor that enables managers and organizations to gain a competitive edge. In this part of the text an overview is given of the ingredients and the thinking that must go into the construction of systems to produce and maintain information that will be used in this new way.

In Chapter 1 the changing role of information in organizations is explained. The accompanying window shows the forces described in Chapter 2 that shape the face and orient the focus of this vital resource whose output will create information that fits this role. Several specific ways to build and components to include in constructing innovative information systems are given in the last chapter of Part 1.

1
THE INFORMATION RESOURCE

1.1 INTRODUCTION

Information is a critical resource of organizations, as fundamental as energy or machines. It is the indispensable link that ties all an organization's components together for better operation and coordination and for survival in an unfriendly competitive environment. Indeed, today's companies run on information.

The objectives of this chapter are:

1. To provide an overview and analyze information.
2. To explain the role of information in organizations.
3. To demonstrate how information is used as a competitive weapon.

1.2 OVERVIEW OF INFORMATION

What is *quality* information and how do you produce it? What kind of information are we concerned about in this text? This chapter will help you answer these questions.

Information Defined

Information is data that have been put into a meaningful and useful context and communicated to a recipient who uses it to make decisions. Information involves the communication and reception of intelligence or knowledge. It apprises and notifies, surprises and stimulates, reduces uncertainty, reveals additional alternatives or helps eliminate irrelevant or poor ones, and influences individuals and stimulates them to action. Especially in businesses, information should give early warning signals and portend the future. The manager who looks only at historical reports is like Marshall McLuhan's man trying to look forward through a rearview mirror.

Information consists of data, images, text, documents, and voice, often inextricably intertwined, but always organized in a meaningful context. The term *data* will be used throughout the text to encompass all the components of information, but it is important to remember that information is more than mere numbers. A simple schematic that represents how we will think of information is shown in Figure 1.1. Notice that data to be processed can be input, stored, or both. Another point to remember is the cycle of information. Data are processed through models to create information; the recipient receives the information and then makes a decision and takes action; this creates other actions or events, which in turn create a number of scattered data that are captured and serve as input; and the cycle starts all over again.

History of the Need for Information

The present is often much more meaningful when we have a better understanding of the past. Indeed, many historians feel that one of the main characteristics of progressive civilizations is their ability to produce and use information effectively. For example, in the Mesopotamian Valley, civilizations flourished as far back as 4500 B.C. An interesting point is that these civilizations kept fairly sophisticated records on clay tablets of various shapes and sizes. These storage devices provided a great deal of information about receipts, disbursements, inventories, loans, purchases, sales, leases, partnership formation and dissolutions, and contracts.

More than 500 years ago, the Inca Indians of South America developed fairly comprehensive information systems with data bases and processing models composed of thousands of knotted strings called *quipus*. The knots on hanging strings, for example, represented the number of people in a village, their duties, the amount of grain in a storehouse, business transactions, poetry, records of battles, and other historical events. An array of knots and different colors con-

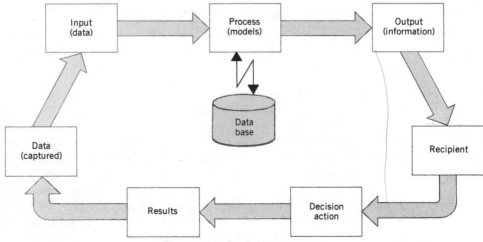

Figure 1.1 The information cycle.

veyed a combination of mnemonics, digits, and narrative information. The people who built these systems were called *quipuamayus*, early forerunners of today's systems analysts. They studied for four years in a "Teaching House," as you may be doing before entering the profession.[1]

In the mid-eighteenth century, pressures to process data increased. The Industrial Revolution removed the basic means of production from the home and small shop and put them in the factory. The development of large manufacturers led to the development of service industries for the marketing and transportation of the manufacturers' output. The increased size and complexity of these organizations made it impossible for any one person to obtain enough information to manage them effectively without enlisting the aid of data processing. Furthermore, with the advent of large factory systems and mass production techniques, the need for more sophisticated capital goods necessitated large investments, and these large capital needs forced the separation of investor (owner) from management (manager). On one hand, management needed more information for internal decisions whereas investors, on the other hand, needed information about the organization and about management's performance.

The Need for Information Today

In the twentieth century, the need to produce more information, available to a wider array of users, is increasing even further. Investors in a business need information about its financial status and its future prospects. Bankers and vendors need information to appraise the performance and financial soundness of a business before making loans or granting credit. Government agencies need a number of reports that disclose financial and operating activities for purposes of taxation and regulation. Unions are interested in the profitability of the organizations in which their members work. The individuals, however, most involved with and dependent on information are those charged with the responsibility of managing and operating organizations, that is, management and employees; their needs range from maintenance of accounts receivable to strategic information for corporate takeover. As a top manager at Sears said, "When you try to keep track of as many things as we do, timely and accurate information is the essential resource to maintain operations and be competitive."

Information Attributes

Many people still tend to equate information with computer printouts. Others state that users are suffering from information overload. Although we may indeed be swamped by printout pollution, memo mania, and misinformation, many users still lack quality information. As depicted in Figure 1.2, the quality of information rests solidly on three pillars—accuracy, timeliness, and relevancy. These are the key attributes of information.

---

[1]For a comprehensive treatment of the history of record keeping, see S. Paul Garner and Marilynn Hughes, eds., *Readings on Accounting Development* (New York: Arno Press, 1978).

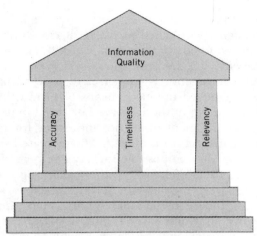

Figure 1.2 Attributes of information quality.

Accuracy means more than one plus one equals two. It means that information is free from mistakes and errors. It means that information is clear and accurately reflects the meaning of the data on which it is based. It conveys an accurate picture to the recipient, which may require a presentation in graphical rather than tabular form.

Accuracy means that the information is free from bias. In some organizations, for example, we discover that middle managers wield great influence over the decisions of top management because middle managers act as "gatekeepers" in passing information between middle (lower?) and top managers. This power over information allows middle managers to manipulate or distort information to ensure that the decisions made reflect their best interests. To reduce the gatekeeping tendency and thereby eliminate bias, we find that organizations employ an independent source to produce and disseminate information directly to each level of management.

Getting information to recipients within the needed time frame is another key attribute of information quality. Clearly, yesterday's newspaper today, variances from standard reported after any corrective action can be taken, or stock quotes a day or two after the fact are normally of little value. Timeliness simply means that recipients can get information when they need it.

Relevancy is the final key attribute of information quality. Very simply, does the information answer specifically for the recipient what, why, where, when, who, and how? For example, the location of a ship may be given as "On her way to Gibraltor." This information may be accurate and timely, but it may also be irrelevant if the recipient wants to know whether or not a ship is passing an intermediate port-of-call. A more appropriate response for this particular recipient may be "At 14:00 hours on December 17, 19X9, she was located at latitude 38 degrees N, longitude 51 degrees W."

Furthermore, what is relevant information for one recipient is not necessarily relevant for another. The relevancy of information from a specific cus-

PUTTING THE SQUEEZE ON DATA GATEKEEPERS

Ron Stafford, IS director at a large insurance company, says, "Top management can assimilate more information from more subordinates with our implementation of a three-tier system that features decision support and executive information systems. The span of control for each management level has increased significantly. We have, therefore, been able to eliminate two layers of middle managers whose only functions were to answer questions about budgets and premiums. This gatekeeping function acted as an unnecessary filter and caused delays.

"Our decision support systems (DSS) and executive information systems (EIS), supported by DBMS, SQL, and 4GLs, permit executives to work directly with professionals and analysts without all the useless gatekeeping.

"Before," Stafford adds, "executives spent hours each week in meetings receiving information from staffers. Now, they get better information from the system without the need for staffers and meetings. They get 'what was, what is, what could be'."

An executive user commented, "I access the data base to monitor the status of re-insurance and subrogation performance. The major value from doing this is that the departments know I do it. If the people below know you are taking an interest, it affects their attitude."

tomer order, for example, will vary among the employees of the company. Those individuals most directly responsible for processing customer orders (e.g., credit clerks, inventory pickers, packagers, shipping clerks) will regard the detail contents of a specific order as necessary information to perform their respective jobs. Individual salespersons will likely be interested in only those orders pertaining to their customers and, perhaps, only the aggregate of all the orders received in a given commission period. The sales manager may be interested in all customer orders but finds these data relevant only when they are reported or presented in reference to quotas, forecasts, or budgets. Accountants view customer orders as data until such time as they represent or are processed into billable shipments, accounts receivables, monthly revenues, and so forth. Personnel in employee relations, research, and engineering routinely do not regard customer orders as relevant to performing their jobs.

1.3 INFORMATION AND THE ORGANIZATION

The essential components of an organization can be thought of in terms of the workplace, the culture, the asset base, and the stakeholders. For an organization to operate smoothly, these components must be oriented toward the same goals and synchronized with one another. Information is the key ingredient that enables an organization to achieve and to maintain a state of unity and harmony. What follows is an explanation of the details of each component depicted in Figure 1.3.

Figure 1.3 The major components of an organization.

The Workplace

The organization is made up of people who are united for a common objective—to create and offer a product or service. For example, a manufacturer converts raw materials to a finished product, a bank provides financial services, and a hospital supplies medical services. The work to achieve organizational objectives is divided among people in accordance with their skills and job goals and then linked together for overall coordination. Work includes physical and mental activities, and in some cases a meshing of both. We, however, discuss the workplace from the viewpoint of operations workers who have a physical orientation and information workers who have a mental orientation.

Operations Workers

These workers are *directly* involved with the manufacture and distribution of products or the rendering of a service. In a manufacturing organization, for example, operations workers are involved in converting raw materials into finished products. Their work can be specifically traced to or identified with the product. They assemble parts into a finished product, operate machines to produce a good, or use tools to work on a product. These are the people who get their hands dirty. Others who do not work directly on a product but are still considered operations workers are forklift operators, toolroom personnel, inspectors, truck drivers, and so on. As the degree of automation in the operations workplace increases, the need for information by this area will grow.

Information Workers

The majority of the labor force in this country works with information. Some estimates indicate that more than half of the work force is involved with information and information processing over 90 percent of the time. Even workers who are directly employed in operations such as operating lathes, running drill presses, driving trucks, or farming are involved in information functions and require information aids.

Accountants, clerks, engineers, lawyers, computer programmers, systems analysts, managers, physicians, librarians, and auditors are all information workers. Information is clearly the major ingredient of their work. The creation, processing, distribution, interpretation, and analysis of information *is* their job. They deal with all kinds of messages, telephone calls, and memos. They study reports, prepare reports, make decisions, act because decisions have been made, conduct or attend meetings, and initiate and follow up activities.

Generally, information workers can be divided into three broad categories: (1) primary users of information, such as managers who use information for controlling, planning, and decision making; (2) both users and providers of information, such as accountants; and (3) information support personnel, such as secretaries, programmers, computer operators, information technology specialists, data base administrators, and systems analysts.

In addition to information workers in the organization, a number of people (some estimate 15 million by the end of this century) work in their homes either as independent contractors (e.g., consultants, accountants) or as employees of an organization. By plugging into the communications network, they are not limited by physical location and, in many instances, can do their work just as well at home as in the traditional office. Their aim, of course, is to gain an idyllic life-style, the best of both the working world and home life. The goal of the organization is to cut costs and increase productivity.

Today, the most labor-intensive part of most organizations is in the area of information workers. Capital equipment to back up operations workers, however, far exceeds support equipment for information workers, despite the proliferation of paperwork and the need for information. Information systems that can eliminate paper bottlenecks and give quick access to information for a variety of users are essential. No doubt expenditures for information technology for information workers will increase significantly in the future.

The Culture

A succinct but revealing definition of organization or corporate culture is that "it is the way we do things around here." For better or worse, it is the social glue that holds the organization together or, in some instances, tears it apart. It is the day-to-day environment as observed and felt by those who work in it. It is the organization's cumulative learning as reflected in promotions, rewards, punishments, and decisions. It is how people have learned to behave in a particular organization. Corporate culture is not written down anywhere; it is not necessarily part of job descriptions; it is not in the procedures manual; it is actually how people really behave and what really goes on in the organization. Corporate culture gives each organization its personality, uniqueness, and meaning. Its power is awesome and often absolute. Without its support, most endeavors are doomed from the start.

Some cultures accept change and encourage innovation and risk taking. Other cultures abhor change and uncertainty and do not want anyone to rock the boat, try untested ideas, or do something different. A really unhealthy culture is one in which the organization is in trouble and the culture does not allow the organization to get help or be helped. Such organizations are, indeed, sick and dying.

What, then, does the organizational culture have to do with information systems? Many organizational cultures have a fortress mentality because of paranoia or because of well-founded fears about information systems. As a result of these anxieties and fears, the culture feels a need to protect itself. In the past, people may have been hurt by trying to cooperate or do something positive. Things blew up in their faces and they are understandably gun-shy. Many of their great expectations turned sour. These people started to reinforce each other about the negative things that have happened, or might happen. No one wants the negativism, yet they do it to one another anyway. To be sure, many fears in the culture come from computers, information technology, and proposed changes in the information system.

Any change in the information system is going to force people to behave differently, to behave in a way that clearly violates cultural norms. No matter what earnest claims systems people or top management (both groups are part of the culture) make about how everyone is going to benefit from a new information system, the system will not be accepted automatically. Indeed, trying to implement such systems changes will generally create tremendous resistance. The culture may be saying that we are used to producing information this way and we do not want any changes or new information technology. Furthermore, a new information system may require the sharing of information between groups, and quite possibly these groups do not trust each other and, therefore, refuse to share information. Some may even feel that the information will be used against them. Moreover, some managers may not want their excuse for poor decisions taken away. The new information system will disarm them of the crutch of saying, "Well, I didn't have the information so how am I supposed to make the right decision?" They do not want a system that holds them accountable![2]

Information system designers cannot significantly alter the cultural norms in an organization, but they can do some things that will make the information system more palatable to the culture and thus get the culture on their side. The best advice for accomplishing this is to get the system's users involved in its development and thereby develop systems that perform as people want rather than people performing as the system wants.

People should not be forced to become computer-literate; computers should become people-literate. The so-called user-friendly systems should be easy to use, nonthreatening, and a true partner in work and problem solving. By the same token, people should not be fooled into believing that working with

[2]Ralph H. Kilmann, "Impact of Organizational Culture on the Implementation of Computer and Information Technology," *Computer and Information Technology Symposium* (Texarkana: East Texas State University, June 23, 1983).

the system is going to be "a piece of cake." They should be aware of the learning curve that they will encounter. The use of homey little names like Apple, Lisa, Peanut, Lotus, and so forth is to some degree misleading (better than calling them Brutus, however). What starts out with friendly name calling, clever and warm "handshaking," can end up in clenched fists and expletives-deleted name calling. If people become involved in systems development and know what to expect, then "technological shocks" should not occur.

To be sure, technology has always set in motion great changes within human societies, from the spear to star wars, from hieroglyphics to holographs, and from human couriers to satellites. So, too, will the implementation of information technology in the culture of organizations.

Many people have fundamental gripes and fears about the new "silicon gods." Developers of information systems will have to be the ones to allay these fears if these systems are to be successful. Information technology, information

---

INFORMATION AND THE CORPORATE CULTURE

As new computer communications tools find their way into organizations, they change not only work flow patterns, but also basic structures and attitudes. Micro-to-mainframe connections have decentralized the control of information power and, as a result, have transformed the way managers and workers think about their roles. From top to bottom, it is at least theoretically possible for everyone to have access to the same information.

The concept of information is also changing. If you only have numbers to work with, you think in those terms. If you spend most of your time communicating, you think in terms of systems that can help you communicate better.

Computer communications are changing how we see knowledge and what we can do with it. Corporate culture is changing as a result of this. Executives can prepare their own briefings without having to wait for someone else to generate reports or cope with another person's interpretation of the facts.

The corporate culture has shifted even more with laptops and remote access to mainframe computers and LANs. The shift is subtle but significant. "Work can be done anywhere," says Peter Dallow, director of administration services for the city of Fort Collins, Colorado.

Dallow says the city's commitment to telecommuting, and connectivity in general, produces better employee attitudes. "People who have access to information through communications technology can see more clearly—and for themselves—what is happening," he says. "While there is more vertical communication, there is also much more lateral information sharing, and things happen more quickly.

Excerpted from Thomas B. Cross, "The Transformation of the Cultural Connection," *Computerworld*, November 16, 1987, p. S18.

models, and information systems are all rational, systematic, based on sound assumptions about workers' duties and about the decisions people make, what information people want, and how they want it—all quite logical. People, however, are not always rational and logical. Information systems designers must move beyond technology and look at the social, psychological, and anthropolitical aspects of the organization and their relationships to the information system. If the designers do not have the support of the culture and its collective will, they will be up against a stone wall and the most technologically correct information system will fail.

Probably all organizational cultures suffer from varying levels of technology phobia. People may feel that they will be overcontrolled and turned into platoons of zombies. They may feel that they will be stuck in dead-end jobs in mental sweatshops. Indeed, spending hour after hour at a keyboard is boring and energy sapping. Research from the workplace already indicates that order entry clerks and others who use computer terminals most of the day suffer extremely high levels of stress.

Offices of the future appear serene and uncluttered with their sleek workstations. But do people really feel serene and competent in these settings? Possibly it would be appropriate to design some informality into such settings. Moreover, is information technology invading personal turf? People should have some feeling of "ownership" to be able to say that "this is my workspace." A strong and well-defined coupling of tasks with the purpose of the job, the group, and the organization should exist. Dividing and subdividing jobs excessively, which in turn leads to "monkey work," should be avoided. Variety in jobs should be implemented to eliminate repetitiveness. Workers need challenges, focused activities, and formal structures, as well as periodic informality and rest. People become bored, even hostile, if forced to carry out routine, repetitive, and uninteresting tasks day after day. Clearly, this is a lesson that is being learned in the auto industry and must be learned by designers of information systems.

DON'T MOVE TOO FAR FROM THE CROWD

"There is nothing more difficult to carry out, nor more doubtful of success, nor more dangerous to handle, than to initiate a new order of things. For the reformer has enemies in all who profit by the older order, and only luke-warm defenders in all those who would profit by the new order. This luke-warmness arises partly from fear of their adversaries, who have the law in their favor; and partly from the incredulity of mankind, who do not truly believe in anything new until they have had actual experience of it.

Machiavelli, *The Prince,* 1513.

"If people don't like an interactive system, it will fail. They'll complain about it, avoid using it, and sabotage it until the beast finally dies.

Author unknown.

The Asset Base

The asset base can be defined in a variety of ways. For example, one could say that an organization's asset base is made up of people, money, machines, material, and methods. Or one can describe assets as tangible (e.g., plant and equipment) and intangible (e.g., patents, copyrights, and trade secrets). We simply show the assets as *financial* and *operational*. In all cases, however, information is needed to keep track of these assets, show how well they are being employed, or indicate how they could be better employed. Indeed, the effectiveness and efficiency of asset use is a key success factor of any organization.

Financial assets are cash or near cash. These assets provide the investment "energy" of the organization. In nonfinancial companies, such as manufacturers, financial assets support operations and provide the means by which the organization can grow and prosper. The information required entails capital budgets and investment analysis, market share, sales forecasts, and so forth.

In financial institutions, such as insurance companies and banks, the primary asset *is* money. For example, an insurance company collects premiums, invests this money, and subsequently pays out money in the forms of claims, death benefits, or annuities. Measurements of how well this money is being used and the profitability of each type of insurance policy are imperative to the success of an insurance company.

Operational assets are all the tangible and intangible assets required to produce and distribute a product or service. In a manufacturing or construction company, these assets include all the inventory; property, plant, and equipment; patents; and so forth. In both profit and not-for-profit service organizations, such as hotels, restaurants, banks, hospitals, governmental agencies, and educational institutions, the asset base has relatively little inventory. Some professional organizations, such as accounting, engineering, and law firms, have small, simplistic asset bases. Their main asset is their professional staff (any organization, however, could say its main asset is its people). But as with all organizations, human assets do not appear on the balance sheet. The flow of information about "assets" in a professional organization, however, is just as important as in other organizations, especially information that deals with time management and scheduling, correspondence, document indexing, minutes of meetings, various reports and contracts, billings, and staff performance appraisal.

Different organizations have different needs for certain kinds of information, but regardless of their type or nature, all organizations need fairly universal information concerning their assets. For example, all need basic accounting information, which includes invoices, cost accounting, payroll, accounts receivable, accounts payable, and various financial and audit reports. All need marketing information, which includes product or service sales analysis, market research, sales forecasts, competitive profiles, and correspondence. Whether one includes workers in the asset base or not, personnel information is clearly needed; this includes employee records and benefits, affirmative action reports, skills inventory, job openings, job descriptions, training and policy manuals, and correspondence. The acquisition of assets includes information, such as purchase orders, reorder points, safety stocks, order quantities, specifications, vendor performance, bid requests, and correspondence. All of this information is fairly universal across all organizations and represents the minimum needed for the proper management, control, and use of assets.

The Stakeholders

A continuous interaction takes place between the environment and all organizations, even those that are closely held. A fairly steady stream of information flows from the environment into the organization and from the organization into the environment. This flow of information involves the stakeholders of the organization.

First, information is needed about the impact of the organization on society and the quality of life of that society. Various segments of society become stakeholders and are concerned with the programs undertaken by government and not-for-profit organizations to accomplish specific social objectives. Many members of society are clearly concerned about organizations' performance in the area of water and air pollution, conservation of natural resources, product or service quality and safety, trade barriers, prices, and employment practices.

Many people, such as stockholders and lenders, have bet their hard-earned money on organizations' success. Financial status and prospects for the future of organizations are also of interest to more and more stakeholders, such as financial analysts, tax collectors, employees, and union representatives. Still others, such as regulatory agencies, are interested in specific operations of organizations. Certainly, key stakeholders are customers, who look to organizations for a dependable source of products or services. One can clearly see both the need and the opportunity in designing information systems with tight couplings to organizations' stakeholders.

1.4 KEY ORGANIZATIONAL FACTORS

Organizational factors play a major role in dictating the kind of information that is produced and how it is communicated. These factors are nature, categories, size, structure, and management style.

Nature

The very nature or purpose of an organization is one major factor contributing to the information requirements of the organization. For example, while the content or specific values of information required in a variety of manufacturers will differ, the manufacturing process dictates a commonality of information requirements concerning planning, scheduling, controlling, and decision making. A real estate firm, an insurance company, or a transportation firm, however, is unlikely to be comparable to a manufacturer in terms of many major information requirements. All organizations are somewhat similar in areas such as payroll, accounts receivable, accounts payable, and purchasing; however, even in these areas such characteristics as retail or wholesale orientation, unionized or nonunionized, and service or product orientation make for substantial differences in information requirements.

If the organization is an automobile manufacturer, does it upsize or downsize its automobiles, does it move manufacturing facilities to foreign lands, and does it diversify into nonrelated industries? If it is an oil and gas company, does it build a new pipeline, increase or decrease exploration and drilling, and build a new cogeneration system? Good strategic planning actually determines the future for the organization.

Where does the information to support strategic planning come from? Much of it, as illustrated in Figure 1.6, is similar to military intelligence in the sense that it comes from sources external to the organization. These sources, among many others, are government reports, demographic studies, trade publications, market surveys, research firms, and general media. This information, combined with internal information from forecasts, interaction with others, and examination of different scenarios, leads the strategic planner through a formulation filter to a final plan.

Tactical and technical planning involves the implementation of the strategic plan. These plans set specific standards, budgets, and quotas for the next year. This kind of planning requires a great deal of internal information concerning accounting, sales, inventory, and production. Clearly, the planning function, to one degree or another, is shared by all levels of management on a fairly continuous basis.

Controlling

In all organizations, varying levels of control information is required. For example, the strategic-level managers may find that if they build their plant in South America, nationalization may occur. They, therefore, may change their plans to build at another site. Tactical-level managers are concerned with items such as budget variances. At the technical level, variances from a number of standards must be reported. For example, "we have an average 20-day delivery

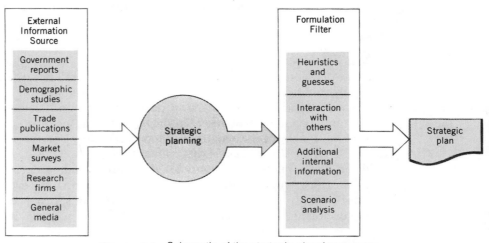

Figure 1.6 Schematic of the strategic planning process.

period, our customer service level in warehouse 1 has dropped to 60 percent, we have an unfavorable material usage variance of $4,000.00, or our average credit collection period has increased to 48 days."

To a great extent, what is actually happening at the tactical and technical levels stems from day-to-day transactions. In fact, the basic raw data necessary to produce control information come from a variety of transactions. Clearly, the actual results of the organization are reflected in these transactions.

The efficient processing of transactions is the key to tactical and technical control. Among other things, the efficient and timely processing of transactions give status information. This information can either represent the status of the transaction itself or reflect the status of the resources affected by the transaction.

Tracking the status of a transaction is a simple control problem that can become complicated in large, complex operating systems. For example, a customer order is received and begins a transactional life that may be measured in minutes, days, weeks, or months. It may involve two or three physical activities, or it may involve several dozen physical activities. Although the total transactions represent the organization's lifeblood, a specific transaction may be considered somewhat insignificant, mundane, and routine. But a query concerning that transaction (e.g., customer order) can result in a significant expenditure of resources to provide an answer. Our concept of how well an organization performs is often based on how well it is able to provide information concerning its transactions. In addition, lost, misplaced, or erroneous transactions can be very expensive to an organization.

The second form of status information is related to the resources that are affected by the processing of transactions. This type of information is similar to traditional inventory or balance sheet information. It satisfies the question, "How much?" Although we commonly think of inventory as being materials, virtually all resources, tangible and intangible, have an inventory status. Thus, appropriate status information reflects machine availability, personnel skills, accounts payable, accounts receivable, customer orders in process, purchase orders in process, budgetary dollars, storage space, and materials.

Decision Making

Some decision problems and conflicts are simple and deterministic and have only minor ramifications. Others are complex and probabilistic and can have a significant impact. Decision making can be routine and well structured, or it can be complex and ill structured. In the broad terms introduced by Herbert Simon, decision making is either programmed or nonprogrammed.[3]

Programmed decision making refers to the process of dealing with well-structured and repetitive decisions. To effect programmed decision making, the decision rules as well as the alternative courses of action pertaining to a decision must be completely defined. In many organizations, programmed decision-making opportunities are defined as standard operating practices, and an algorithm

---

[3]Herbert A. Simon, *The New Science of Management Decision* (New York: Harper & Row, 1960).

is developed to describe how this decision is to be made. The execution of this decision process can be manual or computerized. A great challenge to those designing information systems is to identify programmed decision opportunities and to develop computer programs to execute them.

Routine and repetitive decisions, with the potential for well-defined parameters, lend themselves to the development and implementation of programmed decision making. The payoff of implementing programmed decision making is freeing management for more important tasks.

Nonprogrammed decision making or heuristic decision making, on the other hand, is the process of dealing with ill-defined problems. The problems are usually complex, only a portion of the total set of parameters is known, and many of the known parameters are highly probabilistic. All the talent of a skilled decision maker plus the aid of a well-designed information system are required to make sound nonprogrammed decisions. Expansion of plant facilities, purchase versus lease, and merger transactions, are examples of nonprogrammed decision making. The decision-making process is illustrated in Figure 1.7.

GETTING INFORMATION TO WHERE IT IS NEEDED

"We push the process closer to the decision makers," says Gary Biddle, vice-president of MIS at American Standard. "The real efficiencies come in reaction time and culturally, in the people feeling they're controlling their own destiny—and they are."

Excerpted from Michael Ball, "Distribute or Centralize? Strategies for Support," *Computerworld*, March 21, 1988, pp. 88–91.

Product and Service Differentiation

Product and service differentiation, or the offering of new products or services, includes such things as innovation, access, price, quality, image, benefit, uniqueness, maintenance, warranty, and services. At present, many organizations are being clobbered by better differentiated products or services from foreign competition, especially Japan. Clearly, then, the appropriate strategy for the organization to survive and succeed in a highly competitive world is to increase its productivity and differentiate its products and services. We will discuss productivity in the next section.

In a sophisticated and affluent society with more money to spend, consumer demands shift from more to different. People want style, individuality, and quality. They look for special features, uniqueness in concept, and an attractive design. They want superior performance or service. Copycat products or services are of doubtful competitive merit. Indeed, outdated products and services cannot compete in the marketplace even if they are offered at reduced prices.

In the past, most information systems were designed by persons who lacked a tactical and strategic perspective. Moreover, they viewed the information sys-

ager's video display terminal (VDT). The manager decides in which truck the order will be shipped and enters that number into the computer. The system automatically calculates the size, weight, and shipping charges of the load. Picking and packing labels and documents are then printed, detailing information for that shipment. In some instances, automated order entry and shipping systems like this one have reduced the time it takes customers to get their product from one or two weeks to a day or two.

3. *Airlines.* Airlines must have fairly sophisticated information systems to be competitive today. These systems provide, among many things, faster fare update, international pricing and fare shopping techniques, direct links with hotel and car rental agencies, and banking services. Bonus programs for frequent flyers require computerized data bases. Some of the more progressive airlines have extensions of their information systems embedded in travel agencies. These agencies in turn offer a full range of travel services to customers from seat assignment to hotel reservations. Clearly, the tie-in with travel agencies is intended to increase the airline's revenue.

INFORMATION SYSTEMS HELP AIRLINES PROFITS TAKEOFF

Industry leaders have discovered they can leverage their systems to raise the bottom line in two important ways. They can turn a profit from reselling internally developed software and services, which eventually evens out the cyclical earnings of air transportation. Airlines are counting on their computer systems more than ever to help them stay aloft.

"The purchase of Eastern Airlines and its information services subsidary System One was a crucial part of Frank Lorenzo's strategy for growth and for developing products that differentiate Texas Air from the competitors," says David Hultsman, staff vice-president of technology planning for System One, now Texas Air's information system subsidiary.

Excerpted from Elisabeth Horwitt, "Carrier Land Profits by Empowering DP Units," *Computerworld,* March 7, 1988, pp. 73–80.

---

4. *Hotels.* Some hotels have automated, front-desk systems that offer guests 45-second check-in time. This is an excellent service for bone-weary travelers who dread standing in snail-paced lines, only to find at the other end a desk clerk who is a new employee unfamiliar with check-in procedures. What a hassle! Automated check-in systems process reservations and payments, issue magnetic guest cards, and dispense receipts. They are interconnected to accounting and other hotel operations. To use the system, the guest simply goes to a self-service computer terminal in the lobby. Similar to automatic teller machines (ATM), these terminals are menu-

driven, and they allow the customer to confirm room type, rate, and length of stay. Guests enter their reservation number or personal information if no reservation has been made. After the room is assigned, the guest can board a talking elevator, which announces floors. Furthermore, on the way up to their rooms the guests can check the local weather conditions, current stock prices, and entertainment hot spots on a video display. A magnetic guest card opens the door. In the room, lighting, television controls, air conditioning, and heating are controlled by a console activated by the guest card or by a console panel on the telephone. Moreover, if guests do not want to be disturbed by phone calls, all they have to do is press a do-not-disturb button, and all calls will be recorded for playback later. The do-not-disturb button also displays the same message on the guest's door. In addition, function buttons on the control panel give guests easy access to a variety of hotel services and allow the signaling of emergencies. If the guest chooses, an in-room computer terminal or connection for the guest's personal computer will be provided for link-up with home or office or for stand-alone processing.[7]

5. *Retailers.*   Interactive technology gives retailers unlimited opportunities to provide outstanding customer service. Using "informercials" is a powerful way to present products without time restrictions. The customer can enjoy a leisurely and full explanation of products or services, alternatives, newest features, warranties, and complete demonstrations, in their homes over a television or computer terminal. The customer can use a toll-free number to place a credit card order or use a personal computer connected to the retailer's system. Electronic shopping systems give the retailer an excellent way to market products and differentiate services. Customers are becoming tired of fighting traffic, scouting for parking space, and hassling with rude, uninformed sales clerks. They welcome a "boutique" or "store" in their living room and the ability to order what they want when they want it. Clearly, electronic shopping is a boon to families in which both husband and wife work outside the home and do not have time to shop during the day. Some larger retailers are also extending point-of-sale services into various companies where employees can order from their workplace.

6. *Freight Forwarders.*   A national freight forwarder uses a network of computer terminals as a strategic tool to serve its customers' needs. The company's major clients have terminals in their offices connected over leased lines to the freight inventory system. Clients can reserve space for shipments on planes or ships and can confirm their reservations immediately through the online freight inventory system. The data base enables the company to provide its larger customers with analyses of shipping routes and expense monitoring. The network gives the company an edge over its competitors because of efficiencies and because it can provide customers with status and

---

[7]Also see Susan Blakeney, "Japanese Hotel Boasts 45-Second Automated Check-In." *Computerworld,* October 22, 1984, p. 31.

detailed information. The information system is central to the way in which the company runs its business.[8]

7. *Publishers.* Publishers can now send page proofs to editorial offices in a matter of seconds whether the offices are across the street or across the country. By integrating the functions of computer terminals, which gather data to be typeset, with digital facsimile, high-quality page proofs can be sent quickly anywhere in the country, thereby overcoming significant time delays and logistical problems. Copy can be transmitted day or night to units totally unattended.[9]

8. *Banks.* Early on, many banks realized that information systems were extensions of their services and, therefore, thought of systems in competitive terms. Where once ATMs were few and scattered, today they seem to be almost everywhere. Some banks are going a step farther; they are installing systems that provide online stock and option trading and home banking capabilities through the customers' personal computers. The system permits customers to send orders to the floors of all major stock exchanges and pay for those orders without having to talk to their brokers, or write a check. New ATMs, besides performing all the basic deposit, withdrawal, and account balance inquiry functions, also dispense coins along with currency. These machines cash checks without the need to fill out and put the checks in special envelopes. "For anyone who has ever been stuck in a long line at a bank branch while tellers tried to process the paychecks of employees from a large nearby factory or office complex, the possibility of offloading a good portion of that check cashing activity to an ATM should be very appealing; these in-lobby systems should help banks keep their existing customers and attract new ones."[10] In addition, many banks offer a complete range of data processing and accounting services to their customers.

Productivity

Some organizations, such as fashion designers, gourmet food companies, and health spas, can do much to differentiate their products and services. In fact, such a differentiation is essential to their business. By the same token, these organizations can do little on the productivity dimension. At the other extreme, organizations dealing with general commodities such as agricultural products, crude oil, and metals cannot do much in the area of product or service differentiation, but they can do a great deal to improve productivity. Of the many organizations in the middle are a number such as automobile manufacturers, banks, airlines, insurance companies, and so forth that can do both. Indeed, in these organizations, a thrust in productivity can also augment product and service differentiation.

---

[8]Summarized from "Communications Network Keeps Freight Firm on Track," *Computerworld*, November 26, 1984, p. S/R7.

[9]Summarized from "Solving Logistics at a Page a Minute," *Infosystems*, September 1984, p. 37.

[10]M. William Friis, "Information Systems Changing Banking's Role," *Infosystems*, September 1984, p. 114.

Schlumberger, a premier energy service company, provides a good example of how information technology can be used to increase service and productivity. Schlumberger has developed a family of electrical, acoustical, and nuclear probes that are lowered into wells by a wire cable. Measurements produced by these devices are recorded on long pieces of paper known as well logs and are interpreted by experts skilled at inferring geological information from masses of squiggly lines. Schlumberger's ability to generate new measurements currently exceeds by orders of magnitude the ability of the expert to interpret these measurements adequately. The application of computer expert systems, a subject more fully discussed in a later chapter, now gives Schlumberger's human engineers the interpretive ability they lacked before.

Indeed, the day of the computer-illiterate is almost gone, and as the need for greater productivity increases, information technology will become a natural way for both information and operations workers to enhance and support their performance. The technology will change what is being done as well as how it is being done. It will extend the brainpower of all workers. The quality information produced will tell what is happening in the marketplace, in the office, and on the shop floor—all parts will be tied together. Further, traditional boundaries will be blurred between the factory and the office. Operations workers will become more like information workers, and vice versa. The gap between blue-collar and white-collar workers will dissolve into a powder blue.

Some of the technologies that will be tied together by advanced telecommunications include computers, data bases, automated office systems, computer-aided design and engineering (CAD/CAE), computer-assisted manufacturing (CAM), robots, artificial intelligence and expert systems, computer-based message systems and electronic mail, automated warehousing and inventory control

---

INCREASING LOAN-PROCESSING PRODUCTIVITY

Wells Fargo sought to increase the number of commercial loans that could be processed by lenders in its 23 branch offices, while at the same time increasing the response time to customer-service requests, reducing turnaround time on loan applications, and freeing up more of the loan officer's time for marketing activities.

The bank's systems team developed a local area network (LAN) to support the integrated office support system (IOSS) they designed. Each loan officer has a PC with a variety of applications on the LAN as well as links to mainframe applications.

The IOSS speeds up the process of generating loan documents, reduces response time on customer-services requests, and reduces the number of support staff. The system also provides an additional 10 hours per month of each loan officer's time for marketing activities.

Condensed from "Wells Fargo Backs Office Automation," *PC Week*, July 7, 1987, pp. C/4, C/9.

systems, advanced power equipment, electronic shopping devices, automatic test equipment, security devices, and energy management systems.

Smokestack companies and the so-called Rust Belt are getting new life from the use of robots, automatic test equipment, and CAD/CAE/CAM. Computer-controlled machine tools permit manufacturers to make short-run, semicustom products at costs not much higher than mass-produced products. These companies are also installing automated warehouses and inventory control systems.

Productivity of Operations Workers

Even today, a product is produced for a month or so after management decided to discontinue it; a production facility is held up for weeks because someone forgot to order raw materials; the factory is working on the wrong job, at the wrong time, and producing the wrong amounts; or work load scheduling is unsynchronized. A timely flow of information from the factory to the office and back will help correct these debilitating problems. The shop floor provides work-in-process, cost, inventory usage, and tracking information. The office brings this information together with budgeting, accounting, and marketing information for different levels of management.

The modern factory and operations workspace will be a technology-intensive and an information-intensive environment with a highly skilled work force. The greasy, noisy, dirty, repetitive, and dangerous tasks of the past are on their way to being handled by robots, the steel-collar workers. They will be supervised by a combination of embedded intelligence and human workers who will be housed in glass-enclosed, air-conditioned, soundproof operations workstations. As stated earlier, the operations worker will become more of an information worker and may share office space with engineers, designers, marketing managers, and cost accountants.

A data base will contain data from all parts of the organization. Barriers between departments for data that were regarded as within the domain of only one department will be removed. Design engineers will require word processing features to handle documentation and technical publications. Inventory control and cost accounting will need access to computer-based spreadsheets to determine bill of materials and costs. And so it goes.

Productivity of Information Workers

Meanwhile, back at the office, the profile of information work is eclectic, ad hoc, random, and transaction driven. Probably half of an information worker's time is wasted waiting for something to happen, because of poor scheduling, redundant work, and simple inefficiencies. A clerk may spend a good part of the day looking for a "lost" file. A secretary may manipulate and copy the same thing over and over again to prepare reports. Any change in a report may call for a complete retyping. Salespersons spend 20 to 40 percent of their time selling a prospect or servicing a customer; the rest of their time is spent on paperwork. Executives may spend most of the week traveling to and from a one-day meeting. Most of the people in a bank do nothing but manipulate data. To prepare and distribute a memo by traditional methods costs between $15.00 and $20.00 per memo. Many auditing and accounting tasks could be done more productively by computers.

A relatively small investment in information technology can significantly increase the production of information workers. How should this be done? Put more intelligence and quality information at the fingertips of all levels of management (also professors, physicians, engineers, lawyers, etc.), use teleconferencing where possible, adopt computer-based message systems and electronic mail, provide widely accessible data bases, incorporate both single-use and multiuse personal computers, make liberal use of graphics, apply expert systems and aides-de-camp where feasible, widely embrace word processing facilities, provide time management systems, provide appropriate personnel with paging systems and cellular telephones, make available voice-response systems 24 hours a day, and investigate the feasibility of some employees working at home rather than coming to the office every day.

Clearly, many of the more routine clerical, stenographic, and data processing tasks can be automated to achieve increased productivity and improve the quality of output. To emphasize this point, consider the following example of how a major international bank handles a simple letter of credit request:

> Sorting clerks in the mailroom check the contents of the envelope and send the item on to the bank's letter-of-credit department on the building's 24th floor. Three days later a letter of credit is issued. At least 12 people—a typist, a log-in clerk, a preparer, a signature control clerk, two checkers, the department manager, a central liabilities clerk at the bank's uptown corporate headquarters, a marketing officer who approved the credit, the accounting department, the files unit, and the customer services clerk— have acted on it.
>
> The original source document has been read, reread, checked, and rechecked. It has been crumpled, clipped, stapled, unstapled, rubber-banded in bundles of cards and tickets, stuffed into envelopes, copied, copied from, annotated, and preserved in a cardboard file folder.
>
> The processing of the credit issuance has generated a stack of papers maintained in six files. An offering ticket has gone to central liabilities and to the marketing officer, with a copy for the file; a five-copy fanfold has been typed, split, and its folds dispersed to a variety of destinations; accounting tapes, proof tapes, and other tapes have been punched, rolled, and delivered around the bank; special instructions have been duly noted and recorded in duplicate. A week after the credit is issued, the customer requests that it be amended, starting the process all over again.
>
> Ultimately, this system was put to rest and replaced by a more productive system. A mail robot moves along the aisle, the item is plucked from its slot by an individual sitting in a neat, cockpitlike workstation, where she is typing on a CRT. As she punches the last key, a printer terminal nearby prints out a formal letter of credit. It is mailed that day. She immediately puts the customer's original request and instructions in microfiche and stores it in a small file case on the flat top of her workstation.
>
> Where it once took days, 30-odd separate processing steps, 12 people, and a variety of forms, tickets, and file folders to process a simple letter of

1.17 Explain the impact the U.S. government has had on the data processing requirements of businesses that must file reports to it.

1.18 How have advances in technology changed the nature of work performed by society in general, and how has this trend impacted on the design of information systems?

1.19 Discuss the following comments:

"As far as processing data is concerned, accuracy is a simple matter of getting the math right."

"As long as information is presented in a timely and accurate manner, it will automatically be relevant."

"Ongoing changes in information systems technology will continue to upset established organizational culture."

"Culture? Smulture!" retorted the new supervisor. "We're gonna do things *my* way around here, period!"

"Increasing the quality of information tends to increase the accountability of those decision makers using the information."

"Implementing programmed decision-making models into information systems relieves managers of the responsibility and accountability of the decisions made."

1.20 Analyze the possible implications to the auditor resulting from the compression of information float time and the demands by investors and creditors for more timely financial information.

1.21 Do you agree that accountants will be the most likely candidates to step in and close the information gap? If so, how is the accountant better equipped and positioned than other corporate personnel to meet this objective? If you do not agree, who do you believe could best serve as the chief information officer and why?

1.22 Why is knowledge of the structure and culture of an organization imperative to understanding the information processing function?

1.23 How does more efficient information processing help reduce operating costs?

1.24 From where does an organization derive its culture?

1.25 Why are information needs of top strategic managers not being met as readily as those of technical managers? Because of the lack of sufficient information, strategic managers must often resort to informal methods of information such as intuition and the industrial "grapevine." The ability to do this successfully, perhaps more than any other single skill, separates the proficient executive from the "figurehead" manager. Comment on this.

EXERCISES AND PROBLEMS

1.26 Select an organization, and, using personal knowledge and library research, prepare a brief report specifically describing how that organization is using its information system to achieve a competitive edge over its competitors.

1.27 Determine which of the following business situations can be considered a significant opportunity for programmed decision making. Explain your choice for accepting or rejecting each situation.

1. Strategic corporate planning.
2. Shipping merchandise to customers.
3. Advertising.
4. Hiring a vice-president.

5. Processing payroll.

6. Inventory control.

7. Research and development of new product.

8. Reporting variances between actual and expected values.

1.28 Based on library research and knowledge gained in other courses, prepare a brief report, outlining the statutory requirements of the Foreign Corrupt Practices Act of 1977 as they relate to the preparation of accounting and other financial data. Specifically, how does this law influence the design of the subject entity's information system?

1.29 Businesses, like people, are unique entities. What makes them unique is the organizational culture that develops within each entity. In an attempt to identify some of the characteristics peculiar to an organization, answer the following questions about a firm with which you have had experience.

1. a. Identify the person with whom others consulted about important situations.

   b. If you wanted to make sure a bit of information would be circulated throughout most of the organization, whom would you tell first?

   c. Was there a particular style of dress and grooming, that is, conservative, high fashion, relaxed?

   d. Can you trace any of the grapevines within the organization?

   e. Identify a clique in the firm. What common interest held this clique together?

   f. Describe the working conditions. Was the atmosphere rigid and strict, or flexible and easygoing?

   g. Did top management practice social responsibility in their decision making?

   h. Was there an "informant" in the group?

   i. Did supervisors practice an open-door policy?

   j. What was the general attitude toward customers? Competitors?

   k. Were there any identifiable "taboos?"

   l. Was the management resistant to change, not willing to take risks, and maintaining the status quo, or just the opposite?

   m. List any other unique characteristics of the organization you selected.

2. How did this culture influence the design and operation of the information system?

3. What steps can be taken to change undesirable aspects of an organization's culture, specifically the reluctance to accept a new information system?

1.30 Pablo is one sale short of winning a trip to the Virgin Islands in a contest that ends this evening. He is just about to close a sale for a new copy machine when the prospect asks about a maintenance agreement on the machine. Pablo cheerfully says that as long as his company, Lentex Office Machines, carries that product line, the copy machine will be serviced every six months. He fails to mention Lentex is seriously considering dropping that product in the near future.

Vincent is a regional sales manager for Lentex. In his weekly report to the main office, he shows gross sales figures less selected sales returns and allowances. The balance of the sales returns and allowances are reported to the main office embedded within the Monthly Operational Expenses report.

Since the vice-president of sales, Ms. Martinez, has expressed disgust at the many useless reports she receives, her secretary, June, has been filing away the Monthly Operational Expenses report so as not to bother the vice-president. June also screens all the

VP's calls, and again, not wanting to interrupt her, decides which calls the VP should take immediately and which calls will never get through.

Ms. Martinez is very anxious about the upcoming budget committee meetings in which all the department heads will be required to submit their projections for next year's budget. The latest sales report Ms. Martinez has received from the regional sales managers confirms her fears that sales for the current year will be down 2 percent. When she was hired earlier this year, Ms. Martinez was confident she would be able to increase sales by 3 percent. The president of the firm was counting on Ms. Martinez projecting at least another 5 percent increase for next year. Under a great deal of pressure, Ms. Martinez has decided she will go ahead with a projection of 5 percent increase in sales next year without dwelling on the expected loss in sales percentage this year. She fully expects to work twice as hard next year to make up this year's 2 percent loss and at least half of next year's projected 5 percent.

Required:

a. Define the term gatekeeper. Identify the characters in the above narrative who would fit this profile. Explain the reasoning that supports your selections.
b. Identify other positions in any organization where gatekeepers are prevalent.
c. What procedures could be implemented to eliminate some of the distortion caused by information gatekeepers?

1.31 A state government agency has a contracting department whose job it is to ensure that every contract entered into by that agency and a vendor is in compliance with state purchasing regulations. Ten full-time contracting officers work in the department to process the 7,000 or so contracts issued by the agency each year.

The process of obtaining goods or services begins when a request is received by the department from other "line" departments within the agency. Once a day the supervising contract officer goes through the requisitions received and checks her list of authorized persons in the agency to ensure each requisition is properly authorized. An equal proportion of the properly authorized requisitions received that day are distributed to each contract officer. Sometimes this method of distribution creates delays in the processing of a requisition because the unevenness of the work loads or because an officer might be sick or on vacation.

The state is very concerned that purchases are made only from approved vendors. Each month an updated list of approved vendors and the goods or services they are approved to supply is prepared by the supervising contract officer. The list is then photocopied and distributed to the 10 contracting officers. They, in turn, use this list to request bids from the approved vendors. Often, mismatches between goods and services requested and approved vendors result. This happens because requests for bids are sent to vendors who do not supply the goods or services wanted or because potential approved suppliers of the goods or services do not receive the appropriate request for bids.

At the close date for receipt of written responses to supply specific goods or services, an available contract officer reviews the request for bid, sorts through the bids to weed out those that are not responsive, and usually chooses the least expensive bid. Frequently, contract officers are unfamiliar with the goods or services being requisitioned and have difficulty determining whether the bid is responsive. When this happens, agency departments wind up with unacceptable goods and services.

The last step in the procurement procedure is for the contract officer to prepare a contract for review and signature by the supervising contract officer. Because of the job demands placed on the supervising contract officer, she only has time to perform a perfunctory review of each contract.

Required: Suggest how, with a reliatively small investment in technology, such as a microcomputer for each contract officer, the productivity of these information workers could be significantly increased.

1.32 Pro Products of Cleveland, Ohio, manufactures and wholesales golf bags for men and women. Women's and men's bags differ in the material used in their construction (and therefore the price) and the variety of colors. Basically, women's golf bags are made of a durable, leatherlike material that can be washed to remove stains and retains its color-firm appearance. Men's golf bags, however, are made of leather and hand oiled to preserve their natural color. While the company is constantly seeking ways to make the production process more efficient, the basic style of a Pro Products bag has not changed in the last 10 years. What has changed is the variety of colors offered in response to changes in tastes and to the development of new dyes.

Pro Products also manufactures golf bags for a national chain of sports stores. Bags sold in the sports stores are marketed under the store's private label and do not compete directly with Pro Products own brand because Pro Products brand bags are sold exclusively through pro shops at golf courses.

Required:

   a. Periodically Pro Products must make strategic decisions about new and existing products. List these strategic decisions.
   b. What information does Pro Products need to support its product strategy decisions?
   c. In making tactical planning decisions concerning its sales forecast, what kind of information would be useful to Pro Products?

1.33 Higgins Company, a Dallas-based manufacturer and distributor of a variety of laser printer toner cartridges, views planning and controlling operations as serious activities. In October of each year, the management of Higgins embarks on a month-long series of intensive meetings to prepare their cash flow and income projections for the next fiscal year. Guided by a business plan that spells out the strategies Higgins intends to pursue, and armed with market research data and information on new products and processes development, management begins the planning process by updating the long-range sales forecast and sales plan and, because of the importance of research and development at Higgins, a research and development budget. This forecast and plan drives two other components, the capital budget by project and the one-year sales forecast by product. These planning efforts are completed and distributed by the seventh working day of October.

The next phase of Higgins planning process is to translate the sales forecast into a sales budget. This process takes no more than five working days. From the sales budget a production budget is prepared. The sales and production budgets are then combined to produce the inventory and purchases budget. By the sixteenth day of October, everything is ready for preparation of a projected gross income statement and cash flow projection.

Required: Draw a chart of how these budget components are condensed into summary projections of operating results and cash flows.

BIBLIOGRAPHY

BALL, MICHAEL. "Distribute or Centralize? Strategies for Support." *Computerworld,* March 21, 1988.

BARRETT, STEPHANIE S. "Strategic Alternatives and Interorganizational Systems Implementations: An Overview." *Journal of Management Information Systems,* Winter 1986–1987.

BLAKENEY, SUSAN. "Japanese Hotel Boasts 45-Second Automated Check-In." *Computerworld,* October 22, 1984.

BYLINSKY, GENE. "America's Best-Managed Factories." *Fortune,* May 28, 1984.

"Communications Network Keeps Freight Firm on Track." *Computerworld,* November 26, 1984.

CROSS, THOMAS B. "The Transformation of the Cultural Connection." *Computerworld,* November 16, 1987.

FRIIS, M. WILLIAM. "Information Systems Changing Banking's Role." *Infosystems,* September 1984.

GARNER, S. PAUL, and MARILYNN HUGHES, eds. *Readings on Accounting Development.* New York: Arno Press, 1978.

HORWITT, ELISABETH. "Carrier Land Profits by Empowering DP Units." *Computerworld,* March 7, 1988.

INGLESBY, TOM. "Computing Chrysler's Profitability." *Infosystems,* June 1984.

JARVIS, PAMELA. "Banking's New Glamour Boy—The Chief Information Systems Officer." *Bankers Monthly,* February 1987.

KILMANN, RALPH H. "Impact of Organizational Culture on the Implementation of Computer and Information Technology." *Computer and Information Technology Symposium.* Texarkana: East Texas State University, June 23, 1983.

LAYNE, RICHARD. "Serendipitous Systems." *Across the Board,* April 1987.

MATTHEIS, RICHARD. "The New Back Office Focuses on Customer Service." *Harvard Business Review,* March–April 1979.

PARSON, GREGORY L. "Information Technology: A New Competitive Weapon." *Sloan Management Review,* Fall 1983.

SCHINDLER, PAUL E., JR. "IS Must Change to Survive." *InformationWEEK,* June 1, 1987.

SIMON, HERBERT A. *The New Science of Management Decisions.* New York: Harper & Row, 1960.

"Solving Logistics at a Page a Minute." *Infosystems,* September 1984.

"Wells Fargo Backs Office Automation." *PC Week,* July 7, 1987.

2
THE FUNDAMENTALS OF BUILDING INFORMATION SYSTEMS

2.1 INTRODUCTION

Obviously, the information resource described in the previous chapter requires the building of information systems to produce it. Anything that is built—automobiles, bridges, houses, traffic control systems, or information systems—can be defined in terms of building blocks along with the design forces that affect these building blocks. At a primitive level, six building blocks define the substance of information systems and 10 design forces influence these building blocks' form. The people who design and put together the building blocks in accordance with the design forces are systems analysts. The process that systems analysts follow in doing their work is the systems development methodology (SDM).

Learning these fundamentals sets the stage for you to relate to the other material in this text and to provide you with a springboard to build innovative and sophisticated information systems. The objectives of this chapter are:

1. To describe the building blocks that define any information system, small or large, simple or complex. The use of a building block approach has precedence in other fields, such as architecture, engineering, physics, and genetics. Consequently, that is why we use it in this text as a foundation to the study of information systems.

2. To define the design forces that act on and influence the building blocks. Nothing is ever designed in a vacuum. Systems analysts must, therefore, make sure that what they are designing conforms to external influences—what we refer to in this chapter as design forces.

3. To outline the systems development methodology, a guide and process employed by systems analysts who have the overall responsibility of developing information systems from start to finish.

2.2 INFORMATION SYSTEM BUILDING BLOCKS

No matter what organizations they serve or how they are developed and designed, all information systems are made up of the six building blocks of input, models, output, technology, data base, and controls. As illustrated in Figure 2.1, these building blocks may take on different shapes, values, and content; they may look different and work different; some may support well-designed systems; some may support poorly designed ones; some may be crude; some may be highly sophisticated—no matter. These are the basic building blocks of all information systems. How well they are put together and what kind of information system results is up to the designer—the systems architect. Just like a toy erector set containing a few basic components that, with proper doses of imagination, can be transformed into trucks, airplanes, windmills, ferris wheels, bridges, and even robots and dinosaurs, so too the information system building blocks can be formed into functioning information systems that meet the needs of organizations and their users. Understanding these building blocks, their relationships and couplings, and their logical and physical content, provides the basic knowledge for describing, developing, and designing information systems. At this point, simply for definitional purposes, we will briefly discuss the building blocks. In Part 3, however, a detailed presentation on each building block will be made.

Input Block

Input represents all the data, text, voice, and images entering the information system and the methods and media by which they are captured and entered. Input consists of transactions, requests, queries, instructions, and messages. Generally, inputs follow protocol and format for proper content, identification, authorization, layout, and processing. Entry can be made by means of handwriting, paper forms, recognition of physical characteristics such as hand geometry and fingerprints, keyboards, joy sticks, cats, mice, voice, touch sensors, and optical and magnetic characters and codes.

Today, the most common means of entering transactions and text are bar codes/laser readers and the keyboard, respectively. Often, input efficiencies can be gained by combining input methods. For example, voice input can complement a keyboard to provide commands such as enter, file, or stop, to perform

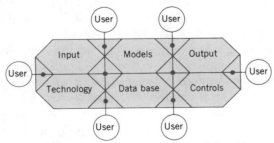

Figure 2.1 The information systems building blocks.

input of numeric codes, or to input messages. An even better way would be to develop voice input systems as a viable alternative to keying. With voice input, the input bottleneck would be substantially reduced. The user probably works better by voice input, because both hands are free for other tasks, and voice input over the phone, for example, is highly efficient because it eliminates the intermediary steps of writing down and rekeying messages. Indeed, one of the major trends in the next decade will be toward voice and handwriting recognition systems, both fixed and portable. Also, a variety of input-efficient devices, such as touch-sensitive screens, respond directly to fingertip pressure. Light-pens, cats, and mice are also available for use with screen displays and graphics.

Models Block

This block consists of logico-mathematical models that manipulate input and stored data, in a variety of ways, to produce the desired results or output. A logico-mathematical model may combine certain data elements to provide an appropriate response to a query, or it may reduce or aggregate volumes of data into a concise report. It may be as simple as

$$Income = Revenue - Expenses$$

The models block also contains a description of some of the more popular modeling techniques used by systems analysts to design and document system specifications. These techniques include decision tables and trees, structured English, data flow diagrams, structured analysis and design technique, traditional flowcharts, Nassi-Shneiderman charts, HIPO, structure charts, Warnier-Orr diagrams, and prototyping.

Output Block

The product of the information system is output—quality information and documents for all levels of management and all users inside and outside the organization. To a large extent, output is the guiding and influencing block of the other blocks. If this block's design does not meet the needs of the user, then the other blocks are of little consequence.

Output is the other end of input and clearly cannot be any better than the input and models used to produce it. Often, input and output are interactive. Input becomes output; output becomes input. A mouthpiece of a telephone is an input device; the earpiece is an output device. A keyboard on a typewriter inputs data; the type font produces output on paper. A user makes a query by means of a visual display unit (VDU) and gets a response; based on that response, another query is made.

Logically, output consists of such things as financial statements, invoices, purchase orders, paychecks, budget reports, answers to queries, messages, commands, results of programmed decision making, scenarios and simulations, and decision rules. The quality of this output is based on its accuracy, timeliness, and relevancy. Moreover, this output must be dealt with in terms of its destination, use, frequency of use, and security.

The preceding discussion is concerned with the *message*. But what about the *medium*? Output can be produced on screens, printers, audio devices, or microfilm. In the past, the main medium of output was stacks of printed reports, called computer printouts. Today, people are choosing other forms of output that are more amenable to their tastes, such as graphics, video, and audio. Because most workers spend 50 to 90 percent of their time dealing with information and communicating, they, indeed, are looking for a wider range of media that comes close to natural human methods of outputting information and communicating with the system and with each other.

The use of large, flat screens for wall displays is becoming popular, especially where graphics and videoconferencing are being used. Also growing in popularity are split screens and other techniques of manipulating and presenting information to make the screen more like a desk and filing cabinets containing many different documents and reports. Other popular output methods include graphic plotters and phototypesetters. Halfway points between paper and screens to present information are microfilm and microfiche. And, of course, voice response and electronic mail systems are ideal ways to output messages; certainly they are outputs that are to the liking of most people because of their attractiveness and convenience.

Technology Block

Technology is the "toolbox" of information systems work. It captures the input, drives the models, stores and accesses data, produces and transmits output, and helps control the total system. It does all the toil and grunt work and binds all the building blocks together. Technology consists of three main components: the computer and auxiliary storage, telecommunications, and software. Telecommunications is the employment of electronic and light-transmitting media to communicate between nodes across distance. Software presents programs that make the computer hardware work and instruct it on how to process the models. Hardware consists of a variety of devices that provide physical support for the building blocks. For example, a terminal serves as an input device for accounting transactions; a central processing unit (CPU) drives the accounting models with appropriate data; printers located at several divisions across the country and linked to the CPU by satellites and earth stations output accounting statements; a magnetic disk in the data base stores accounting master files, journals, and ledgers; and an encryption device helps control the confidentiality of accounting and other sensitive information as it is being transmitted, and also while it is stored in the data base. To be sure, the problem of technological scarcity has been superseded by a problem of choosing the right technology for the job that needs to be done. For today's information system, a wider range of solutions may be applicable rather than only one solution.

At its very core, technology is a substitute for human labor. Of the six building blocks, technology is the most evident. Most information systems today and in the future will be technology based. A common pitfall, however, is an overenchantment with technology while disregarding the information needs of users. Another pitfall is to assume that acquiring and installing a computer and related technology is tantamount to implementing an information system. Nothing could be further from the truth. A computer by itself does not make an information system. Indeed, management has had too many technological boondoggles in which, without forethought or a modicum of systems analysis, they acquired million-dollar computers and then told people in the organization to "use" them. No wonder many computers acquired under such circumstances have been left idle, only to collect dust. Moreover, the systems population has had more than its fair share of technological tinkerers and toy freaks who have little regard for users' needs. On the other side of the coin, however, are a number of information systems concepts that would still be only concepts if not for the advent of technology. Some examples are point-of-sale entry devices and an array of telecommunications equipment, both of which effectively reduce time and space.

Data Base Block

The data base is where all the data necessary to serve the needs of all users are stored. And, again, data may be a combination of voice, images, text, and numbers. The data base is treated from two viewpoints, physical and logical. The physical data base is made up of storage media, such as tape, disk, diskettes, cassettes, magnetic cards, chips, and microfilm. This is how data are actually stored. But another, probably more important problem is how to search for, associate, and retrieve the data stored to meet specific information needs. This, of course, is the logical side of the data base and, if structured correctly, ensures the timely, relevant, and accurate retrieval of information. It also deals with the software component of the system and includes such logical and data associative techniques as indexes, directories, lists, keys, pointers, networks, trees, and relations.

Controls Block

All information systems are subject to a variety of hazards and threats, such as natural disasters, fire, fraud, systems failure, errors and omissions, eavesdropping, inefficiencies, sabotage, and malicious hackers. In many instances, however, the worst abuses to the system come from inadequate operational procedures, incompetent employees, and poor management. Some of the controls that need to be designed into the system to ensure its protection, integrity, and smooth operation are the installation of a records management system; the implementation of traditional accounting controls; the development of an information systems master plan; the creation of a contingency plan; the implementation of personnel procedures, such as background checks, training, rotating jobs, compulsory vacations, and so forth; the preparation of complete and current documentation; the implementation of hardware and software monitors; the establishment of backup systems and offsite storage; the installation of uninterruptible power systems and fire suppression systems; the use of proper programming procedures and controls; and the implementation of a variety of security procedures, devices, and access controls.

2.3 INFORMATION SYSTEM DESIGN FORCES

Leonardo da Vinci, the great Florentine painter, sculptor, architect, and engineer, had the genius and support to create and design a variety of artifacts without constraint. He did not have to satisfy the marketplace, meet parochial needs of users, or worry about costs and schedules; he had sufficient financial support to follow wherever his creative instincts led him. Many of his creations once considered "useless" are today considered masterpieces.

People who have the responsibility for the development and design of automobiles, bridges, buildings, information systems, and so forth do not have the luxury that da Vinci had to "do their own thing." They are, to a large extent, influenced and constrained by a number of *design forces*. To be successful, designers must determine what the design forces are, how they impact on their design projects, and then abide by them, while still incorporating in their work, creativity and innovation. It is, indeed, a complicated balancing act.

Let us use the design of automobiles as an analogy. All automobiles consist of the same building blocks—a body, an interior, instrumentation, and drive controls; wheels and axles; and a power train made up of a power unit, energy source, transmission, and differential. But because of a number of automobile design forces, the form and substance of these building blocks have changed over time. For example, new safety and pollution controls and fuel-economy requirements forced top-to-bottom redesign of cars. Furthermore, some car manufacturers, a number of years ago, paid little attention to radical shifts in market tastes and designed cars that were unacceptable to a large number of consumers. Only after these manufacturers quit designing cars in isolation and started designing them to conform to the design forces did they get back on track and recapture a large share of the market. Awareness of the design forces and compliance with them, to be sure, returned these manufacturers to profitable operations.

Information systems designers must consider 10 design forces that impact on their work: integration, user/system interface, competitive forces, information quality and usability, systems requirements, data processing requirements, organizational factors, cost-effectiveness requirements, human factors, and feasibility requirements. Designers must, in each situation, define design forces in detail and determine their level of impact and their interaction, and sometimes conflict, with each other. A schematic of the design forces and their impact on information systems building blocks is illustrated in Figure 2.2, followed by a definition and discussion of each one.

Integration

Information systems will have to be designed with tighter couplings between the office and the plant. Indeed, the information system will become just as important on the factory floor as in the office. Moreover, connectivity and communications among and between departments must be better within the office and the factory. Information technology will be embedded in the organization and tied together for full synchronization and coordination of operations. The system will no longer be separated functionally and spatially from the workplace. This design

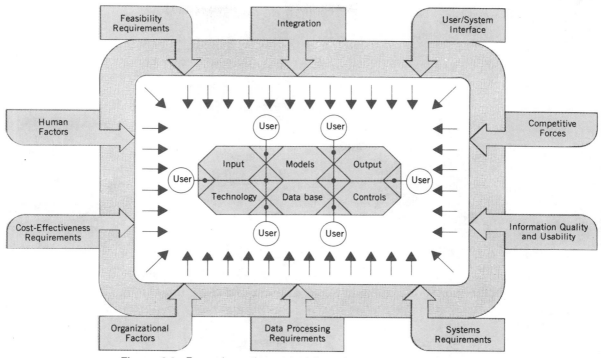

Figure 2.2 Forces impacting on the information systems building blocks.

will result in an information web for the organization. The right hand will know what the left hand is doing, and vice versa. The information web will bring together functions as depicted in Figure 2.3.

The traditional method of designing metal parts, for example, has been to create a series of drawings on paper, develop a prototype, and then make production decisions that led to the manufacture of a specific batch of parts by a platoon of machine tools. In the past, the activities of the designer and those of the production planners and schedulers have been disparate, and the manufacturing sequence was not, therefore, integrated. The developments in computer-integrated manufacturing (CIM) and especially programmable robots, are forcing more integration between designing, planning, scheduling, cost accounting, inventory control, and marketing. With the increase in manufacturing cells, robots, and flexible manufacturing systems, online feedback loops and coordination with all components of the organization are becoming imperative.

Robots will be used more because they (1) increase productivity and the quality of output; (2) eliminate tedious, dangerous, and dirty jobs; (3) have the ability to explore and work in hazardous and hostile environments (e.g., undersea exploration, lunar-based mining and manufacturing, satellite repairs); (4) will benefit from the growing economics of microelectronics; and (5) because of their programmability can be used in a variety of manufacturing processes. Indeed, robots and information systems work well together, and as robots become more

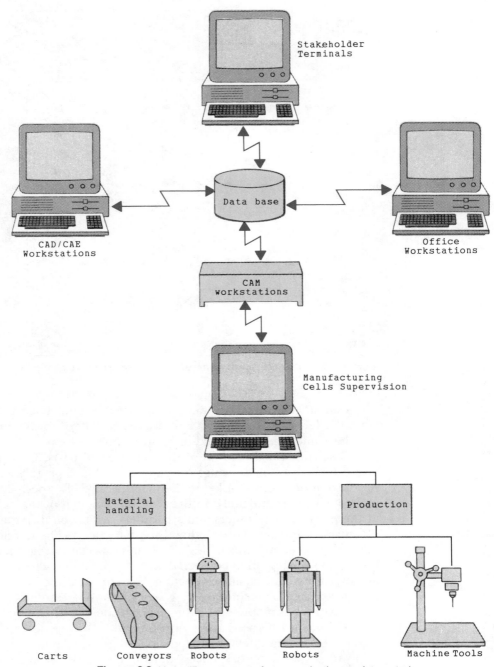

Figure 2.3 How different areas of an organization are integrated.

TECHNO-STRESS   A psychiatrist who specializes in stress-related illnesses in London's financial community says the new deregulated trading environment is particularly difficult to cope with because of the surveillance capability of the new systems. "Dealers are now well aware that their directors, who may be in Switzerland, can tap into their systems and look at how much business they have done." Explains the doctor, who asked not to be named, "This causes stress and paranoia."

According to the psychiatrist, the incidence of stress-related illnesses—which can manifest themselves in many different ways, including loss of appetite for food and sex—has quadrupled since the new systems have been installed.

Condensed from Philip Hunter, "Big Bang a Stress Test," *InformationWEEK*, August 17, 1987, p. 15.

is that of an "office factory" where unskilled workers feed data to the computer and fill in the gaps between automated processes. Work is highly structured and preprogrammed, and piecework rates and machine monitoring are used to control workers.[1] The fear of the sociologist can be overcome because systems that are physically and psychologically comfortable for employees can be designed, if the systems designer effectively deals wtih the human factors.

The human factors area is expansive and sometimes fuzzy, but designers should try to understand and deal with it in order to design systems that work with people, not against them—systems that are easy to use, friendly, and natural. Because the design of the human is fixed, the system's design must be formed to fit it. The aim is to design the system to adapt to the likes, dislikes, habits, skills, and tasks of the user. Systems designed with human factors in mind have a direct, positive, bottom-line impact on productivity. Clearly, as computer and information technology use expands, the need to consider human factors grows.

One key element that should be considered is the ergonomic design of information systems and the physical working environment. A major goal of ergonomics, sometimes referred to as human factors engineering, is to optimize and make compatible the people/system interface, a crucial determinant of the effectiveness of the systems design. Ergonomics brings together the systematic application of techniques from a variety of disciplines, such as physiology, engineering, psychology, and sociology, to enhance the workplace for people. Most of the work of ergonomists in the area of information systems has centered on the person working at a video display terminal (VDT) or a full-blown workstation. To be sure, this is a critical point because as a number of people have said, "Eight hours in front of one of those units will make you goofy."

---

[1]Harry J. Otway and Malcolm Peltu, *New Office Technology* (Norwood, NJ: Ablex Publishing, 1983), p. 120.

Specifically, ergonomists are concerned with acoustics, room climate, lighting that is glare free, decor and wall colors, foot rest, freedom of leg movement, seating height, back support, and safety. Their aim, of course, is to reduce the aches and pains, excessive fatigue, and stress of people working at VDTs.

In addition to the application of ergonomics, the following things can be done to improve both the physical and psychological aspects of systems:

1. *Alternate Areas.* Divide the workplace into two areas: work area and relaxation area. The work area is ergonomically designed so that people can concentrate and get their work done. The relaxation area, however, is a relief or break place designed to bring people together to socialize, unwind, and swap ideas, jokes, and war stories. It accommodates others who want to meditate or simply doodle. Other amenities to humanize the work environment might include physical fitness centers or day care centers. Moreover, systems may be installed to provide employees with electronic shopping and banking conveniences, or anything else that will help reduce the "hassle" factor.

2. *Work Groups.* Those people who work in different departments, such as sales, accounting, personnel, or purchasing, require access to the same basic information (e.g., accounts receivable, accounts payable, price lists, inventory, personnel records). The information system should be designed to bring them together to encourage openness, collaboration, and sharing of work.

3. *User Specification.* Some systems designers, in trying to design a single system to satisfy all potential users, end up creating a system that satisfies no one in particular. Users have different needs; consequently, the system should be designed to fit these needs.

4. *Presentation and Response.* As mentioned several times in this book, people work better with mixed presentations. Therefore, where possible, a combination of forms, text, graphics, video, and sound should be used. To enhance presentation, also use various display and input coding techniques, such as abbreviations (e.g., TX for Texas), colors for different categories of information, icons to indicate categories or locations, and blinking and brightness variation codes to focus attention. In addition, a critical element of performance is the response time. Long delays on tasks that need a quick response can lead to user dissatisfaction and, ultimately, to poor performance. Moreover, the system should be easy to use (e.g., Polaroid camera or elevator), natural, and easy to understand.

5. *Psychological Job Demands.* People should be proud of their work. For those who aspire to it, opportunities should exist for rewarding and challenging work. The system should also accommodate those who are satisfied with routine work. Moreover, connect a task with a purpose—the purpose of the job and of the organization. Give employees autonomy so that they can make decisions about their own work. Also, incorporate variety in the job. As a general rule, the more *toil* we can take out of the job, the better.

6. *Information Resource Center.* Install a "tool room" or "open-shop com-

puter center" where users can come to get the help they need to work with the system. This help may entail more training, a minor change in systems design, or the "checking-out" of a personal computer or other information systems aids. This part of the systems design stresses usability and accessibility of computer services. Employees can come in and do pretty much what they want. They can browse, try things out, ask questions, see demonstrations, play with the latest technology, and, generally, get a better understanding of how the system works and what it can do for them, all within the context of a friendly and helpful environment.

Feasibility Requirements

The TELOS acronym represents the five components of the feasibility requirement.

1. *Technical Feasibility.* To decide technical feasibility, the designer determines if the preliminary design can be developed and implemented using existing technology. Usually, this determination includes the technological expertise that exists presently within the organization, but it may also include an assessment of the technological state of the art outside the organization. As a general statement, technology is far ahead of people's ability to apply it effectively. So, in most cases, technical feasibility from the viewpoint of availability is a nonissue; the ability to acquire, apply, and use it may, however, be very much at issue. Indeed, because technology ties together and supports the other building blocks, the level of access to technology will clearly have a significant impact on how the system is eventually designed.

2. *Economic Feasibility.* This area of feasibility generates a basic question: Does the organization have the funds necessary to develop and implement an information system, given the requirements of other capital projects within the organization? If so, what is the level of financial commitment? Clearly, the level of design and scope are directly related to economic support.

3. *Legal Feasibility.* This factor mandates that no conflicts exist between the system under consideration and the organization's ability to discharge its legal obligations. In this regard the analyst must consider the legal implications arising from applicable federal and state statutes, rules of common law, federal and state administrative agencies (e.g., Internal Revenue Service, Securities and Exchange Commission), and contractual provisions. For example, in considering requirements for records retention, the analyst should know what records must be retained, who must keep them, how long they must be kept, and the level of security required.

4. *Operational Feasibility.* Will the design be based on the organizational environment, existing procedures, and personnel? If not, can sufficient skills be acquired, people trained, and other changes made to make the system operational? If the answer is no, then the system design will have to be changed so that it will be operational within existing conditions.

5. *Schedule Feasibility.* This means that the system's design must be able to become operative within some time frame. If not, the design or the time frame will have to change.

2.4 INFORMATION SYSTEMS DEVELOPMENT METHODOLOGY: THE SYSTEMS ANALYST'S GUIDING LIGHT

The systems development methodology is what systems analysts follow in doing their work. We use the generic term *systems analyst* to describe the person(s) who has primary responsibility for bringing the building blocks together, giving them form and substance in compliance with the design forces to build successful information systems. In a small company, the systems analyst may not only design the information system, but also perform the programming and operate the computer. In a large company, the systems analyst may prepare design specifications that are given to technicians, such as programmers, ergonomists, forms designers, and communication specialists. The systems analyst will coordinate all these specialists' tasks for final implementation of the total system.

Major Phases of the Systems Development Methodology

In Part 4 the systems development methodology is described in detail; a general schematic of it, however, is shown in Figure 2.5. Its major phases are systems analysis, general systems design, systems evaluation, detailed systems design, and systems implementation. The major activities or tasks are included within each phase. The first four phases are directed toward providing specific values for the building blocks. The last phase deals with making the building blocks operational. Some authors, companies, and consultants divide their systems development methodology into different phases or steps from the one presented in this chapter. For example, one author divides the methodology into three steps: systems analysis, systems design, and systems implementation. Some accounting firms use six phases: feasibility, design, programming, testing, training, and implementation. Systems analysts at Holiday Corporation follow seven steps: systems design, software selection or creation, testing, implementation, training, conversion, and postimplementation review.

No matter the number or names of the phases or steps, the systems development methodology rationalizes and routinizes the process of building information systems. It is a step-by-step progression from the very general to the very specific. Its hallmark is its discrete phases. The major goal of the systems development methodology is to reduce false starts, undue recycling, rework, and dead ends. Moreover, it increases the likelihood that the system eventually built and installed is the one the users want and need. But in no way should the systems development methodology stifle creativity or innovation. It provides a guiding light for an information systems journey. How exciting, productive, and creative the systems analyst wants this journey to be is, to a great extent, up to the systems analyst.

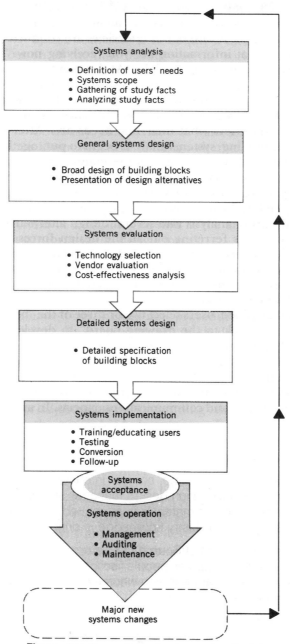

Figure 2.5 The systems development methodology.

The role of systems analysts and their use of the systems development methodology is, of course, a composite picture. In a large organization the information system is a vast, complex entity, and many analysts are involved in designing and implementing only one subsystem of the organization's overall information system. At a given point in time, an analyst might well be executing activities related to more than one phase of the systems development methodology, and these activities must be properly coordinated.

To make the system more effective, the systems analyst will be engaged in a wide spectrum of activities ranging from formal to informal, quantitative to qualitative, structured to unstructured, specific to general, and traditional to revolutionary. In performing these activities, the analyst may use flowcharts, data flow diagrams, decision tables, matrices, graphs, narrative reports, interviews, models, and prototypes. These techniques reinforce one another, and, when viewed in combination, provide the basic tools for systems work.

SUMMARY

All information systems—big or little, advanced or simple, good or bad—are made up of six building blocks: input, models, output, technology, data base, and controls. The way these building blocks are shaped and interwoven and the substance they contain will, to a high degree, be influenced by 10 design forces: integration, user/system interface, competitive forces, information quality and usability, systems requirements, data processing requirements, organizational factors, cost-effectiveness requirements, human factors, and feasibility requirements.

The building blocks do not make a purposeful information system unless they meet the dictates of the design forces and are brought together into a unity. This enterprise is undertaken by systems analysts who use the systems development methodology as their guide, from analysis to determine users' requirements all the way to implementation.

IMPORTANT TERMS

alternate areas	ergonomics
building blocks	feasibility
computer-integrated manufacturing (CIM)	general systems design
	human factors
controls	information resource center
cost-effectiveness requirements	input
data base	integration
data processing requirements	models
design forces	organizational factors
detailed systems design	output

prototyping
psychological job demands
robots
software
systems analysis
systems development methodology
systems evaluation

systems implementation
systems requirements
technology
telecommunications
TELOS
user/system interface
work groups

Assignment

REVIEW QUESTIONS

2.1 List and briefly describe the six building blocks that make up an information system.

2.2 What does input represent? What does input consist of? What are some of the devices for entering input data?

2.3 What determines the quality of output?

2.4 What are some of the media that can be used to produce output?

2.5 Give a definition for each of the components that make up the technology information systems building block.

2.6 The data base can be described in terms of its logical and physical properties. Explain these properties and provide examples of each.

2.7 What five controls should be designed into the information system to ensure its protection, integrity, and smooth operation?

2.8 Every organization and, therefore, every information system, operates within the context of internal and external pressures and constraints. Identify and describe the 10 design forces that influence and help mold the information system.

2.9 Much attention has been given to the speculation that computerized robots will displace a significant percentage of operational workers, thereby upsetting the national economy. In spite of these fears, robot populations continue to increase. Discuss five reasons for the increased use of robots in the future.

2.10 What four attributes can be designed into an information system to affect the quality and usability of the information it produces?

2.11 Identify and explain the significance of the six systems requirements.

2.12 Systems maintenance is an inevitable component of any information system that is expected to provide efficient data processing over an extended period. Give four suggestions for designing more maintainable systems.

2.13 What are the four data processing requirements?

2.14 Discuss some of the specific environmental and physical conditions that ergonomics addresses in trying to optimize the user/system interface.

2.15 What uses can be made of the information resource center?

2.16 Every information system is constrained by five feasibility requirements. List these requirements and discuss how each affects the design of the system.

2.17 The master plan from which a proficient, operative information system evolves is called the information systems development methodology. Describe the five major phases of this methodology. Include in your discussion an explanation of systems prototyping.

QUESTIONS FOR DISCUSSION

2.18 How much influence should information users have in the design of the system?

2.19 All too often, the decision maker is relegated to a position of passive frustration in his or her relationship with the information system that is supposed to serve the user. How will the introduction of microcomputers relieve this condition?

2.20 How will voice communication with the information system improve the user/system interface?

2.21 Engineering computer applications are typically characterized by a large amount of "number crunching." Discuss the computation demands placed on the information system in terms of volume, complexity, and time constraints.

2.22 What is the major goal of ergonomics? From what disciplines does ergonomics draw its techniques?

2.23 If the systems development methodology is correctly applied the first time around, there should never again arise a need to repeat the systems development methodology. Do you agree? disagree? Why?

2.24 As management decides to enhance the information system to meet users' needs better, it must also increase expenditures to acquire new information technology, as well as maintain the old. How would you justify such expenditures?

2.25 Discuss the importance of information systems designers' consideration of the social and psychological aspects of the organization in their designs.

2.26 What is your definition of a user-friendly system, and what changes would you recommend to make present systems more user friendly?

EXERCISES AND PROBLEMS

2.27 Ergonomics relates to the designing of systems components to enhance the user/system interface. Prepare a brief report on some of the improvements that have been realized in the work environment as a result of research in the field of ergonomics.

2.28 One of the building blocks described in the text related to the models that manipulate input and stored data to produce desired results or output. Describe how logico-mathematical models are used in the preparation of a firm's financial statements.

2.29 As part of a new systems development project, John Mark, sales manager for Todco 500 Toy Company, was asked to provide a list of the information he needed to perform his job. John Mark's list is as follows:

1. Sales figures by product, salesperson, and region.
2. Daily, weekly, and monthly sales reports.
3. Complete, detailed sales analysis on all competitors.
4. Name of every person in the United States who has ever bought the types of products Todco sells.
5. Address, phone number, annual income, place of employment, health record, credit record, and tax records for each person in item 4.
6. The name and phone number of every person with a personal computer. I would like to prepare a mail-out to these persons and announce a new toll-free telephone line

from Todco's computer to the individual's PC so that a person can order directly from my sales office.

P.S. Can you have this system operable within three weeks?

> *Required:* Identify the five systems feasibility requirements discussed in the text. Analyze John Mark's information needs in light of these feasibility requirements.

2.30 Select a local organization with a computer-based information system. Examine the system in person and prepare a report detailing the specific components of the system in terms of the building blocks described in the text.

2.31 Odee Boot Company's predominantly manual "paper-and-ink" information system uses two calculators, a typewriter, and a copy machine to generate and update all records. Recently, Odee's only local competitor went out of business, whereupon Odee purchased all the assets of the competitor and anticipates controlling the boot market in the area. As part of a study to determine whether Odee should convert to a computer-based system, you have been asked to prepare an analysis of how the two systems, manual and computer based, compare within each system's requirement category.

2.32 Caralene Industries is a highly successful West Coast supplier of small office electronic security systems. Although the electronic component of its security systems generates the majority of Caralene's revenue, in the last five years an increasing proportion of Caralene's revenue has come from ancillary services related to the activities of security system evaluation, planning, and installation.

Caralene dominates the U.S. market, with its closest competitor having about one-fifth its sales. Much of this competitive advantage can be attributed to Caralene's technologically superior electronic components and its proprietary method for evaluating, planning, and installing electronic security systems.

The vice-president of marketing for Caralene, Joanne Lin, is concerned about threats to Caralene from foreign competitors. Specifically, she wants to ensure that a foreign competitor does not enter and establish a foothold in the U.S. market before Caralene has a chance to react in an effective way to this competitor's entry. She places the design and installation of a surveillance reporting information system as a top-priority item.

> *Required:* Prepare a brief report that lists the types of information to be incorporated into this surveillance reporting system.

2.33 StarCare is a Kansas City–based distributor of farm implement parts. Its customers are repair establishments and farm service centers throughout the Midwest. Working through 12 branch offices management believes that getting the right parts into the customers' hands is the key to StarCare's continued success.

At present, StarCare sales order processing is done by a centralized computer system located in Kansas City. When an order for parts is taken by a salesperson, it is sent to the appropriate branch office, where it is checked for completeness and mailed to Kansas City. When the order is received in Kansas City, clerks process the order and send a copy of it to the warehouse. There the parts wanted by the customer are picked and set aside for shipping via a carrier that delivers to the region where the customer is located. The shipping copy of the order is batched with other shipping notices and processed each night on the centralized computer system. Next day the resulting sales invoices are mailed to the respective customers.

StarCare is considering an alternative sales order processing system. The alternative involves employing portable microcomputers and a telecommunications network. The salesperson upon receiving an order for parts from a customer, would transmit the order to the branch office using the microcomputer's built-in communications capabilities. As part of the transmission process the parts are checked for availability and the order is validated for completeness and accuracy. Each hour the orders received in the last time period would be retransmitted to the central computer in Kansas City.

At the home office, the central computer system would cause a copy of the sales order to be printed at the warehouse and stored on the shipping department's microcomputer. After the parts ordered are picked and shipped, the shipping department clerk uses his or her microcomputer to update the order with shipping data and send it back to the central computer system. By reference to customer accounts receivable records, a sales invoice is prepared and printed hourly. The goal of the alternative system is to mail a sales invoice the same day the order is shipped.

Required: In broad terms, what questions might be asked concerning the feasibility of this alternative design?

BIBLIOGRAPHY

APPLETON, DANIEL S. "The State of CIM." *Datamation*, December 15, 1984.

BECKER, HAL B. *Information Integrity*. New York: McGraw-Hill, 1983.

BROD, CRAIG. *Technostress: The Human Cost of the Computer Revolution*. Reading, Mass.: Addison-Wesley, 1984.

BRUNO, CHARLES. "Labor Relations in the Age of Robotics." *Datamation*, March 1984.

DARROW, JOEL W., and JAMES R. BELILOVE. "Keeping Informed." *Harvard Business Review*, November–December 1978.

DRUCKER, PETER F. *The Practice of Management*. New York: Harper & Row, 1954.

FLYNN, ANITA M. "Gnat Robots." *AI Expert*, December, 1987.

GASSMANN, HANS-PETER. *Information, Computer and Communications Policies for the 80's*. Amsterdam: North-Holland, 1981.

GINZBERG, MICHAEL J., WALTER REITMAN, and EDWARD A. STOHR, eds. *Decision Support Systems*. Amsterdam: North-Holland, 1982.

GORE, MARVIN and JOHN STUBBE. *Elements of Systems Analysis*, 3rd ed. Dubuque, Iowa: William C. Brown, 1983.

GUIMAROES, TOR. "The Evolution of the Information Center." *Datamation*, July 15, 1984.

HARRAR, G., "Information Center, the User's Report." *Computerworld*, December 26, 1983.

HICKS, JAMES O., JR. *Management Information Systems: A User Perspective*. St. Paul, Minn.: West, 1984.

HUNTER, PHILIP. "Big Bang a Stress Test." *InformationWEEK*, August 17, 1987.

HUSSAIN, DONNA, and K. M. HUSSAIN. *Information Resource Management*. Homewood, Ill.: Richard D. Irwin, 1984.

INOSE, HIROSHI, and JOHN R. PIERCE. *Information Technology and Civilization*. New York: W. H. Freeman, 1984.

KANTOWITZ, BARRY H., and ROBERT D. SORKIN. *Human Factors: Understanding People-System Relationships*. New York: John Wiley, 1983.

KAY, SHERYL. "Making It in Manufacturing." *Computerworld*, April 25, 1988.

McQUADE, WALTER. "Easing Tensions Between Man and Machine." *Fortune*, March 19, 1984.

OTWAY, HARRY J., and MALCOLM PELTU. *New Office Technology*. Norwood, NJ: Ablex Publishing, 1983.

PORTER, MICHAEL E. *Competitive Advantage*. New York: The Free Press, 1985.

RUDALL, B. H. *Computers and Cybernetics*. Tunbridge Wells, Kent: Abacus Press, 1981.

because everyone approaches an array of information in a different way and with a different purpose.

The way innovative systems analysts develop information systems is significantly different from that of a mechanist or technocrat. The technocrat's approach is to acquire the technology building block first, then try to find software that is compatible with the technology, and finally try to "force" people to use the "system." On the other hand, innovative systems analysts try to grasp opportunities that users are not even aware of; apply the systems development methodology to exploit opportunities by defining users' needs; then acquire or develop software that meets the needs; and, finally, install a technology building block that is cost-effective, is compatible with the software, and supports the systems design.

3.3 INFORMATION SYSTEM EFFECTIVENESS AND EFFICIENCY COMPONENTS

In this section, we present selected components that make information systems more effective and efficient. These components enable the information system to serve as a filter, as a monitor, as an interactive component, as a knowledge pervasion component, and as an extension component.

Filtering Component

One way to make information systems more efficient, and provide users with more information and less data, is to reduce or filter the amount of detail data provided to each level of decision making, as shown in Figure 3.2. Data are filtered through summarizing and classifying operations that screen out unnecessary detail for a given level of decision making.

As a rule, strategic decision making requires less detail than do either tactical or technical decision making. For example, the president of a large manufacturing organization is certainly concerned with the sales of that organization; however, this concern does not necessarily require a daily listing of invoices; a monthly summary of total sales dollars might be satisfactory. It must be recognized, however, that requirements for detail vary significantly among individuals at the same level of decision making. Ideally, an information system is designed to permit the filtering of selected data elements from the data base

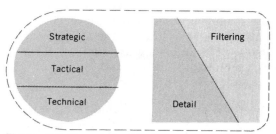

Figure 3.2 The relationship between levels of management and requirements for detail.

so that each decision maker can obtain the level of detail appropriate to his or her individual needs. Traditionally, data are filtered at each superior/subordinate level in an organization. In modern organizations using modern data processing technology, an opportunity exists, however, to include this filtering process as an essential element of the information system.

The filtering component is applicable in large organizations where current information reporting emphasizes providing large detail reports. All forms of transaction reporting lend themselves to filtering, and this can be illustrated with the reporting of cost and sales dollars.

In a construction company, for example, an awareness of actual costs incurred is an important aspect of each manager's job regardless of the manager's position in the organization. The president of the firm is likely to be concerned with the total costs incurred in a given time period. The vice-president responsible for construction might require a further breakdown of total costs into prime costs and overhead costs. Each lower level of management would require a correspondingly higher level of detail concerning costs related to their activities only. In Figure 3.3, we illustrate how the information system can be used as a filter to report relevant construction costs to various levels of decision makers.

Reporting sales activity in a large organization is another area where filtering is effective. In Figure 3.4, a series of reports are shown that describe the sales efforts of a company and the distribution of these reports.

The major advantage of having the information system filter data is that the amount of useless data provided to each decision maker is reduced, and, hence, the organization's resources and management's time are conserved. The disadvantages of having the information system serve as a data filter are that (1) implementation is difficult when the requirements for detail among decision makers at the same level varies, (2) filtered reports do not provide enough action-oriented information, and (3) because the filtered information goes to the decision maker directly from the information system without flowing through subordinates, superior/subordinate relationships are upset. On the other hand, this last disadvantage can become a real advantage because it eliminates the gatekeeping tendencies of subordinates.

Monitoring Component

Using the information system as a monitor dramatically reduces the drudgery in the workaday world. The system does all the work of looking at mountains of data, ferreting out significant variables, continuously comparing actual events with expected events, making thousands of low-level decisions, and keeping track of hundreds of instructions. It is, indeed, the kind of work the system "loves" but the human "hates." The following are some of the ways the information system can serve as a monitor.

Key Variables
The information system is designed to monitor and report the status, trends, and changes of key variables (also called critical success factors, key result areas, and pulse points) that have a significant impact on the total performance and profitability of the organization. The human body's condition and performance,

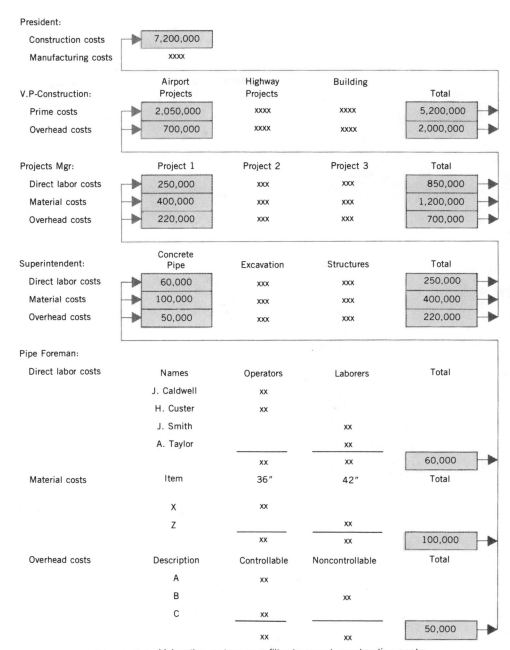

President:

Construction costs	7,200,000			
Manufacturing costs	xxxx			

V.P-Construction:

	Airport Projects	Highway Projects	Building	Total
Prime costs	2,050,000	xxxx	xxxx	5,200,000
Overhead costs	700,000	xxxx	xxxx	2,000,000

Projects Mgr:

	Project 1	Project 2	Project 3	Total
Direct labor costs	250,000	xxx	xxx	850,000
Material costs	400,000	xxx	xxx	1,200,000
Overhead costs	220,000	xxx	xxx	700,000

Superintendent:

	Concrete Pipe	Excavation	Structures	Total
Direct labor costs	60,000	xxx	xxx	250,000
Material costs	100,000	xxx	xxx	400,000
Overhead costs	50,000	xxx	xxx	220,000

Pipe Foreman:

Direct labor costs	Names	Operators	Laborers	Total
	J. Caldwell	xx		
	H. Custer	xx		
	J. Smith		xx	
	A. Taylor		xx	
		xx	xx	60,000

Material costs	Item	36″	42″	Total
	X	xx		
	Z		xx	
		xx	xx	100,000

Overhead costs	Description	Controllable	Noncontrollable	Total
	A	xx		
	B		xx	
	C	xx		
		xx	xx	50,000

Figure 3.3 Using the system as a filter to report construction costs.

Company Sales			
Division	Year to date	This month	
Eastern	$292,000	$ 66,050	Sales dollars, shown by company division; produced for Vice-President of Marketing
Central	284,000	83,100	
Pacific	310,000	101,000	
Total Company	$886,000	$250,150	

Eastern Division			
Territory	Year to date	This month	
New England	$ 58,830	$ 11,250	Sales dollars, shown by territory, for each division; produced for each Division Manager
Mid-Atlantic	73,190	14,100	
Seaboard	42,080	15,800	
Southeast	35,000	12,000	
Northeast	82,900	12,900	
Total Division	$292,000	$ 66,050	

New England Territory			
Salesperson	Year to date	This month	
J. Dee	$ 19,010	$ 3,000	Sales dollars, shown by salesperson, for each territory; produced for each Territory Manager
M. Horish	12,150	4,200	
J. Michaels	11,480	2,300	
J. Lucey	16,190	1,750	
Total Territory	$ 58,830	$ 11,250	

Super Manufacturing			
Product	Year to date	This month	
¼" Drills	$ 350	$ 75	Sales dollars, shown by product, for each customer; produced for each salesperson
½" Drills	790	140	
Sanders	1,150		
Jig Saws	4,580	1,150	
Rip Saws	290		
Others	1,375	$ 75	
Total Sales	$ 8,535	$ 1,440	

Figure 3.4 Using the system as a filter to report sales dollars.

for example, can be determined to a great extent by the monitoring of key variables, such as pulse rate, blood pressure and blood sugar levels and reporting these results to a physician for appropriate action. So, too, the organization has key variables that require monitoring.

Peter Drucker has stated that the key performance areas of an organization are typically market standing, profitability, innovation, productivity, physical and financial resources, motivation and organization development, and public responsibility.[1] Using Drucker's key performance areas as a guideline, examples

---

[1]Peter F. Drucker, *The Practice of Management* (New York: Harper & Row, 1954).

of key variables can be identified, monitored, and reported as shown in Figure 3.5.

Some of these key variables can also be used as predictors. If a leading manufacturer began to buy a large amount of machine tools, for instance, this could indicate future expansion in a particular market. Also, the reporting of key variables helps management zero in on a particular area for action. For example, from lost customer reports, management can formulate a strategy to recapture these customers. The lost customers become "target customers" that require immediate attention and the concern of everyone throughout the or-

---

GETTING THE RIGHT INFORMATION TO THE RIGHT PEOPLE

The management reporting system must provide both operating and financial information, be tailored to the various levels of the firm, include more detail at the operations level, and offer more summary information for senior executives.

For the *operations level,* three main kinds of information are useful: product lines, profitability, expenses and assets. The product line's performance includes responsiveness to customers and measures of product quality and delivery. The operations manager must know whether controllable financial objectives are being met. Materials, operating supplies, energy, and inventory levels are major determinants of line managers' cost performance and should be tracked on a regular basis.

At the *business unit level,* the manager requires less detail than the operations manager. He needs information about various product lines' economic characteristics and operating performance to enable him to make the correct capital investment, pricing, and strategic choices.

At the *corporate level,* management must have information about business units' performance, product line, and product performance to solve significant problems and exploit strategic opportunities. Yet, corporate executives should not be burdened with detail. They must be able to see major issues facing the firm.

Corporate executives should receive four principal kinds of information. The first report should be a summary from the business unit manager that reviews the operation, analyzes results, and addresses significant strategic and management issues. Second, the package should include a limited number of critical success factors the corporate executive can quickly relate to and use to assess performance. Third, financial results should be summarized in a managerial rather than financial accounting format. Finally, there should be a forecast of future expectations.

Excerpted from Robert A. Howell and Stephen R. Soucy, "Management Reporting in the New Manufacturing Environment," *Management Accounting,* February 1988, pp. 22–29.

ganization, including top management. To maintain attention on the lost customer problem and to assist in an effort to recapture them requires a reporting feedback system to be implemented in the information system. A simple report that illustrates this point is shown in Figure 3.6.

This report puts everyone on notice that the goal is not only to recapture lost customers but to increase sales at the same time. On a weekly basis, the results of this effort are reported to all personnel involved (e.g., top management, sales manager, salespeople, and supporting personnel such as shipping and order-entry clerks).

Variances

This form of continuous monitoring compares actual events with planned ones to detect variances. Variances are then compared with a control value to deter-

Key Performance Areas	Key Variables
Market standing	Sales
	Product margin
	New orders
	Lost orders
	Lost customers
Innovation	Number of new products
	New markets
Productivity	Capacity utilization
	Backlogs
	Backorders
	Manufacturing costs
	Yields
Physical and financial resources	Number of pieces of idle equipment
	Number of obsolete inventory items
	Accounts receivable turnover
	Inventory turnover
	Cash flow
	Working capital ratio
	Return on investment
Motivation and organization development	Absenteeism reports
	Number of personnel problems going to arbitration
	Number of personnel attending continuing education programs
	Labor turnover
Public responsibility	Number of employees involved in community programs
	Expenditures for pollution control
	Contribution to charitable organizations

Figure 3.5 Key variables that can be reported by the information system.

TARGET ACCOUNTS

Salesperson	Account Number	First Quarter Sales	Second Quarter Sales*	Third Quarter Sales Goal
Smith	143	$ 9,000	$ 0	$10,000
	156	12,000	0	15,000
Oswald	176	6,000	100	8,000
	290	50,000	200	60,000
	294	24,000	0	30,000
Gatski	179	18,000	0	25,000

*Period in which customers were "lost."

Figure 3.6 Feedback report showing status of recapturing lost customers.

mine if they are significant. If so, the variance is reported to a decision maker for corrective action.

For example, a large manufacturer of metal fasteners develops and maintains standard costs for each of its 23,000 different products. A cost variance report for every product would require more than 1,000 pages. Many of the entries in this report would show that the products are manufactured at, or very close to, the established standard. A much smaller report is produced, however, for products varying more than ±5 percent from standard. Each entry in the smaller report represents a need for either further analysis or action on the part of management.

In this example it can be seen that the time spent by the human in identifying every variance is eliminated. Such monitoring is still accomplished, but now it is performed by the information system, and the system, in turn, reports to the decision maker only those variances that are significant.

Another example of variance reporting is applied to sales reporting of a Northwest wholesaler of cleaning supplies. In this sales organization each salesperson is assigned a sales quota, and the sales manager reviews only those who are well above or below their quota in any given time period. The sales manager assumes that the salespeople are operating satisfactorily when sales are within 10 percent of the quota. In Figure 3.7, the sales performance of the one salesperson has been plotted for 12 months.

This chart shows that our salesperson exceeded the guidelines in the months of February, April, May, and December. Using the variance reporting method, the sales manager receives detailed sales reports on this individual's sales performance only at these times. In the remaining months, the sales manager assumes that this particular salesperson is selling according to expectations. In effect, the sales manager is freed from monitoring reports that contain little, if any, useful information; therefore, he can better use his time and energy where they are most needed.

Although variance reporting (also called exception reporting) is powerful, one should remember that management also needs periodic reports for decision

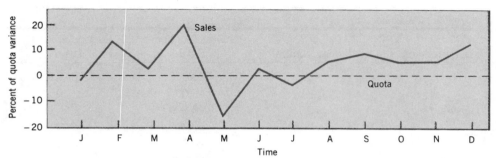

Figure 3.7 A chart illustrating variances from quota.

making. Many managers are more comfortable if they know the overall status or general health of the organization. They feel that receiving information only when something has gone wrong or has fallen outside a predetermined limit does not indicate the gradual buildup of problems. Management must be in an informed position to anticipate situations. To be sure, variance monitoring and reporting does not give anticipative information as key variable monitoring does, but it is quite effective for its intended use.

Programmed Decision Making

As described earlier, a major part of technical decision making, and a small part of tactical decision making, involves routine, repetitive decisions. By designing the information system to monitor events, comparing these events with decision rules, and executing routine decisions, the systems analyst provides human decision makers with more time to spend on nonprogrammed decisions.

Indeed, most organizations offer many opportunities to implement programmed decision making. For example, checking the credit of customers is an important, but repetitive, order-entry process that can be built into the information system. Figure 3.8 illustrates one approach to programming this process. Once the credit manager is relieved of checking each customer order processed, he or she is able to concentrate on those orders that have a problem, such as collection associated with them.

The purchasing function provides still another opportunity for the implementation of programmed decision making. Periodically, a purchasing agent must review all outstanding purchase orders to determine if some form of expediting is required to ensure that the goods are delivered when needed. This process entails an examination of each purchase order and a comparison of the date the purchase is scheduled to arrive with the date when what is ordered is required for use. Both dates are subject to continuous revision. In many organizations, this process can be a tedious task because hundreds or thousands of purchase orders may be outstanding at any one time. Obviously, if the system is allowed to monitor outstanding purchase orders and the decision as to which orders are to be expedited is programmed, much time and effort is saved. Figure 3.9 illustrates one approach to programming this decision-making process.

RAILROAD AUTOMATION Transportation Control System (TCS) is the key to Union Pacific's operation. TCS is a computer-driven system that handles every aspect of freight movement from start to finish. For instance, when a customer orders a car, TCS will find the most appropriate car at the location nearest the shipment's origin point and then issue instructions for movement. Once the car is loaded and switched out, the system traces it, updating the file and then issuing instructions for spotting at destination. The system will also compute billing information. And, since many shipments are repetitive in nature, TCS keeps basic information on file; the shipper needs only to provide his "pattern number" and variable data such as car number and weight and TCS will handle the rest of the transaction automatically.

"Keying Shippers into EDI," *Railway Age,* March 1987, pp. 50–51.

lieving nurses and others from keeping track of each detail. Moreover, the system can perform routine tasks when appropriate, such as producing picking lists for loading medication carts, setting time schedules for the administration of drugs, preparing drug labels, checking for possible harmful effects because of the interaction of drugs, and automatically charging costs against each patient's account.

Patient monitoring systems rely on the computer for continuous surveillance of a patient's vital signs and automatic notification of physiological data for use by trained personnel. Figure 3.10 illustrates a typical medical monitoring system. The first step in the system is to capture data from monitoring devices connected to the patients and convert these analog signals to digital data for computer processing and display. In addition to providing automatic notification, the system stores information for periodic retrieval. Early warning information is given based on various clinical models and trend analysis. Various types of information are displayed periodically at monitoring stations based on programmed decision rules.

In industry, this method of providing information is used to present work assignments to individual workers. For example, when workers complete one assignment, they receive notification of their next assignment automatically from the system. The allocation of other resources is also monitored. In a particular construction company an inventory schedule of heavy equipment is monitored. Periodically a notice is output identifying machines scheduled to be available for another project assignment.

In the preceding examples, the system merely monitors a large file of data and instructions, makes changes in this file, and remembers what to do with all of the data based on predetermined criteria or a schedule. To a great extent, it "taps the human on the shoulder" and helps him or her remember and keep up with instructions and particulars, at any time of day.

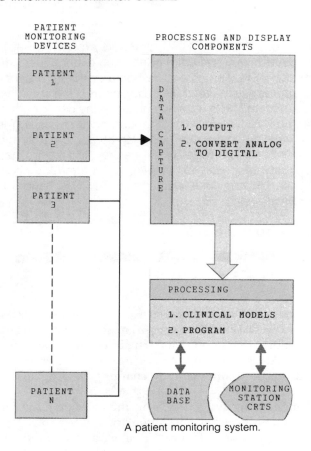

A patient monitoring system.

Interaction Component

The user/system interface is a strong design force that demands direct interaction between the user and the information system. The design and implementation of the interaction component requires a large and fully related data base, sophisticated models, and multifunction input and output devices.

An order-entry process provides a simple example of using the information system as an interaction component. In the order-entry system, the salesperson or desk clerk communicates with the system by means of a terminal. A list of functions available to the user is then displayed. For example, the user may enter a customer order into the file, cancel, alter, or reschedule an order, or obtain an inquiry response relative to sales performance items.

An example of a transaction selection display is illustrated in Figure 3.11. The user makes a selection by depressing the appropriate key. If key 2 is depressed, a list of order-entry functions is displayed. An example of this response is shown in Figure 3.12.

Let us suppose that the user wants to enter details of a customer order. When a "1" key is depressed, the screen shown in Figure 3.13 is displayed. It provides a skeleton consisting of customer name, customer identification num-

CRT Screen

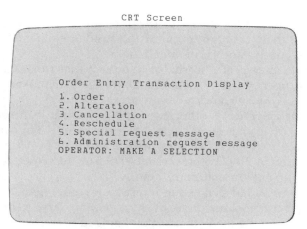

```
Gross Transaction Display

1. Customer record control
2. Order entry control/old customer
3. Billing, taxes, and freight information
4. Sales administration
5. Inquiry
6. Order entry control/new customer
OPERATOR: MAKE A SELECTION
```

Figure 3.11 A display of a transaction selection.

ber, address, date, sales location, salesperson, purchase plan (such as sale or lease), plus the items ordered.

When an entry is completed, the order is checked against other constraints in the system such as credit status and inventory availability. If the final order is accepted by the system, then the order is processed in accordance with predetermined criteria.

CRT Screen

```
Order Entry Transaction Display

1. Order
2. Alteration
3. Cancellation
4. Reschedule
5. Special request message
6. Administration request message
OPERATOR: MAKE A SELECTION
```

Figure 3.12 A display of an order-entry function.

In addition to this menu-style dialogue, question-answer (Q/A) systems can be designed and implemented for a variety of users. With this approach, the system asks a series of questions, the user provides the answers, and at the end of the Q/A session, the system makes recommendations. A simple example of how a portfolio analyst may use this approach follows:

SYSTEM: "What are the names of companies you are investigating?"

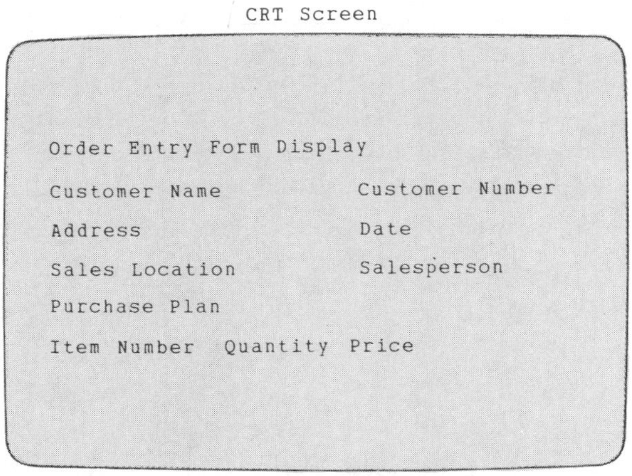

CRT Screen

```
Order Entry Form Display

Customer Name          Customer Number

Address                Date

Sales Location         Salesperson

Purchase Plan

Item Number  Quantity  Price
```

Figure 3.13 A display of an order-entry form

USER: Inputs ticker symbols of companies.

SYSTEM: "What are their credit ratings, high-lows of 19X8 and 19X9, yield, P/E ratios, earnings per share since 19X5, current assets, current liabilities, long-term liabilities, and capital?"

USER: Inputs these variables on a fill-in form.

The system combines these variables with extensive data stored in the data base and processes them through technical and fundamental models to give the user investment scenarios and recommendations.

A banker may prefer a what-if approach that works along the following lines: "If customer = 123 + Code A and present loan outstanding ≤ Y and (last payment date − today's date) ≤ 30 and acid-test ratio > 1.8 : 1 and cash flow ≥ 20 percent of (debt service + other expenses + present loan request), then what is disposition of loan request?" Or a sales manager may want the system to respond to the following: "If sales price is reduced by 15 percent, volume of output increased by 30 percent, variable expenses decreased by 10 percent, what will be the contribution margin of item X?"

A key device that makes the interaction component even more effective and efficient is the workstation. A workstation may serve a single user or a small work group. It can be made to assist all kinds of users, such as nontechnical or technical, occasional or power/production, and single- or multifunctional. The range of workstation capabilities provides effective and efficient aids to managers, accountants, staff, engineers, scientists, production personnel, and clerical workers. The technology can be tailored to meet specific work needs; therefore, workstations are by no means standardized throughout the organization. To be sure, the workstation for a top manager would be different from the workstation designed for an order-entry clerk. The differences lie in the kinds of tasks that the user is expected to perform. Consequently, a workstation may range from a portable PC to a multiple-component, multifunction configuration as illustrated in Figure 3.14.

If the user is interfaced with manufacturing, as well as other operations, the computer-integrated manufacturing (CIM) element of the multifunctional workstation places at the user's fingertips the power to create new designs, simulate their impact on costs, production resources, and engineering standards; quickly modify and sketch new designs, document their dimensions and specifications; and, at some point, actually set in motion the manufacturing process

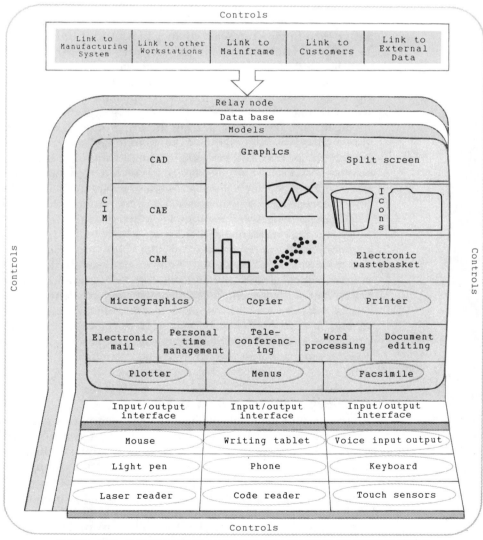

Figure 3.14 A multifunctional workstation with hardware components circled.

to make and assemble the necessary part. Users can do most of this by using a lightpen and screen at their workstation. They may sketch an entire drawing and have the system straighten the lines and add dimensions. The lightpen interacts directly with the image on the screen.

The mouse, writing tablet (which may use an electronic tablet and stylus, and an optical character recognition device to recognize handwriting), voice input/output, alphanumeric keyboard, phone, and touch sensors are used in combination to enter instructions and text, specify positions on the screen, store and retrieve data, send messages to other workstations, and so forth. Various readers are used to input precoded items such as inventory.

The system provides a variety of graphics for output. If the user presses the icon for the filing cabinet, he or she can electronically leaf through the files faster than fingers can search paper files. And if unnecessary documents are to be removed from the system, the user calls the electronic wastebasket. The user can dictate text to word processor operators, then receive the results in manuscript form, edit it, and retransmit for final preparation. At any time, users can open the "mailbox" electronically by speaking or keying in a password. They can also "mail" messages electronically. Physical mail is sent to the workstation by means of a facsimile link from the organization's mailroom. Voice store-and-forward devices help eliminate "telephone tag" and time zone differences. The phone component can provide automatic dialing, redialing, and directory assistance with picture phone service, if desired. Cellular phones and paging components can keep users in touch while they are away from the workstation. Full teleconferencing provides interactive video, audio, and graphic capabilities. Personal time management facilities keep diaries and calendars up to date and help in setting appointments, coordinating schedules, and setting up meetings. This component also automatically provides reminders of coming appointments. Access to outside information can come in many forms, including videotex. Plotters convert digital graphics into hard copy. Or graphics and text can be put on microfilm or microfiche for convenient and efficient storage. Menu selections can be made by an array of push buttons, touch, pen, or voice. All voice input or output is very efficient because it frees the user's hands to manipulate other devices or to monitor other operations. Unquestionably, we will be using more voice input/output in the future.

Knowledge Pervasion Component

A collection of artificial intelligence (AI) techniques, called expert systems, enables computers to leverage the knowledge of experts to help people analyze problems, make decisions, and perform certain tasks. Expert systems have been developed, for example, to assist managers with complex manufacturing and scheduling problems (XSEL), aid physicians in diagnosing diseases (MYCIN), and advise oil exploration crews about drilling problems (DRILLING ADVISOR). By combining the components of knowledge leveraging and monitoring, a valuable resource can be created for any organization involved in complex processing operations.

CAPTURING AND LEVERAGING KNOWLEDGE THROUGH EXPERT SYSTEMS

N L Baroid Company's MUDMAN and Digital Equipment Corporation's XCON perform tasks previously thought too complicated or not routine enough for computers. MUDMAN and XCON are not ordinary computer programs though. They are "expert systems"—programs that mimic the thinking of the human experts who would otherwise have to perform the analysis, design, or monitoring. Through a complicated series of "if . . . then" rules—"If there is a disk drive that has not been assigned and there is capacity for at least one disk drive, then assign the disk drive to the current computer configuration"—such programs allow computers to solve difficult, one-of-a-kind problems.

Growing numbers of managers are asking whether expert systems are right for them, and if so, how they can start using them. Those who want to exploit the new technology can learn from the early users of large, commercial expert systems. Their experience shows that expert systems are indeed a valuable tool for capturing and disseminating skill and knowledge, often to create competitive advantage. But prospective users may be encouraged to learn that despite the fascination with applying the new technology to more sensational tasks like space exploration or warfare, some of the greatest opportunities for expert systems lie in small, everyday tasks like credit verification or capital budgeting analysis.

Excerpted from Dorothy Leonard-Barton and John J. Sviokla, "Putting Expert Systems to Work," *Harvard Business Review,* March–April 1988, pp. 91–103.

A general expert systems schematic is shown in Figure 3.15. It shows the expert system monitoring operations, managing robots, or interacting by natural language with users through a workstation.

An expert system is made up of rules, a knowledge base, and an inference engine. The rules, phrased as IF-THEN statements, represent actions to be taken based on a set of certain conditions occurring. For example, a rule might be phrased as "IF the sky is cloudy (condition), THEN take an umbrella (action)." The knowledge base of an expert system consists of facts about a specific body of knowledge or domain. It also contains rules based on heuristics to limit the need for a complete search of the domain. The inference engine of an expert system chains together appropriate rules and regulates the order in which inferences are drawn, such that new facts are generated from known facts.

The following scenario may soon become common in the practice of medicine. A patient enters a hospital complaining of dizziness and double vision. He is identified by both name and a bar code from a bracelet attached to his wrist. A nurse feeds his symptoms into an expert system that tentatively diagnoses a brain tumor and recommends a nuclear magnetic resonance brain scan. Other tests confirm the expert system's diagnosis. That afternoon the patient undergoes brain surgery with an assist from expert systems and robotics. Later, the physician

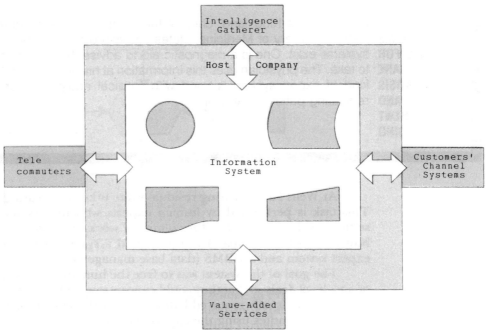

Figure 3.16 The extension component.

on areas where strategic (or tactical) change may yield the greatest payoff to meet or beat the competition. Also, demographic and industrial statistics processed by models can spotlight places where population and industry trends promise to hold the greatest significance as either opportunities or threats. Indeed, strategists wanting to position their companies to cope with the environment or influence it to their advantage, clearly must learn what makes the environment tick.

The need for intelligence can be summarized in the following examples. An executive committee, hot on the acquisition trail, wants a list of potential

BUSINESS INTELLIGENCE The specialized business information now routinely available through public and commercial data bases has transformed pursuit of business knowledge—about competitors, markets, technology—from an occasional luxury to an everyday strategic necessity.

Excerpted from Carolyn M. Vella and John J. McGonagle, Jr., "Spy vs Spy: Competitive Intelligence," *Information Strategy: The Executive's Journal,* Winter 1988, pp. 27–32.

buyout candidates in specific industries accompanied by supporting financial data, forecasts, and comparisons with industry norms. A strategic planner wants to estimate the effect of $20-per-barrel oil on retail sales in oil-producing states. A marketing strategist wants a color-coded map of the number, geographical locations, buying power, and recreational habits of potential customers for a new ski boat.

Intelligence can be gathered from sources such as newspapers, trade journals, government reports, legislative chronicles, industry statistics, demographic studies, marketing surveys, and from the organization's data base. The systems analyst can be effective in providing this information by installing the following procedures:

1. Making publications available for quick dissemination. In some instances, top management may need to research a topic. The system could provide management with information about various topics, ranging from the Industrial Revolution to the 1950 World Series, from the use of biotechnology to the number of cellular phones in the Chicago area, and from the current price of gold on the London market to the number of drilling rigs operating in Alaska.

2. Gathering and summarizing documents from governmental agencies and other groups that affect the organization. Examples of strategic information resulting from this effort include truth in packaging, foreign trade regulations, economic indicators, consumer affairs, foreign exchange rates, tax rulings, stock exchange information, voting trends, cost-of-living indexes, labor trends, projected strikes, and developing technology.

3. Gathering external data, storing it in the data base, and processing it by means of models for reformatting into graphs. Trade associations as well as private organizations provide financial and market data in traditional report form or in a computer-readable format for input to the information system. This type of information shows such things as total sales, market trends, market share, developing markets, and industry averages. For example, census data, readily available from the Census Bureau, can be used to gauge potential markets, to make sales forecasts, to define sales territories, to allocate funds for advertising, to decide on locations for new plants, warehouses, or stores, and to provide general demographic analysis.

Many commercial data bases, most of which are computer based, allow managers to retrieve a variety of data external to the organization. Some examples of these data bases are location, size, and products of plants scattered across the country; statistics of the securities market; abstracts of legislative reports; abstracts of articles from magazines and newspapers; abstracts of medical literature; access to various economic data; appropriate logico-mathematical models and computer programs to drive them; and business ratings.

Often, the systems analyst may designate a physical location or locations where this intelligence is presented. This "place" is usually called a strategic decision center, corporate war room, decision support center, or the intelligence center. Whatever the name, it is a place where top management meet on a periodic basis to discuss issues, receive timely information that relates to these issues, and make strategic decisions. The same result can be obtained, however, by allowing top managers to become involved from their individual offices by means of closed-circuit television and teleconferencing facilities.

Equipment and media, which can be used to support a strategic decision center, include television, video and audio tape, computer output to microfilm (COM), copiers, computers, movie projectors, telecommunications, and color graphs and tables displayed by cathode-ray tube (CRT) devices. Management should be able to access information on its own through access codes provided in a directory. For example, to access the return on investment profile of Division A, an authorized manager simply keys into a terminal the code ROI-A. Return on investment information for Division A, along with trends and comparisons, is displayed immediately in graphical form. Some other types of information (e.g., research material) might require assistance from technical support staff.

Computer vendors offer a variety of terminals and software designed to produce graphics. Users can obtain digital plotters for multicolor, camera-ready output and overhead transparencies, as well as hard-copy devices that reproduce paper copies of the screen at a touch of a button. Technology that uses color liquid crystal displays or electroluminescent panels offers superb graphics resolution, better than that found on home television sets and can generate all forms of graphs in eight or more colors.

Graphs, in the form of bar charts, trend charts, histographs, and pie charts, are convenient and timely instruments for summarizing data in a format that gives management the "big picture." Management can spot trends quickly and get early warning signals. Because graphs filter out extraneous detail they also give strong support to the filtering method.

Customers' Channel Systems

By connecting the company's information system to customers' information systems, the company positions itself strategically to differentiate its products and services significantly from its competitors. Here, systems analysts view information systems design from an entrepreneurial perspective by following a simple marketing credo: "Make sure the system is providing what the customer wants and needs."

All encounters with the company's information system should be helpful and functional. Immediate processing of orders, for example, results in quicker deliveries, better cash flow, and less paperwork. Such customer channel systems enable customers to enter repeat orders and track them through operations.

Videotex can be used to provide product and service information and to announce new products and services, price changes, future promotions, and so forth. Such a coupling builds customer loyalty and establishes smoother relations. In addition, salespeople can gather intelligence about competitors and markets and transmit it to the home office for better strategic planning and decision making. Product information, especially that dealing with design flaws, can be transmitted directly to engineering for redesign.

The simple idea of point of sale has had a tremendous impact on the grocery and retail trade, and its application will continue to expand to other industries (e.g., manufacturing for materials routing and airlines for baggage handling). Laser-scanning registers get customers through the line quicker. The system automatically reorders merchandise directly from the supplier when stock gets low. Some retailers have installed online banking services as well as information kiosks to provide financial and merchandise information. Fidelity Investment, Incorporated, of Boston, for example, opened customer service centers to provide an array of investment information to investors. Walking into a center, investors first encounter kiosks with literature about different services, prospectuses, and applications for each fund. A 90-foot electronic stock ticker flashes overhead displaying the hourly prices of the 35 single-industry funds that make up the Fidelity Select Portfolio. A bank of hotlines are linked to Fidelity's telecommunications network for investors who need additional information.

Value-Added Systems

In the past, many "information systems" were viewed by management and other users as "necessary evils," nothing more than facilities to process transactions and prepare payrolls. A new generation of entrepreneurially minded systems analysts strongly believe that information systems can be valuable resources to the host organization as well as revenue generators. This philosophy is not mere fluff because we are beginning to see the emergence of information systems that have value-added components.

The information system of Weyerhaeuser sells a number of its information processing modules, such as accounting and timber tract management. American Airlines' Sabre System provides complete travel service for fliers as well as processing services for other airlines. United Airlines is now competing with its Apollo System. American Express, long known primarily for its credit card and travel-oriented businesses, is one of a number of major companies that has found great opportunities in providing a wide range of financial services through sophisticated information systems. It has more than quadrupled its business within the last five years. Several years ago, Sears decided that its network and networking expertise was extensive enough to support a profitable business in its own right as a value-added reseller. The company, therefore, created a wholly owned subsidiary to sell communication services to users outside the company who did not have a private network of their own.

Because of aggressive use of information technology, Skandinaviska Enskilda Banken of Sweden can offer to deduct customers' checking account funds and transfer them directly to creditors. They not only pay monthly bills such as mortgages but also handle anything from purchase of stocks and bonds to childcare expenses. In addition, S. E. Banken provides these services for individuals along with a slew of commercial services for business clients from cash management programs to foreign exchange.

S. E. Banken has established its information system as an independent business within a business. This approach frees up systems analysts to look for additional revenue-producing services for old and new customers. They also offer their proprietary systems to banks in Europe and the United States. Their systems analysts' philosophy is: "The world is in real time, therefore all systems should be in real time."[2]

Is it, therefore, any wonder that more and more financial analysts are looking hard at companies' information systems to determine if they are worthy investment candidates?

Telecommuters

A mix of enhanced telecommunications media, hard-disk storage, graphics, computer-based video teleconferencing, and applications software has made a large portion of office work virtually time and space free. Spurred by this vast array of new sophisticated information technology, the business world is extending office networks to include telecommuters (i.e., employees who work outside corporate buildings and who receive and transmit most of their work through workstations and telecommunications media, such as satellites and telephones).

Telecommunications networks and the portability of computers from notebook-size to multifunctional, stand-alone workstations will allow people to do their work wherever they are or want to be—main office, branch office, motel, airplane, or home—especially in the home. Moreover, workstations are being designed to permit the handicapped, the blind, and even paraplegics to operate workstations from their homes and become full-fledged members of the work force.

Two main groups of at-home workers are independents, such as consultants, writers, professionals, and craftspersons, and those people who do not have to go to the office or plant every day to get their work done. Their work can be "telecommuted."

Work away from the office or plant is often more easily arranged in situations in which certain tasks can be performed individually and relatively independently of the work of others. Even in situations in which a sharing of work and coordination is handled electronically, the workers can be eyeball-to-eyeball or miles apart—it makes little difference. Clearly, at-home work gives systems analysts a whole new array of design possibilities because they can expand the boundaries of conventional networks and plug in nodes almost any place they choose.

At-home work, however, may have its drawbacks. If they seldom come in contact with fellow workers, telecommuters can be socially, intellectually, and professionally isolated. In some instances, work and home life simply will not mix unless "home and family" time is separated from "work" time. Also, not everyone has the temperament to work at home. Some people do not have a self-starter button; they need direct supervision and someone to "crack the whip." They need someone to get them organized and give them step-by-step directions. On the management side, some managers cannot break away from the "9-to-5-if-you're-not-at-your-desk-you're-not-working" syndrome. They simply cannot, or believe they cannot, do an effective job of managing their people unless their

---

[2]Janet Fiderio, "MIS Profit, Swedish Style," *Computerworld*, August 10, 1987, pp. 63–68.

TELE- COMMUTING NOT FOR EVERYONE	Telecommuting has been used effectively by some computer programmers as well as people involved in writing, editing, word processing, and data entry. These people usually work alone at tasks that require little space, equipment, or face-to-face contact. Surveys indicate that telecommuters are typically males in their 30s to mid 40s; they are more likely than other workers to be self-employed, and they produce better quality work and suffer from fewer distractions as they work.

Excerpted from Paul Gray, "Examining End-User Computing," *Journal of Information Systems Management,* Winter 1988, pp. 84–85.

people are close at hand and under the manager's wings. And, finally, some labor authorities fear that at-home work will turn our economy into one based on "sweat-cottage" industries where the "boss man" is an electronic pacing monitor.

3.4 SELF-SERVICE INFORMATION SYSTEMS: AN INNOVATIVE DESIGN TWIST

Following the lead of Skandinaviska Enskilda Banken described earlier that established its information system as a business within a business, let's go one step farther and apply an entrepreneurial twist to make "the business-within-a-business approach" a self-service information system (S-SIS). Such an approach follows a do-it-yourself trend established early on by distributed data processing (DDP). It abides by design forces, especially integration, user/system interface, competitive forces, information quality and usability, cost effectiveness, and human factors. From the users' viewpoint, the self-service idea mirrors their self-reliance and self-sufficiency. A significant point made by James Martin, a leading information systems authority, is that over 70 percent of users' needs can be served if these users are given the tools to develop their own applications.

Genesis of Self-Service Information Systems

Because the S-SIS is a business within a business, *all* users are considered system customers. They are treated like any customers of businesses that offer self-service products or services. For example, the self-service supermarket was a creative response to the needs of a growing and more highly urbanized population for a method of distribution that significantly reduces operating costs and selling prices as well as provides a wider assortment of merchandise and services under one roof. The aim of entrepreneurially developed information systems is the same as these marketers', which is to respond creatively to the needs of a growing and more sophisticated population of end users and develop a method of distribution that will significantly reduce operating costs as well as provide a wider assortment of information and task support.

**DECISION
SUPPORT:
A BIG
PAYOFF OF
S-SIS**

Decision support systems (DSSs) are not decision-making systems; they are systems that assist in decision making. A DSS can be used not only for what-if analysis, but to examine different ranges of probability for a given objective or set of conditions. It can be used to determine the sensitivity of a given variable to other variables—before the user decides what to do about it. Working in reverse, a DSS can start with a given condition and help determine which conditions and variables will achieve that objective.

Excerpted from H. Gerald Moody, "Decisions, Decisions," *Information Strategy: The Executive's Journal,* Winter 1988, pp. 43–46.

System customers do not want to ask permission from anyone to use the information system. They want the freedom to use the system as they choose without being intimidated by cryptic protocols or waiting "forever" to obtain access to information. As do customers in a retail store who select the quantity, size, color, and style of the merchandise, systems customers want to be able to access by themselves the appropriate function and quantity and kind of information they need to get their jobs done. The concern of overwhelming the systems customer with too much information or the wrong kind of information becomes irrelevant in a S-SIS.

S-SISs have the qualities of personalization and autonomy. Being built with the concept of connectivity in mind, they are also highly integrated and cooperative. Information from S-SISs travels in all directions throughout the network so decisions can be influenced and acted upon at many different points outside the strict functional boundaries of organizations. Communication flows freely across disparate groups and quasi-political boundaries, and even into stakeholders' organizations.

The Self-Service Information Systems Model

A general model of a S-SIS is illustrated in Figure 3.17. Besides the building block part, which is common to all information systems, the model of a S-SIS contains four other parts, each of which is discussed next.

Taxonomy

The taxonomy makes S-SISs full-fledged, all-inclusive information systems that serve the needs of system customers and stakeholders. Functions that permeate the entire organization are integrated from the shop floor to the executive suite. The system processes transactions necessary for collecting money, paying bills, meeting payrolls, generating quarterly financial statements, and keeping governments' bureaucratic leviathans well fed. But in addition to these traditional processing tasks, it performs a variety of office procedures (some refer to this as office automation) and information processing for technical operations such

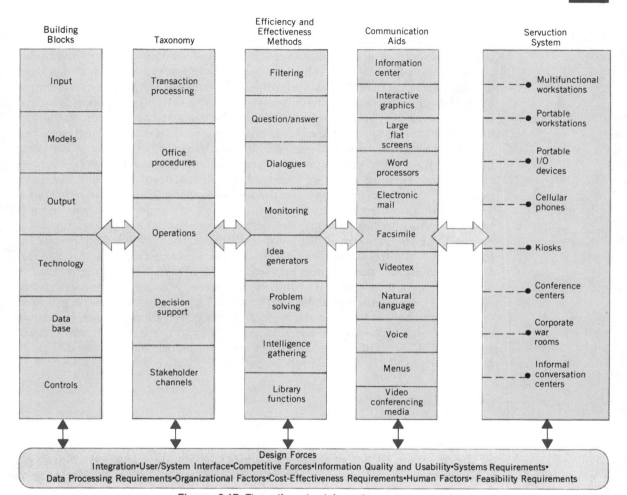

Figure 3.17 The self-service information systems model.

as cost accounting, inventory control, computer-integrated manufacturing, and computer-aided design. It also provides decision support for all levels. This support is based primarily on the model's building block that includes scenario analysis, expert systems, anticipatory models, and the like. Also, a number of channels allow the system to interact with and provide information to a variety of stakeholders.

Efficiency and Effectiveness

Clearly the aim of systems analysts is to build S-SISs that are more efficient, effective, and human serving. To achieve this objective, the systems analyst can bring to bear on the S-SIS several of the components presented earlier in this chapter. For example, one way to make the S-SIS more efficient is to filter the amount of detail provided to each level of decision maker. Another is to incorporate the question/answer component so that users are allowed to pose a number of questions and receive answers and recommendations from the models and data base of the S-SIS or other customers of the system. A similar component lets customers carry on a dialogue with the system and other system customers or stakeholders through bulletin boards, message systems, or expert systems. Implementing the monitoring component reduces the toil in the workaday world because the S-SIS does all the work of looking at gobs of data, ferreting out significant variables, keeping tabs on critical success factors, continuously comparing actual events with expected events, making thousands of low-level decisions, and keeping track of hundreds of instructions. By using the idea generator, customers can enter into the system a particular situation or scenario and receive a number of ideas from other system customers, which in effect is brainstorming through systems. Problem solving is similar to generating ideas except a specific problem is displayed throughout the network and anyone on the network who has expertise applicable to that problem responds. Also, in this context, the Delphi method may be used. Intelligence gathering means that the S-SIS is designed to extend beyond the corporate walls to gather intelligence useful to strategic and tactical decision makers. This intelligence can be gathered from sources such as newspapers, trade journals, government reports, legislative chronicles, industry statistics and standards, demographic studies, and market surveys. This method makes a number of publications and synopses of these publications available to customers according to their research interests.

Communication Aids

Communication aids are those devices and procedures that connect the S-SIS structure to the servuction system. The servuction system is how customers interact with the S-SIS. The communication aids enhance the quality and usability of this interface by fitting a mix of cognitive styles. As a general rule, voice, natural languages and symbols, graphics, and images are more effective ways to communicate information than numbers and text. For the most part, the type of communication in a S-SIS is in the form of a communication aid such as video, graphs, or reports as distinguished from person-to-person communication. The objective, however, is to use the communication aids in ways to emulate the same kind of communication enjoyed in person-to-person communication in either dyads or larger groups.

The information center helps system customers to understand and use the system. Interactive graphics are more amenable to right-brained people and for summarizing mountains of data. Large flat screens are more appropriate for a variety of output, such as demonstration of a new product. Word processing is readily available to help all who have manuscripts, reports, and letters to prepare or to combine material from a number of system customers who are working on the same project. Electronic mail reduces the problems and duration experienced with traditional mail systems. Facsimile and videotex extend customers' ability to both receive and transmit lengthy messages quickly. Natural languages, voice, and menus provide friendly and easy-to-use ways for customers to communicate with the system. Video conferencing media reduce travel time and increase the productivity of a variety of system customers who, in the past, have had to attend a number of meetings remote from where they work.

Servuction System

The servuction system is the interface between customers and the system; it represents the location of the system customers and the way they are served. The use of S-SISs is independent of physical constraints because the servuction system is not a place per se that system customers and stakeholders have to go to be served. They can use the system *wherever they are,* (i.e., in offices, on the shop floor, in the warehouse, at home, in a hotel, or in transit). The servuction system provides a wider array of system customers and stakeholders with the means to interact, cooperate, share, and communicate over short or long distances in a wider variety of forms than was ever possible before.

Office functions will obviously continue, but their physical embodiments in large, fixed office buildings will diminish, if not disappear, because more people will be working from their homes or neighborhood work centers. Time and distance are of little significance and do not pose constraints in the servuction system. Less emphasis on 9-to-5 work will result along with a diminution of the dreaded rush hour and long commute. Moreover, the servuction system will accommodate people who like to work early, those who like to work late, those on an irregular schedule, part-timers, and the handicapped.

Local functionality is provided by a number of devices that directly connect system customers to all that the S-SIS provides. The multifunctional workstation is provided to assist all kinds of system customers, such as managers, accountants, engineers, or clerks. It performs most of the tasks provided by the S-SIS. Portable workstations, other I/O devices, and cellular phones are provided to allow system customers to go practically anywhere and still be connected to the system. Kiosks are open, pavilion-like structures that permit customers to enter so that they can interact with the system in a variety of ways and also receive special training on new applications. Conference centers are obviously connected to video conferencing media and allow customers to hold meetings without traveling to remote locations. Intelligence is presented in corporate war rooms. All aspects of the servuction system are ergonomically designed. But, in addition, it has relaxation or conversation areas designed to bring people together to socialize and unwind. It humanizes the work environment and gives people a chance to discuss common problems in a relaxed atmosphere. Moreover, auxiliary components of the servuction system might include creche facilities for working parents and physical fitness centers. Also, other facilities could be installed to provide system customers with teleshopping, telebanking, or anything else that would help reduce the "hassle" factor.

Connectivity: The Key to S-SISs

Connectivity of geographically dispersed locations is the key to building integrated S-SISs. With the arrival of the integrated services digital network (ISDN) telecommunications standard, unprecedented network capabilities are available on demand, giving system customers convenient, inexpensive access to almost any voice, data, and image service. Indeed, ISDN permits a large and varied portfolio of network capabilities as well as a rich source of accessibility, flexibility, functionality, and ubiquity—the prime payoffs of connectivity.

Moreover, technological developments, such as low-cost very-small-aperature terminal (VSAT) systems combined with high-powered satellites not only add to connectivity but provide networks that are becoming more and more economical. On the heels of this is an imminent explosion in the use of fiber optics with its huge bandwidth, accuracy, security, immunity to interference, durability, and low cost.

SUMMARY

The challenge facing systems analysts today is to develop information systems that assist organizations in competing in the global marketplace. To meet this challenge, the character of the systems they develop must change. Systems analysts should adopt an innovative, entrepreneurial approach to information systems so that harmony and support is created in the workplace. They should view unfilled information needs as an opportunity space populated by potential users. Systems analysts should also strive to make information systems more effective and efficient. One way to do this is by filtering the data so that users are provided with more information and less data. Another way the innovative systems analyst can make an information system more effective and efficient is by incorporating into the system monitoring and interaction components between it and its users.

The time is ripe for innovative systems analysts to enhance the quality of information systems by adding expert system components and by extending information systems beyond the internal boundaries of the organization. Intelligence about the external environment can be gathered and combined with proprietary internal data so executives are better prepared to combat competition. The organization's information system can be connected to customers' information systems so that what it sells can be differentiated from its competitors' products and services.

The next step for innovative systems analysts to take is to treat the information system as a business-within-a-business and develop self-service information systems. These self-service information systems will have the qualities of being fitted to the personalities of users, providing them with a significant increase in autonomy of action. Being built on the concept of connectivity, self-service information systems will also be highly integrated and cooperative.

IMPORTANT TERMS

automatic notification

communication aids

connectivity

corporate war room

customers' channel systems

effectiveness

efficiency

expert systems

feedback

filtering

inference engine

information center

integrated services digital network (ISDN)

intelligence gatherer

interaction

key variables

knowledge base

monitoring

programmed decision making

robotics

self-service information system (S-SIS)

servuction system

telecommuters

unfilled information needs

value-added systems

variance or exception reporting

very-small-aperature terminal (VSAT)

workstation

Assignment

REVIEW QUESTIONS

3.1 What has been the reaction of people in organizations who have been frustrated by irresponsibleness and long development cycles of information systems?

3.2 How do innovative systems analysts view the organization? Based on this view, what activities are supported by information systems?

3.3 What is the mechanist's or technocrat's approach to building information systems? How does the approach of innovative systems analyst differ?

3.4 List five components that can be brought to bear by the innovative analyst to increase the efficiency and effectiveness of the information system.

3.5 What is the major advantage of having the information system filter data? What are the disadvantages of having the information system serve as a data filter?

3.6 List four ways the information system can serve as a monitor?

3.7 In an organizational context, define the phrase "key variables" or critical success factors?

3.8 What is the key device that makes the interaction component more effective and efficient?

3.9 What are the three parts of an expert system? Identify the purpose of each part of an expert system.

3.10 List four ways information systems can be extended beyond the walls of the host organization.

3.11 Identify three ways a systems analyst can adapt the information system to assist management in coping with strategic change.

3.12 What is the major benefit of connecting a company's information system to a customer's information system?

3.13 Define the term "telecommuter."

3.14 Besides the six building blocks common to all information systems, what other parts make up a self-service information system?

3.15 What is the purpose of the servuction system component of a self-service information system?

3.16 What is the key to building integrated self-service information systems? What technological developments have been instrumental in enabling this key element to be applied economically?

QUESTIONS FOR DISCUSSION

3.17 Do you agree that an information system should be designed to report all variances between actual and expected values? Would your answer be influenced by the capability of an information system to act as a filterer of data? Should significant variances be reported to the individuals who are responsible for the variances, their manager, or both?

3.18 "It really doesn't matter what kind of changes are made to our information systems. There will always be too much paperwork and red tape." Comment on this statement.

3.19 "A financial institution has to learn to live with pieces of paper that signify transactions. People and systems can't cope with a paperless world." Do you agree or disagree? Why?

3.20 How will telecommuting offer more handicapped, and otherwise homebound people, the opportunity to become a part of the work force? Also discuss the benefits of telecommuting with respect to travel time to and from work, energy consumption, and wear-and-tear on both vehicles and employees.

3.21 How has the introduction of personal computers into the business world caused information fragmentation in some companies? How could this situation be reversed to realize greater benefits from information systems?

3.22 Point-of-sale (POS) transactions are entered into the information system immediately as they occur. How is this technique important in extending information systems outside the walls of a corporation?

3.23 What can be done to change the attitude that information systems are necessary evils to process transactions and prepare payroll?

3.24 A trend is appearing in large companies toward more interactive information systems with distributed processing capabilities. Can a highly centralized, autocratic information system be compatible with this trend? Explain your answer.

3.25 "Users don't know what they want in a system. They can't articulate their information needs, and, quite frankly, just get in our (the information systems development group) way when we build systems for them." What is wrong with this viewpoint on the role of users as system customers?

3.26 How does connectivity fit into the overall scheme of building integrated self-service information systems?

EXERCISES AND PROBLEMS

The following narrative is used to work exercises and problems 3.27 through 3.30.

    Top Dollar Department Stores, Inc., is considering opening two new stores in the city where the original store is located. Tom Lee, owner, has decided to consolidate the operations of all three stores and to provide necessary data processing, administration, payroll, purchasing, and credit transaction processing from a centralized office.

    Top Dollar currently sells merchandise on a cash-only basis and uses a manual bookkeeping system. Mr. Lee has personally supervised the day-to-day operations of the original store for the past 15 years, having taken over the business from his retired father. Mr. Lee is overly suspicious of his employees, and he believes no one can be trusted, not even his senior employee of 13 years. Only he handles the cash and mans the cash register at all times. He also takes care of the purchasing, payroll, and personnel functions after the store closes. Four sales clerks work at the store attending customers, stocking shelves, and running errands. Mr. Lee counts all inventory himself and has the only key to the store.

Mr. Lee's CPA has advised him to start granting credit to his customers once all three stores are in operation. At first, Mr. Lee was hesitant to agree with the CPA's recommendation, but now, to realize increased sales revenue, he has agreed to grant credit.

The CPA, after studying the information needs of the new organization, recommends complete automation of the business. After endless attempts to persuade him of the wisdom of computerizing the business, Mr. Lee finally agreed to converting to a computer-based system but warned that he would not spend any money on fancy gimmicks or gadgets.

3.27 List and discuss the information requirements created by the decision to start granting credit to Top Dollar's customers, especially in terms of an accounts receivable function.

3.28 Use a diagram to trace credit sales through Top Dollar's individual systems components listed. Provide a brief narrative of what information each component of the system uses and what documents are prepared at each station.

1. Billing clerk
2. Accounts receivable clerk
3. Credit approval clerk
4. Collector
5. Sales clerk

3.29 Draw an appropriate configuration of the system necessary to network the three stores and main office into one complete information system. Assume Mr. Lee's autocratic management style is basically still intact. Explain your choice of network topology.

3.30 1. Discuss how Mr. Lee's management style constrains the development of the information system for the business.
2. Include in your answer an evaluation of the advantages and disadvantages of both centralized and decentralized systems management.
3. In your opinion, will Mr. Lee's managerial attitude enhance or detract from the expected growth in sales? Explain.

3.31 A multifunctional workstation offers a variety of features to complement the skills of the user. The workstation makes the user more efficient by providing quick access to needed information sources. Drawing from the workstation features illustrated in Figure 3.14, design a workstation for each of the following employees.

1. An industrial engineer
2. An administrative assistant
3. A strategic-level manager
4. A secretary

3.32 Assume you have been hired to design a report for Mrs. Ruppy, owner of a recreational vehicle dealership. She would like to have a monthly record of sales in terms of units and dollars. The report should show year-to-date totals for both categories. Additionally, the owner would like to know how the current month compares with last year. She would also like to have variances from quotas highlighted in the report. Finally, Mrs. Ruppy would like all the foregoing data for each of three brands of RVs she sells.

3.33 A manufacturer of electronic environmental controls services more than 100 construction firms throughout the region. The company receives an average of about 12 customer orders a day. The electronic controls are manufactured both to stock and to order. Shipping papers are prepared daily by a computer. The shipping department maintains a hard-copy file of orders to be shipped during the last five days and orders to be shipped, because it is not always possible (or necessary) to ship an order the same day it is received.

A computer-based inventory reporting system produces an inventory status report. This report is available each morning at 8 A.M. and includes production and shipping activity as of 5 P.M. the preceding day. Production scheduling prepares a schedule each Friday indicating the products to be manufactured, the quantity, and the production date for the following two-week period. The customer service department receives 10 to 20 calls a day concerning customer order status and availability of finished goods.

Following are 10 typical questions received by customer service. Indicate which questions can be answered by the available information described previously and which questions require still more information.

1. Has my order of a week ago been shipped yet?
2. How much is my account balance?
3. Can you ship me 30 units of product X today?
4. I placed a customer order a month ago to be delivered next week. Can I cancel my order?
5. Why did I receive only a partial order last month?
6. Has my account been credited for the returns last week?
7. Do you have any of product Y available for shipment this month?
8. Is it possible to substitute product A for product B in my order next week?
9. What is my new salesperson's name?
10. Are you still selling product D?

3.34 The organizational information system is highly sensitive to changes within the organization. Almost all management-initiated change results in adjustments to current information needs. Four such changes are listed. Evaluate the likely impact of the changes on the information system of that organization.

1. A local machine shop is unionized.
2. A department store suspends use of its own credit cards.
3. A manufacturing concern acquires its major supplier.
4. A municipality adds a budget planning department.

3.35 Design a document to record sales transactions for a furniture business. Assume the business provides free delivery within the city limits. Describe how the computer-based information system would keep track of unpaid customer accounts.

3.36 Suggest several key variables you would monitor for control purposes in each of the following businesses:

1. Gasoline station
2. Fast-food restaurant
3. Travel bureau
4. Shopping mall
5. Resort hotel

3.37 The Blue Cab Company serves a large metropolitan area and employs approximately 200 cabs and 500 drivers. Recently, the accounting department reported that insurance coverage for Blue Cab is increasing at a rate 15 percent faster than comparable cab companies throughout the nation. Additionally, revenues as a result of lower cab fares and reduced number of trips have been trailing company forecasts by 17 percent. The president of Blue Cab believes that some of this lackluster performance is due to a less than aggressive policy of evaluating individual drivers' performances. Consequently, the president has requested that a reporting system be designed that would evaluate those aspects of a driver's performance most closely related to insurance premiums and requests for cab service.

The following statistics are made available to you, a systems analyst in the Blue Cab Company:

1. Traffic citations have averaged close to 1,000 a year for the last three years.
2. Cabs are involved in an average of 37 accidents a week, 35 of which are considered minor "fender benders" and 2 of which involve some form of personal injuries claim.
3. Customer service people handle between 5 and 75 customer complaints for long waiting time, abusive language, poor service, and so on. Complaints average about 25 per day. Each reported complaint, accident, and traffic citation is logged by day, by driver, by cab number, and by time of day.

From the data given and using the variances reporting method, develop a monthly report for the president reflecting driver performance.

3.38 Martini and Associates, a corporation operating in southern New Jersey, specializes in verifying claims of individuals and businesses against insurance companies. Most of its business comes from insurance companies that do not have adjusters in the area.

In the last two years the number of insurance claims adjustments has increased fivefold. Henry Martini, the president of the company, is seeking ways for his adjusters, especially those with less than one year of experience, to perform their work more proficiently. He has read extensively about expert systems and wonders if adding this type of component could be of help.

All adjusters carry powerful laptop microcomputers with them when they go into the field. At present the micros are used only to store the claimants' interview data. Often this process presents difficulties for new adjusters because they do not know how different insurance companies will classify and process a claim. As a result, new adjusters either collect the wrong data or incomplete data. When another interview is necessary animosity toward the insurance company is created because claimants think they are being badgered. Moreover, the productivity of the adjuster suffers because of the extra time he or she had to invest in the adjustment process.

> ***Required:*** Suggest how the knowledge pervasion component of expert systems could be applied to the process just described. What might be some of the benefits of such an application?

BIBLIOGRAPHY

ALEXANDER, TOM. "Computing with Light at Lightning Speeds." *Fortune*, July 23, 1984.

BORTHICK, A. F., and O. D. WEST. "Expert Systems—A New Tool for the Professional." *Accounting Horizons*, March 1987.

BRETZ, RUDY. *Media for Interactive Communication.* Beverly Hills, Calif.: Sage, 1983.

CHEONG, V. E., and R. A. HIRSCHHEIM. *Local Area Networks.* New York: John Wiley, 1983.

DIX, JOHN. "Sears to Fuse Private Lines into Unified Net." *Computerworld*, November 12, 1984.

DIZARD, JOHN W. "Machines that See Look for a Market." *Fortune,* September 17, 1984.

FERRIS, DAVID, and JOHN CUNNINGHAM. "Local Nets for Micros." *Datamation,* August 1, 1984.

FRANK, HOWARD, and IVAN FRISCH. "Local-Area Nets: What Matters Most to Users." *Computerworld,* November 5, 1984.

GRAY, PAUL. "Examining End-User Computing." *Journal of Information Systems Management,* Winter 1988.

GROSS, JERRY L. "Components Can Be Added Gradually by Logically Mapping Out Present, Future Uses." *IE,* June 1984.

HABRECHT, HERBERT Z. "Is There a Best Way to Deliver Data Services?" *ABA Banking Journal,* October 1984.

HODGE, BARTOW, ROBERT A. FLECK, JR., and C. BRIAN HONESS. *Management Information Systems.* Reston, Va.: Reston Publishing, 1984.

HOLSAPPLE, CLYDE W., and ANDREW B. WHINSTON. *Business Expert Systems.* Homewood, Ill.: Richard D. Irwin, 1987.

HOWELL, ROBERT A., and STEPHEN R. SOUCY. "Management Reporting in the New Manufacturing Environment." *Management Accounting,* February 1988.

"Keying Shippers into EDI." *Railway Age,* March 1987.

LANCASTER, KATHLEEN LANDIS, ed. *International Telecommunications.* Lexington, Mass.: Lexington Books, D. C. Heath, 1982.

LEONARD-BARTON, DOROTHY, and JOHN J. SVIOKLA. "Putting Expert Systems to Work." *Harvard Business Review,* March–April 1988.

LIPNACK, JESSICA and JEFFREY STAMPS. *Networking.* Garden City, N.Y.: Doubleday, 1982.

LOUIS, ARTHUR M. "The Great Electronic Mail Shootout." *Fortune,* August 20, 1984.

MICOSSI, ANITA. "The Ten-Second Commute." *PC World.* December 1984.

MOODY, H. GERALD. "Decisions, Decisions." *Information Strategy: The Executive's Journal,* Winter 1988.

OTWAY, HARRY J., and MALCOLM PELTU, eds. *New Office Technology: Human and Organizational Aspects.* Norwood, N.J.: Ablex Publishing, 1983.

SACHS, JONATHAN. "Local Area Networks." *PC World,* July 1984.

SINGLETON, LOY A. *Telecommunications in the Information Age.* Cambridge, Mass.: Ballinger, 1983.

TEICHOLZ, ERIC. "Computer Integrated Manufacturing." *Datamation,* March 1984.

VELLA, CAROLYN M., and JOHN J. MCGONAGLE, JR. "Spy vs Spy: Competitive Intelligence." *Information Strategy: The Executive's Journal,* Winter 1988.

WOMELDORFF, THOMAS, "The Pursuit of Data Integration." *Computerworld,* November 12, 1984.

YOUNG, ROBERT E., and RICHARD MAYER. "The Information Dilemma: To Conceptualize Manufacturing as an Information Process." *IE,* September 1984.

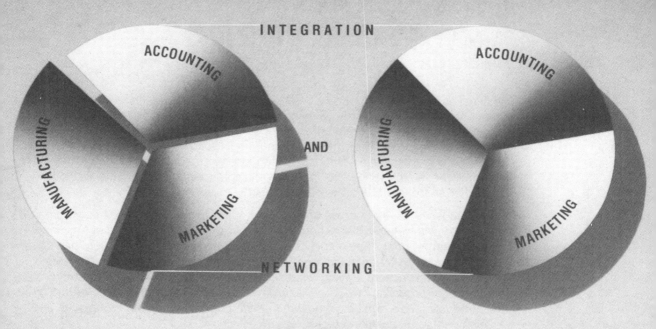

INTEGRATION AND NETWORKING

PART 2

INFORMATION SYSTEMS

DIMENSIONS AND STRUCTURES

Businesses have been traditionally organized along the functional lines of marketing, manufacturing, and accounting. Accordingly, the general character of the information systems that were built to support transaction processing and decision making specific to each of these functions is described in Chapter 4. Although accomplishing their major purpose of supporting these business functions, the information systems tended to be highly compartmentalized, unable to work in concert or share information with each other.

In the 1980s we have observed a new era of management thinking. Integration is the byword, with organizational goal congruency being placed ahead of functional or departmental goal attainment. The old, function-specific information systems are being replaced by or linked together into fully integrated information systems, as shown in the accompanying window. Chapter 5 examines how this trend to integration of organizations' information systems is being further accelerated by the introduction of a number of new manufacturing concepts and techniques and developments in networking technology.

4
FUNCTION-SPECIFIC INFORMATION SYSTEMS

4.1 INTRODUCTION

Traditionally, businesses have been organized along functional lines. A function is an action or process for which a person or activity is specially fitted or used. Marketing is a classic example of a necessary function in any business.

While commonalities run through function-specific information systems, each system also has to be modified and designed to match the industry in which the business operates. For example, an information system that supports the accounting function of an oilwell service company differs in many respects from an information system that supports the accounting function of a hospital. Also, the amount and variety of transactions dictate the degree of simplicity or complexity of the information system needed.

The objectives of this chapter are:

1. To introduce the information systems that support the accounting, manufacturing, and marketing functions.
2. To show how information systems are comprised of a number of subsystems or modules that support the vital subfunctions of accounting, manufacturing, and marketing.
3. To describe the informational outputs of these modules.

4.2 INFORMATION SYSTEMS THAT SUPPORT ACCOUNTING

Information systems that support the accounting function have always played important roles in organizations. As far back as civilization can be traced, groups of people have relied on some kind of system to record obligations and account for goods in storage. Then, entries to accounts may have been recorded on clay tablets or sticks. Today, the purpose of accounting is the same, but accounting data are processed by computers and accounting records are kept on magnetic storage media.

Information System Overview

A typical accounting-specific information system is depicted in Figure 4.1. Discussed in the following sections are each of the information system modules that support accounting subfunctions, as shown in the schematic.

Ledgers, Chart of Accounts, and Journals

The general ledger is the foundation or core of the information system that supports the accounting function. The general ledger contains the chart of accounts necessary to prepare the balance sheet, income statement, and other reports. An abridged chart of accounts is shown in Figure 4.2.

The numbers attached to the accounts are unique codes to aid in control and computer processing. For example, account numbers 100–399 represent assets; 400–499, liabilities; 500–599, equities; 600–699, revenue; and 700–799, expenses. If the systems analyst wants more detail, then another coding scheme could be used, such as 600–689, operating revenue; 690–699, other revenue; 700–749, cost of goods sold; 750–799, operating expenses; 800–850, marketing expenses; 851–899, administrative expenses; and 900–950, taxes, licenses, and fees.

The chart of accounts coding system can be made as extensive and descriptive as the systems analyst chooses. For example, a code of 6104378 could mean 610 for sale of a minicomputer represented by credit sale revenue from minicomputer category; 4 for Division 4; Warehouse 37; and type 8 customer, which is private secondary education. Indeed, such a coding system adds to the flexibility of the information system. Moreover, it is more efficient for computer

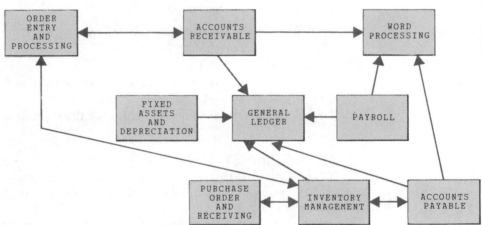

Figure 4.1   Schematic of an information system that supports the accounting function.

CHARTS FOR ALL REASONS Executive Data Systems, Incorporated (EDSI), has launched a business accounting software series for IBM PS/2 and PC compatibles that features charts of accounts for about 60 different businesses ranging from accounting firms to tugboat operators.

Excerpted from Robert Snowdon Jones, "EDSI Accounting Package Features Industry Charts," *InfoWorld*, January 4, 1988, p. 20.

processing. By using these kind of codes, or even more extensive ones, computer programs can quickly sort and extract data from the files and prepare financial statements and a variety of other management reports. In some companies, codes are expanded to over 70 digits to give even greater detail.

The key to designing a chart of accounts is to set up the accounts to reflect the financial operations of the company now and for at least the next three years

BALANCE SHEET ACCOUNTS

Assets	Liabilities	Equities
100 Checking Account	400 Accounts Payable	500 Common Stock
200 Accounts Receivable	405 Notes Payable	580 Retained Earnings
250 Inventory	410 Taxes Payable	
300 Furniture and Fixtures	450 Mortgage Payable	
301 Equipment		
320 Depreciation—Furniture and Fixtures		
321 Depreciation—Equipment		

INCOME STATEMENT ACCOUNTS

Revenue	Expenses
600 Cash Sales	700 Cost of Goods Sold
620 Credit Sales	750 Advertising Expense
	755 Salary Expense
	760 Utility Expense
	770 Depreciation Expense—Furniture and Fixtures
	771 Depreciation Expense—Equipment
	780 Interest Expense

Figure 4.2 Condensed example of a chart of accounts.

ACCOUNTING SOFTWARE

One measure of an accounting system's performance is its range of functionality. High-end systems are typically sold in modules, with each module representing a separate accounting function. Different manufacturers put different functions in their modules. Thus, what one company sells as a general ledger, another may sell as three separate modules: general ledger, spreadsheet interface, and report writer. Another relevant criterion is the availability of particular accounting functions suited to a particular type of business. For example, a strong manufacturing costing capability would be of little use to a service organization.

Excerpted from Richard Morochove, "High-End Accounting Software," *InfoWorld,* April 25, 1988, pp. 43–55.

"WHAT DO YOU MEAN, WE CAN'T PREPARE OUR ACCOUNTING STATEMENTS FROM THE GENERAL LEDGER?"

You might expect that a $19.6 billion organization would use its accounting systems to generate its year-end statement of financial condition. But at the Education Department in Washington, D.C., the general ledger system just isn't up to the job.

A December 1987 audit by the U.S. General Accounting Office identified the following problems with the agency's financial system:

- It cannot accept and record all relevant payroll expenses and liabilities, such as accumulated leave, from its subsidiary payroll accounting system.
- It fails to record information on receivables, such as collections, accrued interest and insurance premiums.
- It cannot accept much of the data from the department's $2.6 billion college housing loans program because of the incompatibility of the systems.

"Education's general ledger system . . . contains unreliable data because of inadequate and inefficient computer systems that support the general ledger and subsidiary accounting systems," the GAO reported.

The situation was so bad that agency officials had to rely on estimates and other records to prepare the annual financial report to the U.S. Department of the Treasury. "Education officials told us that none of the information in the agency's statement of financial condition is drawn from the general ledger," the auditors said.

Taken from Glenn Rifkin and Mitch Betts, "Strategic Systems Plan Gone Awry," *Computerworld,* March 14, 1988, pp. 1, 104–105.

TRADITIONAL ACCOUNTING PACKAGE WITH REPORT GENERATOR

Turbo Paragon is a complete accounting package with all the basic modules. It uses one main input screen for all modules and includes a sophisticated report generator. The menu-driven report writer lets you select data fields for printing. You can choose data on the basis of criteria you specify, perform calculations, and prepare simple graphs to illustrate financial trends.

Excerpted from Richard Morochove, "Midrange Accounting Package Is a Cut Above," *InfoWorld*, February 29, 1988, pp. 55–57.

in the future. Clearly, not all companies are the same and, therefore, do not need the same accounts. For example, a direct marketing company may not have any equipment, so this company would not need an account, such as 301 Equipment. On the other hand, this same company may pay commissions to salespeople. Therefore, an account called, for example, 757 Commission Expense would need to be set up.

When a large number of individual accounts have a common characteristic, it is usual to place them in a separate ledger called a subsidiary ledger. If certain transactions, such as credit sales, become numerous, the need for maintaining a separate account for each creditor is clear. Each subsidiary ledger is represented by a summarizing account in the general ledger called a controlling account. The sum of the balances of the accounts in a subsidiary ledger must agree with the balance of the related controlling account.

Subsidiary ledgers provide data needed for further processing. The accounts receivable subsidiary ledger, for example, produces customer statements and invoices, aged accounts receivable analysis, and customer analyses.

A journal is a chronological listing of transactions. All transactions are initially recorded in a journal and then posted to the appropriate accounts in a ledger. In larger companies with numerous transactions, journals may be specialized. The system is expanded by the systems analyst to replace an all-purpose journal with a number of special journals, each designed to record a single kind of transaction. An enterprise that has many cash transactions may use a special journal for recording cash receipts and another special journal for recording cash disbursements. A company that sells services or merchandise to customers on credit might use a separate credit sales journal designed for recording only such transactions. On the other hand, a business that does not give credit would have no need for such a journal.

Journals control the company's individual transactions by ensuring that all are originally recorded when they occur. If a transaction is later lost or improperly processed, its full details can be checked in the journal. Moreover, many useful reports can be extracted from journals at any time. For example, the treasurer may want to know the level of the capital account balances as of the end of the tenth working day of each month.

ICON APPROACH TO ACCOUNTING Simply Accounting, the latest addition to Bedford Software's accounting line, runs on Apple's Macintosh computer. It is an entry-level accounting package with functions for general ledger, accounts receivable, accounts payable, inventory, payroll, and job costing.

Simply Accounting's screens look like the familiar paper forms you'd produce by hand; this makes it easier to move from a manual to a computer-based accounting system. The main screen displays icons for ledgers for the primary accounting functions as well as the related journals.

When you compare Simply Accounting to higher-priced modular accounting software, it has fewer financial reporting options and an inflexible account structure. For example, in the general ledger, asset accounts must be numbered 1000 to 1999, liabilities 2000 to 2999, and so on. It's a top choice for small businesses who want to start Maccounting.

Excerpted from Richard Morochove, "Accounting Package Has the Basics, Is Easy to Use," *InfoWorld*, March 14, 1988, pp. 53–55.

Accounts Receivable

Accounts receivable arise from sales of merchandise or delivery of services on account and represent claims against debtors, which are generally customers. It is in the accounts receivable module that all customers' accounts are recorded and tracked. A typical profile of the module is shown in Figure 4.3.

When credit sales are made, a variety of data are posted to appropriate customer accounts. When money is received for these sales, the payments reduce customer balances. The accounts receivable module processes invoices, keeps a sales history for each customer, and identifies customers with past-due accounts through a process of aging the accounts receivable.

The accounts receivable module is central to the generation of customer invoices, statements, dunning letters, and mailing labels. A variety of management reports may also be generated based on coding schemes. For example, if sales transactions are coded at a sufficient level of detail, reports may be generated by the information system that identifies sales by customer location, customer type, salesperson, and so forth. Reports produced by the system may rank customers by sales amount and payment history. Furthermore, online inquiries can be made about specific customers. The module can also be designed to maintain sales, cost of goods sold, and salesperson commission figures.

Audit trails are available for both external and internal auditors. These audit trails in the form of audit reports can summarize customer information in customer number sequence, including date and amount of last invoice and last payment, current year-to-date and previous year's sales amounts, and outstanding transactions and account balances. Access to this module can be password protected or use some other security method to safeguard the data.

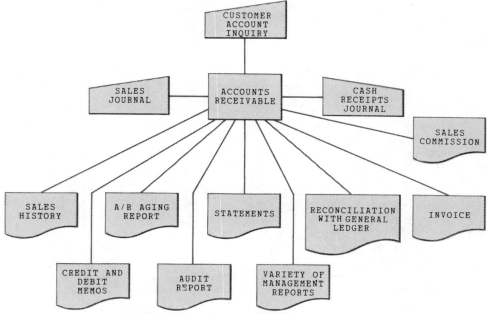

Figure 4.3 An accounts receivable module.

Accounts Payable

Generally, the most common liabilities are recorded in the accounts payable module. This module is like its accounts receivable counterpart except that the debtor-creditor relationship is reversed. A common accounts payable module is depicted in Figure 4.4.

The accounts payable module permits entry of purchases from vendors, editing and verification of invoices, check reconciliation, discount and due-date monitoring of vendor invoices for payment planning, and maintenance of separate ledgers for different companies if necessary. Moreover, this module can produce a variety of reports. It can provide an alphabetical listing of vendors, addresses, telephone numbers, and representatives. The purchase history report provides the date and amount of the last invoice and payment made to each vendor, current year-to-date sales and previous year's purchases, and the number and description of outstanding transactions. Outstanding transactions are grouped into aging categories. This report also provides due dates, discount dates, and past-due invoices. The cash requirements report aids in cash management. Checks are automatically sequenced by vendor name. Advices are recommended to provide details of invoices being paid. Expenses by job, department account number, or any other classification can be made for cost control. Receiving reports are verified against invoices to make sure that the company is receiving what it is being charged for. Shipments returned to vendors are properly credited and corrections made in the accounts. Audit reports contain information similar to the purchase history report and summary information

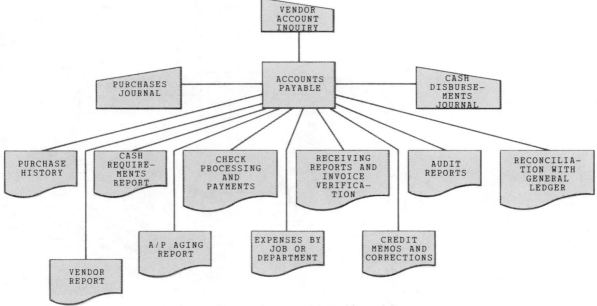

Figure 4.4 An accounts payable module.

from the other reports. This module also interfaces with the general ledger for balancing and control purposes.

Order Entry and Processing

The order-entry and processing module provides the way for customers' orders to get into the system. It can be designed to permit online allocation of inventory at entry time and interface with a number of models (not shown in the figures) for optimum picking and packing procedures, reorder points, safety stock calculations, and forecasting. An order-entry and processing module is shown in Figure 4.5.

Order entry begins the customer's order through the process. Many order-entry and processing modules check credit online, verify product availability, and allocate stock at entry time. They also track active, standing, and future orders, backorders, and orders on hold for credit approval. Order entry's integration with accounts receivable permits the production of an invoice right after the order is entered, or storage of the order data for invoicing at a later date. Order entry can also generate basic operational paperwork, such as bills of lading (a contract between a business and common carrier that describes the shipment, route or mode, consignee, and rates charged for shipping), acknowledgments of customer orders, picking lists (a guide to the person who selects inventory items from a warehouse to fill a customer order), and packing slips indicating the items that make up a particular customer shipment. It provides

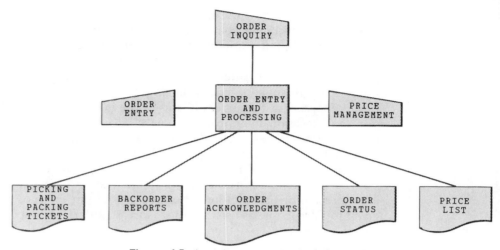

Figure 4.5 An order-entry and processing module.

inquiries on status of orders. It also enables the updating of prices easily. Reports cover general paperwork, price list, and order status.

Inventory Management

Because of the amount of investment and susceptibility of items to misappropriation and misstatement, inventory is one of the most significant assets for many companies. A typical inventory management module is represented in Figure 4.6. This module maintains complete details of items issued and items

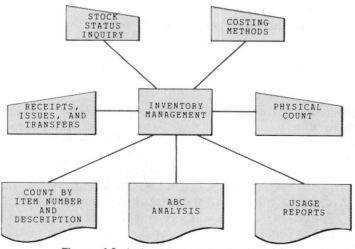

Figure 4.6 An inventory management module.

transferred from one warehouse to another warehouse. Stock status inquiry enables users to know what inventory they have, where it is, and what it costs. The system might use optional costing methods, such as weighted average, first-in, first-out (FIFO), or last-in, first-out (LIFO). Periodically, inventory is counted and reconciled to amounts recorded in the records. All variances are reported for proper investigation and balancing.

Reports provide current counts of the inventory by item number, description, and location if appropriate. ABC analysis divides the inventory into a number of categories, such as A for the most profitable, B for items with average profitability, and C for least profitable. Other categories are provided such as rates of turnover and number of items sold by warehouses. Usage reports list slow-moving items according to user-defined criteria. This report provides early identification of problem items so they can be put on sale. The report can be given to salespeople as an action list. This report also gives overstocked items.

Fixed Assets and Depreciation

Fixed assets often constitute the most significant asset in the balance sheet, and depreciation is usually a material amount in the income statement. But because of the low volume of activity and the long-term nature of these assets, a company's accounting records for fixed assets are not as elaborate as those for other accounts such as accounts receivable, cash, or inventories. A fixed assets and depreciation module is shown in Figure 4.7.

Fixed assets are acquired and are added to a detailed asset ledger. When assets are no longer used by the company, they are retired and deleted from the asset ledger. Often, managers need to know where equipment is being used and the status of such equipment for proper allocation to new jobs as we would find in the construction industry. A variety of depreciation methods, such as straight-line, sum-of-the-years'-digits, or composite-rate methods can be used. Maintenance and repairs are charged to expense as incurred and include the cost of repairing breakdowns.

Reports include depreciation expense for the period, accumulated depreciation, and a list of assets by a variety of categories, such as where used, by type (e.g., all motor graders), by size, by age, and so forth.

Purchase Order and Receiving

This accounting module enables a company to maintain complete purchasing records and ensures the quality, accuracy, and promptness of delivery of purchased items. As is shown in Figure 4.8, it follows the progress of what is ordered from the time of requisition through receipt, inspection, to its placement in warehouses or stores. It also provides a profile of vendor performance showing information such as late and defective shipments matched against standard of all vendors for the current period and for the year to date.

The purchase order and receiving module produces basic paperwork, such as purchase orders, changes to purchase orders, and notices of cancellation of purchases. It reports on the number of items received and their condition. It

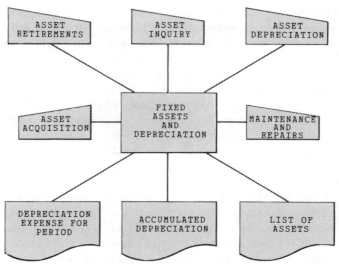

Figure 4.7 A fixed assets and depreciation module.

prepares a report of scheduled receipts by vendor, by item, and by job department.

Payroll

The payroll module handles the complexities of payroll computation, record keeping, payment, and reporting. The module can process the records of hourly, salaried, and piecework employees simultaneously and over a variety of pay frequencies (e.g., daily, weekly, biweekly, semimonthly, four-week, monthly, or

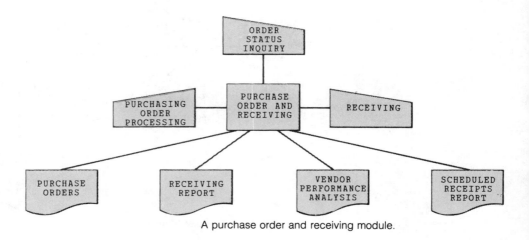

A purchase order and receiving module.

quarterly). It can also accommodate nonstandard earnings such as commissions, bonuses, and tips. A payroll module is outlined in Figure 4.9.

Entries to the payroll module include appropriate tax codes; employee details such as name, department, pay rate, and so forth; deductions such as union dues; reimbursements such as meals or travel; and hours worked, commissions earned, or items produced.

An employee master report is produced that includes information such as employee name, address, Social Security number, department, date of employment, and pay type. Federal form 941 report provides the quarterly tax withholding and liability information required by the federal government. Payroll checks are printed for disbursement. The payroll register summarizes hours worked, gross pay, deductions, tax, and the net pay for the pay period by job or department. The W-2 and 1099 forms are required by the federal government. The unemployment report lists the unemployment tax and insurance contribution made by the company. For each employee, the report lists unemployment insurance amounts for the current month, employee's gross month-to-date and year-to-date earnings, and the amount by which the employee's earnings exceed the wage limit. The withholding report lists employee taxes withheld sequenced by taxing authority and provides totals for each taxing authority and each department. Vacation/sick/compensation time reports include quarter-to-date and year-to-date dollar amounts for vacation, sick time, and compensation, and hours available, hours used, and hours remaining for each employee.

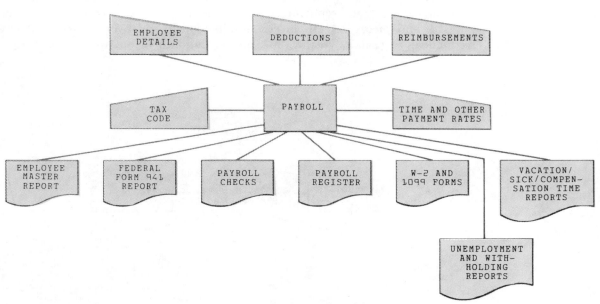

Figure 4.9 A payroll module.

Word Processing

The word processing module is fed by the other accounting information system modules to prepare a variety of letters, documents, and reports. Its functions include cut-and-paste, global search and replace, boiler plate for form letters and other documents, automatic headers and footers, correction spelling, mailing labels, and mail-merge. It includes a number of fonts for bold, shadow, underline, and so forth. It supports any dot-matrix or letter-quality printer. It can also be used to produce a variety of graphics such as histograms, bar charts, line charts, and pie charts to enhance many of the reports.

A DIFFERENT APPROACH TO ACCOUNTING NewViews of Q. W. Page Associates still won't find a place on the shelves of conservative accountants who abhor the way it lets users delete past transactions and lets financial statements get out of balance. Properly installed and used, however, NewViews offers unparalleled flexibility. For best performance, NewViews should be installed on an 80286- or 80386-based machine with a fast hard disk.

NewViews eschews the standard accounting approach, which has a module for each functional area. In New Views, one data base keeps the data for all your financial documents and schedules.

Excerpted from Richard Morochove, "Update of Controversial Accounting Program Counters Critics," *InfoWorld,* January 18, 1988, pp. 53–54.

4.3 INFORMATION SYSTEMS THAT SUPPORT MANUFACTURING

No two manufacturers are exactly the same. Manufacturing can range from highly repetitive to job shop; manufacturing can sell to consumers, other businesses, or the government. Manufacturers may have one plant or multiple plants, and many use several large computers or a single minicomputer. But the one thing all manufacturers have in common is the need for a viable information system that helps them to coordinate and control a variety of operations.

Information System Overview

The goals of the information system that supports any kind of manufacturer are to improve product quality, decrease production costs, reduce engineering development time, and cut set-up and lead time. Moreover, a well-designed information system provides a real-time link between the many applications and automated operations. It ties together all components into a single, streamlined process that extends the product and information flow from concept to design to product completion. A manufacturing-specific information system and its modules necessary to achieve these goals is shown in Figure 4.10.

Master Production Scheduling

The master production scheduling module, which is illustrated in Figure 4.11, provides a formal, systematic way of notifying production what needs to be manufactured over a certain time period. It helps to ensure products will be made and delivered on time and is designed usually to work in a make-to-stock, make-to-order, or assemble-to-order production environment.

Many profit-enhancing factors begin to work when production is planned. Delivery of customer orders is improved, inventory levels are minimized, and efficiencies in the plant take place.

Creation of the master production schedule is derived from a combination of customers orders and sales forecast data. Moreover, the production schedule is monitored against both available resources and known customer orders for adjustment to quantities.

Output from this module gives cumulative lead times required to produce a finished product. It provides contract delivery schedules for both end item and spare part requirements. Inquiries can be made on contracts individually, by group, or for all contracts combined. Simulations of alternative production plans can be generated as contract demands change or new business is proposed. Priorities are set to support contract delivery dates.

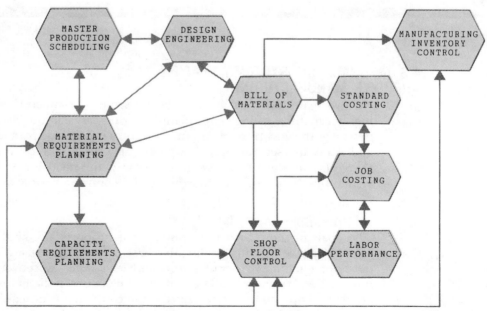

Figure 4.10 Schematic of an information system that supports the manufacturing function.

implosion (in what products and stages are the parts and subassemblies needed) formats. The bill-of-materials module provides cost figures for costing standards. It creates modular bills of materials for products with optional or special features. Standards for scrap and shrinkage are used by standard costing and shop floor management for effective material usage control. Picking lists are printed to facilitate the creation of kits for assembly.

Manufacturing Inventory Control

The manufacturing inventory control module interfaces with bill of materials to set up a list of materials to be made, purchased, or gathered from stores to issue to production. It maintains stockroom and bin locations online. It processes all receipts, issues, and transfers and provides dock-to-stock tracking. If necessary, this module can be designed to interface with an automated storage and retrieval system. This module is outlined in Figure 4.14.

Output from the manufacturing inventory control module includes a complete usage report by inventory code, by description, and where used. On each item, it gives a profile of receipts, issues, transfers, and adjustments. The stock status report gives dock-to-stock information and on-order status. The location report gives item location within a warehouse and between warehouses in a multiwarehouse environment.

Capacity Requirements Planning

The capacity requirements planning module compares projected work loads over time to a viable capacity for each work center or department. It is critical that manufacturers have timely information about each work center's load versus

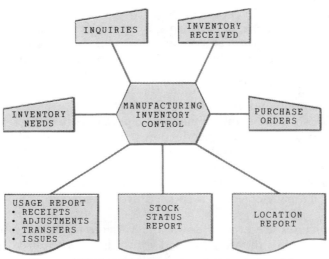

Figure 4.14 A manufacturing inventory control module.

its capacity. Moreover, it facilitates shop floor planning by reporting on both current and predicted orders. This module is presented in Figure 4.15.

The production load report is broken down by work centers or departments. It identifies the production loads by time period, part, order, and operation. If capacity problems are found, what-if analyses can be performed showing the predicted results of alternative schedules. The module measures planned production against actual production over a specified time period. Reports can be in tabular or graphic formats.

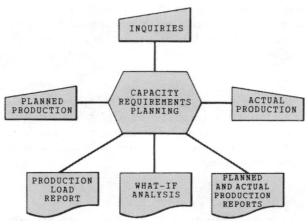

Figure 4.15 A capacity requirements planning module.

Shop Floor Control

The shop floor control module in Figure 4.16 addresses many aspects of the shop floor environment. It maintains shop order routing and operations standard data. It specifies the shops, departments, or work centers through which a manufactured product must flow and the standard hours by operation. Control is provided from the moment an order is released to manufacturing and continues until the order is completed and routed to a finished goods warehouse. Status reports are given at each critical location. Data are transmitted to standard costing for labor, material, and overhead cost analysis.

The shop floor control module helps to ensure that the priorities and plans scheduled by the master production scheduling module and the material requirements planning module are executed on the shop floor. Moreover, work center load profiles are created for capacity requirements planning. Queues and lead times are controlled to avoid bottlenecks and increase shop floor throughput. Clearly, its main objective is to keep products moving smoothly through production.

Processes are broken down and variable inputs are identified. Steps are taken to monitor the variables and adjust them as required. For example, tools are an important input variable. Cutter-tool blades are subject to wear, air-driven

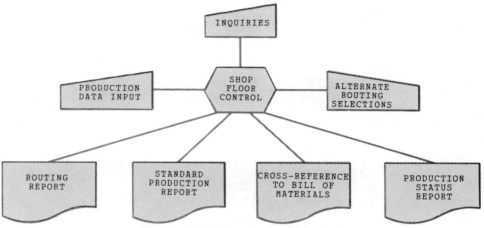

Figure 4.16 A shop floor control module.

torque wrenches must be reset, machine speeds vary, and holding tools grip components slightly differently. The module monitors the variables, as well as the product in process, as it passes through numerous production checkpoints. In this way, a minor variation is spotted and corrected before it influences product output, thus eliminating output that falls outside the specifications.

Routing information includes definition of the operations required to make each product, the tooling required in the process, the work centers or departments involved, and the sequences in which the product flows through these work centers or departments. This report also provides alternate routings as well as a prime routing. Cross-references to bill of materials by work center and operation are given. Another report tracks the status of each order by operation, spotlighting problem areas. The standard production report displays time required for each part or product, set-up time, run time, move time, and queue time.

Standard Costing

The standard costing module contains all cost standards, such as labor rate, labor time, material price, material usage, and various overhead standards. Control prevents some inefficiency from occurring by establishing standards, thereby encouraging employees not to exceed these standard costs. These standards furnish bases for measuring deviations from planned accomplishments. They also provide a means for fixing responsibility. Standard costing also calculates the cost of products. A standard costing module is displayed in Figure 4.17.

The standard costing module collects actual production costs and compares them with standard costs. The main report produced by this module is the standard cost report. In addition to cost of product, this report provides variances from standards. Four basic variances are generally calculated for the prime costs: material usage and material price variances, and labor efficiency and labor rate variances. Further analysis shows the effect of a change in the mix of material

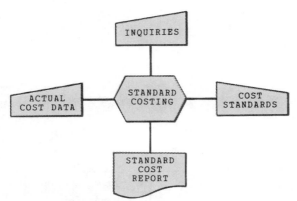

Figure 4.17 A standard costing module.

and labor as well as a difference in the actual yield of finished output compared to the standard yield. Overhead (or burden) costs can be analyzed in several ways. One way is to provide management with volume, efficiency, and spending variances.

In addition to product costing and helping management control variances, information from this module assists in estimating future jobs and preparing bids. Whether job, project, or process, this information also discloses the profitability of products.

Job Costing

The job-costing module is a cost-tracking program designed to meet the needs of manufacturers that operate on a job or project basis. It interfaces with the standard costing module for reporting. It collects costs and allocates these costs and overhead by job or project. Through the standard costing module it provides cost analysis reports by job or project. Also, rate, yield, performance, and quantity breakdowns are included in the variance analysis. Because reporting is performed by the standard costing module, a job-costing schematic is not shown.

Labor Performance

The labor performance module in Figure 4.18 enables management to identify productivity problems and improve use of labor resources. Key inputs to this module are labor rate, yield, and efficiency variances from the standard costing module. Moreover, the labor performance module tracks employee production statistics and monitors the performance of foremen and crew. It provides for incentive pay and supports clock card entry. It reports on salaried employees as well as incentive earnings and provides for entry of regular, overtime, and double-time wages. The main report is the production statistics report that tracks employee production statistics and monitors a crew's performance.

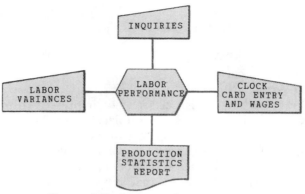

Figure 4.18 A labor performance module.

Design Engineering

The design engineering module creates, organizes, and maintains specifications required to produce a manufacturer's products. Design engineers make heavy use of workstations and computer-aided design (CAD) software. Such a module helps design engineers develop accurate and timely specifications for new products to meet quickly shifting tastes and needs in the marketplace. Moreover, it helps control and track revisions to existing bills of material. A design engineering module is configured in Figure 4.19.

The design specifications report contains data that describe the characteristics of each part and product. In it are alternate and substitute parts that can be used interchangeably in the manufacturing process. This report also reconciles any differences between engineering configurations and production bills of material. Also, the report shows changes to be made to product configurations

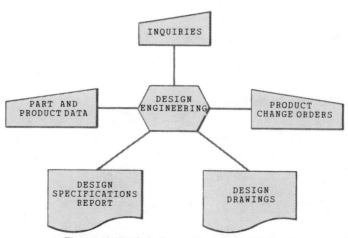

Figure 4.19 A design engineering module.

to support unique customer requirements. Specifications and configurations are supported by computer-generated drawings.

4.4 INFORMATION SYSTEMS THAT SUPPORT MARKETING

Organizations seek ways to get closer to their present customers, develop new customers, and understand the marketplace better. Marketing managers need information to help them anticipate shifting demand for products, increase selling productivity, and keep tight control over sales and distribution expenses. They want to eliminate duplicate, fragmentation, conflict, and waste in the marketing area. Information systems that support the marketing function aid in these efforts.

For too long, marketing has been untouched by information technology. But this is changing rapidly. Today, a new emphasis on information systems that are specific to the marketing function is taking place. Managers are changing marketing from a gut-feel operation to one that is information based. Indeed, they are beginning to realize that an information system is a critical weapon in their struggle for a competitive edge in the marketplace.

Information System Overview

The information system specific to marketing gathers and processes data to provide a variety of reports to marketing managers and personnel concerning their budgets, sales performance, sales force management and needs, marketing research and intelligence, product analysis, advertising and promotion, logistics and distribution, and customer service. A schematic of the information system that supports these subfunctions is presented in Figure 4.20. While it's not shown in the figure, a great deal of the data fed into this information system come

MARKETING WITH TECHNOLOGY Johnny Fisher, senior vice-president of Banc One, has emerged as the foremost coupler of computer technology and marketing in the banking industry. He helped bring the credit card to U.S. consumers, turned on the first automated teller machine (ATM), and filled his bank's coffers by offering DP services to a variety of non-bank entities.

Once the bank had its DP foundation in place for servicing credit cards, Fisher found the potential for enhancements unlimited. He quickly tied the credit card together with the checking account, providing an early example of overdraft protection. Fisher was also an early proponent of video home banking.

Excerpted from Glenn Rifkin, "He Changed the Rules in Banking," *Computerworld*, April 25, 1988, pp. 1, 84–85.

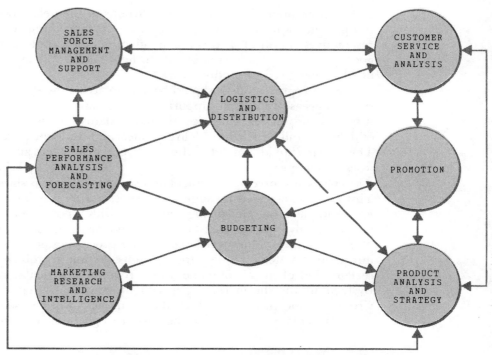

Figure 4.20 Schematic of an information system that supports the marketing function.

from the information systems related to the accounting and manufacturing functions and from external sources.

The information system specific to marketing combines data in the company's data bases with outside data, including economic, demographic, and industry statistics. These data serve as input into a variety of forecast, competitive, and pricing models to supply, within minutes, strategic information that was impossible to provide with manual systems. Moreover, new and improved information systems convert reams of numbers into charts, colorful graphs, and maps that are easy for marketers to understand and digest. Telecommunications, word processors, and electronic mail also enable reports, memos, and product information to be transmitted simultaneously to a number of marketing personnel, salespeople in the field, and even customers.

With this overview of the relationship of information systems to the marketing function, let us turn our attention next to the details of how function-specific information system modules support and work with different marketing subfunctions.

Sales Force Management and Support

Sales managers need information to allocate their sales force intelligently and to determine each salesperson's performance equitably. But of equal importance is the information that supports the "troops in the field," because without the troops, sales will soon dry up. Therefore, making things easier for sales representatives is critical. If a company gives its salespeople a good product at a good price but no sales support, then these salespeople are receiving only half of what they need to produce sales.

Sales representatives should be able to access the system easily and obtain such things as procedural support and information about the quantity of products on hand; prices and price discounts; status information on invoices, time of delivery, and backorders; delivery dates; and complete product specifications. The system should also aid in the timely entry of orders and reduce the paperwork of salespeople.

The sales force management and support module is shown in Figure 4.21. This module, accessed through a sales person's terminal, can help make sales. For example, a manufacturing rep armed with a portable computer can check inventory, give quotes, delivery dates, and place orders from the customer's place of business. Moreover, access to the processing power of the home office information system can help the rep solve technical problems. For instance, a certain kind of metal component may require a particular protective coating. By feeding into the marketing-specific information system data about the environment and process in which the component will be used, almost instantly the representative would have the answer to give the customer about the most

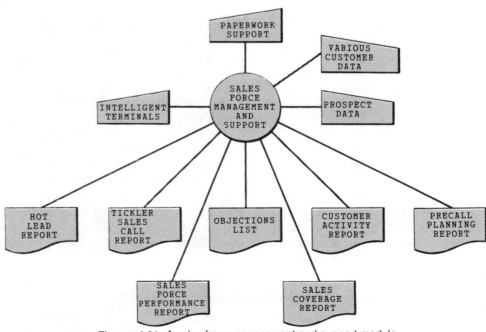

Figure 4.21 A sales force management and support module.

appropriate coating for the component. Clearly, this kind of support gives salespeople the technical edge over competitors.

In another case a hot lead report, which has been prepared from ads, questionnaires, interviews at trade shows, and the like, is supplied by a regional sales office or headquarters information system. Ideally it should contain a list of future prospects; their profiles; and an estimate of the probability, value, and timing of a sale. The faster the sales staff gets the names of the prospects the quicker they can work on these leads.

A tickler sales call report helps in proper timing of a sales call. For example, data are tracked on customer's current products by the information system to estimate when they are likely to need replacing. Or, because most customers voice at least one objection to a deal before making a purchase commitment, the information system could track these objections and prepare an objections list of appropriate counterresponses to the objections.

Under the heading of customer activity reporting, the information system follows customers' activities, such as ordering, shipping, and delivering; open orders; and volume projections based on business peaks and valleys. Associated with the task of customer activity reporting the information system can also produce a report that contains computer-generated maps for optimal territory coverage. Such infomation could be passed on immediately to the sales force on a daily basis. The payoff of these reports is that salespeople can manage their accounts more closely and faster. Menus on a screen present salespeople with different options depending on the kind of precall information they need. They can retrieve information on specific products customers bought in the current month, previous month, and year to date. Order status reports summarize accounts' booking and shipping and indicate any problems involving unfilled orders. Salespeople can also get a quick review of quotas being met or exceeded for each account.

Many salespeople complain that they can't call on customers and prospects because they are drowning in a flood of paperwork. They say, and rightfully so, that they are not paid for preparing reports and other documents, but for calling on customers. To chop away at the mountains of paperwork that robs them of precious selling time, the information system can set up a paperwork interface to help produce letters, memos, and price quotes quicker. Salespeople can use their terminals to key variable data, such as a new customer's name and address, and then access by codes or templates fixed data, such as product descriptions, prices, boilerplate, and the like. Automatic ordering through hand-held terminals also eliminates many of the errors that occur when order forms have to be completed manually.

The sales force performance report is for marketing management to evaluate sales performance of each member of the sales team. This report includes calls made, calls-to-sales ratios, contribution margin on products sold, holding of old accounts, opening new accounts, and meeting sales targets. The sales coverage report lets management know how well new prospects are being covered, how many turn out to be new customers, whether enough leads are being generated, and general territory coverage.

Sales Performance Analysis and Forecasting

Sales performance analysis is a detailed study of the total sales revenue of a company for some period, month, quarter, or year. Management analyzes total sales volume, by product line, by salesperson, by territory, and by customer groups. These sales are then compared with company goals and industry sales.

Forecasting is the estimation of the market size and the company's share of that market. Clearly, an accurate sales forecast is one of the most useful pieces of information a marketing manager can receive because budgets, sales strategies, and sales quotas are influenced by such estimates. Forecasting also helps in the planning and control of manufacturing, logistics and distribution, and advertising and promotion, especially as it is reflected through the budgeting process. A sales performance analysis and forecasting module that supports these subfunctions is portrayed in Figure 4.22.

The sales volume analysis report gives the company's sales volume, the industry's sales volume, and the company's percentage share of the market. Also, sales volume is analyzed by sales territories, customer groups, product lines, and salesperson. The sales profitability report determines the relative profitability of its customers, territories, product lines, salespeople, and other marketing units. For example, marketing managers and salespeople want to know who their best customers are. Based on Pareto's law, 20 percent of the customers may be contributing 80 percent of the profits. As many as 20 to 40 percent of the total customers may be costing the company more to service them than it's worth. This information is needed for a better allocation of salespeople and other marketing resources. As part of this analysis, management may establish budgeting goals, and then study the variations between budgeted costs and actual expenses.

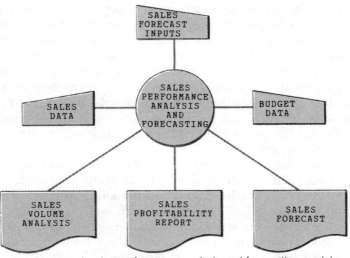

Figure 4.22 A sales performance analysis and forecasting module.

To produce a sales forecast requires a number of inputs, including top-management opinion, a sales force composite, survey of customers, projection of trends, correlation to leading indicators (association between sales and another variable called a market factor—increased summer travel means increase in sales of motel rooms), and the *Sales Management Buying Power Index*. All or part of these inputs are used to produce a sales forecast.

Marketing Research and Intelligence

The marketing research and intelligence module, in Figure 4.23, provides marketing managers with anticipatory or discovery information. Marketing research and intelligence gathering helps define marketing problems and systematically collects and analyzes data to recommend actions to improve a company's marketing activities. It helps managers find new customers and quickly adapt products to meet changing customer requirements and possibly provide value-added services. User-friendly software and large relational data bases help advise marketers on which segments to target. It tells what customers really need, how to price a product and increase sales, which distribution channels to use, and how to get more out of advertising and promotion expenditures.

A significant task of the marketing research and intelligence module is the gathering of primary external data (i.e., new data for a specific problem as opposed to secondary data that have already been recorded). The advent of scannable products (e.g., Universal Product Code), the linking of individual purchases to specific buyers, the control and monitoring of commercials beamed into homes, and the recording of what is watched on TV have increased significantly the power of marketing research and intelligence gathering.

The Universal Product Code is a good example of how information tech-

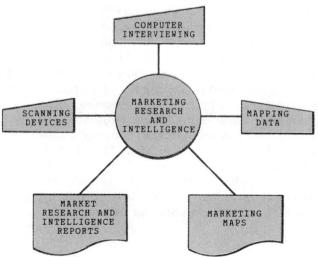

Figure 4.23 A marketing research and intelligence module.

nology is used to portray buying patterns. Some marketers are even talking about placing microchips in magazines that will send signals about what magazines are bought and the pages read. Collecting data at the source has the potential to provide precise insights into shifting preferences and tastes of local and regional markets almost as soon as these changes occur. The marketing research and intelligence module can then convert these huge amounts of primary data into actionable information.

Moreover, computers can be used in the interviewing process. Computer-assisted telephone interviewing (CATI) and direct computer interviewing (e.g., used in malls) are used by researchers to reduce errors and increase interviewing efficiency. These devices can be connected to automatic voice-to-text translators and respondent coding devices. Also, hand-held computers are used to record screening data to replace old tick mark systems.

Mainframe computers have been mapping demographic data for over a decade. Companies such as Federal Express use computers to help make geographically based decisions daily to deploy airplanes and delivery trucks. Such a technique is tailor-made for the information system that supports marketing because marketers are always trying to get the answers to two questions: where and who.

As Federal Express has a need to deploy its resources, marketing managers also have a similar need to deploy their sales force or locate a store. Maps that help solve marketing problems are called thematic maps because they combine geographical data with demographic data and a company's sales or other proprietary research data.[1]

Color-coded maps can help realign sales and service territories. Such companies as Sears, Liberty Mutual, and 3M build sales territories with equal customer potential. Liberty Mutual, for example, builds maps around 25-mile radii overlaid with census and company data to produce a market evaluation score for each zip code. Others use maps to pinpoint telemarketing areas and direct-mail regions to reach potential customers efficiently. Other uses include targeting markets, site location, and what-if analysis.

Specifically, Coca-Cola divides the United States into 5 geographical areas, 22 regions, 90 districts, and 420 bottling areas. Coca-Cola, for example, produced maps daily during the summer it introduced new-formula Coke. Maps checked the share of the population receiving the new product by five-day intervals and segmentary penetration by cans versus bottles and by bottle sizes, as well as tracking new Coke's availability against Pepsi.

Hallmark uses marketing maps to study card distribution by product line and by census tracts in metropolitan areas. Hallmark also tracks sales by economic areas in the nation as a whole. Banks use mapping to decide where to locate automatic teller machines. Retailers use latitude and longitude centroids for postal carrier routes to help pinpoint a store and to plot the characteristics of the population within a radius around the store.

---

[1]Martha Farnsworth Riche, "Computer Takes Center Stage," *American Demographics*, June 1986, pp. 26–31.

Product Analysis and Strategy

Many marketers say that the first commandment of marketing is "know thy customer," and the second commandment is "know thy product." The product analysis and strategy module, depicted in Figure 4.24, helps marketing managers keep the second commandment.

Many companies will get a substantial part of their sales volume and net profit today from products that did not exist a few years ago. The market testing of a new product involves exposing actual products to prospective customers under realistic purchase conditions to see if they will buy it. Results from test markets help a company establish relative product performance and the likelihood of having a winner or loser. Test markets are also used to check other elements, such as price and level of advertising and promotion required to support full commercialization. In attempting to commercialize a product, companies can position it head to head against the competition or seek a differential position.

The new product report includes estimation of potential sales and customer buying habits and motives. Clearly, the key point is that there must be an adequate market demand for the product. All technical problems are reported as well as its ability to fit in with marketing, manufacturing, and financial resources. Timing evaluations are made to determine if the product is too early or too late.

The pricing strategy report helps management meet certain pricing objectives, such as earning a target margin, increasing sales, gaining or holding a target share of the market, and meeting or beating competitors' prices. Key elements that influence management's decision when setting a price are demand for the product, competitors' reaction, and the product's cost. After setting a base price, management may use various techniques to employ different strategies. These techniques are discounts, allowances, interest rates, and freight. When pricing a new product, management can use a skimming, penetration,

Figure 4.24 A product analysis and strategy module.

prestige, price-lining, or odd-even pricing strategy. Cost and profit analysis includes percentage of markup on cost and selling price, markdowns, inventory turnover rates, contribution margin, return on investment, and breakeven analysis.

The product mix report tells management to expand the product mix by increasing the number of lines or the depth within a line or, alternatively, to prune out the product mix by eliminating an entire line or by simplifying the assortment within a line. Another strategy is to alter the design, packaging, or other features of existing products. And still another strategy is to reposition a product relative to competing products or to other products sold by the company.

All products have a life cycle. Conventional stages of the life cycle are introduction, growth, maturity, and decline. But the shape of the product life cycle, the rates of change in sales and profits, and the length and height of the cycles vary greatly among products. Peanut butter, for example, has been in the maturity stage for decades. On the other hand, hula hoops had a short life, but later they were reincarnated containing metal balls to create a swishing noise. The principal goal of the marketing manager is to bring the product into the maturity stage and to keep it there as long as it is profitable. Moreover, marketing managers want to know if the product is in decline and if so to determine how to extend its life cycle as has been done with Gillette razors a number of times since introduction at the turn of this century. Old products in decline with no hope of rejuvenation should be eliminated.

The product life-cycle report helps marketers manage the product through the various stages and to, if possible, anticipate the marketing requirements of the subsequent stage. As already noted, if management receives life-cycle information, then actions can be taken to extend the maturity stage as Colgate did with pump dispenser toothpaste and Procter & Gamble did with leak-resistant disposable diapers. Marketers may find the greatest challenge during the sales decline stage. Management must decide whether to eliminate the product or try to revitalize it with a potent dose of innovation.

Promotion

Having a better product is not enough. Potential customers must be made aware of the product's benefits. That's where promotion comes into play. The company must communicate persuasive messages to the public. As all marketers know, effective marketing requires effective communication. A big part of this communication is composed of four elements, namely; sales promotion, personal selling, advertising, and publicity. Together, they form an effective promotional mix. A promotion module is shown in Figure 4.25.

When setting the amount to be spent on promotion, marketers are often reminded of the old bromide, "If you can't make a splash, don't make a ripple." This adage means go for it all, spend all you can. But marketing managers need better direction than this. A promotion budget gives them that direction. The ingredients of this budget are based on targets, percentage of sales, industry standards, and specific competitors.

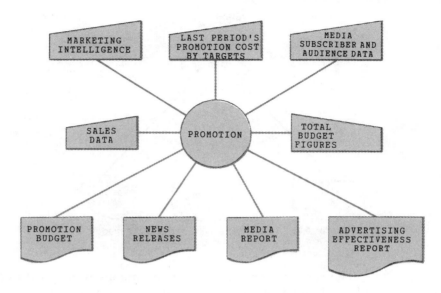

The marketing manager may identify a target, such as a product or customer group and decide to increase by 40 percent the amount of promotion dollars for this target. The percentage-of-sales method is probably the most commonly used technique for setting promotion budgets. If forecasted sales are $1 million and the percentage allocated to promotion is 5 percent, then the promotion budget would be $50,000. Industry standards and specific competitors guide the promotion manager in setting the budget by doing what others are doing. This is called copycat or parity promotion.

The advertising effectiveness report helps to determine who the target audience is, what to communicate, when to communicate it, and what media to use. Afterward, the advertising program should be evaluated for its effectiveness. Surveys are done to determine recall or recognition. The promotion module can also produce news releases for publicity through newspapers and radio. Media report guides management in selecting among alternative media. Ratios such as cost per 1,000 persons reached can be computed by multiplying price of the medium times 1,000 divided by delivered audience. Delivered audience is the total number of people who read the magazine or watch television.

Customer Service and Analysis

When a customer buys a product, it is not an act but a process that has five steps: problem recognition based on a need or want, information search, alternative evaluation, purchase decision, and postpurchase evaluation. At least two of these steps, information search and purchase decision, can be made easier with a customer service and analysis module, as presented in Figure 4.26. In addition to serving the customer, this module also helps marketers to "know thy customer" better.

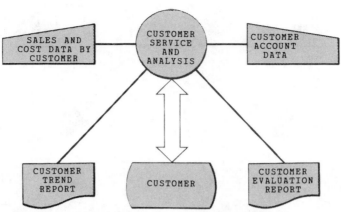

Figure 4.26 A customer service and analysis module.

The customer service and analysis module is designed to interface online and in real time to customers' systems. This computer-to-computer connection can help the customer in a number of ways. Computer-to-computer ordering, often called direct order entry (DOE), is becoming more common. Customers can order from the company's inventory, check items in stock and their prices, and determine delivery lead times. The company can establish data bases and technical problem-solving models and make them available to customers via computer-to-computer linkage whereby they can get a wealth of technical service. Product information and price lists can be made available to customers directly by using facsimile and videotex. Menus can also be made available for a variety of access options.

The customer trend report spotlights such items as active customers with down trends, new customers with up trends, and lost customers. Customer complaints are also cataloged for follow-up. The customer evaluation report gives a complete breakdown of profitability by customer.

Logistics and Distribution

A channel of distribution is the path that products take as they flow from producer to customer. The marketing manager's determination of the structure of channels is a crucial element of marketing strategy. Logistics controls the physical flow of products through the organization and its channels of distribution. The function of logistics and channels of distribution is to provide time and place utility. The goal is to minimize distribution costs while maintaining the level of service specified by customers. To achieve this goal requires precise coordination, accurate forecasts, and complete plans.

Transportation, warehousing, inventory control, materials handling, order processing, and packaging are the key operational elements that relate to the logistics and distribution module. In some organizations, the logistics or physical distribution function is separate from manufacturing and marketing. In this chapter, we include it in with the marketing function for convenience. In any case, logistics and distribution directly affect the success of the marketing program. Therefore, marketing managers should pay close attention to this function, whether they are in direct control of it or not. Logistics and distribution must function as a totality, working in concert with other operating functions of the organization and with external influences that impact day-to-day operations. The logistics and distribution module in Figure 4.27 helps managers to coordinate and operate these vital subfunctions.

A variety of models are used to provide distribution modeling information. This information helps managers locate warehouses, design layouts, and evaluate their present distribution system. The order processing control report allocates stock to fill customer orders, processes backorders, answers order status inquiries, produces shipping reports by invoice, and produces freight and labor charges. The distribution planning report is prepared based on forecasts to schedule loading and traffic routing. Warehouse control provides stock and pallet location and labor performance management. Logistical mapping information selects the shortest practical truck routes between selected points. Models evaluate trade-offs between shortest time routes and shortest mileage routes. This information gives solid support and efficiency to dispatching functions. The fleet management report provides daily information on preventive maintenance schedules, me-

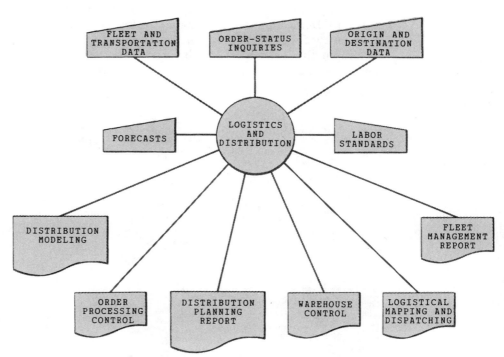

Figure 4.27 A logistics and distribution module.

chanical defects, servicing activity, performance statistics, vehicle history, fuel tracking, truck usage, driver hours, and fuel-tax reports.

Budgeting

The marketing budget is a quantitative expression of a plan of action and an aid to coordination and implementation of marketing operations. The budget is a commitment in terms of money to a forecast to make an agreed-upon outcome happen. The marketing budget is the glue that holds the various marketing components together. It coordinates the company's strategy with personnel and tasks that need to be performed to achieve overall marketing strategy.

Generally, companies adopt a "goals-down, plans-up" approach. Top management sets sales goals. Forecasts are established. Marketing develops proposals and plans to achieve these goals and meet the forecasts. Once approved, the marketing budget is prepared in detail to coordinate facilities and tasks necessary to meet marketing's commitment. A budgeting module is presented in Figure 4.28.

The sales force management and support budget along with other information discussed earlier in this section helps management hire and deploy a sufficient number of salespeople to meet sales quotas. The marketing research budget indicates the amount of money allocated to this area for the forthcoming period.

After setting promotion objectives, the company must decide on how much to spend. Determining the ideal amount for the budget is difficult because there is no precise way to measure the exact results of spending promotion dollars. Several methods, however, can be used to set this budget. As mentioned before, the percentage-of-sales budgeting method allocates promotion funds as a per-

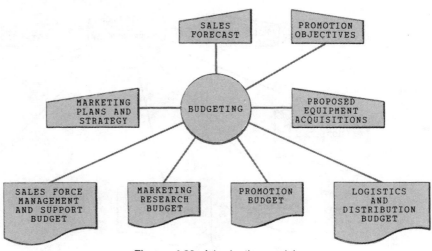

Figure 4.28 A budgeting module.

centage of past or anticipated sales, either in terms of dollars or units sold. Competitive parity budgeting is matching the competitors' level of spending. The all-you-can-afford method allocates funds to promotion only after all other budget items are covered. Task budgeting allocates funds to focus on and accomplish certain tasks. Other budgeting methods may be integrated into this approach. If costs are beyond what the company can afford, then tasks are revised.

The logistics and distribution budget helps management to plan day-to-day physical distribution operations and plan expenditures for the addition of new facilities (e.g., trucks, automated materials handling equipment) and for the replacement of present equipment to secure lower operating costs.

SUMMARY

To support the primary functions of marketing, manufacturing, and accounting, businesses have constructed separate, function-specific information systems. Although the information systems are modified to reflect the industry in which the business is located and the amount and variety of transactions that must be processed, certain commonalities run through these function-specific systems.

Information systems that support the accounting function consist of several modules designed around ledgers, a chart of accounts, and journals. These modules enable a business to process sales and collect money due from customers. The information systems also contain modules that support the functions of purchase order processing and receiving, inventory management, accounts payable, and payroll. Additionally, accounting-specific information systems contain modules to perform word processing and fixed asset accounting.

Although no two manufacturers are exactly the same, most manufacturing-specific information systems consist of a master production scheduling, material requirements planning, and bill-of-materials module. These modules interface with a module to support the design engineering activity.

The module of capacity requirements planning helps decison makers anticipate the strains projected work loads will place on each work center or department over time. The module of manufacturing inventory control interfaces with the bill of materials module so that materials needed in the manufacturing process can be made, procured, or gathered from stores and issued to production. The module of shop floor control interfaces directly or indirectly with the modules of standard costing, job costing, and labor performance.

Marketing managers need information to help them anticipate shifts in product demand, increase selling productivity, and exercise control over sales and distribution expenses. A function-specific system that has modules for sales management and support, sales performance analysis and forecasting, marketing research and intelligence gathering, customer service and analysis, promotion, and product analysis and strategy, provides this necessary information to these managers. Modules for logistics and distribution and budgeting also help managers plan and control marketing operations within the business.

IMPORTANT TERMS

ABC analysis
accounts payable
accounts receivable
audit trails
bill of materials
bills of lading
capacity requirements planning
chart of accounts
computer-assisted design (CAD)
computer-assisted telephone
  interviewing (CATI)
depreciation methods
design engineering
direct order entry (DOE)
fixed assets
forecasting
goals-down, plans-up budgeting
hot lead report
job costing
journals

labor performance
ledger
logistics and distribution
marketing research and intelligence
master production scheduling
material requirements planning
order entry
packing slips
payroll register
picking lists
pricing strategy
product life cycle
production load report
promotion
routing information
shop floor control
standard costing
stock status
universal product code (UPC)
word processing

Assignment

REVIEW QUESTIONS

4.1 Traditionally, businesses have been organized along functional lines. Define the term "function."

4.2 When is a subsidiary ledger appropriate for use in a business? What is the function of a controlling account? What is the purpose of a company having a journal?

4.3 What are the basic transactions that affect accounts receivable? How is the account affected by each transaction?

4.4 List the reports or documents normally produced by the accounts receivable module; by the accounts payable module.

4.5 What are the different types of orders that the order-entry and processing module can track?

4.6 What is a bill of lading? a picking list? a packing slip?

4.7 What four events cause an entry to be made to a detail fixed asset ledger?

4.8 What is the name of the report that provides information on late and defective shipments?

4.9 Describe the contents of the unemployment report and the withholding report.

4.10 What is the objective of the master production schedule? What is the basis for its derivation? What information does it contain?

4.11 What is the purpose of material requirements planning module? In general terms, what is generated by this module?

4.12 Identify the difference between a bill of materials report produced using an explosion versus implosion format.

4.13 Which manufacturing module sets up a list of materials to be made, purchased, or gathered from stores to issue to production? Which gives us information on the status of an order, from the time it's released to manufacturing until it's completed and routed to a finished goods warehouse?

4.14 What report enables management to analyze overhead or burden costs? What three types of variances can be provided for their analysis?

4.15 Which manufacturing module can best help a business develop accurate and timely specifications for new products as well as help control and track revisions to existing bills of materials?

4.16 Define the purpose of a hot lead report; a tickler sales call report; an objections list; a sales coverage report.

4.17 List five inputs needed to produce a reliable sales forecast.

4.18 What are two ways information technology can be employed to portray buying patterns to marketers?

4.19 List the three key elements that influence management when setting a price for a product.

4.20 All products have a life cycle. What are the four conventional stages? How can the life cycle of a product be changed?

4.21 A customer in buying a product goes through a process that has five steps. What are these steps and which can be influenced by the customer service and analysis module?

4.22 Define the function and goal of the logistics and distribution module in a marketing-specific information system.

4.23 What has been called the "glue" that holds together the various marketing components? What are its basic inputs?

QUESTIONS FOR DISCUSSION

4.24 With computer-based information systems, the requirement for journals has all but disappeared. Do you agree or disagree? Why?

4.25 A company's chart of accounts dictates the level of detail it can track products, cost centers, sales productivity, and the like. Why is this statement true?

4.26 A business believes that magazines are the primary media used to promote its products. Why would it be in the best interests of this company's marketing manager to support research investigating the feasibility of embedding microchips in magazines?

4.27 A quality system that supports the module of master production scheduling enhances the activity of production planning. Discuss what other facets of a business improve or work better when management knows what it will produce.

4.28 In small plants, determining the work centers through which a manufactured product must flow and monitoring a product's progress as it is fabricated is unnecessary. Do you agree or disagree? Why?

4.29 How can a sales manager monitor the performance of her six district managers? How can these district managers monitor the performance of the salespersons reporting to them?

4.30 A manufacturer experiences a significant decrease in the orders received for its products. The production manager is not notified of this decrease for three weeks. Which modules would you look to change or remedy this situation?

4.31 What modules in the accounting function are affected by transactions for purchases of raw materials on credit transactions? Checks from credit customers?

EXERCISES AND PROBLEMS

4.32 For each of the following situations, indicate the information needed to solve the problem, the report that might supply such information, and the module that might produce the report:

1. A worker takes two hours to gather items from inventory for a $40 order.

2. An auditor is unsure as to how much of the $178,014 owing the company can be collected.

3. The new marketing manager wants to know if advertising a line of archery in an outdoor sports magazine is effective.

4. Management is concerned its company might not be able to react to changes in the buying patterns of major customers.

5. A marketing manager wonders if a new product will appeal to a certain customer segment.

6. A rush order to manufacture a specialty product for a customer has been received. The plant superintendent is worried that work on goods already started into production will stop because of the attention given the rush order.

7. A mill supervisor is concerned that the electric blast furnace will have to be shut down because too few electrodes were ordered.

8. An hourly employee asks her supervisor to explain why the amount she was paid six weeks ago was so low.

9. A supervisor is suspicious that invoices are being submitted by vendors for goods never received.

10. A sales representative cannot promise a firm delivery date on a make-to-order product to a customer because she does not know the lead time to produce it.

4.33 Electro Co. is a worldwide manufacturer and distributor of process control systems. It has two corporate offices, located in Cupertino, California, and Paris, France. The Paris office is responsible for all plants and sales offices outside the United States. Each corporate office maintains a data base of products it manufactures, orders it takes, and customers in its geographic area of responsibility so that it can provide from a central source such things as product assurance and financial and legal reporting.

Of Electro Co.'s 70 sales offices throughout the world, 39 are located in the United States. Fifteen of its 24 manufacturing plants are located abroad. These sales offices and plants are both originators and receivers of data. For example, customer data originating at sales offices are sent to the appropriate corporate office where they are entered into the data base. Subsequently, a slice of these data is sent to the plant where the process control system for that customer will be manufactured. More specifically, sales orders and changes to those orders are captured at sales offices for subsequent transmission to the corporate office. At the corporate office the orders are entered into the data base and are then sent to the factories for acceptance and delivery acknowledgment.

Customer order, shipment, and backlog status is maintained at corporate headquarters for the purpose of providing information to top management. Delivery information is sent from the plants back to the sales offices so that customer acknowledgments can be prepared.

All invoices are prepared at the corporate offices, although credit and collection functions are decentralized in the sales offices. Biweekly a report is prepared by each sales office regarding the status of its receivables so that financial control can be exercised by the corporate office.

The sales offices are also originators of all data for product records. The corporate office receives and retains a complete product data base and portions of that data base are kept at each plant.

> *Required:* Prepare a table that lists the type of information which flows between the systems that support the sales function, the manufacturing function, and the corporate controllership function.

4.34 Hampton Manufacturing has nine plants located throughout the Northeast. Each of these plants produces a series of extruded plastic products for major toy manufacturers in the United States. The management of Hampton believes it enjoys an advantage over its competition because of its patented, modern, highly efficient production process. In fact, were it not for the attention given by management on the composition and use of Hampton's production facilities, most of Hampton's business would eventually be won by foreign competitors.

Essential to the successful operation of Hampton's plants is the existence of a fixed assets reporting system. This reporting system must provide management with not only detailed operational information about how Hampton's fixed assets are being employed, but also information on which projections for future fixed asset expenditures can be based.

> *Required:* What kind of reports should the fixed asset reporting system produce to provide Hampton's management with the information they need for operational and planning purposes?

4.35 Krackoff Company is a small fabricator of aluminum siding located in Omaha. It employs 80 full-time production workers, who are paid on an hourly basis. The salaried portion of Krackoff's work force consists of 16 supervisory and management people.

Each week a payroll is prepared for Krackoff's production workers. As part of the process of preparing a payroll for the company's hourly workers, data stored on the employee master file are updated. This updating process applies to both hourly and salaried personnel.

During any week two types of data are entered in the payroll system. Time reporting data, which come from the various departments in the company, are keyed onto a magnetic disk by a payroll clerk. As part of this keying process, the time card data are checked by the system for accuracy and reasonableness. Additionally, the payroll supervisor enters data that cause the employee master file to change. These changes could reflect modifications to pay rates because of promotions, increases or decreases in income tax withholding because of the number of exemptions changing, revisions to withholding amounts because of changes in the level of contributions, and changes in basic employee information (e.g., name, address, telephone number).

On Thursday evening of each week, time card and employee master file data are processed, and checks for signature are prepared. On the last Thursday of the month, checks for salaried workers are also produced.

Required: Besides the payroll checks, what other regular reports should be produced by the system that supports the payroll function of Krackoff Company?

4.36 Bob Embry is a senior production supervisor for ChemCo International. He is responsible for managing a 38-person mixing department in ChemCo's Nashville plant. Within the Nashville plant six other departments perform mixing operations for the company's products.

Since taking over the department two months ago, Bob has been concerned over his lack of day-to-day control of operations. On one hand, he is worried that some of his highly productive workers are not receiving adequate compensation. On the other hand, Bob is apprehensive about his inability to identify workers who are not as productive as they might be.

ChemCo International is considering computerizing its shop floor control process. For Bob's department this would entail workers, upon receipt of a batch, entering by voice command the batch number, the mixing process to be applied, the time the mixing operation was started. Upon completion of the mixing process, the workers would indicate the treated condition of the batch and the time it left the department.

Required: Assume that ChemCo will implement this computer project. Lay out a report that would reduce Bob's fears about his department's workers being inadequately or over compensated.

BIBLIOGRAPHY

CASH, JAMES I., and BENN R. KONSYNSKI. "IS Redraws Competitive Boundaries." *Harvard Business Review,* March–April 1985.

COHEN, WILLIAM A. *Developing a Winning Marketing Plan.* New York: John Wiley, 1987.

CUSHING, BARRY E., and MARSHALL B. ROMNEY. *Accounting Information Systems and Business Organizations,* 4th ed. Reading, Mass: Addison-Wesley, 1987.

DOUGLAS, PATRICIA B., and TERESA K. BEED. *Presenting Accounting Information to Management.* Montvale, NJ.: National Association of Accountants, 1986.

GAITHER, NORMAN. *Production and Operations Management,* 3rd ed. Chicago: Dryden Press, 1987.

GERWIN, DONALD. "Do's and Don'ts of Computerized Manufacturing." *Harvard Business Review,* March–April 1982.

GESSNER, ROBERT A. *Master Production Schedule Planning.* New York: John Wiley, 1986.

HUGHES, G. DAVID. "Computerized Sales Management." *Harvard Business Review,* March–April 1983.

JONES, ROBERT SNOWDON. "EDSI Accounting Package Features Industry Charts." *InfoWorld,* January 4, 1988.

MOROCHOVE, RICHARD. "High-End Accounting Software." *InfoWorld,* April 25, 1988.

MOROCHOVE, RICHARD. "Accounting Package Has the Basics, Is Easy to Use." *InfoWorld,* March 14, 1988.

MOROCHOVE, RICHARD. "Midrange Accounting Package Is a Cut Above." *InfoWorld,* February 29, 1988.

MOROCHOVE, RICHARD. "Update of Controversial Accounting Program Counters Critics." *InfoWorld,* January 18, 1988.

MOSCOVE, STEPHEN A., and MARK G. SIMKIN. *Accounting Information Systems,* 3rd ed. New York: John Wiley, 1987.

PINCHOT, GILLORD. *Intrapreneuring.* New York: Harper & Row, 1985.

RIFKIN, GLENN. "He Changed the Rules in Banking." *Computerworld,* April 25, 1988.

RIFKIN, GLENN, and MITCH BETTS. "Strategic Systems Plan Gone Awry." *Computerworld,* March 14, 1988.

SMITH, IVAN C. "Market Analysis: Developing, Using, and Maintaining the Market Intelligence System." In David J. Freiman, ed. *What Every Manager Needs to Know About Marketing.* New York: AMACOM, 1983.

SYNNOTT, WILLIAM R. *The Information Weapon.* New York: John Wiley, 1987.

WISEMAN, CHARLES. *Strategy & Computers: Information Systems as Competitive Weapons.* Homewood, Ill.: Dow Jones-Irwin, 1985.

5

FULLY INTEGRATED INFORMATION SYSTEMS

5.1 INTRODUCTION

In the previous chapter, we described information systems as supporting separate functions of the business (i.e., function-specific information systems). Many companies operate in this highly compartmentalized manner. It appears that the general direction of information systems in the future, however, is toward linking together function-specific information systems into fully integrated information systems (FIIS).

The direction information systems take, however, depends to a great extent on management's philosophy. If management puts the goals of the functions or departments before those of the organization, then its information systems will be disjointed assemblies of subsystems that do not work together very well. If, on the other hand, management follows the adage that "no man is an island unto himself" and strives for goal congruency, then the reality of a FIIS becomes feasible.

In addition to management's attitude toward integration or nonintegration, a number of new manufacturing concepts and techniques that support integration are receiving a great deal of attention by systems analysts. These concepts and techniques include factory automation, computer-integrated manufacturing (CIM), manufacturing automation protocol (MAP), technical and office protocol (TOP), just-in-time (JIT) manufacturing, and manufacturing resource planning (MRP II).

The technology backbone of a fully integrated information system (FIIS) is the telecommunication nodes and links that form network topologies into either local area networks (LANs) or wide area networks (WANs). Moreover, hardware vendors, such as AT&T, DEC, and IBM, are trying to improve connectivity between their own products and products of other vendors for better integration. The jury is still out, however, on how successful they will be in bringing about an information system that has seamless connectivity or full integration.

The general objective of this chapter is to "wire" together much of the material discussed so far, especially the material in the previous chapter. The objectives of this chapter are:

1. To explain why the integration design force will exert a powerful influence on the shape of information systems in the future.
2. To demonstrate a fully integrated information system model by integrating the function-specific information systems presented in the previous chapter.
3. To describe how new manufacturing concepts and techniques are pushing information systems in the direction of more integration.
4. To explain networking and show why it is the key to FIIS.
5. To define network topologies, the specific "data traffic highways" that tie all the components together to form a FIIS.

5.2 ANALYSIS OF THE INTEGRATING FORCE

Integration is a powerful design force because of the increasing need for co-ordination and synchronization of operations inside and outside organizations. The results of integration are displayed in Figure 5.1. To make it work, management must first integrate its basic business functions and then integrate the information systems that support these functions.

Goal of Integration

Organizations should be viewed as total systems themselves made up of inter-dependent functions forming a unified whole. Therefore, the goal of integration as it pertains to information systems is to provide a multilevel, cross-functional flow of information to support this interdependency.

Why is it important to strive toward integrated organizations and information systems? Integration unquestionably fosters a climate of creativity, harmony, and a sense of organizational solidarity. A climate of this type contributes to the organization's pursuit of economic well-being and its ability to withstand competitive forces. In many instances, integration helps to reduce, if not eliminate, negative cultural norms and generally enhances human factors. The result of integration is better communication between departments, which, in turn, improves cooperation, helping to eradicate suboptimization and departmental fiefdoms. Indeed, a free flow of information facilitates better working relationships, increases understanding, precludes barrier building, and supports smoother operations. All the natural interdependencies of information and operations workers are allowed the freedom to operate above the stifling bureaucracies and layers of intermediaries. Furthermore, integration produces synergism, an environment in which the sum of the different parts working

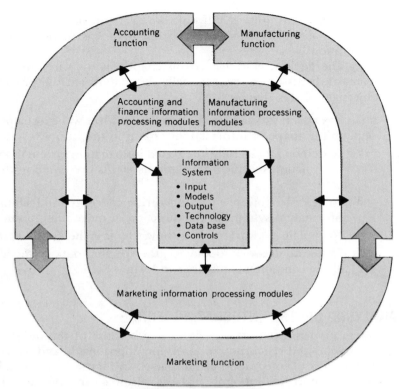

Figure 5.1 A fully integrated information system.

cooperatively has a greater total effect than does the sum of the parts working independently.

Fully integrated information systems mean that users are no longer divided into the "information rich" and "information poor." Therefore, suspicions are reduced and the rumor mills are put out of business. But the goals of integration, while laudable, must be balanced against the threat of breach of data confidentiality, invasion of privacy and "turf," and ownership and the discouragement of individuality, innovation, and creativity. Moreover, many organizations want to give their division managers a great deal of autonomy to foster an entrepreneurial spirit within the organization. But with the offering of autonomy, top management and stockholders still want congruency between the goals of divisions and the goals of the total organization.

Integration Eliminates the Tower of Babel Syndrome

In organizations in which operations do not communicate with one another, marketing may sell one product, manufacturing may make another, and engineering may add unnecessary changes. The following scenario, for example, is more common than most would like to admit: Marketing sells to customer A 10

Integration can be a humbling experience. Many companies that desperately want integrated systems don't know where to begin putting them together. Yet those that have found the gumption to assemble a working integrated system wouldn't go back to doing business the "old fashioned way."

The purpose of integration is twofold. First, departments that can share information resources should be linked together. Second, integration should reduce data redundancy. How many times is a customer's address entered into the system? On quick count: four—once each in accounts receivable, accounts payable, order processing, and shipping and handling. This information should be entered once.

Departments that should be integrated first are those that use "action data"—data that are in need of real-time, simultaneous update forecasting.

It's those departments, such as manufacturing, order processing, traffic and transportation, distribution, accounts receivable and accounts payable, purchasing and inventory that need action data. If products are being sold, produced, depleted, shipped, paid for, replenished, and sold again on a day-in, day-out basis, it's wise to keep this information flowing among the departments on an as-it-happens basis.

Condensed from Cathy Coffman, "Integration or Stagnation," *Automotive Industries,* September 1987, pp. 95–99.

model Xs, which are 6-inch rotary drills with eight-day delivery; Manufacturing makes 12 model Ys, which are $5\frac{1}{2}$-inch rotary drills, three weeks later; Shipping sends this order to customer B, who has never ordered any rotary drills; and Accounting bills customer C. Such a fiasco would be funny if so many negative things did not result from it. First, productivity and service is down the drain. Second, backing this mess out of the system will probably create additional errors and more fiascos. And, third, the competition is going to gain three customers. The sharing and coordination of technical information among operations would have prevented such bungling in the first place.

Besides better coordination between operations, better tactical and strategic decisions are also made when operations "talk" to each other. Marketing detects shifts in customers' tastes and needs and changes in the competition. This information is communicated to Engineering, which, in turn, designs simulations along with material requirements planning and cost analysis for product enhancement to meet the shifting needs of the marketplace. This information is communicated to Manufacturing, which simulates production and loading schedules, production resource planning, and personnel skills analysis. This information is coordinated with capital budgeting for financial analysis.

Here's an example of the way it should work if the system is properly integrated. Assume a salesperson takes an order from a credit customer for an air compressor. First, this transaction's input is put through an edit and validation screen. For example, the order is checked for validity, reasonableness, and accuracy. A credit check is made, and assuming that credit is granted, the compressor requested is either found in stock or is placed on special order. If the compressor is in stock and the order passes validation, the order-entry system updates the appropriate files and a variety of technical documents are automatically prepared, such as an invoice, order acknowledgment, and shipping papers. If the compressor is to be manufactured, the order-entry system produces a transaction that causes the manufacturing system to generate a job order and bill of materials. This order transaction is then used, along with other external data, such as competitive, demographic, industrial trends and ratios, to update a sales forecast. This forecast is used to reformulate budgets, cash flow projections, and production schedules to provide relevant and timely information to users at all levels and across functions.

5.3 A FULLY INTEGRATED INFORMATION SYSTEM MODEL

We will use a manufacturing enterprise to demonstrate a fully integrated information system model. But other nonmanufacturing firms, such as United Airlines with its Apollo system and Sears with its nationwide wide area network,

---

Macola Accounting Software works with both online and batch processing. A convenient windowing facility lets you look up required master file data without exiting the data entry screen. Multiple levels of password protection and extensive audit trail reports protect your data.

To go from a single-user to a network environment, you simply add the package's multiuser run-time module. The system is well suited to many different businesses with varying levels of accounting complexity. Growing companies will not outgrow the software.

Macola offers additional marketing, distribution, and manufacturing modules that can be integrated into the accounting software and form a fully integrated information system. Some of the modules include customer order processing, inventory management and analysis, bill of material processor, materials requirements planning, master production scheduling, and job costing.

Macola on a Novell LAN installation (about $60,000 for hardware and software) gives you functionality equivalent to that of a $250,000 installation.

Excerpted from Susan Davis and Morris W. Stemp, ''Macola Accounting Software,'' *PC Magazine*, September 15, 1987, pp. 220 and 222.

are evolving to FIISs. In any case, FIISs for any kind of organization call for companywide backbone networks that reach and serve all the groups and stakeholders of the organization.

FIIS Ties the Functions Together

A fully integrated information system model is outlined in Figure 5.2. Note how all the major functions presented in the previous chapter are connected to form a FIIS. The major goal of the FIIS is to link all operations from accounting, through manufacturing, to marketing electronically. In most organizations well over half of the total transactions processed are accounting transactions. Many of these transactions impact on other functions of the enterprise and therefore should interact with these functions. By the same token, other functions act as feeder systems to the accounting area, making the total organization a highly interactive and interdependent system.

Manufacturing in Transition

The manufacturing process adds value to a product, and the only way to add value to a product is to do work on it, such as machining it, welding components together, wiring it, painting it, and the like. Activities like moving, setting up, storing, inspecting, scheduling, and expediting increase the product's cost but not its value. Furthermore, a very shocking statistic bandied about by manufacturing experts is that most conventional manufacturers spend less than one percent of their time and money adding value to the product. Clearly, a worthwhile challenge is to develop information systems that help to make those other activities more efficient or decrease the need for them entirely.

Traditional factories with their cumbersome and costly set-up procedures, long lead times, large lot sizes, and huge stocks of inventory are no longer the manufacturing environment to provide productivity and quality that will be competitive in a global market. The aim of new manufacturing processes is to reduce production lead times by 80 to 90 percent; cut manufacturing inventories by 40 to 90 percent; slash direct labor costs by 50 to 60 percent; trim indirect labor by 70 to 80 percent; and virtually eliminate scrap, rework, and the need for warranties. Many watchers of the manufacturing sector say that this industry's new focus will soon put it on the road to manufacturing excellence.

Selected Integrating Elements for Manufacturing

The reappraisal of manufacturing strategy over the last several years has led to the development of a number of techniques and concepts that promise to integrate the manufacturing process and make it more efficient. Some of the more noted ones are discussed in the paragraphs that follow. Be careful, however, not to become entangled in the acronymic jungle while reading this material.

Factory Automation

Factory automation uses machines that are computer controlled. These computer-controlled machines either enhance work done by humans or replace

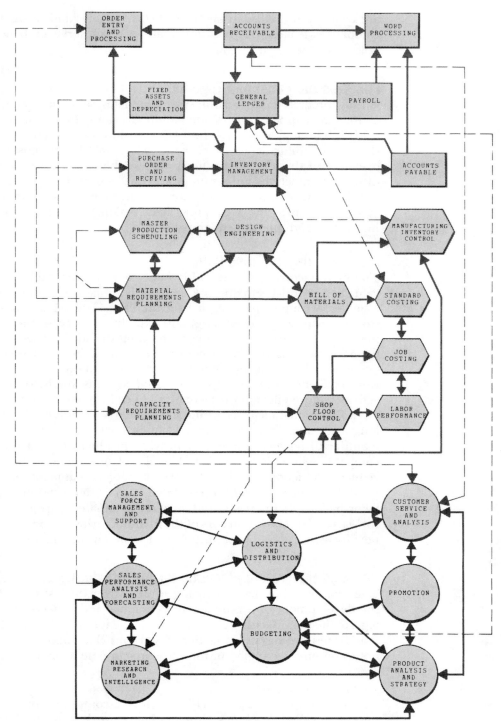

Figure 5.2 A fully integrated information system for a manufacturing company.

workers entirely. In many instances, these machines cost less, are more reliable, and do a better job. Major types of factory automation are:

1. *Computer-Aided Design (CAD)*. Design engineers use interactive workstations to design products, parts, bridges, buildings, and the like.
2. *Computer-Aided Manufacturing (CAM)*. This is an application of the computer to those tasks that come after design. An important part of this operation, for example, would be direct numeric control (DNC) of a cutting machine to cut shapes from a steel plate in the most efficient and scrap-saving manner. Generally, DNC uses a minicomputer.
3. *Robotics*. Industrial robots fill the gap between automation such as DNC and the worker. The principal characteristics of a robot are that it incorporates much of the adaptability and responsiveness of the worker, but in some instances it outperforms the worker. Also robots operate in environments hostile to humans.

Computer-Integrated Manufacturing

Computer-integrated manufacturing systems have become the keystone for "factories of the future." All processes and information flow in the factory of the future are online and in real time to increase productivity and efficiency. In the new world of manufacturing, real-time factory devices, shop floor computers, robots, and controllers are used. All functions of the organization are tied together by a telecommunications network. Automatic data collection devices use scanning and bar code input. Electronic message systems are employed to ensure that valuable time is not lost and problems are handled immediately. For example, product design changes are broadcast throughout the approval chain on screens for approval by "electronic signatures." Other activities are handled in a similar fashion to decrease the generation of paper reports. Note also that CIM is more of a master plan or concept that integrates many of the elements discussed in the paragraphs that follow.

Each workday in the last three years, Allen-Bradley has turned out between 1,000 and 4,000 controllers in electrical industrial motors. AB prices them competitively. It guarantees they'll work according to specifications. And it promises they'll be ready for shipment the day after the order is in.

Allen-Bradley manages to do all this with only four people attending to the entire manufacturing process. The four attendants do light maintenance on the 26 machines on the 45,000-square-foot production line and feed it with raw materials.

Excerpted from Tom McCusker, "Allen-Bradley Tries to Fight Competition by Tooling Up," *Datamation*, March 15, 1988, pp. 33–36.

GM has put $2.6 billion where its mouth is by being the first to use MAP in its highly automated truck factory, which turns out more than 400 trucks daily.

In a pyramid-like structure, various machines from mainframes to PCs are connected by a broadband network using the MAP protocol. An array of pedestal robots apply 98 percent of all the welds. A statistical process control-based vision system measures 40 dimensions on each truck, monitoring the welds, maintaining tolerances, and reporting on discrepancies. Sixty robots apply paint to trucks that have been prepped by vision-camera-guided robots.

Condensed from John Kador, "GM Factory is First to Use MAP," *InformationWEEK,* August 10, 1987, p. 15.

Manufacturing Automation Protocol

Manufacturing automation protocol, developed by General Motors, is a method by which CIM can become a practical reality. MAP is a set of protocols or structure to let the different components in a factory "talk" to each other.

MAP makes it easier to allocate and transfer personnel from one job to another. Data transmission is more accurate and faster. The shop floor gets quality control statistics and variances from standards in real time. Time-consuming preparation and flow of paper documents are reduced. Online connectivity among the shop floor, engineering, cost accounting, logistics, and the sales force accelerates management's ability to solve problems, respond to market needs, and implement changes.

Some manufacturing mavens think that MAP is the hottest thing to hit the factory since the conveyor belt. Champions of MAP view it as becoming the factory communications utility, transparent and easy to use as electricity. Still others think that MAP may become mired in its own complexity, especially with its bewildering array of multivendor connectivity. But some companies, despite the uncertainty, are preparing for MAP by laying broadband networks, a prerequisite for MAP. Several large companies, such as Boeing, IBM, GM, Eastman Kodak, Deere, and others, are using MAP in some pilot plants to tie together equipment from several leading automation vendors. With blessings from these companies, the market for MAP could climb dramatically over the next several years.

Manufacturing Automation Protocol/Technical and Office Protocol

MAP, as we have already learned, is a protocol (or set of protocols) for a broadband communications network to integrate a factory. TOP, an office automation system developed by Boeing, is the same thing used to integrate office procedures. Put MAP/TOP together, and you have the basis for a fully integrated information system, total systems integration from the shop floor to the executive suite.

All enterprises are information driven. But the flow of information throughout many firms is impeded by an array of incompatible components. As we learned in the preceding section, MAP is a solution to this problem in manufacturing. Early on, Boeing saw the same need for a solution in the office and therefore developed the technical and office protocol to support compatibility and connectivity within the office.

A number of years ago, Boeing reenacted the Tower of Babel story. Very few of its computers understood each other. Over three million parts went into building an airplane. To buy, receive, store, locate, and pay for all those parts was a monumental task. Boeing's computers were supposed to help in this task. Instead, they were part of the problem. Everything was fragmented and piecemeal.

Boeing had computers for accounting, inventory control, logistics, production; peripherals to handle communications with divisions; and special workstations for engineers. Some computers operated independently; others were connected to form small groups or "islands of automation." But the total "information system" was scattered and incompatible.

In the early 1980s, Boeing had over 50 mainframes, 450 minicomputers, and 20,000 workstations from more than 90 vendors. Miscommunication and discord were pervasive. Finally, management said, "Enough is enough." A tone was set that fostered an entrepreneurial spirit. As entrepreneurs are inclined to do, Boeing changed this chaos into an opportunity. Thus, TOP was born.

Just-in-Time Manufacturing

Just-in-time manufacturing, a widely used technique in Japan, is exactly opposite to the approach traditionally practiced in the United States, which is mass production of large quantities of products at one time. JIT attempts to minimize inventory costs by receiving a supply of raw materials from the vendor "just in time" for the production run. Small quantities of raw materials are received at a time; perhaps a single vendor's truck arrives at the plant several times a day.

JIT manufacturing, or "Kanban" as the Japanese call it, is designed to eliminate waste, increase productivity, and improve quality throughout the production and logistics process. For example, companies in Japan that use JIT maintain an average inventory of $30 per manufactured unit. For a similar product manufactured in the United States by a company not using JIT, an average inventory of $500 to $600 per manufactured unit is maintained.

One of the goals of JIT is zero inventories (i.e., not only just in time but just enough). Delivery is not made on the day it is needed but provided at the instant it is needed. Therefore, the supplier must deliver defect-free items.

With these kinds of demands placed on suppliers, a long-term partnership between a manufacturer and a supplier must be established. In such a single-source relationship, a clear joint commitment to success exists between the manufacturer and its supplier, whereas in multiple-source supplier relationships, the commitment may not be quite so strong.

JIT manufacturing is not just another automated gimmick—it's a new way of working, and it's hard to achieve. The heart of JIT is better information delivery to factory designers, project schedulers, and foremen. All end users with a need to know have direct access to the data base.

"We build to customer orders, not to stock," explains Jerry Molter, systems analyst responsible for building manufacturing support data bases for Steelcase, Incorporated. "We have reduced manufacturing lead time on many items by two days. We've also reduced our inventories."

Excerpted from G. Berton Latamore, "Getting in Touch with JIT," *Computer & Communications Decisions,* February 1988, p. 28C.

Workers on a JIT line are trained in each other's work and are expected to inspect the work-in-process before they perform their task. If defects are identified, the worker hits an emergency switch to stop the conveyor and the problem is solved on the spot. Nothing is ever set aside to be examined or reworked later. This procedure places a severe burden on the work force, but by doing it this way, the production team learns all the possible sources of defects and eventually learns to produce zero-defect products.

"Jidoka," another Japanese term, is also an important concept of JIT. Jidoka makes problems apparent. For example, JIT removes the safety cushion of buffer stocks and changes other procedures, which may have been hiding problems. These problems can be any number of things from poor quality and high scrap rates to machine down time and late supplier deliveries. Indeed, JIT mavens are emphatic that JIT is not just an inventory program, but that it uncovers weaknesses that may have been going on for years. Or, putting it another way, JIT does not tolerate any weaknesses or sloppy habits in the manufacturing process.

While JIT manufacturing has risks, these are diminishing because of better linkage between manufacturers, suppliers, and carriers. Moreover, these par-

Chicago-based Navistar has some materials delivered only four hours before they are needed. Navistar's JIT program, which includes electronic links with suppliers, has helped reduce inventories by $80 million in its first year of operations.

Excerpted from A. T. Sadhwani and M. H. Sarhan, "Electronic Systems Enhance JIT Operations," *Management Accounting,* December 1987, pp. 25–30.

ticipants are gearing up and changing methods for JIT implementation. At a GM plant, 300 truck docks are located around the perimeter to expedite delivery of supplies to its work centers. Railroad companies are offering minitrain services to meet JIT delivery schedules of major manufacturers. Trucking companies collect materials from several suppliers in a clustered area to make a full truck load, then deliveries are made to the JIT manufacturer's plants two to four times a day. Side-loading trailers are used for loading and unloading efficiency. Manufacturers, suppliers, and carriers regularly exchange information via computers on production schedules, delivery dates, and shipment notifications. Through this regular information interchange, operations can be coordinated precisely between all parties.[1]

Manufacturing Resource Planning

Manufacturing resource planning (MRP II) had its origins in the 1960s as material requirements planning, a computer-based method of scheduling and ordering manufacturing inventories. MRP answered four questions: What are we going to make? What do we need to make it? What do we have on hand? What else do we have to get? Later, MRP II added the elements of translating the operating plan into financial terms and providing managers with the ability to ask "what-if" questions.

MRP II goes beyond managing production, purchasing, and inventory. It considers cash flow and returns on investment and ties together accounting, man-

Manufacturers have long recognized that linking the factory floor to financial, warehousing, and distribution systems decreases inventories and production lead times and speeds delivery to customers. The manufacturing resource planning loop has since expanded, however, to include higher-level management decision making, more sophisticated tracking and more data collection links, as manufacturers develop corporatewide computer-integrated manufacturing strategies.

Vendors agree that future enhancements and additions to MRP systems will continue to expand the limits of the loop to leverage CIM strategies to more links to what Tom Carney, product line manager for Xerox, calls "the world of CIM"—engineering, computer-aided designs and manufacturing systems, robotics, and automated guided vehicles—lie ahead.

Excerpted from Barbara Francett, "Expanding the MRP Loop," *Computer & Communications Decisions*, February 1988, p. 28A.

[1]A. T. Sadhwani, M. H. Sarhan, and Roger A. Camp, "The Impact of Just-in-Time Inventory on Small Businesses," *Journal of Accountancy*, January 1987, pp. 118–132.

ufacturing, marketing, and logistics planning into an overall company plan that can be executed and monitored. It is a management concept that becomes the basis of a company strategy.

Some companies are combining MRP II with JIT. Proponents of this integration say that the two concepts work together like hand-in-glove or rack-and-pinion. With this approach, it is no longer practical to develop information systems as loosely related sets of functionally specific subsystems.

5.4 FULLY INTEGRATED INFORMATION SYSTEMS FOR NONMANUFACTURING COMPANIES

Manufacturing is not the only industry that can profit from FIIS. Following are several examples of how other industries can benefit.

1. *Banking.* The three main applications in banking are demand deposits, loans, and savings. One customer may have several savings, checking, and loan accounts scattered across several bank branches. All activities of the customer are cross-referenced in the data base. The benefits of this integration are (a) standardization of procedures and customer service across all branches, (b) the ability to extend banking services within easy access of customers at any time, day or night, (c) increased marketing opportunities for the bank in selling additional services to customers, and (d) more timely and comprehensive customer information for management analysis.

2. *Insurance.* The insurance agent in the field—in the local office or in a prospect's home—feeds into the system through a portable terminal a number of parameters about the prospect, such as age, marital status, salary, number of dependents, and so forth. Models built into the information system analyze these parameters and within seconds transmit to the terminal an insurance program that fits the prospect. Also, the data base can be designed to provide a variety of ways to access data about present policyholders, such as by policyholder name and address, by policy claims, by policy renewals, by insurance representative identification, by geographic territory, and by rating. All policy information is available to all offices of the insurance company.

3. *Utilities.* Information systems that serve this industry consolidate all data relating to each customer, such as (a) name and address, (b) appliances installed, (c) maintenance history, (d) gas or electricity consumption (current and history), (e) account details (current and history), and (f) installment plan account details. Access to this information from online terminals enables the utility company to answer readily customers' queries regarding their account status, gas or electricity billing, and installment plan account status. Furthermore, a customer service system is built on this information, allocating maintenance technicians to satisfy requests for service and repair of appliances.

4. *Medical Industry.* The information system records all visits made by the patient to the clinic or hospital, the diagnosis made on each visit, and

treatments. A complete medical history is thus established for access by all authorized persons. Moreover, a patient profile can be maintained that details drugs the patient is currently on and any possible allergies or side effects from other drugs. The system also monitors for drug interaction and drug regimen.

5. *Law Enforcement.* A data base contains information that relates to convicted criminals. Typical entries include aliases, personal characteristics, modus operandi, and previous convictions. Personnel at online terminals are able to access this data base when given any of several items of information. Possible relationships between particular crimes and the modus operandi and characteristics of various criminals can be identified. Crime patterns and likely time and location of incidences can be drawn from the system for better crime control. On the judicial side, information systems monitor the progress of each case and periodically prepare action reports. These action reports include lists of persons being held for no apparent reason, cases that are ready for trial but have not been placed on the calendar, and persons whose probation periods have elapsed but have not been officially terminated. The system also provides numerous written reports that assist the criminal justice officials in preparing a case for trial, scheduling each event of the trial, and preparing local and state statistical reports.

5.5 NETWORKING: THE KEY TO FIIS

Networks are, indeed, the links that bind people and machines together, making it possible for them to share work, facilities, information, and ideas. The installing of mechanical conveyor belts in offices in earlier times to move work from one station to another was an attempt at networking. Today, when users of PCs swap floppies, they are building a network. When such haphazard networking becomes too inefficient and awkward to handle the traffic, the technology building block, which includes telecommunications hardware and software, is implemented. This technology permits instantaneous interaction between persons, groups, and systems or any combination thereof, thus opening up a broad vista of integrating and interfacing possibilities. As our transportation networks carry products to the remotest corners of the country, so too will emerging telecommunication networks carry information to *all* users with equal efficiency. It will support information and operations workers as electrical or fuel energy supports engines and machines.

A Simple Network Example

In simple terms, the network permits one computer to work with a file stored on another computer, to print a report on another computer's printer, or to send a message to a co-worker who is working on another computer. An example of how this is done is illustrated in the following case:[2]

---

[2]Taken from Jonathan Sachs, "Local Area Networks," *PC World*, July 1984, pp. 69–75.

It's 8 A.M. Monday when service manager George Smith arrives. George tells his PC to print an inventory record that it prepared overnight. A customer calls, reporting that his tractor is broken and must be fixed immediately. George can do it, but he may not return in time for a staff meeting that Bob Anderson, the general manager has planned. Bob is not in, so rather than run upstairs to leave a note, George sends a message from his PC. When Bob's secretary comes in, the message will be waiting.

George wants a copy of the broken tractor's service record. It's in his PC, but his printer will be tied up for half an hour. No problem; he prints the service record on his "second printer," which is attached to a PC in the showroom. The showroom printer has just finished producing the service record as George enters the room. He tears off the report and is out the door.

Salesperson Sue Wright, meanwhile, answers a phone inquiry. Does Green Equipment stock a pump for a milking machine that it sold last year? "One moment, I'll check," Sue says. The service department keeps the parts inventory, but obtaining inventory information is, again, no problem. Sue searches a file on the showroom PC's "third disk drive," which is actually located on the service department's system. She learns that the part isn't in stock but can be delivered in three days. "Is Thursday OK?" she asks. The caller says that it is. Sue has just made the day's first sale.

Linda Tolliver, Bob Anderson's secretary, clocks in. She's been helping the bookkeeper put old sales data into computer files for financial projections. Much of the work has been done since she last looked at the project; the bookkeeper must have worked on it late last week. The files are on Linda's PC, but they have been read by the bookkeeper's PC as though they were on his computer's "third disk drive."

Bob Anderson arrives. "Any messages?" he asks. Linda finds the message from George. "Have an emergency repair call; may not be back for the meeting. Reschedule?" Bob asks Linda to check every employee's calendar. The calendars are scattered throughout Green Equipment's computers, but they're easy to review; a scheduling program collects them automatically. Linda notes that everyone is available Tuesday at 10 A.M., and Bob approves that time. Linda updates all the calendars, which "return" to the computers from which they came. Linda drafts a memo announcing the change and, from her PC, sends everyone a copy.

Most businesses, large or small, could certainly use a network like the one described here. In many offices today, however, you will find people constantly running around the office exchanging floppy disks with other workers, or milling around *one* printer, waiting for their output.

Network Components

The basic components of networks are nodes and links. Nodes are units that can accept data input into the network or output information, or both. Subnodes act as relay devices that manage information between input and output nodes. They act as front-end or back-end information traffic controllers that provide polling and queuing tasks. Links are channels or paths for the flow of information between input/output and relay nodes. A growing number of nodes and links offer the systems analyst a number of configuration possibilities. Nodes and relay nodes can be anything from a printer to a facsimile device, from a PC to a giant mainframe, and from a modem to a multiplexer. Link media can be terrestrial (wire or cable), microwave, laser, optical, or satellite, with either an analog or digital transmission mode.

Networks can grow from very simple to a network of networks, called metanetworks. Some may look like an upside-down tree, ring, or star; others may resemble a badly knotted fishnet. Indeed, a "correct" or "standard" model does not exist. As we will see later, the network must fit the organization and abide by the design forces. As for now, view Figure 5.3, a general illustration of a metanetwork.

5.6 NETWORK TOPOLOGIES: DATA TRAFFIC HIGHWAYS

Topology is the interconnecting arrangements or configuration of nodes in a network. Network topologies can "look" like anything from a string with a knot in one end to a plate of spaghetti. The best network for a particular situation

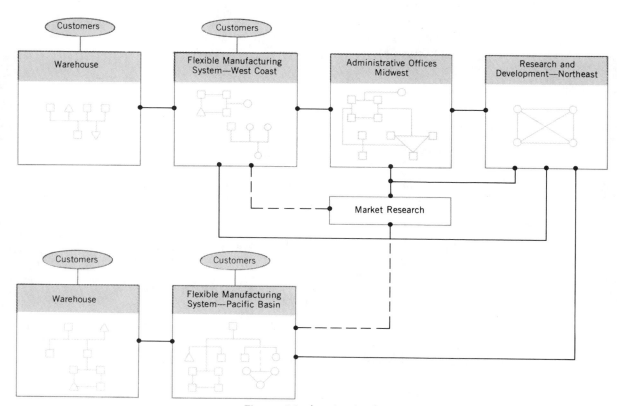

Figure 5.3 A metanetwork

is chosen from the basic topologies of the star, hierarchical tree, loop, bus, ring, and web, all of which are illustrated in Figure 5.4.

Topologies Defined

1. *Star.*   All communications are routed to and handled by a major, central node. Generally, the central node does most of the processing and is responsible for switching all messages between outlying nodes, such as a mainframe in a time-sharing environment. Most, if not all, of the outlying nodes have minimal stand-alone capabilities and perform fairly uniform tasks.

2. *Hierarchical Tree.*   This topology looks like an upside-down tree and is characterized by intermediate nodes between communicating nodes, in which the intermediate node operates in a store-and-forward mode. Applications of this topology may have a mainframe at the top of the hierarchy, serving as the coordinator and controller of computing, minicomputers at intermediate levels performing analysis and data management, and microcomputers at the lower levels performing basic input/output functions.

3. *Loop.*   The loop topology is often used to interconnect a series of similar-sized nodes doing similar work, such as a group of order-entry clerks or word processors. Each node in the loop must be capable of all the communications functions of the network. Some network designers also call the loop topology "daisy chaining," because of its one-to-another mode of communication.

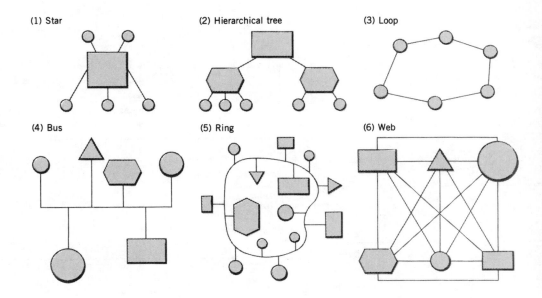

(1) Star   (2) Hierarchical tree   (3) Loop

(4) Bus   (5) Ring   (6) Web

4. *Bus.*   A bus network assigns portions of network processing and management to each node. Hardware nodes can range from small, portable terminals to large computers. This topology is common in local area networks serving one site, such as in one building or office complex. Each node has access to a common communications line (the bus), but the individual nodes perform widely varying tasks—from word processing, transactional processing, and general accounting to analysis and strategic planning.

5. *Ring.*   The ring is a combination of loop and bus topologies but is more similar to a bus. If an individual node on the ring crashes, either no effect or a small degree of degradation on the total ring network is felt because, unlike the loop topology, the failed node is not directly in the communication path.

6. *Web.*   A web is the spaghetti topology of networks. Each node in the network is connected to each other by means of a dedicated link. Fully connected nodes possess as many links as there are nodes. A web that has N nodes, has $N(N - 1)/2$ links. Web topologies are used where the network needs to be dense and tightly coupled, such as in a system that controls a space launch.

Note that it is not necessary to hardwire or permanently connect all the nodes of any of the preceding topologies. Indeed, in any network a few of the nodes are usually wireless or loosely coupled. For example, cellular phones and other mobile devices can be used in designing effective networks. Moreover, all kinds of hybrid topologies are possible, using one topology to fit one part of the organization and others for other parts. For example, Figure 5.5 illustrates this point. The ABC organization is served by an information system metanetwork made up of (1) the bus that serves accounting and administrative functions, (2) the loop that is for clerical and word processing tasks, (3) the star that supports research and design engineering, and (4) the ring that aids production and quality control. All the subtopologies are connected by a bus topology to form the metanetwork.

Topology Selection

The decision as to what network topology to use promises to be as interesting and controversial in the near future as it has been in the recent past. To be sure, today's information technology permits the systems analyst to design any topology he or she desires. But as in nearly all cases, the main question is not technological feasibility but organizational culture and factors discussed earlier in this text. It is, however, somewhat incongruous to design a ring topology with stand-alone nodes distributed throughout an organization if the organization is highly structured, with a centralized, bureaucratic management and an insular culture, and is committed to that style. A highly centralized organization would presumably be better off using some form of star or hierarchical topology that provides it with a centrally controlled system, which mirrors its management style.

ABC Organization

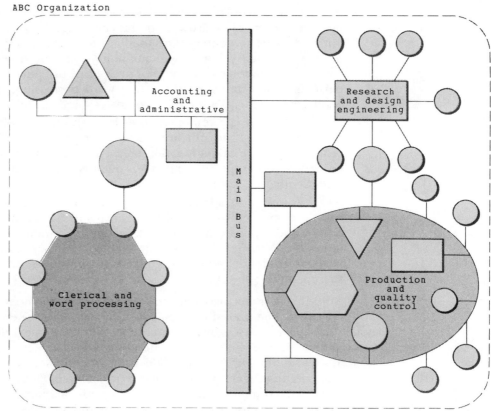

Figure 5.5 A metanetwork made up of a hybrid of basic network topologies.

Unless an organization wants to overhaul its culture and style completely, the information system must be mapped into the organization to achieve balance and harmony. The system must *fit* the organization. With this in mind, we provide in Figure 5.6 the cultural and organizational factors that influence the choice of topologies. Because loop and web topologies are special cases, we have deleted them from this analysis.

The top bar represents the topology choices. All the dashed lines running through the vertical arrow represent the organizational factors and indicate their influence on the topology selected. If a preponderance of the factors in any organization are similar to those pointing to the left, then a star or hierarchical topology is appropriate. If most of the factors point to the right, then the topology chosen should be a bus or ring. The two strongest influences on topology selection are management style and organizational culture. But if the direction is unclear, or some of the factors vary from one area of the organization to another, the systems analyst may choose a combination of topologies for the design of the total information system, thereby fitting specific topologies to specific situations, and, at the same time, achieving total integration.

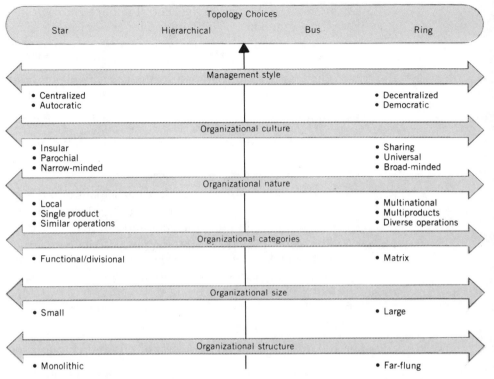

Figure 5.6 How organizational and cultural factors can influence the choice of network topologies.

Topology Advantages and Disadvantages

The following are the *advantages* of star and hierarchical topologies:

1. Controls are easier to implement and monitor.
2. In some instances, with the use of large mainframes as the central hub, economies of scale can be achieved.
3. Standards in policies, programming, and building blocks can be more easily implemented.
4. The malfunction of a remote device does not affect other devices.
5. Generally, it is more reliable.

The following are the *disadvantages* of star and hierarchical topologies:

1. The central mainframe is the processor, controller, and gateway for all the other nodes in the network. If this central node fails, all the other nodes are effectively out of commission. In the future, to make star and hierarchical topologies meet the widening and varying needs of the organization, mean time between failure (MTBF) must be measured in years, and mean time to repair (MTTR) must be measured in minutes.

2. Because of the size of the central node, significant inefficiencies can occur when a member of outlying nodes are not using the system.
3. In some instances, stringent standards and monolithic design can become a barrier to quick responsiveness to user needs.
4. The total system is limited by the capacity of the central node.
5. This topology is generally more expensive to install.

The following are the *advantages* of bus and ring topologies:

1. They are good topologies for supporting integration of all functions.
2. They increase direct user access, and greater stand-alone capabilities are distributed to the point of need.
3. The possibility for greater user participation in design exists.
4. User expertise and confidence in using the system are increased, presumably resulting in more efficient and effective use of technology.
5. The ability to share computing power, data base, input/output operations, and models increases, thereby improving productivity and avoiding significant degradation of the total system because of crashes at one or two nodes of the system.
6. Customizing systems nodes to fit user needs precisely are facilitated.
7. Generally, the installation costs are lower.

The following are the *disadvantages* of bus and ring topologies:

1. They tend to allow redundancies in all of the building blocks to creep into the system.
2. Generally they are more difficult to manage and control.
3. Because some of the nodes are small, it is difficult to attract technicians to work in a "small shop" environment and, therefore, skills may not be available to remote nodes.
4. If the organizational factors and culture were misread, or if they change, a tendency could be set in motion toward fiefdom-building and fragmentation, exactly what one was trying to avoid in the first place. Indeed, the topology begins to break down if cooperation and compatibility between nodes begin to diminish.
5. If the bus or ring network backbone is broken, then the whole system is disabled.

SUMMARY

This chapter has explained why organizations are changing from highly compartmentalized, function-specific information systems to fully integrated information systems. Because of the integrated nature of these systems, a climate of creativity and organizational solidarity has been created, a freer flow of communication between departments has occurred, and a synergism among the interacting functional units has resulted.

As well as an increase in emphasis by management on integration, new manufacturing concepts that support integration are receiving attention. These concepts and techniques include computer-integrated manufacturing, manufacturing automation protocol, just-in-time manufacturing, and manufacturing resource planning. Coupled with developments in telecommunications nodes and links, and attempts by hardware vendors to improve the connectivity of their products and products of other vendors, the time is right to move in the direction of large-scale development of fully integrated information systems.

IMPORTANT TERMS

bus topology

computer-aided design (CAD)

computer-aided manufacturing (CAM)

computer-integrated manufacturing (CIM)

factory automation

fully integrated information system (FIIS)

hierarchical topology

jidoka

just-in-time (JIT) manufacturing

kanban

loop topology

manufacturing automation protocol (MAP)

manufacturing resource planning (MRP II)

networking

ring topology

robotics

star topology

technical and office protocol (TOP)

web topology

Assignment

REVIEW QUESTIONS

5.1 What is the goal of integration as it pertains to information systems?

5.2 Why is it important to strive for integrated organizations and information systems?

5.3 A freer flow of information results from integration. What does this freer flow of information facilitate?

5.4 Fully integrated information systems mean users are not divided into the "information rich" and the "information poor." List the negative practices or situations that could occur as a result of introducing FIIS.

5.5 How can the manufacturing process be made more efficient? State the goals of new manufacturing processes on four dimensions.

5.6 List six techniques and concepts that promise to integrate the manufacturing process and make it more efficient.

5.7 What are the three major types of factory automation?

5.8 What is the difference between CAD and CAM?

5.9 Why might it be more appropriate to use robots than people in the manufacturing process?

5.10 What are the characteristics of computer-integrated manufacturing (CIM) systems?

5.11 Define the technique of manufacturing automation protocol. What is an essential prerequisite for MAP? How does technical and office protocol correspond to MAP?

5.12 How does just-in-time manufacturing contrast to traditional manufacturing processes in the United States? What is JIT manufacturing designed to do?

5.13 For a JIT manufacturing process to work, what kind of relationship must be established between a manufacturer and its supplier? What is expected of the workers on a JIT production line?

5.14 What elements did manufacturing resource planning add to material requirements planning?

5.15 What are the basic components of newtorks? Define each component.

5.16 What are the six basic network topologies? What network topology is most appropriate with a centralized management style? a multinational organization? a matrix form of organization? an extremely small-sized organization? a monolithic organizational structure?

5.17 List five advantages of the star and hierarchical network topologies. List five disadvantages.

5.18 What network topologies tend to support integration of all functions, increase direct user access, and allow for greater user participation in design?

QUESTIONS FOR DISCUSSION

5.19 How does networking fit into the overall scheme of fully integrating the information system?

5.20 Does information system integration extend to information users who are external to the organization? If so, how would such a system be designed to handle input/output requirements of these external users?

5.21 As individual departments are integrated into the organization's information system, the risk of invalid or inaccurate input/output increases, the maintenance cost of the system escalates, and security and other controls are extended over a larger control area, subjecting them to dysfunction. How can management justify these marginal costs, and what measures can systems designers employ to reduce the risk of invalid data?

5.22 "Fully integrated information systems are like a straightjacket to me. It used to be that I could run my own show. Now with these systems I can't." What arguments can be made to counter this manager's attitude?

5.23 "What do you expect us to do? The left hand doesn't know what the right hand is doing. Sales promises delivery dates that cannot be met because the wrong materials are ordered by purchasing." What alternative information systems environment might hold the potential to solve this executive's problem?

5.24 Modernizing a factory's production facility is only half the answer to achieving manufacturing excellence. What is the other half of the answer and what is its aim or intent?

5.25 How would you argue the point that just-in-time manufacturing is more than an inventory program?

5.26 "We have had MRP for a long time in this organization. It seems to me that if we really want to benefit, we need to leap forward with something new instead of inching ahead with a variation of MRP called MRP II." Why is this statement selling short the capabilities and benefits of MRP II?

5.27 "Integration techniques and concepts are fine for the factory, but most of them cannot help our hospital provide a better level of service more efficiently." Point out why this view might be somewhat myopic.

5.28 Discuss the pros and cons of adopting a loop and bus topology for a local area network.

EXERCISES AND PROBLEMS

5.29 Spar Craft is a Los Angeles producer of custom aluminum masts and booms for sailboats. When Spar Craft was founded in 1927, all of Spar Craft's masts and booms were designed by its founder and one other associate, made of wood, and constructed by a group of craftsmen who used hand tools. With the change in the composition of masts and booms from wood to aluminum, most of Spar Craft's manufacturing operations were converted to automatic machines. These changes were necessary to keep Spar Craft competitive in the industry and resulted in higher-quality booms and masts with an extended useful life.

One aspect that has not changed in the last 62 years is Spar Craft's design process. Individual designers still sit at their desks and formulate rigging characteristics using manual methods. Once the design specifications are determined, they are written up and given to various production supervisors to be used as guides in the manufacturing process.

Required: Spar Craft's management is interested in modernizing the design process used so that they may remain competitive in all aspects of their business. Prepare a brief report of how factory automation might be profitably applied in this situation.

5.30 Ajax Manufacturing produces precast concrete products for customers within a five-state area. While sales of Ajax's products have remained strong over the three years, profits have declined dramatically. Ajax's management believes one major reason for this decline has been the lack of coordination among the company's various functional areas. Specifically, based on a study done by consultants of a "Big Eight" CPA firm, Ajax's marketing, production, and accounting functions, frequently appear to be working in opposite directions.

Ajax's management has stated that at the time these systems were implemented, the focus was on employing technology to support each of these major functions. Although the systems have evolved and have been enhanced over the years, integration has totally been ignored.

Required: What arguments could be made in favor of a FIIS for these function-specific systems of Ajax?

5.31 A fully integrated information system brings together function-specific information systems of the organization. Pick a manufacturing company of your choice that is big enough to have distinct accounting, marketing, and production functions. Analyze this company in terms of the modules within it that would serve as interface points for a FIIS.

5.32 For each of the following descriptions, indicate whether a ring or star network topology would be appropriate and the reasons for your recommendation:

1. A medical supplies distributor maintains a central warehouse in Omaha for supplying items to dealers in medical supplies in the Midwest.

2. A motel chain has its headquarters in San Antonio, Texas, and has approximately 35 motels in Texas, Arkansas, and Oklahoma.

3. A pulp and paper manufacturer has processing plants in Eugene, Oregon, and Tacoma, Washington. Sales and distribution are done from its headquarters in Portland.

4. A New York–based precious gem distributor has international offices in Paris, Tokyo, Montreal, and Mexico City.

5. A Philadelphia consumer electronics manufacturer and distributor believes its essential to achieve close coordination between its home office and its manufacturing plants in Eastern and Western Pennsylvania, its three distribution centers, and its eight warehouses.

6. A regional travel bureau has nine offices scattered throughout Southern California.

5.33 Savers Bank originated in Annapolis, Maryland. Beginning in the 1980s Savers initiated an aggressive policy of broadening its market by buying local banks on Maryland's Eastern shore. Today, Savers Bank has 11 banks operating under its name.

Savers was the first bank in Annapolis to automate its account processing. In 1978 it purchased a large computer and linked 15 cashier and officer terminals to it. Because of the demand on funds for Savers expansion program, large-scale automation of its other branch banks has not proceeded at a rapid rate. In fact, the bulk of customer transaction processing in the branch banks is still done using accounting machines.

Required: What kind of network topology would be appropriate to help Savers Bank modernize its branch bank processing?

BIBLIOGRAPHY

AGGARWAL, S. C. "MRP, JIT, OPT, FMS." *Harvard Business Review,* September–October 1985.

COFFMAN, CATHY. "Integration or Stagnation." *Automotive Industries,* September 1987.

"Datapro Communications Solutions." *DataPro 70.* Delran, NJ.: Datapro Research Corporation, 1986.

"Datapro Dictionary of On-Line Services." *DataPro 70.* Delran, NJ.: Datapro Research Corporation, 1986.

"Datapro Reports on Data Communications." *DataPro 70.* Delran, NJ.: Datapro Research Corporation, 1986.

DAVIS, SUSAN, and MORRIS W. STEMP. "Macola Accounting Software." *PC Magazine,* September 15, 1987.

FITZGERALD, JERRY, and TOM S. EASON. *Fundamentals of Data Communications.* New York: John Wiley, 1978.

FORD, F. N., W. N. LEDBETTER, and B. S. GABER. "The Evolving Factory of the Future: Integrating Manufacturing and Information Systems." *Information & Management,* February 1985.

FRANCETT, BARBARA. "Expanding the MRP Loop." *Computer & Communications Decisions,* February 1988.

GAND, HARVEY, and MILT COOK. "Choosing an MRP System." *Datamation,* February 1986.

GUNN, THOMAS. "The CIM Connection." *Datamation,* February 1986.

JELINEK, MARIANN, and JOEL GOLDHAR. "The Strategic Implications of the Factory of the Future." *Sloan Management Review,* Summer 1984.

KADOR, JOHN. "GM Factory Is First to Use MAP." *InformationWEEK,* August 10, 1987.

LATAMORE, G. BERTON. "Getting in Touch with JIT." *Computer & Communications Decisions,* February 1988.

McCUSKER, TOM. "Allen-Bradley Tries to Fight Competition by Tooling Up." *Datamation,* March 15, 1988.

SACHS, JONATHAN. "Local Area Networks," *PC World,* July 1984.

SADHWANI, A. T., and M. H. SARHAN, "Electronic Systems Enhance JIT Operations." *Management Accounting,* December 1987.

SADHWANI, A. T., M. H. SARHAN, and ROGER A. CAMP. "The Impact of Just-in-Time Inventory on Small Businesses." *Journal of Accountancy,* January 1987.

STALLINGS, WILLIAM. *Data and Computer Communications.* New York: Macmillan, 1985.

PART 3

CONTROLS

INPUT   MODELS   OUTPUT

INPUTS

OUTPUTS

DATA BASE

TECHNOLOGY
PLATFORM

CONTROLS

INFORMATION SYSTEMS

DESIGN OF INFORMATION SYSTEM BUILDING BLOCKS

In Chapter 2, you were introduced to the building block approach to the design of information systems. It was argued there that all information systems, irrespective of their complexity, are made up of six building blocks as shown in the accompanying window.

In this part of the text, each of these building blocks will be described in detail. Chapter 6 examines the building block of input, the starting point of the information process. Chapter 7 discusses the models building block. In this chapter, you will be shown some of the more popular models and modeling techniques used by systems analysts. Chapter 8 looks at the output building block, the end product by which users judge the information system.

Chapters 9, 10 and 11 present the technology building block. This block, comprising the computer and its auxiliary storage, telecommunications, networking, and software, enables systems analysts to build powerful and innovative information systems.

The logical and physical components of the data base building block are described in Chapters 12 and 13. Part 3 concludes with a comprehensive description of the controls that can be built into the information system to protect it from hazards, threats, and the introduction of errors.

6

INPUT

6.1 INTRODUCTION

Input is where the whole information process starts. The raw material of information are data that occur from transactions, events, orders, and inquiries, all represented by voice, images, text, numbers, letters, and special characters or symbols. Obviously, an information system is no better than the data that it is fed—GIGO (garbage in, garbage out). But some pundits believe that with an increasing dependence on information technology, this classic acronym may develop a new meaning—garbage in, gospel out. Either expression, indeed, engenders a caveat for proper input design, the subject of this chapter.

Specifically, the objectives of this chapter are:

1. To present an overview of how transactions are input and processed by the system.
2. To describe and illustrate how to design paper forms, the carrier of most input data.
3. To provide guidelines for the design of electronic forms, a new way to improve productivity and efficiency.
4. To present explanations and illustrations of codes and to demonstrate how they are used to identify, process, and retrieve data.
5. To cover the many data entry devices available to the systems analyst.

6.2 INPUTTING AND PROCESSING TRANSACTIONS

The key considerations concerning the input of data are data identification, layout, and timing. Following is an example and overview of these considerations.

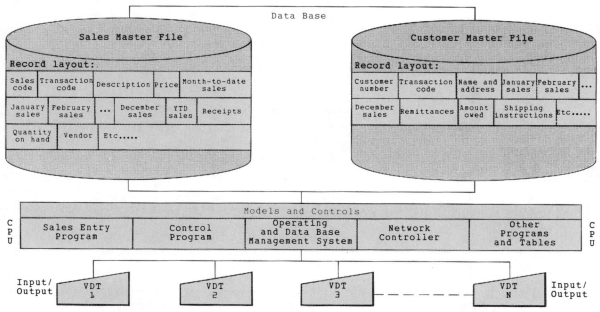

Figure 6.1 How a transaction is input into a system and processed.

Anatomy of a Sales Transaction

A sales transaction provides a good example of how transactions are entered into a system and processed. Building blocks of the system are shown in Figure 6.1. The control program restricts usage of the sales entry program to authorized users by requiring entry of a password. If a valid password is entered, the sales entry program is released for processing. The transaction is then input for appropriate updating and processing. The sales entry form layout is shown below:

SALES ENTRY LAYOUT

Name of Data	Data Start in Character Position	Number of Digits
Sales code		
Store number	1	3
Department number	4	2
Salesperson number	6	2
Inventory number	8	5
Transaction code*	13	1
Amount	14	9
Customer number	23	6
&#8942;	&#8942;	&#8942;

*1 = add record; 2 = delete record; 3 = change price; 4 = inventory receipts; 5 = update sales; 6 = change description; 7 = change customer; 8 = sales credit.

The following steps explain how a sales transaction is processed:

1. A transaction is entered into the buffer memory of a visual display terminal (VDT) by an operator, by filling in the zones of a form display on the screen. Note that input could also be handled by keying from a paper form (source document) or by a menu-driven system. In any event, the operator releases the transaction to the system when it is completed and verified.

2. The operating system and data base management system (OS/DBMS) transfers the contents of the VDT buffer after being released by the control program. The OS/DBMS then gives control to the sales entry program.

3. The sales entry program reads the codes and customer number (if the transaction changes the customer file). Upon request, the OS/DBMS fetches appropriate records from one or both files by following certain hardware file addresses and data association techniques. Once found, the record(s) is (are) transferred to main memory of the processor.

4. After performing many housekeeping, editing, and control details, the OS/DBMS returns control to the sales entry program at the point where it left off and resumes execution.

5. Instructions of the program, controlled by codes, perform appropriate processing and updating of the record(s).

6. The updated record(s) is (are) written over the contents in the old record(s).

7. After completing this input, the OS/DBMS returns control to the network controller to poll for another transaction, triggering a repetition of the process.

Batch Versus Direct Input

Data, such as the preceding sales transaction, are input into the system in one of two ways: batch or direct. Batch input simply means that transactions are accumulated (batched) for some period of time—a day, week, month, quarter, or fiscal period. Direct input means that data concerning an event or transaction are input into the system *when it occurs*. Whether batch or direct input is used depends on the requirements of users and the timeliness of output produced. Payroll data, for example, may be batched; inventory control data requires direct input. Moreover, because of added validation and automatic testing procedures embedded in direct systems, accuracy increases significantly.

Batch input usually involves capturing and filling in paper forms (source documents), and then converting data from these forms to computer input media by a keying or scanning operation. Keying alternatives are key-to-card, key-to-tape, key-to-disk, and key-to-floppy. Scannable forms are processed by magnetic ink character recognition, optical character recognition, holographic, or laser devices. These scanning devices are also known as *source data automation*. In any case, these devices can support either batch or direct input.

The leitmotiv of most systems analysts and users alike is to develop better ways to input data directly into the system with direct input; data created by an inquiry, event, or transaction is input and processed immediately. Airline reservation and point-of-sale (POS) systems are good examples of direct input.

Source data automation, VDTs with keyboards or touch screens, and voice-recognition devices, represent methods by which direct input can be made.

Whether input is batched or made directly, it must follow some form or layout and be identified by codes. Forms may be zones and blanks on paper or cards or the same layout displayed on a VDT. Codes made up of numbers, letters, and special characters ensure proper identification of data input, processing, retrieval, and coordination with other data and processes in the system. The purpose of the following sections is to discuss and illustrate how these tasks are achieved.

6.3 FORMS ANALYSIS AND DESIGN

Events take place—people apply for a job, are hired, and fired, patients are admitted to hospitals, students enroll in universities. Transactions occur—customers order products, purchases are made from vendors, items are transferred from work-in-process to finished goods inventory, credit card sales are made, deposits are made at banks, stocks are bought and sold. Actions are taken—jobs are started into production, funds are released for projects, authorization is given to build a structure, trucks are dispatched, and goods are loaded and shipped.

In some industries, the form *is the business,* such as insurance policies, stock certificates from brokers, mortgage documents, or loan agreements. Forms that support a business include work orders, and requisitions for materials. Support forms are what we are primarily concerned with here.

Guidelines for Forms Analysis

The form is used as a tool to get work done and enter data into the system. The 18 basic forms functions are as follows:[1]

To acknowledge	To identify
To agree	To instruct
To apply	To notify
To authorize	To order
To cancel	To record
To certify	To report
To claim	To request
To estimate	To route
To follow up	To schedule

Furthermore, forms grant authority, help ensure control, provide an audit trail, and serve as auxiliary or backup files. In performing forms analysis, you must determine what data you are trying to capture, how data will be classified

---

[1]Belden Menkus, "Designing a Useful Form," *Business Graphics,* September 1972, p. 32. Used with permission.

and entered in the form, who captures the data and for what purpose, who gets a copy and what should appear in various copies, under what conditions the form will be filled out and how it will be handled, and for how long it will be filed. You want to make sure that the form captures the correct data and initiates the appropriate action or procedure. Also, you want to make sure that the right number of copies are specified, thus avoiding useless copies, that the form does not require unnecessary steps, that it does not overlap other forms, and that present forms could not do the job just as well.

All these examples require that data be captured and classified to represent these events, transactions, and actions and that these data be input into the information system to keep up with everything and make sure that everything is carried out systematically. Forms—paper, cards, icons, or displays on VDTs—are the media that perform this function.

Guidelines for Paper Forms Design

Even today, in organizations with advanced information technology, paper forms are still the primary vehicles used to get data into the system. For years, experts have predicted the imminent demise of paper forms; it simply has not happened. Paper use and production continue to grow at a rapid pace. Clearly, paper forms are still key tools of information systems design. Indeed, most organizations literally run on paper. It, therefore, behooves systems analysts to learn more about the analysis and design of this important and pervasive data capture medium. Following are some guidelines that help do this:

1. *Paper.*   A number of factors must be considered when selecting the paper to support your form: (1) the length of time the form will be kept, (2) the appearance of the form, (3) the number of times it will be handled (e.g., average of six times per day for one month), (4) how it will be handled (e.g., gently, roughly, abusively, folded and carried by the user), (5) its environmental exposure (e.g., grease, dirt, heat, cold, moisture, acids), (6) the method of filling in the blanks used (e.g., handwritten or machine prepared), and (7) its security against erasures.

   The *kinds* of paper are (1) *bond,* which is high-quality paper and is usually durable enough for most forms; (2) *ledger,* which is a heavier weight bond paper, usually 24 to 44 pounds, is very durable, is easy to fill in by pencil, ink, or machine, and can be filed for long periods of time; (3) *bristol* (also called *index*), which is even heavier, usually 60 to 220 pounds, and is used for card forms; (4) *thin* (or onionskin), which is a lightweight bond, usually 8 to 10 pounds, and is often used as parts of a multipart form (also called a manifold set); (5) *duplicating* paper, which is used for reproduction; and (6) *safety* paper, which cannot be erased without leaving an obvious mark. The weights of paper are based on 500 sheets of paper measuring 17 by 22 inches.

   The *grades* of paper, from the lowest to the highest and from the least to most expensive, are (1) mechanical wood pulps, (2) sulfite, from number 1 through number 4, and (3) rag paper, from 25 percent content to 100 percent content. Generally, most single-part forms are prepared on number 3 or 4 sulfite, 12 to 20 pound weight. For better durability and appearance, number 1 or 2 sulfite with a heavier weight is used. The same applies for manifold sets, except that some of the parts will generally be of lighter weight, usually 8 to 12 pounds. When forms must have excellent appearance, will be handled often under adverse conditions, and must be kept indefinitely, then 100 percent rag paper with 16-pound or better weight is recommended.

2. *Size.*   The most common size form that will fit standard equipment, file forms, filing cabinets, typewriters, and so forth is 8½ by 11 inches. Try to make your paper forms this size. If you want a smaller paper form, then specify one-half the standard length, or 8½ by 5½ inches. For card forms, the standards start with 8 by 10 inches. A half-card form is 8 by 5 inches. Nonstandard sizes can create a number of problems in preparing, handling, and filing forms. Moreover, because suppliers stock standard sizes, using an off-standard size can increase the cost of paper and cards dramatically.

3. *Color.*   The use of color can help in identifying, routing, and controlling copies of a manifold set. Some colors, however, are more readable than others, especially for carbon copies. The most readable colors are yellow, buff, goldenrod, and light pink. Colors to avoid are blue, red, brown, and dark green.

4. *Title.*   The form should contain a name that tells what it *is* and what it *does* as shown in Figure 6.2. Make the title as long as necessary to describe clearly how the form is to be used. If the form is used by others outside the organization, also include the organization name and address.

5. *Numbering.*   Use a number to identify the form uniquely, and place the number in the lower right or lower left margin where it will not be torn or obliterated when the form is stapled. Place the form number in the same position on all forms. The number can include initials for further identification. For example, TD may stand for truck division, and the number

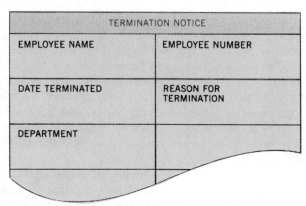

Figure 6.2 A form with titles.

742 may identify a sales order form as in TD-742. If the form is revised later, an alpha suffix can be added to the number—TD-742-A. If it is revised again, the second revision would be represented by TD-742-B, and so on. Also, edition dates can be appended to indicate if the current edition is being used. In addition to a number that identifies the type of form, serial numbers, usually placed at the upper right, are often used for accounting control, audit trail, and logging purposes.

6. *Pagination.* When a form consists of multiple pages, such as three pages, pagination should be indicated as "page 1 of 3," "page 2 of 3," and "page 3 of 3." Generally, page numbers are placed in the upper right corner.

7. *Spacing.* Horizontal and vertical space requirements are determined by the amount of data to be entered and the printed captions. The method used (handwriting or machine) determines the amount of space that should be allowed for fill-in data. Horizontal spacing is based on the number of characters written per inch. Vertical spacing is based on the number of writing lines per inch. Twelve characters of elite type and 10 characters of pica type can fit into 1 horizontal inch on standard typewriters. Accordingly, $\frac{1}{10}$ inch allows space for either elite or pica type. Adding an extra space prevents crowding. A standard typewriter types six vertical lines of elite or pica type on an inch of paper. Therefore, $\frac{1}{6}$ inch should be allowed for each line of typing. Using this measurement, a form is adjusted in the machine for the first line of typing and no further adjustments are necessary. All-purpose spacing, hand or machine, is 3 lines to the inch on all horizontal lines, and 5 characters to the inch for vertical spacing; this is also called "$\frac{3}{5}$ spacing." Most people can easily write five characters within a 1-inch space. If you have a space in which a maximum of two characters are to be written, then a space of $\frac{2}{5}$ inch is provided.

8. *Zoning.* Zones divide the form into logical blocks that contain related data, as shown in Figure 6.3.

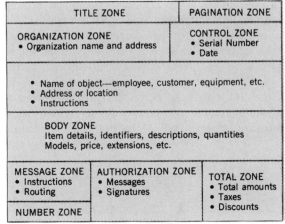

Figure 6.3 Zoning.

9. *Captions.*   These are the words printed on the form that tell *who* fills it out, and *what* data are to be placed there. The key is to use specific, unequivocal captions. For example, "date" is often a caption, but date can mean date ordered, date shipped, or the date the form is filled out. Another consideration in addition to printing definite captions on the form is the position of the caption. If the caption serves as a column heading, then it should be positioned at the center of the column. Other captions can be placed above the line, below the line, before the line, after the line, or above or below a box. Probably the best place to set the caption, however, is the upper left corner of a rectangular space, or box, as shown in Figure 6.4. Other caption formats are illustrated in Figure 6.5.

10. *Instructions.*   Try to make your forms self-instructing rather than providing detailed instructions on how to fill out the form on a separate document or in a procedures manual. Only in a very few instances should such detailed instructions be necessary. Definitive captions are the key to making forms self-instructing [e.g., NAME (LAST, FIRST, & INITIAL)]. If you need further instructions, however, then place such instructions at the top of and within the zone to which they relate. If the instructions apply to the entire form, place them at the top of the form so that the user will see the instructions *before* filling out the form. Routing instructions (e.g., send buff copy to accounting department), however, should be placed at the bottom of the form.

11. *Manifolding.*   In forms design, manifolding simply means that multiple copies are made with one writing. Most manifolding forms are action forms, such as sales orders, invoices, statements, bills of lading, purchase orders, shipping orders, and receiving reports. Moreover, usually a number of people and functions are involved in the action that is initiated, such as shipping goods to a customer. Therefore, it is imperative that this action be started in several places at once and be coordinated throughout the process.

Also, with multiple forms, zoning is required so that the user can fill in the first page of the form and have the same data appear on all or select copies of the set. For example, on a receiving report, you want the quantities to appear on the copy for accounting and inventory control, but you do not want the quantities to appear on the copy for the receiving department because you want to force the receiving clerk to count the items received. If you show the quantities, the receiving clerk may be tempted simply to check off the items without actually counting them. As another example, a manifold set of forms to ship an order to a customer is made up of invoice copies, shipping orders, bill of lading copies, acknowledgment, packing

1. NAME	2. STUDENT NUMBER	3. DATE ENROLLED

Figure 6.4 Box captions.

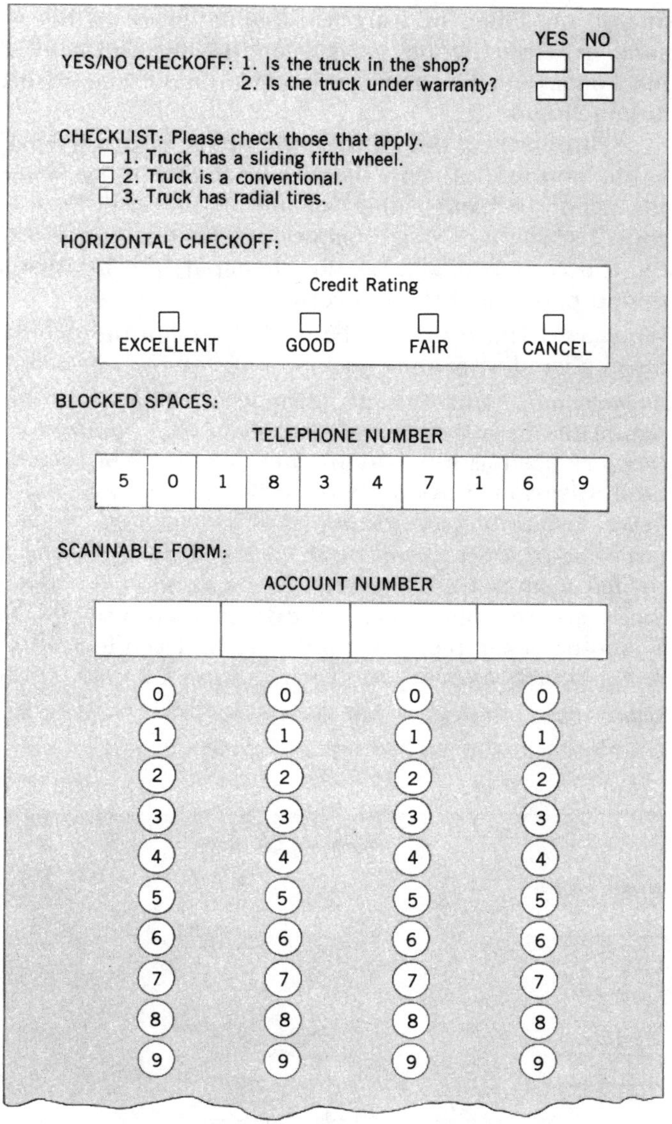

YES/NO CHECKOFF: 1. Is the truck in the shop?
                 2. Is the truck under warranty?

YES NO
☐   ☐
☐   ☐

CHECKLIST: Please check those that apply.
    ☐ 1. Truck has a sliding fifth wheel.
    ☐ 2. Truck is a conventional.
    ☐ 3. Truck has radial tires.

HORIZONTAL CHECKOFF:

Credit Rating

☐   ☐   ☐   ☐
EXCELLENT   GOOD   FAIR   CANCEL

BLOCKED SPACES:

TELEPHONE NUMBER

| 5 | 0 | 1 | 8 | 3 | 4 | 7 | 1 | 6 | 9 |

SCANNABLE FORM:

ACCOUNT NUMBER

| | | | |

0   0   0   0
1   1   1   1
2   2   2   2
3   3   3   3
4   4   4   4
5   5   5   5
6   6   6   6
7   7   7   7
8   8   8   8
9   9   9   9

Figure 6.5 Caption formats.

slip, and a mailing label. Although some of the data will appear in all copies, other data will appear in only certain copies. For example, only the customer name and address would appear on the mailing label, not prices and quantities. By zoning and using carbons, you can make data appear or not appear on selected parts in the manifold set. For example, all the shipping data are in one zone on all the forms; address data are in another; item numbers, quantities, descriptions, prices, and extensions are in another;

and so on. Then by using a combination of carbon cutouts and carbon spots at selected zones, varied lengths and widths of sheets, and printed blockouts, data, like magic, will appear on selected forms and not on others, as you choose.

Moreover, if one of the copies must be a heavy paper stock, it should be the bottom (last) copy because each carbon has a cushioning effect and the typing or handwriting becomes lighter and harder to read with each copy. Use a lighter-weight paper for copies below the original. For example, the top copy could be 12-pound paper, the intervening copies 8- or 9-pound paper, and the last copy 22-pound paper.

12. *Windows.*   If a form is to be mailed, design the mailing address so that it fits in a window of the envelope, thus saving one writing step.

13. *Turnaround.*   Turnaround forms are produced as output from the processing of one system; when returned to the organization that created them, they are used as input to another process. The turnaround form can be used in various ways to increase the efficiency of and eliminate errors in input. Utility bills are examples of turnaround forms. Also, many organizations produce turnaround forms when a product is received and recorded in an inventory system. As the product is removed from inventory, the forms are input to record the depletion transaction. Some organizations, as another example, pay employees and vendors with checks that are in reality punched cards, used later as input for cash reconciliation purposes.

14. *Sequencing.*   Layout of the data elements should be in a logical sequence

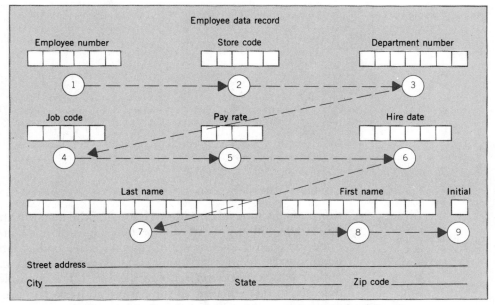

Figure 6.6 A properly sequenced source document for data entry.

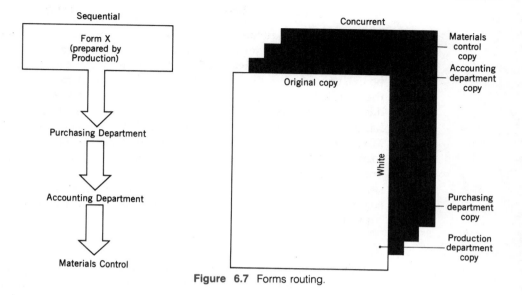

Figure 6.7 Forms routing.

that the user can easily follow. A good example[2] of proper sequencing is presented in Figure 6.6.

15. *Routing.*   The distribution or routing of forms can be either sequential or concurrent, as shown in Figure 6.7. The particular approach used to route a form is important because it deals with (1) the action to be initiated, by whom, and when; (2) the number of forms required; (3) the total through-put time; (4) use of manifolding, carbon, and zoning techniques; (5) preparation time and costs; and (6) inputting, filing, and retention procedures.

Guidelines for Electronic Forms Design

Many systems analysts use a combination of page layout software, high-resolution graphics, microcomputers, and laser printers to create, process, and manage electronic forms. The form on the screen is an exact image of a preprinted paper form.

Paper-intensive businesses have been looking for ways to improve productivity and efficiency by inputting and moving data electronically. When Metropolitan Life, for example, started its new computer-based forms management system, it learned for the first time that it had more than 51,000 active and inactive forms stored in rows and rows of file cabinets. Using a manual means to encourage standardization and prevent duplication was all but impossible. In fact, before going to a computer-based forms management system, Metropolitan was almost strangled by its own paperwork.

---

[2]This example is from Marvin R. Gore and John W. Stubbe, *Computers and Informatino Systems,* 2nd ed. (New York: McGraw-Hill, 1984), p. 215.

Overview of Electronic Forms Compared to Paper Forms

The use of paper forms calls for typewriters, pens and pencils, correction fluid, and filing cabinets. Generally, the steps to design, create, process, and manage paper forms include design, print, store, locate, forms fill-in, distribute, keyboard, process, distribution of results, and back to storage. With electronic forms, these steps can either be combined or simplified. Forms fill-in, data entry, and data processing become one step. Distribution to other users in the network is handled electronically. Only one electronic form image is stored per application. Moreover, with paper forms, the data that fill the blanks become part of the form. With electronic forms, the user fills in the form and the data and form are together on the screen and printout (if a printout is necessary), but the system treats them as separate files. Distribution of electronic forms can be made electronically through the telecommunications network, via diskettes, or by hard copy from a laser printer.

Forms Mapping and Printing

A form map or a zone format (see Figure 6.8) is displayed for the forms designer to use in creating a specific forms design. Interacting with the software, the designer tells the system what to do with the data entered in each blank. Mapping also directs the form where to send data for other applications.

If a user needs to print a form, the system automatically merges the electronic form with data that have been entered. The system can print manifold sets of forms or single blank forms on demand. A laser printer can use a variety of typefaces for design enhancement. The style and size of the data can be varied to taste. What-you-see-is-what-you-get (WYSIWYG) when the form is printed.

Smart Electronic Forms

The electronic form's intelligence is created by the form's mapping software. Smart forms process data on the form, show users how to fill-in the form, provide

DESIGNING FORMS ELEC-TRONICALLY Graphics Development International offers two electronic forms software products: FormEasy and FormScan. FormEasy is designed to work with laser printers for the creation of forms and nonintensive desktop publishing. The product provides a moderately capable word processor, good font and print-attribute handling, and a graphics tool kit that facilitates on-screen line and box drawing for forms creation.

Its companion product, FormScan, allows forms to be scanned in and altered on screen, and it can link to data files for merge printing. It will accept scanned input and display it on screen, allowing the user to cut and paste parts of the form to new locations or other forms.

Excerpted from Jon Pepper, "Pair of Powerful Software Tools Keeps Business True to Forms," *PC Week*, March 15, 1988, p. 70.

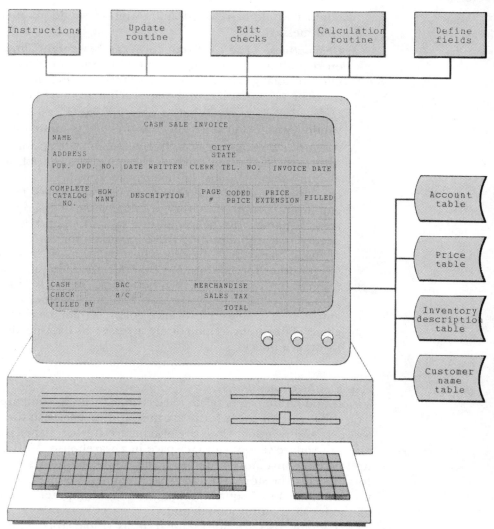

Figure 6.8 How constant tables and routines can increase input efficiency.

online messages and instructions, and transmit the data to other related forms and applications if necessary. Some specific examples follow.

1. *Define Fields.* A field definition specifies the field's length and type of data it contains—text, numbers, dates, percentages, and currency. If a field is defined as eight numbers and a user enters nine numbers or a character other than a number, an error message appears in a window telling the user what is wrong and how to correct the error.

2. *Limit Checks.* The forms designer can establish limits on a field. If net weight for a van cannot exceed 48,000 pounds, for example, any higher

number would be rejected and a window would automatically display the limit message.

3. *Calculations.*   The electronic form can be "taught" how to add total costs on requisition orders, for example. In a sales order, it can add individual sales for total gross sales, compute taxes, retrieve the proper discount, and calculate net sales due, and place each item in its proper space.

4. *Online Instructions.*   When a user gets stuck, a "help" key brings up a window with detailed instructions on what is wanted in that blank.

5. *Automatic Data Retrieval or Transmission.*   Ideally, only the data that vary with each transaction, such as the quantity ordered, hours worked, and quantity shipped, must be filled in or keyed. Data that remain relatively constant over some time period, such as customers' names and addresses, employees' names, inventory prices, inventory descriptions, tax rates, and account names, can be stored in a table (file) and retrieved by a code as needed. Clearly, inputting these constants for each transaction is a waste of time. The system can also export data for use by other applications or trigger other forms work. For example, the filling-in of a customer's order triggers the preparation of other forms, such as shipping and acknowledgment forms. The system can also pull together other forms. For example, to assemble an insurance policy, certain data are keyed in about the client. This input automatically accesses all data needed to complete the insurance policy.

Payoff of Electronic Forms

Visible and hidden costs relate to electronic forms as compared to paper forms. The visible costs of paper forms are the out-of-pocket costs for paper, typesetting, artwork, and printing. Costs are also incurred when paper forms require thousands of square feet of storage space in a warehouse. Moreover, money is tied up in a large inventory of paper forms. Only one form's map of the electronic form needs to be stored, and the space required for all electronic forms requires no more than 4 or 5 square feet (e.g., a microcomputer and hard disk can store all the forms most businesses use).

Hidden costs are not as apparent as visible costs. Nonetheless they eventually impact the company's bottom line. Some of these hidden costs that can be reduced by using electronic forms are as follows.[3]

1. *Cost of Running Out.*   When a company runs out of paper forms, operations are halted. Electronic forms never run out. Supply always equals demand.

2. *Forms Obsolescence.*   Needs change, laws change, and suddenly many paper forms aren't worth the paper they are printed on. Electronic forms eliminate this waste entirely. Investment in printing and storage is not wasted.

---

[3]Electronic Form Systems™ "Seven Hidden Costs of Every Form Your Company Uses. And How to Stop Paying Them," 2395 Midway Road, Carrollton, Tx. 75006.

3. *Inefficient Forms.* Pressure always exists to keep a paper form the way it is, even when it's not as useful as it could be. To create a new form costs money, so it's better to leave well enough alone. But it's easy to revise an electronic form to meet changing conditions and give users exactly the form they need.

4. *Using the Wrong Form.* Murphy's law of forms is: If the wrong form can be used, it will be. With electronic forms, controls determine who uses a form, which form they use, and what they use it for. When a form is revised, employees have to use the new one because the old one is no longer available. Use of forms can be restricted to certain people or departments by password control. Nobody will confuse two forms because they look alike. People request a form by name and number, and that is the form the computer gives them.

5. *Forms Management and Enforcement.* When a company uses thousands of different forms, manging them is a large and expensive task. With electronic forms, the creating, managing, and processing of every form is brought into a single, integrated system. Summaries of how many times a form has been used, how long since a form was revised, and what the current revision looks like are available. "Bootleg" forms disappear.

6. *The Speed Limit of Paper.* Every process in a company is subject to the speed limit of paper forms. Filling out electronic forms takes less time. The cursor stops at each blank, guiding the user in a logical order. Help windows are available for each blank if needed. The form can do calculations and enter the results in another blank. The form can automatically pull in data from other files. Data in one form can trigger the system to pull all the other forms to make up a set.

7. *Handling Data Twice.* With paper forms, someone fills in the form, and then someone reads data off the form and inputs the data into the computer. Electronic forms end this duplication because data capture for the form and data capture for the computer are one.

8. *Data Float.* Data float is a function of time. It is the result of paper float, the time it takes a paper form to get from point A to point B. Electronic forms virtually eliminate data float because data are input and transmitted electronically.

6.4 CODING CONSIDERATIONS

Codes provide a means of classifying data, entering data into the system properly, keeping track of data, and retrieving data in different ways to provide a variety of information. Codes are used to identify people, equipment, accounts, events, and transactions. In this section, available coding symbols and some considerations of code design are discussed.

Coding Symbols

In selecting a given code format, you must consider the character set available. Analysts have a large number of symbols at their disposal. They have numbers, letters, and special characters (e.g., dollar sign, colon, period). Numbers are by far the most widely used symbols in coding systems, however, especially where electromechanical and electronic equipment are used. Computers work efficiently with large, contiguous strings of numbers, whereas people have difficulty remembering and processing numeric codes of more than 6 to 10 digits.

A *numerical* code provides up to 10 classifications for each digit in the code. *Alphabetic* codes provide up to 26 classifications for each position in the code. Codes that use both numbers and letters are called *alphanumeric*.

When calculating the capacity of a given code for covering all situations while still maintaining the code's uniqueness, the following formula applies: $C = S^p$, where C is the total available code combinations possible, S is the number of unique characters in the set, and p is the number of code positions. For example, a three-digit code with the characters 0 through 9 would have $1000 = 10^3$ unique code combinations. If the alphabetic characters O, Z, I, S, and V were eliminated from the permissible character set of an alphanumeric code of length two, then 961 (31^2) unique code combinations would be available.

Although numeric, alphabetic, and alphanumeric codes comprise the majority of coding structures used in information processing today, future systems will most likely provide for data coded in special symbols understandable only to special scanning or sensing devices. Symbolic coding structures seem appropriate in many POS applications in which vast amounts of data are available but quite costly to collect with present input methods and procedures.

Code Design

Many possible arrangements of digits, letters, and characters can be designed into codes. A great deal of thought, however, must go into the coding scheme if it is to satisfy a variety of users. The following considerations should be kept in mind when designing codes:

1. The coding scheme must logically fit the needs of users and the processing method used. An arbitrary code, such as PDQ, assigned to represent an accounting class, is confusing to users.

2. Each code must be a unique representation for the item it identifies. An inventory item number or employee identification code, for example, must identify one and only one inventory item or employee.

3. The code design must be flexible to accommodate changing requirements. It is too costly and confusing to change the coding structure every few months or years. The coding structure should not be so extensive, however, that part of it will not be used for a number of years. For example, if a 16-digit code will handle all processing needs for three or four years, then it would be too costly to set up a code larger than 16 digits. A basic trade-off exists in the length of the code. Normally, the shorter the code, the less the cost of classification, preparation, storage, and transmission. On the other hand, the longer the code, the better the translation, and the wider the variety of data retrieval, statistical analysis, and information processing.

4. As discussed before in this text, a particular transaction can affect many parts of the information system's data base. For example, an order from

a customer triggers changes in inventory, sales, accounts receivable, purchasing, and shipping, and requires credit checks. Therefore, a code structure must be designed to be meaningful in all related situations. Codes must pertain to the overall functions of the organization. It might not be feasible to design one code structure that would take care of all the requirements for each individual function or subdivision in the organization. The structure, however, must be broad enough to encompass all functions and provide a basic cross-reference for any additional special-purpose codes for a variety of processing requirements.

5. Standardization procedures should be established to reduce confusion and misinterpretation for persons working with the code structure. Some of the procedures that can be easily standardized in most systems are as follows: (1) Elimination of characters that are similar in appearance. The range of permissible characters to be used should be selected on the basis of their dissimilarity to other characters. For example, the letters O, Z, I, S, and V may be confused with the digits 0, 2, 1, 5, and the letter U, respectively. (2) Gaps in code numbers should be avoided where possible. (3) Days and weeks should be numbered. For example, days are numbred one to seven and weeks are numbered consecutively beginning with the start of the fiscal period. (4) The use of a 24-hour clock alleviates the AM/PM confusion. (5) Dates should be designed by digits using the Year Month Day format YYMMDD (in which September 18, 1990, becomes 900918) or using the Julian calendar dating system. The MMDDYY format is also favored by many.

6. Where possible, letters that sound the same should be avoided (e.g., B, C, D, G, P, and T, or the letters M and N). In alphabetic codes or portions of codes having three or more consecutive alphabetic characters, avoid the use of vowels (A, E, I, O, and U) to prevent the inadvertent formation of recognizable English words. In cases in which the code is structured with both alphabetic and numeric characters, similar character types should be grouped and not dispersed throughout the code. For example, fewer errors occur in a three-character code in which the structure is alpha-alpha-numeric (e.g., WW2) than in an alpha-numeric-alpha sequence (e.g., W2W).

7. The layout of the code itself should have parts that are of equal length. For example, a chart of accounts code should read 001–199 (for assets), not 1–199.

8. Codes longer than four alphabetic or five numeric characters should be divided into smaller segments (sometimes called *chunking*) for purposes of reliable human recording and rememberability (it makes no difference to the computer because the computer likes to process contiguous data). For the human, 726-49-6135 is more easily remembered and more accurately recorded than 726496135.

9. In instances in which a code is an essential element in processing information, particularly when financial control is involved or humans are required to transcribe this code repeatedly, its accuracy is verified by using a check digit. The *check digit* is generated when the code is initially assigned

to a data element and, in fact, becomes part of the code itself. The check digit is determined by performing a prescribed arithmetic operation on the number. In subsequent processings, this same arithmetic operation is performed to ensure that the number has not been recorded incorrectly.

A check digit guards against typical errors such as the following:

- Transcription errors, in which the wrong number is written, such as 1 instead of 7.
- Transposition errors, in which the correct numbers are written but their positions are reversed, such as 2134 for 1234.
- Double transposition errors, in which numbers are interchanged between columns, such as 21963, for 26913.
- Random errors, which are a combination of two or more of the foregoing, or any other error not listed.[4]

The modulus 11 check digit method is the most frequently used method to generate check digits. Three different approaches to using modulus 11 are:

1. Arithmetic progression.

Account number:		1	2	3	4	5
		×	×	×	×	×
Multiply by:		6	5	4	3	2

Add result of multiplication:
$$6 + 10 + 12 + 12 + 10 = 50$$

Subtract 50 from next highest integer multiple of 11:
$$55 - 50 = 5$$

Check digit = 5
New account number: 12345-5

2. Geometric progression.

Account number:		1	2	3	4	5
		×	×	×	×	×
Multiply by:		32	16	8	4	2

Add result of multiplication:
$$32 + 32 + 24 + 16 + 10 = 114$$

Subtract 114 from next highest integer multiple of 11:
$$121 - 114 = 7$$

Check digit = 7
New account number: 12345-7

3. Prime number weighting.

Account number:		1	2	3	4	5
		×	×	×	×	×
Multiply by:		17	13	7	5	3

Add result of multiplication:
$$17 + 26 + 21 + 20 + 15 = 99$$

[4]From *Systems Analysis,* Alan Daniels and Donald Yeates, eds. Copyright National Computing Centre, 1969. Adapted by permission of Sir Isaac Pitman and Sons, Limited. Reprinted by permission of Science Research Associates, Inc.

Subtract 99 from next higher or equal integer multiple of 11:

$$99 - 99 = 0$$

Check digit $= 0$

New account number: 12345-0

It has been determined statistically that modulus 11 with prime number weighting, a method developed by Frieden, Inc., will detect all transposition and transcription errors. It should be pointed out that under any modulus 11 system a percentage of all numbers will have a "10" as a check digit. When this occurs, the letter X is used in lieu of 10, or the number is not included in the sequence of permissible codes.

Although most commonly the check digit becomes the last digit of a number, such placement is not imperative. As long as the check digit is placed in a constant position, most pieces of equipment can verify the correctness of the number whatever the position of the check digit. In a manual or semiautomatic operation, many advantages are gained by separating the check digit from the main number by means of a hyphen, because it is much easier to sort and read the account number. In the case of fully automatic equipment and computers, the placement of the check digit should depend on the type of equipment used and the system to be employed.

Now let's take a simple example to show how the check digit works. Assume that you open an account at Fourth National Bank, and you are assigned the number 1234. Further assume that the bank uses a prime number weighting, modulus 11 check digit system. Your account number would then become 12341, as follows:

$$
\begin{array}{ccccc}
1 & 2 & 3 & 4 & 1 \\
\times & \times & \times & \times & \\
13 & 7 & 5 & 3 & \\
\end{array}
$$

$13 + 14 + 15 + 12 = 54$, subtract 54 from the next highest multiple of 11;

$$55 - 54 = 1$$

Now assume that next week you deposit \$1000 and somebody transposes your account number to read 13241. The system, rather than posting your deposit to someone else's account, would catch the error and automatically display it for correction. The error is detected as shown:

$$
\begin{array}{ccccc}
1 & 3 & 2 & 4 & 1 \\
\times & \times & \times & \times & \\
13 & 7 & 5 & 3 & \\
\end{array}
$$

$13 + 21 + 10 + 12 = 56$, and the next highest integer multiple of 11 is 56;

$$66 - 56 = 10; \quad 10 \neq 1$$

6.5 TYPES OF CODE STRUCTURES

Codes can be formatted in a variety of ways, and selecting a specific code structure is critical. The choice of code structures is fairly extensive. In this section, several code types used in a number of organizations are discussed, and an attempt is made to indicate the advantages and disadvantages of each. In practice, the systems analyst might select a code structure that is some combination of the following codes.

Sequential Code

A *sequential* (or *serial*) *code* represents a one-for-one consecutive assignment of numbers to such items as payroll checks, account numbers, inventory items, purchase orders, and employees. Any list of items is simply numbered consecutively, usually starting with one. For example, a sequential coding scheme for inventory items might be structured as follows:

```
001     WRENCHES
002     HAMMERS
003     SAWS
  .        .
  .        .
  .        .
678     VALVES
```

The advantages of a sequential coding scheme are:

1. It is the most commonly used scheme, because of its simplicity.
2. It is short and unique.
3. It provides a simple way of locating records or documents on which the code appears, assuming that the requestor knows the code.
4. It is simple to administer.

The following are the disadvantages of a sequential code:

1. It has no logical basis. It contains no useful information about the item except its order in the list.
2. It is inflexible because it cannot accommodate changes. Additions can be made only at the end of the numerical sequence. Vacant number codes must either remain open or wait for reassignment at a later date.

Frequently, the term random number code is mistakenly applied to the sequential code just described. The difference between a sequential and a random code is the number list from which the code values are assigned. The *random code* is drawn from a number list that is not in any detectable order or sequence. Computer programs are available to produce these random number lists. Each additional item to be coded is given the next number in the random list. This method forces the coder to look up the next number on the list because the coder has no logical way to predict what the next number will be when the last-used number is known. In a sequential list, if 200 were the last number assigned, the next one would be 201; in a random list it might be 163. This forced look-up is supposed to reduce errors in coding, but in actual practice it tends to introduce problems of control. Properly controlled sequential lists have proved less error prone than have random lists.

Block Codes

The *block code* classifies items into certain groups in which blocks of numbers (or letters) are assigned to particular classifications. The block representing a particular classification must be set up on the basis of an expected maximum utilization of that block.

A typical example of a block code is the zip + 4 code developed by the U.S. Postal Service. This coding scheme uses a nine-digit code divided into blocks as follows:

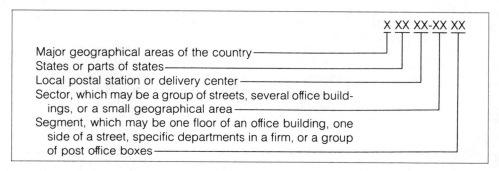

The Postal Service has established approximately 22 million codes. These have been recorded on magnetic tape and are free of charge on request from the Postal Service. The same material is also available on microfilm or microfiche from several commercial sources. With this kind of data base, large mailers can automate the mailing process and enjoy large cost savings.

Another example of a block code is illustrated in Figure 6.9. The equipment is classified into meaningful categories so that a code number identifies certain attributes of a particular piece of equipment. For instance, in the equipment file, those bulldozers on a rental contract and held by the airport divison can be determined by accessing all records with a "2" in position 1, a "3" in position 2,

Code Number	Code Position			
	1	2	3	4
1	Truck	Lease	Service contract	Airport division
2	Bulldozer	Purchase	No service contract	Highway division
3	Grader	Rent	—	—
4	Pile driver	—	—	—
5	Crane	—	—	—

Figure 6.9 Block code structure for equipment.

and a "1" in position 4. Or we can retrieve any information or make any statistical analysis desired, just as long as the code contains the requisite classifications.

Now for a final example of a block code, simply look at the back cover of this book, or any other book, and you will find an International Standard Book Number (ISBN), which consists of 10 digits divided into the following four blocks:

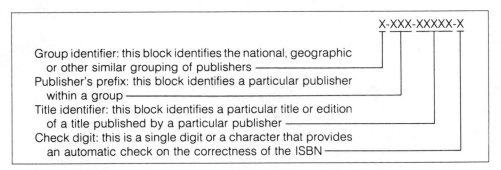

As noted, the publisher's prefix designates the publisher of a given book, but publishers with a large output of books are assigned a short publisher's prefix. On the other hand, publishers with a small output of books are assigned a longer publisher's prefix. To accommodate this scheme, the group identifier is shortened or lengthened accordingly. For example, Australia, Canada, Rhodesia, the Republic of South Africa, the United Kingdom, and the United States are assigned 0. Indonesia is assigned 979. If Indonesia, or another smaller country (e.g., Nigeria 978), has publishers with large outputs in the future, the ISBN would have to be revised.

Now, using ISBN 0-471-88832-X, let us show how the check digit system can be applied to block codes. The check digit is calculated using modulus 11 with weights 10-2, substituting X in lieu of 10 where 10 occurs as a check digit. This method means that each of the first nine digits of the ISBN is multiplied by a number ranging from 10 to 2, and the sum of the products plus the check digit must be divisible, without remainder, by 11. For example,

$$
\begin{array}{ccccccccc}
0- & 4 & 7 & 1 - & 8 & 8 & 8 & 3 & 2 - X \\
\times & \times & \times & \times & \times & \times & \times & \times & \times \\
10 & 9 & 8 & 7 & 6 & 5 & 4 & 3 & 2 \\
\end{array}
$$

$$0 + 36 + 56 + 7 + 48 + 40 + 32 + 9 + 4 + 10 = 242$$

As 242 can be divided by 11 without remainder, 0-471-88832-X is a valid ISBN.

Advantages and Disadvantages of Block Codes

The advantages of block codes are as follows:

1. The value and position of the numbers have meaning.
2. The coding structure is amenable to information processing, in that data items can be easily retrieved, manipulated, analyzed, and sorted.

3. A category of the code can be expanded easily.

4. Whole categories can be added or deleted.

The disadvantages of a block code are as follows:

1. The code length will depend on the number of attributes classified. As a result, codes can become quite lengthy.

2. In many instances, the code will contain spare numbers (e.g., in our equipment example attributes 2, 3, and 4 have spare slots); however, this condition may not always represent a disadvantage.

3. Block codes used as identifiers or record keys pose significant systems maintenance problems when they require modification.

Hierarchical Block Codes

Hierarchical block codes are developed on the basis of ascending significance. Conventionally, this structure starts with the most general, or most significant, aspect of the item as the leftmost group of characters and moves toward the right as subclasses or less significant aspects are classified.

For example, the clearing of checks through the Federal Reserve check-clearing system uses a coding system developed by the American Bankers Association. This code uses a combination of standardized magnetic ink characters, which include 10 digits (0–9) and 4 special symbols. These characters are printed at the bottom of the document in specific areas, as illustrated in Figure 6.10.

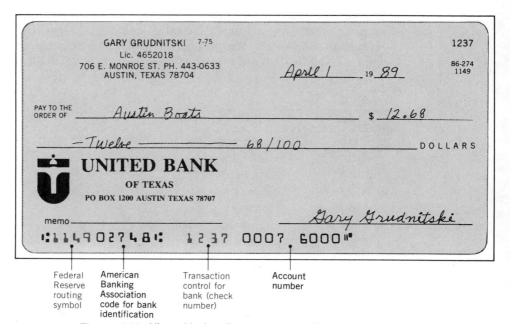

Figure 6.10 Hierarchical coding structure used by the banking system.

The transit number code is printed near the left edge of the document (or check). This classification uses 11 characters: 4 digits for the transit number, 5 digits for the American Bankers Association number, and a beginning and ending transit number symbol. The next classification represents, in order, the transaction code and the customer account number. The rightmost characters, which are not part of the coding scheme per se, represent the dollar amount of the document (not shown in the illustration).

The charts of accounts for accounting systems are numbered for appropriate classification, to permit indexing, and for use as posting references. A simple chart of accounts for a small organization is set up so that the first digit indicates the major division of the ledger in which the account is entered. Accounts beginning with 1 represent assets, 2 are liabilities, 3 are capital, 4 are revenue, and 5 are expenses. A second digit indicates the position of the account within its division. For example, cash is coded as 11, accounts payable as 21, John Smith—Capital as 31 and Mary Jones—Capital as 32, sales as 41, supplies expenses as 51, and so forth. For a large organization with many divisions, plants, and warehouses, it is not unusual for each account number to have four or more digits. For example, finished goods (coded 124 in the asset category), stored in warehouse 1 on floor 3, may be coded as 12413.

Decimal Codes

Decimal codes, such as the Dewey decimal coding system, are basically hierarchical block codes in which the group of digits to the left of the decimal point represents the major classification and the digits to the right of the decimal point denote the subclassifications. The Dewey decimal system classifies books by dividing them into 10 main knowledge groups. Each of these 10 main groups is broken down into more specialized areas. For example, class 600–699, applied science, is subdivided into 10 special classes. And each of these divisions, in turn, is further subdivided. The numbers 630–639, for example, represent agriculture and are subdivided into such classes as field crops, garden crops, dairy products,

Code	Field of Knowledge
600	Applied science
610.7	Health care
610.73	Nurses and nursing
610.732	Private duty nursing
610.733	Institutional nursing
610.734	Public health nursing
610.735	Industrial nursing
610.736	Special nursing
610.736.1	Psychological

Figure 6.11 Segment of the Dewey decimal coding system.

and so on. Using the area of applied science, as an example, this system can be subdivided into meaningful relationships in the field of nursing, as shown in Figure 6.11.

In addition, two similar areas may be related by linking two separate code numbers. For instance, human anatomy in the area of teratogenesis, coded 611.012, can be linked to biochemistry under human physiology, coded 612.015, by use of a hyphen, resulting in 611.012–612.015, which signifies that the designated book or article treats the first subject area from the viewpoint of the second.

Bar Codes

The example in Figure 6.12 represents a bar code used in the grocery industry. This *bar code* is a computer-readable representation of the Universal Product Code (UPC), a voluntary 10-digit coding system used to identify manufacturers and their products. The symbols can be easily read by a scanner and converted by the computer into numbers that represent a particular code. The bars themselves merely represent the number code.

Each participating manufacturer is permanently assigned the first 5 digits of a 10-digit number. The number is similar to the sequential code discussed earlier. The last 5 digits (on the right) uniquely identify a particular manufacturer's product. For example, the manufacturer's number for Kellogg is 38000. Kellogg, in turn, assigns 01620 to Special K cereal in the 15-ounce box. Similarly, Hunt's tomato paste in the 6-ounce can is 2700038815, in which 27000 is Hunt's unique manufacturer's number and 38815 is the product's unique number. By changing the bar widths and spaces between the bars, all variations of products and sizes manufactured can be accommodated. In a supermarket application, the computer matches the code to the correct price, product type, size, and other data already stored in the computer's data base. The results of each transaction are displayed and printed on a receipt at the same time. A typical receipt is shown in Figure 6.13.

This kind of POS system enables users to reduce checkout time; increase inventory control; eliminate the need for price marking individual items; improve resource and shelf allocation; reduce the probability of human error, pilferage, and fraud through cash register manipulations; and generally produce a broader range of more timely information to a variety of users.

Figure 6.12 A bar code.

BAR CODE'S USE IS EXPANDING

Bar coding has revolutionized data entry and collection procedures. As more companies reduce inventory stocks, automate production processes, and electronically interchange financial data, automatic identification techniques such as bar coding becomes absolutely essential.

When a fully integrated bar code network is in place, accounting reports that once lagged production by days and weeks can now be prepared in a matter of minutes.

There are five general types of reading equipment: hand-held light pens, stationary fixed beam scanners, stationary moving beam scanners, hand-held lasers, and imaging array readers. All readers work on the principle of illuminating a bar code symbol and converting the reflected light pattern into an analog signal that is decoded and then digitally processed. As bar coding equipment costs continue to decline, application opportunities increase, and their interface with accounting procedures becomes more frequent.

Timely scanning of bar-coded information is essential for Xerox's sophisticated MRP system that determines the quantity, frequency, and location of parts replenishment of all of its assembly lines and workstations.

Fully integrated bar code systems now can assume nearly every aspect of an accountant's scorekeeping responsibilibies.

Excerpted from Thomas Tyson and Arian T. Sadhwani, "Bar Codes: Speed Factory Floor Reporting," *Management Accounting,* April 1988, pp. 41–46.

A large number of effective applications of bar codes exist in other areas. For example, materials control personnel use bar-coded labels and scanners in an integrated, online scheduling production control system. Each representative bar code is attached to specific components and subassemblies, which are monitored as they pass through production. These bar code labels contain mnemonic codes and color codes (e.g., red means chassis, blue means motor block), discussed next, for human reading and identification. Such a system provides an accurate count and control of materials. It also provides timely performance, scheduling, and tracking information.

In some large manufacturing and distribution organizations, data entry problems have been significantly reduced by using bar codes for product identification and installing computerized conveyor belts. The warehouse employees load products onto the conveyor. As various products move along the belt, they are automatically scanned, identified, and routed to the connect spur of the conveyor, where they are loaded for shipment. Data on the product and its movement are also input into the system.

National shoe companies with thousands of retail outlets use POS terminals that read bar codes. Sales data are automatically input into a centralized ac-

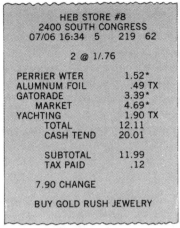

Figure 6.13 A typical grocery receipt produced by a bar-coded system.

counting system. In addition to performing general accounting, the system also provides sales performance information, identifies fast- and slow-moving items, and generates replenishment and pick orders. These kinds of systems provide vast improvements in accounting and stock control over earlier systems that batched sales tickets for a week or so before processing.

In other applications, bar codes are attached to windows on the sides of cars to identify authorized staff members for hospital parking lot control systems, in which remote scanners read the bar code to activate entry and exit gates. Bar codes are attached to luggage in some airport terminals (e.g., Miami) for proper routing of luggage.

An endless number of possibilities exist for using bar codes. For example, libraries can use them for circulation control. The dispensing of valuable resources, such as tools, equipment, and drugs might be more effectively accounted for and controlled using bar codes.

Mnemonic Codes

A mnemonic code is characterized by the use of either letters or numbers, or letter-and-number combinations that describe the item coded. The combinations are designed to aid memorization of the codes and association with the items they represent. For example, a Peterbilt cabover truck with 180-inch wheel base, 13-speed transmission, 3406 Caterpillar engine, 3.75 Eaton rear end, and radial tires, that is owner-operated may be mnemonically coded as PETE-CO-180WB-13SP-3406CAT-3.75E-RAD-OO.

Some problems are connected with the use of mnemonic codes to identify long, unstable lists of items. Wherever item names beginning with the same letters are encountered, there may be a conflict of mnemonic use. To overcome this, the number of code characters is necessarily increased, thus increasing the likelihood that the combinations will be less memory-aiding for code users. Also, because descriptions may vary widely, it is difficult to maintain a code organization that conforms with a plan of classification.

Mnemonic codes are best used for identifying relatively short lists of items (generally 50 or fewer, unless the list is quite stable), coded for manual processing in which it is necessary that the items be recognized by their code. A common problem, however, is that the code is likely to be misapplied when specific code values are subject to change and users rely too heavily on memory. Thus, to be coded effectively with mnemonics, entity sets must be relatively small and stable.

Phonetic Codes

The coding of names represents a significant problem in building information systems. One problem with the use of names is that some names appear frequently whereas others are nearly unique. Duplication of entries can occur. An even more serious problem is that the spellings of names are not consistent. A coding technique that helps to reduce these problems to some extent and bring together all similar sounding names is the Soundex code developed by Remington Rand. The code contains one letter followed by three digits and has the form A123. The steps in deriving this code are as follows:

1. Given any name, the first letter occupies the first position of the code.
2. All nonalphabetic characters are eliminated.
3. The frequently unvocalized consonants H and W are removed.
4. The vowels A, E, I, O, U, and Y are removed.
5. Numbers are assigned, as shown by the following list, to the remaining letter. This procedure is performed from left to right until three numbers are obtained. If the name is short and has insufficient consonants to generate three numbers, then zeroes are inserted to fill. The code now contains one letter plus three digits, or a four-position code.

Code Number	Letters to be included
1	B F P V
2	C G J K Q S X Z
3	D T
4	L
5	M N
6	R
0	Insufficient consonants

(Note: The digits 7, 8, and 9 are illegal in this scheme. Also, two or more adjacent identical digits are combined, such as SQ = 2, SC = 2, LL = 4, and MN = 5.)

6. Example: By the preceding rules, the name BURCH is coded as B620, but this code also represents BIRCH. The code for GRUDNITSKI is G635, the same as the code for the name GRATON.

```
B U R C H
B  6 2 0 ──→ ( ZERO FILL )
G R U D N I T S K I
G 6   3 5
```

The purpose of the Soundex code is to provide an approximate, if not exact, location of the name even though differences in spelling may exist. By this technique, names that sound the same will be given the same code number, or very closely related code numbers, regardless of minor variations in spelling. When sorted in order, the names will be adjacent, or nearly so, in the file. If a name code identification includes several names in its category, each of these names is then examined in detail to obtain the exact match required. When the identity of an individual has to be resolved, secondary information, such as address, birthdate, birth place, and profession, may still be required.

Color Codes

In manual information systems *color codes* are used to help identify records fast and efficiently. Color-coded devices for identification and control have always been available; they were not used extensively in the past, but today they are being used more frequently. Color coding has many benefits, including increased filing accuracy, speed in storage, and retrieval, increased security and control, and automatic indication of misfiles.

Applications include using color to file by year, by department, by project, by accounting use, and so forth. Color by year (e.g., 10 color stripes, one for the last digit in each year) speeds the transfer of data to inactive files and helps avoid misfiling one year's data with another (inadvertent filing of a red-year record in a blue-year file is easily detected). Color by department helps avoid misdirection of information. Color by accounting use helps to separate information by function. For example, all incoming accounts receivable might go into green folders, accounts payable into red folders, and credit memos into blue folders.

Colors are also used for filing sequences. In such a system a different color is assigned to each digit, 0 through 9. Color coding for alphabetic filing is just as easy. Groups of letters are assigned specific colors. For example, in a doctor's office, small clinic, or neighborhood health center, alphabetical filing may be practical, eliminating the need for a cross-reference index. A variety of simple color-code systems are now available for alphabetic filing, including self-labeling systems with A–Z self-adhesive labels, precolor-coded alphabetic systems, and alphanumeric systems for larger volumes of records.

Folders are not the only record repositories that benefit from color. The use of computer printouts can be simplified considerably by using a color-coding system. Nylon post binders are available in a wide range of materials and colors, and users can create many different codes based on the nature of the information. Color can also enhance security in the use of computer reports. Reports can be cycled by color so that when a green report is delivered to a department, an old green report must be turned in. Similarly, color can be used to see that only authorized personnel have access to certain computer reports. If all payroll reports were in red binders, for example, then someone from sales authorized to get only blue sales binders could not easily walk off with confidential payroll information.

The integrity of any storage and retrieval system depends on the ability to find any given record when it is needed. When any record card or folder is removed from the file, a signal or outmarker should be put in its place so that anyone else needing the same information will know where it is and when it was removed. Color outcards are vivid and obvious. Color can also be used to denote which day, week, or month applies to out-of-file material. It can help in spotting material that should have been returned earlier and initiating corrective action.[5]

6.6 INPUT METHODS

In earlier times, the major method used to capture and input data was the keypunch. Today, input methods can be selected from a wide range of possibilities. Greater consideration can now be given to the abilities and preferences of individuals and to how and where they do their work. Today's systems analysts are, indeed, concerned with the friendliness of the system, its ease of use, its naturalness, its understandability, and its helpfulness. Systems analysts must carefully select the appropriate devices and interfaces to address ergonomics, human factors, productivity, and systems efficiency and effectiveness.

The following input methods represent the devices that can be used to capture and feed data into the system. Some of the devices, such as keypunches, although nearing obsolescence, are still used in many installations today. They are used for inputting high volumes of data but are not very efficient and are not ergonomically designed. Other methods, such as scanning devices, input data directly into the system, thus reducing bottlenecks and increasing the system's overall performance. Still others, such as touch-sensitive and voice technology, permit users to interact with the system in a natural way through menus and language commands.

The Keyboard

The most common way to input data, especially text, is to use a keyboard. This method is likely to be the dominant method into the 1990s. In yesteryear, the keyboard was associated with punched-card equipment; today, it is usually associated with a VDT.

The keyboard provides a fairly efficient means of inputting data for some

---

[5]Condensed from "The Wonderful World of Color Makes Records Management Easier," *Information and Records Management*, October 1976, pp. 23–27.

applications, such as entering large volumes of text or transactions. In other applications, such as in manufacturing, where a worker's hands are dirty and occupied by assembling or some other task, the keyboard can be an impediment to capturing and inputting data. Early on, keyboards were used in grocery stores for entering sales. Today, using keyboards at supermarket checkout counters creates bottlenecks.

Because the keyboard remains the major means of entering data, however, specialists are experimenting with alternatives to gain keying efficiencies. Several vendors offer a keyboard that at first looks scrambled but is supposedly easier to use than a conventional QWERTY keyboard; it is called a DVORAK keyboard. This keyboard places the most frequently typed characters beneath the fingers that rest on the home row, reducing the amount of movement required to type. Some ergonomists predict that typing speeds can be improved by 30 or 40 percent once an operator becomes accustomed to this keyboard. If these predictions are true, then it would be advantageous for production users, such as data entry and word processing operators, to use the DVORAK keyboard.

Keypunching

Keypunching is a classic way of preparing data for input, but its use is in decline. An operator uses a machine called a keypunch to transcribe data from a source document (paper form) to punched cards. The keyboard of a keypunch is similar to that of a standard typewriter (QWERTY). Once the cards are punched, their accuracy is checked in a rekeying operation on another machine called a verifier. Any incorrectly punched cards are removed from the input being prepared and rekeyed. Finally, the punched cards are placed in the hopper of a card reader that is connected to the computer system. The data are input into the system for processing.

Keyboard-to-Storage

The keyboard-to-storage technique consists of several workstations (VDTs) connected to a minicomputer or programmed controller that collects the data input, verifies it, provides various other functions, and writes it on tape or disk for processing. Some of the functions that this kind of data entry system performs are the following:

1. Keyed-in data are input to an edit program to filter out errors.
2. VDTs provide sight verification for the operator; if an error is made, backspacing and deletion allows the operator to correct the error quickly.
3. Operators can work at higher keying rates than is possible with keypunches.
4. Productivity statistics for monitoring and checking operators' efficiency are supplemented by means of a program in the system.
5. Check digits and batch totals are prepared automatically.
6. Certain reasonableness checks and relevancy checks are made.
7. True modular input of data is allowed because blocks of data are merged together into proper sequence for further processing.

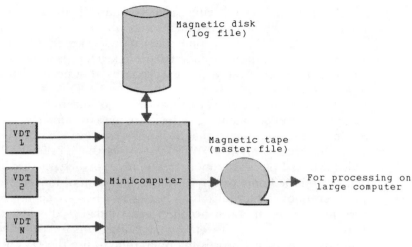

Figure 6.14 A keyboard-to-tape system.

The typical keyboard-to-storage system is referred to as key-to-tape or key-to-disk. It consists of a low-cost minicomputer, direct-access intermediate storage, and magnetic disk, tape, floppy disk, or cassette for final output. Most manufacturers of these systems offer 8 to 64 workstations per system. Studies indicate that at the present cost levels, disregarding any other benefits, a system has to replace from 10 to 14 keypunches before a key-to-tape system becomes cost-effective. With falling prices, the same basic system may be cost-effective in the near future at a five or six keypunch level. A key-to-tape system is shown in Figure 6.14.

Keyboard-to-System

With the keyboard-to-system alternative, data are keyboarded through the VDT connected directly to the computer system. This alternative is common in airline and hotel reservation systems. In some applications, operators are not involved in entering transactions, such as when customers transact their banking business on automated teller machines (ATMs).

Often, the list of choices or entries offered to the user is menu driven. Also, the user may be guided step by step, by messages or prompts that appear on the screen. Some, if not all, of the data may be entered by devices other than a keyboard, such as a touch screen, which is discussed later.

Computer-Readable Forms

Magnetic ink character recognition (MICR) and optical character recognition (OCR) devices represent advances in data input in several areas. These devices help to reduce the data preparation tasks, such as keyboarding, by capturing data in a computer-readable form at its source, also called source data automation. For example, the U.S. Postal Service is automating the processing of first-class letter mail by installing high-speed optical character readers and bar code scanners in postal facilities throughout the country. After the OCR device has read the address, it will automatically print a bar code representing that zip code on the bottom of the mail piece, for use in further automated processing. Also, source data automation is being used increasingly in business information systems.

Magnetic Ink Character Recognition

The magnetic ink characters enscribed at the bottom of a personal check serve as direct input to the computer system. These characters provide an efficient means of processing an ever-increasing volume of checks with speed and accuracy. Blank checks are originally supplied with certain identifying information printed on each check in MICR characters. The data include both the account number of the customer and the unique bank number assigned to the bank location handling that customer's account. The characters appear to be printed in ordinary black ink, but the ink contains finely ground particles of iron oxide.

When a check is cashed or deposited at a bank, employees at the bank receiving the check must ensure that the amount for which the check is written is encoded on the check in MICR characters. A keyboard-type device known as a magnetic character enscriber is used to do this encoding. The checks are then read by a magnetic character reader/sorter, which first magnetizes the characters and then reads them electronically. The checks are physically sorted by bank number so that they can be returned to their home banks. At each home bank, they are again read by a magnetic character reader/sorter. This time, they are sorted into account number sequence so that they can be returned to customers with monthly bank statements. The bank statements are prepared from data transmitted to magnetic tape or disk during the sorting.

Such a process increases productivity because the data need not be transcribed from source documents—the check itself is the input form. Another significant factor is that only the amount of the check and whether it is to be debited or credited to a customer account must be recorded after the check is received at a bank.

Optical Character Recognition

One of the oldest computerized data entry methods is OCR. Data recorded on paper in optically readable symbols can serve as direct input to the system. The symbols can consist of a wide variety of forms: marks, bars, numbers, letters, or special characters of certain type fonts and ordinary handwriting. Many OCR readers work by scanning the text and converting black and white variations into electrical signals, which are then compared with a pattern of known character dot-matrix images. More advanced and flexible systems analyze each character into topological and geometric properties, such as loops, concavities, and line segments. This approach permits the OCR reader to recognize a variety of type fonts intermixed within a document or book and to cope with substandard print containing fragmented, broken, or joined characters.

Optical Marks

This is the simplest form of OCR. Optical mark or mark sense recording reads optical data, such as pen or pencil marks made in predetermined locations on paper forms. After the marks have been made, the forms become input to an optical mark reader connected to the computer system. Examples of optical mark recording are multiple-choice tests, surveys, and questionnaires. Optical mark data may also be used for sales orders, inventory control, payroll, and so forth.

Optical Characters

Some OCR readers can read characters printed in any of a wide variety of type fonts. A good example is the use of a "crash imprinter" for credit card invoices. Even greater versatility is available through the use of devices that can read handwritten characters. Handwriting input, however, will be more widely applicable when equipment can more easily read lowercase as well as uppercase letters and also connected, natural handwriting.

Bar Codes

The Universal Product Code (UPC) is a classic example of bar codes. These codes appear on consumer products for facilitating checkout and for other control and analytical purposes. The bars are read by a hand-held reader or "wand" or by a fixed scanner. Data are input directly for price retrieval and calculations, printing of customer receipts, general information processing, and programmed decision making. As discussed earlier in this chapter, the use of bar codes is expanding.

Other Methods

A number of other methods are available and show some promise as input alternatives. These include (1) computer input microfilm, (2) images, (3) keypads, (4) the mouse, (5) penpads, (6) hand-held terminals, (7) touch, and (8) voice.

1. *Computer Input Microfilm.* With the use of computer input microfilm, forms are filled in by hand and are microfilmed using high-density recording and later read into the computer system for processing. This system is applicable when extremely high volumes of data are processed on a batch basis.

2. *Images.* So-called imaging systems expand the kinds of data that can be fed into a computer system. An imaging system can scan a piece of paper, or even a three-dimensional object, and store an image of it. Handwritten notes, drawings, and photographs on a scanned page can all be stored as an image.

3. *Keypads.* A telephone keypad can be used to enter a variety of data, such as customer numbers and product codes. Data can be entered anywhere there is a phone.

4. *Mouse.* Everyone is familiar with the mouse. It assumes some of the keyboard's functions by replacing a series of typed commands with a single button. By moving the mouse on a table, users position the cursor over commands listed on the screen. One tap on the mouse's button executes the command. With the mouse, the user does not have to remember complex commands or bother with keying them. The mouse is very simple to use, but sometimes simplicity means a sacrifice of sophistication and even functionality. An experienced, high-volume operator, for example, who is totally comfortable with the keyboard may view the mouse as a hindrance.

5. *Penpads.* Advanced character recognition systems, called penpads, accept handwriting for data input either as is, or in cooperation with traditional keyboard entry. The penpad consists of a digitizer, a tablet, a stylus, and a connection to the computer. The digitizer tells the computer where the stylus is positioned on the tablet surface. The device can input anything that is drawn or formed by hand, such as notes, sketches, and diagrams. Many people believe penpads or tablets have definite advantages over both the keyboard and the mouse. Ergonomists state that the mouse, for example, is unnatural because it does not use the strong, flexible muscles of the operator's hand and wrist to create subtle detail. Instead, it forces the use of long muscles in the arm, shoulder, and back to drag the object across a flat surface. Tablets can be used to point to objects or menu entries, to trace drawings from paper, and as an accurate drawing device for computer graphics. The mouse basically points. In some installations, penpads are replacements for the mouse and keyboard.

6. *Track Balls.* A track ball is a sphere mounted in a housing. The user rotates the sphere in any direction by pushing it. Some are integrated with keyboards. Track balls have the advantages of high resolution, ease of location by touch alone, and unlimited motions.

7. *Joysticks.* Computer joysticks are levers that can be moved left or right, forward or back. Many commercially available joysticks have low accuracy and resolution. Joysticks are of two types, proportional and binary. Proportional units send the computer a number representing the displacement from center in each axis. Binary units indicate which of four or eight directions from center the stick is displaced. Generally, the joystick is not applicable for input design in most business information systems.

8. *Hand-Held Terminals.* Portable desk entry units are used by route salespersons for route accounting, preparation of sales tickets, and inventory control. At the end of the day, all data are fed into the central computer for further processing. At some hospitals, nurses use hand-held terminals as electronic scratchpads. They download relevant patient data from a central system to their terminals before making their rounds. During the rounds, they use, update, or add to these data. Once the rounds are complete, the data in the terminals are fed back into the computer. Hand-held terminals are, indeed, useful to those who needs computer power at their fingertips, wherever they are. Radio-linked terminals, whether hand-held

or mounted on vehicles, provide interactive communications in real time. Radio systems are especially attractive to manufacturers and distributors (e.g., route drivers in the beverage distribution industry).

9. *Touch.*   Touch-sensitive screens and other devices represent ways to enter data by touching a position on the screen, a symbol, or a descriptor on a pad. Touch technology involves touch-sensitive screens, conductive membranes, and capacitive and infrared scanning beams. For some users, touch is the easiest, most natural, and efficient way to input data. For commodity traders, for example, time is of the essence. Before touch screens, traders had to fill in a form and send it via a conveyor belt to another section, where data entry clerks keyed data from the form into the system. This entire process took 15 or more minutes. Today, a trader handles hundreds of transactions a day. With touch-sensitive screens, deals are entered within seconds of their completion. Touch technology is also helpful to executives who do not want to type. Moreover, the durability of touch screens makes them useful in workplaces such as laboratories and factories. They operate well even if they are dirty, whereas keyboards malfunction. Factory workers are often intimidated by the keyboard and fear that they will mess up something. Touch-screen technology is effective in combating this problem.

10. *Voice.*   A number of devices are now available for both voice input and output, and the applications are expanding. On the floor of a commodities exchange, a transaction between two brokers is completed. The reporter speaks into a wireless microphone, "September gold, four-five-six-two-three." A visual confirmation is given and he says, "Go." This input has been captured for further computer processing. Voice terminals are used in parts management and quality control where hands and eyes are busy elsewhere. A quality control inspector wearing a microphone can follow a checklist on a screen and orally input physical characteristics of the product. These data processed by the system, in turn, update inventory and provide timely performance reports for management. Packages in distribution centers are routed by voice commands. Normally, voice recognition systems are discrete, which means that the speaker must pause for a fraction of a

---

CHOICE OF ALTERNATIVE INPUT DEVICES

- *Standard Keyboard:* Used for high volume text entry.
- *Mouse:* Facilitates precise and more natural cursor control than keyboard.
- *Trackball:* A substitute for a mouse when desktop space is limited.
- *Lightpen/Touch Screen:* Offers direct command selection for casual or infrequent users.
- *Digitizing Tablet:* Allows users to sketch or trace drawings.

Excerpted from "Variety of Data-Entry Devices Can Make the User's Job a Snap," *PC Week,* January 26, 1988, p. 40.

second between each sound. Moreover, each user must train the system through repeated utterances to recognize his or her particular enunciation of sounds. Also, voice systems usually have a limited memory capacity (vocabulary) of words. Other advanced systems are speaker-independent. They can understand any user regardless of the user's accent, dialect, and inflections. Moreover, they permit data and command entry in a naturally spoken stream of words, numbers, or phrases without artificial pauses, with a 99 percent recognition accuracy. Voice-input units are available with vocabularies ranging from 15 to more than 1000 words.

SUMMARY

Input is the raw material of information systems, in which the quality of input has a direct bearing on the quality of output. In some instances, data are accumulated on paper forms over a period of time and then input into the system. In other applications, data are input directly into the computer as soon as they occur.

One of the key vehicles used to capture and input data is the paper or card form. Many operations of a business would literally stop without forms. Good forms design demands (1) selection of appropriate paper; (2) use of standard sizes and colors; (3) full definition by the use of titles, numbering, pagination, spacing, zoning, captions, and instructions; (4) manifolding and proper routing; and (5) application of efficiency techniques, such as windows, turnarounds, and constant tables.

One way for companies to improve efficiency and productivity is by inputting and moving data electronically. Electronic forms simplify and reduce the many steps used in paper forms. When forms-mapping software is used in conjunction with an electronic form, a smart electronic form can process data on the form, show users how to complete the form, and send the data entered to other related forms and applications.

Codes represent efficient means of classifying, identifying, inputting, and retrieving data. Coding symbols consist of numbers, letters, special characters, and symbols. Good coding design demands efficient and flexible code structures, the use of standard characters and formatting, and the application of check digits when the code is a critical part of the input. Code structures include sequential, block, decimal, bar, mnemonic, phonetic, and color structures.

Input methods represent a number of devices by which data are captured and input into the system. These devices include keypunches, keyboard-to-storage, keyboard-to-system, magnetic ink character recognition, optical character recognition, computer input microfilm, images, keypads, mouse, penpads, track balls, joysticks, hand-held terminals, touch, and voice.

IMPORTANT TERMS

alphabetic code

automatic data retrieval or transmission

bar code

magnetic ink character recognition (MICR)

manifolding

mnemonic code

batch input

block code

bond

bristol

check digit

chunking

coding capacity

color code

computer input microfilm

data float

decimal code

digitizer

direct input

duplicating paper

DVORAK keyboard

electronic forms

envelope windows

form map or zone format

forms analysis

half-card

hand-held terminals

hierarchical block code

images

joysticks

keyboard-to-storage

keyboard-to-system

keypads

keypunching

ledger

limit checks

mouse

numerical code

onionskin

optical character recognition (OCR)

optical marks or mark sense

pagination

penpads

phonetic code

point-of-sale (POS)

QWERTY keyboard

random code

random errors

routing

safety paper

sequencing

sequential code

smart electronic forms

soundex code

source data automation

touch-sensitive screens

track balls

transcription errors

transposition errors

turnaround document

Universal Product Code (UPC)

voice input

what-you-see-is-what-you-get
   (WYSIWYG)

zoning

Assignment

REVIEW QUESTIONS

6.1 Distinguish between batch and direct input.

6.2 Assume you are performing forms analysis. Identify at least 10 functions that paper forms are supposed to perform.

6.3 List at least five factors that should be considered when selecting the type of paper to be used for forms.

6.4 Briefly discuss at least 10 of the 15 guidelines for forms design.

6.5 List the five functions performed by smart electronic forms.

6.6 What are the hidden costs of paper forms that can be reduced by using electronic forms?

6.7 Define the term "check digit," and list examples of the typical errors it is designed to guard against.

6.8 Define sequential codes and block codes, and give the advantages and disadvantages of each. How are bar codes used in a point-of-sale system?

6.9 Describe some of the functions performed by keyboard-to-storage input devices, and discuss the advantages of using these systems.

6.10 Briefly describe the function of each of the following input devices:

1. Computer input microfilm.
2. Images.
3. Keypads.
4. Mouse.

6. Track balls.
7. Joysticks.
8. Hand-held terminals.
9. Touch systems.

6.11 Discuss and give an example of the use of magnetic ink character recognition as an efficient data input method.

6.12 Explain how optical marks, optical characters, and bar codes are used as part of an optical character recognition input system. Provide examples as part of your explanation.

QUESTIONS FOR DISCUSSION

6.13 Electronic mail, point-of-sale devices, voice input/output, and computer output to microfilm are examples of how data can be manipulated efficiently without the use of reams of paper. Some experts have suggested that continued advancements in those electronic data transmission systems will eliminate the need for paper in the office of tomorrow. Discuss the role of paper-based components, such as forms and printouts, within an electronically based information systems environment. Will electronic devices ultimately make paper in the office obsolete? How will these changes affect the clerical and secretarial worker?

6.14 Forms design guidelines give advice on the placement of related data items on a paper form; the proper use of spacing, captions, and titles; and the numbering of forms. How can these guidelines be incorporated in the design of electronic forms appearing on CRT screens? How will the instructions for completing the form differ for paper forms and for electronically represented forms?

6.15 A frequent complaint among consumers is the increasing depersonalization of individuals by assigning them code numbers, such as customer account numbers, social security numbers, and employee numbers. Now, instead of Mr. John Doe, we have F328-XL-200. Has this coding practice dehumanized business transactions? What impact might this alienation have on persons whose responsibilities center on customer service or public interaction? Should businesses attempt to reduce the amount of coding of personal data items to appear more sensitive to the customer?

6.16 The DVORAK keyboard scheme places the most often typed characters beneath the fingers that rest on the home row, thus reducing the amount of movement required to type. It would seem logical to incorporate this new, more efficient keyboard scheme into all video display units for quicker input. What problems may be encountered in implementing this strategy, especially among typists already trained on the current QWERTY keyboard?

6.17 "All the information in the world is useless to the decision maker if he or she receives it in a form that is unclear, unorganized, illegible, out of sequence, or confusing." Comment on the importance of proper forms design and control in the overall setting of the information system.

6.18 The phrase "computer error" has been used to a great extent to explain away problems and inaccuracies prevalent in business transaction recording. How much of this error is actually human error instead of computer error? How will the amount of erroneous information be affected by the use of data input technologies such as machine-readable forms, touch screens, and voice recognition? If reducing the level of human involvement in the input phase tends to reduce input errors (and, therefore, processing and output errors), does it seem logical that eliminating the human component from the input phase is the ultimate goal of data input technology? Comment.

6.19 The increased speed and efficiency of new data input devices suggest that greater quantities of data will be stored in computer-based processing systems. Without doubt, much of this increased level of record keeping will involve the collection of highly personal information by both businesses and the government. What issues does this trend raise in terms of invasion of privacy? How much information is "enough" when it concerns an individual's private records? Are we, in effect, creating an uncontrollable information monster that will monitor our every action? Discuss.

6.20 One of the goals of data input technology is to capture as many transactions as possible at the point of occurrence. Unfortunately, many recordable events occur away from online data input devices. For example, breaking news stories occur throughout the world and need to be recorded quickly for text processing. Many sales contracts are offsite from the main store or warehouse, yet orders must be processed and filled quickly. How will increasingly portable computers equipped with modems allow more direct data input? Discuss other advantages afforded by "briefcase" computers. Can you think of any significant disadvantages?

EXERCISES AND PROBLEMS

6.21 Using library research, identify and briefly describe three organizations that are currently using direct data input through the use of point-of-sale, touch screen, voice recognition, or some other form of direct entry system.

6.22 Discuss the significance of the following guidelines in designing effective and efficient forms:

1. Paper.
2. Size.
3. Color.
4. Title.
5. Numbering.
6. Pagination.
7. Spacing.
8. Zoning.
9. Captions.
10. Instructions.
11. Manifolding.
12. Windows.
13. Turnaround documents.
14. Sequencing.
15. Routing.

6.23 Design a functional payroll check with stub that meets the forms design guidelines outlined in the chapter.

6.24 Using the three different approaches to modulus 11 listed below, calculate a check digit for the account number 23621.

    1. Arithmetic progression beginning at 2.

    2. Geometric progression beginning at 2 and doubling.

    3. Prime number weighting beginning at 3.

6.25 Use the Soundex coding system to prepare a code name for each member of your immediate family.

6.26 Visit your local post office, supermarket, or bank and prepare a brief report explaining how this institution uses computer-readable forms, such as magnetic ink character recognition and optical character recognition.

6.27 Examine any three of the coding schemes found on the documents listed below and report on the meaning of each code position, as well as any recommendations to improve the effectiveness of the coding scheme.

    1. Payroll stub.

    2. Personal check.

    3. Credit card statement.

    4. Coding on magazine subscription label.

    5. Library catalog card.

    6. University course code.

6.28 The emphasis on automotive safety has resulted in Detroit automobile manufacturers having to recall millions of automobiles for real and potential safety defects. Often the potential safety problem is related to a certain part made in a specific plant or during a specific time period. Obviously, if the automobile manufacturer could determine which automobiles had which parts, needless expense could be eliminated in many recalls. Moreover, structural defects in older cars could also be addressed, as they were determined. One suggestion offered by safety experts is the development of an identification number that could be imprinted on a metal plate and attached to each automobile. This number would be recorded by a dealer on all new sales and by the owner on all subsequent resales.

    Using the above ideas and any additional assumptions or ideas of your own, prepare a proposal for a coding structure to be used by the automobile manufacturers.

6.29 Plutronics, Inc., is an electronics component manufacturing firm. Plutronics purchases electronic components from a variety of suppliers, and then assembles these components into signal converters and modulators for use in the communications industry. The company uses four manufacturing plant/warehouse complexes in four cities to serve its nationwide clientele. Each complex purchases independently from suppliers of its choice at going rates to satisfy its own production needs. This practice has resulted in varying qualities of end products, inefficient buying practices, and frequent stockouts.

    A recent study has recommended the creation of a centralized purchasing function at the company's headquarters. This new department will be responsible for receiving requisition orders from the four warehouses, processing purchase orders to a variety of vendors and suppliers, and accounting for the actual receipt of goods at the warehouse site by means of receiving reports.

    As manager-elect of the new purchasing department, design the purchase requisition, purchase order, and receiving report necessary to effect the new purchasing system.

6.30 You are a systems analyst for the Bayou State Insurance Company of Ruston, Louisiana. Your job, among other things, is to design a coding structure for the Automobile Claims

File. Following are items of the file that must be coded:

1. Identification of cities and towns in Louisiana.

2. Personal injury protection deductible coverage:
   full coverage
   $250 deductible name insured
   $500 deductible name insured
   $1,000 deductible name insured
   $2,000 deductible name insured
   $250 name insured and members of household
   $500 name insured and members of household
   $1,000 name insured and members of household
   $2,000 name insured and members of household

3. Bodily injury limits:

5/10	50/100
10/20	20/50
15/30	100/300
20/40	Excess of 100/300
25/50	All other

4. Medical payments limits:

$500	$3,000
750	5,000 and over
1,000	All other
2,000	No medical payments

5. Property damage:

$ 5,000	$ 50,000
10,000	100,000
15,000	300,000
25,000	All other
35,000	No property damage

6. Property damage coverage:

Full coverage	+	Option 1
Full coverage	+	Option 2
Full coverage	+	Option 3
Deductible	+	Option 1
Deductible	+	Option 2
Deductible	+	Option 3
Full coverage		
Straight deductible		

Design a coding scheme to classify properly and make the foregoing items more manageable, meaningful, and amenable to processing.

6.31 The Macy twins have decided to open a television repair store to complement their father's TV and stereo retail outlet. Since Mac Macy is more familiar with the actual repair work, he will be the repairman and Stacy Macy will be responsible for ordering and stocking parts, and for general office work.

Most of the customers will be referrals from Mr. Macy's TV and Stereo Center. The Macy twins plan to provide free pickup and delivery service to these customers. As each TV is brought to the shop, a service work order detailing the work to be done is prepared and left with the customer. Frequently, customers are interested in obtaining an estimate of the cost of repair and when the work will be completed. They also often ask about a rental TV while theirs is in the shop.

As the work is performed, the costs of parts and labor are recorded on a copy of the service work order. When the TV set is delivered or picked up by the customer, a copy of the service order serves as the bill. The customer can then pay the invoice by cash, check, or credit card. A 60-day guarantee is included with each service order.

After you have designed and installed Mr. Macy's computer system, he asked you to help his children out by designing a format for the service work order document. Also determine how many copies of the service work order document should be prepared and for what reason.

6.32 A national furniture maker specializes in the production of furniture for use in the education industry. The four major products include office desks, individual student desks, laboratory tables, and specialized work areas, such as computer workstations for student training and drafting tables. The number of styles within each product category are 12, 4, 10, and 5, respectively. The company services its widespread clientele by dividing the sales area into 9 regions, with each region divided into 6 to 12 districts each assigned to an individual salesperson. Currently, 1500 customer accounts can be categorized into 7 major customer types.

Using the given data requirements, design a sales code to enable management to analyze sales transactions more efficiently. Indicate the meaning of each digit in the code.

6.33 Identify violations of forms design in the following form.

Please place customer number here	⇒	DO NOT STAPLE

Form to Return Merchandise
(Must first be approved by Manager)   Date: _____

Price $ _____   08261

Signature: _____   Date: _____
Customer's Name and Address

Comments:

Doesn't the customer not have the receipt?

Initials: _____   Y   N

⟨DO NOT FOLD⟩
Steps:
1. Sign first two copies
2. Give one copy to customer, second copy to general account
3. Send third copy to manager for signature

DO NOT WRITE
IN THIS SPACE

For Accounting
ONLY

If second request, sign form.
35-A-ZF

_____
Signature

Customer's credit card # _____

6.34 A transaction code has been developed for the Bow Shirt Company, as follows:

Position / Digit	1 Sleeve length	2 Neck size	3 Shirt color	4 Style	5 Material	6 Market	7–8 Market region*	9–10 Outlet†	11 Salesperson	12 Quantity‡
1	28	14	White	Monogram	Cotton	South	Dallas	Neiman-Marcus	P. Newman	XXXX
2	30	14½	Ivory	Tapered	Polyester	West	Little Rock	Godchaux	J. Danelli	
3	32	15	Lime	Sport	Silk	Midwest	Memphis	Goldrings	T. Gretz	
4	34	15½	Gray	Dress	Other	Northeast	New Orleans	Holmes	C. Griffin	
5	36	16	Blue	—	—	—	Birmingham	Palais-Royale	M. Kotecki	
6	38	16¼	Orange	—	—	—	Jackson	—	B. Cushing	
7	40	17	Shale	—	—	—	Atlanta	—	J. Mandel	
8	42	17½	Pink	—	—	—	Richmond	—	E. Summers	
9	44	18	Yellow	—	—	—	Charlotte	—	J. Mathern	
0	Short	—	—	—	—	—	—	—	K. Larson	

*Market regions are sequence codes (00–99) within the market.

†Outlets are sequence codes (00–99) within the market region. Example: Market: South; Market region: Dallas; Outlet: Holmes is 10104.

‡Represents actual quantity—cannot exceed 9999.

In addition, cost and sales price is coded

Last two letters in code = cents.

```
1 2 3 4 5 6 7 8 9 0
B O W S H I R T L N
```

What follows is a partial list of transactions for September:

CODE	QUANTITY	COST CODE	SALES PRICE
23241301038	400	BWN	OLH
43222102044	300	OIR	SLH
55422307740	250	WNN	HLT
45422124937	500	WOI	ISN
45422236783	275	WOI	ISN
44423173047	800	OLN	HIL
43534407451	750	OTL	HRL
75741380415	450	SNH	RLH
53633407082	600	WNH	IOL
33422410121	950	OTH	HRH

Please answer the following questions based on the partial list of transactions for September:

1. What is the most popular color of shirt nationwide? in the Northeast?
2. What is the revenue obtained from the item having the partial code of 23241?
3. Which salesperson produced the largest dollar sales? Which salesperson sold the most shirts? Which salesperson produced the largest profit?
4. What market is the most profitable?
5. What market purchases the most shirts having 16-inch necks?
6. How many shirts having 36-inch sleeves and 18-inch necks did J. Mandel sell in this period?
7. How many shirts having 36-inch sleeves and 16-inch necks were sold during September?

6.35 Listed next are 10 typical applications in a manufacturing organization, with a brief description of their functions. Additionally, 10 business transactions are listed. For each transaction, indicate the potential logical relationship to each application.

Applications

1. *Purchasing.* Prepares a purchase order to be sent to a vendor. Keeps track of purchase orders placed.
2. *Inventory control.* Keeps track of current inventory status for raw materials, work in process, and finished goods.
3. *Production scheduling.* Assigns people, machines, and material according to customer orders received or an inventory replenishment plan.
4. *Machine utilization.* Keeps track of machine usage in terms of hours available, hours running, and hours down.
5. *Accounts payable.* Keeps track of monies owed by the organization for products and services received from vendors. Prepares a check for payment.
6. *Accounts receivable.* Keeps track of monies owed to the organization for products/ services provided to customers. Prepares invoices and statements.
7. *Bill of material.* Maintains the composition (recipe) of each finished good item, in terms of the type and quantity of raw material or subassembly material.
8. *Sales reporting.* Maintains a record of sales to customers by various selling units.
9. *Payroll.* Processes time cards to prepare paychecks for employees. Maintains records concerning various deductions from gross pay to calculate net pay.

10. *Personnel.*   Maintains employment records for each employee including a variety of descriptive information, job performance, and salary history.

Transactions

1. Receipt of a customer order.
2. Receipt of a raw material.
3. Receipt of an invoice by a customer.
4. Notification of an employee change of address.
5. Notification of a customer change of address.
6. Realignment of sales territories.
7. Physical shipment of goods to a customer.
8. Notification of a substitute raw material.
9. Machine repair report.
10. Receipt of returned goods.

6.36 A bank data base contains several files, one of which contains a complete customer profile. This file is stored on magnetic disk and is accessible by bank tellers by means of online inquiry devices. One way to access this file is with an abbreviated alphanumeric code. The last name of the customer is abbreviated by a computer-generated key based on eliminating certain letters and replacing others with phonetic symbols. Using this method, as outlined in the text, code the following names: RODRIGUEZ, BROWN, JOHNSON, COHEN. Would you code the names, RODRIGEZ, JONSON, and COHAN the same? If not, then how would you access, say, FRED COHEN, if you also have a FRED COHAN in the files?

6.37 Old Briar Patch, Inc., is a major corporation that acts as a holding company for numerous smaller corporations engaged in the distillation, blending, bottling, and distribution of spirits. Old Briar Patch controls 45 corporations, sells 6 basic spirit types (gin, bourbon, scotch, Canadian, etc.), sells under 60 different brand names, bottles 26 sizes (from small one-drink bottles to gallons in various increments), engages in both domestic and export business, offers many special packages (Christmas, Father's Day, etc., as well as wooden crate, cardboard carton, and similar variations), and distributes in up to 1000 subclassifications of geographical area. Develop a product/customer combination code.

The product code should uniquely identify each product sold and, in addition, provide for statistical analysis by financial account, spirit type, brand, size, market, area sold, and so forth. Also, the combined customer code indicates at least three items, such as the major area within domestic and export class, the subclass within major area and the customer serial code within area subclass. [Adapted from Van Court Hare, Jr., *Systems Analysis: A Diagnostic Approach* (New York: Harcourt Brace Jovanovich, 1967), pp. 501–503.]

6.38 Abernathy Computers is a new company that sells microcomputer hardware to customers in the Columbus, Ohio area. Approximately 80 percent of its sales are to individuals, with companies making up the remaining portion of the business.

The eight employees of Abernathy Electronics were hired by Sam Abernathy, the owner of the company, because of their background in electronics. Sam believed the paperwork to run the business was a necessary evil, and it was something he would take care of on the weekends with his home-grown microcomputer accounting system. As might be expected, after the first two months of operation, Sam found he lacked the records he needed to figure out what was going on in the business. In particular, because he had no record of returns or the corresponding credits given customers, he had no idea how much of his revenue was real.

"What I need is some way to account for hardware returned by customers. I would like to know what was returned, when, and the reason it was returned. Because several of our customers have accounts with us, their account number should also be identified. Last, for control purposes, I would like to know who authorized the credit to our accounts receivable."

Required: Prepare a credit memo form for Abernathy Computers, taking into account Mr. Abernathy's needs.

BIBLIOGRAPHY

BASSETT, ERNEST D., DAVID G. GOODMAN, and JOSEPH S. FOSEGAN. *Business Records Control,* 5th ed. Cincinnati: South-Western Publishing, 1981.

BURKE, HARRY E. *Handbook of Bar Coding Systems.* New York: Van Nostrand Reinhold, 1984.

DANIELS, ALAN and DONALD YEATES, eds. *Systems Analysis.* Palo Alto, Calif.: Science Research Associates, 1971.

GORE, MARVIN R., and JOHN W. STUBBE. *Computers and Information Systems,* 2nd ed. New York: McGraw-Hill, 1984.

HARE, VAN COURT, JR. *Systems Analysis: A Diagnostic Approach.* New York: Harcourt Brace Jovanovich, 1967.

HOWITT, DORAN. "Buying Plane Tickets On-line." *InfoWorld,* June 25, 1984.

MAEDKE, WILMER O., MARY F. ROBEK, and GERALD E. BROWN. *Information and Records Management.* Encino, Calif.: Glencoe, 1981.

MATTHIES, LESLIE H. *Forms Design: Applied Principles.* Colorado Springs: Systemation, 1969.

MCGEEVER, CHRISTINE. "Graphics and Digitizers." *InfoWorld,* September 3, 1984.

MENKUS, BELDEN. "Designing a Useful Form." *Business Graphics,* September 1972.

PELTU, MALCOLM. *A Guide to the Electronic Office.* New York: John Wiley, 1981.

PEPPER, JON. "Pair of Powerful Software Tools Keeps Business True to Forms." *PC Week,* March 15, 1988.

POWERS, MICHAEL J., DAVID R. ADAMS, and HARLAN D. MILLS. *Computer Information Systems Development: Analysis and Design.* Cincinnati: South-Western, 1984.

RICH, ELAINE. "Natural-Language Interfaces." *Computer,* September 1984.

ROMAN, DAVID R. "Building Up Your Personal Computers, Part II. Data-Input Devices." *Computer Decisions,* March 1984.

SENN, JAMES A. *Analysis and Design of Information Systems.* New York: McGraw-Hill, 1984.

"Seven Hidden Costs of Every Form Your Company Uses." Carrollton, Tx.: Electronic Form Systems, 1987.

TELESCA, RICHARD J. "Aetna Plans for 'No Fault' OA." *Datamation,* April 15, 1984.

"The Wonderful World of Color Makes Records Management Easier." *Information and Records Management,* October 1976.

TYLER, MICHAEL. "Touch Screens: Big Deal or No Deal." *Datamation,* January 1984.

TYSON, THOMAS, and ARIAN T. SADHWANI. "Bar Codes: Speed Factory Floor Reporting." *Management Accounting,* April 1988.

"Variety of Data-Entry Devices Can Make the User's Job a Snap." *PC Week,* January 26, 1988.

WAGSTAFF, BILL. "Data-Entry Update." *Computer Decisions*, May 1984.

WIEDERHOLD, GIO. *Database Design*, 2nd ed. New York: McGraw-Hill, 1983.

WOOD, LAMONT. "Directing the Flow of Goods." *Computer Decisions*, September 15, 1984.

WOOD, LAMONT. "Ringing in the New Retail Technology." *Computer Decisions*, September 15, 1984.

ZIENTARA, MARGUERITE. "Touch Screens: Here to Stay?" *InfoWorld*, April 27, 1984.

7

MODELS

7.1 INTRODUCTION

Models are a form of abstraction or representation of reality. They are usually a simplification of the real thing. In information systems, the systems analyst must construct a number of models for several purposes. One purpose may include developing a set of procedures for personnel to follow to perform certain tasks. Another is to analyze systems and develop design "blueprints" of proposed systems, and, later, document the system. Still another purpose is to develop logico-mathematical models to convert data into information. For example, a string of numbers representing the ages of a population (data) manipulated by summing the ages and dividing by the number of people in the population gives the average age (information).

The general objective of this chapter is to present some of the more popular models and modeling techniques used by systems analysts. The specific objectives are:

1. To include several logico-mathematical models. These models are included only to demonstrate the role that they and other similar logico-mathematical models play in information systems development.
2. To present several of the more popular systems analysis, design, and documentation models.

7.2 LOGICO-MATHEMATICAL MODELS

In this section a brief description is provided of a few, widely used logico-mathematical models. The purpose of these descriptions is to help you gain a proper perspective on where these models apply in the development of information systems, rather than make you an expert on building or implementing these models.

Bookkeeping Model

The bookkeeping model is an equation that sets up a procedure for classifying, recording, and reporting financial transactions of an organization. It can be stated as follows:

$$\text{Assets } (A_t) = \text{Liabilities } (L_t) + \text{Contributed Capital } (CC_t)$$
$$+ \text{ Retained Earnings } (RE_t)$$

Each category represents some financial amount at some point in time. All transactions are classified and recorded in such a way that the total assets equal the sum of the liabilities, contributed capital, and retained earnings.

Retained earnings, at some point in time (usually stated at the end of an accounting period), is the algebraic sum of the retained earnings of the previous period, RE_{t-1}, the earnings for the period, E_t, and the dividends declared during the period, D_t. This equation is stated as:

$$RE_t = RE_{t-1} + E_t - D_t$$

Earnings are determined by matching the inputs for the period with the outputs for the period. In business organizations, the inputs are measured in terms of revenue (R), and the outputs are measured in terms of expenses (EXP) required to generate this revenue. Income tax (TAX), is not recognized as an expense per se but as a social cost of doing business. The equation for earnings is stated as:

$$E_t = R_t - EXP_t - TAX_t$$

Cost-Volume-Profit Model

Costs react on the basis of activity. Costs can be divided into the two basic behavior patterns of variable and fixed. Where variable costs react in direct proportion to changes in activity, fixed costs remain the same within a specified range of activity.

By knowing cost behavior, we can simulate earnings that might be obtained with changes in the level of activity or volume by the following equation:

$$E = (SP - VC)X - FC$$

After subtracting fixed costs, FC, earnings, E, are equal to the difference between the unit selling price, SP, and the unit variable cost, VC, times the number of units sold, X.

The cost-volume-profit relationship provides a useful way to simulate the profit factors of any organization. The factors that increase profit are:

1. Increased selling price per unit.
2. Decreased variable cost per unit.
3. Increased volume.
4. For a multiproduct company, a change in its product mix.

A typical question from management may be: What would the profit picture look like if we decreased selling price by 5 percent, variable cost remained constant, and we increased volume of sales by 20 percent? A variety of questions such as this, proposed by management, could generate information to enhance planning and decision making.

Budget and Performance Analysis Models

A budget is a plan of action, expressed in quantitative terms, that covers some specific time period. The key concept of a budget is structuring it in terms that equate to the responsibility of those charged with its execution. In this way the budget is used not only as a planning device but also as a control device. Budgets are of three types:

1. An operating budget showing planned operations for the forthcoming period.
2. A cash budget showing the anticipated sources and uses of cash.
3. A capital budget showing planned changes in a variety of fixed assets.

Budget is a macro concept whereas standards are micro concepts. For example, the standard cost per labor hour may be $5. The budget for 20,000 hours would show a total labor cost of $100,000. The standard itself is a predetermined estimate of what performance should be under stated conditions. In preparing performance information based on standards, we can use three formulas:

Quantity variance = (Actual quantity − Standard quantity)

× Standard cost per unit

Cost variance = (Actual cost − Standard cost) × Actual quantity

Total variance = Quantity variance + Cost variance

Net Present Value Model

The net present value model can be used to help management make decisions about investment proposals if such a proposal can be reduced to monetary amounts. Stated simply, neglecting nonmonetary considerations, an investment proposal is acceptable if the present value of its earnings or cost savings equals or exceeds the amount of the investment required at some desired rate of return.

For example, suppose that management is thinking of purchasing a computer system for $200,000. The useful life of the computer is five years. The cost savings for the first year are $36,000 and for each of the next four years, $100,000. The minimum desired rate of return is 30 percent. Neglecting other quantitative or qualitative considerations, should management purchase the computer?

In the example of Figure 7.1, the net present value of $−5716 means the investment has not earned what it should at a minimum desired rate of return of 30 percent. Therefore, the investment is undesirable. If the present value

	Present Value	Cost Savings Streams				
	Present Value of $1 Discounted at 30%		1	2	3	4	5
Annual cost savings						
$36,000 ×	.769	$ 27,684	$36,000			
100,000 ×	.592	59,200		$100,000		
100,000 ×	.455	45,500			$100,000	
100,000 ×	.350	35,000				$100,000
100,000 ×	.269	26,900					$100,000
Present value of future						
cost savings		$ 194,284				
Initial Investment	1.000	−200,000				
Net present value		$− 5,716				

Figure 7.1 Application of the net present value model to an investment decision.

226

were positive or zero, the investment would be desirable because its return either exceeds or meets the desired minimum.

Network Model

PERT (program evaluation and review technique) is an example of a network model used for planning and controlling projects with well-defined activities and events. PERT is based on a network composed of activities that take time to accomplish (see, for example, Figure 7.2). Between the activities are instantaneous events, which designate the completion of each activity. Probably a better interpretation indicates that events represent a start or finish of the activities.

The activities are placed on a network and are represented by arrows. Generally, arrows flow from left to right. The following are four rules to follow when placing an activity on the network:

1. It must be determined if any activities logically precede the activity that is under consideration.
2. It must be determined if any activities are logically concurrent with the activity under consideration.
3. It must be determined if activities are logically subsequent to the activity under consideration.
4. Events must be clearly defined relative to their beginning and end.

The activity time should be estimated by someone knowledgeable about the particular processes. The three time estimates furnished are as follows:

1. *Most Likely Time.* How long do you expect it would take to complete this particular activity?
2. *Optimistic Time.* What is the minimum possible time in which this particular task or activity can be completed?
3. *Pessimistic Time.* What is the longest time this particular activity or task has ever taken?

The goal in getting three subjective estimates is to use them to calculate a single weighted average, or mean time, and variance. This average or mean time is called the expected time of the activity. Briefly, the three time estimates are related to the expected time and standard deviation by the following formulas:

$$t_e = \frac{O + 4M + P}{6}$$

$$\sigma_{t_e} = (P - O)/6$$

where:

O = optimistic time estimate

M = most likely time estimate

P = pessimistic time estimate

t_e = expected time (weighted average)

σ_{t_e} = standard deviation of t.

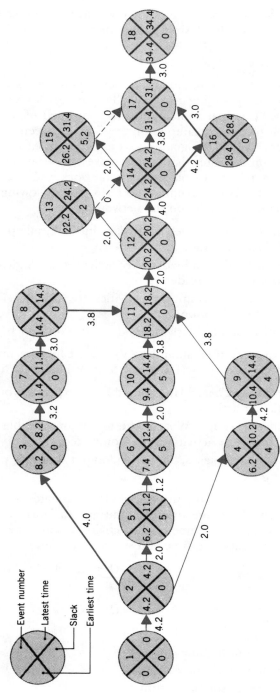

Figure 7.2 Network showing earliest and latest time and slack. The heavy line represents the critical path.

These formulas are based on the assumption that the time estimates approximate a beta distribution.

Critical events on the network are those that have zero slack time. Slack time equals the completion deadline (T_D) less the earliest event time (T_E). The latest event time is the latest time that an event can occur without disrupting the project. The earliest event time is the earliest time that an event can occur. A heavy line connecting the critical events represents the critical path for a network. An increase in time along this path will extend the completion date by the same amount. A decrease in time along this path will shorten the time to completion by the same amount or change the critical path.

Decision Model

The elements of a simple decision model consist of actions, outcomes, probabilities of outcomes, and utilities. Let us define the following:

$$A = \text{set of alternative resource commitments, or actions } (a \in A)$$

$$O = \text{set of future states or outcomes } (o \in O)$$

$$p(o) = \text{set of probabilities that describe the outcome occurrence}$$

$$U(o, a) = \text{utility of an outcome occurring given the selection of an}$$
action. If an expected utility approach is taken, then the alternative with the highest expected utility would be selected.

$$E(U/a^*) = MAX \sum_{a \in A} [U(o, a) \cdot p(o)]$$
$$a \in A \quad o \in O$$

An example may make this model clearer. Suppose you are a raw material inspector for the Swill Wine Co. Your job is to either accept (a_1) or reject (a_2) incoming shipments of grapes. The shipments can either meet standards (o_1) or be substandard (o_2). From past experience you know that the probability of a substandard shipment is .2. Conversely, you know that the probability a shipment will meet standards is .8. Now suppose further that the following utility matrix, in terms of dollars, is applicable:

Actions	Outcomes	
	o_1	o_2
a_1	2	-4
a_2	0	1

Then the expected dollar utility for the alternative resource commitments is as follows:

$$E(U/a_1) = U(o_1, a_1) \cdot p(o_1) + U(o_2, a_1) \cdot p(o_2)$$

$$= \$2(.8) + (\$-4).2$$

$$= \$1.60 - \$.80$$

$$= \$.80$$

$$E(U/a_2) = U(o_1, a_2) \cdot p(o_1) + U(o_2, a_2) \cdot p(o_2)$$

$$= \$0(.8) + \$1(.2)$$

$$= \$.20$$

Maximizing over alternatives leads us to choose action a_1, that is, to accept the shipment.

Many different types of questions can be answered within this decision framework. One of the most interesting is, "What would be the most you would pay for correct information about the contents of a shipment?" Let us answer this question by again referring to our example.

Suppose your "perfect" information source was a trained German shepherd dog, who by sniffing the crate could tell with certainty whether or not the grapes were substandard. Your expected utility function would now be:

$$E(U) = U(o_1 \, a_1) \cdot p(o_1) + U(o_2, a_2) \cdot p(o_2)$$

$$= \$2(.8) + \$1(.2)$$

$$= \$1.60 - \$.20$$

$$= \$1.80$$

Notice that the probabilities of the outcomes have not changed. What has changed is that you are no longer making incorrect decisions. You should be willing to pay up to $1.00 ($1.80 − $.80) per crate sniffed for this canine's services.

7.3 DECISION TREES AND DECISION TABLES

Decision trees and decision tables have been used as models by others in areas of engineering, biology, and computer science for a long time. They, however, also possess certain characteristics that make them applicable for information systems modeling.

Decision Tables

A decision table is a matrix of rows and columns that shows conditions and actions. The general form of a decision table is depicted in Figure 7.3. The upper half of the table contains the decision conditions, which are expressed in areas called *stubs* and *entries*. Condition stubs are those criteria the decision maker wishes to apply to his or her logical model. To incorporate these criteria into a decision table, the criteria must be phrased to follow the word *IF*.

The lower half of the table contains the actions to be taken when the specified conditions are satisfied. To incorporate actions into the table, the actions must be structured to follow the word *THEN*.

Combining the conditions with the actions results in *IF* (these conditions exist), *THEN* (perform these actions). A simple, self-explanatory example is illustrated in Figure 7.4.

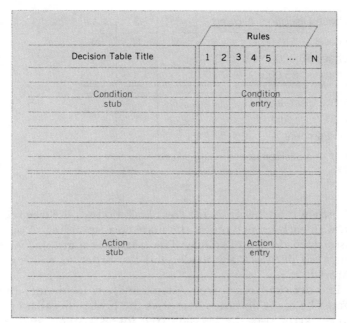

Figure 7.3 A skeleton structure of a decision table.

Decision Trees

A decision tree is a model of a sequence of decisions or conditions (see, for example, Figure 7.5). Each decision made depends on the current value of the variable being tested and all previous decisions that have been made. The tree appears horizontally with the root at the left. The root indicates the first decision and corresponds to the first decision variable. The outcomes of the decisions

REASONS FOR MODELING The reasons for building an information systems model are very similar to the reasons for building any model. Properly done, a model "declutters the mental workplace" so that the modeler can focus on what is really important. The model lets the modeler "see the forest." By using computer-aided software engineering (CASE) package, the model can be analyzed in a variety of ways before the final design is selected.

Another reason for building a model is to ensure that there is valid and complete communication between users and systems analysts.

Paraphrased from Jon Stonecash, "Declutter the Mental Workplace with an Information Model," *Data Management*, December 1987, pp. 22–28.

Purchase Discounts Allowed	1	2	3
Purchase > $10,000	Y	N	N
Purchase $5,000 to $10,000		Y	N
Purchase < $5,000			Y
Take 5% discount	1		
Take 3% discount		1	
Pay full amount			1

Figure 7.4 A decision table showing purchase discount procedures.

are shown as branches from the root. Each node of the tree represents a decision point, with each branch out of the node corresponding to one possible value of the associated decision variable. The tree gives a graphic view of the variables tested, what decisions are made, and the order in which decision making is performed.

The decision tree forces systems analysts to identify the actual decisions that must be made and thus decreases the probability that critical decisions will be overlooked. Also, the decision tree forces systems analysts to consider the sequence of decisions.

7.4 STRUCTURED ENGLISH

The English language used to describe procedures and specifications can contain a number of ambiguities. Structured English, however, is a narrative notation that can be used to define procedural logic and promote clarity. Structured

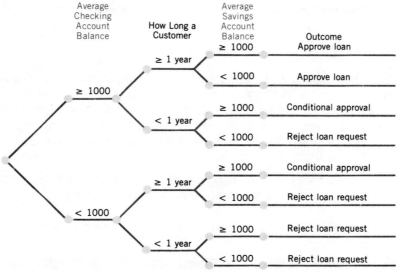

Figure 7.5 A decision tree describing the granting of personal loans.

English, therefore, is an excellent tool for describing procedures both for humans and computers. Even though it is a programming-like language, structured English purists believe it should be independent of any programming language.

Structured English is hierarchical and uses indentation to show its structure. Its keywords for controlling flow are: ELSE, ENDIF, REPEAT WHILE, FOR ALL, REPEAT UNTIL, END, ENDFOR, and EXIT, and for logic are AND, OR, GT (greater than), LT (less than), GE (greater than or equal to), and LE (less than or equal to). Undefined adjectives and adverbs are not permitted unless defined in the data dictionary. Keywords that make up the data dictionary are capitalized. General comment lines are indicated by a beginning asterisk and a terminating semicolon.

Structured English will be applied later in this chapter. For now, perhaps the following example will reveal its usefulness.

```
ORDER ENTRY:
*Process customer and item file;
 FOR ALL orders
     Access CUSTOMER record;
     IF CUSTOMER NUMBER is valid
         Access ORDER form;
     ELSE
         Issue "invalid customer code" message;
         STOP ORDER ENTRY;
     ENDIF;
     FOR ALL items ordered
         Access ITEM record;
         IF ITEM NUMBER is valid
             IF QUANTITY ON HAND GE QUANTITY ORDERED
                 Enter ORDER;
                 Decrease QUANTITY ON HAND by
                     QUANTITY ORDERED;
             ELSE
                 Access BACKORDER form;
                 Write BACKORDER;
             ENDIF;
         ELSE
             Issue "invalid item code" message;
         ENDIF;
     ENDFOR;
     Access SHIPPING DOCUMENT form;
     Enter shipping data;
     Print documents;
 ENDFOR;
EXIT ORDER ENTRY.
```

Pseudocode is a technique used to model program logic. Like structured

English, it uses English statements, but these statements are formed to follow closely the syntax of a particular programming language, such as COBOL and FORTRAN. Therefore, pseudocode is oriented to the programmer, whereas structured English is designed for both programmers and general users.

7.5 DATA FLOW DIAGRAMS (DFDs)

A data flow diagram (DFD) is a model that describes the flows of data and the processes that change or transform data throughout a system. A palette of symbols used to form DFDs is depicted in Figure 7.6. Symbols may be taken from a pallete on a screen of a computer-aided systems engineering program or prepared manually by using a template. Automating the process of drawing and maintaining data flow diagrams improves significantly their usefulness.

Two popular varieties of DFDs are bubble charts, which use circles to represent processes and curved data flow lines, and rectangles with rounded corners and straight data flow lines. The first kind is associated with Ed Yourdon and Tom DeMarco. The second kind uses the symbols shown in Figure 7.6 and

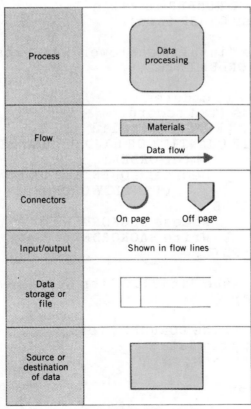

Figure 7.6 Symbols palette for data flow diagram.

PRECISE THINKING AND COMMUNICATIONS THROUGH DIAGRAMS

Good, clear diagrams play an essential part in designing complex systems and developing programs. Philosophers have often stated that what we are capable of thinking depends on the language we use for thinking.

If only one person is developing a system design or program, the diagrams that he uses are an aid to clear thinking. When a number of people work on a system or program, the diagrams are an essential communication tool. Given an appropriate diagramming technique, it is much easier to describe complex activities and procedures in diagrams than in text. A picture can be much better than a thousand words because it is concise, precise, and clear. It does not allow sloppiness and woolly thinking.

A systems analyst, like a carpenter, needs a number of different tools at his workbench. Many systems analysts in the past have drawn one or perhaps two types of diagrams. In early training courses, flowcharts were the only type of diagramming taught. We believe that a well-trained systems analyst should be comfortable in the use of a wide array of diagramming techniques.

Excerpted from James Martin and Carma McClure, *Diagramming Techniques for Analysts and Programmers,* Englewood Cliffs, N.J.:Prentice Hall, 1985.

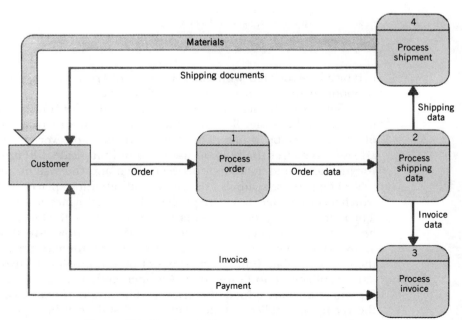

Figure 7.7 High-level DFD of an order processing system.

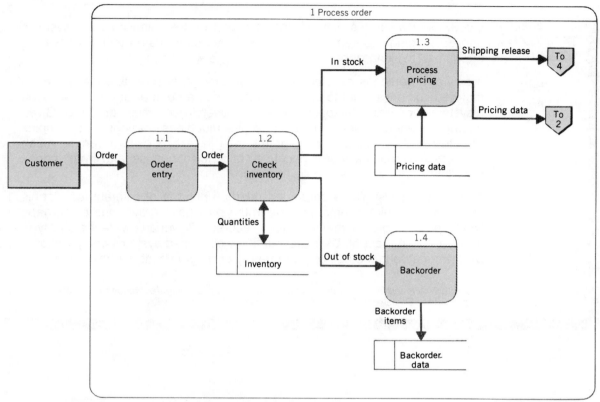

Figure 7.8 A detailed DFD of the "process order" box.

is typically associated with Chris Gane and Trish Sarson. All these people are proponents of structured analysis and design.

Some still debate whether symbols should be round, square, oval, or rectangular, and whether flow lines should be straight or curved, and raise a variety of other cosmetic issues. The relevant issue, however, is the application of DFDs—no matter the symbols used—to communicate different models to users for increased understanding between them and the systems analyst.

The process symbols are used to indicate those places within the system at which incoming data flows are processed or transformed into outgoing data flows. The name of the process is generally written inside the block. Numbers can also be used for reference and sequencing. Material flows are shown by the broad arrow. Data flows are shown by arrows marking the movement of data through the system. A data flow can be thought of as a pipeline transporting packets of data from source to destination. An open-ended rectangle represents a logical file where data are added or retrieved. The origin of data is called a source, and the recipient is called a sink. Sources and sinks can be a person, organization, or even another system. Such external entities are represented by rectangles.

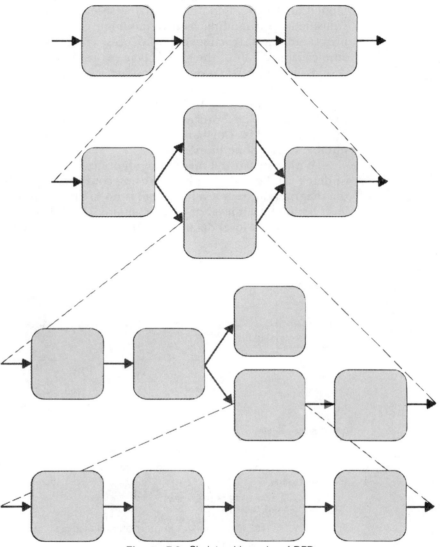

Figure 7.9 Skeleton hierarchy of DFDs.

For example, a customer is an external entity and a source of sales orders. In essence then, a DFD represents the system boundaries, external interactions, processes, and data flow. The DFD is a logical model and therefore does not identify disks, tapes, printers, computers, or any other physical devices.

DFDs are constructed in a top-down manner. Figure 7.7, for example, is a top-down model of an order processing system. It outlines the system being considered in an easy-to-understand way. The model presented in Figure 7.8 is an explosion of the "process order" box. Process boxes can be repeatedly exploded or decomposed until each lowest-level process box represents functions equivalent to a module of programming code (i.e., about 50 to 100 lines of programming instructions). This process creates a total hierarchy (see, for example, Figure 7.9) of the system being considered.

By creating DFDs on a computer, it is easy to build such hierarchies. Analysts and users can easily enlarge a diagram by an EXPLODE menu or implode a process box by using IMPLODE. Each page or screen of the DFD hierarchy should include 7 ± 2 process boxes because it's believed that people's short-term memories (STMs) can handle 7 ± 2 chunks more easily (e.g., Social Security numbers, telephone numbers).

With a structured method of identification and numbers, increasing levels of detail can be added without causing confusion. The degree of complexity of the diagrams at each level of detail is no greater than is that at the next higher level because each level of detail contains 7 ± 2 processes.

The lowest-level detail of DFDs are used by programmers for developing

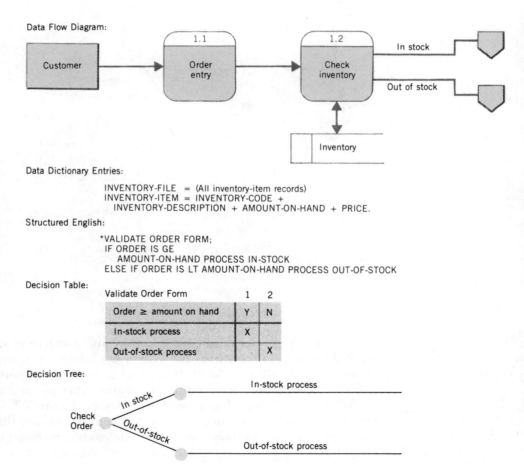

Data Flow Diagram:

Data Dictionary Entries:

INVENTORY-FILE = (All inventory-item records)
INVENTORY-ITEM = INVENTORY-CODE +
    INVENTORY-DESCRIPTION + AMOUNT-ON-HAND + PRICE.

Structured English:

*VALIDATE ORDER FORM;
IF ORDER IS GE
    AMOUNT-ON-HAND PROCESS IN-STOCK
ELSE IF ORDER IS LT AMOUNT-ON-HAND PROCESS OUT-OF-STOCK

Decision Table:

Validate Order Form	1	2
Order ≥ amount on hand	Y	N
In-stock process	X	
Out-of-stock process		X

Decision Tree:

Figure 7.10 A completely documented detail process.

the software that supports the applications. Supplementary techniques, such as a data dictionary, structured English, decision table, and decision tree, are used to provide additional information to both users and programmers. All these techniques are presented in one, simple example in Figure 7.10.

7.6 STRUCTURED ANALYSIS AND DESIGN TECHNIQUE

The structured analysis and design technique (SADT) originated by Douglas T. Ross uses a rectangle as the basic symbol as presented in the left bottom corner of Figure 7.11. SADT's goal is to produce models of the system that can be analyzed and reviewed by all users and other parties during development of the system.

A box represents a function or activity that transforms data. Each of the four sides of the box has a meaning associated with it. The left side of the box is where input data arrives from other activities. The right side is where output leaves to be used by other activities or recipients. The top of the box represents the controls of the activity. The bottom is where the mechanism or particular technology is used by the function or activity to perform its task. Describing the mechanisms are not necessary in a SADT model. An arrow represents data and its flow. Each arrow is labeled with a noun.

SADT analysis proceeds in a top-down manner, first presenting an overview of the system, then exposing details, one at a time, where each detail is related to higher and lower levels. Whenever a box is exploded or decomposed, everything inside the box is included, and everything outside is excluded. The boxes

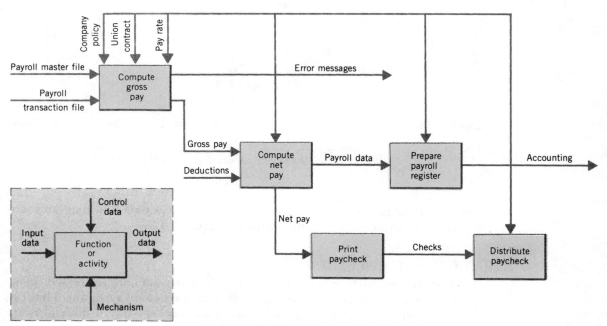

Figure 7.11 A SADT model of payroll processing.

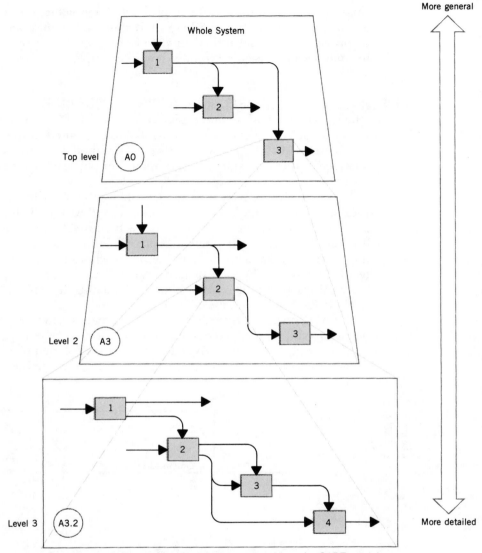

Figure 7.12 Skeleton decomposition of a SADT model.

have the same parent-child hierarchical relationship as data flow diagrams. For a general example of this relationship, see Figure 7.12.

7.7 TRADITIONAL FLOWCHARTS

Traditional flowcharts graphically illustrate how the data are processed. Flowcharts show the input, output, and processes for a system or program. They can be used to display varying levels of detail. Two general types of flowcharts are

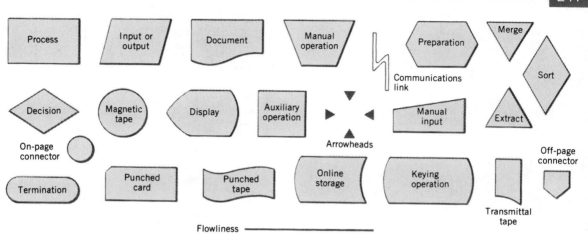

Figure 7.13 Conventional flowchart symbols.

systems flowcharts, which illustrate the general overview of the systems application, and program flowcharts, which present details of the program logic.

The symbols used to build flowcharts are depicted in Figure 7.13. Some of the symbols such as arrowheads and flowlines are used for both data flow in a system and computer programs. Most of the systems-related symbols, however, resemble physical media, such as magnetic tape, online storage, punched cards, punched tape, document, manual input, or operations, such as keying, display, merge, extract, and sort. The common symbols used to prepare program flowcharts are process, input or output, decision, preparation, termination, arrowheads, and connectors.

Systems Flowcharts

The systems flowchart provides a general model of the systems application. It is a physical summarization of all the input and output processed and produced by all the sequences of procedures and processes involved. Meaningful names are written within each flowchart symbol to aid understanding. Also, specialized symbols, annotation, and cross-referencing should be used whenever they will help the reader to understand the flowchart more easily.

Figure 7.14 illustrates a simple systems flowchart that depicts the processing of customer orders. The input is the customer order. The data base consists of two online files, the inventory master file and the customer master file. The process is where the program logic is executed, which will require a program flowchart to describe. The output consists of a number of printer-generated reports.

Program Flowcharts

A program flowchart models the program logic. It graphically represents the types of programming instructions, as well as the sequence and logic of those instructions, as they appear in a program. A program flowchart serves as a guide

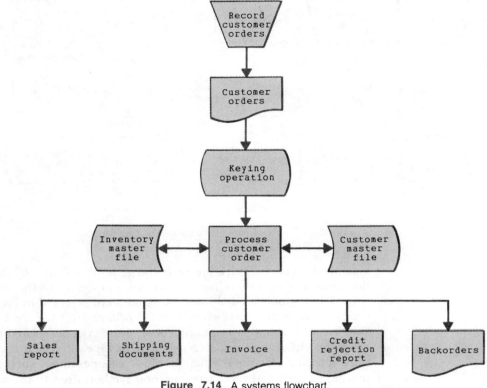

Figure 7.14 A systems flowchart.

used by programmers to code the program. It is also used as a means of illustrating to users, managers, and auditors how data are processed. And, later, when the program has to be changed to handle new systems requirements, the program flowchart serves as documentation for the maintenance programmer.

Figure 7.15 demonstrates a simple program flowchart that processes payroll. It also uses the five most commonly used symbols. Program flowcharts begin and end with terminal symbols. Most program flowcharts contain one or more loops (see on-page connector 2). All symbols should contain written identification.

In situations where programs are lengthy and complex, macro-level program flowcharts are prepared first to give an overview. Then, if the macro-level logic is correct, micro-level program flowcharts are then prepared for the lowest detail. For example, the program flowchart in Figure 7.15 could be considered a macro-level flowchart wherein micro-level program flowcharts would be prepared for the two process blocks.

Generally, a complete flowchart package is far too large to fit on a single page. Off-page connectors are, therefore, used to join the logic between pages. When many flowlines are required on a page, on-page connectors are used to reduce the "spaghetti." Entry and exit connectors should be consistently posi-

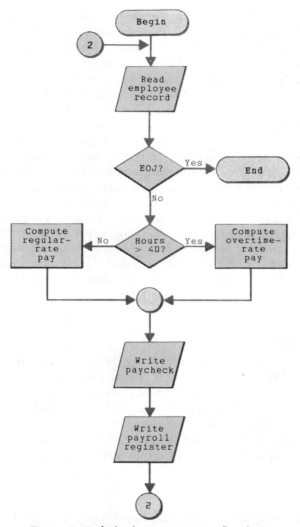

Figure 7.15 A simple macro program flowchart.

tioned with respect to the symbols to which they are attached. The general flow should be from top to bottom and from left to right.

Flowcharts: A Dying Breed
Early on in the information systems field, systems and program flowcharts were widely used. Their popularity over the years, however, has diminished considerably. For those who prefer a structured, hierarchical approach to systems development and program design, traditional flowcharts are not used at all. Opponents of traditional flowcharts believe a better alternative is the data flow dia-

gram. They state that DFDs are more efficient and provide the structured-modular-hierarchical approach to systems design.

The very nature of systems flowcharts tends to get the "cart before the horse." They encourage a physical model of the system before overall logical requirements are considered. This approach leads to the inappropriate sequence of acquiring the hardware first, then developing or buying software, and finally, determining user requirements. Such an approach is analogous to "fire, aim, ready" rather than the more logical "ready, aim, fire."

Program flowcharts are difficult to draw and maintain manually. Software packages, however, are available to help generate flowcharts. But these packages represent a Catch-22 because the program flowchart should be prepared before the program code is written. The flowcharting packages, on the other hand, require the program code to generate the flowchart. In either case, program flowcharts that represent programs of over 5,000 instructions become clumsy and increase the complexity that they are supposed to reduce. Moreover, the way program flowcharts are constructed tends to encourage the use of the undesirable GO TO statement. Alternatively, hierarchical diagramming models such as DFDs and the use of structured English encourage modular, GO TOless programming.

7.8 NASSI-SHNEIDERMAN CHARTS

Nassi-Shneiderman charts force the programmer to structure programs that are top-down, modular, and GO TOless. These charts are named after their originators. I. Nassi and B. Shneiderman, who set out to replace traditional program flowcharts. N. Chapin uses a similar diagram, called the Chapin chart. Both authors' charts are referred to as box charts or structural charts. These charts are used primarily to describe detail program logic. Generally, one box per page or screen represents the logic of a program module.

Basic Symbols

Four basic symbols make up Nassi-Shneiderman charts. These are sequence process, condition decision process, case decision process, and iteration process.

Figure 7.16 General form of a sequence process.

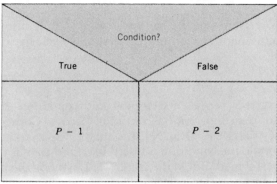

Figure 7.17 General form of a condition decision process.

Sequence Process

The process itself is represented by a rectangular box. Within this large box, several processes are performed in sequence. Examples would include initialization of values, input and output activities, write headings, and calls to execute other procedures. A sequence process is shown in Figure 7.16.

Condition Decision Process

Figure 7.17 illustrates the condition decision process. The top half of the process box is divided into three triangles to show a decision. The bottom half shows actions taken. The middle triangle contains the condition to be tested. The left and right triangles represent the true and false parts of the IF-THEN-ELSE decision process, respectively. The bottom half is divided into the true process box, P-1, and the false process box, P-2. If the condition is true, P-1 is executed. If the condition is false, P-2 is executed.

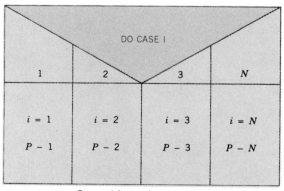

Figure 7.18 General form of a case decision process.

Case Decision Process

The condition decision process can be extended to a case decision process in which a decision is made from multiple, mutually exclusive choices, as portrayed in Figure 7.18.

Iteration Process

The iteration symbol represents looping and repetition of operations *while* a certain condition exists or *until* a condition occurs. Consequently, iteration is indicated by DOWHILE or DOUNTIL symbols displayed in Figure 7.19. In the DOWHILE symbol, the condition is tested first, and then if the condition is true, the process is performed. But in the DOUNTIL symbol, the process is performed first, and then the condition is tested.

The iteration symbol shows the scope of the iteration, including all processes and decisions contained within the loop. The left-hand part of the symbol indicates the path that the iteration follows until the conditions controlling the iteration are satisfied.

Brief Example

An example of the Nassi-Shneiderman chart when the symbols are put together is illustrated in Figure 7.20.

General Comments

Nassi-Shneiderman charts can serve as an alternative to traditional flowcharts and structured English. Nassi-Shneiderman charts are easy to read and convert to program code. They are, however, difficult to draw, especially if a module has a great many nested IF statements. They do not link to a data dictionary, and they cannot be used at a higher level to show the general structure of a program. In addition, error routines are hard to illustrate.

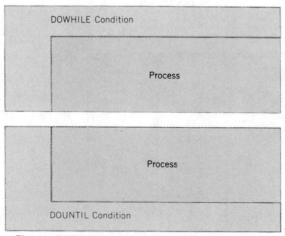

Figure 7.19 General form of the interation process.

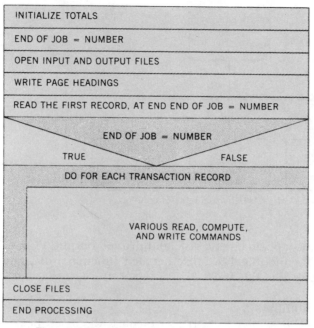

Figure 7.20 A simple Nassi-Shneiderman chart.

7.9 HIERARCHY PLUS INPUT PROCESS OUTPUT

IBM developed HIPO (hierarchy plus input process output), a diagramming technique that uses a set of diagrams to show the input, output, and functions of a system or program. It serves both as an analysis and design tool and as documentation for the system.

HIPO involves the use of two types of diagrams: (1) a hierarchy diagram or a visual table of contents (VTOC) that shows how the modules of the application fit together and (2) an overview or detail functional diagrams that show the input, processing, and output for each module.

Visual Table of Contents

Figure 7.21 illustrates a visual table of contents. Each box can represent a system, subsystem, program, or program module. Its purpose is to display the overall functional modules and reference the overview and detail HIPO diagrams. The modules are in increasing detail. Depending on the complexity of the application, two to six levels of modules are typical.

Functional Diagram

The functional diagram, either at an overview or detail level, consists of an input box, a process box, and an output box. One functional diagram is created for each module in the VTOC. Traditional flowchart symbols represent media, such

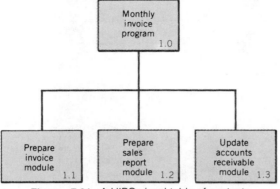

Figure 7.21 A HIPO visual table of contents.

as magnetic tape, magnetic disk, and printed output. Figure 7.22 is a functional diagram for module 1.0. More detailed functional diagrams can be prepared for modules 1.1, 1.2, and 1.3.

General Comments

The VTOC is similar to a structure chart (discussed next). The overview and detail functional diagrams are similar to a data flow diagram. Generally, HIPO diagrams are more difficult to prepare than are DFDs.

During the analysis and general design phases, VTOCs are prepared to define in general the program modules necessary to handle user requirements. During the detailed design phase, the systems analyst prepares more detailed diagrams to describe each module that will be converted to program code. In this way, decomposition continues until a function has been reduced to its most basic activities.

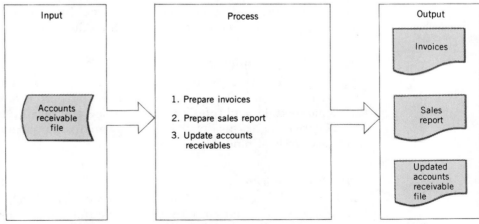

Figure 7.22 An overview functional chart for monthly invoice program (1.0).

HIPO facilitates a top-down design. It does not replace flowcharting, but supplements it. It is generally regarded as a good technique for smaller, simpler applications. It is criticized, however, for lacking the characteristics that would permit it to be useful for complex systems. For example, HIPO diagrams become cluttered and difficult to read when an application involves a large number of processes and input and output steps. Narrative description must be used for conditions, loops, and any linkage to and definition of data structures.

7.10 STRUCTURE CHARTS

A structure chart displays the overall systems application structure, as shown in Figure 7.23. Each rectangle represents a module—a named, bounded, contiguous set of executable program statements. The name in the module summarizes the transformation performed by that module and its subordinates. Invocation of one module by another, a call from a superior to a subordinate, is represented by a directed arrow known as a connection. An information flow across the connection is known as a data couple and is represented by an open circle at its tail. This represents data used in the problem. A control couple, or flag, is shown by a solid circle at its tail. This arrow indicates control data used by the program to direct execution flow, such as an error flag or end-of-file switch.

A large number of software vendors have developed interactive graphics packages that create, edit, and maintain structure charts. These diagrams can be drawn on the screen of a personal computer and linked to a data dictionary, the same as data flow diagrams.

Only one module is at the top of the structure chart. This module is called the root (also called the coordinate module). Control is passed from the root down the structure level by level to other modules. Control is always passed back to the invoking (superior) module. Therefore, when the program finishes executing, control returns to the root module.

The return of data from an invoked, or called, subordinate module to the invoking, or calling, superior module is implicit unless overriden by relationships

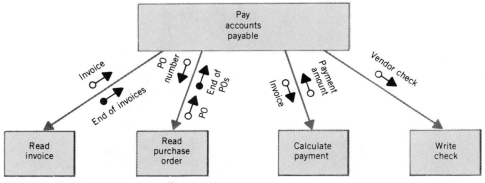

Figure 7.23 A structure chart.

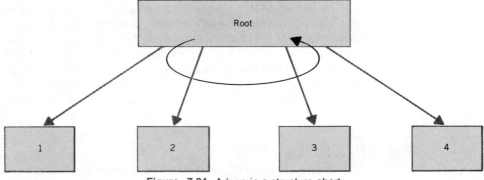

Figure 7.24 A loop in a structure chart.

explicitly shown between peer-level subordinates or between a subordinate and a superior that is not the direct superior of the subordinate module. In the normal case, execution begins at the root module and passes to the first subordinate, back to the root, to the second subordinate, back to the root, to the third subordinate, and, finally, back to the root.

Optional steps and loops may be indicated by using appropriate symbols. For example, in Figure 7.24, steps 2 and 3 are executed two or more times in succession for each iteration of steps 1 through 4. Figure 7.25 shows an optional step as indicated by a decision symbol. In this case, steps 1 and 3 are mandatory, whereas step 2 is conditional.

7.11 WARNIER-ORR DIAGRAMS

Jean-Dominique Warnier developed a logical construction of a program. Later, Kenneth Orr extended this basic concept to include systems design. Today, this structured analysis and design tool is called a Warnier-Orr (W-O) diagram. It uses graphical displays consisting of a hierarchy of brackets to portray activities

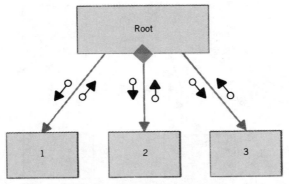

Figure 7.25 An optional step in a structure chart.

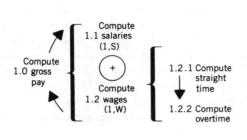

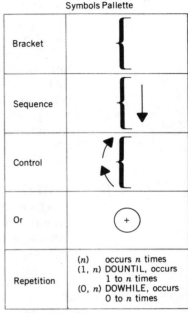

Figure 7.26 A W-O diagram with symbols palette.

or data elements. Some people describe the diagram as a hierarchical chart or structure chart turned on its side, while others describe it as an alternative to structured English or pseudocode. Figure 7.26 illustrates a W-O diagram and defines the symbols used.

Creation of the W-O diagram starts with the identification of the output or processing requirements and then works backward to determine the steps and combinations of input needed to produce them (see, for example, Figure 7.27). It can serve as an alternative to a HIPO, structure, Nassi-Shneiderman

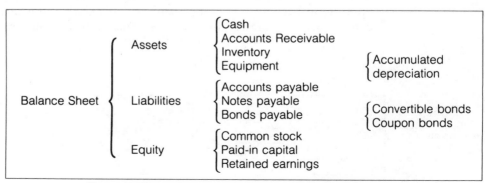

Figure 7.27 Example output defined by input in a W-O diagram.

or SADT chart, and structured English. W-O diagrams can represent hierarchical data structures or reports as well as computer programs in which each bracket in the W-O diagram becomes a module in a computer program.

W-O diagrams are simple in appearance and easy to understand. The sequence of working backward from output required to necessary inputs ensures that the application will be requirements oriented. Generally, W-O diagrams are preferred over HIPO diagrams, except that HIPO diagrams relate data to processing, whereas W-O diagrams do not. W-O diagrams also do not indicate conditional logic as well as other detail-level diagramming techniques. They are better suited to small applications.

7.12 PROTOTYPING

An information systems application prototype is a physical model of the application that acts much like a car model used to test a new car before it goes into production. This mock-up of a proposed systems application provides early feedback to the systems analyst from users about the viability of the model.

The prototyping process is presented in Figure 7.28. Based on perceived user's requirements, a prototype is built to provide a first-cut model that establishes an unambiguous beginning. User requirements are matched against the model. If it does not meet these requirements, then the first prototype is "thrown away" and another is built, or a slight modification is made depending on the user's requirements. This heuristic, hands-on process continues until agreement is reached and a prototype is accepted. This solution prototype is implemented, or it provides specifications for its own replacement.

Prototyping is an engineering approach to "build a little, test a little," before building the final system. This approach gets rid of most of the design glitches before they have a chance to become part of the production system. Moreover, during each iteration, the user can "kick the tires" before deciding on which model to "buy."

The user/system interface design force is prominent in prototyping. The results of tight coupling among the user, systems analyst, and systems models narrows the gap between what users say or think they want from the system and what they actually get. The user is brought directly into the process so that the application becomes his or her project. This closer interface permits users to communicate accurately their requirements to the systems analyst. On the other

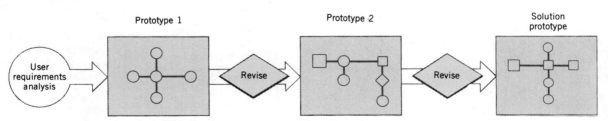

Figure 7.28 Prototype iteration until solution prototype is achieved.

side, this communication and interaction improves the systems analyst's ability to translate user requirements into a functioning system.

An unrestricted user/system interface is especially applicable with strategic- and tactical-level users because their requirements often cannot be specified clearly and totally in detail at first. With prototyping, these users can "discover" their needs. The user tries something, then sees what happens, then modifies, then tries something slightly or significantly different, then sees what happens, and so on until the user gets what he or she needs.

This user and systems analyst interaction provides instant feedback and allows the user to see his or her results immediately and modify the model as many times as is necessary before finalization. The traditional steps of analysis, design, programming, and testing are combined into one interactive flow with the user being the key focus.

The first step in prototyping may be to map out a plan on paper. Next, a data flow diagram may be used to indicate data flow. Finally, the user and analyst may work at a workstation to create examples of output on a screen. If a report is laid out one way, the user may ask to look at it in another way, or elements may be added. This way, the user can play with the application *before* it is implemented.

The prototype should include as much detail on building blocks as possible. Input and especially output should be defined along with supporting technology, data base, and controls. Also, if applicable, the prototype should show how it interfaces with other applications. Parts of the prototype may be described by using other models, such as data flow diagrams, decision tables or trees, flowcharts, and structured English.

Generally, prototyping is best used in the development of applications that are poorly defined. Also, prototyping is appropriate in one-on-one or one-on-a-few small applications that require a tight user/system interface. One could probably find many other applications of prototyping, even if the models are merely worked out on paper. To be sure, in almost any situation, prototypes enhance visualization and communications.

SUMMARY

A model is a form of abstraction of reality. Models help systems analysts in the design and documentation of information systems. Logico-mathematical models are quantitative representations of reality. They are implemented in systems to support an organization's transactional processing functions and provide it information to support vital planning and control activities. The first part of this chapter contains a brief description of a few of the more widely used logico-mathematical models.

System analysts apply a variety of modeling techniques in the development and documentation of information systems specifications. A decision table is an important design tool that helps systems analysts to state rules and develop models. In its simplest form, a decision table is the tabular representation of the logical process of *if* this occurs, *then* do that. A decision tree is a model of a sequence of conditions wherein each decision made depends on the current value of the variable being tested and all previous decisions reached.

One excellent vehicle for describing procedures to people and computers is structured English. Another, called pseudocode, is often used to specify procedural models in a form close to an actual programming language.

Data flow diagrams are models that document the flow of data and processes. At their most detailed level, data flow diagrams are used by programmers to document application software.

The goal of the structured analysis and design technique (SADT) is to create models of the information system that can be analyzed and reviewed by users during systems development. SADT analysis proceeds in a top-down manner, first presenting an overview of the system, then exposing a successively greater amount of detail as portions of the model are exploded.

Flowcharts have been the traditional way to illustrate system or program inputs, outputs, and processes. Over the years, however, their use has constantly diminished. In fact, for those who prefer a structured, hierarchical approach to systems development and program design, flowcharts are not used at all.

The box chart technique developed by Nassi-Shneiderman and Chapin is used primarily to describe detailed program logic. This technique and a design tool called Warnier-Orr (W-O) diagrams also serve programmers as an alternative to traditional flowcharts and structured English.

A diagramming technique that sets out the input, output, and functions of a system or program is HIPO (hierarchy plus input process output). HIPO is really the integration of a hierarchy diagram or a visual table of contents (VTOC) and a set of functional diagrams showing the input, processes, and output for each module. A structure chart is a viable alternative to HIPO, especially if a systems analyst has access to one of the many interactive graphics software packages that create, edit, and maintain structure charts.

Prototyping is a process that gives the systems analyst early feedback from users about the viability of a system. From a list of user requirements a first-cut model of the system is built. An iterative process ensues wherein the prototype is "used and abused" and modified until the requirements of the user are met. The final prototype then becomes the actual system or it serves to provide the specifications for a more traditionally implemented system.

IMPORTANT TERMS

bookkeeping model	Nassi-Shneiderman charts
case decision process	net present value
computer-aided systems engineering (CASE)	program evaluation and review technique (PERT)
condition decison process	program flowcharts
cost-volume-profit model	prototyping
critical event	pseudocode
data flow diagram (DFD)	sequence process

decision model

decision table

decision tree

functional diagram

hierarchy plus input process output (HIPO)

iteration process

logico-mathematical models

slack time

structure charts

structured analysis and design technique (SADT)

structured English

system flowcharts

visual table of contents (VTOC)

Warnier-Orr (W-O) diagram

Assignment

REVIEW QUESTIONS

7.1 What is meant by cost-volume-profit analysis?

7.2 What are the three components of variances used in preparing performance information based on standards as stated in the chapter?

7.3 What are the four elements of a decision model?

7.4 Define the purpose of a decision table? What is contained in each quadrant of a decision table?

7.5 What does the root of a decision tree represent? Each node?

7.6 What are structured English's keywords for controlling flow? How are they identified?

7.7 What is the purpose of each of the six symbols found in a data flow diagram?

7.8 How many processes should be drawn on one page or screen of a data flow diagram? Why?

7.9 A box in the structured analysis and design technique represents a function or activity that transforms data. What does an arrow to or from each of its four sides mean?

7.10 What symbols are used in all traditional flowcharts? used commonly in systems flowcharts? used commonly in program flowcharts?

7.11 What are the reasons for the decline in popularity of systems and program flowcharts?

7.12 What is contained in the top half of a Nassi-Shneiderman decision process box? the bottom half? How is the top half subdivided? How is the bottom half subdivided?

7.13 What are the two diagrams of the HIPO technique? What is the purpose of each diagram?

7.14 Identify the types of arrows used in structure charts and define what each represents.

7.15 Relative to other modeling techniques, when should W-O diagrams be used? When would it be disadvantageous to use W-O diagrams?

7.16 What is the basis on which a first-cut prototype is built? How might the solution prototype be used?

QUESTIONS FOR DISCUSSION

7.17 Explain the importance of the net present value method when evaluating investment alternatives.

7.18 Horizontal bar charts and other charting techniques offer operations managers macro control over projects, whereas PERT offers micro control. Explain why this is true.

7.19 "We always have used and will continue to employ flowcharts as the only technique to document program logic." Explain why this unnecessarily narrow view may be detrimental to the efficiency and effectiveness of this organization's systems development efforts.

7.20 "Decision trees are the best technique to ensure all critical decision alternatives are considered." Do you agree or disagree with this statement? Why?

7.21 "I like W-O diagrams except that their flow is opposite to other tools and their focus is on processing." Why does this statement have merit?

7.22 Discuss some practical rules that might govern the construction of data flow diagrams.

7.23 "Prototyping leads to a second best system." Under what circumstances might this statement be true? What can be done to prevent this from happening?

7.24 Program flowcharts, Nassi-Shneiderman diagrams, and structured English or pseudocode are alternatives to document program logic. For each technique, what set of conditions would favor it over the other techniques?

EXERCISES AND PROBLEMS

7.25 Last week, the programmer responsible for maintaining the weekly payroll program was fired when it was discovered he had been fishing the three days he called in sick. The following terse comments are the only evidence of documentation for a section in the program called COMPUTE CURRENT PAY:

"If the id on a time reporting transaction and an employee master record match, check to see if hours worked exceed 40. If necessary, calculate overtime pay. Then, calculate taxes and deductions. Write the results to the master record and read a new master and transaction record."

"If transaction id is greater than master id, write master record because there wasn't any transactional data for that employee. On the other hand, if the master id is GT the transaction record id, someone goofed! It's likely Personnel hasn't added this employee to the master file. Anyways, write the transaction to the error file and hope you get a match when the next transaction record is read."

"P.S. If either file comes to an end, control is transferred to the routine called END-OF-FILE."

> ***Required:*** Because of the criticalness of this part of the program, your boss has requested you prepare documentation for it using a graphical (Nassi-Shneiderman) and nongraphical (structured English) technique.

7.26 Milan deGesta celebrated New Year's day 1801 by being thrown into an underground dungeon known as the "Pit of Doom." The pit was not a nice place—even for vermin. It was totally dark and isolated from everyone. Three times a day deGesta's keepers lowered his meager rations down to him on a conveyor. With not a moment to spare, deGesta would grope for his food before the conveyor was silently hauled up.

Over six years later, deGesta was liberated from the pit. Although his liberators expected him to be mad, he was not only sound of mind but could tell them the day, month, and year of his release. In his cell they found only the clothes he wore when he was confined, a few stones, a large can, a box, and a leather bag.

> ***Required:*** Using structured English, devise a system to keep track of calendar time. Hint: You might put stones in a shoe to record the delivery of a meal, stones in the can to signify days, stones in the box to indicate months, and stones in the bag to denote the passage of years.

7.27 Mettling Manufacturing would like to write checks for vendor invoices once a week. They envision the process of reading invoice records arranged by vendor number, calculating the discount if appropriate, and printing the check. Accompanying each check is a stub. The check stub lists the amount and invoice number of all invoices covered by the check.

Required: Prepare a Warnier-Orr (W-O) diagram for Mettling's check writing process. Also prepare a functional chart for this process.

7.28 Construct a decision tree and a decision table that represents a salesperson's commission table. The four rules are as follows:

1. If fewer than 400 units are sold, then the salesperson's commission is 1 percent of total sales.

2. If between 400 and 499 units are sold, then the salesperson's commission is 2 percent of total sales.

3. If 500 or more units are sold, and the salesperson has been with the company more than one year, then the salesperson's commission is $3\frac{1}{2}$ percent of total sales.

4. If 500 or more units are sold, and the salesperson has been employed by the firm for one year or less, then his or her commission is 3 percent of total sales.

7.29 Fred and Flo Flawn operate a summer camp. The camp consists of 14 week-long sessions beginning in June. The campers of Camp Flawn can choose from such activities as soccer, boating, computer programming, archery, and other outdoor programs. Applications from prospective campers are reviewed for completeness by the Flawns as they are received. The applications are also used to update the activity lists. These lists are kept by activity (e.g., roller skating) and by week (e.g., week 3 of 14).

Required: Prepare a data flow diagram for Camp Flawn's camper application processing.

7.30 Waggener Realtors is in the process of installing an electronic mail system for its agents. After a year of studying the benefits of electronic mail, Ferd Waggener, the company's owner, has decided the only issue that remains is how many micros will be a part of the system. In an attempt to model the payoffs of adopting different sized systems, an analyst has prepared the following table:

SIZE OF SYSTEM	HIGH ACCEPTANCE	LOW ACCEPTANCE
20 micros	$200,000	$ − 20,000
15 micros	150,000	20,000
10 micros	100,000	60,000

Required:

1. Assume you are totally ignorant of how high or low the level of acceptance will be to the electronic mail system. Using an expected value approach, how many micros would you recommend?

2. What is the *most* you would pay for an information source that told you with perfect reliability a 40 percent chance of high acceptance exists and a 60 percent chance of low acceptance exists?

3. What is the *most* you would pay for a perfect information source?

7.31 The payroll system at Bartholemew Laboratories was originally installed in 1973 and has been functioning reasonably well ever since. With the latest changes to the tax laws, Bartholemew's director of personnel has requested you to document the existing system.

Based on interviews with payroll clerks and a review of the current system's programs, you have discovered the following facts:

1. Tax summary information is extracted from the employee payroll file. It, together with a check, is periodically sent to the IRS.
2. Employee time reporting data, once validated and sorted, are used along with the tax file and employee master file to compute the amount paid to Bartholemew's employees.
3. The personnel department frequently makes changes to the employee master file.
4. Current pay and deductions for each payroll are applied to the employee payroll file. This file is then used to print the checks and year-to-date summaries for each employee.

   Required: Prepare a visual table of contents and data flow diagram for Bartholemew's current payroll system.

7.32   decision table for the following procedure:

1. If the quantity ordered for a particular item equals or exceeds the minimum discount quantity and the order is from a wholesaler, give the customer a discount and make the shipment. This presumes that sufficient quantity is on hand to fill the order.
2. If the quantity ordered is less than the discount quantity, bill at regular rates and make the shipment even if the customer is a wholesaler. Do the same if the sale is retail.
3. If quantity on hand is not sufficient, bill as above, ship what can be shipped, and backorder the remainder of the order. It must be emphasized that, in this situation as well, even if the discount quantity is ordered, the discount is not given if the customer is a retailer.

7.33   the following table, determine the probability of path a-c-d-e-j-l-m of the RATS project taking longer than 20 weeks.

Activities	Optimistic Times	Most Likely Times	Pessimistic Times	Expected Times of Duration	Variance
a. Preliminary propulsion design	3	4	5	4.00	0.11
b. Preliminary flight system design	5	6	8	6.17	0.25
c. Static tests I	2	2	3	2.17	0.03
d. Propulsion design modifications	1	2	3	2.00	0.11
e. Static tests II	1	2	3	2.00	0.11
f. Flight tests I	2	3	5	3.17	0.25
g. Flight system design modifications	2	3	4	3.00	0.11
h. Flight tests II	3	3	6	3.50	0.25
i. Demonstrate to customer	3	3	3	3.00	0
j Materials and components costs	5	6	8	6.17	0.25
k. Labor and overhead costs	3	6	9	6.00	1.00
l. Process bid package through company	2	2	2	2.00	0
m. Deliver bid package to customer	1	1	1	1.00	0

Note: Time is given in weeks.

BIBLIOGRAPHY

BAYLIN, EDWARD N. "System Diagramming Methods: Which Works Best?" *Journal of Information Systems Management*, Summer 1987.

BOAR, BERNARD. "Application Prototyping: A Life Cycle Perspective." *Journal of Systems Management*, February 1986.

DeMarco, Tom. *Structured Analysis and System Specification.* New York: Yourdon Press, 1979.

Edwards, Perry. *Systems Analysis, Design, and Development with Structured Concepts.* New York: Holt, Rinehart, and Winston, 1985.

Gane, Chris, and Trish Sarson. *Structured Systems Analysis: Tools and Techniques.* Englewood Cliffs, N.J.: Prentice Hall, 1979.

Gould, F. J., and C. D. Eppen. *Introductory Management Science.* Englewood Cliffs, N.J.: Prentice Hall, 1984.

Kauber, Peter G. "Prototyping: Not a Method but a Philosophy." *Journal of Systems Management,* September 1985.

Martin, James, and Carma McClure. *Diagramming Techniques for Analysts and Programmers.* Englewood Cliffs, N.J.: Prentice Hall, 1985.

Naumann, J. D., and A. M. Jenkins. "Prototyping: The New Paradigm for Systems Development." *MIS Quarterly,* September 1982.

Stonecash, Jon. "Declutter the Mental Workspace with an Information Model." *Data Management,* December 1987.

Sumner, Mary, and Jerry Sitek. "Are Structured Methods for Systems Analysis and Design Being Used?" *Journal of Systems Management,* June 1986.

Yourdon, E. "What Ever Happened to Structured Analysis?" *Datamation,* June 1, 1986.

Yourdon, E., and L. Constantine. *Structured Design: Fundamentals of a Discipline of Computer Programs and Systems Design.* Englewood Cliffs, N.J.: Prentice Hall, 1979.

8

OUTPUT

8.1 INTRODUCTION

Generally speaking, systems analysts are better at acquiring and installing information technology and developing models than they are at packaging and transmitting information to end users—the reason that information systems are built in the first place. It makes very little sense to install a million-dollar computer and have it spew piles of paper and flash numbers on screens that no one wants or uses. Output is the building block that really puts the "user in the system." It is the point where end users meet the system. It is, indeed, the moment of truth for the systems analyst.

The general objective of this chapter is to emphasize output as the information system's product. Therefore, for this product to be useful to end users—the information system's "customers"—it must be designed to fit end users' needs, both in form and in substance. The specific objectives are:

1. To describe how the human processing system and the form and substance of output come together to determine the output's usability.
2. To demonstrate how to design analytical, notice, equipoised, variance, comparative, and ratio reports.
3. To explain the value and application of graphics in output design and to display appropriate examples.
4. To describe the various computer output media.

8.2 DESIGNING OUTPUT FOR USERS

Understanding the information-using characteristics and needs of end users and how to package and present output for them represents challenging design tasks influenced by user/system interface and human factors design forces. To abide by these strong design forces, systems analysts must consider three elements: (1) the human processing system, (2) form of output, and (3) substance of output. Form implies the arrangement or packaging of output (i.e., how the information is presented). Substance implies content of the output and its quality. All these elements working together determine the usability of output.

Use a chef as an analogy of a systems analyst. The chef must understand the needs and tastes of his or her patrons. Then raw food such as beef, poultry, or vegetables is cooked to create the meal, which is the substance. How the meal is presented, however, may be as important as the meal itself. Presentation, for example, includes arrangement of the food on dishes, color of the food, seating arrangement, and the like. How the chef puts all this together will determine the level of acceptance of his or her output.

Human Information Processing System

At the user/system interface, the output from the information system flows into the human information processing system through one or more of the visual, auditory, or, possibly, kinesthetic senses, as shown in Figure 8.1. Information systems output, once recognized by the human, interacts with short-term memory (STM) and, possibly, long-term memory (LTM). If the output is of no con-

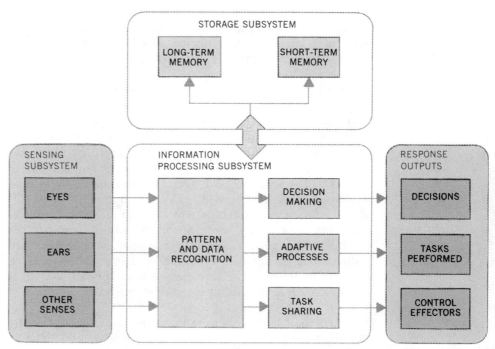

Figure 8.1 Human information processing system. (Adapted from Charles H. Flurscheim, editor, *Industrial Design in Engineering.* Springer-Verlag, Berlin, 1983, p. 36.)

sequence, it is simply lost. If it is meaningful but transitory in nature, for example, a prompt to perform a task, it never reaches LTM. It is simply held in STM for a few seconds and vanishes.

STM's capacity is limited to about seven units of information plus or minus two. Information units may be symbols, numbers, or groups of symbols and numbers called chunks. Before LTM can absorb information from STM, three conditions must be met: information must be stored in STM for more than one second, full attention must be given to it, and it must go through an adaptive and learning process. Response outputs from the human processing system are decisions, tasks performed, and control effectors that influence other processes.

Form: Output that is Appealing to Users

The output of the information system entering the human processing system must appeal to the visual, auditory, and, possibly, kinesthetic senses. Although we have presented an outline of the human processing system for reference and insight, much of it still remains a "black box." Enough research and consultation has been done, however, to give systems analysts at least a clue as to what appeals to this black box. And, in some instances, common sense is sufficient. For example, designing auditory signal output in a noisy environment would clearly be frustrating to the user.

For the visual sense, the principal sense for which systems analysts design, users tend to prefer graphics and patterns over text and numbers to aid both STM and LTM. Graphics seem to improve problem solving and decision making. Also, it appears from a number of observations that most users want paper reports to augment video display units' ephemeral screen.

Moreover, some scientists divide users' cognitive styles into left-brain or right-brain. Left-brain people are linear, analytical thinkers. Sometimes they are referred to as "numbers people." They, therefore, need detail and numbers. Right-brain people are spatial, lateral thinkers. They desire information in the form of images and patterns. They are often referred to as "big-picture people."

In businesses, one could surmise that most people operate somewhat equally from both sides of the brain. Therefore, this would indicate that these users would need an equal mix of graphics and tabular reports. Presentation methods that seem to have special appeal to all users involve dynamic three-dimensional multicolored displays accompanied by sound. Such presentations show changing relationships, which, in turn, release intuitive faculties to discover new relationships and generate ideas. Also, color is important to most users because it possesses a high informational state. Indeed, with the use of color, animation, flashing cues to highlight changes, and dynamic or static graphics, systems analysts can present output that appeals to both right- and left-brain users to analyze, to evaluate, to see threads of continuity, to recall from LTM, and to "get the picture."

To assist end users in tapping the full potential of the system, a carefully designed user/system interface should be accessible, friendly, and simple. Messages and commands should be understandable to experts as well as to novices, and be easy to use. For example, acronyms and mnemonics help managers in

Gould's graphics strategic decision support center to access information on everything from sales performance and inventory turnover to changes in balance sheet items. Managers tap three-digit codes into a 12-button pad, in which SEX retrieves sales figures and MUD inventory data. Various other acronyms and mnemonic codes access over 75 other categories.

Substance: Output that is Essential to Users

Substance of output is its basic message; it is the information content. The output, if properly designed, has specific meaning to the user because it fits the user's knowledge, skill, and tasks. As stated in Chapter 1, quality output is derived from attributes such as (1) *accuracy*—the output is free from mistakes and errors based on source data that are verifiable; (2) *timeliness*—the output reflects the most current situation and data; and (3) *relevancy*—the output has significant bearing on the matter at hand and the decision to be made. Appropriate technology must be installed and networked to support these attributes, especially timeliness. Adequate controls help to ensure accuracy. And performing proper systems analysis will help create output that is relevant.

When designing output, some systems analysts may tend to equate quality with quantity. A request for a new report may result in a "dump-the-date-base" approach with hopes that something of substance will appear. Or producing "one more report" may be viewed as building better information systems. Normally, this is not the case, as many executives and others recognize the fact that a "fungus of overreporting" grows uncontrolled in a number of organizations.

Before designing output, for paper or screen, the systems analyst should

---

WHY DO THEY KEEP PRINTING THAT STUFF? Many of the reports and schedules produced by management accountants are no longer necessary. For example, when a company was battling bankruptcy it created Schedule 345, a weekly cash receipts and disbursements report for the purpose of keeping the CEO informed of the daily cash position. Today, the prosperous company with millions in cash still spends hours putting it together and no one uses it.

Most manufacturing companies still have one-third to one-half of their production reporting schedules focusing on labor efficiency and utilization. Fifteen years ago, when labor was 30% to 40% of total cost, the reports were relevant. Today, labor is 5% to 10% of total cost and the production manager is not concerned with labor utilization, but quality, delivery, scrap, inventory, and cycle time. Is the source of the production manager's management information the accounting department? No, accounting reports often are relegated to the circular file. The production manager's information comes from his own PC.

Excerpted from Robert A. Howell and Stephen R. Soucy, "Management Reporting in the Manufacturing Environment," *Management Accounting*, February 1988, pp. 22–29.

understand clearly the purpose of the information, what decisions are being made, what job is to be performed, what process is being monitored, and so forth. Better systems work may even call for the elimination of some reports and the consolidation of others. Indeed, when designing output, more is not always better.

Usability: The Final Test for Output

If systems analysts understand the human processing system, and present output in the proper form containing quality substance, then end users will find the output usable. Usability is the ultimate test for output.

Users should be able to get the output and understand it instantly without any special training or instructions. Output should be easily accessible and easy to read. The user must be able to "see" the content quickly. For example, too much accuracy can actually obscure the substance of the output by including numbers three or four places to the right of the decimal point for financial values, especially if such values were based on estimates to begin with. Such "accuracy" is viewed as contrived complexity. Furthermore, page after page of single-spaced computer printouts without headings and breaks can contain timely, accurate, and relevant information but be so overwhelming in volume and complexity that they discourage the recipient from even looking at the pages. Indeed, one of the major reasons that many users have turned to personal computers is so they can produce output that they can use and understand—output that fits them and their needs.

But systems continue to produce reams of printouts for almost any application. Most users, however, do not need gobs of numbers; they need output they can quickly grasp. Therefore, the usability of output from the viewpoint of the user is probably "calculated" intuitively by the following "formula:"

Net usability of output = Benefits obtained from the information

   − (Effort + Aggravation + Frustration in obtaining the information)

If the user has to pore over and reprocess many numbers, is irritated and disappointed in the process, and only gains a small amount of quality information, then the output will not be used. How, then, can the usability of output be increased? The following material will help answer this question with specifics.

8.3 OUTPUT DESIGN RULES AND SELECTED EXAMPLES

As we learned in Chapter 6, paper is still a dominant form of inputting a variety of transactions. So, too, is paper the medium of choice for output. Following are some guidelines that make paper reports more usable and meaningful. Of course, these guidelines are also applicable for screen or micrographic output.

Rules for Construction

The following are rules that aid in better constructed reports:

1. Trying to digest information in one lump is difficult. Divide the report into meaningful chunks. For formal reports, use at least three main sections:

(a) report headings, which include the report title and columnar headings, (b) report body with repetitive detail lines, and (c) report footings, which contain summary, subtotal, or total lines.

2. Use good-quality paper heavy enough to make the letters and numbers stand out. Generally, white bond paper, 20-pound weight, will do the trick. For output that requires high durability, such as permanent documents and master forms, instructions and manuals, charts, address and parts lists, and other frequently handled documents, use nontear material, which resists not only tearing but also staining and soiling.

3. Maintain at least 1-inch margins all around.

4. Use plenty of spacing between lines, and use block letters and underlining for highlights. If possible, use different colors. But do not overdo the amount of differentiation by these techniques.

5. Use legible, nondistracting type. Avoid script and types with fancy lines and flourishes.

6. If the sequence of a list is random, or arbitrary, use bullets (•) or dashes (—). If the order is important, use Arabic numerals (1, 2, 3 . . .). Also, try to order data according to its importance.

7. Place detail data in an appendix and build an easy-to-use pointer system to direct the user to this detail as needed.

8. If appropriate, add a summary and table of contents.

9. Break the report vertically and use plenty of labels, titles, headings, and legends, to help the user understand the details. Otherwise, the meaning of disparate numbers is often lost.

10. Present both vertical and horizontal comparative data. Also, use ratios where appropriate.

11. Try to include in the report answers to questions that will likely be asked when the report is reviewed.

12. The objective of producing usable output is to transfer quality information from STM to LTM. Mnemonics can be the key that puts information into LTM and gets the information back out again.

Reports Examples

Following are some selected examples of output reports that stress form, substance, and, of course, usability.

Analytical Report

The analytical report in Figure 8.2 represents a breakdown of three projects as to their payback period. This report enables the user to understand immediately which project is best, how much it costs, the method of evaluation, and the magnitude of any differences among projects. If other return-on-investment methods (e.g., present value analysis) are to be used to analyze these projects, then similar reports can also be readily prepared.

This analytical report example combines a tabular report and a bar chart on the same page. The bar chart gives the payback period for each project while

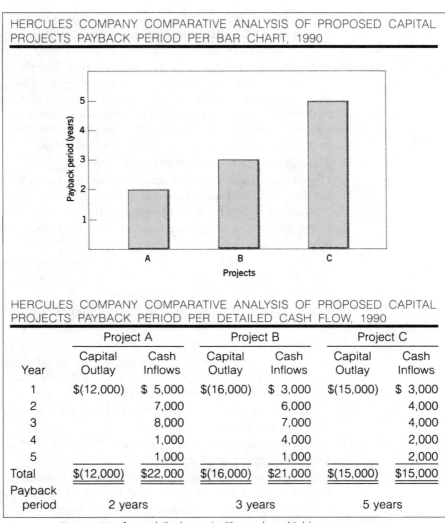

HERCULES COMPANY COMPARATIVE ANALYSIS OF PROPOSED CAPITAL PROJECTS PAYBACK PERIOD PER BAR CHART, 1990

HERCULES COMPANY COMPARATIVE ANALYSIS OF PROPOSED CAPITAL PROJECTS PAYBACK PERIOD PER DETAILED CASH FLOW, 1990

Year	Project A Capital Outlay	Project A Cash Inflows	Project B Capital Outlay	Project B Cash Inflows	Project C Capital Outlay	Project C Cash Inflows
1	$(12,000)	$ 5,000	$(16,000)	$ 3,000	$(15,000)	$ 3,000
2		7,000		6,000		4,000
3		8,000		7,000		4,000
4		1,000		4,000		2,000
5		1,000		1,000		2,000
Total	$(12,000)	$22,000	$(16,000)	$21,000	$(15,000)	$15,000
Payback period	2 years		3 years		5 years	

Figure 8.2 An analytical report with graph and table on same page.

the tabular report presents the capital outlay and cash inflows for each year. The bar chart gives the "big picture"; the table gives the "detail."

In this text, we have to use brief examples because of space constraints. In a real-world situation, however, the data for our example would probably be much more involved. If this is the case, then for many recipients, especially those who want the "big picture," a better presentation would be to display the bar chart first followed by the tabular report on another page(s).

Notice Report
This kind of report signals to the recipient that something needs attention. For example, quality control of products is of paramount importance to meet or beat

the competition. A good, usable quality control report is a weapon to help do this, as shown in Figure 8.3. The report is simple and to the point. It does not tell the whole story; it simply points out clearly and succinctly that a problem exists that needs immediate investigation. Other information will be forthcoming to deal with the problem more completely.

Another example of a notice report is the automatic display of flash totals. Based on time, amount of sales, or any other trigger point, certain output is flashed on a screen to let the recipient know the current status of various events. Sales figures for several leader items are flashed every half-hour during a clearance sale, for example. In fact, this kind of reporting is tailor-made for the monitoring component (described in Chapter 3) in which the system is programmed to monitor and report key variables or critical success factors such as late orders or shipments, turnovers, backlogs, and yields.

Equipoised Report

Output of an equipoised report is counter-balanced. All sides of the situation at hand are given equal weight; an equipoise exists between opposing or interacting elements. For example, both worst- and best-case scenarios, which help planners judge a project's riskiness, are valuable information for the planning process. An example of such a report is illustrated in Figure 8.4.

This report is prepared for management, who is planning a leveraged buyout of Cielo Vista Publishing, a company that publishes a small regional magazine. The report shows that under the worst conditions, the buyout target would suffer a loss of $150,000 for FY 19X7; under ideal conditions a profit of $170,000 for FY 19X7 would be generated. If management needs additional information on expenses and wants to know how estimates were calculated, this detail is readily available from appendix material. Or the system may also produce a most likely scenario. At any rate, management "sees" all sides of the project under consideration.

QUALITY DEFICIENCY REPORT

PRODUCTS WITH RETURN RATES GREATER THAN 3 PERCENT FOR MONTH ENDED MAY 19X9

Products	Return Rate (%, Based on Sales)
Gizmo	5.9
Widget	6.2
Shoreline	6.8
Stretcher	9.4

Figure 8.3 A notice report.

CIELO VISTA PUBLISHING WORST BEST CASE SCENARIOS ($000) APRIL 20, 19X6

	For Fiscal Year (FY) 19X7	
	Worst Case	Best Case
Advertising revenue	$1000	$1500
Operating expenses	850	960
Gross margin	150	540
Selling expenses	200	250
Administrative expenses	100	120
Profit (loss)	($150)	$170

Figure 8.4 An equipoised report.

Variance Report

This kind of report shows a variance or divergence from a standard, plan, or benchmark. It is similar to a notice report in the sense that it warns that something is or is becoming out of control. The variance report should include the variance, the reason for the variance, the action being taken to correct any unfavorable variance, and the time required to correct it. A word of caution, however, is in order. Variance reports should not be used as an excuse to conduct witch hunts or as a means of beating line managers over the head. The emphasis is on the

GO-GO COMPANY
PERFORMANCE REPORT
PURCHASING DEPARTMENT
FOR MONTH ENDED JUNE 19X7

Item Purchased	Quantity Purchased	Actual Price	Standard Price	Difference in Price	Total Price Variance
A	3000 lb	$4.00/lb	$3.80/lb	$.20/lb U	$600 U
B	1000 gal	$9.00/gal	$8.50/gal	$.50/gal U	$500 U

Reason: Could not buy in economic quantities for discounts.
Action: Coordinating with production to accept larger quantities.
Result: Actual prices will meet standard prices next month.

Figure 8.5 A variance report.

LITTLE COMPANY
COMPARATIVE BALANCE SHEET—HORIZONTAL ANALYSIS
FOR FISCAL YEARS 19X8 AND 19X9

	19X8	19X9	Amount	Percent
Assets				
Current assets	$ 40,000	$ 60,000	$20,000	50.0
Plant and equipment	200,000	250,000	50,000	25.0
Total assets	$240,000	$310,000	$70,000	29.2
Liabilities				
Current liabilities	$ 20,000	$ 30,000	$ 10,000	50.0
Long-term liabilities	50,000	20,000	(30,000)	(60.0)
Capital	$ 70,000	$ 50,000	$(20,000)	(28.6)
Common stock	$150,000	$200,000	$ 50,000	33.3
Retained earnings	20,000	60,000	40,000	200.0
Total liabilities and capital	$240,000	$310,000	$ 70,000	29.2

Figure 8.6 Comparative horizontal analysis applied to balance sheets.

SURETHING INCORPORATED
COMPARATIVE INCOME STATEMENT—VERTICAL ANALYSIS
FOR FISCAL YEARS 19X8 AND 19X9

	19X8		19X9	
	Amount	Percent	Amount	Percent
Sales	$120,000	103.0	$160,000	101.2
Sales returns	4,000	3.0	2,000	1.2
Net sales	$116,000	100.0	$158,000	100.0
Cost of goods	86,000	74.1	100,000	63.3
Gross income	$ 30,000	25.9	$ 58,000	36.7
Selling expenses	$ 14,000	12.1	$ 15,800	10.0
Administrative expenses	8,000	6.9	11,060	7.0
Income before taxes	$ 8,000	6.9	$ 31,140	19.7
Income taxes	4,000	3.4	14,000	8.9
Net income	$ 4,000	3.4	$ 17,140	10.8

Figure 8.7 Comparative vertical analysis applied to income statements.

SOLVENCY RATIOS

Current Ratio:			Acid-Test Ratio:		
	19X8	19X9		19X8	19X9
Current assets	$500,000	$600,000	Quick assets:		
Current liabilities	300,000	250,000	Cash	$100,000	$150,000
Working capital	$200,000	$350,000	Investments	150,000	120,000
			Receivables	150,000	260,000
Current ratio	1.7:1	2.4:1	Total	$400,000	$530,000
			Current liabilities	$300,000	$250,000
			Acid-test ratio	1.3:1	2.1:1

ASSET MANAGEMENT RATIOS

Accounts Receivable Turnover:			Inventory Turnover:		
	19X8	19X9		19X8	19X9
Net sales on account	$1,500,000	$2,000,000	Cost of goods sold	$900,000	$1,200,000
Receivables (net):			Beginning of year	$140,000	$ 100,000
Beginning of year	$ 200,000	$ 150,000	End of year	100,000	260,000
End of year	150,000	260,000	Total	$240,000	$ 360,000
Total	350,000	410,000	Average	$120,000	$ 180,000
Average	$ 175,000	$ 205,000	Inventory		
Accounts receivable turnover	8.6	9.8	turnover	7.5	6.7

PROFITABILITY RATIOS

Return on Shareholders Equity:			Price-Earnings Ratio:		
	19X8	19X9		19X8	19X9
Net income	$ 100,000	$ 140,000	Market price per share	$18.00	$22.00
Shareholders equity			Earnings per share	$ 1.40	$ 1.60
Beginning of year	$ 700,000	$ 800,000	Price-earnings ratio	12:9	13:8
End of year	800,000	900,000			
Total	$1,500,000	$1,700,000			
Average	$ 750,000	$ 850,000			
Rate	13.3%	16.7%			

Figure 8.8 How ratios can be used to improve usability of accounting reports.

control function and participating with line managers to correct significant variances. An example is shown in Figure 8.5.

Comparative Reports

Balance sheets and income statements represent periodic formal reports that summarize thousands of transactions and data elements into output for a variety of users. These reports follow conventional classification and layout, but their usability is somewhat limited when considered individually and in only one dimension. Users can often gain a clearer picture by seeing comparisons. One way to do this is to make a *horizontal* analysis. The amount of each item on the most recent report is compared with the corresponding item on one or more earlier reports. The increase or decrease in the amount of the item is then listed, together with the percentage of increase or decrease. This analysis can be applied to almost any kind of report, but balance sheets for 19X8 and 19X9 are used for an illustration in Figure 8.6.

A percentage analysis can also be used to compare component parts with the total within a report. This is called *vertical* analysis, and its application is shown in Figure 8.7. In using an income statement, for example, each item is stated as a percentage of net sales.

Ratio Reports

Ratios help managers and other users evaluate a variety of relationships and activities. For example, accounting ratios help managers evaluate solvency, asset management, and profitability. Such ratios can be added to balance sheets and income statements to help spotlight a number of key success factors. Examples of a few of these ratios are presented in Figure 8.8. This figure shows how ratios can vastly improve the usability of accounting reports.

8.4 SAYING IT WITH GRAPHICS

If having precise and detailed readings of output is critical, conventional reports and tables must be used. Graphs and charts, however, can be used in a number of situations in which gobs of numbers can be turned into "pictures" with which the user can quickly "see" the problem or situation. With graphic presentations, such cliches as "one picture is worth a thousand printouts" and "seeing the problem is tantamount to solving it" apply. Indeed, with today's information technology, two-dimensional or three-dimensional graphs can be easily prepared using a galaxy of colors. But all graphics are not necessarily good graphics.

Value of Graphics

The problems of too much data and not enough information can be solved with graphics. A number of studies indicate that graphics for data analysis and presentation can shorten business meetings, double a person's ability to communicate ideas, and make information over ten times easier to absorb.

The gigabit bandwidth of the eye and cortex system permits much faster perception of geometric and spatial relationships. By transforming thousands of numbers into graphics, end users can see the unseen. Clearly, the purpose of output is not the numbers but insight into the numbers. Images may evoke intuition that mere numbers cannot or portray anomalies hidden in the numbers. Moreover, the brain simply cannot absorb gigabits of data each day. Staying with a numbers' format, therefore, causes a great deal of "information" to be lost.

A Hewlett-Packard study indicates that we communicate at about 1200 words per minute, and with images, the rate increases to 40 million words per minute.[1] Therefore, enabling executives to interact with two- or three-dimensional graphics in a strategic decision support center, or workers to use color-coded icons displayed on screens for operational instructions, increases efficiency of both users and the information system itself.

Graphics: A Window to Data, Words, and Events

Well-designed graphics reveal meaning of the data clearly. Look at the four x, y columns of data at the top of Figure 8.9. Do these data give you any insight, or do they all look fairly similar? Now, look at the four graphical displays of these data at the bottom of Figure 8.9. See how the relationship and behavior of these data are clearly revealed by the charts.[2]

Graphics: The Power to Explain

An effective way to enhance the explanation power of time-series displays is to add spatial dimensions to the design of the graphic, so that data are moving over space in two or three dimensions as well as over time. Two excellent space-time-story graphics are Charles Minard's graph, showing in simplicity and clarity the essence of Napoleon's ill-fated Russian campaign of 1812. The second one is a computer-generated time-space graphic that shows the levels of three air pollutants in southern California. Both are depicted in Figure 8.10.[3]

Napoleon's Russian campaign graph, at the top of Figure 8.10, tells with brutal eloquence the devastating losses suffered by France. Beginning at the left, on the Polish-Russian border near the Niemen River, the thick band shows the size of the army (422,000 men) as it invaded Russia in June 1812. The width of the band indicates the size of the army at each place on the map. In September, the army reached Moscow, which was by then sacked and deserted, with 100,000 men. The path of Napoleon's retreat from Moscow is depicted by the darker, lower band, which is linked to a temperature scale and dates at the bottom of the chart. It was a bitterly cold winter, and many froze on the march out of Russia. As the graphic shows, the crossing of the Berezina River was a disaster, and the army finally struggled back into Poland with only 10,000 men remaining. Also shown are the movements of auxiliary troops, as they sought to protect the

---

[1]Joel Orr, "Business Turns to Graphics," *Infosystems*, November 1980, p. 57.

[2]The data and graphs taken from F. J. Anscombe, "Graphs in Statistical Analysis," *American Statistician*, February 1973, pp. 17–21.

[3]Material on Minard's graph and the air pollutants graph summarized from Edward R. Tufte, *Visual Display of Quantitative Information* (Cheshire, Conn.: Graphics Press, 1983), pp. 40–42.

	I		II		III		IV	
X	Y	X	Y	X	Y	X	Y
10.0	8.04	10.0	9.14	10.0	7.46	8.0	6.58
8.0	6.95	8.0	8.14	8.0	6.77	8.0	5.76
13.0	7.58	13.0	8.74	13.0	12.74	8.0	7.71
9.0	8.81	9.0	8.77	9.0	7.11	8.0	8.84
11.0	8.33	11.0	9.26	11.0	7.81	8.0	8.47
14.0	9.96	14.0	8.10	14.0	8.84	8.0	7.04
6.0	7.24	6.0	6.13	6.0	6.08	8.0	5.25
4.0	4.26	4.0	3.10	4.0	5.39	19.0	12.50
12.0	10.84	12.0	9.13	12.0	8.15	8.0	5.56
7.0	4.82	7.0	7.26	7.0	6.42	8.0	7.91
5.0	5.68	5.0	4.74	5.0	5.73	8.0	6.89

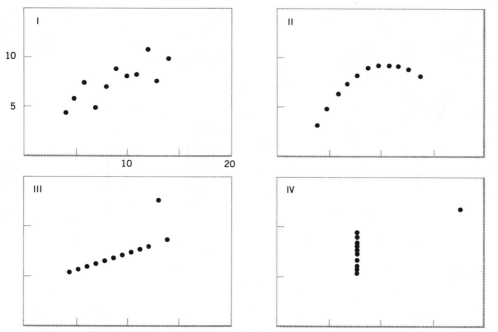

Figure 8.9 How underlying patterns of tables of statistical data are revealed in graphs.

rear and the flank of the advancing army. Charles Minard's graphic tells a rich, coherent story with its multivariate data, far more enlightening than just a single number bouncing along over time. Six variables are plotted: the size of the army, its location on a two-dimensional surface, direction of the army's movement, and temperature on various dates during the retreat from Moscow. Tufte considers this Minard classic one of the best graphics ever drawn.

Napoleon's Russian Campaign Graph

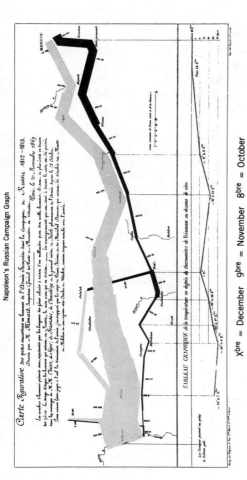

X^{bre} = December 9bre = November 8bre = October

Southern California Air Pollutants Graph

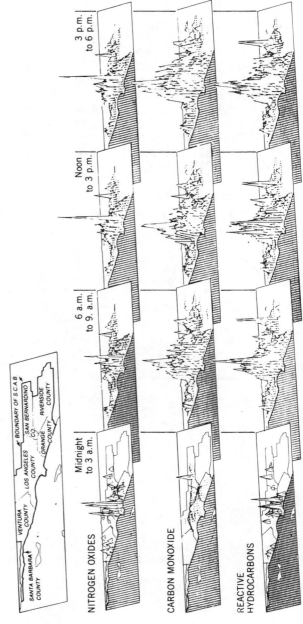

Figure 8.10 Two space-time-story graphics.

The air pollutants graphic, at the bottom of Figure 8.10, displays the levels of three air pollutants located over a two-dimensional surface of six counties in southern California at four times during the day. Nitrogen oxides (top row) are emitted by power plants, refineries, and vehicles. Refineries along the coast and Kaiser Steel's Fontana plant produce the postmidnight peaks shown in the first panel; traffic and power plants (with their heavy daytime demand) send levels up during the day. Carbon monoxide (second row) is low after midnight except out at the steel plant; morning traffic then begins to generate each day's ocean of carbon monoxide, with the greatest concentration at the convergence of five freeways in downtown Los Angeles. Reactive hydrocarbons (third row), like nitrogen oxides, come from refineries after midnight and then increase with traffic during the day. Each of the 12 time-space-pollutant slices summarizes pollutants for 2400 spatial locations (2400 squares five kilometers on a side). Thus 28,800 pollutant readings are shown, except for those masked by peaks.

Graphical Integrity

An old saying is, "charts lie, and liers chart." In some instances, graphics do misrepresent the underlying data. For example, in Figure 8.11, two charts are

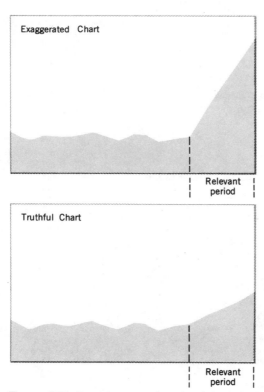

Figure 8.11 Two charts used to reveal the same data.

presented. The top one is an approximation of a chart depicting some unfavorable economic data. It was taken from one of the most popular newspapers in this country. The preparer of this chart apparently wanted to exaggerate this economic bad news, thus the tremendous spike. The direction was correct, but the magnitude was highly exaggerated. A chart that reveals the data more accurately is shown at the bottom of the figure.

But graphics are simply another tool that can be used to display output. They can be used or misused the same as words and statistics. Graphics are no more vulnerable to exploitation by liars than any form of communications. Because graphics carry such a large amount of information, it is, however, important that they accurately reflect their underlying data. Graphics should tell the truth about data, not distort the data.

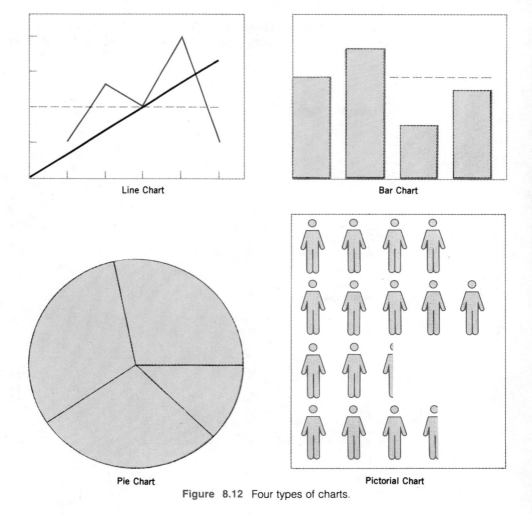

Line Chart

Bar Chart

Pie Chart

Pictorial Chart

Figure 8.12 Four types of charts.

Chartjunk: Too Much of a Good Thing

Chartjunk is interior decoration, overly busy grid lines, excess ticks, redundant representations of the simplest data, and moiré vibrations.[4] It is paraphernalia added to graphics that doesn't tell the user anything new or different. Moreover, it may actually decrease the usability of a particular chart. Graphics stand or fall on form and substance, not on chartjunk. Chartjunk is like weeds in a garden; it should be pulled out.

8.5 SELECTED CHART EXAMPLES

Charts are a special form of graphics, and they are becoming an increasingly important element in information systems design. Charts can be classified as line charts, bar charts, pie charts, and pictorial charts. Figure 8.12 illustrates each of these four types of charts. Figure 8.13 lists the advantages and disadvantages of each type.

Line Chart Examples

A typical sales report may include thousands of numbers listed in columns that continue over several pages. A condensed version of a sales report is shown in

	Line Charts	Bar Charts	Pie Charts	·Pictorial Charts
Advantages	1. Shows time and magnitude of relationships well.	1. Good for comparisons.	1. Good for monetary comparisons.	1. Very easily understood.
	2. Can show many points.	2. Emphasizes one point.	2. Good for part versus whole comparison.	2. Easily constructed.
	3. Degree of accuracy adjustable.	3. Accurate.	3. Very easily understood.	
	4. Easily read.	4. Easily read.		
Disadvantages	1. Limited to less than four lines without adding complexity.	1. Limited to one point.	1. Limited usage.	1. Limited usage.
	2. Limited to two dimensions.	2. Spacing can mislead.	2. Limited precision.	2. Limited precision.
	3. Spacing can mislead.		3. Tends to oversimplify.	3. Tends to oversimplify.

Figure 8.13 Advantages and disadvantages of the four types of charts.

[4]Ibid., p. 121.

GEMINI COMPANY
SALES BY PRODUCTS (UNITS)
FOR YEAR ENDED DECEMBER 31, 19X8

	Product A	Product B
JAN	900	1700
FEB	1000	1900
MAR	1400	1000
APR	1200	2000
MAY	1800	900
JUN	1600	1000
JUL	1700	800
AUG	2100	700
SEP	2200	600
OCT	1800	900
NOV	1500	1000
DEC	1200	2000

Figure 8.14 A typical sales report.

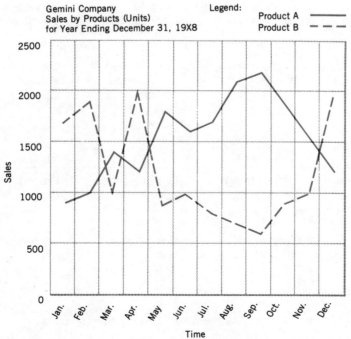

Figure 8.15 A line chart showing sales of products A and B.

REPORT OF NET INCOME OF ADOBE WELL SERVICE BEFORE AND AFTER ACQUISITION OF DELTA DRILLING FOR 19X8 and 19X9

Adobe Well Service's net income was between $240 million and $320 million in the first two quarters of 19X8 prior to the acquisition of Delta Drilling in the third quarter. Since then, quarterly net income from Adobe's traditional servicing business has declined steadily to a level of over $50 million in the fourth quarter of 19X9. With quarterly income ranging between $150 million and $250 million, Delta has more than doubled Adobe's net income during 19X9.

Figure 8.16 A typical report.

Figure 8.14. Immediately following this conventional report, in Figure 8.15, is a line chart that reflects these data. The difference is that most people can quickly grasp the magnitude of relationships between products A and B over time. The results would look the same whether thousands of numbers were plotted or only a few, as shown in the sample sales report. In either case, management can quickly see sales patterns.

For another example of how a line chart is helpful in streamlining clutter, look at Figure 8.16, which represents a typical text report. Then see how the

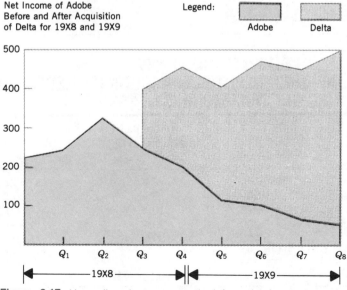

Figure 8.17 How a line chart presents the information in a text report.

line chart in Figure 8.17 helps to clarify and show clearly the results of net income both before and after acquisition of Delta.

Bar Chart Examples

It is generally recognized that the older an account receivable is, the greater the probability it is uncollectible. The analysis of accounts receivable provides management with valuable information regarding probable cash inflow and the general effectiveness of the credit department. Figure 8.18 illustrates a typical uncollectible accounts receivable report. In Figure 8.19 a bar chart reflects the data in this report.

Now, if management wants an accounts receivable aging report by customer, a graphical presentation would not be appropriate; a tabular report would be necessary. Such a report is shown in Figure 8.20.

Many kinds of comparisons can be shown clearly with bar charts. For example, look at Figure 8.21, which illustrates the use of a bar chart to compare actual sales with budget and to compare sales by managers. Clearly, Brown and Smith are performing well above budget. Moreover, they are far outstripping Jones and Adams. It appears that Adams has significant problems. Such output might not be quite as clear if one had to "go into the numbers."

Accounting Statement Presentation

Accountants have tried for years to make their financial statements more usable for a variety of recipients. The use of bar charts (or pie charts) may be a way to help in this endeavor. Following are two figures that show how this can be done. Figure 8.22 illustrates an income statement presented in bar chart form. Figure 8.23 does the same for the balance sheet.

QUIXOTE COMPANY
ESTIMATION OF UNCOLLECTIBLE ACCOUNTS RECEIVABLE
AS OF DECEMBER 31, 19X9

Age	Amount of receivable	Percent estimated to be uncollectible	Amount of doubtful accounts
Current	$30,000	2%	$ 600
1–30 days past due	20,000	5%	1,000
31–60 days past due	12,000	10%	1,200
61–90 days past due	8,000	20%	1,600
Over 90 days past due	5,000	30%	1,500
Total	$75,000		$5,900

Figure 8.18 An uncollectible accounts receivable report.

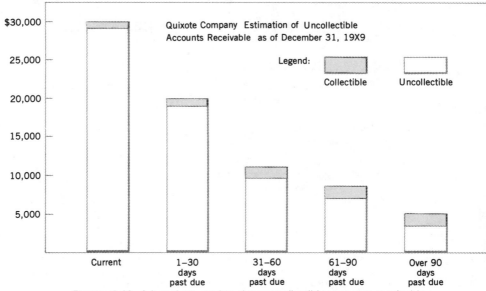

Figure 8.19 A bar chart used to show uncollectible accounts receivable.

QUIXOTE COMPANY
ANALYSIS OF ACCOUNTS RECEIVABLE
BY AGE AND BY CUSTOMER
AS OF DECEMBER 31, 19X9

Customer	Total	Current	1–30 days past due	31–60 days past due	61–90 days past due	Over 90 days past due
Aaron, Herb	$ 500	$ 500				
Baker, Bill	1,500	300	$ 900	$ 300		
Charli, Barry	1,200			600	$ 400	$ 200
Dingle, Sue	4,000	2,000	1,500	500		
.	.	.	.	.	.	.
.	.	.	.	.	.	.
.	.	.	.	.	.	.
Zeno, Zeb	1,000				400	600
Total	$75,000	$30,000	$20,000	$12,000	$8,000	$5,000
Percent	100%	40%	27%	16%	10%	7%

Figure 8.20 Why a tabular report is needed to show clearly analysis of accounts receivable by age and by customer.

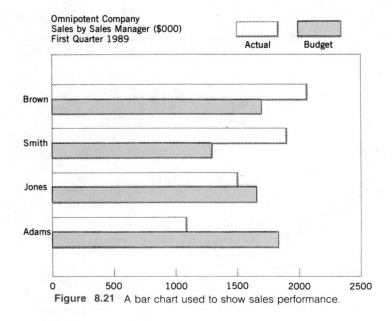

Omnipotent Company
Sales by Sales Manager ($000)
First Quarter 1989

Actual   Budget

Figure 8.21 A bar chart used to show sales performance.

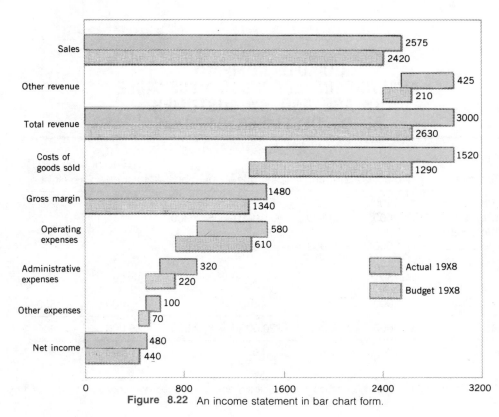

Figure 8.22 An income statement in bar chart form.

December 31, 19X8

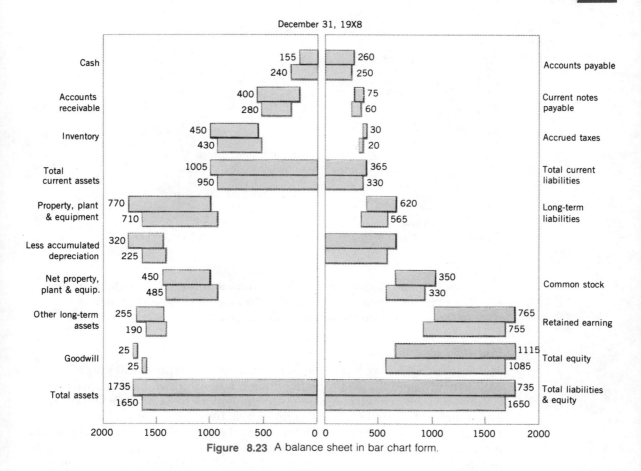

Figure 8.23 A balance sheet in bar chart form.

Pie Chart Example

Few will argue with the proposition that a graphics image on a computer screen has more impact and is more memorable than text and numbers in most situations. This proposition holds true not only for line and bar charts but also for pie charts. In its simplest form, a pie chart is a circle that has been segmented into two or more pieces, like slices of pie—hence the name. Each "slice of the pie" represents a different component of the whole, and the size of each is proportional to its contribution to the whole. For example, government economists or politicians may show the proportion of a country's economy devoted to various programs, such as defense spending, social security, and education. The proportional amount is immediately apparent to any viewer. Indeed, the visual impact is strong and memorable.

An example of how a pie chart can be used is shown in Figure 8.24. Echo Bay Company has two divisons that handle four products. Note that Division A sells a proportionately larger share of products 1 and 2 than does Division B.

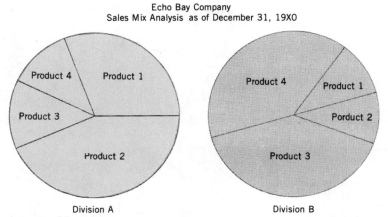

Figure 8.24 Pie charts used to show sales mix by divisions and by products.

If products 1 and 2 have much higher contribution margins than products 3 and 4, where such products are used as "loss leaders," management may try to change the proportions significantly in Divison B.

Matrices and Tables

Matrices and tables are a cross between conventional reports and graphics. Generally, they are applicable for highlighting relationships and giving instructions. Assume that the general equipment superintendent for a construction company has completed a survey of all equipment scattered over several projects. His responsibility is to report to the home office the general condition of this equipment for capital budgeting and maintenance plans. A general summary of his findings may be presented as shown in Figure 8.25. This matrix gives top management the "big picture," which can be clarified with more detailed information.

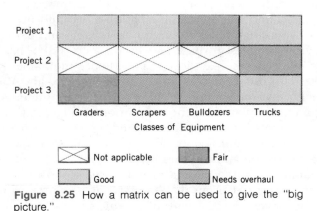

Figure 8.25 How a matrix can be used to give the "big picture."

Also, bear in mind that color codes could be used where cells colored red could mean "overhaul," green "good," orange "fair," and black "not applicable."

8.6 OUTPUT DEVICES

Will the output be displayed on a screen, printed, or plotted on paper? What is the purpose of the output? What is its final disposition? Will it have one-time or continuous use? Is it high volume or low volume? Will it be a periodic report for a number of users, or is it special-request or inquiry output? If it is for one-time display, a screen is sufficient. If the volume is high and needs to be filed for a long period of time, then a micrographics system or a printer is applicable. If documents are distributed to scattered locations, then facsimile devices may be appropriate. To enhance communications between a number of people in the organization, computer-based message systems and teleconferencing are used. To extend the systems outside the organization, videotex devices hold a great deal of promise.

Improvements are being made to screen and printer devices. For example, faster and quieter printers are being introduced at lower costs. Screens are becoming flatter and larger, with large wall displays becoming commonplace. Screens at workstations use splits and windows to make the screen seem more like a desktop containing many different documents. Graph plotters can copy high-resolution, multicolored graphics off the screen for hard-copy presentations. A halfway point between using paper and screens to output information is microfilm and microfiche. A technique that will challenge traditional computer output devices, such as screens and printers, is audio output. This can be achieved by synthesized voices or by recording a person's selected words and phrases and then using the computer to string them together to generate the appropriate output.

Printers

The traditional, and some people believe the most effective means of outputting the results of the information system, is the hard-copy output of a printer. In recent years, great advances have been made in printers, and today they can be broadly classified as impact and nonimpact.

1. *Impact.* This kind of printer includes dot-matrix, daisywheel, line, and chain. They all cause a print hammer to strike the paper to form the character, as a typewriter. They are capable of speeds from 10 to more than 800 characters per second. These printers can produce letter-quality output.

   Dot-matrix printers create characters through combinations of dots in a 5- by 7-inch or larger matrix. These printers use a wire matrix printhead whose nibs strike a ribbon to transfer a character on paper.

   For most word processing and general office work, printing is done by *daisywheel* printers. These use a flat plastic disk with petal-like projections, each containing an embossed character, as on a typewriter print bar.

PRINTING OF CONTRACTS IS EASY AND EFFICIENT

"As our membership grew, assembling contracts from preprinted policy pages stored in our issue unit's "pigeon holes" became too expensive—not only in terms of time errors but also of the dollars spent on preprinting and warehousing those pages," says Dennis Birkholz, systems analyst at AAL, a large life insurance company.

AAL is using Xerox 9700 laser printing systems in conjunction with mainframe-based page-composition software, also from Xerox, to create, store, and print customized insurance contracts electronically. When a contract is to be printed, the system merges appropriate boilerplate text, AAL's digitized logo, signatures, and variable subscriber information. Then, the laser prints out the tailored policy.

"Our subscribers reside in all 50 states, and each state has requirements that are always changing," Birkholz says. "When we were preprinting policy pages, they quickly became obsolete, and warehousing and printing expenses mounted accordingly. Since we can now demand print our contracts, those problems are a thing of the past. Responding to new legal requirements is simply a matter of keying in the changes."

Condensed from "Top Life Insurer Streamlines Contract Production with Laser Printing Systems," *Data Management,* December 1987, pp. 14–16.

Line and *chain* printers print an entire line of text at one time, generally using a drum or chain to create the hard-copy output. They usually operate at speeds from 200 to 3,600 lines per minute and are for high-volume output.

2. *Nonimpact.* These printers include thermal, laser, ink-jet, ion deposition, heat transfer, and electrophotographic. Thermal, laser, and ink-jet printers have wide commercial application. As a matter of fact, laser printing is one of the most rapidly developing technologies. These printers print high-quality text and graphics. Their print speeds range from 6 to 150 pages per minute and cost as little as $1500. *Ink-jet* printers are low-volume printers that are applicable to general office work. Ink-jet technology produces output of photographic quality and multiple colors. They are durable and dependable with mean time between failure (MTBF) ratings of more than 6000 hours and mean time to repair (MTTR) ratings of less than 15 minutes. Generally, nonimpact printers require little maintenance. They create text and graphs with superb resolution, and they eliminate the irritating rat-tat-tat-tat of impact printers.

Plotters

Plotters convert output signals from the central processing unit into lines and curves that are "drawn" on paper. Plotters are of two types: pen and electrostatic.

LASER
PRINTERS

A laser printer, to a great extent, works like an office copier. The computer transmits a series of eight-bit codes, each group representing one character to be printed. A processor in the printer converts that group to a pattern of dots that define the actual character to be printed and passes this information to a small semiconductor laser that flashes on whenever a dot is signaled. A rotating mirror causes the pulsing laser beam to scan the width of a rotating drum or belt.

The light striking the photosensitive drum or belt produces an electrical charge; the charged positions of the drum or belt attract powdered toner. When the drum comes into contact with the paper, the toner is transferred to the paper through a combination of pressure and heat. Excess toner is collected into a cleaner magazine.

Special features of laser printers are:

- High speed—over eight pages per minute.
- Quiet operation, a major blessing in work areas.
- Excellent resolution.
- Availability of a variety of type faces, fonts, and styles, including sideways printing, or "landscape" printing, to use the industry jargon (normal vertical page printing is correspondingly called "portrait" printing).

Excerpted from Lee Green, "Laser Printers Now Letter-Perfect," *InformationWEEK*, August 10, 1987, pp. 25–26.

1. *Pen Plotter.* The pens (or styluses) can be nylon tips, ball point, liquid ink, or liquid ball. A number of pins can be used to give a mix of colors. In the *flatbed* plotter, the paper remains stationary on a table, with bidirectional movement to draw the path of both X and Y axes. In the *drum* plotter, the paper is wrapped around two drums or rollers; the drums rotate the paper back and forth. The pens ride on a track, enabling them to move from side to side over the image area.
2. *Electrostatic Plotter.* This plotter uses nonimpact printer technology to prepare plots on paper that rotates at a fixed rate. The ouptut is in black and white.

Computer Output to Microfilm (COM)

The need to preserve records and the need to reclaim storage space are always in conflict, especially with a paper records system. For example, a stor for a small company may require 1000 to 1500 square feet with boxes of paper records piled head high. Not only do these paper records take up space, but it is difficult to find needed records quickly and easily. And after records are retrieved and used, it is equally difficult to put them back into the boxes where they belong. This mess can be converted to a micrographics system requiring about 4 square feet and immediate access to records.

First instituted for archival storage as an alternative to paper files, micrographics systems are being used more and more. This technology has been around for a long time to help reduce the volume of paper, but now with new links to computers and telecommunications, the technology makes producing, locating, and retrieving records easier. The retrieval speed on computer-assisted retrieval (CAR) equipment is much greater than with old manual methods. COM can be used to store widely distributed reports and frequently accessed documents. Its use will certainly increase, because microfilm cost is only 15 to 20 percent of the cost of computer paper, and film or fiche uses only 2 percent of the filing space required for hard-copy storage. No doubt, COM and CAR have great potential as powerful tools for information processing. A complete micrographics system is shown in Figure 8.26.

COM and CAR are excellent applications for documents that are voluminous, must be kept for long periods of time, must be updated periodically, and also must be used to respond to random inquiries. Banks need to store customer information for a number of years and give reports on account status. The same kind of need exists in hospitals, insurance companies, and the like. Many publications, such as airline schedule guides, are output on microfilm for use by reservation clerks, travel agents, and others. Parts lists and bills of material in manufacturing organizations can also make good use of COM and CAR.

Facsimile

Facsimiles are copies of graphic or various documents transmitted electronically from one location to another. No rekeying of data or redrawing is needed.

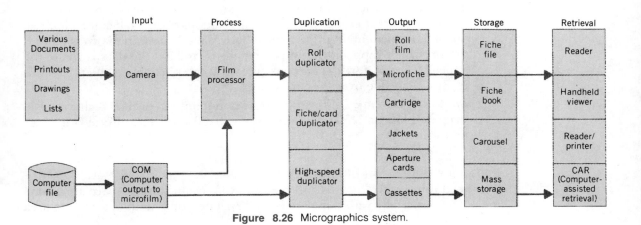

Figure 8.26 Micrographics system.

Almost any text, drawing, chart, or formal report can be sent by facsimile devices with little difficulty.

The appeal of facsimile, also called fax, is that it is fast, accurate, and, in most instances, cost-effective. A typical machine consists of a photocopier equipped with a scanner. The device scans a document, converts the images to electronic impulses, and sends the images across telephone lines or satellites to a remote fax that reconverts the impulses to hard copy.

The advantages of this technology are obvious. Unlike its chief competitor, electronic mail, which can send only messages that have been keyed into a workstation, fax can send duplicates of any documents without rekeying. Even signatures duplicated by fax are legally binding.

Fax equipment is both reliable and durable, with MTBF of more than 4000 hours. It is flexible. Disputed bills, legal documents, or drawings, can be sent to regional offices in minutes, and the sender can retain the original copies. Mail or private couriers may take several days. Clearly, fax is suitable for organizations that have to send a lot of diagrams, charts, pictures, signatures, or other images that cannot be easily transmitted over computer terminals; it is also suitable when time is of essence.

Computer-Based Message Systems

Telephone tag is one of the most frustrating aspects of doing business by phone and is clearly one of the biggest problems of communications. Studies show that

PC AND FAX: A PERFECT MARRIAGE Facsimile transmission, or fax, has emerged as the hottest new technology to sweep through the business world since the personal computer. The worldwide installed base of fax equipment increased 50 percent last year alone, from 2 million to more than 3 million units.

Hotter still is the prospect of welding those two technological stars, fax and the PC. By uniting their individual strengths, the new alloy, PC-to-fax, is destined to revolutionize business communications.

Stripped to its essentials, fax is the convenience of sliding a sheet of paper into a machine in one office and having a duplicate crawl out of a machine in an office halfway across the world a minute later.

A perfect communication medium for cultures using pictograph-oriented writings, fax is growing fastest in the Far East, Japan in particular.

The need to move quickly to graphics as simple as signatures on contracts or as elaborate as computer-aided design (CAD)-generated schematics is fueling the fax demand in the United States.

Excerpted from Winn L. Rosch, "PC-to-Fax: A Revolution in the Offing," *PC Week*, January 26, 1988, p. 38.

four out of five calls do not reach the intended recipient. Instead, the caller reaches a secretary, or worse, no one.

To remedy the problem, organizations are installing different computer-based message systems to create continuous communication, regardless of differences in time zones and office hours. Every message, whether voice or text, is handled through the user's workstation, independent of secretaries or message centers. An integrated system ties directly into the private branch exchange (PBX). The calling party has the option of leaving a detailed private message or transferring to the company operator to relay information requiring immediate attention. Both senders and receivers can access the system 24 hours a day, 7 days a week.

Typical applications are invitations to and scheduling of meetings, feedback and status reports, for your information (FYI) notes, thank you notes, reminders, directives and announcement of policy changes, legal and financial announcements, introduction of new products and services to customers and employees, notification of price or service changes and quotes, announcement of sales promotion to field employees, and flash sales bulletins to customers. Techniques that help support these applications and others are the following:

1. *Electronic Mail.*   This method can substitute for telephone calls as well as conventional paper mail. Electronic mail systems have dramatically reduced the time lag involved in sending traditional mail. Electronic mail networks can be set up within a building, spread around a city, or distributed throughout the country or the globe. Companies send shipping documents to their distribution centers for immediate attention. Big accounting firms, with international offices, shuttle reports back and forth between offices. When job opportunities open up, these firms broadcast the kinds of skills or work experience needed over the network.

2. *Voice.*   How to communicate between dispatchers and drivers on the road is a continuing problem for trucking firms. A computerized voice message system stores messages that are available 24 hours a day. Drivers dial an 800 number and leave messages by entering a code or password. Recorded messages are retrieved in the same way. The conduit of voice mail systems is the telephone. Such voice mail systems are a logical extension of text-based systems. Voice mail can save money in several ways. It can cut telephone bills by reducing the number of calls necessary to deliver messages. It can allow callers to leave detailed messages. It is a boon to people in the field, such as salespersons. It can eliminate the flood of message slips. A significant amount of a manager's time is spent on the telephone. Even a small percentage reduction of this time can contribute to better productivity. Integrating voice mail with other media will increase the effectiveness of managers and other employees even more.

3. *Cellular Telephone.*   In areas where cellular phone service is offered, the service area is divided into cells. Each cell has its own antenna for receiving and transmitting signals. As cars move from one cell to another, computers at a central switching station transfer calls from one antenna to another. The calls are then patched into local phone systems like ordinary calls.

VOICE MAIL At the core of a voice-messaging system is a computer with three unusual abilities: the ability to turn the sounds carried by a telephone wire into digital data files that can be manipulated—copied, duplicated, moved, deleted—as any other computer file; the ability to turn those files back into sounds; and the ability to recognize and respond to telephone Touch-Tones.

A voice-mail system typically allows a user to:

- record a voice message and send it to one or many users;
- listen to a voice message sent to his or her mailbox by another user;
- answer an incoming message;
- forward a message to another user, with or without a covering voice message;
- file a message for future reference; and
- "flip through" incoming or filed messages, "fast forward" or "rewind" them, and otherwise manage the collection of voice recordings.

According to William Spain, voice-industry analyst with Probe Research, of Parsippany, N.J., voice-mail systems hold a major attraction to companies who have a lot of people frequently on the road, or where time differences are an obstacle to communications. Basic message exchange, as well as features such as distribution lists to transmit the same voice message to many recipients, are particularly valuable in such contexts.

Excerpted from John Helliwell, "Corporate Voice Mail Seen Changing Business," *PC Week*, August 11, 1987, pp. C34–C35.

Cellular phones are truly portable. A caller from anywhere can link up with the system to receive information on inventory availability, price changes, sales orders, and so forth. Eventually, cellular telephones will be interconnected through a national network.

Audio Output

The form of audio output is either the actual or simulated human voice. Audio or voice output reverses the process discussed in Chapter 6. To output a message from a computer-based system, a microprocessor selects the right words from a digitized data base or vocabulary of words, strings them together, and converts them to analog signal for final output. Also, the computer may have a sound generator, or speech synthesizer, which simulates human speech, male or female, variable pitch and loudness, appropriate pauses, and even local accents.

Applications of audio output are commonplace. For example, audio response is being used on a regular basis with the telephone company and stock market quotation services. It can supplement visual display in computer-assisted instruction and aid in teaching and translating foreign languages. It can help to validate input of transactions. It can confirm an event or process. It can caution or remind. Most banks use audio output to provide account balances to tellers.

Teleconferencing

Teleconferencing is a business meeting or an event aired over satellite relay or telephone lines that permits employees, customers, managers, job candidates, and others who are geographically separated to view text, data, graphics, and images and to interact with one another in real time while sitting at their workstations or in a teleconferencing station. Teleconferencing is especially useful for those who hate to travel and write extensive reports and letters.

A significant potential of teleconferencing is its improvement of information workers' productivity. Everyone involved in a project can meet at once and answer all questions without confusion or hearsay and reach a consensus without spending excessive time away from the job. Normally, it is impossible to get a number of people together at one location and one time. Moreover, for those who can attend, money spent on airfares, hotel rooms, and meals can be saved. It will, however, not replace all face-to-face meetings. Sales calls, arbitration meetings, first contacts with colleagues, and the like are often more effective if done in person.

A subset of full-blown teleconferencing is one-way video and two-way audio. Images and voices of the presenters are transmitted to an audience who can be heard but not seen, like some popular call-in TV shows. Viewers call in with questions for the presenters. This method is applicable for ad hoc announcements, such as the launching of a new product or service, a promotion and advertising program, or a speech or seminar.

As a side note, some experts have stated that incidents like the nuclear mishap at Three Mile Island in 1979 could have been prevented, or at least handled better, had some of the findings and subsequent events been relayed to a variety of involved parties. Indeed, billions of dollars could have been saved. It is interesting to see that the Nuclear Safety Analysis Center has installed a teleconferencing system. Today, the system permits utilities to interact with each other every day about a number of issues.

Videotex

Videotex is the interactive communication of text, numbers, and graphics, accessed by any computer, including personal computers, or a television set and a telephone. A personal computer that is already in place can be used as a videotex terminal, giving videotex access to a broad, ready-made audience. This device, therefore, represents an ideal means for an organization to extend its system into the hands of present or potential customers for teleshopping or other services.

Although videotex is in its infancy, many applications are already working. Interactive services are available from financial organizations, banks, mail order firms, cable TV, and news and information services such as Dow Jones.

Output includes weather maps, bulletin boards, charts of stock prices, latest stock quotes, late-breaking news and sports, and so forth. Some banks offer complete video-financial packages, which range from demand deposit accounting to stock purchases. Customers can check their account status from their home and transfer money from one account to another. From retailers and mail order firms, customers can shop, browse, get up-to-date information about any product or service, see a demonstration of it, determine its specifications and price, and place an order. From a travel agency, customers can view travel brochures and locations and book travel arrangements. It appears now that entrepreneurs will increase the use of videotex, especially in the area of tele-shopping.

SUMMARY

Usability, the final test of output, can only be achieved by ensuring that the output has sufficient information content and that it is presented in a form suitable to the visual, auditory, and kinesthetic senses of the end user. If the output is in report form, then design rules must be applied to make the reports more readable and attractive. Also, reports should call to the user's attention conditions that need immediate action, present all sides of a project, measure performance, evaluate, disclose comparisons, and show relationships.

In addition to conventional reports, output can be effectively presented using graphs and charts, such as line, bar, pie, and pictorial charts. In many situations, usability of output can be increased significantly with charts because recipients can quickly see a "picture" of the output and are often able to make better decisions quicker.

A variety of output devices help facilitate usability of output in addition to augmenting communication between a number of users and improving their productivity. These devices include impact and nonimpact printers, plotters, computer output to microfilm, computer-assisted retrieval, facsimile, computer-based message systems, audio output, teleconferencing, and videotex.

IMPORTANT TERMS

analytical report

audio or voice output

cellular telephone

chartjunk

comparative report

computer output to microfilm
  (COM)

computer-assisted retrieval (CAR)

daisywheel printer

dot-matrix printer

electronic mail

equipoised report

facsimile (FAX)

graphics

horizontal analysis

impact/nonimpact printer

inkjet printer

laser printer

left-brain/right-brain	teleconferencing
long-term memory (LTM)	variance report
notice report	vertical analysis
plotter	videotex
ratio report	voice message system
short-term memory (STM)	

Assignment

REVIEW QUESTIONS

8.1 What three elements must the analyst consider when designing output for users?

8.2 Define the terms "form" and "substance" as they pertain to output.

8.3 People's storage system is comprised of long-term memory and short-term memory. What must happen for information to go from STM to LTM?

8.4 What kind of information is preferred by "left-brain" people? "right-brain" people?

8.5 Briefly discuss the 12 rules for constructing meaningful and usable reports.

8.6 Describe the main features of analytical, notice, equipoised, variance, comparative, and ratio reports.

8.7 Discuss both the advantages and the disadvantages of the four different types of charts.

8.8 List and briefly discuss the different types of impact and nonimpact printers available to meet the output needs of organizations. Also describe the two primary types of plotters.

8.9 Explain how computer output to microfilm can be used as an efficient output medium. Under what circumstances is this method best applied?

8.10 Describe the use of facsimile in the transmission of graphs and documents. List the advantages offered by this output medium.

8.11 Although car phones have been in operation for many years, only a select few people have been able to take advantage of the benefits of these systems because of limited technology. The latest wave of mobile telephone systems, however, promises to make mobile phones available to the general public. With the use of cellular technology, these new systems will even allow phone calls from airplanes to be dispatched to a business phone. Explain how this system works and give an example of how this technology can be integrated with the existing information system.

8.12 How can teleconferencing make information workers more productive while at the same time reducing a company's business meeting–related expenses?

8.13 List four applications and four outputs of videotex.

QUESTIONS FOR DISCUSSION

8.14 Amy was eagerly anticipating receipt of the first copy of the newly designed sales analysis report. As regional sales director, Amy had been frustrated by the insufficient and disorganized sales analysis reports she was receiving. The situation deteriorated to the point that she no longer bothered to try to interpret the data contained in the report. However, three weeks ago she was informed that a new information system had been installed at the company's main office. After completing a short information needs questionnaire, Amy had submitted a request for a redesign of the useless sales analysis document.

Upon receipt of the redesigned report generated by the new information system, Amy was greatly impressed with the abundance of detail data provided in the report. Complete data were provided on each product's sales in every region under Amy's jurisdiction. The report even presented what products were sold by each salesperson, at what price, and to which customer. Amy was sure she could now make valid marketing decisions based on the exhaustive data provided on her new sales analysis report.

Recently, Amy stormed into the information services department (ISD) with an armful of computer printouts and threw the entire stack of sales analysis reports onto the ISD manager's desk. Amy angrily explained to the manager that she could not spend every weekend trying to sort through the mountains of detail to find a few vital sales statistics needed to make product and marketing decisions. The lack of readily available data had already caused the closing of two stores in Amy's district and she was getting a lot of heat from her bosses. Amy gave the ISD manager four days to come up with a usable report, and she threatened to file a complaint against him to the vice-president.

Discuss how Amy's information problems might have been resolved at the very beginning. Comment on Amy's attitude that more data are better data. Who has ultimate responsibility for the contents of any report?

8.15 Discuss the concept of the cost-effectiveness constraint in terms of preparing individually customized reports to every supervisory-level employee.

8.16 Many large companies have developed in-house report-generating languages that will allow their executives to draw from a common data base and generate highly customized reports for decision making. These languages are typically very simple to use with only a few, easy-to-understand commands. As a busy executive, would you be willing to learn to use this type of report-generating system? How would you justify using your very valuable (and expensive) time typing on a keyboard to obtain needed information?

8.17 The purpose of management-by-exception reporting is to disclose inefficient operating performance so that management can initiate corrective action. However, these decision makers frequently develop a narrow, negative perspective when their primary source of information is provided on an exception basis. Comment on the necessity for management-by-exception reporting to also reflect favorable operating performance for which no corrective action is necessary.

8.18 "Many of the newest data output technologies like teleconferencing, voice output, and videotex are nothing more than executive playthings. These media bring status and a flavor of sophistication to the user but are, in reality, superfluous toys that are rarely used with any consistency. Frequent hardware breakdowns force the company to revert to the old, reliable forms of communication, especially paper and pencil." Comment on the attitude of the speaker. Is that point valid?

8.19 As more sophisticated information transmission and dissemination technologies are developed, many experts fear the demise of the long-honored face-to-face business encounter. Already, teleshopping makes interaction with a human unnecessary; automated bank tellers respond in monotone, robotlike voices with a cold, unfeeling "thank you" for using their services; dialing for directory assistance connects the caller with a series of prerecorded, computerized digits which are replayed for the caller to hear; the Internal Revenue Service even uses a computerized dialing system that employs a computer-simulated voice to inform taxpayers of unresolved issues on their tax returns. Some experts contend that if these trends continue, customers, employees, and other end users will feel alienated from a perceived uncaring, synthetic organization that does not understand end users' needs. Do you agree with these allegations? What steps would you recommend to overcome, or at least counteract customers' feelings of alienation? How should employees using media such as teleconferencing be trained to appear more interested and concerned about the other party?

8.20 Accountability increases in direct proportion to increases in the amount of quality information available to the responsible decision maker. In light of this statement, can you describe circumstances under which an individual may actually prefer insufficient, inaccurate output from the information system? Does the lack of quality information really excuse an individual from his or her responsibility?

8.21 An organization's information processing system must also produce quality output for use by individuals external to the firm, such as creditors, investors, suppliers, and regulatory agencies. Because of this demand on the system, competition exists between internal reporting and external reporting for use of the scarce processing resources available to a company. Which of these two applications should receive priority? Under what circumstances? Discuss the implications of ignoring either reporting application.

8.22 Nonprofit organizations such as most hospitals, universities, and civic organizations, as well as governmental entities, require quality output just as much as for-profit organizations. This is especially true when compliance reporting is conditional to the existence of the nonprofit entity. Discuss how reporting requirements and other output forms of nonprofit organizations and for-profit businesses differ. In what ways are they similar?

8.23 Perhaps one of the best known and most easily recognized output reports of any organization is its annual report. Discuss how these general-purpose financial statements meet the needs for information about the reporting entity to customers, stockholders, employees, creditors, governments, and suppliers.

EXERCISES AND PROBLEMS

8.24 As head teller at the First National Bank, you are responsible for monitoring the professional behavior of 23 tellers and cashiers. Complaint cards are avalaible for customers to fill out on any teller they feel is rude, sloppy, or otherwise unpleasant. Every month, you are required to report to your manager every teller that has exceeded a 5 percent complaint threshold. In addition, you are required to report any flagrant or significant disciplinary problems in your report to management. This month, each of six tellers accounted for at least 5 percent of the total complaints received. One teller missed four consecutive workdays without permission. Another teller came up $700 short in his cash box and has been reprimanded for this offense before.

Required: Prepare a notice report for your manager that clearly and neatly organizes the problem areas he or she should investigate. Use good form and implement as many of the guidelines as possible for constructing reports presented in the chapter.

8.25 Webber Industries, Inc., uses a standard cost system in its production plant to monitor the efficiency of its operations. The engineering department has determined through time-motion studies that operations A, B, and C in the assembly department should take 2.5, 5, and 3 hours, respectively, to complete. Information obtained from employees' work cards shows the following times expended to complete each operation mentioned.

Worker I.D.	Time Expended in Operations (hours)		
	A	B	C
1	2.25	5.25	3.00
2	2.00	5.75	3.00
3	2.50	4.75	2.75
4	3.50	5.75	3.75
5	3.00	5.25	3.25

Required: Prepare a variance report comparing the average hours expended on each operation by all workers against the standards prepared by the engineering department. Use good form and highlight significant variances, if any. Be sure to show the net variance for the assembly department as a whole and label variances favorable or unfavorable.

8.26 Obtain the annual report of a company in which you are interested. Make sure the report shows comparative data for at least two years. Find and anaylyze the financial statements in the report, then do the following:

1. Perform a horizontal analysis for any two years of the report.
2. Calculate any three ratios (e.g., current ratio, acid test, inventory turnover, debt to equity) with which you are familiar.
3. Submit a well-organized report showing the horizontal analysis and the ratios calculated.

8.27 Using library resources and other research sources, prepare a report on one of the commercial electronic mail services. Include in your report a general explanation of how these systems operate and what benefits they offer.

8.28 Charlie, sales manager for Columbo Enterprises, Inc., left a memo on your desk while you were away. He would like to meet with you and discuss the design of a document to report on the activities of his sales force. Before you meet with Charlie, however, you would like to think about specific questions to ask him concerning not only the actual format of the report but other reporting considerations as well.

Required: Prepare a list of at least 10 significant questions concerning the generation of this new report that you would want to ask Charlie before starting work on the document.

8.29 Jim McKelvick is reponsible for preparing financial projections for his firm. Jim relies heavily on sales forecasts provided by Nancy Acorn of the marketing department. Sam Snickle, in accounting, provides Jim with pro forma financial statements, specifically highlighting projected future expenditures. Marion Alcanter supplies all standard production costs, prepared by the engineering department. Moses Tinsley, in tax, has advised Jim on the tax implications inherent in his projections, especially pointing out that several material unresolved tax issues are currently pending with the IRS.

Once Jim has gathered all the necessary data, he compiles the information using a sophisticated computer-based processing system that provides extremely accurate results. Upon presentation of his projections to the board of directors, Jim becomes involved in a dispute with Peter DeOlvo, manager of production. Peter contends that Jim's external financing projections for capital improvements are "way off" and will imperil the company by placing it in a state of undercapitalization. In response, Jim confidently picks up his copy of the report and points out to Peter, and the others, that the new information system installed by the company is so sophisticated that built-in input/output controls would catch any error immediately and generate an error log. "What's more," Jim boasts, "the system is so accurate it computes every digit to at least 13 places to the right of the decimal point." This fact is readily apparent, as figures appear throughout the bulky report with multiple decimal places. Jim concludes that his figures are correct and charges Peter with trying to obtain additional allocations for his department's free-wheeling spending.

Required: Briefly discuss the viability of Jim's argument. What fact is he completely ignoring? How does the term "spurious precision" relate to this case? Do you believe Jim's financial forecasts should be accepted as the sole decision-making tool for planning, or should his report be trashed? Briefly analyze the purpose of this type of output, including its benefits and limitations.

8.30 Using business periodicals and newspapers, annual reports, and feasibility studies or any other useful library sources, gather one sample of each of the following graphics: line chart, pie chart, bar graph, and pictorial charts. Prepare a report on each type of graphic and include the following:

1. A complete interpretation and analysis of the content and message of the graph.

2. An evaluation of the effectiveness with which the graphs present the data as well as the intended message.

3. Any recommendations you would make to improve the effectiveness of the chart. Would you use the same media to express the message? If yes, why? If no, explain why not?

8.31 Although computer report generation generally services the managers of an organization, and colorful graphics are the current "main attraction" produced by the information system, computer-generated forms are, for many firms, the unheralded backbone of a smoothly operating information system. Simple, plain, everyday forms do not receive a great deal of attention from managers and are thus relegated to a lower status than are reports and colorful graphics. No organization, however, would even attempt to survive through a day without the computer-generated forms that sustain the very life of the business.

Forms are a type of control that verify proper authorization to perform a variety of routine but vital tasks within an organization. Following is a list of tasks that occur in a typical firm. What form would you want as proper authorization to perform each task?

1. To arrange for the purchase of goods for your company at the best price.

2. To write a check, except for signature, in payment of a company bill.

3. To post debits to customers' accounts.

4. To assign work to factory operators in your department.

5. To release operators of cash registers at the end of their shift.

6. To repair broken machinery.

7. To disburse petty cash.

8. To assemble the items ordered by a customer and prepare them for delivery.

9. To issue materials and supplies to employees for use in their work.

10. To prepare the payroll summary each week.

8.32 You are a systems analyst employed by a data processing service bureau. One of the specialties of your organization is to provide a data encoding service to other organizations in the area in addition to supporting your own operations. Much of this effort involves large jobs in short time periods. The goal of your organization is to provide a firm cost estimate for each job to the prospective customer. You employ approximately 100 data entry operators, both full and part time. The manager of the service bureau has requested you to design an information system that will assist him to plan and control the data entry operations. You have investigated the situation and determined the following:

1. A sampling of work indicates that three primary factors are related to the time (and therefore cost) needed to complete a job: (a) the experience level of the operator, (b) the number of strokes per document, and (c) the format of the source document from which the data are entered.

2. You have classified operators as trainees, juniors, and seniors. A trainee is considered to have a productivity factor of 75 percent, a junior 100 percent, and a senior 125 percent.

3. Source documents are classified as either formatted or mixed. A junior operator can key 10,000 strokes an hour from a formatted source document and 8,000 strokes an hour from a mixed document.

4. The keyboards are linked to a microcomputer, which can account for the number of strokes keyed in a job. When the operator indicates end of job, the micro will create a record that contains the number of strokes keyed for that job.

5. Approximately 40 percent of the data entry work done by the service bureau is repetitive.

6. The service bureau has a medium-sized computer with complete processing capabilities.

   Requirements: In your design proposal, include the following:

1. An analysis of a simple planning model that could be used.

2. The information outputs available for users in both planning and controlling activities.

8.33 After two hours, the young systems analyst left the office of the chief toy designer shaking his head.

"I thought I knew what she wanted in a project support system when I went into her office two hours ago. You see, in the information systems department, we have this very complete, well-tested project control system. In fact, it has been used for the last 10 years by all senior analysts to control projects. It provides all the data you would ever want. It can produce tables that tell you what was done or what is planned by person and by time period. It even has an extensive language interface so the user can program a variety of 'what-if' questions."

   Required: Explain why the nature of this project control system was likely foreign to the chief toy designer.

BIBLIOGRAPHY

ANTHONY, ROBERT N., JOHN DEARDEN, and NORTON M. BEDFORD. *Management Control Systems,* 5th ed. Homewood, Ill.: RICHARD D. IRWIN, 1984.

ANSCOMBE, F. J. "Graphs in Statistical Analysis." *American Statistician,* February 1973.

BOOKER, ELLIS. "Computers Help You Win the Game." *Computer Decisions,* September 15, 1984.

BRETZ, RUDY. *Media for Interactive Communication.* Beverly Hills, Calif.: Sage, 1983.

BROWN, MAXINE D. "Mainframe Business Graphics." *Datamation,* May 1, 1984.

CASTAGNA, RICHARD E. "The Information Trail." *Infosystems,* April 1984.

COLBY, WENDELIN. "The Big Picture." *Infosystems,* October 1984.

COOPER, MICHAEL S. "Micro-Based Graphics." *Datamation,* May 1, 1984.

DIETRICH, MARK and JENNIFER STROTHERS. "Toward a Graphics Standard." *PC World,* November 1984.

EIDSON, STEVAN. "Videotex Hardware Heralds Another Node—The Home." *Data Communications,* June 1984.

FLURSCHEIM, CHARLES H., ed. *Industrial Design in Engineering.* Berlin: Springer-Verlag, 1981.

GREEN, LEE. "Laser Printers Now Letter-Perfect." *InformationWEEK,* August 10, 1987.

HELLIWELL, JOHN. "Corporate Voice Mail Seen Changing Business." *PC Week,* August 11, 1987.

HOWELL, ROBERT A. and STEPHEN R. SOUCY. "Management Reporting in the Manufacturing Environment." *Management Accounting,* February 1988.

JARETT, IRWIN M. *Computer Graphics and Reporting Financial Data.* New York: John Wiley, 1983.

JOHNSON, JAN. "Videotex Hits the Office." *Datamation,* June 15, 1984.

KAY, SUSEN S. "How to Choose Electronic Mail." *Infosystems,* June 1984.

KELLER, ARNOLD E. "COM and Information Resource Management." *Infosystems,* April 1984.

LIVINGSTON, DENNIS. "Computer Conferencing." *Datamation,* July 15, 1984.

LOUIS, ARTHUR M. "The Great Electronic Mail Shootout." *Fortune,* August 20, 1984.

MCLEOD, RAYMOND, Jr. *Management Information Systems,* 2nd ed. Chicago: Science Research Associates, 1983.

MITZNER, MELANIE. "Drowning in Data? Help Is on the Way." *Computer Decisions,* June 15, 1984.

NEWELL, ALLEN, and HERBERT A. SIMON. *Human Problem Solving.* Englewood Cliffs, N.J.: Prentice Hall, 1972.

ORR, JOEL. "Business Turns to Graphics." *Infosystems,* November 1980.

RAND, ALEXANDRA J. "Producing Viable MIS Reports." *Infosystems,* June 1984.

ROBEY, D., and W. TAGGUNT. "Human Information Processing in Information and Decision Support Systems." *MIS Quarterly,* June 1982.

ROSCH, WINN L. "PC-to-Fax: A Revolution in the Offing." *PC Week,* January 26, 1988.

THIEL, CAROL TOMME. "Teleconferencing—A New Medium for Your Message." *Infosystems,* April 1984.

"Top Life Insurer Streamlines Contract Production with Laser Printing Systems." *Data Management,* December 1987.

TUFTE, EDWARD R. *The Visual Display of Quantitative Information.* Cheshire, Conn.: Graphics Press, 1983.

UHLIG, RONALD P., ed. *Computer Message Systems.* Amsterdam: North-Holland, 1981.

WHIELDON, DAVID. "Computer Graphics: Art Serves Business." *Computer Decisions,* May 1984.

9

TECHNOLOGY: THE COMPUTER AND AUXILIARY STORAGE

9.1 INTRODUCTION

Computers and other information technology are not, by themselves, information systems. Together, they represent a building block that enables systems analysts to build modern, sophisticated information systems. Before systems analysts can wisely use this predominant building block, however, they must understand its basic parts and functions.

The objectives of this chapter are:

1. To define the central processing unit and describe how it works.
2. To categorize computers by size, cost, power, and application.
3. To stress the concept of full connectivity and compatibility between computers.
4. To present four very important auxiliary storage technologies, namely, magnetic tape, magnetic disk, mass storage, and optical disk.

9.2 THE CENTRAL PROCESSING UNIT

The heart of any computer configuration is the central processing unit, or CPU. Although systems analysts are not expected to have a working knowledge of the internal circuitry of the CPU, it is important for them to understand the principal functions performed by the CPU.

Components of a Computer System

A schematic of a computer system, emphasizing the CPU, is illustrated in Figure 9.1. The schematic shows the following six components:

1. *Input.* The data to be processed and the instructions for processing are made available to the central processing unit by means of input media of the type described in Chapter 6.

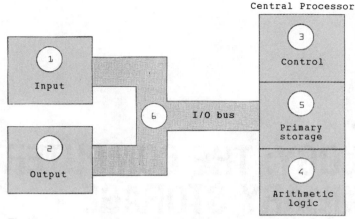

Figure 9.1 Schematic of a computer system, emphasizing the central processor unit.

2. *Output.*   The final results of data processing within the central processing unit are written on various output media referred to in Chapter 8.

3. *Control Unit.*   The control unit directs and coordinates the entire computer system in carrying out program instructions. It is like an orchestra conductor in that it does not execute the instructions itself but instead directs other parts of the computer system to do so. The control unit tells the input media what data to enter and when to enter the data; the primary storage section where to place the data; the arithmetic logic unit what operation to perform, where the data are found, and where to place the results; and what output media to use and what data will be written on the output media.

4. *Arithmetic Logic Unit.*   The arithmetic logic unit, or ALU, is the calculator of the CPU. It contains the circuitry to perform the arithmetic operations of addition, subtraction, multiplication, and division; and the logical operations of equal to ($=$), greater than ($>$), and less than ($<$) on the data.

5. *Primary Storage.*   Just before a program is processed, the control unit places its instructions and data related to those instructions in primary storage, also called main storage, internal storage, or memory. After being processed, the data are kept in primary storage until they are ready to be released to the output unit.

6. *Bus.*   A bus is a collection of wires or lines for carrying data. A bus transports data from input to primary storage, between components of the CPU, and from primary storage to output.

Executing a Program

As a computer program is executed, the control unit gets an instruction, examines the instruction to determine what operation is to be done, and then turns control over to the ALU. This sequence of steps is done during a period called the *instruction time,* or *I-time.* The actual performance of the operation by the ALU occurs during a period called the *execution time,* or *E-time.* Together, these two time periods comprise the machine cycle time.

Figure 9.2 illustrates this two-part, four-step machine cycle. It shows the control unit retrieving the program instruction from primary storage and then decoding the instruction and making the data needed available to the ALU. It also shows the ALU performing the actual operation on the data and returning the results of that operation to the control unit for storage.

Processor Primary Storage

The basic unit for storing data in primary storage is a *bit* (binary digit). It has two states, an "on," or 1, and an "off," or 0. To represent numbers and characters, bits must be combined. A *byte* is a unit consisting of eight bits. Each byte in primary storage has a unique address, analogous to a mailbox in a post office. These addresses identify the location where one or more bytes of data are stored and from which one or more bytes of data are accessed.

When computer manufacturers state the size of their processor, they are referring to the size of its primary storage. The size of a processor's primary storage helps to determine the maximum size of programs and the maximum amount of data available for processing at any one time.

A kilobyte (KB) denotes the size of primary storage of small computer processors. Although a kilobyte actually represents 1024 bytes, it is common for systems people to round off a KB to 1000 bytes. Storage may also be expressed in megabytes, or millions of bytes. The abbreviation for megabytes is MB.

In advertising computers, some vendors use the term *word* rather than byte to define the number of bits that comprise a unit of representation. This is

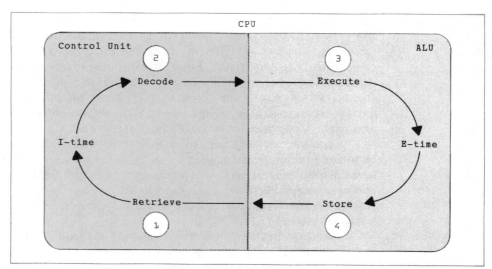

Figure 9.2 The parts and components of a machine cycle.

unfortunate because the length of a word is not standardized and therefore varies from one computer to another. For instance, a small computer may have a word length of 8 or 16 bits, whereas a larger computer may have a word length of 32 or 64 bits.

Primary computer memory is also described in terms of ROM, RAM, PROM, EPROM, and EEPROM. *ROM,* or *read-only memory,* contains programs and data permanently built into the processor's memory by the manufacturer. The contents of ROM can be accessed and used, but they cannot be changed. For example, the ROM of most small computers contains a program to interpret BASIC program instructions.

RAM, or *random-access memory,* is the internal memory available to users to store their data and programs. Users can access data from RAM, make changes to the data, and, because RAM is not permanent (i.e., its contents can be altered by users), write over the original data.

PROM, or *programmable read-only memory,* is a close relative of ROM. It is like ROM in that its contents can be read but not changed by a user's program: it is unlike ROM in that its contents are not built in when the processor is made but instead created by a special type of "programming" done by either the manufacturer or technical specialists in the user's organization. The added flexibility gained with PROM can become a liability if an uncorrectible mistake is programmed into the PROM unit. To overcome this drawback, *EPROM,* or *erasable programmable read-only memory,* has been developed. With EPROM, any portion can be erased by exposing it to ultraviolet light and then reprogrammed. *EEPROM* is electrically erasable read only memory.

Processor Speed

The time for a computer to execute an instruction or complete machine cycle is referred to in unique units of time. On one end of the time spectrum, a small "slow" computer may take as long as a fraction of a *millisecond,* or one-thousandth of a second to execute an instruction. In the middle of the time spectrum are most modern computers, which can execute instructions in *microseconds,* or one-millionth of a second. The very fastest of the large computers are at the other end of the time spectrum. Their processing speed is measured in *nanoseconds.* A nanosecond, or one-billionth of a second, is the time light takes to travel from the top of this page to its bottom. Or, equating time to distance, if you think of a nanosecond as a mile, then 1 second is the equivalent to 2000 trips to the moon and back. A picosecond is a trillionth of a second.

Another common way to specify the speed of a processor is in terms of how many million instructions it can execute in 1 second (MIPS). For example, a small computer might have a processing speed of 0.5 MIPS, whereas a superfast processor might be able to execute 500 MIPS. Expectations are that the so-called fifth-generation computers will operate at speeds of BIPS, or billions of instructions per second.

Speed depends on two factors: word size and clock speed. Word size or bytes represent the number of bits that are manipulated during a complete cycle. A word is either 2 or 4 bytes (16 or 32 bits) long, where the word length is characteristic of the particular computer. On 32-bit machines, the half word of 16 bits is often an important data unit and sometimes the double word (64 bits on a 32-bit machine) is significant. Normally, however, the word is the largest number of bits that all the other parts of the computer can work on as a unit. An 8-bit processor can manipulate 8 bits, or 1 byte, of data at a time. A 16-bit processor can manipulate 2 bytes at a time, a 32-bit processor can manipulate 4 bytes at a time, a 64-bit processor can manipulate 8 bytes at a time, and so forth. Generally, but not always, a 64-bit processor is faster than a 32-bit processor, and a 32-bit processor is faster than a 16-bit processor, and a 16-bit processor is faster than an 8-bit processor.

Clock speed is the number of electronic pulses the chip can produce each second, and this is measured in megahertz (MHz). For example, 25 MHz is 25 million times per second. Assume that one instruction is executed every 25 pulses on a 25-MHz processor. The machine, therefore, could process 1 million instructions per second. It would be classified as a 1 MIPS machine.

Assigning a million of instructions per second ratings reflects only raw CPU power. Total systems measurements are complicated by differences in operating systems and factors, such as input/output, data base management systems, and hierarchy of storage used.

9.3 MAINFRAMES, MINIS, AND MICROS

Mainframes typically cost more than $1 million and serve more than 150 users. Medium-sized computers (superminis and superminimainframes) cost in the $100,000 to $1 million range and serve 20 to 150 users. Minicomputers cost less than $100,000 and serve less than 10 users. An information system for a small proprietorship, such as a local merchant, is adequately supported by a microcomputer costing less than $1,000 and supporting several users.

Scientific systems use high-speed, compute-intensive computers, including supercomputers, superminicomputers, and vector processsing machines. These "big iron" supercomputers can cost several million dollars.

Mainframes

The largest, fastest, and most expensive computers are called mainframes. These are the center of processing in large organizations. Mainframes are able to interface with large data bases and support a variety of peripheral devices— magnetic tape drives, magnetic disk drives, optical scanners, laser printers, VDUs, and even other computers. Mainframes are also intended to service many users' needs at one time.

Mainframes typically operate on 64 bits at a time, have several hundred megabytes of primary storage, and operate at processing speeds measured in nanoseconds. Support from mainframe vendors normally consists of around-the-clock maintenance service, extensive documentation, and a complex and sophisticated array of supporting software.

The large, powerful commercial mainframes have performance ratings of more than 80 MIPS. Typical example of these "big boxes" are IBM's 3090 (IBM's next big box is SUMMIT), National Advanced Corporation's (NAS) AS/XL, and Amdahl's 5890. In the supercomputer market are Cray Research's Y-MP and Cray-3 and ETA Systems's ETA-10. NEC and Fujitsu are starting to make inroads in the supercomputer market.

Superminis and Minis

Some noted vendors in both the mid- and small-range category are IBM's 9370, Honeywell Bull's DPS 7000 or DPS 8000, NCR's Tower 32/800, and DEC's VAX 8800. IBM's AS/400, formerly code-named Silverlake, and its new operating system, OS/400, provides a new mid-range platform and fairly easy migration for System/36 and System/38 users. AS/400 may also be positioned as a replacement for the once much-heralded 9370. In the supermini and mini categories are Hewlett-Packard's HP 3000 Series 930, Data General's MV/15000, and Harris Corporation's HCX series. Within these computers, there are different models, varying in performance, primary storage, and the number of devices that can be attached to each.

A PIECE OF TECHNOLOGY TRYING TO FIND ITS NICHE

IBM has been clear enough about the various roles it wants the 9370 to play. Slated to be a key component of IBM's three-tiered distributed computing architecture, the mid-range system will act as the liaison between the vendor's traditional Systems Network Architecture (SNA)-based mainframe hierarchy on one hand and networks of IBM Personal Computers and Personal System/2s on the other.

Within that framework, the 9370 is designed to function in a wide range of roles: as communications gateway, local-area network (LAN) server, data base machine, network management node, and liaison to other vendors' systems.

Excerpted from Elisabeth Horwitt, "What's Still Missing from the 9370," *Computerworld*, November 18, 1987, pp. 25–29.

These computers are very versatile because they fit wherever they are needed. They can serve as small mainframes, or as departmental processors, or as a prominent node in a large network. Their rack-mounted design eliminates special environmental requirements and also makes it easy to expand processing power or storage. They have floating-point hardware, which improves performance for compute-intensive applications.

Many of these computers are no larger than a two- or three-drawer filing cabinet. Cables are housed within the racks. Such a small "footprint" enables these computers to fit easily and unobtrusively in offices and other crowded workplaces. Moreover, no special environmental facilities are required such as false flooring or a separate climate-controlled "cold room."

Typically, these computers contain primary storage in the 10- to 30-MB range with direct-access storage device (DASD) capacity measured in gigabytes (GB). Their speeds are rated between 1 and 50 MIPS.

Workstations are special-purpose computers with the power of minis. Workstations can be configured with 16 or more megabytes of primary storage, several gigabytes of mass storage, floating-point 32-bit processors, and 1- to 20-MIPS performance. These workstations feature high-resolution, multicolor monitors. Graphics processors provide two- and three-dimensional transformations. Applications for these workstations include computer-assisted design (CAD), computer-assisted manufacturing (CAM), artificial intelligence development, financial services, prototyping, computer-aided publishing, and computer-assisted software engineering (CASE). Apollo Computer and Sun Microsystems are two popular workstation vendors.

Micros

Microcomputers of today are equivalent to minicomputers of yesterday in processor speed and performance. They include larger, high-resolution screens, rapid updating, and multiuser and multitasking capabilities. The Intel 80386-based or Motorola 68020-based 32-bit microcomputers are approximately 250 percent faster than is the old IBM PC AT. The Intel 80486 microprocessor will be four times faster than the 80386. Motorola's 68030 microprocessor, a 32-bit chip, is twice as fast as Motorola's 68020. The 68030 is completely compatible with the 68020 instruction set and with software developed for the 68020. The 68030 adds several features, including on-chip instruction and data caches and dual address and data paths. The chip also supports multiuser, multitasking operation. Additional support products for the 68030 include a math coprocessor, a C language compiler, and an emulator module. The 68040, the next-generation microprocessor, will be announced within the next several months. Microcomputers process in the low MIPS.

Concept of Connectivity and User-Oriented Computers

Users want to plug a computer in and run applications on it without worrying about incompatible data, codes, program instructions, or design of other devices on the network. They want plug-to-plug compatibility, or full connectivity, without using adapter cards. Users are demanding an ability to share applications across multiple processor lines without having to customize at each machine level.

This Utopian state has not been achieved quite yet, but computer vendors are trying to provide cross-systems consistency across their product lines and compatibility with other vendors' products. This seeking of connectivity and applications portability has not come too soon because some major computer vendors have allowed incompatible operating systems, communication protocols, hardware architecture, and even within their own product lines, to grow like Topsy over the years to a point close to compatibility chaos. Those vendors who use a single, common architecture have already achieved compatibility within their product lines, and, to some extent, within multivendor environments.

Successful computer vendors in the future will provide customers with a compatible family of computers that start small and grow in performance all the way to the top of the line while providing a wide range of choices. The technology will serve equally well compute-intensive and input/output-intensive environments. The technology will be easy to install, compact, and also compatible with equipment from other manufacturers. Moreover, users who have large investments in software will feel secure in rapid technological change because when the computer system changes or expands, the applications software portfolio will be preserved.

9.4 AUXILIARY STORAGE TECHNOLOGY

Data processing in organizations implies large amounts of data being stored and constantly updated. Even if all the data about an organization's accounts payable, accounts receivable, inventory, and payroll could fit into the internal memory of the CPU, the storage of that data would likely be extremely expensive. For this reason auxiliary storage devices are used.

In this section we will discuss four popular auxiliary storage technologies—namely, magnetic tape, magnetic disk, mass storage, and optical disks. Within the treatment of magnetic tape, streaming tape and tape cartridge technology will also be discussed. The presentation of magnetic disk will include an examination of floppy and Winchester disk technology. Following this discussion is a presentation of storage hierarchy as it relates to magnetic disk. After mass storage is described, a treatment of optical disk technology is presented.

Magnetic Tape

Tape technology is used for processing, backup, journaling, archiving, and interchange. The characteristics of traditional tape technology follows.

Magnetic tape is a popular medium for storing voluminous amounts of data. It is a sequential medium and, in the past, has been widely used in batch processing environments.

1. *Physical Characteristics.*   Data are recorded on 7-, 8-, 9-, or 10-channel tape in the form of magnetized spots. Tape widths are normally $\frac{1}{2}$ inch, although some tapes are $\frac{3}{4}$, 1, and 3 inches in width. Some new tapes are being marketed that record data in a fashion similar to videotape (i.e., data are recorded across the tape rather than along it). This technique allows bits to be much smaller and closer together. Some manufacturers claim that packing density is 40 times greater than on regular tape. Usually, reels hold 2400 to 3600 feet of magnetic tape; however, shorter tapes are sometimes used.

2. *Coding Scheme.*   The recording of data on magnetic tape is similar in concept to sound recording. Magnetic tape for data processing, however, records numbers and alphabetic and special characters. These data are recorded on tape in channels or tracks, as shown in Figure 9.3.

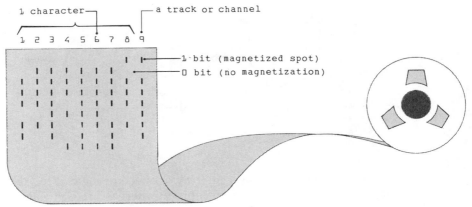

Figure 9.3 Data encoded on magnetic tape.

3. *Density.* The density of magnetic tape is represented by the number of characters or bits recorded per inch (BPI). High-density tapes can record up to 6,250 BPI.

4. *Transfer Rate.* The transfer rate is determined by the speed of a tape drive unit and the density of characters recorded per inch. The tape drive unit functions in much the same way as a home tape recorder (i.e., the tape is wound from one reel to another, passing through a read/write unit where it can be read repeatedly without destroying the data stored). New data can be written over the old data, when desired, and the tape can be rewound and backspaced. If the speed of a tape unit is 112.5 inches per second and the characters per inch are 800, then the data transfer rate is 90,000 characters per second (CPS). The common speeds of tape units are 18.75, 22.5, 36, 37.5, 75, 112, 125, and 200 inches per second. Some manufacturers use vacuum systems rather than capstan systems. These vacuum systems literally suck the tape from one reel to another at speeds of 1,000 inches per second.

5. *Blocking Records.* Each record that is written on tape is separated by a blank ($\frac{1}{2}$ inch, $\frac{3}{4}$ inch, and so on, according to the particular tape system), referred to as an interblock gap (IBG). The IBG has three purposes: (1) it separates a record or block, discussed below, (2) it allows enough space for the tape unit to reach its operating speed, and (3) it allows enough space for the tape unit to decelerate after a read or write operation.

The IBG contains no data. For example, if a recording density is 1,600 BPI, this means that a $\frac{1}{2}$-inch IBG could hold 800 characters of data. The storage of records on a tape, with each record separated by an IBG, is shown in Figure 9.4.

Tape economy is realized by combining the records into a block of records by a blocking factor of N, where N equals the number of records within each block. The block itself becomes a physical group of characters separated by IBGs

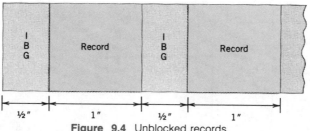

Figure 9.4 Unblocked records.

and the data records within the block become logical records. A block is therefore said to be a tape-recording concept, whereas a record within the block is a logical record, or a data processing concept. Figure 9.5 represents records with a blocking factor of 5.

The concept of transfer rate is a little misleading because, as a tape unit reads blocks of logical records, it stops each time it comes to an IBG. Consequently, when blocks are being read or written, a certain amount of time is spent at each IBG. The total amount of time required to read or write a given number of blocks is equal to the sum of the time spent reading or writing the data plus the time spent starting and stopping at the IBGs. To realize the effect that start/stop time has on reading and writing speeds, consider the following example:

Tape density = 1,600 BPI
Tape unit speed = 75 inches per second
Therefore, stated transfer rate = 120,000 characters per second
Number of blocks on tape = 8,000
Blocking factor = 10 where each logical record contains 30 characters; therefore, each block contains 300 characters or a total of 2,400,000 characters.
Number of IBGs = 8,000
Size of IBG = $\frac{3}{4}$ inch
Time to pass over IBG = 0.010 second
Therefore, total start/stop time = 8000 × 0.010
$$= 80 \text{ seconds}$$
Total time for reading data = 2,400,000 ÷ 120,000
$$= 20 \text{ seconds}$$
Therefore, total time to read all records = 80 + 20
$$= 100 \text{ seconds}$$

I B G	Logical record 1	Logical record 2	Logical record 3	Logical record 4	Logical record 5	I B G

Figure 9.5 Records with a blocking factor of five.

$$\text{Effective transfer rate} = 1,200,000 \div 100$$
$$= 12,000 \text{ characters per second}$$

Consequently, it takes 80 seconds to start and stop the tape, and only 20 seconds to read the data. A waste of tape space and, accordingly, of processing time results. To reduce this waste, more records should be placed in a block. If the blocking factor is 40, then the number of IBGs would be reduced to 2,000 from 8000. The total time to read the records is 20 seconds for reading data plus 20 seconds (2000 × 0.010), or 40 seconds. When an installation has thousands of tape reels, reducing wasted space becomes quite significant.

Streaming tape drives entered the data processing market in 1981 as an inexpensive backup for magnetic disks. They read and write data in a continuous stream by using microprocessor-controlled technology to pass the small, 13-byte IBG without really stopping or starting the tape drive. Thus, streamers are able to fill 97 percent of the ¼-inch tape with data, whereas traditional start/stop drives, with their much larger IBGs, use only about 35 to 70 percent of the tape.

Streaming tapes offer higher tape speeds and transfer rates, and greater capacities than start/stop models. Streaming tape drives operate at 200 inches per second, versus the 30 to 60 inches per second typical of start/stop drives. Data transfer rates for streamers are as high as 380 KB per second. In contrast, nonstreaming tape transfer rates rarely exceed 30 KB per second. Finally, because of their exceptional tape utilization, streamers can pack up to 100 MB into one tape.

The one obvious constraint on the attainment of optimal performance of streaming tape technology is the need for a continuous flow of data. In the event the stream of data is broken, the drive must undergo a relatively slow repositioning movement before it is ready to accept data again.

Tape cartridge media are set in an enclosed plastic cartridge that is about one-fourth the size of a standard tape reel. The total tape system features a thin-film read/write head and chromium dioxide tape media, which combine to provide a data density approximately six times the current 6250 BPI standard. Data transfer rates are greater than 3 MB per second. Tape units are under microprocessor control, which enable high-speed searches. Tape motion under the control of two reel motors eliminates the need for vacuum columns, vacuum switches, and the capstan motor associated with traditional tape systems.

Digital audio tape (DAT) (also called Data DAT, or DDAT) is a new medium that is generating interest as a high-capacity data storage alternative. DDAT provides gigabyte storage with transfer rates of up to 10 MB. DDAT promises to be an ideal medium for archival files and storage backup.

Magnetic Disk

A magnetic disk system is typically referred to as a direct access storage device (DASD). It is made up of a stack of rotating metal platters on which records are stored. Direct access to any record can be made without having to read through a sequence of other, irrelevant records. This direct access capability allows random entry of transaction data and random inquiry into the file from a user. The different disk models range from 5 to 100 disk platters per unit measuring from 1.5 to 3 feet in diameter.

The illustration in Figure 9.6 portrays a disk unit in which 10 of the 12 surfaces are used for recording data. Each surface is divided into 404 tracks, which are analogous to flattened, circular sections of magnetic tape. Each track has a capacity of 13,030 bytes. The read/write mechanism positions the read/write heads over a separate track, which forms a vertical cylinder. Because each surface consists of 404 tracks, we can see that the disk unit is composed of 404 concentric cylinders. In Figure 9.6, the read/write heads are positioned over the tracks that make up cylinder 013.

In Figure 9.7, we have four 3100-byte records stored on cylinder 013, track 02. Each record on the track is numbered sequentially. Therefore, each data record is preceded by a small address record.

With these addresses, it is possible to access directly any desired record stored on the disk. Note that records are separated by gaps, similar to an IBG on magnetic tape. Because the addresses and gaps require a portion of the track, it is impossible to store a full 13,030 bytes of data on a track when more than one record per track is stored. As the number of records per track increases, the number of gaps and addresses increases, causing the data per track to decrease. For example, if the record size is 500 bytes, then the track capacity would be 20 records, for a total track capacity of 10,000 bytes of data.

The disk pack rotates clockwise on a spindle as the access mechanism moves in and out. The speed with which data are read or written depends on two factors plus read/write head selection and data transfer. These factors are:

1. *Access Mechanism Movement Time.* This is the time it takes for the access assembly to move the read/write heads to a specified cylinder (called seek time or access time). The access movement time is based on the number

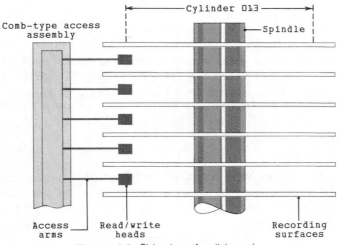

Figure 9.6 Side view of a disk pack.

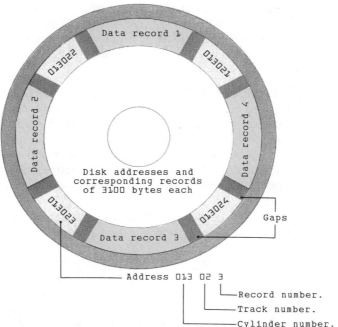

Figure 9.7 Four 3100-byte records stored on disk showing an address for each record.

of cylinders the read/write heads travel over to reach the one specified and the speed of the mechanism itself. The movement rate is not uniform because the mechanism is electromechanical and does not move at a constant speed (notice the movement of the player arm of a record; the naked eye can detect a somewhat irregular movement). The read/write heads are fixed in position over each track for some disks. In this case, the seek time consideration is eliminated.

2. *Read/Write Head Selection.* After the access mechanism has been properly positioned on the specified cylinder, the head that is to read or write is switched on. This switching is electronic and the amount of time, therefore, is negligible in all cases.

3. *Rotational Delay.* Before data are read or written, the proper location on the track must rotate under the read/write heads. The time spent in rotating to a proper alignment of the read/write heads with the specified location is called *rotational delay.* For the IBM 3380 Disk Storage Facility, a full rotation requires 8.3 milliseconds (msec). If, after positioning the access mechanism over the desired track, the desired record has just passed, then the rotational delay is a full 8.3 msec. If, on the other hand, the desired record has just reached the read/write head, the rotational delay is zero. For timing calculations, an average rotational delay of 4.15 msec is used.

4. *Data Transfer.* After the disk has rotated to its proper location, the record

can be read or written. The time required to transfer the record between the disk pack and main storage is the transfer rate, which is a function of rotation speed, the density at which the data are recorded, and the length of the record transferred. The transfer rate of a 3380 unit is 3 MB per second.

In timing a read or write operation, the actual direct accessing therefore consists of access mechanism movement time, rotational delay (using average time), and data transfer rate. The total time for a complete processing job also requires consideration of additional factors such as program processing time, access method processing time, and control program time. For example, again using the IBM 3380 as the storage medium, Figure 9.8 presents an approximate timing summary to read a thousand 5000-byte records randomly distributed over an entire disk pack.

In 1973, IBM introduced *Winchester* disk technology. Today, Winchester disks offer more storage capacity for their price than any other magnetic storage medium.

A Winchester's disks, read/write heads and access mechanism are contained in a hermetically sealed head disk assembly (HDA), in which air is continuously circulated and filtered. This hermetically sealed HDA eliminates the problem of head crashes caused by read/write heads touching particles created by contamination. Thus, no preventive maintenance, such as changing air filters or cleaning and aligning read/write heads, is required and the MTBF is improved significantly. Winchester disks are also able to achieve higher data transfer rates than removable disks. This is a result of two factors. First, because of the ability of a Winchester head to position itself close to the surface of the disk (only 19 microinches from it), greater bit packing densities and greater track densities are possible. Second, because of the improved head design and a better bit definition, Winchester disks can be rotated at faster speeds than their removable counterparts.

Identified in Figure 9.9 are some pertinent characteristics of typical Winchester disks that one might find attached to a mainframe and a microcomputer.

Because of their low-cost, random-access storage capability, *floopy disks* have become the most popular magnetic storage medium for small computers. Floppies are punched out of a polyester film coated with an iron oxide compound. The flat, circular floppy rotates freely within a jacket that is intended to prevent

Per record:	
Average access time	16.00 msec
Average rotational delay	4.15 msec
Data transfer time	1.70 msec
Total	21.85 msec
1000 records—21.85 seconds	

Figure 9.8 A timing summary.

Characteristic	IBM 3380	Tandon TM 705
Disk size (inches)	14	5.25
Capacity (MB)	1,520	50.1
Average access speed (msec)	16	39
Number of data surfaces	15	5
Price ($)	116,050	1,950

Figure 9.9 Characteristics of a typical Winchester disk associated with a mainframe (IBM 3380) and a microcomputer (Tandon TM 705).

both loss of data and damage to the floppy. The jacket has access and index holes to accommodate the read/write head which actually touches the magnetic surface and the data timing transducers of the floppy disk drive.

The 8-inch diameter floppy of 1972 has shrunk to the standard 5.25-inch floppy of today (3.5-inch microfloppies are also available). We have seen the single-sided floppy give way to the double-sided floppy; the 48-tracks-per-inch floppy has been replaced by the 96-tracks-per-inch floppy. The average access time for a typical floppy is approximately 80 msec. A floppy can hold up to 2 MB of data. The typical floppy disk costs less than $1; the price of a floppy disk drive is around $200.

Semiconductor Disk

Semiconductor (or solid-state) disks are available that emulate the way conventional magnetic disks operate. Solid-state devices store data on memory chips rather than on magnetic disks. Vendors claim that these semiconductor disks provide seven to ten times the performance of conventional rotating disks systems.

In addition to storing gigabytes of data, these disks also contain local intelligence for file access and input/output control and battery backup, a feature designed to preserve stored data throughout a one- to three-hour power failure.

Storage Hierarchy Relative to Magnetic Disk

The chief aim of a well-designed computer configuration is to move data to and from storage devices quickly for optimal response time (less than 5 seconds) and throughput in today's highly interactive environments. But strides in mainframe processing power have greatly exceeded advances in conventional magnetic disk technology. Consequently, the performance gap between the processor's primary storage and channel-attached devices has created serious input/output bottlenecks.

To narrow the gap and enhance overall performance, the systems analyst can adapt a storage hierarchy patterned after the one displayed in Figure 9.10. The trade-off is cost for speed. High-speed buffer and primary storage serve the processor directly with performance-critical data. Expanded storage is non-addressable primary storage that is a tiny bit slower than is the processor's

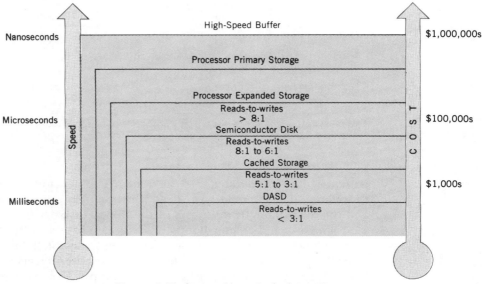

Figure 9.10 Storage hierarchy for interactive media.

primary storage. It resides in the computer's primary storage bus, which means that access to data is made without waiting for communications between storage devices and processors. Semiconductor disks are built from RAM chips. Cache for DASDs is controller-based storage that contains frequently used pages that are provided without the need for a disk read. Both expanded storage and semiconductor disks provide alternatives to the more established method of speeding up disk input/output through the use of cached DASD. But choosing either option is not clear cut. As with most things in systems development, it requires the consideration of a number of trade-offs.

DISK-CACHING APPLICATIONS For a relatively small segment of the PC market, where high-capacity, high-performance disk drives are standard equipment, effective disk caching can be even more critical to overall systems performances. Particularly for disk-intensive applications such as network file servers, multiuser systems, computer-aided engineering and design (CAE/CAD) workstations and desktop-publishing systems, disk caching is almost achieving acceptable disk performance. The bottleneck between data on the disk and the central processor becomes increasingly apparent with the high-speed 80386-based systems.

Excerpted from Susan Janus, "Effective Caching Critical to Disk-Intensive Uses," *PC Week,* February 2, 1988, p. 128.

Expanded storage completes a page transfer in microseconds. This is much faster than external disk and cache devices, which require scheduled input/output operations and take milliseconds to transfer a page. Expanded storage is about 10 times faster than semiconductor disks and costs about twice as much. Cost savings result in a response time of less than 5 seconds for the end user and reduced cost per input/output per second.

Obviously, more efficient use of processing power is achieved by limiting the number of input/output transactions queuing up at DASDs. To implement an appropriate storage hierarchy, data usage patterns should be ascertained by using either hardware or software monitors (e.g., IBM's Systems Management Facility, SMF). As a rule of thumb, the more critical the data set and the more times it is accessed compared to the times it is updated (reads-to-writes ratio), the faster the storage it should reside in. For example, a data set with a 2:1 reads-to-writes ratio should reside in a DASD. On the other hand, a data set with a 12:1 reads-to-writes ratio and accessed often for a variety of tasks, for example, is probably a candidate for expanded storage residence.

Mass Storage

Although magnetic tape is being replaced by disk units, large data files, backup files, and seldom-used files still need to be stored on a low-cost, medium-to-slow access medium. One such system is Control Data Corporation's 38500 Mass Storage System (another is IBM's 3851).

This system is intended for processing large active files within an environment where performance and equipment costs are the key criteria for evaluation. The storage capacity of the system ranges from 16 billion to more than a trillion bytes. A maximum of 5, and an average of 2.5 seconds, is required to access data.

The Control Data 38500 system is built around magnetic tape cartridges. Each enclosed cartridge contains a 150-inch-long, 2.7-inch-wide magnetic tape, capable of storing up to 8 million bytes of data. Within a single-file unit, 2052 tape cartridges are clustered in beehive fashion. To retrieve data, an X-Y selector is positioned at the addressable location, the cartridge is picked by the selector, and the cartridge is then moved to a tape transport. At the transport, the cartridge is opened, and the tape is unwound fully and inserted into vacuum columns. It can then be moved past the read/write station at approximately 129 inches per second, effecting a data transfer rate of more than 800,000 bytes per second.

Optical Disk

One of the most significant current developments in storage technology is optical disk. This technology can be divided into the following three categories:

1. *Compact Disk/Read-Only Memory (CD-ROM).* CD-ROM disks are made of reflective metal. Data are recorded in digital form by creating a series of microscopic pits and adjoining spaces arranged in spiraling tracks. Each disk contains 16,000 tracks per inch, and each disk is approximately $4\frac{1}{2}$

inches in diameter. A disk can hold over 600 MB of data. As a supplement to a processor's ROM and online data bases, storage capacity begins to approach gigabytes.

POSTAL SERVICE GOES TO CD-ROM   In what is said to be the largest nationwide installation of compact disk-read-only memory technology in a production environment, the U.S. Postal Service has unhooked its mainframe-based ZIP code retrieval system and replaced it with more than 400 CD-ROM drives. Officials state the project is saving as much as 50 percent in online transactions costs.

Excerpted from James A. Martin, "Postal Service Ousts Mainframe Application for CD-ROM Scheme," *Computerworld*, March 7, 1988, p. 116.

---

2. *Write Once, Read Many (WORM).*   WORM disks do not require the special mastering procedures of CD-ROMs. Data from video scanners, keyboards, optical character recognition equipment, and other devices can be recorded on WORMs. Access time of WORMs is greater than magnetic disk but less than microfilm. Normally, 12-inch, 8-inch, or 5¼-inch WORMs are stored in jukeboxlike systems. A jukebox is a rack system that allows several hundred optical platters to be mounted into a rack that is connected to a central controller for access and reading. The result is hundreds of gigabytes, even terabytes (TB), of online storage within a single system. Storage-intensive companies that have high document-imaging needs are big users of WORM systems. Any document in the system can be accessed in less than 30 seconds.

3. *Erasable Optical Disks.*   Most erasable disks are recorded using lasers to heat magnetized areas coated with various metals. The magnetism provides polarity in the sections, which can then be read with another laser. Data are erased by shooting an even more powerful laser at the disk, which reverses the magnetism. These disks may be used as alternatives to traditional magnetic disks or for backup.

SUMMARY

Technology is an important building block of information systems. In this chapter we have talked about its components as being the central processing unit and magnetic auxiliary storage devices.

The heart of a computer system is the CPU. Its main functional components are a control unit that directs the system in carrying out instructions, an arithmetic logic unit that acts as a calculator to the CPU, and a primary storage or internal memory unit that holds data and instructions. To execute an instruction,

THE EASY WAY TO STORE GARGANTUAN AMOUNTS OF DATA

WORM, CD-ROM, and erasable optical disks provide vast expanses of storage space that leave hard disks and cartridge tapes far behind. Although all three types of optical drives use a low-power laser to read data from a spinning removable disk, they differ in other technological ways, and each is best suited for different applications.

A WORM optical drive allows the end user to write data permanently onto a disk coated with a special reflective material. Once the data are stored on the disk, it can never be erased or changed without physically destroying the disk. This makes WORM storage ideal for backup and archiving applications that require that files never be altered.

Currently, there are no standards for WORM disks, and each manufacturer uses a different cartridge size and/or different format.

Although CD-ROM disks encode data much as WORM disks do—as a series of tiny pits in the disk surface—the machinery used to burn those pits into the platter of CD-ROM is much more expensive, partly because it works faster. For this reason, CD-ROM disks are "mastered" at a central location, and are used to distribute large amounts of data that will not require frequent updating.

Unlike WORM drives, all CD-ROM drives use the same disk size and format, and any disk can be read by any manufacturer's drive.

Erasable optical systems are based upon a hybrid technology known as magnetic optical (MO), although other ways to provide erasable optical storage are also being tested in research and development labs.

An MO drive takes advantage of the fact that the magnetic properties of any material can be changed more readily when the substance is heated to a certain temperature.

The material used to coat the surface of an MO disk is chosen partly because it shows this magnetic response at the relatively low temperature a small laser can generate, and also because it reflects laser rays differently depending upon how much it is magnetized.

To write a data bit, the drive's laser heats a tiny, precisely defined point on the disk's surface while a magnetic flux is simultaneously applied.

Condensed from Steve Cummings, "Mass-Storage Devices Differ in Technology and Target Varied Uses," *PC Week,* March 15, 1988, p. S22.

OPTICAL-DISK TECHNOLOGY ENDING THE PAPER CHASE For certain kinds of businesses—such as banks and insurance firms—where the volume of documents to be processed and stored is staggering, analysts and users say optical technology is the enabling factor in the development of systems designed specifically to manage heavy paper traffic.

This application has created a unique niche for optical storage, quite apart from the controversy raging over optical vs. magnetic technology for conventional data storage. The systems designed for this application area do not store data. Rather, they are designed to store many digitized images of entire documents.

"A bank can't take a request for a $500 credit on a Mastercard, put it through 12 people and make a profit," says Scott McCready, optical-disk systems analyst. "Document-processing systems can cut those costs dramatically."

"Many think of archiving and 'back of the house,' but that's not where the real action is—it's in accounts payable, order fulfillment, claims processing, and the like," says Richard Zeck, senior analyst.

Excerpted from Susan Janus, "Optical-Disk Technology Could Help Put a Stop to Paper Chase," *PC Week*, February 2, 1988, p. 79.

the control unit must involve all the functional components either when an instruction is retrieved, when it is interpreted, or when the instruction's actions are carried out.

In the future, successful computer vendors will provide customers with a compatible family of computers that starts small and grows in performance all the way to the top of the line. Today's microcomputers equal yesterday's minicomputers in speed and performance, being capable of performing more than a million instructions per second. Superminis and minicomputers can serve as small mainframes or as departmental processors. Because of their size they can fit easily into offices and other crowded workspaces. Mainframes serve the most sophisticated and complex of an organization's applications. Mainframes are associated with megabytes of internal memory, nanosecond processing speeds, and around-the-clock vendor maintenance support. They are intended to service many users' needs at one time.

Processing in organizations implies storage and constant updating of large amounts of data. This is the domain of four auxiliary storage technologies: magnetic tape, magnetic disk, mass storage, and optical disks. Although the characteristics of magnetic tape have changed little over the years, streaming tape and tape cartridge technology are new adaptations. Winchester, floppy, and semiconductor disk technology have brought new capabilities and measures of economy to magnetic disk technology. Optical disks, in the form of read-only

WORMS FOR BIG DATA   Robert A. Zeek, a senior projects analyst at Pfizer, Inc., in Groton, Conn., is not operating under any optical illusions about the performance of write-once read-many (WORM) online storage disks. He says that compared with IBM 3380-type Winchester technology, WORM disks perform like an out-of-tune family station wagon. However, the clunky disks hold a key advantage for the pharmaceutical research in which Zeek is involved. Once data are written to disk, they can never be erased or overwritten. "We don't see magnetic [disks] as even being in the ball game, because we want write-once," Zeek says. "We don't want erasable. We don't even want erasable optical." Among the data Pfizer stores on its WORM disks are graphs of the spectrum of a chemical. Prior to optical disks, computer comparisons of these graphs could date back only about six months. Now the company can store data on optical disks dating back several years. For that reason, data security is of the utmost importance.

"We want to know that we can compare that for years to come," Zeek says. Pharmaceutical companies are not the only users turning to WORM disks rather than magnetic disks for data security purposes. Banks, insurance companies, and government agencies are taking advantage of the permanence and removability of the relatively young technology, despite its shortcomings in access speed. "To these industries," says analyst Ray Freeman, president of Freeman Associates, Inc., a Santa Barbara, Calif., storage research firm, "it is preferable that the data can't be altered in order to provide a permanent audit trail."

These organizations can also overcome the relatively slow performance of WORM disks by using high-end magnetic disk systems to act as a cache memory to achieve the much-improved access of Winchester technology. WORM disks access data at an average access time of about 100 msec, at least five times slower than most Winchester disks.

Barbara Sehr, "They May Be Slow, They May Be Heavy, But Sometime WORMs Work Best," *Computerworld*, November 16, 1987, p. 77.

memory and write once, read many, are one of the most significant recent developments in storage technology.

IMPORTANT TERMS

access mechanism movement time
address
arithmetic logic unit (ALU)
auxiliary storage

billions of instructions per second (BIPS)
bit
bits per inch (BPI)

blocking

bus

byte

cached storage

central processing unit (CPU)

compact disk/read-only memory (CD-ROM)

control unit

cylinders

digital audio tape (DAT)

direct access storage device (DASD)

E-time

electronic erasable programmable read-only memory (EEPROM)

erasable optical disk

erasable programmable read-only memory (EPROM)

floppy disk

footprint

gigabytes (GB)

I-time

input

interblock gap (IBG)

kilobyte (KB)

magnetic disk

magnetic tape

mainframe computer

mass storage

megabyte (MB)

megahertz (MHz)

microcomputer

microsecond

millions of instructions per second (MIPS)

millisecond

minicomputer

nanosecond

output

picosecond

primary storage

programmable read-only memory (PROM)

random-access memory (RAM)

read/write head

read-only memory (ROM)

rotational delay

semiconductor disk

streaming tape drives

tape cartridge

terabytes (TB)

tracks

Winchester disk

word

workstations

write once, read many (WORM)

Assignment

REVIEW QUESTIONS

9.1   Name and describe the six components of a computer system.

9.2   Define the following terms:

CPU	KB/MB/GB/TB
ALU	ROM/RAM/PROM/EEPROM/EPROM
I-time/E-time	bit/byte
milli/microsecond	nano/picosecond
MIPS/BIPS	megahertz
BPI	IBG

DAT   track/cylinder
CD-ROM/WORM

9.3 State briefly how instructions are stored and executed.

9.4 List the basic types of primary computer memory and state the distinguishing characteristic of each.

9.5 Explain the factors that cause the speed of two processors to be different.

9.6 List five ways to distinguish mainframes from other classes of computers.

9.7 What does the concept of connectivity mean when used in context of different sized computers?

9.8 How does blocking result in reducing processing time of data stored on magnetic tape?

9.9 What promises to be an ideal magnetic medium for archival files and storage backup?

9.10 What factors affect the speed with which data are read from or written to magnetic disk?

9.11 Why are Winchester disks able to achieve higher data transfer rates than removable disks?

9.12 What is the basic difference between CD-ROM and WORM?

QUESTIONS FOR DISCUSSION

9.13 Discuss whether or not data can always be expressed as a series of bits.

9.14 Discuss whether a manager needs to know how computers work or just how to use them.

9.15 Compare the capabilities of a CPU interacting with main memory with those of a person handling data with a pencil and scratch pad.

9.16 Report on the performance of some newly announced storage device. Why is storage capacity so important in a computer system.

9.17 Calculate the number of characters of data about each person on earth that could be stored on an IBM 3380. What might it cost to gather and enter all these data? Does a risk to individual privacy exist because of such a capability? What will prevent this possibility from becoming reality?

9.18 Some experts believe that each new generation of computers revolutionizes the computer industry and eventually changes the way we do things. What effects will the next generation of computers have on the computer industry and what effects will be felt by society?

9.19 Discuss how reference data stored on CD-ROM and accessed through microcomputers might replace an alternative method whereby these same data are stored in a large centralized data base and accessed over telecommunication lines via special terminals.

EXERCISES AND PROBLEMS

9.20 In designing a file it has been determined that there will be 75,000 records and that each record is 200 bytes. Calculate (a) records per track, (b) number of tracks required, and (c) number of cylinders required. Assume the model of disk pack available has 200 cylinders, each cylinder has 10 tracks, and each track has a maximum capacity of 16,000 bytes.

9.21 Access motion time is negligible if a file is being processed in sequence. The significant time, in this case, is rotational delay and data transfer. If the full rotational delay is 8.5 milliseconds per track and the data transfer is 1,882 KB, then, using exercise 9.20, calculate the time required to read all the records.

9.22 A disk pack has 200 cylinders. There are 10 recording surfaces or tracks, and each track can store a maximum of 16,000 bytes (characters). What is the maximum capacity of each cylinder? What is the maximum capacity of the disk pack?

9.23 There are 200 cylinders in a disk pack. Each cylinder has a maximum capacity of 320,000 data bytes. If there are 20 recording surfaces, what is the maximum capacity of each track?

9.24 Assume that a tape drive has a transfer rate of 60,000 bytes per second and a start/stop time at each IBG of 10 milliseconds. If this tape drive is to read 15,000 records and each record is 50 characters in length, how long will it take? This exercise, so far, represents 15,000 unblocked records. Suppose, however, that the 15,000 records to be read were blocked, 10 to a block. How would this blocking affect the total time to read the records from the tape?

9.25 A nine-track tape has a density of 6,250 BPI and a tape unit speed of 60 inches per second. The number of blocks on the tape is 6,000, the blocking factor is 4, and each logical record contains 25 bytes. The size of the IBG is 0.75 inch and the time to pass an IBG is 0.012 seconds. Calculate (a) stated transfer rate, (b) size of each block, (c) total number of bytes, (d) total start/stop time, and (e) total time for reading data.

9.26 Assume the availability of 2,400-foot magnetic tape reels with 6,250 BPI density. Further assume 200-byte logical records, blocked 5, 0.00016 inches per character, and a .60-inch IBG. On a 2,400-foot reel, 28,440 inches are available for storing working records (2,400-foot reel minus 30 feet of combined header and trailer records). Calculate the physical and logical records per reel.

9.27 A 4.5-MB document stored on hard disk is to be backed up to a tape cartridge. The cartridge has 150 feet of ¼-inch tape. The data cartridge is capable of holding 100 KB per foot of tape. How much space will the document use of the data cartridge?

BIBLIOGRAPHY

CAPRON, H. L., and BRIAN K. WILLIAMS. *Computers and Data Processing*. Menlo Park, Calif.: Benjamin/Cummings, 1982.

CUMMINGS, STEVE. "Mass-Storage Devices Differ in Technology and Target Varied Uses." *PC Week*, March 15, 1988.

HELMS, HARRY, ed. *The McGraw-Hill Computer Handbook*. New York: McGraw-Hill, 1983.

HORWITT, ELISABETH. "What's Still Missing from the 9370." *Computerworld*, November 18, 1987.

JANUS, SUSAN. "Effective Caching Critical to Disk-Intensive Uses." *PC Week*, February 2, 1988

JANUS, SUSAN. "Optical-Disk Technology Could Help Put a Stop to Paper Chase." *PC Week*, February 2, 1988.

KROENKE, DAVID M. *Business Computer Systems*. Santa Cruz, Calif.: Mitchell, 1981.

KULL, DAVID. "Busting the I/O Bottleneck." *Computer & Communications Decisions*, May 1987.

MANDELL, STEVEN L. *Computers and Data Processing Today*. Saint Paul, Minn.: West, 1983.

MARTIN, JAMES A. "Postal Service Ousts Mainframe Application for CD-ROM Scheme." *Computerworld*, March 7, 1988.

MEYER, EDWIN W. "To Preserve and Protect." *PC Products*, December 1985.

SARDINAS, JOSEPH L. Jr. *Computing Today*. Englewood Cliffs, N.J.: Prentice Hall, 1981.

SEHR, BARBARA. "They May Be Slow, They May Be Heavy, But Sometime WORMs Work Best." *Computerworld*. November 16, 1987.

SEHR, ROBERT. "Need for Winchester Backup Pushes Floppies to Higher Densities." *Mini-Micro Systems,* April 19, 1984.

SEIDMAN, ARTHUR H., and IVAN FLORES, eds. *The Handbook of Computers and Computing.* New York: Van Nostrand Reinhold, 1984.

SIMPSON, DAVID. "Tape-Drive Market Rebound Moves to Fast Forward." *Mini-Micro Systems,* April 19, 1984.

SIMPSON, DAVID. "Streaming-Tape Cartridge and Cassette Drives Extend Back-up Abilities." *Mini-Micro Systems,* February 1984.

SUTTON, DAVID, "Removable-Cartridge Winchester Triples Performance-to-Volume Ratio." *Mini-Micro Systems,* March 1984.

WHITE, RON. "Strength in Silence." *PC Products,* August 1986.

WHITE, RON. "The Optical Alternative." *PC Products,* May 1986.

10
TECHNOLOGY: TELECOMMUNICATIONS AND NETWORKING

10.1 INTRODUCTION

Telecommunications is the use of electronic and light-transmitting media to communicate between nodes across distance. Today's telecommunication networks provide the links that move massive volumes of data across the hall or across oceans in seconds.

The essence of telecommunications is its compression of time and space; it virtually eliminates "information float." With satellite communication, for example, it makes no difference whether two or more nodes on earth are close together or far apart; transmission 100 miles is the same as 1000 miles. Access of a node to the system is independent of its location. Moreover, the movement from analog to digital as opposed to analog links permits the integration of all forms of information communication within a network, including voice, facsimile, video, graphics, micrographics, and text. Today, satellite communications is replacing wire channels; optical fiber, with bandwidths in the gigabit region, is replacing copper in the conduction of signals.

Sound telecommunications and networking strategy is a key element for building successful information systems. Indeed, usefulness of an information system can be greatly enhanced by the comprehensiveness and robustness of its telecommunication network.

The objectives of this chapter are:

1. To define the basic, traditional telecommunication components.
2. To explain line configuration and utilization.
3. To describe the most common communication media and discuss guidelines for media selection.
4. To present an analysis of network architectures, standards, and protocols.

5. To illustrate and explain local area networks (LANs) and show how they are connected to other LANs and wide area networks (WANs).

10.2 BASIC TELECOMMUNICATION COMPONENTS

Figure 10.1 illustrates the basic components of a traditional telecommunications system. These are terminals, modems, channels, communications processors, and a host computer.

Terminals

Terminals in data communications configurations represent devices that enter data into and take information out of the system. Although we usually think of terminals in terms of video display units (VDUs) having keyboard-generated input and screen output, terminals may contain far more intelligence.

Intelligent terminals are used to extend the power of the central computer and accept data at its origin and perform some level of processing. Many intelligent terminals include microcomputers, which can be used for different purposes based on how they are configured and programmed. For instance, by

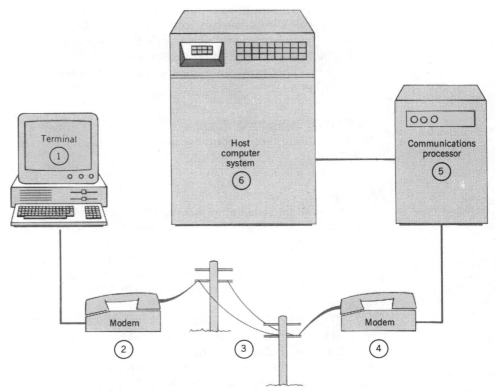

Figure 10.1 Basic components of a traditional telecommunications system.

using one set of peripherals and programs, a remote job entry (RJE) system is developed, and by using a different set of peripherals and programs, a data entry system, such as a remote key-to-disk system, is created.

With the advent of lower costs and greater availability of computers and data communication systems, the use of RJE systems has become cost-effective for small users that cannot economically justify having their own data processing systems.

Modems

A modem is a device for electronically converting digital signals to analog signals and vice versa. A modem (a word formed by combining *mo*dulation and *dem*odulation) is necessary because computer hardware produces and receives digital signals, whereas most communication lines handle only voice or analog signals.

The sequence of modulation/demodulation is illustrated in Figure 10.2. This figure shows the modulator portion of a modem converting a terminal's digital pulses, represented as 1 and 0 bits, into analog, or wavelike signals acceptable for transmission over communications lines. The demodulator at the other end of the communications line reverses the process. It converts the analog, sine wave signals back into 1 and 0 bits that are acceptable to a computer at the other end of the communications line.

Low-speed modems are capable of handling up to 600 bits per second (bps). They interface with voice-grade lines. Medium- and high-speed modems operate in the 1,200- to 3,600-bps range and 4,800-bps to 19.2-Kbps range, respectively. The most common types of microcomputer modems work at 300 or 1,200 bps.

Traditional Telephone Channels

Traditional telephone channels can be described under the following classifications.

Line Speed

Channels can be classified as low, medium, or high speed. Low-speed channels, which were originally developed for use with teletypes, operate at speeds of up to 1200 bits per second (bps). Medium- or voice-grade lines carry transmissions of 2400 to 9600 bps. The carrying capacity in the upper range of a voice-grade line can be attained only by conditioning, or electronically balancing the line. High-speed lines operate at speeds of up to 1.544 million bits per second (Mbps) or more.

T-spans are high-capacity digital channels that support transmission speeds of 1.544 Mbps and greater. These channels include T-1 (1.544 Mbps), T-1C (3.152 Mbps), T-2 (6.312 Mbps), T-3 (44.736 Mbps), and T-4 (274.176 Mbps). The major T-1 users comprise two categories. The first category includes carriers that use T-1 channels as high-capacity "pipes" to provide access into their own networks. The second category includes users with large telecommunication

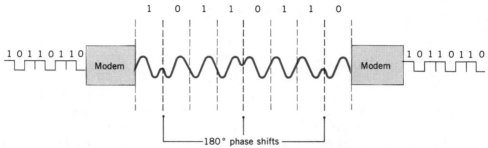

1 0 1 1 0 1 1 0

180° phase shifts

Figure 10.2 A terminal's digital pulses being modulated, transmitted, and demodulated.

budgets, such as *Fortune* 500 companies and government agencies that use T-1s as basic components in their private wide area networks. For local or intercity T-1s, companies use them for private voice networks. T-2s or T-3s used as intercity components of a private network are a rarity outside state or federal government networks. Many telecommunication experts believe that T-spans will help to provide a smooth migration to the integrated services digital network (ISDN), a telecommunications standard discussed later in this chapter.

Switched/Nonswitched

A line can be either switched (also called dial-up and public) or nonswitched (also called leased, dedicated, and private). Switched lines use the public telephone network. They are available as long as the connection is made, and their cost varies according to mileage, time of day, and duration of the connection. Because each switched connection may actually involve a unique combination of lines, the electronic characteristics of the line are not guaranteed. Consequently, to achieve high transmission rates on the switched network, any required conditioning must be done with modems. Such modems rapidly determine the characteristics of the lines, compensating for them at the start of a connection and then continuously during the connection, as changes in the combination of lines occur.

Nonswitched lines offer users several cost alternatives. The first cost alternative is flat rate. The flat rate nonswitched line allows unlimited usage. Its cost is entirely related to its distance. The measured rate nonswitched line is a second alternative. Its cost structure is like that used by the direct distance dial network in that rates are a function of the duration, time of day, day of week, and distance. A third nonswitched line cost alternative is tapered rate. The basis of tapered rate pricing is a graduated schedule that relates decreased costs per time segment to increased usage.

Analog/Digital

The public telephone system has been basically analog from the beginning because it was originally built to handle voice communications. But in recent years, the Bell operating companies (BOCs) have begun changing their systems to digital. More about this change from analog to digital is presented later in this chapter.

Mode

Depending on the terminal equipment and the application, communication channels can be arranged for operation in one or more of three basic transmission modes. *Simplex* transmission mode is transmission in one direction only. Simplex transmission would be adequate if, for example, a terminal at a remote location were used only for entering and reporting data on the climate conditions, inventory levels, or order status to a centralized processor.

Half duplex allows transmission in both directions but not at the same time. Half duplex would be an appropriate transmission mode if an application requires a retail store to report its sales data to corporate headquarters during the day and to receive stock information related to those sales from its corporate headquarters at night.

With *full-duplex* mode, transmission can be made in both directions at the same time. It gives applications the most flexibility and, correspondingly, is the most expensive of the three transmission modes.

Asynchronous/Synchronous

Data transmission is either asynchronous or synchronous. The operations of these two types of transmission are contrasted in Figure 10.3. Asynchronous transmission is the slower of the two. With *asynchronous* transmission, signal elements (bits) are transmitted to indicate the start and stop of every byte of

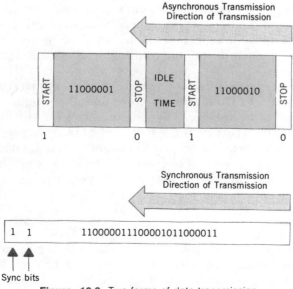

Figure 10.3 Two forms of data transmission.

data. With *synchronous* transmission, the receiving equipment is synchronized in time with the sending equipment. Synchronization is established by passing a predetermined group of "sync" characters between the sending and receiving devices when transmission is initiated and periodically thereafter to maintain synchronization.

The Second Modem

This modem demodulates the analog signal on the communication line to a digital signal acceptable to the processing hardware.

Communications Processor

A communications processor is a multifunctional, program-controlled computer dedicated to communications. It serves three major functions: front-end processing, intelligent switching, and concentration.

As a *front-end processor,* the communications processor removes the overhead associated with message handling and network control from the host processor. Thus, the host processor is free to do what it does best—application and data base processing. As an *intelligent switch,* the communications processor performs such functions as message sequencing, message assembly and disassembly, and transmission error control. Finally, in its role as a *concentrator* the communications processor polls the devices connected to it. When a communications line is free, the first device ready to send or receive data is given control of and retains the line for some specified time period. It may also concentrate data from other concentrators or front-end processors in the network.

Host Computer

The host computer is the hub of the communications configuration. Most host computers are mainframes.

10.3 LINE CONFIGURATION AND UTILIZATION

No matter the type of communications channel, the speed at which data are transmitted, or whether simplex, half-duplex, or full-duplex mode is used, terminals, channels, and data processing hardware must be arranged in some type of line configuration. Following is a discussion of two major types of line configurations: point to point and multidrop. Preceding the discussion is an examination of the multiplexer, another piece of communications equipment for improving line utilization.

Multiplexers

The two most widely used types of multiplexers in today's communications applications are *time division multiplexers* (TDMs) and *statistical time division multiplexers* (STDMs). With conventional TDMs the multiplexer serves a group of terminals in a fixed order. This means that each terminal is given a turn at sending and receiving bits, bytes, or packets of data. TDMs take what is offered

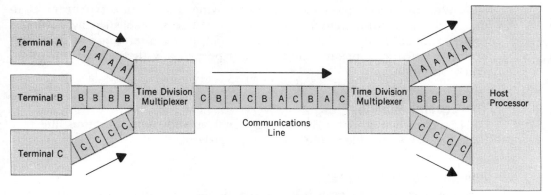

Figure 10.4 Transmission with time division multiplexing.

from each terminal and put it in a specifically allocated time slot on the high-speed transmission line. The data from one terminal, therefore, is interleaved with data from another terminal. This interwoven data stream can be seen in Figure 10.4.

At the other end of the transmission line is another multiplexer. It recognizes which time slots contain particular data. It unweaves the bits, bytes, or packets of data and routes them to the appropriate device at their original transmission rate.

By taking time division multiplexing one step farther, a STDM gives better service to the terminals and results in better line utilization than a TDM does. A STDM detects which of the terminals currently want to send or transmit data and serves only them. A STDM provides, in essence, variable rather than fixed time slots, so that more than one bit, byte, or packet of data can be accepted from a specific terminal before a STDM goes on to the next active terminal.

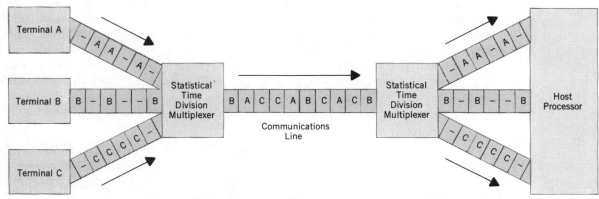

Figure 10.5 Transmission with statistical time division multiplexing.

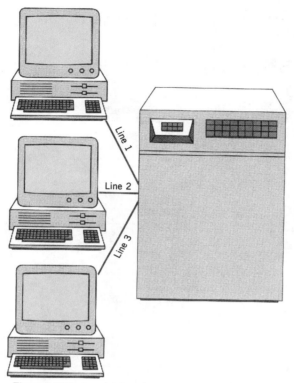

Figure 10.6 A point-to-point communications network.

The data stream for statistical time division multiplexing is illustrated in Figure 10.5.

Point-to-Point Lines

In a *point-to-point* communications network, each terminal sends data to and receives data from a computer by means of an individual line linking it directly to the computer. Figure 10.6 illustrates a point-to-point communications network.

A point-to-point communications network, where no terminal shares a line, is appropriate if constant, high-speed data transmission and response are necessary. This might be the case, for example, if the function of one computer system is to collect, process, and then transmit data to a larger computer system on a continuous basis. The costs of a point-to-point network are obviously substantial because a line and two modems must be allocated to every terminal in the network.

Multidrop Lines

Often a single terminal connected to a dedicated line is not active for enough time to justify its own separate line. An alternative to high-cost, underutilized

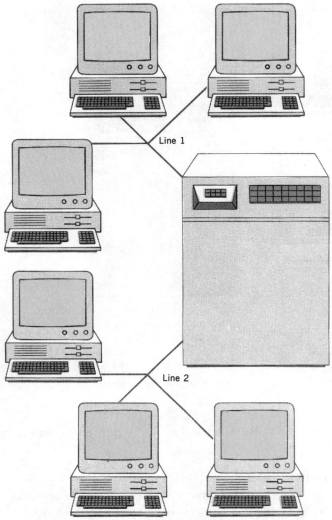

Figure 10.7 A multidrop communications network.

point-to-point connections is to connect several terminals to the same line, as shown in Figure 10.7. Because terminals are "dropped off" the communications line, this configuration is called a *multidrop*.

When a multidrop line is used, only one terminal on the line can send data at any one time. It is like a party line, insofar as if one person is in the midst of a call, all others on the party line must wait for that person to hang up before they can call out. It is unlike a party line, however, in that more than one terminal on the multidrop line can receive data at the same time.

The doubling up of lines and modems makes a multidrop configuration significantly less costly than a point-to-point communications network. Although a multidrop's terminals may be "busied out" during certain peak periods, a multidrop line configuration is normally sufficient for multiple terminal inquiry systems, especially if each inquiry can be stated briefly (i.e., in less than 5 seconds).

10.4 COMMUNICATION MEDIA

The most popular media types used to create telecommunications networks are twisted-pair wires, coaxial cable, fiber optic cable, terrestrial microwave, and satellite. Each is discussed in turn followed by an analysis of baseband and broadband signaling.

Twisted Pair

Twisted pair uses two standard wires that are separately insulated and twisted together. The twisted pair is protected by an outer layer of insulation called a jacket. Twisted pair is relatively inexpensive and easy to install. Because it is the same type of cable used in telephone systems, the same cable may be used for forming the information systems network. The disadvantage of twisted pair is its narrow bandwidth. If transmission rates are in excess of 1 Mbps and cable runs are greater than 500 meters, twisted pair is a poor medium. Shielded twisted pair is more precisely made than regular twisted pair and can support both higher transmission rates and longer cable runs, up to 10 Mbps and over 1000 meters, respectively.

Coaxial Cable

Coaxial cable is made up of one wire, called a conductor, surrounded by a stranded shield that serves as a ground. The conductor and the ground are separated by thick insulation, and the entire cable is protected on the outside by an insulating jacket.

Coaxial cable is available in a wide variety of types and thicknesses. Thicker coaxial cable carries signals longer distances than does thinner cable, but thicker cable is more expensive and less flexible than thinner cable. Thicker coaxial cable may not be usable, however, in installations where cable must be pulled through existing cable trays or conduits with limited space or around tight corners.

Fiber Optic Cable

Fiber optic cable uses either plastic or glass fiber medium to carry light signals. Although plastic is more durable with respect to bending, glass provides a lower attenuation (i.e., loss of power) of the transmitted signal. Glass also has a wider bandwidth and permits higher data transfer rates than plastic.

The transmitter is the electrical-to-optical converter. The receiver is an optical-to-electrical converter. Optical cables range from simple, 1-fiber cables to complex, 18-fiber jacketed cables. An 18-fiber cable can provide nine full-duplex transmission channels. Various specially constructed cables can be manufactured to order by vendors.

Fiber optic cables offer many advantages over cables with metallic electrical conductors. Fiber optics have a wider bandwidth than do metallic conductors. Data rates of up to 10^{14} bits per second have been achieved on ultrapure fiber optics, whereas telephone twisted pair are typically limited to between 9600 to 14,400 bps. Moreover, fiber optics permit voice, video, and data transmission to be merged on one conductor.

Fiber optic cables can be laid in noisy electrical environments because optical energy is not affected by electromagnetic radiation. Fiber optic cables do not generate cross-talk because they do not generate electromagnetic radiation. Therefore, multiple fibers can be routed in one common cable. Optical fiber transmission has a lower bit-error rate than do corresponding metallic cable systems. Typically, only 1 in 100 billion bits of data transmitted by fiber optic is an error. The error rate for the next best medium, such as broadband coaxial, is 1 in 10 billion bits.

Because of low attenuation, fiber optic cables can be extended without the need for repeaters as is generally necessary with metallic cable systems. The absence of sparks makes fiber optic cables especially suitable in dangerous industrial environments, such as munitions factories, petrochemical product sites, refineries, chemical plants, and grain elevators. Because no electrical energy is transmitted, most building codes allow fiber optic cable to be installed without being run through a conduit. Also, the need for a common ground is eliminated.

The absence of radiated signals makes tapping virtually impossible. If tapping were attempted, it would be readily noticeable because a light signal loss would occur.

SECURITY OF FIBER OPTIC Equifax also needed an extra level of security it believed was available only with fiber optics. "Since two of the floors in the building would be leased to other companies, we wanted to make sure that there wouldn't be the opportunity to tap into our data cable," says Beth Springer, information systems consultant with Equifax.

"Including fiber as a part of its wiring topology also provided Equifax with the opportunity to incorporate numerous networks on a single cable. With the use of the Fiber Distributive Data Interface (FDDI)," she said, "it's possible to network Ethernet, IBM's Token-Ring and broadband CSMA networks and hook them all together."

Excerpted from Tony Pompili, "Mix-and-Match Cabling Plan Yields Savings," *PC Week*, January 5, 1988, p. C24.

Fiber optic cables are smaller and lighter than are metallic cables of equal transmission capacity. Fiber optic cable have the same tensile strength as steel wire of the same diameter and are more corrosion resistant than any metals.

Signals on electronic cabling must be retransmitted every mile or so by repeaters. Fiber optic cables can carry unrepeated signals over 150 miles without the aid of repeaters. This ability allows mainframes located miles apart to communicate with each other at the same high speeds at which they process data internally. For the global network user, AT&T offers a digital service, from the United States to Japan, a 7175-mile fiber optic cable. For example, American Airlines' Sabre reservation network uses it to connect with travel agencies and airports in Japan. In the long-haul domestic market, a number of carriers, in an attempt to compete against AT&T, have pooled their resources to form the national telecommunications network (NTN), a predominantly fiber optic–based network reaching most of the largest U.S. cities.

The major disadvantage of fiber optic is cable splicing. When fiber optic cables are spliced, each fiber end must be aligned precisely to permit the maximum amount of light to be transmitted between spliced fibers. This alignment is time consuming and costly. Technologically, the most significant limiting factor of fiber optic cable involves the connections between it and electronic devices, such as computers and printers. Signals carried by fiber optic cables must be converted by transceivers from light signals to electric signals to be understood by processing hardware. When the electronic hardware is ready to transmit, electric signals have to be converted to light signals.

Fiber optic cable can be used for the network backbone of many organizations for many reasons. First, because of its huge bandwidth capacity, once it

FDDI TO THE RESCUE FDDI accommodates high-performance workstations. These devices have such high transmission demands that a mere six to 12 nodes can serve to overload an Ethernet system. As a short-term expedient, managers can break the networks into smaller chunks, but they prefer to interconnect the machines. Companies with diskless workstations, which have their own heavy communications demands, also are high on the list of potential FDDI customers.

Other FDDI interests include mainframe-to-mainframe connections and interconnections among LANs. The latter FDDI application is of considerable interest to PC users and managers planning networks. FDDI is designed to take advantage of the strengths of fiber optics without being penalized by the technology's major limitations.

FDDI is based on token ring design with two fiber rings that interconnect all nodes. The two rings carry signals in opposite directions, providing redundancy, so one component failure will not shutdown the whole network. The backup ring can be used continually or switched on only in the event of a failure.

Excerpted from Jeff Hecht, "FDDI: Next-Generation LAN Promises Fast Links, Reliability," *PC Week,* June 9, 1987, pp. C1, C35–C37 is in place, a company would probably never have to lay cable again. Second, the life of fiber optic cable is estimated to be over 50 years with virtually no maintenance. A third reason why a company might adopt a fiber optic alternative is because the price disparity between fiber optic and coaxial cable has narrowed to the point where fiber optic may be the least expensive option for many companies that require high data rates and the integration of voice, data, and video.

In addition to its many advantages already enumerated, optical fiber is gaining great impetus for a network backbone from the fiber distributed data interface (FDDI), a standard supported by international standards groups including American National Standards Institute (ANSI). FDDI provides a 100-Mbps fiber optic network that contains two specifications, one for the physical layer and one for medium access control. FDDI accommodates up to 1,000 physical connections and a total fiber path of well over 100 miles. It uses a token passing access scheme and is based on a ring topology. Capacity allocation is controlled by a technique referred to as timed token rotation, whereby each device or station on the network keeps track of how long it has been since it last saw the token. When it next sees the token, the station seizes it and sends synchronous or asynchronous messages. This kind of technique provides good support for a variety of interactive and bulk data transfer applications.

Microwave

Microwave transmission technology is being used more and more for building private networks. Newer microwave systems operate in the 18- to 23-gigahertz (GHz) range of the electromagnetic wave spectrum, although all waves above the 1-GHz mark are considered microwaves.

Microwave offers features that often make it more attractive than cable-based local systems, especially in metropolitan areas. An 18-GHz microwave band can carry several 1.5-Mbps channels that support voice and data transmission simultaneously. Moreover, installation is much quicker than with cable-based systems. Space is no longer a problem because typical microwave antennas are less than 18 inches in diameter and the associated electronic gear can fit into a weatherproof box less than 24 inches square. Operators of microwave systems, however, still need a license from the Federal Communications Commission.

Maximum usable distance is one of the main differences between bands. Users of the 2-GHz band can transmit as far as 30 miles between stations. On the 18-GHz band, the maximum distance is about 15 miles. On the 23-GHz band, the optimal distance is about 3 miles.

Microwave antennas are more efficient the higher the frequency. As a result, the higher-frequency bands can use smaller antennas. Antennas for a 2-GHz system are 6 feet to 8 feet in diameter; a 23-GHz system can use antennas a little larger than a car headlight.

The trade-offs for microwave are that frequency bands in the 2-GHz to 6-GHz range are the most difficult to license, require the largest antennas and towers, provide the longest links (up to 30 miles), and have the most interference problems. Frequency bands of 18-GHz and 23-GHz are easiest to license, require the smallest antennas and towers, provide the shortest links (as little as 3 miles), and have the fewest interference problems.

The path traveled by the microwaves not only must be a clear line of sight, but there must be enough clearance above terrain, buildings, or other obstructions to accommodate wavelengths. Microwave energy travels in wavefronts that can be affected by obstacles along the route. The space above and below the line of sight, called Fresnel zones, must be kept clear of obstructions for optimal system performance.

Satellites

Satellites, called "birds" by the aerospace industry, are becoming increasingly significant tools for transmitting data as alternatives to traditional terrestrial circuits, especially leased telephone lines. Distance means nothing to a satellite, as their receiving and transmitting cone can cover a district office, city, state, or continent. Moreover, one message can be broadcast once to hundreds or thousands of receivers. Error rates are about 1 in 10 million bits transmitted.

SATELLITE NETWORKS Large data networks based on satellite technology are built around two different kinds of ground stations: a few huge, powerful, costly hub stations and many less expensive, much weaker Very Small Aperture Terminals (VSATs) that have dishes less than six feet in diameter. In such a configuration, "The hub shouts and the VSATs whisper," said Frank Zimmerman, manager of systems applications for GTE Spacenet Corp. of McLean, VA.

Because each VSAT can communicate only with the hub, VSAT technology is well suited for many-to-one network communications. Satellite networks typically are alternatives to multidrop leased ground lines.

John Helliwell, "The Hub Shouts While the VSATs Whisper in Satellite Networks," *PC Week*, July 21, 1987, p. C33.

Ku band (11 GHz to 14 GHz) and very small aperture terminal (VSAT) earth-to-satellite dishes offer cost-effective options for data transmission. VSATs are easier to install and suffer less from atmospheric impedance than do older C band (4-GHZ to 6-GHz) dishes. Data rates for Ku band run anywhere from 1.2 Kbps to 1.544 Mbps and beyond with one-half-second propagation. Generally, a good response is 3 to 4 seconds. No wonder that some telecommunications experts are dubbing satellite communications and fiber optics as the "dynamic duo."

Baseband Versus Broadband

Baseband and broadband are the two basic approaches to signal transmission. Baseband uses the entire available bandwidth to form one channel. Digital signals are serialized and transmitted directly on the link without being modulated. DEC's Ethernet is a complete physical and electrical characterization of a baseband network using coaxial cable. The advantages of baseband are (1) it is popular (used by DEC's Ethernet and IBM's Token Ring); (2) it is an accepted standard; (3) it is relatively cheap to install and maintain; (4) its choices for media include twisted-pair wires, coaxial cable, and fiber optics; (5) its high data rates can be supported (1 to 10 Mbps); and (6) it is easy to make connections. The disadvantages of baseband are (1) it can only be used for short distances not to exceed $1\frac{1}{2}$ miles, (2) it is susceptible to cross-talk and other noises typical of wire and cable (shielding of the baseband cable can be installed in the noisiest areas of the site to lessen this disadvantage), and (3) it has no real-time voice or video.

Broadband subdivides the available bandwidth into discrete bands permitting simultaneous transmission of multiple signals. Coaxial cable is especially applicable to broadband transmission because of its large bandwidth capacity. Radio frequency modems are required to modulate transmissions onto appropriate channel carrier frequencies and to ensure that they do not interfere with each other. Community antenna television (CATV) systems have used broadband transmission successfully over coaxial cable for years. The advantages of broadband are (1) it has an exceptionally wide bandwidth, which can be split into multiple channels; (2) a broadband coaxial cable can simultaneously support multiple carriers for data, voice, and video transmission; (3) broadband is often used as a "backbone" to which small departmental local area networks are connected for interdepartmental communications; and (4) it has a range of up to 30 miles. Broadband's disadvantages are (1) it doesn't have a set of standards, so it requires more design expertise; (2) it requires much more maintenance support for the radio frequency components; (3) broadband connections are costly and the system has to be retuned when connections are made; and (4) broadband is not widely adopted yet.

Media Selection

The preceding discussion of media and signaling indicates the wide range of media types and capabilities. To select the appropriate media or hybrid, it is important to perform sufficient systems analysis to determine current and projected communications requirements, points of access, and bandwidths.

If distributed processing is limited and simple networking is anticipated, twisted-pair media connected to a dial-up public telephone system may be adequate. Extra pairs of cable are commonly run when a telephone system is installed offering the possibility that the extra pairs can be used for data.

The caveat for traditional telephone communications is that voice transmissions are much more tolerant of media flaws than are data transmissions. Even today, portions of the telephone system consist of analog equipment not very well suited for data transmission. For example, noise on the line may be only irritating during a telephone conversation; the same noise may cause a number of severe problems for data transmission.

If, on the other hand, the proposed information system will be fully integrated, requiring channels to carry voice, video, and data throughout the organization, then a combination of fiber optic, coaxial cable, satellite, and microwave may be in order.

No doubt that most organizations will use broadband media in the future. Furthermore, fiber optic will probably be preferred over coaxial cable. When the telephone system converts to an integrated digital network, twisted pair will be a viable option.

10.5 NETWORK ARCHITECTURES, STANDARDS, AND PROTOCOLS

Someone once said, probably facetiously, the great thing about standards is that there are so many of them. This wag was probably talking about telecommunication standards because of the existence of so many network architectures, standards, and protocols. A large number of computer vendors and standardization groups are each trying to achieve computer interconnection through universal acceptance of their respective computer network architectures and protocols.

Communications between network facilities and vendor products can be compared to communications between representatives at the United Nations—the need for many translators. Indeed, some telecommunications experts estimate that over 25 percent of the total available computer power is being used to provide conversion systems between disparate elements in networks. Caught within this maze of competing network standards are frustrated systems analysts, not sure which vendor and media to select. No doubt that those systems analysts who successfully standardize all their information system on a common network architecture will build information systems that produce a strong competitive and productivity advantage.

General Definitions

The architecture of a network defines the functions that the network and its nodes perform. Network protocols provide the basic rules of formatting and handling data that are transmitted from one part of the network to another, and to overcome problems of incompatibility between different devices that are connected to the network. Closely related to architectures and protocols are network standards promulgated by various national and international standards bodies, and even some vendors, whose purported aim is the achievement of mutual compatibility between architectures and protocols, thus creating an "open systems environment."

In accordance with the network architecture, the functions of a network and the protocols that implement them operate at seven different levels and layers. At the lowest level are the physical transmission protocols concerned with linking and routing. At the middle level are transport, session, and presentation protocols responsible for end-to-end transmission and data conversion. At the top level are application protocols that handle end-user functions.

The Standards Jumble

Each of the major mainframe and minicomputer vendors markets its own proprietary network architecture. Major examples include IBM's systems network architecture (SNA) and DEC's DECnet. While each provides roughly the same basic networking functions, they are still incompatible with one another, except by the use of gateways.

SPEAKING IN DIFFERENT TONGUES

Imagine living in a country where the populace spoke English, the courts used French, schools taught in Spanish and civil servants used Russian. The resulting confusion closely approximates the problems of a multiple-architecture (heterogeneous) LAN. Although there is movement to establish a common language built around SAA (Systems Application Architecture) and APPC (Advanced Program-to-Program Communications), the realization of the dream is still years away. Today, connectivity among mixed-computer architectures adds to confusion and can slow the development of work-group productivity.

Organizations with a major investment in computer systems want everything tied together. Files created on the corporate mainframe can be transferred to the PCs for massaging, and files from the PCs can seamlessly transfer to Macintoshes for desktop publishing. Everyone can choose the best computer for the applications he or she is performing. The concept is so inviting that it fogs the harsh reality: mixed systems are a pain to design, administer, maintain and use.

Excerpted from Del Jones, "Homogeneous vs. Heterogeneous LANs: Mixed Architecture Isn't the Answer," *PC Week*, January 26, 1988, p. C41.

The incompatibility between vendors is not by accident because vendors seek to lock users into their systems and software. Going their own way among vendors has a long history. For example, back in the mid-1960s, IBM successfully countered the existing standard for a coding scheme, the American Standard Code for Information Interchange (ASCII), with its own binary synchronous communication representation, the extended binary coded decimal interchange code (EBCDIC). This means a terminal transmitting in ASCII has to go through a conversion process to communicate with IBM products.

Various standards groups such as the Consultative Committee for International Telephone and Telegraph (CCITT) and the International Standards Organization (ISO) are specifying a collection of architectural layers and protocols to allow communication between the products of different vendors. For example, an important packet-level protocol is CCITT's X.25 protocol. Or, another example, the open system interconnection (OSI) reference model promulgated by ISO is a seven-layer architecture of protocols that has become one of the "standards" for interconnecting systems, products, and networks of different manufacturers.

The Department of Defense has specified its own network architectural protocols called transmission control protocol/internet protocol (TCP/IP). General Motors has developed manufacturing automation protocol (MAP), Boeing has developed technical office protocol (TOP), and electronic data interchange (EDI) is based on ANSI standards. Furthermore, a model that is likely to become the standard base for transmission of data is integrated services digital network (ISDN).

If all vendors eventually adopt a total standard, true multivendor networking will become a reality. What is more likely to happen, however, is that major vendors will continue promoting their own proprietary network architectures among their own products, while at the same time offering portions of OSI architectural protocols, and TCP/IP, MAP, and TOP, in gateway products for communication in mixed-vendor environments. Also, it is expected that most terminals, processors, and communication devices will become ISDN compatible.

Open System Interconnection Model

In 1977, the International Standards Organization created the Open System Interconnection Subcommittee to develop an open system interconnection reference model to serve as a framework around which a series of standard protocols could be defined. The result is displayed in Figure 10.8, which represents a total system network architecture. "Open" means that it enables any end user to communicate with another end user without being constrained by equipment of a particular vendor. It is hierarchical, meaning that a layer connects only with layers immediately above and below it.

The telecommunications network must perform a number of functions to enable connected devices to send and receive messages. All these functions are defined within the seven layers of the OSI model. One of the advantages of separating network functions into architectural layers is that it provides mod-

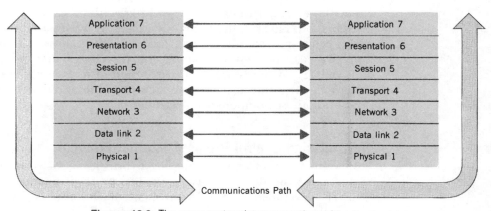

Figure 10.8 The open system interconnection reference model.

ularity for easy facility changes. A given architectural layer may only communicate with the adjacent layers immediately above and below it, therefore ensuring that modularity and independence of architectural layer functions are preserved.

Layer 1 is the physical layer that deals with hardware specifications. It is responsible for electrical, mechanical, and procedural interfaces with the actual transmission medium (e.g., twisted pair, coaxial), including such parameters as voltage levels, number of pins required (e.g., on RS-232C, RS-449, or X.21 connectors), and circuit activation and deactivation. Layer 2 is the data link layer. It provides error detection and correction and flow control. It provides error-free messages to layer 3. Typical data link level protocols are X.25, high-level data link control (HDLC), synchronous data link control (SDLC), and binary synchronous control (BSC). Layer 3, the network layer, is responsible for the efficient routing, addressing, and "packetizing" of data through the network. Layer 4, the transport layer, is responsible for communication between the transmitting and receiving devices. It is the keystone of standardized computer communications and is often referred to as the host-to-host or end-to-end layer because it includes all the facilities needed to manage the flow of messages from source to destination across simple or complex networks. It insulates the upper three layers from the telecommunications nuts and bolts, thereby permitting communication facilities to change without requiring modification to upper-layer procedures.

Layers 1 through 3 are hardware based with layer 4 being both hardware and software based. Layer 5, the session layer, is for message delivery and reception. It manages the interchange between the user and a process on another machine in an orderly manner. It is responsible for initiating, maintaining, and terminating each session between end users. Because the session layer is usually handled by the host computer's operating system, it would be easy for the session and transport layers to merge into a single layer.

Layer 6, the presentation layer, manipulates the data for presentation to the application layer so that applications may exchange data irrespective of each application's representation of that data, such as different character codes (e.g., EBCDIC to ASCII), encryption and decryption, screen formatting, and data compression. Layer 7, the application layer, provides a set of utilities for application programs that interface directly with the end user. It also includes functions like password authentication, user directories, and file transfer.

As OSI advances, the modular design of its layered architecture makes it easier to incorporate and integrate new protocols and new technologies, without disrupting those components already in place.

Transmission Control Protocol/Internet Protocol

Users and vendors typically employ hybrid levels of protocols from the OSI model and from the transmission control protocol/internet protocol standard. TCP/IP, developed by the Department of Defense, addresses the third and fourth layers in the seven-layer OSI model. TCP/IP opens a transparent data "pipeline" between end network nodes and ensures that data are routed properly and delivered without errors. This physical transport of data is achieved by either a LAN or WAN using the X.25 packet-switching interface. One of the weaknesses in the OSI model is its inability to tie together different networks. The strength of TCP/IP lies in its abilities to route data between different networks (e.g., X.25, Ethernet, and Token Ring) and to manage networks that include thousands of nodes. Some refer to TCP/IP as the "superglue that can connect all the devices together."

Manufacturing Automation Protocol
Technical Office Protocol

Another important development in standardization of systems network architectures has been the manufacturing automation protocol, developed by General Motors, and the technical office protocol developed by Boeing. As mentioned in Chapter 5, the objective of MAP is to define a local network and associated communication protocols for computing resources, programmable controllers, and robots within a plant or factory complex. MAP uses the OSI model, especially the transport layer, as its reference. It uses the token bus network, generally the preferable protocol in a manufacturing environment. MAP requires a broadband instead of a baseband network. Broadband is necessary because of its ability to handle voice and video as well as data transmission. Moreover, broadband networks possess high tolerances needed in a factory environment.

A few adjacent devices can be easily hard-wired together using twisted-pair wiring, but in a manufacturing plant, where many different devices are spread over thousands of square feet, a single coaxial broadband cable provides easy connection and allows greater flexibility. Growth in operations can result in a spaghetti of wires, taking up space and making diagnosis of network problems difficult, if not impossible. With twisted pair, each time a device is added, additional cabling costs are incurred. Moreover, broadband can handle synchronous or asynchronous devices concurrently and connect devices with different data rates. MAP products are, therefore, easier to install and interchange because of fewer wires and less wiring time.

TOP supports compatibility and interconnectivity within the office. MAP/TOP together provide full integration of a manufacturing organization's information system.

Systems Network Architecture

IBM's systems network architecture, introduced in 1974, was the first commercially available computer network architecture. Since that time, IBM has announced SNA-compatible software products for all of its mainframe operating systems, and front-end processors. While SNA once supported only host-centered, tree-structured network topologies, it is now possible to build a packet-switching network, such as X.25, with a web topology out of SNA products. It allows multiple routes between network users.

Like the OSI model, SNA is a seven-layer architecture. These are (1) physical control that connects nodes physically and electronically, (2) data link control that transmits error-free data along the circuits, (3) path control that routes data in packets between source and destination, (4) transmission control that paces data exchange to match data processing rates at source and destination, (5) data flow control that synchronizes data flow between source and destination, (6) presentation service that formats data for different nodes, and (7) transaction service that provides specific application services for the end user.

Most of IBM mainframe installation now uses SNA networking. Because SNA is so widely used, it has become a de facto networking standard. Therefore, a large number of vendors have developed SNA gateway products that permit non-IBM products to participate in SNA networks. Moreover, IBM has further strengthened its SNA strategy by incorporating it into its systems application architecture (SAA). SAA was primarily the result of some unique problems faced by IBM in linking up its many disparate computer families. Because SNA is the basis for development of IBM's future as well as current network products, it

---

NETWORK COMPETITORS

DECnet's architecture forgoes the endless designation of node types—Physical Units—that occur within SNA. "In IBM parlance, we have one logical unit and one physical unit," quips Steve Wendler, a DEC marketing manager. DEC emphasizes that the same DECnet software can reside on an Ethernet LAN or WAN using the X.25 protocol set as a subnetwork.

A key element in DEC's network strategy is software that provides links to SNA, allowing a DEC processor to emulate an IBM cluster controller. "DEC's links to SNA are as good as, if not better than, IBM's," says Barry Gilbert, vice-president of Market Information Center. DEC wants users to see DEC processors as extensions of the SNA network.

DEC's VMS operating system provides a single platform for application development. IBM's response to DEC's single platform is Systems Application Architecture (SAA). With SAA, IBM will provide a single programming interface.

According to Paul Rampel, president of Orion Network Systems, VMS is not suited to high-powered online transaction processing.

Dave Terrie, president of Newport Consulting, questions whether DEC's single-platform approach will do the vendor more harm than good. "For nearly a decade, DEC has followed its network-based single-architecture philosophy religiously," says Terrie. "Today, relying solely on VAX/VMS is as inappropriate for DEC as a multiple-architecture midrange strategy was for IBM."

The message: To succeed as network suppliers, both vendors will need to provide a broader range of solutions, and neither can afford the luxury of relying on the past.

Condensed from Gary Stix, "Peer Pressure," *Computer & Communications Decisions,* January 1988, pp. 58–60.

provides users with a stable architecture that they can adopt over long periods of time.

DECnet

DEC's DECnet is designed to help users of DEC's computer systems and terminals create integrated networked information systems. DECnet has the following eight layers, which are in many respects comparable to those of the OSI model: (1) physical link, (2) data link (both layers are similar to OSI, and they jointly handle Ethernet low-level protocols and communication with X.25 networks), (3) routing that provides communication paths for data packets between source and destination, (4) end-to-end communication, (5) session control, (6) network application that performs commonly used application functions, (7) network management that provides modules for network maintenance, and (8) user layer that provides application services for end users.

DECnet can connect local area networks and wide area networks and also link the LANs at different sites of an organization. It can provide gateways between DEC networks and those of other vendors. For example, it can connect DECnet networks with SNA networks. In addition, DECnet is in the process of changing to conform to the OSI model.

Electronic Data Interchange

A large number of diverse companies are implementing electronic data interchange, a set of ANSI-based communication standards. These standards enable a number of business transactions, such as ordering, billing, and paying, to be conducted between companies electronically.

EDI standards provide strong support for computer-to-computer ordering, discussed earlier in this book, because of electronic document exchange. Company A orders parts from company B; B transmits acknowledgment, shipping documents, and invoice to A; A receives goods by a freight carrier and checks goods against the invoice; A remits payment to B through bank wire transfers. This total transaction has been performed without any flow of paper forms, currency, or checks, and without the use of telephones.

ELIMINATING PAPER FORMS EDI is fast becoming a necessity for doing any business at all in many industries. "EDI is overtaking us like a steamroller, and we'd better be a part of it," said Robert Crowley, chairman of The Electronic Data Interchange Association.

There are few areas of commerce where EDI has not begun to take hold.

Excerpted from Don Steinberg, "Electronic Data Interchange Use Moves from the Few to the Many," *PC Week*, December 15, 1987, pp. C1, C4.

Integrated Services Digital Network

Today's large corporations typically use several separate communications networks to carry messages of different kinds. The most common is the telephone network, which provides analog lines for the local loop, requiring modems for digital-to-analog and analog-to-digital conversion at each end. The same organization might also be connected to a packet-switched network such as Arpanet or Telenet for computer communications; a private network of satellites, microwave, and fiber optics; and a telex network for international communications. With integrated digital services network, all messages will be transported over

---

EDI: ENDING THE COMMER- CIAL PAPER CHASE

"Doing business without EDI will soon be like trying to do business without the telephone," Edward R. Lucente, IBM vice-president, told attendees at the annual meeting of the Electronic Data Interchange Association (EDIA). "No EDI, no business."

General Motors gave its suppliers until 1987 to get online with EDI or go offline with GM. More often, a company that has implemented EDI uses the carrot of more orders or the stick of less orders to convince a doubter that paper is out and EDI is in.

"The question now is not whether to do EDI," Steve Korn, GE's manager of EDI product marketing says, "but how and when."

In the end, EDI won't determine whether the business lives or dies. "You can do all the EDI work you possibly can and have the best EDI vendor in the world," says Doug Fisher, vice-president of marketing for Yellow Freight. "But you're still selling your service. In our case, we're still selling where the rubber meets the road. If we don't deliver that, EDI won't matter."

The Transportation Data Coordinating Committee (TDCC), a group of EDI users, established four ground rules for EDI:

- It must provide generalized interface data standards and formats that will be responsive to users' needs for intercompany computer-to-computer transactions;
- Interface capability must be insensitive to internal computer equipment and programs of the interchange parties;
- EDI should leave to the using parties the selection of the option of communications speeds and services;
- It should have a capability of providing documents, when required, as a by-product of integrated database transactions.

Excerpted from Willie Schatz, "EDI: Putting the Muscle in Commerce and Industry," *Datamation,* March 15, 1988, pp. 56–64.

one "pipeline" instead of many separate ones. ISDN is intended to provide a common interface and a unified, global telecommunications network accessible by large and small companies, and even households through the telephone company's central office. Eventually, ISDN promises an easy-to-use interface, similar to plugging in an applicance that uses electricity provided by the local utility.

ISDN SIMPLIFIES CONNECTIVITY

Although Integrated Services Digital Network (ISDN) allows the U.S. Bank of Portland (Ore.) to conduct many connectivity-related applications, the true value of ISDN is that it provides a consistent way of doing what previously required a multitude of products and technologies, according to Earl Vogt, manager of the telecommunications services department at the bank.

"Most of what ISDN accomplishes can be done using existing products, but using one technology in place of many eliminates the need to constantly relearn and rethink how connectivity facilities are implemented," Mr. Vogt said.

ISDN's consistent approach to voice and data connectivity has paid off in several ways, particularly in the way connections between PCs and mainframes are implemented.

In an employee's office, for example, ISDN requires only one PC add-in board, software, and one ISDN twisted-pair wire to provide full connection to telephones or to a PC transmitting either asynchronously or synchronously to a mainframe.

Before ISDN, two telephone lines, one coaxial cable, a modem, a synchronous emulation board and software were required to accomplish the same connections.

ISDN has also made it easier for U.S. Bank to implement connections to a host computer at corporate data centers.

Condensed from Eric Hindin, "ISDN's Unified Front Solves some Big Headaches by Simplifying Training and Networking Tactics," *PC Week,* January 12, 1988, p. C47.

ISDN essentially replaces the old-fashioned circuit-based, hierarchical telephone and telegraph networks. It eliminates the need for coaxial cable, modems, multiplexers, and multiple networks because everything will run on ordinary telephone wire. Ideally, ISDN will allow an end user to plug a device into the network anywhere in the world and achieve virtually instant communications with any other device in the network, regardless of manufacturer. Two end users miles apart, for example, can discuss the contents of a graph on a screen and make changes to it in real time. A credit-granting employee in a small business can make online credit card checks with a remote computer without tying up the telephone for sales orders. Compared to conventional methods of transmission, ISDN technology offers simplicity of operations, increased data integrity, and higher transmission speeds. Moreover, it provides the base for an interesting portfolio of voice, video, and data services, such as teleconferencing, electronic mail, and automatic dialing.

10.6 NETWORKING WITH EMPHASIS ON LOCAL AREA NETWORKS

The first announcement on a local area network was made jointly by DEC, Intel, and Xerox in 1980. And by the announcement of the companies, a local area network along with its proprietary name of Ethernet was born. Since that time, a large number of other LANs have been announced by a variety of vendors.

The three most common network topologies are bus, ring, and star. DEC has its Ethernet bus, IBM has its Token ring, and AT&T has its Starlan star. So, one may argue that DEC is "Captain of the bus," IBM is "Lord of the ring," and AT&T is "Agent of the star." But hybrids have also evolved. For example, MAP uses a token system with a bus topology.

Although differences between LANs are great, they all share a number of common characteristics:

1. A LAN provides the facility through which processors, auxiliary storage, facsimile devices, printers, intelligent copiers, phototypesetters, telephones, and video devices are interconnected to communicate with one another. Some LANs interconnect hundreds of devices.

2. The purported aim of all LANs is to enable organizations to realize large productivity gains and cost savings through the inherent efficiencies of resource sharing. A LAN is a peer-to-peer communications network because all the devices on the network have equal access to all network facilities.

3. Because they are privately owned and installed so as not to interfere with the communications of other networks, LANs are not subject to the jurisdiction of federal or state regulatory agencies.

4. Generally, LANs are limited to a single building or a complex of buildings, although some devices on the network may extend up to 50 miles. This means that a LAN can connect communication devices located on different floors of a building, adjacent buildings, and in the same city.

5. Typically, transmission rates are between 1 and 10 Mbps. Some LANs, however, employ transmission rates well in excess of 10 Mbps. As you may suspect, the faster the data rate, the more the LAN costs.

6. Bus and ring topologies use a shared cable. This means that no two messages can be on one cable in the same place at the same time without colliding with each other, causing destruction of both messages. Devices must somehow transmit messages according to an access scheme by taking turns at using the cable. The main cable access scheme for a bus is contention; for a ring it is token passing. A star uses a central switch to control access.

Bus Topology

The linear bus topology is a simple design with a single length of cable, known as the bus or trunk that is shared by all devices on the network. See, for example, Figure 10.9.

The cable is terminated at both ends. Any device wishing to join the bus taps into the cable at the nearest convenient point via a T-connector, transceiver, interface cable (sometimes called a stub that is normally no more than 6 feet long), and a controller. Typically, the bus is coaxial or fiber optic cable.

Probably the most common contention access scheme for a bus is carrier sense multiple access with collision detection (CSMA-CD). It is probabilistic because users access on a first-come, first-served basis. For a device attempting to

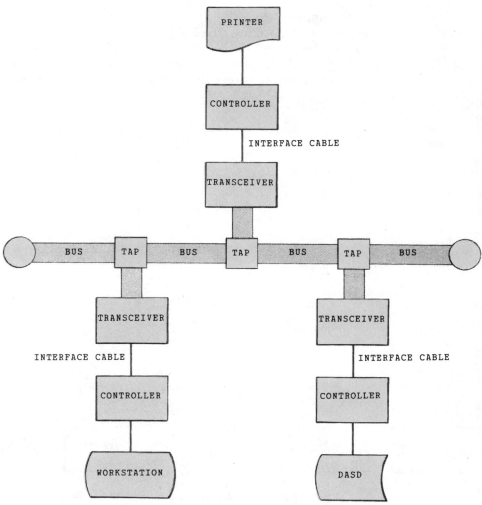

Figure 10.9 A LAN bus with connected devices.

communicate, it first listens for other traffic. If it senses none, it attaches a header to the front of the message being sent and listens for the header to come back. If all is clear, the message is sent. If a collision occurs, it will wait and try again. A retry algorithm reduces the likelihood that after a collision, two stations will transmit retries simultaneously. To lessen the volume of data collisions on the network, systems analysts can partition the network into subnetworks.

In a CSMA-CD network, devices must contend with one another for access to the data communications pathway. Therefore, during periods of heavy demand, performance falls, and the actual network speed is significantly lower than the specified network speed. Contention schemes were designed to function best where network traffic is spread evenly among all devices. Often, however, this is not the case in many installations. To help reduce the probability of losing packets of data, multiple receive buffers can be installed to hold overflow messages.

Ring Topology

Figure 10.10 illustrates a typical LAN ring. Each device is connected to the ring by an access connector, which is connected to a repeater that is actually on the ring. Typically, transmission media are coaxial cable, fiber optic, or twisted pair.

The repeater regenerates signals and passes them on to the next device in

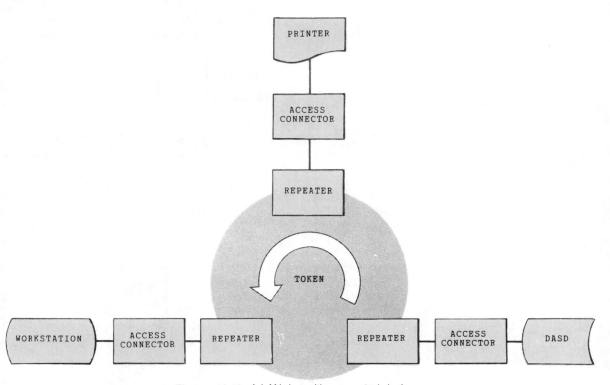

Figure 10.10 A LAN ring with connected devices.

the ring. The access box acts as an interface between the device and the repeater. Generally, a unique device, called a monitor or server, is attached to the ring, or other networks, to monitor and manage the network. Servers will be discussed in a later section.

Traffic in a ring usually flows in one direction only. Each ring device receives messages from one of its neighbors and sends messages to its other neighbor. Although several ring protocols are used, the token ring is the most popular. The token circulates around the ring carousel-like whenever all devices are idle. When a device wants to send a message, it seizes the token and removes it before it transmits. The amount of data that may be transmitted during possession of the token is limited so that all devices can share the cable equally. After it has completed transmitting its message, it releases the token.

Token passing is a deterministic access scheme. Because of the prescribed rules for using the token, it is possible to anticipate the interval between transmissions of a particular device. Certain factory automation applications, such as process control and robotics, can only be managed properly by a deterministic access scheme. MAP, for example, uses a token bus architecture, in which messages move along a linear, not circular, path. Computers, robots, and other machines are linked together along a strand of coaxial cable. The machines communicate by passing an electronic envelope (token) rapidly back and forth. A computer can tell each of the robot painters in the network the model, style, and color of the next car they must paint. A token bus such as MAP is a hybrid, using a bus topology with a token passing access scheme.

Other hybrids are also evolving. In most networks, the links are much more reliable than the network interfaces. Therefore, an approach to improving reliability of rings is to localize all interfaces within a central control and mainte-

TOKEN RING VERSUS ETHERNET "For bigger and busier LANs, token ring is the top achiever in efficiency, maintainability, and transmission media flexibility. The key to a token-ring network's efficiency is its token-passing access method, which guarantees that every node on a token-ring network will have access to the network in a predictable time period. CSMA/CD (carrier sense multiple access/collision detection) networks, on the other hand, fail under heavy loads and become slower as more nodes are added."

Howard Saliven, chairman and founder of Proteon, Inc.

"Because of its acceptance as an industry standard, Ethernet enjoys a number of advantages. In the performance area, Ethernet is king. Over the years, Ethernet has been optimized by LAN system vendors to accomplish reliable, high-performance transmission. And Ethernet has been a key in the communications link between the engineering labs and commercial office systems."

Edward Cooper, manager of marketing programs, Excelan, Inc.

nance closet. Several ring network vendors, including IBM, have taken such a star-shaped ring approach.

Star Topology

More and more "smart" buildings are being constructed that include a telecommunications backbone of fiber optic or coaxial cable and a digital private automatic branch exchange (PABX). Data, voice, and video communications; energy management; building and grounds security; heating and air conditioning; and other similar needs are handled as utilities. A PABX-controlled network provides a real alternative to bus and ring LANs.

The star topology is arranged like a star with cables radiating from a central hub, in this case, a PABX (PABX is also called a computerized branch exchange, CBX). The star uses no shared cables; each device has its own dedicated cable, as depicted in Figure 10.11.

Once digital services arrive as specified by the integrated services digital network standard, then the digital PABX can easily handle voice, data, and video on existing telephone wiring, that is, the existing twisted pair. The telephone handset will be transformed into a data terminal. The distinction between LANs and wide area networks will become blurred because the digital PABX acts as the controller and hub of the network and provides easy-to-access gateways to other networks, both public and private.

As more terminals and computers are networked and distributed to both internal facilities and external elements (e.g., stakeholders and outside data bases), switching capabilities of a digital PABX become apparent. It eliminates modems and integrates voice, data, and video traffic, and it is capable of switching this traffic among a variety of equipment including data terminals, intelligent copiers, word processors, files, telephones, computers, and facsimile.

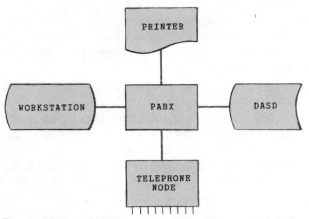

Figure 10.11 A PABX-based star LAN with connected devices.

PBX ALTERNATIVE Digital PBX systems have great agility in linking networks in several buildings. While LAN vendors such as Novell are just now developing or debuting products to allow two or more LANs to be interconnected, digital PBX manufacturers have always provided such capabilities.

Most PBXs are capable of being joined remotely via dedicated circuits or public data networks. This process creates the impression that all users are connected to the same PBX. All users can take advantage of all the features provided by any PBX linked via those dedicated circuits. Rolm, for example, provides interfaces that convert digitized voice or data to T1 format, or to X.25 format.

T1 links specify information-transmission speeds of 1.54 Mbps, and are commonly used by large corporations to bypass local telephone company switching offices in linking remote computers and telephones with each other. X.25 is the standard protocol used by most public and private networks designed specifically for data transmission.

Condensed from Eric Hindin, "Digital PBX Systems Have Long Lead over LANs in Link Agility," *PC Week*, January 12, 1988, p. C16.

LAN Topologies Compared

The star is more acceptable to a centralized management philosophy. The ring and bus are more amenable to a decentralized management philosophy.

Cable fault detection in a star network is simple because each device has its own cable. A fault at one device will not affect other devices. The network will continue to function. Also, with other topologies, each device attached to the network takes a portion of the bandwidth. In a star, each device's cable is dedicated to it. Therefore, as each device is added to the network, the aggregate bandwidth increases. This approach requires more cable and is therefore more costly. If, however, devices are in close proximity, then a star may match or exceed the economy of other topologies.

If the central controller, such as a digital PABX fails, then the whole system is down. Generally, such a situation is unlikely because of the robustness of digital PABXs. Their mean time between failure (MTBF) is measured in years. Network performance, however, is still limited by the capacity of the central PABX.

Generally speaking, the star is the most reliable and expensive topology. The ring is the least reliable because if any network device fails or if there is a break anywhere in the network, the entire LAN is disabled. But the ring is least expensive. The bus is a compromise in both reliability and cost. Because traffic travels in both directions in most buses, a break does not necessarily disable the network, but multiple breaks cause some devices to be unavailable to others. Also, because devices are attached to rather than integrated into the bus, the failure of a device does not affect the rest of the network as it would with a ring topology. Normally, a bus network is not significantly more expensive than a ring network.

Of the two major access schemes in use today, token passing and CSMA-CD, token passing networks provide better user response time, faster data transfer, and the ability to support larger networks. With a digital PABX, switching messages can be handled on a priority or first-come, first-served basis. The PABX gives greater flexibility in access, message switching, and interconnection of devices.

Network Servers

In many LANs, network and peripheral management functions are centralized and handled by special-purpose computers called network servers. Such servers are generally common to all three LAN topologies. A file server, for example, regulates access to magnetic disks and processes requests to shuttle logical files from one device to another. The disk server, therefore, enables network participants to share disk files. Printer servers work the same way.

The choice of a network server can materially affect the performance of a LAN. Even though the network server does not perform application processing, its work load may be extremely high. Every time a device requests access to a hard disk, printer, or other resource controlled by the server, it must receive and process the request and then return a reply.

SERVING THE LAN "We use two file servers per network to smooth out the processing load as well as to provide backup and recovery," said Frank Bruno, manager of special projects and a vice-president at Home Federal.

The Compaqs have IBM Token-Ring Adapter IIs installed. All PS/2s have Token-Ring Adapter/As installed.

"At the beginning of each work day, both file servers contain the same files and data. Each server has primary responsibility for a different subset of files," Mr. Bruno said.

Mainframe access is obtained through the gateway PS/2s, which run the IBM PC 3270 Emulation Program version 3, and have synchronous modems which connect to Home Federal's San Diego mainframes.

Excerpted from David Strom, "Bank's LAN Links Regional Loan Centers," *PC Week*, July 28, 1987, p. C9.

When several requests arrive at the server at the same time, the server places the requests in a queue and answers them in sequence. While the network server is processing requests, it must also handle administrative tasks, such as managing the request queue, denying access to secured files, sending acknowledgment messages to users, and maintaining a variety of indexes and directories. A file server can also provide store-and-forward services that eliminate LAN tag, the equivalent of telephone tag.

A server should have the capacity to handle a number of requests received simultaneously and thus prevent a throughput bottleneck. Clearly, the throughput capacity of the server must match the needs of the LAN. If a LAN's applications make frequent index and directory updates, the indexes and directory, along with frequently used data sets, can be kept in cache memory of the server. This arrangement will normally produce improved performance.

LANs versus WANs

LANs as we already know are networks that are either contained inside a single building or site whose farthest device is not more than 40 to 50 miles, but typically not more than 1 or 2 miles. Wide area networks cover larger regions having distances between nodes of hundreds or even thousands of miles.

WANs include public-switched telephone networks, circuit-switched data networks, and packet-switched data networks. Generally, WANs are mixed-media networks, using a combination of terrestrial lines and satellites.

Bridges and Gateways

To realize their full potential, LANs and WANs must be able to communicate with other LANs and WANs. Such communications are achieved through bridges and gateways.

BRIDGING LANs

Networks using CSMA/CD (carrier sense multiple access/collision detect) technology, such as Ethernet networks, are subject to more collisons and retransmissions. Nodes on token-passing networks are subject to longer delays in receiving the "token" as the number of stations on the network increases.

Therefore, an important reason for bridging networks is to increase performance. A bridge can make a large network into several smaller networks. Within each network, the amount of traffic is low enough that response time is acceptable, and since most of the communication is between the workstations and network resources of members of the affinity network, little data needs to cross the bridge.

Some speed lost is in crossing a bridge due to the overhead of the bridge itself. But data crosses the bridge only rarely, on those occasions when a user on one side of the bridge needs a resource or data that is on the other side.

Excerpted from Roger Addelson, "What Constitutes the Ideal Bridge?" *PC Week,* August 11, 1987, pp. C27–C28.

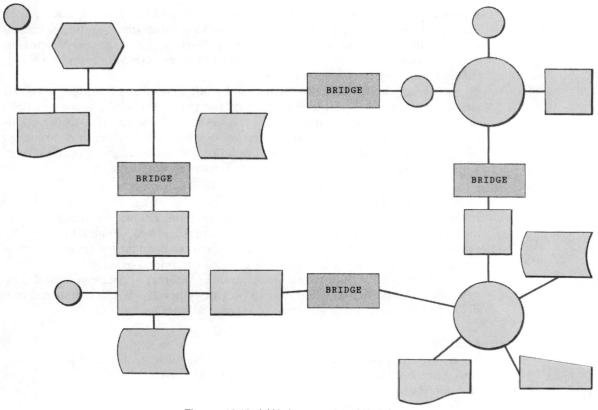

Figure 10.12 LANs interconnected by bridges.

A bridge allows one LAN to connect to other LANs, forming a configuration of LANs within the premises of an organization, as illustrated in Figure 10.12.

Most organizations need more than one type of LAN. For example, strategic-level executives may need a broadband star LAN to handle voice, video, and graphics for strategic decision support systems. The accounting department may need a baseband ring LAN for data transmission only. The shop floor may need a broadband bus LAN. Generally, it would be necessary for all these LANs to be interconnected.

GATEWAYS TO GREATER PROCESSING POWER A financial services company installed multiple gateways to provide brokers and office staff with LAN access to 56 mainframes and information services. Gateways included asynchronous, bisynchronous, X.25, and IBM 3270.

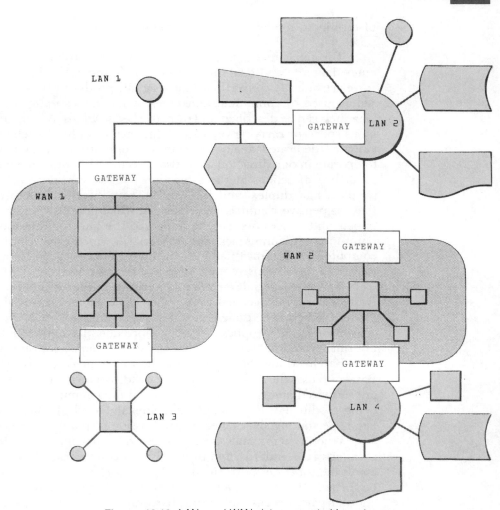

Figure 10.13 LANs and WANs interconnected by gateways.

A gateway links a variety of networks. Figure 10.13 shows a typical topology of interconnected networks of varying kinds, displaying the structure of a metanetwork, whose components consist of several LANs and WANs. All kinds of computers and other information processing devices are attached directly to both LANs and WANs.

SUMMARY

The second technology building block is telecommunications and networking. Telecommunications is the use of electronic and light-transmitting media to communicate between nodes across distance. It has been traditionally comprised of terminals, modems, channels, communications processors, and a host computer.

Terminals in a data communications configuration represent devices that enter data into and take information out of the network. A modem is a device for electronically converting digital signals produced by a computer to analog signals used by communications lines. A modem can also reverse this process. Channels can be described under many classifications. A channel can be classified by its speed or carrying capacity. A line can be either switched/dial-up or non-switched/dedicated, analog or digital. Communications channels can be arranged to operate in one direction only, two directions but only one direction at a time, or in two directions at the same time. These transmission modes are called simplex, half duplex, and full duplex, respectively. To improve utilization of these expensive channels, multiplexers, which interleave data to and from terminals and processors, can be added to the line configuration. In place of a point-to-point communications network, in which each terminal is linked to a computer by an individual line, several terminals can be connected to one line to form a less expensive multidrop line configuration.

The most popular media comprising telecommunications networks are twisted-pair wires, coaxial cable, fiber optic cable, terrestrial microwave, and satellite. Fiber optic cables offer many advantages over twisted-pair wires and coaxial cable. Fiber optics can carry more data, have lower bit-error rates, and are smaller and lighter than metallic cables of equal transmission capacity.

Baseband and broadband are the two approaches to signal transmission. Baseband uses the entire available bandwidth to form one channel. Digital signals are serialized and transmitted directly on the communications channel without being modulated. Broadband subdivides the available bandwidth into discrete bands permitting simultaneous transmission of multiple signals.

When systems analysts build a network, they must be concerned about the architecture, standards, and protocols of that network. They must be concerned about the functions performed by the network and its nodes, and how data will be formatted and handled when transmitted from one part of the network to another part. Because numerous hardware vendors and groups have proposed different network architectures and protocols, no universally accepted network standards exist.

Common network topologies of local area networks are the bus, ring, and star. On one end of the spectrum, the star topology is the most expensive and reliable topology. It is also the most acceptable LAN topology to a centralized management organization. On the other end of the spectrum, the bus topology, preferred by a decentralized management organization, is less expensive and less reliable than the star topology. No matter what the topology in place, however, LANs can be combined with other LANs and joined to wide area networks by means of bridges and gateways.

IMPORTANT TERMS

American National Standards
Institute (ANSI)

American Standard Code for
Information Interchange (ASCII)

analog system

asynchronous transmission

attenuation

baseband

Bell operating company (BOC)

bits per second (BPS)

bridge

broadband

bus network topology

C band

carrier sense multiple access with collision detection (CSMA-CD)

coaxial cable

community antenna television (CATV)

computerized branch exchange (CBX)

concentrator

conditioning

Consultative Committee for International Telephone and Telegraph (CCITT)

DECnet

digital system

electronic data interchange (EDI)

extended binary coded decimal interchange code (EBCDIC)

fiber distributed data interface (FDDI)

fiber optic cable

flat rate

front-end processor

full-duplex mode

gateway

gigahertz (GHz)

half-duplex mode

host computer

integrated services digital network (ISDN)

intelligent switch

intelligent terminal

International Standards Organization (ISO)

Ku band

line speed

local area networks (LANs)

manufacturing automation protocol (MAP)

measured rate

microwave

million bits per second (Mbps)

modem

multidrop

National Telecommunications Network (NTN)

network servers

nonswitched/leased/dedicated/ private line

open system interconnection (OSI)

point-to-point network

private automatic branch exchange (PABX)

protocols

remote job entry (RJE)

ring network topology

satellite

simplex mode

smart building

star network topology

statistical time division multiplexer (STDM)

switched/dial-up/public line

synchronous transmission

systems network architecture (SNA)

T-spans

tapered rate

technical office protocol (TOP)

telephone channels

time division multiplexer (TDM)

token ring

transmission control protocol/ internet protocol (TCP/IP)

twisted pair

very small aperture terminal (VSAT)

visual display unit (VDU)

wide area networks (WANs)

Assignment

REVIEW QUESTIONS

10.1 What is the purpose of terminals in a data communications configuration? the purpose of modems?

10.2 What are low-speed channels? voice-grade lines? T-spans?

10.3 List the cost alternative offered users of nonswitched lines.

10.4 What is the difference between the three types of basic transmission modes?

10.5 Contrast the two types of data transmission.

10.6 What is the primary function of a front-end processor? an intelligent switch? a concentrator?

10.7 How does a statistical time division multiplexer differ in its operation from a time division multiplexer? What does it do better than a TDM?

10.8 How does a multidrop communications network differ from a point-to-point communications network? What economies are achieved by a multidrop over a point-to-point network?

10.9 What is the upper limit in carrying capacity and cable runs of twisted pair? of shielded twisted pair?

10.10 Describe the material composition of coaxial cable.

10.11 List six advantages of fiber optic cables over cables with metallic electrical conductors. What is the major disadvantage of fiber optic cable?

10.12 What features often make microwave more attractive than cable-based systems?

10.13 Define the two approaches to signal transmission. List three advantages and disadvantages of each approach.

10.14 What factors play a role in selecting appropriate media for a telecommunications network?

10.15 Define what is meant by the terms "network architecture" and "network protocols."

10.16 What is the open system interconnection model? What does each of its layers represent?

10.17 Contrast the seven layers of IBM's systems network architecture to the eight layers of Digital Equipment's DECnet.

10.18 What is intended to be provided by integrated services digital network?

10.19 List six common characteristics shared by local area networks.

10.20 Describe how a device is connected to local area networks under a bus topology; a ring topology. Describe the mechanism each topology uses to accept a message from a device on the LAN.

10.21 Compare the star to the ring network topology.

10.22 What is the function of network servers in LANs?

10.23 How is one local area network connected to another LAN? How can these LANs be connected to a wide area network?

QUESTIONS FOR DISCUSSION

10.24 Discuss the issues to be considered in designing a data communications network.

10.25 What factors do you think will turn the integrated services digital network into reality?

10.26 Assume a centralized management organization. Discuss the difficulties that could occur if an improper network topology is chosen. Discuss the difficulties that could occur if an improper network topology is chosen and a decentralized management philosophy exists.

10.27 Discuss how several LAN participants could share a large data base of software programs.

10.28 Debate the merits and disadvantages of every executive in a company having a workstation hooked to a departmental LAN. How would the debate change if a proposal were on the table to connect the departmental LANs and give every workstation access to a WAN?

10.29 Discuss the factors that would cause the different vendors and groups to move in the direction of agreement on a common network architecture standard.

10.30 "Instead of purchasing dumb terminals for users, our department has switched to PCs with hard disks. When not being used as terminals the PCs can be employed as stand-alone processors." Comment on the wisdom of this statement.

EXERCISES AND PROBLEMS

10.31 Bigtime Hauling is a transporter of steel pipe throughout the Southwest. Big City, Bigtime's headquarters, serves three offices located in Armstown, Crown, and Dreadville. The management of Bigtime Hauling is considering installing a communications network between the locations so that the company's dispatching and reporting information processing can be speeded up. To aid in analysis of alternative configurations, a systems analyst at Bigtime has provided the following information:

1. Big City is 670, 572, and 633 miles from Armstown, Crown, and Dreadville, respectively. Crown is 196 and 70 miles from Armstown and Dreadville, respectively.

2. Dial-up charges are 65, 55, and 60 cents per minute from Big City to Armstown, Crown, and Dreadville, respectively. Charges to Armstown and Dreadville from Crown are 25 and 15 cents per minute, respectively.

3. Switching equipment for multidrop lines can be leased for $1,325 per month.

4. Communications time between headquarters and Armstown, Crown, and Dreadville is estimated to be 60, 50, and 40 hours per month, respectively.

5. Dedicated lines can be leased on a monthly basis. The costs for the first, second, third, and fourth hundred miles is $3.75 per mile, $3.40 per mile, $3.25 per mile, and $3.20 per mile, respectively. For every mile over 400, the cost to lease a dedicated line is $3.00 per month.

Required: Compute the monthly cost of the following alternatives:

1. A point-to-point configuration with switched lines between the head office in Big City and each of the other offices of Bigtime.

2. A point-to-point configuration with dedicated lines between the head office in Big City and each of the other offices of Bigtime.

3. A multidrop configuration with switched lines between Armstown, Crown, and Dreadville. The switching equipment would be located in Crown, and Crown would be connected to Big City via a dedicated line.

4. A multidrop configuration as described except with all dedicated lines.

10.32 Your department is contemplating installing a local area network for its professors and other instructional support staff. At this time the only issue to be resolved is the transmission medium to be used for the LAN. Specifically, twisted-pair, broadband coaxial cable, and fiber optic cable are being considered. Based on a library search, prepare a list of the characteristics of each transmission medium. So that comparisons can be made, use the categories of topologies supported, bandwidth, immunity to noise, ease of installation, ease of expansion and reconfiguration, and cost.

10.33 Trains are still run the way they were 50 years ago. Control dispatchers, who have sole control over the movement of trains, issue something called "train orders." These train orders are written instructions sent from a central base and picked up by train crews at certain points along a route. For example, a train order might tell a crew to leave Minot, North Dakota, at midnight, travel 100 miles south, and then wait on a siding for a northbound train to pass.

The problem with this system is the lack of feedback. The southbound train might barrel ahead at full throttle to the designated stopping point. There, it might wait for hours if the northbound train sharing the track is running late.

Required: How might computers and telecommunications be combined to improve the efficiency of running a railroad?

10.34 Currently, Atkins Wholesalers, located in Alpha, transmits its entire, 500-MB, updated inventory data base to Beta, the site of its other major distribution center. The updated inventory data are carried on a 56-Kbps leased line, which is able to transmit the data at a rate of 100 MB every 3.9 hours. The monthly cost of this 1000-mile communications link is $2,925.

The management of Atkins is considering the option of substituting WORM optical disks in place of the expensive communications line. Based on a preliminary investigation, a systems analyst at Atkins has determined WORM disks, which hold up to 1 GB of data, can be bought in quantity for $75 each. Moreover, a WORM drive can be purchased from the same vendor for $7,500. To distribute the WORM disks to the center of Beta, the U.S. Postal Service's Express mail would be used. The cost of this overnight service is $10.35.

Required: Assume a three-year time horizon. Compare the costs of the transmission link and WORM optical disks using an update frequency of 22 and 30 days per month for Atkins' data base.

10.35 To make reservations and seat assignments for individuals' airline flights, travel agents use workstations in their offices in cooperation with a remote airline host mainframe computer. After logging onto the network, the agent identifies the customer's flight number, then sends the necessary data to the remote host for processing. The host, in turn, provides information to the agent about the type of plan involved and the seats available for that flight. Based on this information, the agent can readily book reservations, enter and check locally maintained accounting data, and then return the selection information to the airline's host computer. There it will be stored and then retrieved by the airline for its use.

Required: In broad terms sketch the computer configuration and network facility at the airlines and at the travel agency.

10.36 Lone Star Bottling is located in Austin, Texas, and has two warehouses located in Sweetwater, Texas, and Fort Stockton, Texas. Lone Star has decided to install a telecommunications network to link its home office processor to PC terminals in its warehouses. The distance between Austin and Sweetwater and Austin and Fort Stockton is 300 and 500 miles, respectively. The distance between warehouses is 400 miles. A systems analyst at

Lone Star has provided you with the following data:

1. The home office expects to communicate with the warehouse in Sweetwater and Fort Stockton approximately 45 and 35 hours per month.

2. Line charges between Austin and Sweetwater and Austin and Fort Stockton are $.85 and $.90 per minute.

3. The cost of a multidrop is $350 per month and a multiplexer can be leased for $650 per month.

4. Lines can be rented for $5.00 per mile for the first 200 miles, and $4.00 a mile thereafter.

> **Required:** Compute the total monthly cost of (1) a point-to-point network that links Austin to the warehouses by leased lines; (2) a point-to-point network that links Austin to the warehouses by switched lines; (3) a multidrop network that links Austin to Fort Stockton via the warehouse in Sweetwater; and (4) a multiplexed network, with leased lines, that links Austin to a multiplexer located half way between the warehouses.

10.37 The demands for access to the corporate data center computers come from four user groups of a major chemical company. The first major user of the corporate data center's resources is the accounting department. It typically sends small transaction data blocks over leased lines to the mainframe computers. These batch transmissions are typically done during off-peak hours. While the accounting department is located in the same building as the data center, it is beyond the maximum allowable distance for local attached terminals.

Processing plant personnel are a second group of users who demand substantial resources from the corporate data center. These users connect to the corporate mainframes via LANs, terminals, and minicomputers. This group performs mostly online processing.

The chemical company's engineering organization connects to the corporate data center via its departmental minicomputers it uses for number "crunching." The engineering group relies on the mainframe for the permanent or temporary storage of data that can be extracted for further analysis at some later time.

The fourth group of users who rely on access to the corporate data center's computers is corporate management. They are connected by a LAN so data bases and programs used throughout the company can be shared.

> **Required:** Draw the network topology of the chemical company's corporate data center and its four major user groups.

BIBLIOGRAPHY

ADDELSON, ROGER. "What Constitutes the Ideal Bridge?" *PC Week,* August 11, 1987.

"All About Communications Processors." *DataPro Reports on Data Communications.* Delran, N.J.: DataPro Research Corporation, April 1987.

"All About Modems." *DataPro Reports on Data Communications.* Delran, N.J.: DataPro Research Corporation, March 1987.

"An Overview of Communications Software." *DataPro Reports on Data Communications.* Delran, N.J.: DataPro Research Corporation, May 1987.

"An Overview of Data Communications Standards." *DataPro Reports on Data Communications.* Delran, N.J.: DataPro Research Corporation, December 1987.

BLAUMAN, SHEL. "Developing a User-Oriented Networking Architecture." *Data Communications,* May 1987.

BOLICK, LAWRENCE J. "Telecommunications Standards Arrive." *Datamation*, October 1985.

COOPER, EDWARD B., and PHILIP K. EDHOLM. "Design Issues in Broadband Local Networks." *Data Communications*, February 1983.

DURR, MICHAEL, and DWAYNE WALKER. *Micro to Mainframe*. Reading, Mass.: Addison-Wesley, 1985.

EDMUNDS, ROBERT A. *The Prentice-Hall Encyclopedia of Information Technology*. Englewood Cliffs, N.J.: Prentice Hall, 1987.

FLYNN, LAURIE. "IBM Changes Its Strategy on Protocols." *InfoWorld*, February 16, 1987.

HECHT, JEFF. "FDDI: Next-Generation LAN Promises Fast Links, Reliability." *PC Week*, June 9, 1987.

HELLIWELL, JOHN. "The Hub Shouts While the VSATs Whisper in Satellite Networks." *PC Week*, July 21, 1987.

HERMAN, JAMES G., and MARY A. JOHNSTON. "ISDN When? What Your Firm Can Do in the Interim." *Data Communications*, October 1987.

HINDIN, ERIC. "Digital PBX Systems Have Long Lead over LANs in Link Agility." *PC Week*, January 12, 1988.

HINDIN, ERIC. "ISDN's Unified Front Solves Some Big Headaches by Simplifying Training and Networking Tactics." *PC Week*, January 12, 1988.

JONES, DEL. "Homogeneous vs. Heterogeneous LANs: Mixed Architecture Isn't the Answer." *PC Week*, January 26, 1988.

"Local Area Networks." *DataPro Reports on Data Communications*. Delran, N.J.: DataPro Research Corporation, December 1987.

MADRON, THOMAS W. "Broadband vs. Baseband." *Computerworld*, November 25, 1985.

MADRON, THOMAS W. *Micro-Mainframe Connection*. Indianapolis, Ind.: Howard W. Sams, 1987.

"Manufacturing Automation Protocol (MAP)." *DataPro Reports on Data Communications*. Delran, N.J.: DataPro Research Corporation, April 1987.

MOREL, CHARLES. "LAN Gateways: New Opportunities for PC-to-Host Connectivity." *Data Communications*, October 1987.

"Multiplexers." *DataPro Reports on Data Communications*. Delran, N.J.: DataPro Research Corporation, September 1987.

"Optical Fiber System Economics." *DataPro Reports on Data Communications*. Delran, N.J.: DataPro Research Corporation, February 1986.

PETTI, RICHARD. "LAN/WAN Integration." *Telecommunications*, September 1987.

POMPILI, TONY. "Mix-and-Match Cabling Plan Yields Savings." *PC Week*, January 5, 1988.

PRUITT, JAMES B. "The Real Case for Microwave." *Computer & Communications Decisions*, August 1987.

RUDOV, MARC H. "Wanted: Concerned Users to Join ISD (R)evolution." *Data Communications*, June 1985.

SCHATZ, WILLIE. "EDI: Putting the Muscle in Commerce and Industry." *Datamation*, March 15, 1988.

STEINBERG, DON. "Electronic Data Interchange Use Moves from the Few to the Many." *PC Week*, December 15, 1987.

STIX, GARY. "Peer Pressure." *Computer & Communications Decisions*, January 1988.

STIX, GARY. "Multivendor Networks Now." *Computer & Communications Decisions*, May 1987.

STROM, DAVID. "Bank's LAN Links Regional Loan Centers." *PC Week*, July 28, 1987.

11

TECHNOLOGY: SOFTWARE APPLICATION AND DEVELOPMENT

11.1 INTRODUCTION

A perfect definition of software probably does not exist. A systems maven once said that hardware is something you can stub your toe on; software is everything else. But in some instances what was once considered software has now become embedded in hardware called firmware.

In this chapter, we use software to represent the entire set of programs, procedures, and related documentation of the information system. Further, we divide software between computer-oriented software and human-oriented software.

The objectives of this chapter are:

1. To present computer-oriented software and discuss how it controls the computer.
2. To discuss software languages and differentiate between those that are computer oriented and those that are human oriented.
3. To present human-oriented software and demonstrate how it is evolving to satisfy the many needs of end users.
4. To discuss the use of computer-aided software engineering (CASE) systems and demonstrate how such systems generate human-oriented software.

11.2 COMPUTER-ORIENTED SOFTWARE

When a computer is acquired, the user is buying not merely hardware but also a means of meeting his or her needs through application programs, without having to be too concerned about the internal operations of the computer. This internal operations interface, called the *operating system,* drives the computer in the most efficient manner.

367

The Operating System and Its Components

The operating system consists of an integrated system of complex, sophisticated programs (usually written in machine or assembler language) that supervise the operations of the CPU, control input/output (I/O) functions, translate assembler and compiler languages into machine language, and provide a host of other support services.

The key components of the operating system are control programs that include a supervisor, an I/O control system, data communications control, an initial program loader, and a job control program.

The *supervisor* is similar to a traffic cop in that it directs I/O activities and handles interrupt conditions, job scheduling, program retrieval, and primary storage allocation. The *I/O control system* handles I/O scheduling, I/O error corrections, and other data management functions.

Data communications control programs are included in systems that use a network of data communication channels and remote terminals. They perform such activities as data input, automatic polling, queuing and interrupt handling for competing terminals, message switching, and inquiry and transaction processing.

The *initial program loader (IPL)* is a small control program that loads the supervisor control program from a systems residence device (e.g., a magnetic disk) into primary storage when the computer begins operations. *Booting* is the term most often used when describing initial program loading of a microcomputer.

The *job control program's* function is to prepare the computer system for the start of the next job by executing job control language (JCL) statements.

Multiuser Operating Systems

When several programs vie for the same computer resources, the operating system must decide which program will be executed next, what peripheral devices will be needed by the program, how much internal memory the program will require, and how the program will be protected from inadvertent interference from other programs. Following is a discussion of how operating systems deal with each of these issues.

1. *Processor Management.* The group of programs for processor management are particularly important when resources of the computer must be shared. This requirement for resource sharing stems from two sources: multiprogramming and time-sharing.

   Multiprogramming is the execution of two or more programs concurrently by the computer. What concurrent processing means is that two or more programs are active within the same time frame but do not use the same computer resource at exactly the same instant (simultaneous processing). With multiprogramming, a group of programs take turns using the processor; first, one program is run for a while, then another is run for a while, then another, and so on.

   Multiprogramming is event or interruption driven in that programs share computer resources on the basis of significant events occurring in the programs. For example, in the course of being executed, a program instruction might call for the computer to read data from an auxiliary storage device. Through the operating system, this activity is pursued by the program relinquishing control of the CPU to a second program. The CPU may then proceed to execute instructions of that second program until it, too, is interrupted. Then, if the data for the first program have been obtained from the auxiliary storage device control, the operating system may shift control back to the first program. Thus, in a multiprogramming environment programs appear to be executed simultaneously from beginning to end, when in fact they are being interrupted constantly, as the computer switches from program to program.

Time-sharing is like multiprogramming in that resources are shared, but the basis for sharing is time driven rather than event driven. In a time-sharing environment, the operating system controls users by allocating them slices of processor time. In a 2 millisecond (msec) time slice, for example, a user is free to perform whatever operations are required. At the end of the time slice, the resources are abruptly taken away from that user and given to another user. This time slicing is ideal for applications such as making airline reservations and point of sale, when many users must be connected to the processor simultaneously but each requires only a small amount of CPU time.

The software of the processor manager includes interrupt handlers, a dispatcher program that switches the processor from one program to another, and routines that prevent several programs from using the same resource simultaneously and causing a systems error to occur.

2. *Memory Management.* A memory manager is a set of programs that manage the memory contents of a system. Memory management includes the assignment of programs to memory locations and the movement of program segments and data to and from internal memory and external storage devices.

The memory managers of many operating systems use a technique called *virtual storage.* The basic idea behind virtual storage is the dynamic linking of internal storage to auxiliary storage so that it appears to each of the many users who are simultaneously using the system that a very large amount of memory is at his or her disposal. This is accomplished by breaking up and scattering parts of a program or the data associated with a program both in internal memory and on auxiliary storage devices (e.g., magnetic disk) so that the "virtual" effect of much larger internal storage is given. This is illustrated in Figure 11.1. Normally, only the instructions and data necessary for immediate processing will be located in internal storage in the form of *pages* or fixed size segments (e.g., 2 or 4 KB). With this approach, jobs are loaded into partitions or regions of auxiliary memory. Then, during processing, pages of instructions and data are transferred between auxiliary storage and internal memory according to the immediate needs of each job.

3. *Virtual Machine.* A still more powerful procedure than virtual storage is *virtual machine,* illustrated in Figure 11.2. With a virtual machine (VM) system, each user has the illusion of commanding an entire computer, including a processor, primary storage, and an array of input/output de-

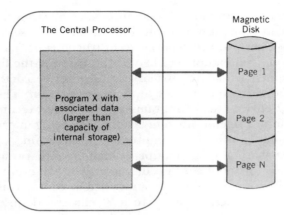

Figure 11.1 The virtual storage concept.

vices. All the virtual machines are, however, implemented by a single, real computing system. This approach provides a higher degree of isolation between users than does virtual storage because the virtual machines are logically independent. The virtual machine structure operates in a fashion similar to multiprogramming and time-sharing.

Proprietary Versus Nonproprietary Operating Systems

As discussed earlier, proprietary operating systems are developed by hardware manufacturers to run on and manage a specific computer. Typically, the operating system cannot be changed or enhanced by the user. This arrangement

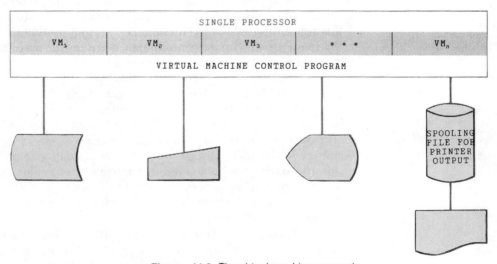

Figure 11.2 The virtual machine concept.

encourages use of the vendor's equipment. IBM and DEC are two manufacturers that market proprietary operating systems.

Multiple virtual storage (MVS) is IBM's largest and most complex operating system. It is intended primarily for use on IBM's recent mainframe computer systems. Although MVS supports batch, transaction, and time-sharing modes, it excels in a centralized, batch processing environment. Virtual machine is a general-purpose operating system that offers excellent time-sharing facilities. It can be used on IBM's new mainframe processors as well as some of its older machines. A virtual machine has software and simulated hardware resources that run in a real computer under VM. A virtual machine can do almost anything a real machine can. VM is perhaps the most versatile IBM operating system. Virtual machine/virtual storage extended (VM/VSE) is an operating system that enables a machine to be used as a mainframe at the departmental level or as a node connected to IBM's more powerful mainframes. IBM's OS/2 is an operating system for their PS/2 product line.

DEC's VMS operating system is purported to be based on an all-in-one approach to operating systems design. VMS also provides gateways to an IBM environment. But, as a proprietary operating system, DEC's offering is tied solely to DEC equipment.

Nonproprietary operating systems are developed to run on a variety of hardware products and provide an industry-standard environment. For nonproprietary operating systems, the industry leaders are AT&T and Microsoft. The Unix operating system, which is sponsored primarily by AT&T, is one of the most popular industry-standard operating systems. Microsoft's MS-DOS and OS/2 are popular operating systems for desktop hardware.

UNIX OR NOT TO UNIX The market is coming around to the Unix operating system. Hardware is getting more and more capable of the kind of applications for which Unix is attractive.

It's in your best interest to buy equipment that runs an industry standard operating system, if there is such a thing. Look at how many Unixes there are, and look at the brouhaha over the AT&T/Sun collaboration to unify Unix, which others claim is an attempt to turn Unix into a proprietary operating system.

Yes, sooner or later we'll be Unixed in the business world. And there'll be two versions—the AT&T/Sun version and All Others. My guess is that in the commercial world, Unix will come in an application at a time—since business users want solutions more than tools, and the battle between OS/2 and Unix will be fought in the software development community.

Condensed from John Gantz, "Unix Finally Catching on in the Commercial Market," *InfoWorld*, March 21, 1988, p. 44.

Work is underway to merge Unix and MS-DOS into one operating system for a one-solution approach to building fully integrated information systems (FIISs) without being encumbered with single-vendor restrictions. Many systems analysts applaud the evolvement toward industry-standard operating systems because they have the flexibility to specify equipment without having it tied to a single, proprietary operating system. This flexibility supports the distribution of a variety of hardware throughout the network and compatible linkages to other systems. Furthermore, an industry-standard operating system reduces the time and investment in applications software changes when the next generation of hardware is acquired. Also, many off-the-shelf applications can run immediately without major adaptations.

BIG-TIME OPERATING SYSTEM

OS/2 is the first operating system for grown-up personal computers. Its introduction means that programmers will be able to set new standards of excellence with grown-up applications.

OS/2 is potentially the most important PC software product since the introduction of the PC itself. Applications that take full advantage of OS/2 have not been written yet.

Current users of DOS have a relatively smooth upgrade path to OS/2. OS/2 uses the same file system, so data files created by DOS applications can immediately be used by the OS/2 versions of these programs. Most of the familiar DOS commands are duplicated under OS/2.

Some people are not happy that OS/2 is only for 80286- and 80386-based machines. Also, they are disappointed that OS/2 offers no advantages over DOS for existing DOS applications, and that OS/2 is a multitask but not a multiuser operating system. In those environments that require a multiuser operating system, several variants of UNIX are available and are obviously preferable to OS/2 for this purpose.

Excerpted from Charles Petzold, "OS/2 a New Beginning for PC Applications," *PC Magazine,* April 12, 1988, pp. 273–281.

Key characteristics of an industry-standard operating system are:

- It is machine independent and therefore does not dictate the kind of hardware used.
- It contains an extensive library of common functions that reduces the time and expense for development of individual applications.
- It contains a standard application software interface, thus reducing complexity and the need for special training.

- It includes monitoring features that provide operating and accounting statistics to help manage the total system and allocate costs.
- It provides a wide variety of telecommunication options.
- It contains sophisticated and reliable security control and access features.

11.3 SOFTWARE LANGUAGES

Software languages represent sets of expressions (often called code) that are interpreted or translated into executable programs run on a computer. One can find in software languages the variety one finds in human languages at the United Nations.

BUILDING YOUR OWN SOFTWARE Big Eight accounting firms have been among the first corporations to set up costly in-house software-development groups. These firms are investing millions of dollars to develop this proprietary software as a means to differentiate their services from their competitors', increase the productivity of their professionals and, they hope, to increase profits.

Trevor Stewart, director of PC software development and a partner at one of those firms, Deloitte, Haskins & Sells in New York, is managing his firm's efforts to create software that automates the work load of its accounting professionals.

"Our motivation is to provide the best services we can to our clients," Mr. Stewart said. "So, we need to make the best software available to our professionals, who are accountants, not software jocks."

"Much of the software Deloitte requires in order to perform its services isn't commercially available," Mr. Stewart said. "When it is, there are often subtle differences in the way an audit takes place that would be lost with a commercial software package. Fifty percent of the software used throughout the firm was developed in-house," he added.

Excerpted from Kathleen Doler, "In-House Software Seen as Next Productivity Boon," *PC Week,* June 30, 1987, p. 10.

As depicted in Figure 11.3, some languages are oriented toward the computer, such as machine language or assembler language. Third-generation languages (3GLs) are somewhat computer oriented but are mostly developed to solve business problems in terms that humans understand. Fourth-generation languages (4GLs) and query languages were developed for use by nontechnical end users. The ultimate human-oriented language would be one in which humans could communicate directly with the computer in everyday, conversational language.

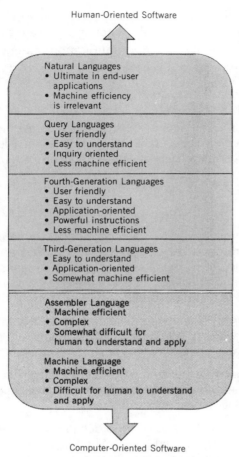

Human-Oriented Software

Natural Languages
• Ultimate in end-user applications
• Machine efficiency is irrelevant

Query Languages
• User friendly
• Easy to understand
• Inquiry oriented
• Less machine efficient

Fourth-Generation Languages
• User friendly
• Easy to understand
• Application-oriented
• Powerful instructions
• Less machine efficient

Third-Generation Languages
• Easy to understand
• Application-oriented
• Somewhat machine efficient

Assembler Language
• Machine efficient
• Complex
• Somewhat difficult for human to understand and apply

Machine Language
• Machine efficient
• Complex
• Difficult for human to understand and apply

Computer-Oriented Software

Figure 11.3 Computer-oriented and human-oriented software indicated by software languages.

Machine Language

Machine language is binary code that the computer interprets directly. For humans, this language is tedious to write as it requires a programmer to keep track of storage locations of data and instructions in the form of strings of 0's and 1's. Machine language is efficient for the computer but very inefficient for the programmer and end user, and it is rarely used today to develop applications software.

Assembler Languages

Assembler languages were developed in the early 1950s to lessen the tedium and quicken the slow development process caused by having to write programs in machine language. Assembler languages are made up of mnemonic operation codes and symbolic addresses that human beings remember more easily than machine codes and addresses. These instructions, however, must be translated into machine language that the computer understands. This translation is performed by an assembler program, which converts the mnemonic operation codes and symbolic addresses of instructions (the source program) into machine-processible form (the object program).

Programs developed from assembler languages are highly efficient in terms of storage space use and processing time. The disadvantages are that assemblers are cumbersome to use and require a high level of skill to use effectively.

Third-Generation Languages

Probably the two most popular third-generation languages (also called compiler or procedural languages) are COBOL and FORTRAN. Both use English-like sentences and mathematical expressions familiar to people. They are relatively computer independent, easy to write, easy to read, and easy to maintain, at least, when compared to assembler languages. Moreover, both languages, especially COBOL, are widely used and supported. Some programming experts estimate that over 80 billion lines of COBOL code are in use worldwide. Third-generation languages require a large amount of storage for their compiler. Moreover, many users believe that programs based on 3GLs are more difficult to write than most people realize. Also, in many installations that do not prepare current and comprehensive documentation, COBOL is difficult to maintain. Numerous undocumented changes to a COBOL program over the years results in a real bucket of spaghetti-like code that nobody understands, not even the original programmer, assuming that he or she is still available.

Still, COBOL continues to thrive. The establishment of new standards by the American National Standards Institute (ANSI) and the development of new products and restructuring tools that help automate the production, documentation, and maintenance of COBOL code all work together to give COBOL a new lease on life.

COBOL IS HERE TO STAY   Thanks in part to the PC revolution, COBOL seems to have caught a second wind and appears ready to get down to business as never before. PC COBOL compiles are the choice for COBOL work.

COBOL functions as a global language. People in many countries have found the language of business is English, also the language of COBOL.

COBOL programs developed on PCs are going to be universal programs that run on all types of machines. COBOL continues to include a strong commitment to application tools.

Excerpts from Art Campbell, "PC COBOL is in Business," *Software Magazine,* February, 1988, pp. 43–46.

Fourth-Generation Languages

COBOL has come under siege in the last few years from a variety of 4GLs, such as ADS/Online, Mantis, Focus, Natural, Ramis II, Ideal, and Nomad2. These 4GLs were developed to simplify and automate the tedious programming required by 3GLs to generate reports and manipulate files.

These 4GLs are used primarily for prototyping, generating ad hoc reports, and building simple systems. They are normally not used to build large, complex systems, because 4GLs may actually require more effort than traditional 3GLs. The 4GLs possess macro verbs and expressions in which one 4GL expression equivalently represents a large number of 3GL statements and therefore accomplishes many tasks when executed. But this "power" may limit and frustrate the fine-tuning and step-by-step processes often required in complex applications.

Generally, 4GLs were developed to replace 3GLs, especially COBOL, and to enable end users to do their own programming. So far, this has not happened to the extent first imagined, although many instances exist where real productivity gains have been realized from using 4GLs. What all this means is that both 3GLs and 4GLs can coexist and be productive. For new, user-specific applications, 4GLs can be used extensively. For large, complex data processing applications, COBOL may be the language of choice. Therefore, combining the two approaches will bring balance to systems development.

MISAPPLICA-TION OF 4GL   In 1985, New Jersey's Division of Motor Vehicles system bit the dust. Not only was the systems plan ill-defined, but the system was written in a 4GL which was unable to perform the heavy production load of the system. Consequently, over a million New Jersey drivers were unable to register their cars or registered them incorrectly. The snafu cost the state nearly seven million dollars.

Query Language

A query language is used in conjunction with a data base management system (DBMS). A query language is very similar to 4GLs and is often classified as such. A good example of a relational query language is IBM's Query By Example (QBE). More will be said about QBE later in this chapter.

Natural Language

Clearly, the ideal way for end users to interact with the information system is through the use of their everyday language without the aid of programmers and without special training. To develop a computer to understand natural languages and respond in the same manner on a large scale is probably impossible because of the inherent ambiguity of natural languages.

Natural languages are comprised of four elements. Syntax represents how words are used to form phrases, clauses, or sentences. Semantics relate to the inherent meaning. Intent is the purpose that the end user had in mind. Dialect is how the same language is distinguished by features of vocabulary, grammar, and pronunciation. Some limited voice systems have been developed that are syntactically correct. Very little has been done, however, that treats semantics, intent, and dialect.

IS HYPERCARD FOR REAL OR ALL HYPE?

According to Apple, Hypercard will revolutionize the way PCs are used. Hypercard does not fit into any of the standard categories of PC software: It's not a spreadsheet or text editing program. It's not graphics or communications, although it can include both. And it's definitely not a database management system.

Hypercard, available now, is a new way to organize information using associative, rather than logical, links. Within Hypercard is Hypertalk, an object-oriented development language with which small databases, or "stacks," can be built. Each stack can represent any group of information the user deems relative, including a combination of text, graphics, and sound. Links between objects within the stacks are determined by the user. Links between objects stored on different stacks are also determined by the user.

It is the way the links are made that makes Hypercard different. The logic is determined by the user; if, for example, horses remind you of pigs, you can draw a link between the two. The significance is that the linkages between objects reflect the user's associations rather than those of the software developer.

Condensed from "Hypercard Steals the Show," *InformationWEEK*, August 17, 1987, p. 14.

11.4 HUMAN-ORIENTED SOFTWARE

Human-oriented software is directed to the job that needs to be done or problem to be solved from the viewpoint of the human, especially the end user. In essence, software written in human-oriented languages tells the computer what to do in terms that people can easily understand. Application and service software are the categories of software that meet human needs.

Sources of Application and Service Software

Two sources for developing and acquiring application and service software exist. In-house, customized development is the general approach. The alternative approach is to acquire software packages (also called canned programs) that are widely marketed by vendors.

In-House Software

Typically, application software and, in some instances, service software are developed by a programmer (also called software engineer) who works for the host company to implement a specific application or perform a service. Examples of application programs include accounting, budgeting, payroll, and order entry. More than likely, these homegrown application programs are written in the COBOL language. But they can also be written in FORTRAN or other procedural languages such as Pascal, BASIC, PL/1, C, or RPG. Ad hoc applications may be written by a programmer or an end user in a 4GL such as Focus or Nomad2.

Vendor-Supplied Application Software

Application software programs that are developed and marketed by computer manufacturers and independent software vendors are directed toward serving the needs of many users across organizations. Applications of this type are spreadsheets, word processing, desktop publishing, electronic mail, statistical and financial packages, and budgeting. Also, function-specific software packages are marketed, such as accounting systems, fleet management and dispatching systems, marketing systems, and manufacturing systems. Another dimension of vendor-supplied application software is industry-specific, such as accounts receivable processing packages for dentists or accounts receivable and inventory management programs for marinas.

BETA SOFT-WARE MAY BE BUGGY

In the tradition of vaporware, preannouncements, and dribbleware, the software industry is witnessing another controversial marketing technique—the release of incomplete programs to paying customers. This software is sometimes referred to as betaware because it is still in beta testing.

"Beta software is still buggy, and I feel very uncomfortable paying money to get something still buggy," says Richard Werbin of Chase Manhattan Bank.

"Users have no business using beta software unless they are experienced software users and are testing the program as a beta site," agrees Glenn Hoffman, who provides technical support for Addison-Wesley.

Excerpted from Rachel Parker, "Release of Incomplete Programs Stirs Debate," *InfoWorld,* February 8, 1988, p. 29.

Service Software

Service software includes a number of programs such as the following: (1) subroutines consisting of a set of instructions that perform some common, subordinate function within another program and that can be called in by that program when needed; (2) librarian programs that catalog, control, and maintain a directory of programs and subroutines that are stored on the library (usually magnetic disk) of the computer system; (3) utility programs, a group of programs that perform various housekeeping functions such as sorts and merges, and file and memory dumps; and (4) various other services and aids such as simulators, emulators, statistical recording and reporting, and debugging tools.

Expert Systems Shells

Human experts have a set of heuristics and a structure to their knowledge base upon which these heuristics operate. The knowledge base engineer, or systems analyst, elicits the human expert's knowledge base along with the heuristics adopted to solve problems or make decisions and "clones" this competence into a computer-driven knowledge base. The inference engine takes a specific problem to be solved or a decision to be made and leads them through the relevant logic and rules to a final solution or decision.

In some applications, the knowledge base engineer helps human experts to structure their knowledge. In other applications, human experts do this themselves. They merely provide the expert systems in the shell statements, in simple English language, such as the following:

```
What is your goal?
Goal:  To dispatch trucks.
Rule:  Dispatch trucks to haul drill
         pipe for hot loads.
       IF the call is for drill pipe
       AND the drill pipe is for deep-well rigs
       AND the arrival time is less than 24 hours
       AND the distance is greater than 800 miles
       THEN dispatch two-driver unit with
         48-foot heavy-duty trailer.
```

In the truck dispatching example, only one rule is illustrated. In a real application, hundreds or thousands of rules may be formulated to model a full-blown truck dispatching expert system.

For another example, one of the many rules in MYCIN, a medical diagnostic expert system, is:

```
IF the infection is meningitis
AND the subtype of meningitis is bacterial
AND only circumstantial evidence is available
AND the patient is at least 17 years old
AND the patient is an alcoholic
THEN there is suggestive evidence that
    diplococcus pneumoniae is an organism
    causing the meningitis.
```

When knowledge base engineers are used, the cloned knowledge base and inference engine are coded in a language such as C, resulting in a robust and complex expert system. When knowledge base engineers are not used, the expert systems shell itself must be much more sophisticated because the human expert, although very knowledgeable in a specific field, is typically not competent in computer languages and the intricacies involved in actually developing the expert system. Therefore, the expert systems shell must have the ability to accommodate the human expert directly through an interface that enables the expert to regurgitate what he or she knows by a fill-in-the-blank method. Human experts know how to structure their knowledge; they simply have to have a user-friendly method by which they can transfer their knowledge to a cloned knowledge base.

Generally, expert systems shells perform a variety of additional tasks. Word processors edit and produce necessary narrative for review and hard-copy documentation. Spreadsheets process any matrix of numeric values, if needed. The expert system is typically connected to a DBMS for access to a relevant set of data for decision making or problem solving. For example, the truck dispatching expert system example previously mentioned would need to be connected to a data base containing data entities and attributes revealing available trucks, trailers, and drivers for automatic dispatching.

11.5 HOW TO INCREASE FLUENCY AT THE USER/SYSTEM INTERFACE

Over the years many languages and methods have been developed to enable end users to communicate easily with the information system. COBOL and 4GLs such as Focus and Ramis are English-like programming languages. For mathematical modeling, APL (A Programming Language) is a symbolic programming language that speaks the language of mathematicians. Statistical languages such as SAS and SPSS are amenable to statisticians. Icons, metaphors, and templates are used as communication methods for computer language illiterates.

In the following sections, we present specific examples of some of the more popular languages and communication methods and focus on how they increase the fluency of users, such as: menus, windows, Query By Example, 4GL, and functional interface (FI). We will end with a discussion on trends in languages.

Menus

Menus provide users a simple and familiar form to retrieve information and interact with the system. Users are shown options from which they make choices.

The menu in Figure 11.4 displays the options for preparation of financial statements. Any or all of the first three reports can be generated by entering the appropriate letters, and the session can be ended. Or the fourth option can be invoked by entering D. This option provides a five-year financial statement's comparative and ratio analysis.

Typically, a main characteristic of menus is to lead the user through a series of menus that provide a range of responses. In some instances, the series of

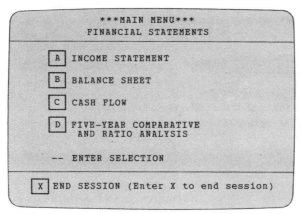

Figure 11.4 A main menu for financial statements.

menus are designed in a top-to-bottom manner in which users move from generalities to specifics. In other instances, the series provide alternatives.

An accounting menu software package, in addition to providing output such as that indicated in the previous example, would also provide menus to make journal entries and perform other accounting procedures. For example, in Figure 11.5 are (a) the general journal main menu and the selection of (b) the menu that permits the user to "post" transactions to the general journal.

In developing menus, the systems analyst can use a menu-dialogue chart very similar to a structure or hierarchical chart discussed in Chapter 7. A menu-dialogue chart, displayed in Figure 11.6, coordinates and depicts the sequence and choices of menus.

The user retrieves the main menu that provides a number of options relating to parts inventory. If the user wants to enter a sales transaction, delete an inventory item, or increase its quantity, option 1 brings up the transaction menu. Or a user may simply need to know the quantity on hand of a particular item. Option 3 from the main menu would permit this kind of query. If a user is viewing the report menu and wants the system to generate a sales report by branches, then option 1 in the report menu is selected. Other similar options are available as illustrated in the menu-dialogue chart.

Where menus are used extensively, the systems analyst should also prepare a menu catalog for users to understand what kind of menus are available. An example of this kind of catalog is illustrated in Figure 11.7.

Windows

Windows are fictional devices, so users don't have to use the entire screen as one window. Window software can produce windows in the screen that are shingled (overlapping), tiled, or pop-up, each of which can display data, instructions, or forms.

Windows are a convenient way of moving blocks of data, graphs, or text.

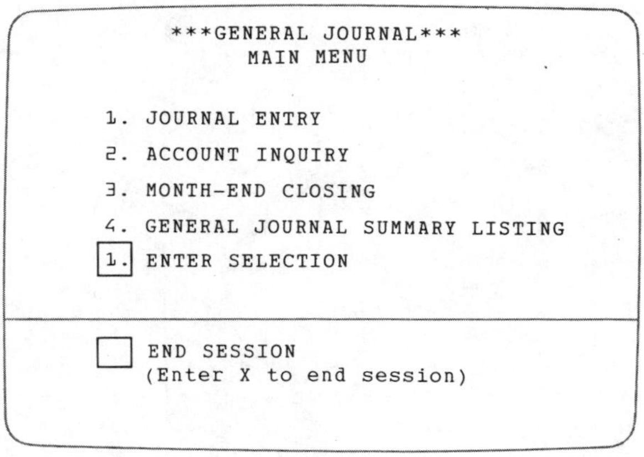

```
        ***GENERAL JOURNAL***
              MAIN MENU

      1.  JOURNAL ENTRY

      2.  ACCOUNT INQUIRY

      3.  MONTH-END CLOSING

      4.  GENERAL JOURNAL SUMMARY LISTING

     [1.] ENTER SELECTION


     [ ]  END SESSION
          (Enter X to end session)
```

(a) General journal main menu screen.

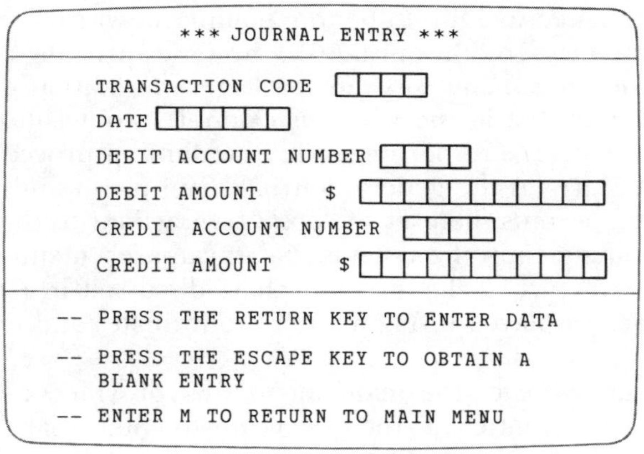

```
          *** JOURNAL ENTRY ***

      TRANSACTION CODE  [    ]
      DATE [      ]
      DEBIT ACCOUNT NUMBER  [    ]
      DEBIT AMOUNT       $ [         ]
      CREDIT ACCOUNT NUMBER  [    ]
      CREDIT AMOUNT      $ [         ]

   -- PRESS THE RETURN KEY TO ENTER DATA

   -- PRESS THE ESCAPE KEY TO OBTAIN A
      BLANK ENTRY

   -- ENTER M TO RETURN TO MAIN MENU
```

(b) Journal entry input screen.

Figure 11.5 How menus are used in series.

Windows can form work spaces for users to edit or enter data. Most window software provide the following kinds of windows: (1) title window, (2) instruction and message window, (3) flag window used to call attention to the uses by pointing at a specific line in one of the other windows or highlighting the location of an error or problem, (4) escape window used to suggest how users can exit the current application or function or how they can go back to the main menu or another menu, and (5) main body window used to display the key output or input new data and to display menu options.

Query by Example
With Query By Example, also called Query By Forms (QBF), the user sitting at a terminal is presented a skeleton table on the screen similar to the one in Figure

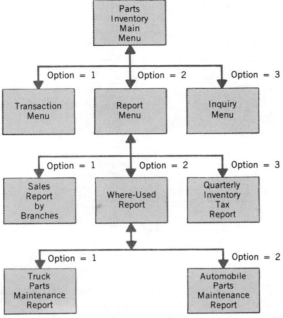

Figure 11.6 A menu-dialogue chart.

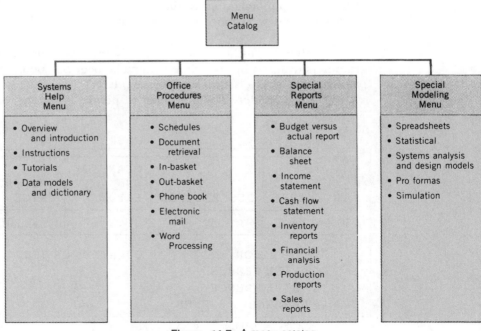

Figure 11.7 A menu catalog.

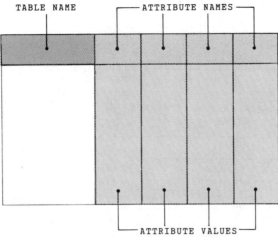

Figure 11.8 General form of QBE.

11.8. The user fills in the spaces for table name, attribute name, and attribute values to express a query or give a command.

The user writes P. to identify those attributes that are printed on a report or displayed on a screen. If, for example, a user wants a list of all wrenches by description in warehouse B with quantity on hand greater than 24 and a selling price of more than $10.00, the QBE entry would appear as shown in Figure 11.9. The output generated is a list that shows description and quantity on hand of all wrenches with more than 24 in stock and a selling price greater than $10.00.

Another fill-in-the-form example is the selection of male COBOL programmers ordered by last name who make over $50,000. The QBE entry that produces this query is shown in Figure 11.10.

QBE is considered by a number of people as a nonprocedural query lan-

INVENTORY	DESCRIPTION	QUANTITY ON HAND	SELLING PRICE
Wrenches	P.	P. > 24	> 10.00

DESCRIPTION	QUANTITY ON HAND
24" PIPE WRENCH	32
36" PIPE WRENCH	26
12" CRESCENT WRENCH	41

Figure 11.9 A query using QBE.

EMPLFILE	NAME	SKILL	SEX	SALARY
	P. LAST NAME	COBOL	M	> 50000

Figure 11.10 Query to retrieve male COBOL programmers by name who earn over $40,000.

guage, but users can perform some procedures, such as updates, arithmetic operations, linkage of several tables, insertions, and deletions. For example, assume that a company wants to insert Adams, a new systems analyst at a $50,000 salary; delete Bundy, an accountant; and update Carr, a systems analyst with a 10 percent increase in salary. How this would be done in QBE is illustrated in Figure 11.11.

4GL and Its Old Nemesis, COBOL

The traditional interface between the end user, such as a marketing manager, and the information system is staff personnel, information systems manager, systems analyst, application programmer (e.g., COBOL), and various technicians, with development time measured in weeks or months. As alluded to earlier in this book, the ideal user/system interface is one in which the user without the need for special training interacts with the system directly with application time measured in seconds or minutes. In this environment, the systems analyst would be more concerned about design of the total information system with appropriate networks, data bases, controls, models, and interface points in which end users could "get at" the information they need any time they need it. The systems analyst would be only incidentally concerned with day-to-day operations and the generation of special reports. End users would become their own "programmers."

To gain an appreciation of the traditional user/system interface gap and how this gap can be bridged by a 4GL, look at Figure 11.12. Here we demonstrate what it takes simply to list employees in department B using COBOL and a 4GL. Looking at this figure, you should be able to envision the amount of COBOL

EMPLFILE	NAME	SKILL	SEX	SALARY
I.	ADAMS	SYSTEMS ANALYST	F	50000
D.	BUNDY	ACCOUNTANT	M	45000
U.	CARR	SYSTEMS ANALYST	M	55000 x 1.1

Figure 11.11 QBE insert, delete, and update operations performed in one table.

```
COBOL Program to List Employees of Department B by Name

IDENTIFICATION DIVISION.
PROGRAM-ID.   NUMBER EMPLOYEES DEPARTMENT B.
AUTHOR.   SYLVIA NORDSTRUM.
ENVIRONMENT DIVISION.
CONFIGURATION SECTION.
SOURCE-COMPUTER.   IBM-370.
OBJECT-COMPUTER.   IBM-370.
INPUT-OUTPUT SECTION.
FILE-CONTROL.
      SELECT EMPLOYEE-FILE ASSIGN TO SYS10
      SELECT OUT-FILE ASSIGN TO PRINTER
DATA DIVISION.
FILE SECTION.
FD EMPLOYEE-FILE
      RECORD CONTAINS 21 CHARACTERS
      LABEL RECORDS ARE STANDARD
01 IN-RECORD
      05 EMPLOYEE-DEPT-CODE                 PIC X.
      05 EMPLOYEE-NAME                      PIC A(20).
FD OUT-FILE
      RECORD CONTAINS 132 CHARACTERS
      LABEL RECORDS ARE OMITTED
01 PRINT-RECORD
      05 FILLER                             PIC X(10).
      05 PRINT-NAME                         PIC A(20).
      05 FILLER                             PIC X(102).
WORKING-STORAGE SECTION.
01 EOF-SWITCH                               PIC X.
PROCEDURE DIVISION.
      MOVE "N" TO EOF-SWITCH
      OPEN INPUT EMPLOYEE-FILE
      OPEN OUTPUT OUT-FILE
      PERFORM READ-FILE UNTIL EOF-SWITCH
            IS EQUAL TO "Y"
      CLOSE EMPLOYEE-FILE OUT-FILE
      STOP RUN
READ-FILE.
      READ IN-RECORD
            AT END MOVE "Y" TO EOF-SWITCH
      IF EOF-SWITCH = "N"
            AND EMPLOYEE-DEPT-CODE = "B"
            MOVE EMPLOYEE-NAME TO PRINT-NAME
            WRITE PRINT-RECORD
```

4GL Program to List Employees of Department B by Name

```
      READ EMPLOYEE-FILE
      LIST EMPLOYEE BY NAME
      IF CODE = "B"
```

Figure 11.12 A 3GL and a 4GL used to write the same program.

code that has to be written for just a mildly complex application. With a 4GL, only 10 percent or less instructions are required and development takes much less time at a fraction of the cost. Indeed, many computer language mavens state that a language should not be called a 4GL unless its user develops the application in 10 percent of the time it would require to write the same application in COBOL.

Most 4GLs today are positioned as either ad hoc report writers or large production application languages. As mentioned earlier in this chapter, the ability of 4GLs to tackle big applications has not been widely tested, whereas COBOL, FORTRAN, and other 3GLs have already proven their big-project mettle. In fact, systems personnel involved in a large application for an industrial state tried to use a 4GL with catastrophic results. Cause and effect, however, are difficult to determine. The systems design could have been flawed, or, possibly, the people writing in the 4GL were not adequately trained. In any event, one should not embark on a large 4GL systems project without investigating thoroughly the 4GL's ability to handle all the complexities and meet the data processing requirements design force. Moreover, the syntax of 4GLs is just as difficult to learn as the syntax of other languages such as 3GLs, and the mere ability to string together programming statements does not make one a professional programmer.

Functional Interface

Generally, when we refer to a user or end user, we mean people who are not systems professionals and who perform a variety of tasks, make decisions, plan, and control business operations, all of which require interaction with the information system. In this section, however, we designate the application programmer as a user at the user/system interface, which we refer to in this section as the functional interface (FI).

The functional interface is a program inserted between the application programs and the data base management system, as illustrated in Figure 11.13. The DBMS receives FI statements generated by CALLs in the application programs. The DBMS executes the statements and returns the results to the FI, which formats the final response and passes it to the appropriate application program to be used for additional processing or displayed or printed with other information.

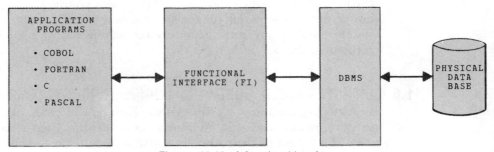

Figure 11.13 A functional interface.

The payoff of using FI are shorter and simpler application programs. Data structures remain independent of application programs. Application programmers don't have to learn the DBMS language. Generally, the DBMS can change without the need to change application programs because the FI makes the DBMS independent from the application programs and vice versa. The FI may or may not require reprogramming, but even if it does, changing the FI is significantly less expensive and time consuming than is changing the application programs.

Trends in Human-Oriented Languages

As always, the general trend of language and systems development is toward a goal of natural user/system interfaces where all users from casual to heavy production can converse fluently with the information system in their own language. For now, the goal of end-user programming, even for the casual user, has just about been achieved as we discovered in the preceding material.

Two major paths toward this goal are 4GLs and DBMSs, especially relational ones. For a long time, 4GL and DBMS paths were separated, but today they are converging. Some 4GLs use Structured Query Language (SQL), the de facto relational language or hooks (interfaces) in their language for hosting SQL.

Many 4GLs such as Nomad, Ramis, and Focus support relational technology. They use SQL and also have their own front-end languages to access relational data bases for complex relationships for which SQL may not be as efficient. Some 4GLs are also incorporating expert systems shells and menu architectures.

Another interesting path toward a natural user/system interface are software packages that automate systems development and generate native machine code or code in a 3GL. The user of this software is the systems analyst who develops models by "painting" them on a screen, which the software package automatically converts to programming code. The kind of software is the subject of the next section.

Probably within the next few years it will be difficult to separate DBMS vendors from 4GL vendors as more and more of the same features are incorporated into one powerful software package. These features are systems development software that includes modeling techniques and electronic forms design capabilities, automatic code generators, screen painting and graphical facilities, nonprocedural access languages, and a variety of end-user tools. Currently, some systems analysts are recommending the acquisition of a DBMS and 4GL and combining the best of both worlds.

11.6 COMPUTER-AIDED SOFTWARE ENGINEERING SYSTEMS

In many organizations, a crisis exists in both new software development and old software maintenance. Some companies report that their systems people spend over 70 percent of their time on software maintenance and that new software development is backlogged for two or three years. Computer-aided software engineering systems promise to eliminate this crisis. CASE systems include

DesignAid, Data Structured Systems Development (DSSD), Excelerator, Maestro, and Foundation.

CUSTOM-DESIGNED SYSTEMS WITH CASE Tools for custom-built, proprietary products are commonly lumped together as CASE, for Computer-Aided (or Automated) Software (or Systems) Engineering. In industry parlance, "upper CASE" deals with system design; "lower CASE" deals with turning the design into code that can actually be run on a computer.

Excerpted from Esther Dyson, "Strategic Software," *Forbes,* May 2, 1988, p. 114.

CASE Overview

CASE systems are extensive and sophisticated software packages of tools that help to design, develop, manage, and maintain software projects—a virtual "software factory." A bewildering array of CASE products are in the market. A few are somewhat limited in scope and performance; others are comprehensive. Figure 11.14 represents a generic model of CASE systems. Typically, a CASE system, implemented on a workstation (also called a workbench), establishes

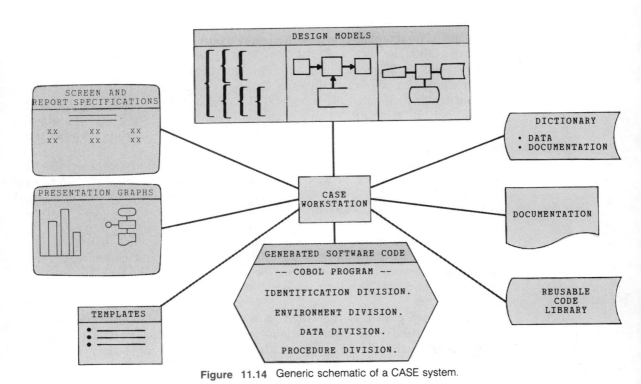

Figure 11.14 Generic schematic of a CASE system.

structures and relationships, tracks and logs changes, checks for consistency, explodes or implodes design models, automatically generates software code, and integrates and documents the final design in one location in both electronic and hard-copy form.

Software engineers perform at a workstation, similar to a hardware engineer using a computer-aided design workstation. The software engineer translates user requirements into a completed systems design.

Often, the software engineer determines desired outputs first by prototyping report specifications on the screen, then by working "backward" to final design. A variety of software automation tools and models work together to aid the software engineer to create, upgrade, or rewrite software packages or help develop a large-scale information system.

Instead of sketching out design models manually, system flowcharts, data flow diagrams, Warnier-Orr charts, structure charts, HIPOs, decision tables, and structured English, are prepared electronically. The software engineer uses a mouse to fetch from a symbols palette, lines, arrows, icons, and characters that make up a particular design. This feature eliminates laborious manual drawing and redrawing of these models. Therefore, changes in user requirements can be accommodated quickly and efficiently.

Screen and report painting facilities provide an easy-to-understand user/system design interface. Easy-to-use presentation graphics are used to show management proposed configurations of people, terminals, file media, networks, reports, and other processes and objects in real time. What-if and brainstorming scenarios can be easily implemented.

Templates are included in some CASE workstations and are invoked by command. The templates contain the generic portion of various constructs in a particular language such as COBOL or FORTRAN. FORTRAN constructs include arithmetic If, block command, Do, Do While, Else If, and Go To. The software engineer fills in specific variables, expressions, or statements applicable to a particular program. The templates also contain placeholders in uppercase letters, such as "If EXPR." These placeholders are replaced with the variables, expressions, or statements or possibly other templates, depending on what the software engineer wants the program to do.

The dictionary contains all the information about the system design. It includes data structures, process logic, models, menus, and graphs. Using this facility, software engineers can quickly review and update the system. Moreover, by capturing the systems specifications and design in one central place, redundancies and inconsistencies are eliminated.

As the system evolves, the documentation is always "in sync" with the latest changes. Therefore, documentation is always complete and current. A word processing component can generate hard-copy specifications any time it is needed. Such a facility is also helpful later when the system has to be modified due to future changes.

The chief payoff of the CASE system is automatically generated ANSI standard software code. Thus, the laborious task of manually writing COBOL code is eliminated. The program produced is ready for operation because it mirrors the design specifications.

Arguments for Using CASE

Writing, updating, and maintaining software has always been one of the most expensive and time-consuming bottlenecks in information systems. Anything that reduces this bottleneck certainly deserves, if not full utilization, at least consideration. Therefore, a strong case can be made for CASE.

The arguments for using CASE systems are the same as those for CAD systems. They increase productivity and quality of work. The software is generated in a top-down structured manner in accordance with ANSI standards. This leads to easier-to-maintain systems, thus reducing time dedicated to routine maintenance and increasing resources for new systems development. Documentation is always current and comprehensive thereby eliminating missing, incomplete, ambiguous, and out-of-date documentation found in some organizations where CASE systems are not used.

Strict methodologies of CASE systems impose a design discipline on software engineers. Discipline reduces design errors and omissions, which, in turn, reduces rework costs. The newly developed applications software is reliable, on time, and within budget. Furthermore, because of standardization and informative documentation, chances are good that code generated for one application may be reused in another application, therefore, reducing the inherent costs of duplication and reinventing the wheel for each new application.

Software development productivity rates can increase significantly by the extensive use of reusable software components, standard program forms, and standard implementation methods. Moreover, reusable software can reduce the risk of applications failure because it has already been used elsewhere and has presumably met all tests during operations.

Each reusable software component is indexed, described, and maintained in a library. Typically, these software components are organized by application type and by function within application type so they can be easily identified and retrieved for reuse.

SUMMARY

Software consists of operating systems, languages, application and service programs, and development packages. All these software components are intended to make the technology of a computer system do what users want it to do.

Operating systems of a computer supervise the functions of the processor, control the computer systems input/output functions, and provide several other important support services. Operating systems become extremely large and complex when they must function in environments where several programs and users are vying for one resource at the same time. Virtual machine is one way of dealing with this issue. With a VM system, each user has the illusion of commanding the entire computer, including the processor, main memory, and all necessary input/output devices.

Early languages were strictly oriented to a few programmers who were capable of expressing in the language of the computer how it was to do tasks. Programming became much easier with the advent of English-like, third-generation languages as exemplified by COBOL. Today, fourth-generation languages, query languages, and natural languages allow users to interact with the computer without the aid of programmers or extensive training. In fact, the amount of end-user programming has increased because of language and communications aids such as menus, windows, query languages (e.g., Query By Example), and functional interfaces.

Application and service programs are a major component of the software used daily by organizations. These programs can either be developed internally or acquired from software vendors. Normally, application software developed internally is more highly customized to the operations of the organization than is packaged software.

Writing, updating, and maintaining software has always been one of the most expensive and time-consuming activities in systems development. Computer-aided software engineering is a set of computer programs that allows a software engineer to translate user requirements into a completed system design. With CASE, systems design can be done more efficiently, with fewer errors and inconsistencies than using manual and paper and pencil methods.

IMPORTANT TERMS

assembler	natural language
booting	operating system
computer-aided software engineering (CASE)	packages
	pages
data communications control program	query by example (QBE)
	query by forms (QBF)
expert systems shell	query language
fourth-generation language (4GL)	service software
functional interface (FI)	supervisor
I/O control system	third-generation language (3GL)
initial program loader (IPL)	time-sharing
interrupt	utility program
job control language (JCL)	virtual machine (VM)
knowledge base engineers	virtual machine/virtual storage extended (VM/VSE)
menus	
multiple virtual storage (MVS)	windows
multiprogramming	

⇨ Assignment

REVIEW QUESTIONS

11.1   List and define the five key components of the operating system.

11.2   Define the term "multiprogramming." How is time-sharing the same as but yet different from multiprogramming?

11.3   What is the basic idea behind the virtual storage technique to memory management? What is the functional role played by pages in this approach to memory management?

11.4   Define the virtual machine approach to multiuser operating systems. How is it different from the virtual storage approach?

11.5   What are the two leading nonproprietary operating systems? What companies developed these operating systems?

11.6   List the six key characteristics of an industry-standard operating system.

11.7   List three characteristics of first-, second-, and third-generation languages.

11.8   What are the primary uses of fourth-generation languages?

11.9   Describe the four elements that comprise a natural language.

11.10 What are the three dimensions on which vendor-supplied software can be categorized? Give two examples of each category of software.

11.11 Define the four general types of service software.

11.12 List four ways to increase the fluency of users to communicate with computer systems.

11.13 What are five different kinds of windows provided by most window software?

11.14 What form is presented when a person uses Query By Example?

11.15 Why can end users become their own programmers when a 4GL is used instead of a programming language such as COBOL?

11.16 Define the term "functional interface." What is the payoff of using FI?

11.17 What functions are typically performed by a computer-aided software engineering system? List three arguments for using a CASE system when developing information systems.

QUESTIONS FOR DISCUSSION

11.18 Why do so many 4GLs exist? If 4GLs are supposed to make programming easier for the average person, why not have just one standard?

11.19 Operating systems for the desktop computer, such as O/S 2, are moving in the direction of mainframe operating systems in terms of complexity. Explain why this statement is unfortunately the case.

11.20 No matter how fast 4GLs and natural languages evolve, such workhorses as COBOL and C will always be used. Do you agree or disagree with this statement? Why?

11.21 "When examining COBOL program code generated automatically by a CASE system, the code tends to be significantly less than optimal in terms of processing efficiency." Comment why this claim might be true.

11.22 What improvements must be made to expert systems shells so that their application can be mastered by human experts?

11.23 "Menus were supposed to help me do my job. Quite frankly they are not doing the trick because too often I get lost in the extensive hierarchy of menus and cannot get to the menu I want." Discuss the types of aids that might be provided to this frustrated user.

11.24 Comment on the proposal to have one standard operating system for all mainframes, minis, and microcomputers. What about one standard with the ability of particular vendors to offer optional enhancement to the standard to take advantage of the way their hardware is designed and operated?

11.25 Someday, there will be an assembler language for the technical people, a 3GL for the application programmers, and a common natural language for users who want to query the information system. Comment on the possibility of this forecast coming true.

EXERCISES AND PROBLEMS

11.26 Part of the Personnel Department's data base for Able Company consists of a table of employee information. This table called EMPLOYEE is made up of the attributes NAME, EMPLOYEE__NO, DEPT__NO, MANAGER, SALARY, and OVERTIME.

> ***Required:*** Prepare a blank table skeleton and fill in the spaces for the table name and attribute names. Then, complete the QBE entry to satisfy each of the following queries and processing:

1. Print all the information for those employees credited with overtime wages.
2. Print the employee name for employees who work in department number 06 and earn more than $10,000 in salary.
3. List the employees numbers and salaries of all employees who have the last name of Burch and also work for the manager named Burch.
4. Update the data base to show the hiring of a new employee named Cane who is assigned the employee number 602.
5. Update the data base to reflect a salary of $25,000 being paid to the employee 602.

11.27 What is missing from the following general ledger main menu?

```
GENERAL LEDGER MAIN MENU
1.  JOURNAL ENTRY INPUT
2.  ACCOUNT INQUIRY
3.  MONTH-END CLOSING
4.  DEMAND REPORT
5.  GENERAL LEDGER SUMMARY LISTING
ENTER OPTION NUMBER > ___
```

11.28 Obtain the documentation for an expert systems shell of your choosing. From the documentation determine its ability to exchange data with data base management systems and electronic spreadsheets. Assess the expert systems shell's ability to help a novice user construct rules using a fill-in-the-blanks method. Determine if a user has the facility of a text editor to aid in his or her modification of the rule base. Finally, evaluate whether the shell can interface with other software written in a procedural language.

11.29 Carl Cline, the company's ace programmer, has a problem. It seems that before a new multiuser operating system called virtual storage was installed, Carl often bragged about the efficiency of his sheet calibration program, which was written in FORTRAN. Now, because his program takes three times as long as before to run to completion, Carl ducks in corners to avoid facing other programmers. A sample of the program code for the sheet calibration program follows:

```
            1000 I = 0
Page 12     1010 J = 10000
            1020 I = I + 1
            1030 SUMG2 = SUMG2 + G(I)**3
            1040 IF (I.LT.J)GO TO 1020
Page 13     1050 I = 0
```

> ***Required:*** Explain to Carl exactly what is happening and what he can do to remedy or minimize the problem.

11.30 All disciplines are surrounded by myths; the field of data processing is no exception. And software, abstract as it is, makes for a bountiful environment in which myths can thrive and become entrenched. The following is a list of 10 great myths of data processing. Write one or two paragraphs for each statement explaining why it is, indeed, a myth.

1. Software represents a growing proportion of total data processing expenditures.
2. Software is (necessarily) expensive.
3. Software must follow hardware.
4. Software outlasts hardware.
5. Software needs continuing change.
6. Software productivity can be enhanced.
7. Software product manufacturers are more efficient producers.
8. Software must satisfy the user.
9. Modern software systems require a data base management system capability.
10. Software is the result of programming.

BIBLIOGRAPHY

ABBEY, SCOTT G. "COBOL Dumped." *Datamation*, January 1984.

CAMPBELL, ART. "PC COBOL is in Business." *Software Magazine*, February 1988.

CAPRON, H. L. *Computer Tools for an Information Age*. Menlo Park, Calif.: Benjamin/Cummings, 1987.

CASE, ALBERT F., JR. *Information Systems Development: Principles of Computer-Aided Software Principles*. Englewood Cliffs, N.J.: Prentice Hall, 1987.

DOLER, KATHLEEN. "In-House Software Seen as Next Productivity Boon." *PC Week*, June 30, 1987.

DYSON, ESTHER. "Strategic Software." *Forbes*, May 2, 1988.

GANTZ, JOHN. "Unix Finally Catching on in the Commercial Market." *InfoWorld*, March 21, 1988.

GREMILLION, LEE L., and PHILLIP PYBURN. "Breaking the Systems Development Bottleneck." *Harvard Business Review*, March–April 1983.

"Hypercard Steals the Show." *InformationWEEK*, August 17, 1987.

MARTIN, JAMES. *Application Development Without Programmers*. Englewood Cliffs, N.J.: Prentice Hall, 1982.

PARKER, RACHEL. "Release of Incomplete Programs Stirs Debate." *InfoWorld*, February 8, 1988.

PETZOLD, CHARLES. "OS/2 a New Beginning for PC Applications." *PC Magazine*, April 12, 1988.

SORTI, J. J. "The Query Management Facility." *IBM Systems Journal*, Summer 1984.

STEWARD, DONALD V. *Software Engineering with System Analysis and Design*. Monterey, Calif.: Brooks/Cole, 1987.

The Arthur Young Practical Guide to Information Engineering. New York: John Wiley, 1987.

12
DATA BASE: DATA MANAGEMENT AND ORGANIZATION CONCEPTS

12.1 INTRODUCTION

The data base is the key building block in designing information systems. It is the prime integrating force of the information system within an organization. A good fit must be achieved between the processing and decision-making needs of the organization and the structure and composition of the data base. If this is not accomplished, the design efforts expended by the systems analyst on the other building blocks will be wasted.

This is the first of two chapters on this important building block. The two chapters are an overview of data organization and data base management systems. After studying these chapters, you should understand generally how file and data base systems work and specifically how to make effective use of these systems.

This chapter begins by discussing the basic concepts of data management systems. The second part of the chapter presents the differences between conventional data organization systems and data base systems emphasizing the relative benefits of both types of systems. The last part of the chapter identifies basic data organization techniques and contrasts the applications of each type of organization.

The objectives of this chapter are:

1. To introduce the basic tasks of data management within an information system.
2. To present the differences between a conventional data storage system and a data base management system, emphasizing the advantages and disadvantages of the two approaches to data retrieval.
3. To describe how computers retrieve data through the interaction between

application programs, a data base management system, the operating system, and actual data.

4. To identify the three basic data organization techniques and discuss how to choose the best technique for a given application.

12.2 DATA MANAGEMENT CONCEPTS

In a large, complex organization, many users simultaneously require access to information. Users may include executives, department managers, accounting and auditing personnel, salespersons, manufacturing supervisors, programmers, and other persons who need to survey information about the organization. A data base consists of data items organized into records and files in a way intended to meet users' information requirements. Users gain access to the information derived from the data base through the function of data management.

Data management is the process of storing and retrieving data. Data management is composed of three basic tasks: (1) describing the real-world organization and interrelation of data in a standard data definition, (2) physically storing data in a specific format on a given storage medium, and (3) retrieving the stored data in a way that provides valid information to the users of the system. It is the responsibility of the systems analyst to design a system that will effectively complete the three tasks of data management.

Data Descriptions

Data represent real-life physical objects. A sales clerk may often need to know how many 3" × 4" × 20' pieces of angle iron are in inventory. It would be impractical to have to go to the warehouse and count the number of items every time a customer asks how many pieces are on hand. Instead, the clerk accesses data that represent the objects, angle iron inventory.

Objects for which we store data are referred to as entities. An entity may be a tangible object, such as an employee, customer, or an inventory item. An entity could also be an intangible object, such as an event, a software project, or a divisional profit center. In the preceding example, the entity is an inventory item.

An entity has certain attributes that we may wish to record. For an inventory item, we probably want to keep track of such attributes as the inventory number, description, size, price, unit of measure, and quantity on hand. Each attribute has a value that could be associated with it and a physical data representation of that attribute value. Figure 12.1 presents an example of how data attributes are applied to actual entities.

An analyst identifies all data attributes for an entity that will be needed to provide information to users. Sometimes this task can be accomplished by looking at the reports and inquiries of a system. For example, suppose a user requests information concerning the relation of the HOURLY PAY RATE to the JOB CLASSIFICATION for a specific department. The systems analyst then knows that attributes for HOURLY PAY RATE, JOB CLASSIFICATION, and DEPARTMENT NUMBER will have to be created and maintained.

Entity	Data Attribute	Sample Data Attribute Value	Data Representation (Maximum Length)
Customer	Customer number	12345	5 Digits
	Customer name	Nept. Inc.	30 Alphanumerics
	Amount owed	01400.00	7 Digits with 2 decimal places
	Credit limit	10000.00	7 Digits with 2 decimal places
Employee	Employee number	135	3 Digits
	Employee name	J. Smith	20 Alphabetics
	Department number	764-B	5 Alphanumerics
	Hourly pay rate	07.00	4 Digits with 2 decimal places
	Job classification	Systems analyst	20 Alphabetics
Inventory item	Item number	117JP	5 Alphanumerics
	Size	$2 \times 2 \times 20$	6 Alphanumerics
	Description	Angle	10 Alphabetics
	Price	00.80	4 Digits with 2 decimal places
	Unit of measure	Each	4 Alphanumerics

Figure 12.1 Data attribute descriptors.

In some instances, data will be calculated from existing attribute values. For example, the credit manager may want to know the names of all customers who have an AMOUNT OWED within 20 percent of their CREDIT LIMIT. The system must subtract the value of AMOUNT OWED from the value of CREDIT LIMIT and divide the result by the value of CREDIT LIMIT.

Frequently, systems analysts must anticipate the need by users for some data attributes. For the employee entity in Figure 12.1 a systems analyst might add attributes such as EDUCATION, TRAINING, and DATE OF LAST PROMOTION. These attributes may not be needed for any current inquiry, but they would probably be relevant for future information needs. The analyst must know enough about the entity to suggest extra attributes to users when defining the data description of a system.

Physical Data Organization

The attributes displayed in Figure 12.1 have to be physically stored in a specific format on a storage medium to be retrieved by users. The format of the attributes includes their size and data organization. Organization refers to the physical order of entities on a storage medium. The media used to store data come in a variety of physical forms. Paper file folders, index cards, microfilm, magnetic tape, magnetic disks, and optical disk can all be used to store data.

For example, let's design the physical data organization for the customer entity. We will use 3″ × 5″ index cards as our storage medium. On a given card we will write each of the data attribute values for a single customer. Because our card has a size limitation, we have to make the maximum length of our attribute values small enough to fit on the card. We also have to decide which physical order to use to stack the cards. The type of retrieval required for the data dictates the type of physical data organization that should be used. Simply stacking the cards one after another by customer number would be using a sequential organization. To retrieve information about a specific customer, we have to search through all the cards preceding that customer.

A more efficient data organization is to sort the cards by the customer name attribute and then use larger cards interspersed with the customer cards to represent the location of each letter of the alphabet. This form of data organization is referred to as indexed sequential organization. To retrieve a customer record, we first reference the larger card containing the alphabetic character that relates to our customer name, and then sequentially search through the cards from that point until we locate the correct customer. We will discuss physical data organization alternatives in more detail in the third part of this chapter.

Retrieving Stored Data

Once the attributes and physical organization are defined for an entity, users can then retrieve information about the entity. For example, let's imagine that the credit manager of an organization who uses the data organization just described wants to know by name all customers with account balances greater than $1,000. A credit clerk could simply start at the first card comparing the AMOUNT OWED attribute value of each customer with the $1,000 parameter, and for every AMOUNT OWED attribute value greater than this parameter, write down the appropriate CUSTOMER NAME attribute value to give to the credit manager. This type of retrieval is termed sequential access.

Another type of retrieval is also available. If the credit manager wanted to know how much CUSTOMER NAME "Nept, Inc." owed, the manager could go to the indexed cards and, after locating the index card for "N," simply look through the cards beginning with "N" until locating the correct customer. This type of retrieval is termed random access.

12.3 COMPUTERIZED DATA MANAGEMENT

Computers are excellent devices to perform data storage and retrieval because of their speed and storage capacity. Data management tasks are not performed differently with a computer, only more efficiently. Using a computerized data management system to satisfy the examples used in this section, the systems analyst still is responsible for performing two tasks. The systems analyst has to describe the data attributes for each entity and design the physical data organization. The computer would be used to retrieve efficiently the data in a format desired by users. Two approaches to computerized data management are (1) traditional file processing environments and (2) data base management environments.

Traditional File Processing Environments

Traditional file processing environments are process-oriented systems. Data flow from one program to another. Data files are created to satisfy specific processing needs. For example, if the purchasing department wants to keep track of purchase orders, then a purchase order file would be developed with only the data needed to generate the output required by the purchasing department. Each application program or system that is developed contains data designed to meet only the needs of a particular department or group of users.

Figure 12.2 depicts a traditional file system for an automotive parts distributor and service organization. Each file is accessed separately by application programs. This system works effectively until data have to be shared between applications. Suppose the manager of this organization wants to find out what date a part needed for a specific customer will be received from a vendor. This inquiry requires three different files to be accessed. In addition, a program has to be written to open the three files, search for the required information, and produce the output.

Data Base Management Environments

In a data base management environment, the focus is on data rather than on the procedures used to process the data. The data base is created separately from the programs that access the data. Data are considered to be a shared resource in this environment. The data resource is physically implemented so that it can be shared by several users.

Figure 12.3 shows a data base management environment for an automotive organization. Notice that each program interfaces with the data base management system rather than directly with the data. The data base management system is responsible for providing access to all the data in this example.

Data Retrieval in the Two Environments

The traditional file processing environment accesses data directly from information exchanged between the application program and the operating system. A data base management environment requires the use of a data base management system. A data base management system (DBMS) is a set of specialized programs designed to describe, protect, store, and access a data base.

The functions of a DBMS are the following:

- Define all data used in the system and specify the relationships among data separate from the application programs that access the data.
- Provide a method to add, delete, and change data within the data base.
- Protect the data resource so that it is secure, reliable, consistent, and correct.

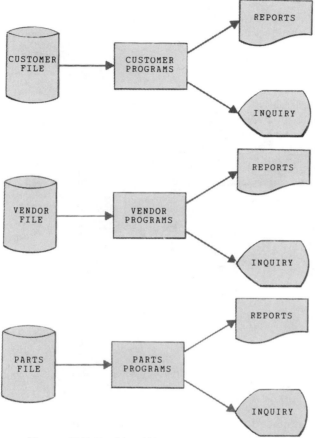

Figure 12.2 Traditional file processing environment.

- Provide for data sharing between multiple users of the data base.
- Allow data retrieval in a language understandable by the users of the system.

Figure 12.4 depicts the difference in data access between a traditional file processing system and a data base management system. In a traditional file processing system, data retrieval occurs as follows:

1. The application program requests a record to be read from a data file. The application program contains information about the organization of the file, how the file will be accessed, what physical device the data are located on, and the exact field structure of the file.
2. The operating system causes the data to be accessed, read, and transferred to a buffer in main memory.
3. The operating system transfers the data to the work area for the application program.

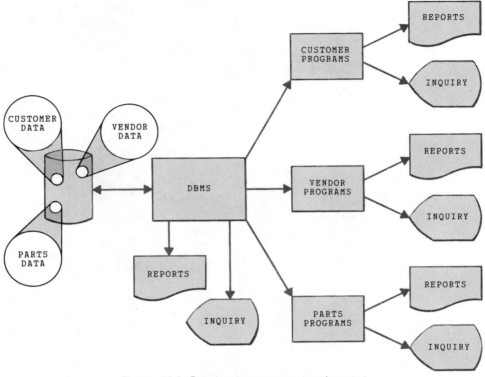

Figure 12.3 Data base management environment.

4. The application program processes the data.

In the data base management system, data retrieval occurs as follows:

1. The application program requests a record to be read from the data base.
2. The DBMS verifies that the data have been previously defined within the data base. The DBMS identifies the location of the data. (This process will be discussed further in the next chapter.)
3. The DBMS requests that the operating system read the data.
4. The operating system causes the data to be accessed, read, and transferred to a buffer in main memory used by the DBMS.
5. The DBMS transfers the data from its buffer to the work area of the application program. The DBMS also provides status information to the application program, such as "record not found."
6. The application program processes the data.

Benefits of the Data Base Management Environment

A cursory examination of these two systems might make you think that a DBMS does nothing but add extra steps. The extra steps added with a DBMS actually

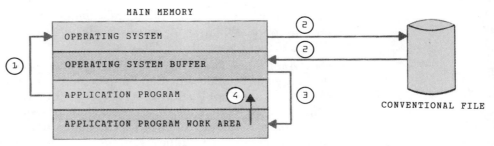

(a) Data retrieval in a traditional file processing environment

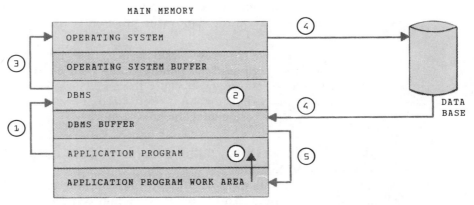

(b) Data retrieval in a data base management environment

Figure 12.4 Data retrieval methods.

make it simpler for users to retrieve data. The data base environment offers a number of important advantages compared to the traditional file processing environment. A few of the major benefits are discussed in the paragraphs that follow.

1. *Improved Data Integration.* In a data base management system, data are organized into a logical structure that allows multiple relationships to be defined between data entities. Look back at Figure 12.3. Suppose a user wants to know how many customers currently need a given part. This relationship could quickly be accomplished by the DBMS.

2. *Increase the Accessibility of Data.* Data accessibility is a user's ability to get needed information from the data base. A DBMS usually contains a high-level query language, such as Query By Example (QBE), that allows data to be obtained from the data base without having to write an application program in, for example, COBOL.

3. *Improves Data Control.* A data base consists of an integrated set of files. Data redundancy can be minimized because the data resource is controlled by a single set of programs. As a result, data inconsistencies are less likely. For example, a company using a data base management system would

typically store the part description and quantity on hand of an inventory item only once. When an update is made to this item, the changes are available to every user of the data.

4. *Ease of Application Development and Management.* Studies show that once a data base has been designed and implemented, a programmer can code and debug a new application at least two to four times faster than with traditional files. With a data base management system, the programmer does not have to be aware of the actual structure, organization, and location of a file. Removing these duties from the application programmer reduces the cost of software development. An organization can change the data structure of the data base without having to modify the application programs that access the data. This function reduces program maintenance costs.

5. *Improved Data Security.* Data security prevents unauthorized access to data. Most organizations require some form of protection against unauthorized access to data. Because the DBMS can control access to data entities, the security function is centralized and easily implemented with the use of a data base management system.

When Should an Organization Consider a Data Base Management System?

Certain factors about an organization indicate the applicability of a data base management system. An organization should consider using a data base management system if:

- Application needs are constantly changing. An organization pursuing new markets or developing new product lines will have different data requirements from an organization that has a more static product.
- Ad hoc and intermittent inquiries will be required from the data base management system.
- Many departments use essentially the same data to satisfy their information needs.
- A need exists to reduce programming lead times and decrease program development costs.
- A need exists to improve the consistency of data.

Not all organizations should adopt the data base management system approach to data management. An organization should use a traditional file processing environment if:

- Very little need exists to share data between users.
- The organization operates in a static internal and external environment. An organization experiencing little to no change usually requires only very standardized transaction processing. This processing is most efficiently completed with a traditional file processing system.
- Data planning cannot be coordinated across departmental boundaries. A

traditional file system does not require that separate departments work together to plan their future data needs. The use of a DBMS forces an organization to collaborate to create the structure of the data base.

A data base management environment requires that an organization make a substantial capital investment in DBMS software. A large investment in time is also required to structure and input data into a data base format. In addition, a DBMS runs most effectively if one person or department is responsible for the overall planning and implementation of the data base. A systems analyst must examine an organization to make sure that the data base management system will provide the best data management alternative.

12.4 DATA ORGANIZATION ALTERNATIVES

Data are stored in files for access by a data retrieval system. Figure 12.5 presents an overview of the hierarchy of data storage on a computer system. Both data base management and traditional file processing environments require data to be physically stored on a secondary storage device. The actual physical data storage is the same in both environments. The rest of this chapter will be devoted to a discussion of the concepts related to this physical data organization.

The three basic file organizations are sequential file organization, direct file organization, and indexed sequential file organization. These three basic

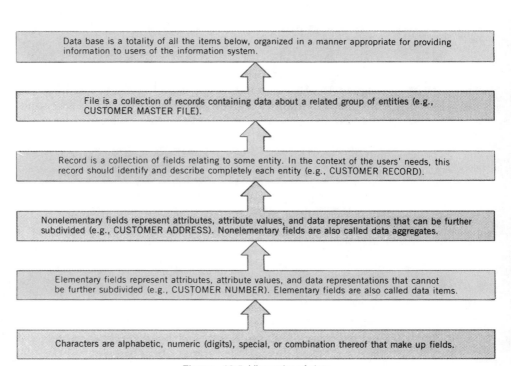

Data base is a totality of all the items below, organized in a manner appropriate for providing information to users of the information system.

File is a collection of records containing data about a related group of entities (e.g., CUSTOMER MASTER FILE).

Record is a collection of fields relating to some entity. In the context of the users' needs, this record should identify and describe completely each entity (e.g., CUSTOMER RECORD).

Nonelementary fields represent attributes, attribute values, and data representations that can be further subdivided (e.g., CUSTOMER ADDRESS). Nonelementary fields are also called data aggregates.

Elementary fields represent attributes, attribute values, and data representations that cannot be further subdivided (e.g., CUSTOMER NUMBER). Elementary fields are also called data items.

Characters are alphabetic, numeric (digits), special, or combination thereof that make up fields.

Figure 12.5 Hierarchy of data.

organizations are not the only ones available. Other organizations have been developed, but if you understand the principles, advantages, and disadvantages of each of these, you will have a strong basis for understanding how data management and organization systems function.

Sequential File Organization

The simplest way to organize a collection of records that make up a file is to use sequential organization. Records are stored one after the other without concern for the actual value of data contained in the records. The first record is placed in the first position of the file, the second record is placed in the second position, and so on until all records are placed in the file. Records can also be sorted into a prespecified order within sequential file organization.

With sequential organization of data records, records are placed on the file using a key or code for sequencing (e.g., inventory item sequence). Usually before changing or updating the sequential file, all new items are first *batched* (grouped) and *sorted* into the same sequence. To access any data record in the sequential file, all records preceding the one in question must first be passed. That is, to access record number 1000, the system must read past 999 records. An insertion of a data record means creating a new sequential file.

The sequence of the file is usually chosen according to some common attribute called a *key*. The sequence of a file may be changed by selecting a different key and sorting the stored records according to the values of the new key. In Figure 12.6(A), a file containing data about the customers of an organization is sorted according to the numerical values associated with the field CUSTOMER NUMBER. If the field CUSTOMER NAME were used as a key, then the stored records would be physically rearranged in the file illustrated in Figure 12.6(B). In some cases, using one data attribute as a sorting key is not sufficient to identify a given stored record. In this case, one or more additional data attributes would be joined together to form the key. Figure 12.6(C) shows the same file sorted in ascending order according to the values of the data attribute SALESPERSON NUMBER. Notice that two stored records exist with the value of SALESPERSON NUMBER equal to 14. To ensure a unique sequence, the data attribute CUSTOMER NAME is joined to SALESPERSON NUMBER and the values of CUSTOMER NAME are placed in ascending order.

Sequential organization is an efficient method of data organization if a large volume of records and a reasonably high percentage of records are being processed each run. Sequential organization is applicable to preparing reports that must meet such information requirements as retrieving all stored records in ascending order by CUSTOMER NUMBER. It is not suited for information requests such as "retrieve only the record where CUSTOMER NUMBER is equal to 176." In both situations, all of the stored records must be accessed, but for the second request, the first six records accessed are of no value. So sequential organization offers rapid access to the next record in a file if the basis for retrieval is the same as the basis for the physical ordering of the file. In an information system meeting a variety of information needs, this is seldom the case.

Customer Number	Customer Name	Salesperson Number	
123	BARCO	21	
138	AJAX	14	
142	ACME	16	
144	TURF	14	(A)
151	BEACON	26	
170	SALZ	15	
176	CEZON	28	

Sort Key

142	ACME	16	
138	AJAX	14	
123	BARCO	21	
151	BEACON	26	(B)
176	CEZON	28	
170	SALZ	15	
144	TURF	14	

Sort Key

138	AJAX	14	
144	TURF	14	
170	SALZ	15	
142	ACME	16	(C)
123	BARCO	21	
151	BEACON	26	
176	CEZON	28	

Sort Key

Figure 12.6 Sorting a file in different sequences by using different sort keys.

If a group of stored records must be processed using more than one key to satisfy information requests, the stored records are sorted into different work files. The contents of each file are the same, but the ordering is different for different purposes. This duplication of files wastes storage space and processing time.

Sequential file organization is effective for high-volume, high-activity rate files that do not have to be accessed in a random manner. Sequential file organization can be used with both magnetic disk and magnetic tape storage media. One major disadvantage of sequential file organization is that a user cannot directly access an individual record in the file. The next two file organization methods differ in one critical way from sequential file organization. Both of the next two methods permit random access of records within the files.

Direct File Organization

Direct file organization allows random access to records within files. This task is accomplished by a relationship between the key field of the record and the physical location of the record on a secondary storage device. Direct organization infers a direct relationship between a key field and storage location. Direct file organization is based on maintaining a predictable relationship between a record's key field value and its location on a secondary storage device. Two different predictable relationships can be maintained: direct conversion and hashing.

Direct Conversion

Direct conversion allows records to be found quickly because the access mechanism needs to be moved only once. With direct conversion every possible key value must correspond to a unique storage address. Hence, the *range* of the key value dictates the number of physical storage locations that must be reserved for the data file. Figure 12.7 illustrates a procedure that converts a key value to a physical address.

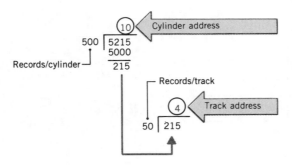

Figure 12.7 A procedure that converts a key value to a physical address.

Suppose we wish to establish a file of data records for the telephone exchange 471. If the last four digits of the telephone number were the primary key, then we would need 10,000 physical storage locations to hold the data records (i.e., 471-0000 to 471-9999). Suppose further that each track of a disk could hold exactly 50 records and that a cylinder had 10 tracks, each holding 500 records. Doing a few calculations tells us that we need 200 tracks or 20 cylinders to hold our data.

The cylinder address of any record relative to where our file begins is the quotient produced by dividing the last four digits of the key by 500. The remainder is divided by the records per track, 50, to determine the track address. Again, the quotient of our second division is the track where our data record is located. For the telephone number 471-5215, you should obtain the relative cylinder address 10 and the relative track address 4.

Direct conversion usually means that the file is not completely filled with data records. Consider the situation in which a Social Security number is the key to a personnel file. One billion storage locations must be set aside because the keys have a possible range of from 000-00-0000 to 999-99-9999. If 10,000 records are in the file, utilization of the assigned memory is 0.001 precent. This poor utilization of storage space can be overcome by adopting a conversion method called hashing.

Hashing

The *hashing* method (also called algorithm, randomizing, or transformation method) converts a key into a relative physical file address. Here the range of keys in a file is compressed into a smaller range of physical addresses. The main difficulty encountered with hashing is the problem of *synonyms* (records whose keys randomize to the same physical address). To minimize synonyms that cannot be written where they belong (*overflow* records), two techniques are used. With the first technique, hashing is to a track address rather than a record address. In this way not every synonym will produce an overflow. A second technique is to select a hashing algorithm that distributes records evenly over the file. Of the many algorithms available, the most popular appears to be *prime number division*.

Using the *prime number division* technique and randomization to a track address, suppose that 6,000, 200-byte records are to be addressed to a magnetic disk having a 5,000-byte-per-track capacity. Therefore, 240 tracks would be required if all the records were evenly distributed. Because this ideal is seldom attained, more storage space, say, 20 percent or a *loading factor* of 83 percent (240/288), is added to handle synonyms. Now the total space allocated is 288 tracks. This means that if an even distribution of records to tracks was actually attained, approximately 21 out of the 25 possible storage locations of each of the 288 tracks would be occupied.

A prime number close to, but less than, 288 is now chosen, say, 283. The prime number of 283 is then divided into a record's key value, say, 1457. The quotient is discarded and the remainder of 042 is the relative address of the track for this record. An overflow condition will occur if more than 25 records happen to randomize to relative track address 042 (i.e., have a remainder of

42). Overflow may be handled by placing overflow records on another track of the same cylinder or by providing separate storage cylinders that are independent of the overflow record's track address.

Another example of hashing[1] that uses 25 percent more storage space to handle synonyms, is illustrated in Figure 12.8. A maximum of two records are stored on each track. Tracks 29 to 32 hold *overflow synonyms*. Overflows are loaded on these tracks in the order in which they occur.

Indexed Sequential File Organization

Indexed sequential file organization is an attempt to retain the advantages of sequential file organization while still permitting random access to records. An indexed sequential file is actually two files: (1) a file containing the data sorted in order by a key field and (2) a file containing a series of indices used to access the data.

Indexed sequential file organization allows both sequential and random access of records within the file. It allows sequential processing to begin at the first (or any other) record in the file and processes as many other subsequent records as desired. Alternatively, the organization also allows a user randomly to obtain a selected record by searching through a series of indices.

We locate data using an indexed sequential method by creating a separate physical file, which is made up of an index entry for every nth data record rather than every data record. It is first searched sequentially until the approximate location of the data record we are seeking is determined. Then, beginning at the location in the data file indicated by the index entry, the localized portion of the data file is searched sequentially until a match to the key value desired is found.

Let us work through an example showing how this procedure is applied to locating data. The six entries in the index of Figure 12.9 indicate the ordered names of persons in the data segment or sublist. For example, suppose we wished to retrieve the data record having the key value "LARSON." We would begin by sequentially searching the index starting with the record having the key value "BARNES." The record "LARSON" may be in the first sublist. We know that it is not in the first sublist only when the second key value in the index "DEITRICK" is read. As we sequentially search through the index, we determine that if the record with the key "LARSON" exists, then it must be contained in the sublist headed by the data record with the key value "KELLOGG" (i.e., "KELLOGG" < "LARSON" < "NEWMAN"). Control is then transferred to relative address 19, the location of the data record "KELLOGG." The sublist of the actual data file is searched sequentially until, finally, a match is found at relative location 21.

Indexed sequential file organization should be used when it is necessary to access data both sequentially and randomly. An indexed sequential file will not access sequentially as quickly as will a sequential file. It will also not access

---

[1]Adapted from James Martin, *Computer Data-Base Organization*, 2nd ed. (Englewood Cliffs, N.J.: Prentice Hall, 1977).

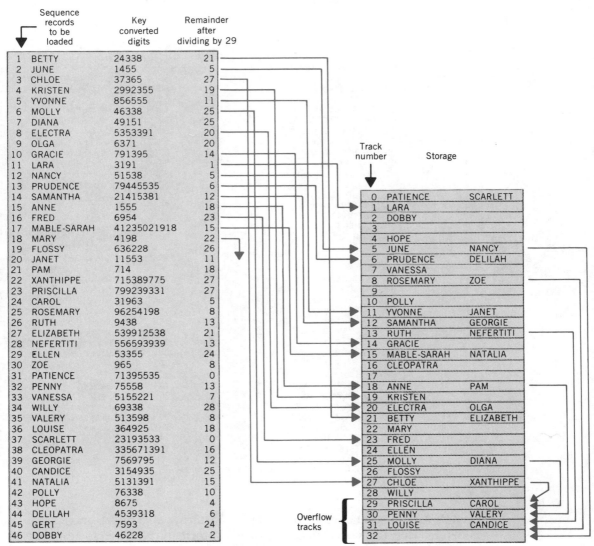

Figure 12.8 Records stored using a hashing algorithm.

randomly as quickly as a direct organization file. The biggest advantage of the indexed sequential organization is its flexibility.

SUMMARY

Authorities refer to the data base as the foundation building block of the organization. It is vital that the structure of the data base matches the processing requirements and decision-making needs of the organization's users.

Data management tasks can be performed manually or by a computerized system. The tasks involved in data management include defining the organi-

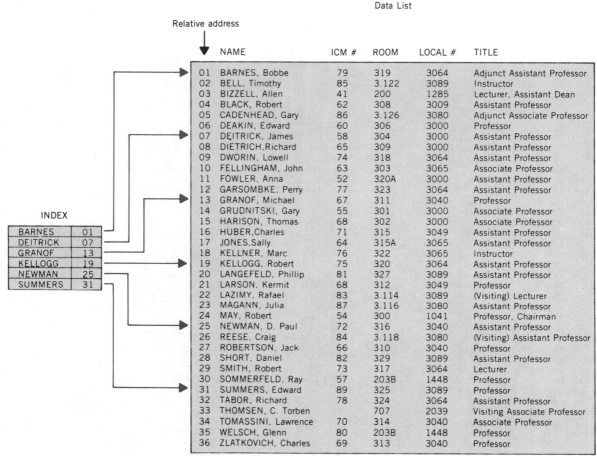

Figure 12.9 Data records searched indexed sequentially.

zation's data in a standard format, physically storing data on a storage medium, and retrieving the stored data to provide information to users within the organization.

Traditional file processing and data base management environments are available to serve as computerized data management systems. Both environments effectively complete the tasks of data management and have relative advantages and disadvantages. A data base management system is a better choice than a traditional file processing system if an organization requires integrated data, is in a dynamic marketplace, shares a lot of data between departments, and has a need to reduce programming lead times and decrease program development costs.

Both data base management systems and traditional file systems require that data be stored on a physical secondary storage device for data access. Three methods to organize data on a secondary storage device are sequential file organization, direct file organization, and indexed sequential file organization. The chapter discusses the relative advantages and disadvantages of each approach to file organization.

IMPORTANT TERMS

attribute

attribute value

batch

data base management system (DBMS)

data description

data management

direct conversion

direct file organization

entity

hashing algorithm

indexed sequential file organization

loading factor

overflow synonym

random access retrieval

sequential access retrieval

sequential file organization

sort

sublist

synonym

Assignment

REVIEW QUESTIONS

12.1 What are the three tasks of data management?

12.2 Contrast the terms "data entity" and "data attribute." Give two examples of data entities and list at least five data attributes for each of your sample data entities.

12.3 What is physical data organization? How does physical data organization affect the efficiency of data retrieval?

12.4 What types of computerized data base management systems are currently available?

12.5 What is a data base? What is a data base management system?

12.6 List five functions of a data base management system.

12.7 Summarize the advantages of a data base management system in comparison to a traditional file processing system.

12.8 What extra steps are involved in data retrieval using a data base management system rather than a traditional file processing system?

12.9 What are the relative advantages and disadvantages of sequential organization? direct organization? indexed sequential organization?

12.10 In a hashing context, what is a synonym?

12.11 What are the steps in locating data using an indexed sequential organization?

QUESTIONS FOR DISCUSSION

12.12 "Every organization maintains a large data base. The problem confronting both management and the systems analyst today is how to organize this data base so that it can be more effectively utilized." Discuss fully.

12.13 "The data base is the underlying and basic component of an information system." Discuss fully.

12.14 "Every organization should purchase a data base management system to do their data management tasks." Decide whether you agree or disagree with this statement and present an argument supporting your position.

12.15 "Data base management systems take computer resources away from application programs and decrease the overall throughput of the system." Discuss this statement.

12.16 "We installed a DBMS six years ago on our mainframe computer. We used our existing file structures and programs, simply converting them to a data base format so that we could convert systems as quickly as possible. We can't seem to get any integrated data from the system. Data base management systems don't work any differently from traditional file systems and are a waste of time and money." Discuss this situation and speculate as to why the organization involved is not able to retrieve integrated data from their data base management system.

12.17 "To sift out the information wanted from a sequentially organized file, a great deal of sorting of data normally is required, and if only a small percentage of the records are affected in a processing run, then many records are read unnecessarily." Comment on this statement.

12.18 "I can furnish any information you want from my batch processing system. It may take me a little longer, but I can still perform any information processing tasks that they can perform in those fancy direct access systems." Comment on this statement.

12.19 "Although data files with direct organization are applicable in many situations, most organizations do not use this technique to organize their data files." Discuss fully.

12.20 "Many data files are organized in an indexed sequential manner because the analyst who designs the files isn't sure how the files will be accessed in the future." Is this a good idea?

12.21 "Many data files are organized sequentially because the analyst who designs the file does not understand what factors must be evaluated when choosing a file organization approach." Discuss why this statement may be true.

EXERCISES AND PROBLEMS

12.22 Interview a manager from a local organization (preferably someone knowledgeable about data processing) that is large enough to utilize a computer for processing data and information, or review the literature for a report or article that describes the data processing activities in a particular organization. The objectives of your efforts are to determine (1) what data are contained in the computer-accessible data base, (2) to what extent this data base is integrated, (3) what the philosophy of the organization as it related to the development of information systems is, (4) what the goals of management concerning future expansion of the data base are, and (5) what the present hardware configuration is. Prepare a report describing your findings.

12.23 Using your own experiences and some library and field research, identify the types of data files and records likely to be found supporting the following organization's operations (ignore considerations such as payroll, inventory control, miscellaneous accounting, and so forth):

1. A personnel recruiting agency.
2. An independent credit bureau.
3. A dating and escort service.
4. A dog breeders association.
5. A custom/antique jeweler.

12.24 From journals and magazines related to information and data processing, research one or more data base management systems being offered for purchase. Evaluate these packages in terms of the capabilities and functions they propose to perform.

12.25 Listed in this exercise is a series of documents and reports prepared by various types of organizations. Evaluate these information outputs and determine the following: (1) what type of data files must be maintained to produce the output, (2) what data could be entered once for many uses, (3) what data must be entered each time the document is produced, and (4) what relationships exist, if any, among the data files you have identified.

1. An employee paycheck.
2. A year-to-date sales report by customer.
3. A purchase order for raw materials and miscellaneous supplies.
4. An invoice to customers for purchases.
5. An analysis of records of work performed, against a planned work schedule.
6. A check to vendors.

12.26 An inventory contains 25,000 different items. Information about quantity on hand of each item is stored in a sequential list. A user may determine the quantity on hand of a particular item by keying in the item number by means of a terminal connected to the computer. The requested number is accessed through a sequential search. Can you suggest a better way?

12.27 A disk has a capacity of 7,200 bytes per track. Thirty-six hundred 200-byte records are to be mapped with a 75 percent loading factor. How many record locations are required? How many tracks are required? Select a prime number for division.

12.28 What track address will be assigned to a record with a key of 29864? Assume that (1) the file contains 40,000 records, (2) 500 records can be placed on a track of a disk, (3) an 80 percent loading factor is desired, and (4) a hashing technique is to be used.

12.29 The Coriolanus Center Stage Theater is considering automating its information system. The theater produces live dramatic productions in a large year-round resort community. Productions are presented six days a week (Mondays are "dark") throughout the entire year. Thursday through Sunday, two performances are given each day. The theater currently seats 2,000 in a theater-in-the-round setting. Ticket prices vary depending on the performance, location of seat, and discount available for the patron. Students and senior citizens receive standard discounts and large groups may receive special pricing from a standard group calculation. The theater company schedules performances approximately three months in advance of the production date. About 15 different productions will be available for ticketing at any one point in time.

1. The theater company would like to automate box office operations. Identify the entities for a box office system. Define the attributes for each of the entities identified. Don't worry about overlap between the attributes of different entities.
2. Would you use a traditional file processing system or a data base management system for this application? Why?
3. Group your data attributes into records. Group your records into files. Identify key values for each record.

4. Which file organization method(s) would you choose for this application?

5. The theater company would also like to create a marketing system at the same time as the automated box office system. The company wants to know what type of patrons frequent the theater and what kinds of production are most profitable. Management is also considering installing a season ticket system. Would you need additional entities in your system? What entities would you add and what attributes would be needed for those entities?

6. Would you use a traditional file environment or a data base environment for the combined box office system and marketing system? Did you change you mind from question 2?

7. What kind of inquiries do you imagine management would make in the marketing system? Did you include all the entities needed to make managerial inquiries?

12.30 Red River Billing Service handles the billing operations for a number of businesses in the local community. Red River has over 50 billing clients that it processes on a monthly basis. Overall, there are approximately 150,000 customer master records maintained and about 70,000 to 80,000 of these are updated nightly. At the end of the working day, credit sales slips are transported to Red River from the various businesses. Red River enters the information nightly from each credit sales slip using key-to-disk technology. Once a month, on a cyclical basis for each client, Red River sends out bills to its clients' customers. Red River also accepts payment from their client's customers and processes the payments as they arrive.

Red River delivers information to each client weekly about the bills that it has processed. This information includes total sales, number of transactions, listing of bills sent, and number of customers. In addition, Red River reports sales statistics, credit exceptions, aging of accounts receivable, and abbreviated income statements. Their current computer system was purchased six years ago. Over the six-year period, the number of transactions has increased about 20 percent.

1. Red River is a profitable company and wants to keep current in its use of computer technology. The company is considering the adoption of a data base management system. Would you recommend the use of a data base management system?

2. All files in the system are sequentially organized at this time. Would you recommend a change in file organization?

12.31 The See-Clearly Optometry Group is an optometry office composed of seven optometrists. The doctors provide a full-service optometric office, including vision evaluations, contact lens, and glass correction. The doctors are working in a very competitive environment because their services are available from a variety of different sources. Currently, all data processing in the office is done manually. The doctors want to install a computerized billing system and an inventory system for glasses and lenses.

1. Identify the data entities that would compose a system for See-Clearly. Define the data attributes for each entity. Attempt to group your data attributes into record structures. Group your records into data files.

2. Would you use a traditional file processing system or a data base management system for this application? Why?

3. Which file organization method(s) would you choose for this application?

12.32 MoParts, an automotive parts dealer, maintains six warehouses scattered throughout the Southwest. MoParts carries an inventory of 30,000 different items, each of these items identified by a 12-digit part number. MoParts management wants to record each transaction affecting each item, as it occurs, so that if any one item in inventory reached or exceeded the reorder point, the buyer(s) would receive an out-of-stock notification. In broad terms, provide a sketch of the computer configuration and description of the system you would suggest to the management of MoParts for implementation. Specify type of file media and data organization to be implemented.

12.33 A large manufacturer of children's toys is considering the implementation of a marketing information system to assist its sales force. Approximately 300 salespeople work out of 15 branch offices throughout the continental United States and Canada. The goal of the system is to have customer sales history files online at central headquarters, in St. Louis, which can be accessed by remote terminals at each branch office during normal business hours. New customer orders and shipments received from each branch office nightly will update the sales history file that same night.

Approximately 30,000 customers' records are on file at any one time. Fifty customers are added, and 20 customers are deleted, daily. History data are maintained for 13 months by product for each customer. Each customer's master record has 100 characters of descriptive data. The average number of product records per customer is expected to be 20, each having 70 characters of information. Finally, projections indicate that the volume of order and shipment records updating the history file will be 3,000 nightly.

Prepare a brief report describing the structure of the required data base you would propose.

12.34 A systems study has been completed in a large company that manufactures and markets various types of paper for the printing industry. This study initially was intended to identify the information requirements related to the purchasing function but was subsequently expanded to include the accounts payable function as well. The justification for expanding the study was based on the similarity of the data required in the data base to support each function.

The study identified the need for purchasing to maintain three files: (1) a vendor master file containing name, address, purchasing terms, and miscellaneous descriptive data; (2) an open purchase order file containing all of the data related to purchase orders placed but not yet completed; and (3) a history file of purchases made in a two-year period, by product, by vendor. At the time of the study, these files were maintained in a manual system.

The accounts payable department on the other hand required the following files: (1) a vendor master file containing the descriptive data necessary to produce and mail a check for purchases received, (2) a file of invoices from vendors received but not yet paid, and (3) a one-year history file of paid vendor invoices. Currently, accounts payable maintains a manual vendor master and open invoice file.

The company leases a medium-sized computer with both magnetic tape and disk storage available. Approximately 20 percent of all purchases are considered rebuys from an existing vendor. At any point in time there are 3,000 active vendors, 5,000 open purchase orders, and 1,500 open invoices, and the company places 40,000 purchase orders annually.

Required:

1. Identify the data entities and data attributes for the system.
2. Should the company purchase a DBMS or use the currently available file processing system? Why?
3. Which attributes are shared among the entities? Group your identified attributes into files.
4. What storage media should be used for each data file?

5. How should each file be updated, and which department is responsible for keeping the file current?

12.35 Oatman Publishing wants to be able to access its personnel records directly yet still process them sequentially for the purpose of generating a monthly payroll. Accordingly, Oatman Publishing has decided to adopt an indexed sequential organization method for these records. Oatman Publishing currently employs 113 people, and its employee identification numbers run from 001 to 113. The manager of systems development has told you this data file will be ordered by employee identification number.

> **Required:** Construct the entries for the index file so that the personnel records can be accessed directly. Assume an index entry contains the key of the first record in a data segment or sublist. Additionally, explain the steps necessary to access the personnel record of employee number 035 directly.

12.36 For each of the following situations, indicate the most suitable data file organization and the reason for your selection:

1. A regional motel chain maintains a computer reservation system for each of its motels. On an ongoing basis, changes are made to the "room records" to reflect arrivals of new occupants and their expected departure date and daily room, food, and other charges.

2. A local speed shop maintains an inventory master file of 5,000 records. Each day an average of 1,200 records are updated to reflect customer sales and parts receipts. Monthly, less than 100 parts are either added to or deleted from the file. An inventory "want" list is printed every day of parts that have fallen below their reorder point.

3. An athletic club has approximately 1,100 members. Each month, member records are updated to reflect the monthly fixed dues and variable charges (e.g., massage, charges to the health bar) and member payments. At this time, records of new members are added to the file and billings are prepared.

4. Approximately 115 jobs are on the shop floor at any given time. As each job passes through a workstation, its record is updated with time and material added. So that in-process jobs can be monitored closely, shop supervisors and planners require a daily listing of all jobs on the floor. On average, 20 new jobs are completed and started each day.

BIBLIOGRAPHY

DATE, C. J. *An Introduction to Data Base Systems*, 4th ed. Reading, Mass.: Addison-Wesley, 1986.

EVEREST, G. C. *Database Management: Objectives, System Functions, and Administration*. New York: McGraw-Hill, 1985.

MARTIN, DANIEL. *Advanced Database Techniques*. Cambridge, Mass.: MIT Press, 1986.

MARTIN, JAMES. *Computer Data-Base Organization*, 2nd ed. Englewood Cliffs, N.J.: Prentice Hall, 1977.

SALZBERG, BETTY JOAN. *An Introduction to Data Base Design*. Orlando, Fla.: Academic Press, 1986.

WALTERS, RICHARD F. *Database Principles for Personal Computers*. Englewood Cliffs, N.J.: Prentice Hall, 1987.

13

THE DATA BASE MANAGEMENT SYSTEM

13.1 INTRODUCTION

This is the second of two chapters on data management systems. The previous chapter concentrated on the basic concepts of data management systems. In Chapter 12 we discussed the three tasks that must be completed by all data management systems, presented the two approaches to computerized data management systems, and explained how data are physically organized on secondary storage devices. The purpose of this chapter is to explain in more detail the principles of the second approach to computerized data management systems: data base management systems (DBMSs).

We begin by defining a data base and explaining the software components that compose DBMSs. Next, we present a framework that makes it a little easier to understand the structure of a DBMS. Then we present an overview of the individual framework components. We end with a discussion of the two approaches to designing an organization's computerized data management system.

You won't become an expert in data base technology reading this chapter. DBMSs are complex software packages that require specialized training to use fully. You will, however, become more data base literate and be better able to work with a data base administrator to design an information system that uses a data base.

The objectives of this chapter are:

1. To present a framework for understanding the technology of DBMSs.
2. To explain the components of a DBMS and how they are used to store, relate, and retrieve data.
3. To understand how to design the data structures used in an information system from a process-oriented and an information-oriented perspective.

13.2 PURPOSE OF A DATA BASE ADMINISTRATOR AND DBMS

Storing data is fairly easy. Retrieving specific data in a format that meets different users' information requirements is another matter entirely. The most important point to understand about data bases is that the data within a data base must be integrated and related to each other by the use of coordinated key fields to meet users' requirements. Some systems analysts try to meet these requirements in a traditional file processing environment. Others use a DBMS. In many companies, the DBMS works even better if a data base administrator helps to structure and maintain data.

Traditional File Processing Environment Revisited

Figure 13.1 presents an example of a set of three files used to process purchase orders in an organization: a file for purchase orders, a file for inventory items, and a file for vendor information. These three files could be considered a purchasing data base. Look at the key fields needed to interrelate the three files. The item number links together the purchase order file and the inventory item file, while the vendor number links together the purchase order file and the vendor information file.

A data base can be implemented through a traditional file management system, but it is very difficult to maintain and manipulate the key fields that are required to produce data integration. Also, in a traditional file system, data retrieval must be done on a record-by-record basis through the use of a third-generation programming language, such as COBOL, BASIC, FORTRAN, or Pascal.

Imagine writing a program to access selectively a specific purchase order with the file system displayed in Figure 13.1. Each of the files should use either indexed or direct file organization, both of which allow random access. All three files would have to be declared in the program. The programmer would have to read the purchase order file, the vendor information file, and the inventory item file randomly to get the required data for the inquiry.

Sample Purchase Order File

ORDER NUMBER	VENDOR NUMBER	DATE ORDERED	DATE NEEDED	SHIPPING LOCATION	SHIPPING INSTRUCTIONS	ITEM 1 NUMBER	ITEM 1 QUANTITY	ITEM 1 PRICE	ITEM 2 NUMBER	ITEM 2 QUANTITY	ITEM 2 PRICE

Sample Inventory Item File

ITEM NUMBER	ITEM DESCRIPTION	ITEM LOCATION	QUANTITY ON HAND	ECONOMIC ORDER QUANTITY

Sample Vendor Information File

VENDOR NUMBER	VENDOR NAME	VENDOR ADDRESS	VENDOR CITY	VENDOR STATE	VENDOR ZIP CODE	TELEPHONE NUMBER	CONTACT NAME

Figure 13.1 Sample purchase order file system.

In many organizations, the data contained in these files might already be located in other files. It's likely that an inventory item file already exists for inventory applications. So, it's possible that the item number might not be a key field and that the file might not be organized in a manner that permits random access. If this were true, the programmer would have to reorganize the file to use it for the purchasing application and then reorganize it again to use it for other applications.

Need for a Data Base Administrator

In a traditional file environment, data integration is done in individual programs by individual programmers. The responsibility for the maintenance of key fields, the choice of file organization, and the access of data are in the hands of the programmers. This means that separate individuals have the power to structure the data base for their own needs.

Many times, individuals do not communicate with each other to discuss the best structure of data for the whole organization. Instead, individuals structure data for a single application or group of applications. A data base environment should have a single person, or group of people, in charge of the structure of the data base. This function is called data base administration, and the person in charge is termed a data base administrator.

The data base administrator is responsible for working with analysts and users to complete the following tasks: define data, model data, design data bases, ensure proper data integrity, monitor the efficiency of the data base, and evaluate different DBMS technologies. Surveys have shown that assigning a specific person as data base administrator increases the overall effectiveness of a DBMS.

Software Components of a DBMS

A data base management system is a set of specialized programs designed to describe, protect, store, and access a data base and overcome the limitations of traditional file processing. A DBMS allows data organization and integration decisions to be centralized. If a data base is designed, implemented, and maintained correctly, a DBMS can help an organization increase its ability to respond to changing information needs.

A DBMS has two major generic software components:

1. *Data Base Control System.* The DBCS software interfaces with user application programs to retrieve data from the data base. It processes data retrieval actions such as READ and WRITE commands from programs. Contained within the DBCS is the data manipulation language (DML). The DML is the set of commands issued by an application program used to retrieve and change data base data. Figure 13.2 provides an example of a set of DML commands to find the names of all female employees with salaries greater than $45,000.

```
SELECT EMPLOYEE-NAME
FROM    EMPLOYEE-FILE
WHERE   SEX = "FEMALE" AND SALARY GREATER THAN 45000
```

Figure 13.2 A set of data manipulation language statements.

2. *Data Base Storage System.*   The DBSS software manipulates the data files needed to store the data within the data base. It establishes and maintains both the organization of data and the links between interrelated data. Contained within the DBSS is the data definition language (DDL). The DDL is the vocabulary used to define the structure of the data base. The DDL contains terms for defining records, fields, key fields, and relationships between records.

The DBCS and the DBSS work together to provide all the functions of a DBMS. The following description is a very brief overview of how the two software components work together. The DBCS receives commands in a predescribed DML format from an application program being run by a user. The DBCS processes the commands and turns them over to the DBSS. The DBSS searches through the available data structures as predefined with the DDL. The DBSS locates the needed file and record. The DBSS then turns over the information to the operating system for actual data retrieval from a secondary storage device.

13.3 FRAMEWORK AND DIAGRAMMING TECHNIQUES FOR UNDERSTANDING DATA BASE LEVELS AND RELATIONSHIPS

Understanding data base levels and DBMSs can be difficult. The task of understanding is easier if you break it down into smaller pieces. The framework shown in Figure 13.3 was developed in 1975 by the Standards Planning and Requirements Committee (SPARC) of the American National Standards Institute (ANSI). It is referred to as the ANSI/SPARC data base reference model. Following this presentation are sections on the entity-relationship and Bachman diagramming techniques that are used to define entity relationships.

Framework Showing Levels of Data in a Data Base

The middle set of boxes in Figure 13.3 defines the four levels, or views, of data in a data base. The left side of the figure describes the people who have contact with each level of data. The right side of the figure defines what the level means. It's important to understand that the only level of data that actually exists is the lowest level, or physical data organization. Physical data organization was explained in Chapter 12. All data have to be stored on a secondary storage device for access by a DBMS. The other three levels depicted in the model are simply images used to understand the structure of a data base better.

The external level is the one viewed by users of a data base. It is the portion of the data base oriented to the needs of one or more application programs.

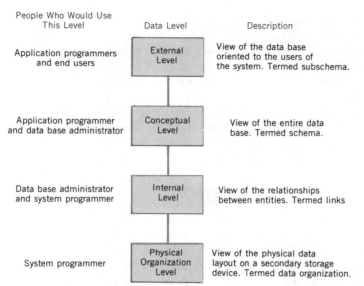

Figure 13.3 ANSI/SPARC reference model: four levels of data in a data base.

This level is frequently called a subschema. The subschema is sometimes referred to as a local view because it is a narrow or single view of the data base.

The conceptual level defines the entire data base at an abstract level. This level includes all the entities in the data base and the relationships among the entities. The conceptual level is frequently called the data base schema.

The internal level is a definition of specific interrelationships between actual records. This level describes how records are interrelated. For example, a DBMS may use pointers or indexes to interrelate data.

The lowest level is physical data organization. Physical data organization includes the grouping of records into actual data files and the data organization of those files.

Entity-Relationship Diagramming Technique

An entity-relationship (ER) diagram has three elements: (1) entities, (2) relationships, and (3) attributes. An entity is a person, place, object, or concept about which data are stored. Typical entities of a manufacturer are employees, suppliers, accounts receivable and payable, equipment, and inventory. Some entities that describe a bank are customers, mortgage loans, buildings, and demand deposits.

Entities are similar to nouns in English and attributes correspond to adjectives. Relationships are similar to verbs. Only entities have attributes. The ER diagramming technique using these elements enables systems analysts to attach attributes to entities and define relationships between entities thus resulting in a simple and easily understood data base model or schema of any system.

Construction of ER Diagrams

The ER model is conceptual, independent of machines or physical constraints. Rectangles represent entities and diamonds and connecting lines show relationships.

Once the entities are identified, the relationship between any two entities is designated as (1) one to one (1:1), (2) one to many (1:M), or (3) many to many (M:N). Notations for these designations are displayed in Figure 13.4.

Some analysts use lines without any notation and place the appropriate designations above the lines. If the relationships are M:N or obvious, some analysts do not use any notations. The diamond-shaped boxes between entities contain verbiage that describes something meaningful about the relationship, such as "is made by," "supplies," "pays," and "produces." This verbiage is optional, but generally recommended.

After the entities and relationships between them have been defined, the ER diagramming process moves to assigning attributes that describe the entities. Every entity has some basic attributes that characterize it. A customer, for example, may be described by such attributes as customer number, name, address, and credit code. A student may be described by name, student number, major, and classification. The assignment of these attributes results in a data model that can be used in data base design.

ER Examples

Figure 13.5 illustrates an ER diagram that models a sales transaction. It shows clearly the entities and relationships involved in a sales transaction from an accountant's viewpoint. The attributes that describe the INVENTORY entity form a data model. Other data models (not shown in the figure) would also be developed for the other entities.

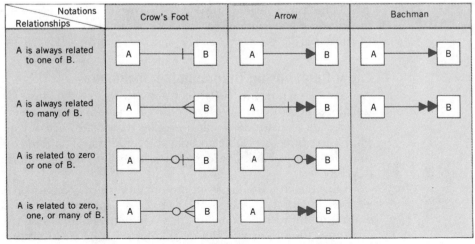

Figure 13.4 Alternative notations to show entity relationships.

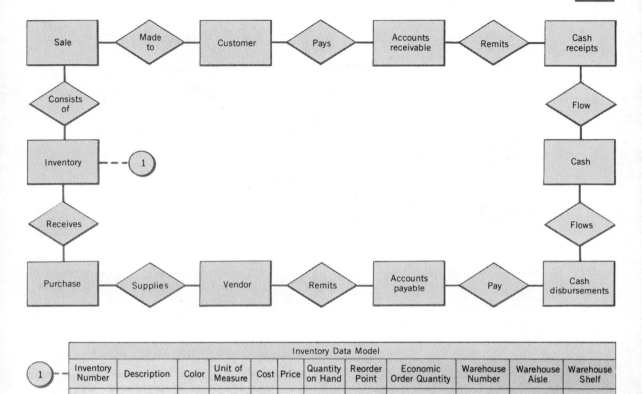

Figure   An ER diagram that models a sales transaction from an accountant's viewpoint.

An ER diagram can be easily drawn to reflect a sales transaction from the viewpoint of a marketing manager. Figure 13.6 demonstrates this, including a data model of the CUSTOMER entity.

The systems analyst can work with users such as accountants, marketing managers, warehouse supervisors, plant managers, and any other users to construct ER diagrams and determine if all necessary entities and relationships are included that pertain to their job, and if users' requirements can be met. The data models derived in the ER diagram clearly show users' data that will be contained in the data base to meet their inquiry and reporting requirements.

Users need not know that certain schema and subschemas are shared by different users. For example, the creation of one ER diagram for the customer entity may be sufficient for all users.

Bachman Diagramming Technique
Figure 13.7 is a graphic portrayal of a portion of a university data base integrated or linked together by the Bachman diagramming technique. This technique uses three rules discussed in the following material.

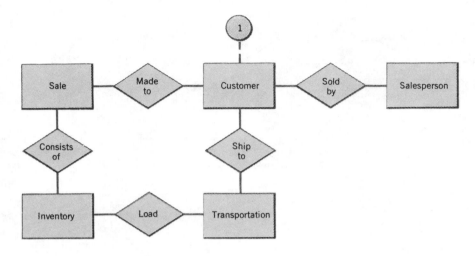

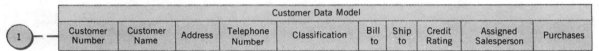

Figure 13.6 An ER diagram that models a sales transaction from a marketing manager's viewpoint.

1. *Each Entity is Displayed in a Horizontal Rectangle.* Our data base contains four entities: SCHEDULED CLASS, FACULTY MEMBER, STUDENT, and ROOM. Notice that the data attributes for a given entity are gathered into groups and are placed in adjacent horizontal rectangles in Figure 13.7. For example, the SCHEDULED CLASS entity has the following attributes: class number, section, faculty number, enrollment, room number, meeting

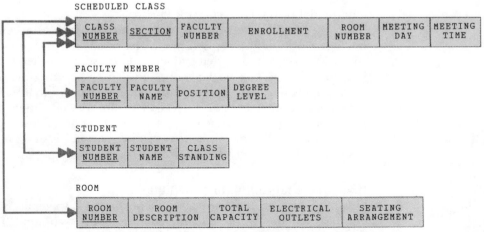

Figure 13.7 Bachman diagram of sample university data base.

day, and meeting time. The name of the entity appears above the first data attribute. Notice that the name FACULTY MEMBER appears above the attribute faculty number in the diagram. No two entities have the same name.

2. *Primary Keys are Underlined.*   An attribute used to identify a specific record is called a primary key. Data values must be unique within a data attribute for that data attribute to qualify as a primary key. For example, the attribute class number could not qualify as a primary key if multiple sections of a class were scheduled. Both the class number and the section need to be used together to form unique data values. Together, the class number and the section act as the primary key. Attributes are underlined to show they are part of the primary key.

3. *Relationships Between Entities are Shown with Lines.*   Lines and arrows are used in the diagram to show how separate entities are related to each other. Entities can be related in one of three different ways: one to one (1:1), one to many (1:M), or many to many (M:N). These relationships are shown graphically through the use of a single or a double arrowhead. A single arrowhead indicates one to one, a single arrowhead and double arrowhead shows one to many, and a double arrowhead at both ends designates a many-to-many relationship.

For example, in Figure 13.7, you can see that every class scheduled is taught by only one faculty member. Faculty members, however, can teach more than one class. The relationship between FACULTY MEMBER and SCHEDULED CLASS is 1:M. One student can take many classes. One class can be taken by, many students. As a result, the relationship between STUDENT and SCHEDULED CLASS is M:N. This single diagram is very useful for understanding the structure of the data base.

Introduction to Following Sections

The next three sections will discuss in detail the three abstract images of the data base: the external level, the conceptual level, and the internal level. The partial data base of a hypothetical university established in Figure 13.7 serves as our example.

13.4 EXTERNAL LEVEL OF DATA

The external level of data is viewed by users of the DBMS. Most users are not aware of the contents of the whole data base. Instead, users see only a portion of the data base.

Subschema and the Data Manipulation Language

A programmer writing a program that lists the names of students enrolled in a class would only view the subschema containing the entities SCHEDULED CLASS and STUDENT. If a faculty member wished to see a list of student names he or she teaches, the subschema used would contain the entities SCHEDULED

CLASS, STUDENT, and FACULTY MEMBER. If a report had to be generated listing all classes that were scheduled, the subschema used would only contain the entity SCHEDULED CLASS. A DBMS allows different subschemas to be used when writing programs or doing online inquiries through the data manipulation language.

Each DBMS vendor sells a unique DBMS and with the DBMS, a unique DML. The ANSI/SPARC reference model was not designed to standardize the DML of DBMSs. Instead, the ANSI/SPARC reference model shows that a way must exist for users of the system to view data.

Structured Query Language

A data model of any kind is useless without a suitable language to represent and manipulate the model. In this chapter, we have presented and emphasized the relational data model on which most current data base management systems are based. The relational model and several variations thereof are based on set theory and a formal language called the relational algebra.

Relational algebra consists of a collection of operations over relations. These operations are the usual set operations: Cartesian product, union, intersection, and difference. Also included are projection, restriction, join, and division operations. These operations are essential for stating queries.

Relational algebra is not, however, suitable for the typical end user because many people are not fluent in this formal language. Therefore, structured query language (SQL) was developed to serve as a practical, English-like language amenable to most users. But the logic of structured query language is the logic of set theory and the relational algebra.

SQL STATUS It has been described as everything from a data processing panacea to the modern equivalent of snake oil, but Structured Query Language (SQL) is emerging as the de facto standard, not to mention the official ANSI standard. Any data base product that does not incorporate SQL today has missed the boat.

Opposition to SQL exists. A number of data base experts maintain that SQL is less than it's cracked up to be.

"The demand for SQL is something the journalists dreamed up," says Adam Greene, a dBase trainer and consultant. He points to strong early interest by the dBase community in Migent's Emerald Bay, which currently does not have SQL capabilities.

Excerpted from Scott Mace, "Developers Feel Impact of SQL on Database Connectivity," *InfoWorld*, April 25, 1988, p. 22.

The most fundamental concept of SQL is called the query block of which the basic form is:

```
SELECT (list of attributes)
FROM   (list of relations)
WHERE  (qualification expression)
```

The first two clauses, SELECT and FROM, define the operation of projection. The WHERE clause is a logical expression that also contains specification of the restriction and join operations. The query block as a whole represents an arrangement of the projection, restriction, and join operations of the relational algebra. These are the operations that we will demonstrate using SQL.

To demonstrate the query block of SQL, we will provide example queries for the following relational accounting personnel schema:

```
EMPLOYEE(EMP_NO, NAME, CLASSIFICATION, SALARY,
  DEPT_NO)
DEPARTMENT(DEPT_NO, NAME, CITY)
CLIENT(CLIENT_NO, PROJECT)
```

An example of a projection that displays an alphabetical listing of accounting employees and their department is shown by the following SQL statements that query our example schema:

```
SELECT    NAME, DEPT_NO
FROM      EMPLOYEE
ORDER BY  NAME
```

An example of a restriction that displays a table of employees' names in alphabetical order who are auditors having salaries greater than $60,000 is specified in SQL as:

```
SELECT    NAME
FROM      EMPLOYEE
WHERE     CLASSIFICATION = "AUDITOR"
AND       SALARY > 60000
ORDER BY  NAME
```

Example of a join that displays a table of employees' names and location of their departments is:

```
SELECT  EMPLOYEE.NAME,DEPARTMENT.CITY
FROM    EMPLOYEE,DEPARTMENT
WHERE   EMPLOYEE.DEPT_NO = DEPARTMENT.DEPT_NO
```

In addition to performing the preceding operations, SQL contains standard functions, such as AVG (the average value), SUM, COUNT, MAX (the maximum of a set of values), and MIN (the minimum of a set of values). The result of the following SQL query, for an example, is the average salary of tax accountants:

```
SELECT   AVG(SALARY)
FROM     EMPLOYEE
WHERE    CLASSIFICATION = "TAX ACCOUNTANT"
```

Many people regard SQL as strictly a query language. But SQL allows other functions to be performed on the data base, such as insert, delete, and update. Selected examples are:

```
DELETE   EMPLOYEE
WHERE    EMP_NO = 1270
```

which removes employee 1270 from the data base. A 20 percent increase in employee 940's salary is handled this way:

```
UPDATE   EMPLOYEE
SET      SALARY = SALARY * 1.2
WHERE    EMP_NO = 940
```

Relations must also be created and SQL also permits this. The following statement creates a relation of foreign offices and specifies its attributes,

```
CREATE TABLE FOREIGN
  (DEPT_NO(INTEGER,NONULL),
   NAME(CHAR(15)VAR),
   CITY(CHAR(30)VAR))
```

in which DEPT_NO is the set of integers (INTEGER) and undefined values of this attribute are not permitted (NONULL). NAME is the set of sequences of characters (CHAR) with variable (VAR) length but not to exceed 15. Attribute CITY is similarly specified.

Another feature that improves the user/system interface is SQL's ability to be embedded in a host language such as COBOL or FORTRAN. Or these host languages can use CALL statements to access SQL functions.

13.5 CONCEPTUAL LEVEL OF DATA

The conceptual level of data describes all the entities in a data base and depicts general interrelationships between entities. The conceptual level, or schema, has two purposes:

1. To represent required data accurately and completely.
2. To provide an easy-to-understand schema for users, programmers, and people who will maintain the data base structure.

Models are a way to visualize abstract data relationships in a data base. At the conceptual level, three major data models are used to represent data relationships: hierarchical, network, and relational. These three data models tend to be connected directly to the capabilities of a specific DBMS. Some DBMSs have the same limitations as the three models discussed in the sections that follow.

Hierarchical Data Model

The hierarchical data model is a familiar structure. The personnel department of an organization displays positions of authority through the use of a hierarchical organization chart. Genealogists use a schema called a tree to show ancestral descent of a person, family, or group. Programmers use hierarchy charts to depict the structure of control within a program.

The hierarchical data model represents data as an upside-down tree of interconnected entities. The top node of this model is termed the root. Other nodes branch out from the root. No single occurrence of a node may have more than one node on its upper level. In an organization chart, this means no employee can have more than one supervisor, but a supervisor can have an unlimited amount of employees.

Figure 13.8 depicts the university data base using the hierarchical data model. This data model demonstrates a 1:M relationship between STUDENT and SCHEDULED CLASS and a 1:1 relationship between SCHEDULED CLASS and FACULTY MEMBER and SCHEDULED CLASS and ROOM.

To find out how many classes a student is taking, we simply move, or

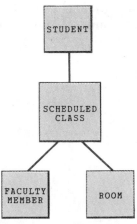

Figure 13.8 Hierarchical data model.

navigate, through the STUDENT entity to the SCHEDULED CLASS entity to determine the classes being taken by a given student. It is harder to find out which room is being used by a given class. With this model, we would have to select a specific student, access the class for that student, and then have access to the room for that class.

Figure 13.9 is another picture of the university data base using the hierarchical model. In this model, the same relationships exist, but it would be easier to locate the room for a given class.

The hierarchical model is usually easily understood by people using the data base. This model, however, cannot be used to represent completely all data bases. Hierarchical models are well suited for representing data bases that have 1:1 and 1:M relationships among entities. In addition, this model works if every node is linked to only one higher level (i.e., parent) node. If a data base has M:N relationships, such as the relationship between STUDENT and SCHEDULED CLASS, or requires a node to have multiple parents, then another data model is more appropriate.

Network Data Model

Any entity in a network may be related to any other entity in an endless number of ways. The network model does not have the strict one-parent rule that governs the hierarchical model.

A network may be simple or complex. A simple network is depicted in Figure 13.10. The added entity, AUDIO/VISUAL EQUIPMENT, could be connected to ROOM, FACULTY MEMBER, or SCHEDULED CLASS.

A network is called complex if it contains M:N relationships. The university data base contains a M:N relationship between STUDENT and SCHEDULED CLASS. Figure 13.11 explodes the STUDENT/SCHEDULED CLASS relationship to show that many different students could be enrolled in many classes. The network model for this relationship is shown in Figure 13.12.

Complex network models can be used to show all possible relationships between entities in a data base. Network models, however, can quickly become difficult to understand. Visualize a networked model with 50 entities. Now visualize some M:N relationships between 50 entities. See how such a networked model can become too complex to comprehend.

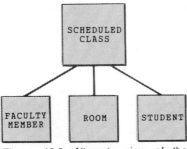

Figure 13.9 Alternate view of the hierarchical data model.

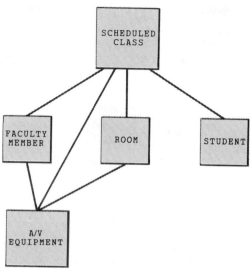

Figure 13.10 Simple network data model.

Relational Data Model

The relational data model can depict all relationships between entities. It is also fairly easy to understand. A relation is a two-dimensional table that represents each entity. Each column is analogous to a data attribute. Each row represents a record.

RELATIONAL DATA MODEL: ANSWER TO TODAY'S INFORMATION NEEDS

A need for the collection and distribution of information has existed since the beginning of recorded history. Today, however, more and more users need more and more information in more and more ways.

To satisfy these demands, a DBMS must be flexible and adaptable. As the most widely accepted model for representing information flexibility, the relational data model is the logical base for a modern DBMS architecture.

Excerpted from Software AG Brochure, "Advanced Information Management," n.d.

The university data base is shown using the relational model in Figure 13.13. The tables shown in Figure 13.13 have the following properties:

1. Each entry in the table represents one data field.
2. Each column contains values about the same attribute and each column is assigned a unique name.

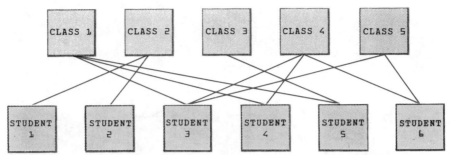

Figure 13.11 Exploded view of a complex network for M:N relationship of STUDENT and CLASS.

A BANK'S USE OF RELATIONAL DATA BASE

Think of the phone book as a data base with three data elements, name, address, and phone number. It is indexed two ways, alphabetically in the white pages and by businesses in the yellow pages. Given a name, it is easy to look up an address or phone number. Given a business category, it is easy to locate individual firms. Those are the types of queries the phone book was designed for. Imagine, with a paper phone book, trying to find out how many people live within a certain distance of a bank. It is probably an impossible task.

To Mark G. Barmann, president and chief executive officer of First Interstate Services, that represents the difference between conventional data bases and relational data bases. He says, "A conventional data base is great when it comes to answering queries it was designed for. But ask a conventional data base to answer an unconventional question and you will quickly find you have a limited ability to lash together what you need."

Condensed from Paul E. Schindler, Jr., "MIS Is Motivated at First Interstate," *InformationWEEK*, August 3, 1987, p. 34.

3. Each row is distinct, in other words, one row cannot duplicate another row for selected attribute columns.

4. Both the rows and the columns can be viewed in any sequence at any time without affecting the information content of the relation.

We can use a shortened notation to represent relational tables abstractly. The five relations shown in Figure 13.13 can be written in the notation shown:

SCHEDULED CLASS(CLASS NUMBER, SECTION, FACULTY
                NUMBER, ENROLLMENT, ROOM NUMBER,
                MEETING DAY, MEETING TIME)

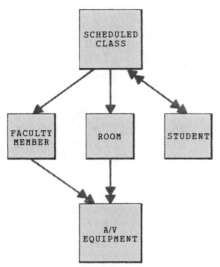

Figure 13.12 Complex network data model.

```
FACULTY MEMBER(FACULTY NUMBER, FACULTY NAME,
               POSITION, DEGREE LEVEL)
STUDENT(STUDENT NUMBER, STUDENT NAME, CLASS STANDING)
STUDENT-CLASS(STUDENT NUMBER, CLASS NUMBER, SECTION)
ROOM(ROOM NUMBER, ROOM DESCRIPTION, TOTAL CAPACITY,
     ELECTRICAL OUTLETS, SEATING ARRANGEMENT)
```

The name of the entity is left of the first parenthesis. Each attribute is listed within the parentheses and separated by commas. The primary key for each relation is underlined. As previously discussed, primary keys must be unique attributes used to differentiate data values within an entity.

One way to determine which attributes can serve as primary keys is simply to search the attributes looking for the one or ones that make each row unique. For example, in the STUDENT-CLASS entity, the data values in the attribute class number alone are not unique. The class number and the section together is not unique. Only when you also add the student number to the class number and the section, do you have a unique primary key. As a result, the primary key is composed of the student number, the class number, and the section.

Using a relational model frequently requires adding additional entities and attributes to the data base. In Figure 13.13, a new entity called STUDENT-CLASS was added to the data base. This entity was needed to show the M:N relationship between student and class.

The relational model is able to show intricate data relationships, similar to the ability of the complex network data model. Compared to the network model, however, it is easier to understand and diagram.

SCHEDULED CLASS Relation

CLASS NUMBER	SECTION	FACULTY NUMBER	ENROLLMENT	ROOM NUMBER	MEETING DAY	MEETING TIME
CS 250	1	1222	50	BB110	T/TH	9:30
CS 250	2	1222	73	BB110	M/W/F	9:00
CS 250	3	1287	104	BB106	T/TH	4:30
CS 485	1	1287	34	BB109	T/TH	11:00
CS 451	1	1287	37	BB109	T/TH	2:30
CS 251	1	1256	45	BB110	M/W/F	11:00

FACULTY MEMBER Relation

FACULTY NUMBER	FACULTY NAME	POSITION	DEGREE LEVEL
1256	PIERSON	ASST. PROFESSOR	PHD
1222	SMITH	ASSOC. PROFESSOR	PHD
1287	WOOSTER	LECTURER	MBA

STUDENT Relation

STUDENT NUMBER	STUDENT NAME	CLASS STANDING
3551414	CORDWHILER	JUNIOR
2241534	KENTON	SOPHOMORE
3325671	JORDENS	SOPHOMORE
3314533	VERDUGO	SENIOR
2211111	MARKS	GRADUATE

STUDENT–CLASS Relation

STUDENT NUMBER	CLASS NUMBER	SECTION
3314533	CS 250	2
3314533	CS 485	1
2211111	CS 451	1
3551414	CS 451	1
3551414	CS 485	1

ROOM Relation

ROOM NUMBER	ROOM DESCRIPTION	TOTAL CAPACITY	ELECTRICAL OUTLETS	SEATING ARRANGEMENT
BB110	STANDARD CLASS	100	5	ROWS
BB106	LECTURE HALL	500	7	STADIUM
BB109	STANDARD CLASS	65	4	ROWS
BB104	STANDARD CLASS	45	4	CIRCULAR

Figure 13.13 University data relational model.

RELATIONAL DBMS WAS THE ANSWER FOR ALLERGAN, INCORPORATED

"We wanted to store data one time in one place, not 15 times in 15 places," says Mike Garrison, senior director of strategic systems planning and development. This required data integration not only from existing systems but also from those that would be added as Allergan acquired new systems.

The move to a relational DBMS was fully supported by users at Allergan. "Our production people now trust their terminals totally to monitor quality and collect data for reports," Garrison says. "They can format and combine data in ways that were impossible before we went the relational DBMS route."

Excerpted from Patrick Flanagan, "A Relational DBMS Vision," *Computer Decisions,* March 1988, p. 20C.

13.6 INTERNAL LEVEL OF DATA

The conceptual level of the ANSI/SPARC model shows the possible interrelationships among data entities. You saw how entities could be associated together through the abstract conceptual data models. But some way must exist actually to link data together to form the associations shown in the conceptual level. The internal level describes in detail how data entities are actually connected.

Sorted Files

A standard sequential file is the simplest way to store and associate data. Imagine two of the university entities, SCHEDULED CLASS and FACULTY MEMBER stored in two separate sequential files. Figure 13.14a represents the two files.

Imagine trying to produce two different reports from these files. To produce a list of the class number, section, meeting time, and faculty name would require the SCHEDULED CLASS file and the FACULTY MEMBER file to be ordered by class number. To produce a list of the faculty name, class number, and enrollment would require the FACULTY MEMBER file to be ordered by faculty number and the SCHEDULED CLASS file to be ordered by faculty number and class number.

The two files cannot be in two different orders at the same time. The traditional solution is to sort the files for the first report, then sort the files again and generate the second report.

What happens if both reports are wanted at the same time? In this case, the data have to be copied into extra files. Figure 13.14b shows the two files copied and sorted into three files. The SCHEDULED CLASS file becomes two files: the first sorted by class number and the second sorted by faculty number and class number. The FACULTY MEMBER file stays in the same order.

The results of all of this work are duplicated data files that waste disk space. A solution to this problem is to associate or link together data in the files. Connecting the data in the files will make it look as if the files are sorted in two different orders at one time. Two different methods used to do this are linked lists and inverted files (or indexes), the subject of the next two discussions.

```
┌─────────────────────────────────────────────────────────────────────────────┐
│ SCHEDULED CLASS File                                                          │
│                                                                               │
│ CLASS               FACULTY                    ROOM      MEETING    MEETING   │
│ NUMBER    SECTION   NUMBER     ENROLLMENT       NUMBER    DAY        TIME      │
│ CS 250    1         1222          50           BB110     T/TH          9:30   │
│ CS 250    2         1222          73           BB110     M/W/F         9:00   │
│ CS 250    3         1287         104           BB106     T/TH          4:30   │
│ CS 485    1         1287          34           BB109     T/TH         11:00   │
│ CS 451    1         1287          37           BB109     T/TH          2:30   │
│ CS 251    1         1256          45           BB110     M/W/F        11:00   │
│                                                                               │
│ FACULTY MEMBER File                                                           │
│                                                                               │
│ FACULTY     FACULTY                              DEGREE                       │
│ NUMBER      NAME        POSITION                 LEVEL                         │
│   1256      PIERSON     ASST. PROFESSOR          PHD                          │
│   1222      SMITH       ASSOC. PROFESSOR         PHD                          │
│   1287      WOOSTER     LECTURER                 MBA                          │
└─────────────────────────────────────────────────────────────────────────────┘
```

Figure 13.14a Sequential data files.

Linked Lists

Linked lists use extra embedded fields called pointers to associate records. The pointer field contains the relative record number of the next record in the list. A relative record number is the number of the record starting from the beginning of the file.

Figure 13.15a is an example of the SCHEDULED CLASS file in order by class number using a series of pointers. Figure 13.15a shows what the file might look like spread out on a disk device. The records would probably be scattered over the surface of the disk.

The class pointer field contains the relative record number of the next record needed to link the list of records in order by class number. In Figure 13.15a, the first class in class number order would be CS 250 section 1. This record happens to be relative record number 2. The second class in class number order would be CS 250 section 2. This record happens to be relative record number 6. To link these two records together, the class pointer for relative record number 2 contains the data to point to relative record number 6. This link is graphically shown in Figure 13.15a with a curve and an arrowhead. Notice that the curve is drawn from the class pointer for relative record number 2 to the beginning of relative record number 6.

The embedded pointer links the records together in class number order. Any number of links can be added to represent different logical orders of data.

Figure 13.15b is an example of the SCHEDULED CLASS file in order by class number and also in order by a combined key field of faculty number and class number. This linkage is achieved by adding an extra field, a faculty pointer,

SCHEDULED CLASS File Sorted by Class Number

CLASS NUMBER	SECTION	FACULTY NUMBER	ENROLLMENT	ROOM NUMBER	MEETING DAY	MEETING TIME
CS 250	1	1222	50	BB110	T/TH	9:30
CS 250	2	1222	73	BB110	M/W/F	9:00
CS 250	3	1287	104	BB106	T/TH	4:30
CS 251	1	1256	45	BB110	M/W/F	11:00
CS 451	1	1287	37	BB109	T/TH	2:30
CS 485	1	1287	34	BB109	T/TH	11:00

SCHEDULED CLASS File Sorted by Faculty Number and Class Number

CLASS NUMBER	SECTION	FACULTY NUMBER	ENROLLMENT	ROOM NUMBER	MEETING DAY	MEETING TIME
CS 250	1	1222	50	BB110	T/TH	9:30
CS 250	2	1222	73	BB110	M/W/F	9:00
CS 251	1	1256	45	BB110	M/W/F	11:00
CS 250	3	1287	104	BB106	T/TH	4:30
CS 451	1	1287	37	BB109	T/TH	2:30
CS 485	1	1287	34	BB109	T/TH	11:00

FACULTY MEMBER File Sorted by Faculty Number

FACULTY NUMBER	FACULTY NAME	POSITION	DEGREE LEVEL
1222	SMITH	ASSOC. PROFESSOR	PHD
1256	PIERSON	ASST. PROFESSOR	PHD
1287	WOOSTER	LECTURER	MBA

Figure 13.14b Sorted files needed to produce the required reports.

to each record. The class pointers link together the records in class number order. The faculty pointers link together the records in faculty number/class number order.

Notice that the links are the same from relative record 2 to relative record 6. At relative record 6, the class pointer links to relative record 3 and the faculty pointer also links to relative record 5. The class pointer then links relative record 3 to relative record 5. The faculty pointer then links relative record 5 to relative record 3. This is because the two orders are not the same and must be represented differently. In Figure 13.14b, two separate files were required to represent two different orders. In Figure 13.15b, one file is maintained with two extra fields in each record. The pointers that represent the necessary order are used to retrieve the records from the file.

Inverted Lists

One of the drawbacks of linked lists is processing speed. It can take a long time to search through the linked records before finding a specific record. Another method of data linking, inverted lists, speeds up the search process.

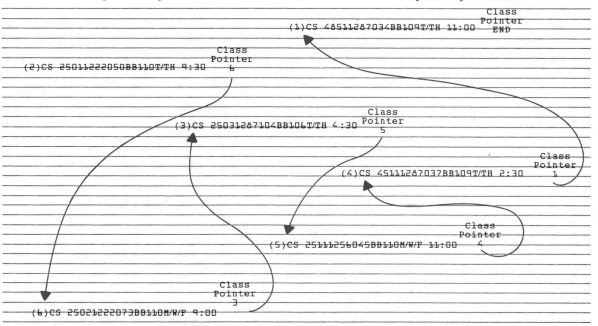

Physical layout of SCHEDULED CLASS File on a secondary storage device

Figure 13.15a SCHEDULED CLASS file linked together in class/section order.

An inverted list is just a copy of the list which has been sorted. Inverted in this context means sorted. Figure 13.16a is an inverted list for the SCHEDULED CLASS file in order by class number. Notice that the only data maintained in the inverted list are the key field and the number of the actual record. Figure 13.16b is an inverted list for the SCHEDULED CLASS file in order by faculty number and class number.

Both linked and inverted lists are data structures used in a DBMS to interrelate data items. Inverted lists can be processed more quickly than linked lists. Inverted lists, however, take more disk space than linked lists.

Variations of the linked list are the two-way linked list and the ring. Variations of the inverted list include trees and B-tree structures. These structures have the same basic principles as the ones described. They are more complex renditions of the linked and inverted lists providing faster and more secure forms of data association.

13.7 APPROACHES TO DATA ANALYSIS

The previous sections of this chapter helped you to understand why data have to be interrelated to be used in an organization. You were also made aware of how a DBMS relates data in a data base. The four different levels of data showed you how data are both abstractly and actually connected within a data base.

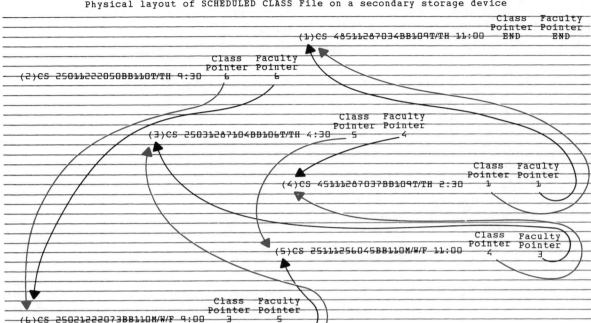

Physical layout of SCHEDULED CLASS File on a secondary storage device

Figure 13.15b SCHEDULED CLASS file linked together by both class/section and faculty pointers order.

A systems analyst has to determine the data needs of an organization. It is the job of the analyst to figure out what data are needed and how the data will be linked together. This job is sometimes called data analysis. Data analysis is not always an easy task. An analyst must anticipate the future needs of an organization and create a data base that will be flexible enough to change over time. Two basic approaches to data analysis are process oriented and information oriented.

CLASS NUMBER	SECTION NUMBER	RELATIVE RECORD NUMBER
CS 250	1	2
CS 250	2	6
CS 250	3	3
CS 251	1	5
CS 451	1	4
CS 485	1	1

Figure 13.16a An inverted list representing class/section order.

FACULTY NUMBER	CLASS NUMBER	SECTION NUMBER	RELATIVE RECORD NUMBER
1222	CS 250	1	2
1222	CS 250	2	6
1256	CS 251	1	5
1287	CS 250	3	3
1287	CS 451	1	4
1287	CS 485	1	1

Figure 13.16b An inverted list representing faculty/class/section order.

Process-Oriented Approach

A process-oriented approach to data analysis is concerned with the flow of data through a specific set of processes. An analyst uses the process-oriented approach by examining the output and processing of a given application to determine the data needs of the system.

Using the process-oriented approach, a systems analyst looks at all reports, display screens, calculations, and decisions needed for an application. Flowcharts and data flow diagrams are drawn to understand the flow of the system better. From this information, the systems analyst begins to devise the data needed to create the application. Data fields are identified and record formats are derived. Key fields are noted and associations are made between different record formats.

This approach should sound familiar. The process-oriented approach is the traditional method to complete the task of data analysis.

The process-oriented approach works very well if a systems analyst knows in advance the output from a system. It also works very well if the data from each set of applications are essentially separate. This approach is effective for applications such as accounts payable, accounts receivable, payroll, and inventory control. Each of these applications usually has a very static set of processes and output.

But what if you are trying to design a system where no one knows exactly what the system should produce? What if you are attempting to design a marketing system that analyzes demand for a product by a series of variables such as geographic location, economic indicators, or customer attributes? What if you don't know in advance what those variables will be? What if your user isn't exactly sure what reports will be created? What if the display screen formats will probably change every few months? You will have to use a different approach to data analysis.

Information-Oriented Approach

The information-oriented approach to data analysis treats the data as separate resources from the processes that use the data. The processes are important, but the first focus of the analyst is on the data that are in the system and the information they will produce. An analyst who uses the information-oriented approach sits down with users of the system to determine what data should be part of the data base.

We will develop a sample system to explore the information-oriented approach to data analysis. Our sample system will be a manufacturer of consumer appliances called the Freestone Corporation. Freestone is a manufacturer of appliances such as dishwashers, stoves, refrigerators, washing machines, dryers, toasters, and food processors.

Freestone requires its customers to send in a form to activate the guarantee for each appliance that it sells. From these forms, the company will develop a data base of information for service validation and marketing research. The people in the Marketing Department at Freestone are interested in analyzing the patterns in which people buy appliances. For example, what is the possibility that someone who has bought a dishwasher will buy a food processor within the next 18 months? In which geographic areas do specific products sell best? Where do the higher-priced models sell? The Marketing Department wants the flexibility to do a variety of different inquiries on the data in the system.

The analyst would have to interview the marketing personnel and service personnel to determine the data needed for this system. Figure 13.17 is a list of potential data items that could be used in this system.

The next step is for the analyst to identify the data entities of the system. This is a difficult process to complete. New systems analysts tend to put all the data items into a single entity. A systems analyst should produce a structure that can be easily modified, has minimal data redundancy, and can be linked together where necessary.

In this case, a single entity encompassing all the data items identified in Figure 13.17 will produce a great deal of data redundancy. The Freestone Corporation is assuming that some customers will buy more than one product. If customer data (such as address, city, state, and zip code) have to be repeated every time a customer purchases a product, then the data base will contain redundant data. Repeating product data (such as product description, cost, and warranty type) for every product purchased will also produce redundant data within the data base.

To prevent data redundancy, three entities are created for this application: CUSTOMER, PRODUCT, and PRODUCT PURCHASE. The CUSTOMER entity will contain all customer-related data, while the PRODUCT entity will contain

Date of Purchase	Serial Number	Customer Name
Customer Address	Customer City	Customer State
Customer Zip Code	Customer Area Code	Product Model
Product Type	Product Description	Product Cost
Product Companion	Purchase Price	Customer Sex
Customer Income	Customer Marital Status	Customer Family Size
Warranty Type	Warranty Length	Product Color
Date of Warranty	Product Introduction Date	Product Advertising Code

Figure 13.17 Potential data items for the warranty data base. (These data items do not appear in any specific order.)

CUSTOMER ENTITY	PRODUCT ENTITY	PRODUCT PURCHASE ENTITY
Customer Name	Product Model	Serial Number
Customer Address	Product Type	Date of Purchase
Customer City	Product Description	Purchase Price
Customer State	Product Cost	Date of Warranty
Customer Zip Code	Product Companion	Product Color
Customer Area Code	Warranty Type	
Customer Income	Warranty Length	
Customer Marital Status	Product Introduction Date	
Customer Family Size	Product Advertising Code	
Customer Sex		

Figure 13.18 Data items grouped by entity.

all product-related data. The PRODUCT PURCHASE entity will record individual purchases of a product by a customer. Figure 13.18 arranges the data items listed in Figure 13.17 by the newly identified data entities.

Figure 13.19 shows the entities grouped into a Bachman diagram. The systems analyst must decide what types of relationships exist among the entities. For example, a customer may make many purchases, so the relationship between CUSTOMER and PRODUCT PURCHASE is 1:M. A given type of product may be purchased many times, so the relationship between PRODUCT and PRODUCT PURCHASE is also 1:M.

Any one of the conceptual models could be used for this application because the system is relatively small and contains only 1:M relationships. The relational data model, however, is more flexible than the other two data models because it permits more potential links between entities. Because we don't know exactly what output will be required from this system, the relational model is the most appropriate data model to use.

The relational notation for this data base schema is shown in Figure 13.20.

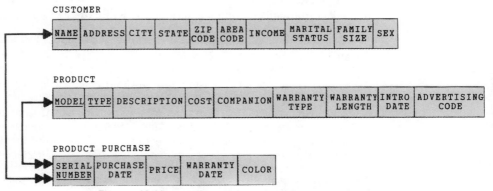

Figure 13.19 Bachman diagram for the warranty data base.

```
CUSTOMER(CUSTOMER NUMBER, NAME, ADDRESS, CITY, STATE, ZIP
         CODE, AREA CODE, INCOME, MARITAL STATUS, FAMILY
         SIZE, SEX)
PRODUCT(MODEL, TYPE, DESCRIPTION, COST, COMPANION,
        WARRANTY TYPE, WARRANTY LENGTH, INTRODUCTION DATE,
        ADVERTISING CODE)
PRODUCT PURCHASE(SERIAL NUMBER, CUSTOMER NUMBER, MODEL, TYPE,
                PURCHASE DATE, PURCHASE PRICE, WARRANTY
                DATE, COLOR)
```

Figure 13.20 Relational notation for warranty data base.

Using the relational model, attributes are added to some or all of the entities so that the entities can be linked together. For example, a customer number is added to the PRODUCT PURCHASE entity so that the CUSTOMER entity can be referenced when necessary. In addition, model and type attributes are added to the PRODUCT PURCHASE entity so that a link can be made to the PRODUCT entity.

Key attributes are underlined in the relational model notation. A key field makes each row in the model unique. In Figure 13.20, customer number is the unique identifier for the CUSTOMER entity. Model and type create a unique key for the PRODUCT entity and serial number and customer number are the attributes that form the key for the PRODUCT PURCHASE entity.

The information-oriented approach to data analysis has the following advantages:

1. The data determined with this approach can be used for a variety of processes. The data base is flexible. Once appropriate data bases are in place, applications can be created quickly with high-level DMLs.
2. End users who have access to the data base can create their own reports and display screens.
3. This approach creates a data base that can be modified more easily at a later date than a data base created with a process-oriented approach.

The information-oriented approach has the potential to build a more fully integrated data base than the process-oriented approach. Some organizations, however, do not create all their information systems at one time. Instead, systems are usually developed slowly as they are needed by an organization.

SUMMARY

A data base is a collection of data items organized in a manner intended to meet users' information requirements. The traditional approach to data base analysis and design has produced a traditional file environment. This environment consists of a separate file or set of files for each application. Two fundamental difficulties with a traditional file environment are:

1. It limits the ability to integrate data from one application to another application.
2. It increases the amount of redundant data that must be stored, in different sets of order, to meet the needs of systems users.

A data base management system is a set of specialized programs designed to describe, protect, store, and access a data base. Using a DBMS, an organization has the ability to centralize the design and control of all data used by all users. The functions of data definition, modeling, design, and control are termed data base administration. These functions are best accomplished when assigned to a single person or department termed a data base administrator.

DBMSs are very complex software packages that take a great deal of training to understand fully. One of the easiest ways to understand a DBMS is to use the ANSI/SPARC reference model to break a DBMS down into a series of "views" or "levels." A DBMS contains four levels: an external level, a conceptual level, an internal level, and a physical data organization level.

The external level is that part of the DBMS viewed by end users and application programmers. It is composed of a data manipulation language that is used to extract data from the data base. The conceptual level is that part of the DBMS viewed by application programmers and data base administrators. It is composed of the data definition language that is used to model the data base. The three primary industry-used data models were discussed in the chapter. The internal level is that part of the DBMS viewed by data base administrators and systems programmers. It is composed of the DDL that is used to express specific links between data items. Two methods of data linking were discussed in the chapter. The physical data organization level is that part of the DBMS viewed by systems programmers. It is composed of actual data placement on secondary storage devices. Three organization methods were discussed in Chapter 12.

An analyst is responsible for working with a data base administrator to design the data requirements for an information system. An analyst can take two approaches to the problem of data analysis: a process-oriented approach or an information-oriented approach.

The process-oriented approach focuses on predefined output and basic data processing requirements of the organization. An information-oriented approach focuses on the data items stored in the data base and their relationships and linkages to provide a variety of ad hoc and yet unknown information requirements. Frequently, both approaches are used by systems analysts to meet the requirements of all users because often a systems project contains aspects of both approaches.

IMPORTANT TERMS

Bachman diagram

complex network

data base administrator

data base control system (DBCS)

data base management system (DBMS)

data base storage system (DBSS)

data definition language (DDL)

data manipulation language (DML)

entity relationships

entity-relationship (ER) diagram

hierarchical data model

inverted list

join operation

linked list

network data model

pointer

primary key

projection operation

relational data model

restriction operation

schema

simple network

sorted file

structured query language (SQL)

subschema

Assignment

REVIEW QUESTIONS

13.1 What is a data base? What is a data base management system?

13.2 What is meant by the term "data integration?"

13.3 What is a data base administrator? List some of the functions of data base administration.

13.4 A DBMS has two general software components. What are these two components? Describe the functions of the two components.

13.5 Define what is meant when a data item is called a "primary key."

13.6 Why was the ANSI/SPARC reference model for data base management systems developed? What is its function?

13.7 List the rules for drawing a schema with a Bachman diagram.

13.8 What data organization methods compose the lowest level of the ANSI/SPARC reference model?

13.9 List and briefly describe the four levels of data as described in the ANSI/SPARC data base reference model.

13.10 Define the data base management system components DML and DDL. What is the purpose of a DML? What is the purpose of a DDL?

13.11 How does an end user communicate with a DBMS?

13.12 How does an application programmer work with a DBMS?

13.13 What is a data base schema? What is a data base subschema?

13.14 Who is responsible for developing the data base schema in an organization?

13.15 How are one-to-one, one-to-many, and many-to-many relationships designated in entity-relationship and Bachman diagrams?

13.16 Differentiate between an ER diagram and a Bachman diagram.

13.17 What are the relative advantages/disadvantages of the hierarchical data model? the network data model? the relational data model?

13.18 What is the difference between a simple and complex network?

13.19 How are data entities linked together in a data base management system?

13.20 How are data entities linked together in a traditional file environment?

13.21 Which type of data linking is faster, linked lists or inverted lists? Why?

13.22 Why does a data base management system require the use of indexed or direct physical data organization?

13.23 Compare and contrast the process-oriented approach and the information-oriented approach to data analysis.

13.24 Why does the information-oriented approach to data analysis produce a more integrated data base than the process-oriented approach?

QUESTIONS FOR DISCUSSION

13.25 "Today we design a data base; a few years ago we designed files. The activities are still the same, whatever you choose to call them." Discuss.

13.26 "We spent nearly three years and $100,000 and have still not identified everything that should be in our data base." Discuss.

13.27 "Most organizations operate under a great deal of pressure that emanates from competition. This pressure tends to limit the amount of time available for planning and the execution of plans. The pressure of competition forces quick decisions and quicker action. How does an organization meet its competition? By offering a good product at reasonable cost and by maintaining a high level of customer service. This last aspect can be achieved by providing answers to questions concerning a multiplicity of matters, such as order status, scheduled shipment date, method of transportation, inventory availability, pricing schedules, change orders, and so forth." Comment on this statement, especially as it relates to the design of the data base.

13.28 "A data base design that will satisfy the needs of every organization is a mirage. We don't read about engineers trying to build one manufacturing process to fit every organization." Discuss this rationale.

13.29 "All files that are used for information purposes require some sort of inversion." Do you agree with this statement? Why?

13.30 "The concepts related to retrieving data from a file are the same whether the file contains payroll data, purchasing data, or production data. It doesn't seem to make much sense, reinventing the wheel for each system designed in each organization." Discuss this rationale.

13.31 "Before the average organization attempts to implement an integrated, online data base, they will have to acquire personnel with a greater understanding of communication hardware and software." Explain.

13.32 "I can use the hierarchical data model to show any relationship between data items in a data base. All logical structures can be expressed ultimately in a hierarchical arrangement." Comment on the validity of this statement.

13.33 "Sequentially organized files have no place in the modern data base environment." Do you agree or disagree with this statement? Why?

13.34 "A major part in the design of any information system must be the study of how data should be organized and structured." Discuss this statement.

13.35 "It takes too much time to create a conceptual model of the data in an information system. Most companies prefer to get a system working rather than invest time in planning a system." Under what conditions may this statement be true? Under what conditions may it be false?

13.36 "Systems analysts should fully understand the technology of data association to design the data for an information system properly." Discuss fully.

13.37 "Our organization does not need a data base administrator because all of our programmers are very capable and can function as programmers/analysts." Comment on this statement.

13.38 "Data base administrators are too expensive to hire and are not needed once the data base has been designed and implemented." Comment on this statement.

13.39 How does a data base management system contribute to the flexibility of information systems?

13.40 Analyze the accompanying figure. Discuss whether it is a hierarchical or network model and explain why.

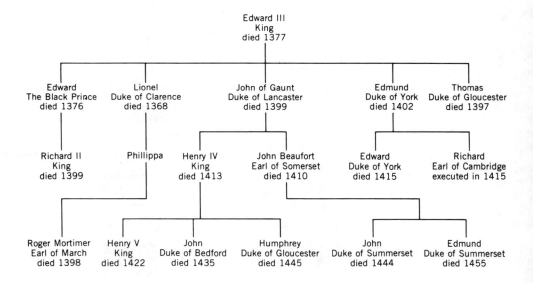

EXERCISES AND PROBLEMS

13.41 Draw a schema for each situation given to represent the following data attribute descriptions:

1. Each employee of the company has certain attributes, such as employee identification, employee name, and employee address. Employees may have worked at one or several jobs. Each job has a title and a starting date. Finally, in each job an employee may have one or more hourly rates and starting dates.

2. A bank has many customers, each of whom is identified by his or her name, business address, and home address. A customer may have one or more checking accounts and one or more saving accounts. Each account has an account number and a balance. Finally, debit and credit transactions make up an account. A transaction contains a date and a dollar amount.

13.42 Study the following two network models. Using relational notation, convert the network models into a single relational model.

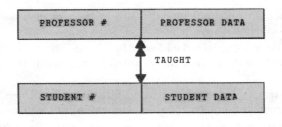

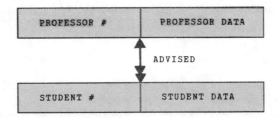

13.43 Prepare an entity-relationship and a Bachman diagram for the following representation:

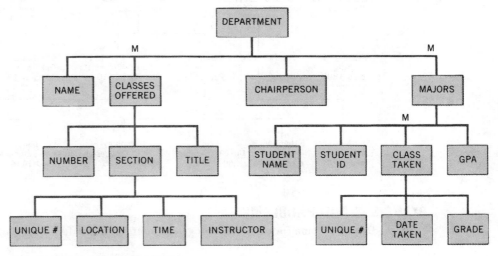

Note: M means a one-to-many relationship.

13.44 Use relational notation to model the following tables:

PROFESSOR-ID	PROFESSOR-NAME	DEGREE-FROM
56	Black	Minnesota
58	Deakin	Illinois
63	Huber	Stanford
74	Robertson	North Carolina
87	Tabor	Florida

STUDENT-ID	STUDENT-NAME	GOAL
462	Falk	Ph.D
690	Haegele	MPA
694	Kowalczyk	MPA
700	Slade	Ph.D
723	Wilkerson	Ph.D

STUDENT-ID	COURSE
462	ACC 380
690	BL 382
700	BL 382
462	ACC 380
690	ACC 380
694	ACC 382
690	BA 384T
700	BA 384T
700	ACC 380
723	ACC 380
723	ACC 382

Imagine the following questions being asked of this data base:

1. Obtain the professor identification number for all professors who taught student 462.

2. Obtain a list of names of all professors who taught student 462.

3. Obtain a list of the professor names and identification numbers for all professors who taught students whose goal is a Ph.D.

Would the model you devised be sufficient to answer these questions? Would you have to add extra attributes in the current relations to answer these questions? What attributes would have to be added? Would you have to add extra relations to answer these questions? What relations would have to be added? Formulate a new relational model to allow for the inquiries just detailed.

13.45 Prepare an entity-relationship (ER) and a Bachman diagram for the following representation:

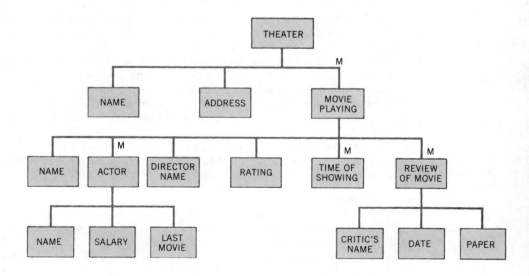

13.46 Use relational notation to model the following tables:

ITEM

ITEM	NAME	WEIGHT
26	WINCH	8
38	TURNING BLOCK	4
52	ROD RIGGING	35

SUPPLIES

ITEM-#	SUPPLIER-#	QUANTITY
24	2	125
26	4	46
38	1	51
52	3	104
52	2	33
91	1	19

SUPPLIER

SUPPLIER-#	CITY	NAME
1	NEWPORT	SCHAFFER
2	BRISTOL	COMET
3	MIAMI	BARLOW
4	SAN DIEGO	TRAX
5	VANCOUVER	FAULTLESS

13.47 The Northern City Blood Bank has hired you to establish an information system. The Blood Bank is located in a city of 150,000 people serving three local hospitals. The Blood Bank provides all blood storage and collection services for the three local hospitals. People donate or sell blood to the Blood Bank, and then the bank, in turn, types and sells the blood to the local hospitals. The Northern City Blood Bank is a nonprofit organization.

The bank has to keep track of all blood including type, amount, date donated, and expiration date. The Blood Bank would like to install a computer system to help keep track of blood so that when a hospital calls with specific needs, the bank can immediately respond. In addition, managers of the Blood Bank envision having a system that will be able to tell them which types of blood are needed most often. Management would like to be able to see if there are any patterns of blood usage by date, type, and hospital.

Managers of the Blood Bank would also like to keep track of blood donors. It would like to be able to send out cards asking people to donate blood again. People can donate blood after a fixed time has passed since their last donation. Management would also like to keep a special list of people with rare blood types so that the people can be contacted in emergency situations.

Required:

1. Should you use the process-oriented or information-oriented approach to complete the data analysis for this application? What additional information would you have to know to use the process-oriented approach?

2. Using the information-oriented approach to complete the data analysis, make a list of all the data attributes you think would have to be maintained to satisfy the requirements stated.

3. Identify unique entities from the attributes, and group the attributes together under the entities.

4. Draw a schema of the data base using a Bachman diagram.

5. Using relational notation, make a conceptual model of your data base.

13.48 Quickstone Newspapers is a company that owns 12 small newspapers covering seven states. The newspapers are primarily advertising instruments allowing local people to sell their products to each other. The newspapers also provide local news as well as very limited national and international news coming from wire services. Each newspaper has a computer. The home office for Quickstone also has a computer. The computers are all minicomputers from the same vendor; however, the management of Quickstone has chosen not to communicate between computers. Each newspaper currently has a circulation system, a payroll system, an accounts payable system, and an accounts receivable system. The home office completes combined financial reporting from magnetic tapes that are mailed from each newspaper location. The company is extremely profitable.

Management is very unhappy with the current accounts receivable programs and wants to redesign the system. The programs are inaccurate, billing some customers twice and not billing other customers. The current programs do not produce any kind of management reporting such as aged accounts receivables reports, or receivable analysis. The programs were written by an in-house programmer 10 years ago and the source code was lost in a fire 5 years ago.

The management of Quickstone would like a new accounts receivable system. Management feels that one system would work very well for all newspapers, because each newspaper is managed the same way and has the same mission.

Required:

1. Do you think that one set of programs and data structures would be suitable for the different newspapers owned by Quickstone?

2. Should you use the process-oriented or information-oriented approach to complete the data analysis for this application?

3. What additional information would you have to know to use the process-oriented approach?

4. Would the data from this application have to integrate with the data from the currently existing applications?

5. Should you use a DBMS for this application?

13.49 Royal Motors is an automobile dealer specializing in high-priced and limited-production vehicles. Royal Motors is located in a large metropolitan area. The company currently has a minicomputer to handle accounts receivable, accounts payable, payroll, general ledger, and financial reporting applications.

The company carries lines of Jaguars, Rolls Royces, and Ferraris. In addition, automobiles are obtained for Royal Motors from car auctions and special sales that occur both in this country and internationally. The company has two people who spend all their time traveling, frequenting sales looking for vehicles to purchase. Some vehicles are purchased for a specific customer, while other vehicles are purchased for inventory.

The management of Royal Motors realizes the company is operating in a business environment that requires a great deal of attention to customer concerns. Management would like to install an information system to help identify customer desires and match those desires with available vehicles. The management would like to build an extensive customer and inventory data base. This data base would be used by the two buyers to match customer needs to vehicles available for sale. In addition, the data base would be used by salespeople to develop mailing lists and to serve customers better by providing personal information about customers for conversation when they visit the Royal Motors' showroom.

Required:

1. Using the information-oriented approach to data analysis, identify all the data attributes that should be maintained for this application.
2. Identify unique entities from the attributes, and group the attributes together under the entities.
3. Make a list of at least five inquiries that would be required from this system. For example, how many people are interested in a 1953 General Motors Corvette? a blue Corvette? a Corvette of the model years between 1954 and 1957?
4. Using the hierarchical data model, draw a conceptual model of your data base.
5. Use relational notation to draw a conceptual model of your data base.
6. Imagine that you have the choice of the type of linking performed by the internal level in the DBMS. What type of internal link, as learned in this chapter, would you feel most suited this application? (Usually, the only choice you have is to pick a DBMS that uses the type of linking you feel is most efficient. Once you buy a DBMS, your choice is essentially complete.)

Gilda O'Hara, president of Pleasure Travel of Miami, Florida, wants to establish a data base of her customers and the travel arrangements they have made through her agency. She would like to be able to maintain historical data on her customers' travel arrangements, including their comments on the accommodations. Ms. O'Hara would like to distinguish her travel agency from its competitors by having a system that enables her agents to give personal follow-up for every booking. Last, Ms. O'Hara wants to achieve a better understanding of the clients' vacation preferences so she can send them personalized promotional material about various vacation packages.

After interviewing Ms. O'Hara you determine that she wants to track data about the following four entities:

* Customers
* Trips
* Trip segments (e.g., flights)
* Accommodations (e.g., hotels, car rentals)

After preparing a Bachman diagram for Pleasure Travel, you realize that customer to trips is a one-to-many relationship, trips to trip segments is a one-to-many relationship, and trip segments to accommodations is a one-to-many relationship.

Required: Use the relational notation to model these four entities.

BIBLIOGRAPHY

DATE, C. J. *A Guide to the SQL Standard.* Reading, Mass.: Addison-Wesley, 1987.

DATE, C. J. *An Introduction to Data Base Systems,* 4th ed. Reading, Mass.: Addison-Wesley, 1986.

DATE, C. J. *Relational Database: Selected Writings.* Reading, Mass.: Addison-Wesley, 1986.

DICKINSON, JOHN. "Relational Databases." *PC Magazine,* June 24, 1986.

DURELL, WILLIAM. *Data Administration.* New York: McGraw-Hill, 1985.

EVEREST, G. C. *Database Management: Objectives, System Functions, and Administration.* New York: McGraw-Hill, 1985.

FINKELSTEIN, RICHARD. "Joining Tables Using SQL." *Data Base Advisor,* December 1987.

FLANAGAN, PATRICK. "A Relational DBMS Vision." *Computer Decisions,* March 1988.

KROENKE, DAVID. *Database Processing.* Chicago: Science Research Associates, 1983.

LANG, GARY, and ROBERT BYERS. "SQL in Perspective." *Data Base Advisor,* September 1987.

LITTON, GERRY M. *Introduction to DataBase Management: A Practical Approach.* Dubuque, Iowa: William C. Brown, 1987.

LOOMIS, MARY E. *The Database Book.* New York: Macmillan, 1987.

MACE, SCOTT, "Developers Feel Impact of SQL on Database Connectivity." *InfoWorld,* April 25, 1988.

MARTIN, DANIEL. *Advanced Database Techniques.* Cambridge, Mass.: MIT Press, 1986.

MARTIN, JAMES. *Managing the Data Base Environment.* Englewood Cliffs, N.J.: Prentice Hall, 1983.

MARTIN, JAMES, *Computer Data-Base Organization,* 2nd ed. Englewood Cliffs, N.J.: Prentice Hall, 1977.

MCCARTHY, W. E. "The REA Accounting Model: A Generalized Framework for Accounting Systems in a Shared Data Environment." *The Accounting Review,* July 1982.

MCCARTHY, W. E. "An Entity-Relationship View of Accounting Models." *The Accounting Review,* October 1979.

MCFADDEN, FRED F., and JEFFREY A. HOFFER, *Data Base Management.* Menlo Park, Calif.: Benjamin/Cummings, 1985.

SALZBERG, BETTY JOAN. *An Introduction to Data Base Design.* Orlando, Fla.: Academic Press, 1986.

SCHINDLER, PAUL E., Jr. "MIS Is Motivated at First Interstate." *InformationWEEK,* August 3, 1987.

Software AG Brochure, "Advanced Information Management," n.d.

SPEZZANO, CHARLES. "Database Managers." *Byte,* Summer 1987.

VASTA, JOSEPH A. *Understanding Data Base Management Systems.* Belmont, Calif.: Wadsworth, 1985.

14

CONTROLS

14.1 INTRODUCTION

The five building blocks of input, models, output, technology, and data base provide the form, content, and function of computer-based information systems. The controls building block ensures their protection from a variety of potential hazards and abuses. Moreover, a proper mix and level of controls support effectiveness and efficiency of operations and the integrity and accuracy of data processing. In extreme situations, controls may even ensure the very survival of the information system and therefore the survival of its host company. Indeed, surveys reveal that 9 out of 10 companies that rely on computer-based information systems collapse after a significant loss or interruption of their information system.

If the information is worth processing and transmitting, it is worth processing and transmitting correctly and efficiently and, at the same time, protecting the information from a variety of hazards and abuses. Moreover, the number of laws and regulations will surely increase in the future to safeguard the confidentiality of sensitive information.

The objectives of this chapter are:

1. To portray the real-world environment that computer-based information systems operate in and thereby set the stage for a comprehensive presentation on the controls building block.

2. To present a complete analysis and discussion of basic computer controls.

3. To establish a hierarchy of security hazards and detail the physical security devices and procedural security techniques that safeguard computer-based information systems from these security hazards.

4. To delineate controls for a PC environment.

5. To discuss briefly traditional paper records and accounting controls.

6. To present a methodology to determine an optimum mix of controls.

14.2 THE REAL-WORLD ENVIRONMENT

Information systems operate in an environment that is full of pitfalls. Like it or not, information systems are vulnerable to a variety of threats and abuses from people both inside and outside the organization; from natural disasters; from undependable and faulty services, supplies, and workmanship; and from everyday incompetencies and inefficiencies.

The Basic Trade-Off

The up side to information systems is the distribution of technology and information flow to personnel throughout the organization and to a variety of stakeholders outside corporate walls. Microcomputers and telecommunications gear are as widely dispersed and common as telephones. Massive amounts of messages are transmitted over public airwaves.

The main goal of such well-designed information systems is greater enduser access and usability. These integrated, user-oriented information systems not only contribute to the strategic success of organizations, but also to their survival because each function in businesses relies on the possession and use of information of one kind or another to perform its tasks.

The down side to this kind of access, however, is that signals emanating from electronic equipment can be easily received by other unauthorized electronic equipment. In short, the greater the access, the greater the vulnerability.

Major Points of Vulnerability

Knowing where and what the major vulnerable points of information systems are assists the systems analyst in effecting a controls strategy. These points are, as one might expect, in the five building blocks already described.

Input can be erroneous, delayed, or manipulated, therefore, requiring a number of input controls. Many of the models are application program driven. This can work in favor of the system because a variety of processing controls can be embedded in these programs to help eliminate processing errors.

The dark side is that programs can contain Trojan horses, a group of instructions embedded in an application program that looks harmless but performs unauthorized functions while the host program performs valid functions. Some application programs may also contain viruses or logic bombs, a group of unauthorized instructions triggered to act based on a specified condition. For example, a logic bomb inserted in a payroll program by a programmer checks to see if the programmer has missed a paycheck. If so, this condition indicates that the programmer lost his job. The logic bomb is automatically triggered to perform some malicious act like erasing files.

Superzap is a utility program used in most IBM computer centers. It is a universal access, "break glass in case of emergency" utility program that bypasses

VIRUSES THAT MAKE SYSTEMS SICK In recent years, a series of computer "viruses" has contaminated PCs, hard disks, and data files, inspiring several companies to develop "vaccines," in the form of hardware and software schemes.

The insidious computer virus is generally a small piece of program code that's self-propagating and is triggered by some event or specified time. The least harmful of these viruses simply springs a joke on the unsuspecting user. The deadliest, and unfortunately the most common, are intended to do some harm, such as reformatting a hard disk. The author of such a program is known, in polite terms, as a computer "hacker." Such hackers most often loose their malicious, virulent strains chiefly to destroy data, according to several security-products vendors and users.

"The threat of viruses is the most serious of any computer abuse that we have seen to date," said Kenneth Weiss, founder of Security Dynamics.

Like its medical counterpart, a computer virus spreads. It latches onto operating system code or PC applications software commands, eventually displaying brash messages or DOS errors, before dealing its deadly blow of destroying data and infecting other programs.

Some security authorities recommend the use of read-only storage devices such as CD-ROM to protect software programs. The programs stored on CD-ROM are safe from being altered.

Excerpted from Linda Bridges, "Software, Hardware, 'Vaccines' Stem Threat of Deadly Computer Viruses," *PC Week*, March 8, 1988, p. 13.

all controls to change or disclose any contents of the computer. A program wielding such power is dangerous in the wrong hands. Strong access control securing it from unauthorized use is therefore imperative.

Loss of the data base can be disastrous to any business. Backup controls are especially applicable to this key building block. Output from the system can be copied or stolen, therefore access controls are needed to restrict the distribution of sensitive output.

All the technology is subject to possible abuses, mishaps, and malfunctions. Consequently, a host of controls is needed for this building block. A relatively new threat in this area is caused by telecommunications, which opens the information system to eavesdropping and wiretapping. Encryption devices are applicable here.

The Criminal Element

Criminals exploit the vulnerable points of information systems to get what they want. Today, high-tech crime is a fact of life because a great deal of money can

VIRUS STRAINS My mother always hoped I'd become a doctor—actually a brain surgeon. Since I work with electronic "brains" every day, I always thought that was as close as I would come to "doctoring" anything, but the recent flare-up of interest in software viruses, infections, cures, antidotes and inoculations might change all that.

The notion of software "hacking" isn't new, having been born just five minutes later than software. But as we've grown increasingly dependent upon the expensive programs and precious data stored in our machines, the cost of a computer failure, whether accidental or deliberate, has skyrocketed. Factor in the notion of someone deliberately destroying your irreplaceable data and you have a hot situation indeed! Multiply this by the unwitting and infectious spread of this destruction throughout the far-reaching tendrils of an entire organization or community's computer usage, and the cost of such deliberate sabotage can be incalculable.

Excerpted from Steve Gibson, "Computer Viruses Express Themselves in Many Ways," *InfoWorld*, April 18, 1988, p. 32.

be made and the probability of getting caught and having to "pay for the crime" is low.

Computer thieves, even if caught, are not prosecuted in many cases. Some experts estimate that 80 to 90 percent of computer crime cases, especially those dealing with internal fraud, are not even reported. It is estimated that untold billions of dollars are lost annually to white-collar computer crime. As a result of all of this, it is no wonder that computer crime continues to increase.

While crime is not new, the use of computer and information technology to commit it is relatively new and is spreading. Law enforcement officials are learning new jargon from computer rip-off artists, such as superzapping, Trojan horses, viruses, logic bombs, and data diddling.

Today's criminals understand that most money transfers are electronic. They also realize that information is a form of big money, other assets, and power. In the banking industry, for example, bank robberies à la Bonnie and Clyde average $4,000; old-fashioned fraud averages $30,000; but computer-based fraud averages over $600,000.

Technology makes criminal abuse easier because, as alluded to earlier, easier access for legitimate users makes it easier for unauthorized users to get access to the system if proper controls are not implemented.

Clearly, the proliferation of terminals; the expansion and integration of telecommunication networks; the availability of low-cost, high-performance electronic gear; and micro-to-mainframe connectivity have greatly increased the power of those with criminal intent. A high-tech criminal can copy a company's data base and programs from a remote location, modify them, and transmit them back to the mainframe without a trace.

RISING TIDE OF COMPUTER CRIME

According to a published survey of executives responsible for computer security, Ernst & Whinney found that over 80 percent of the corporations and agencies represented by these executives had suffered financial loss as a result of computer security problems.

More significantly, over 70 percent of these executives said that the risk of computer fraud has increased in their firms during the past five years—roughly the period since IBM introduced the PC.

To explain the role of the microcomputer in the rising tide of computer crime, Ernst & Whinney noted that the PC has radically increased the level of computer literacy of many employees. This increase in knowledge of computer strengths and weaknesses has been coupled with a movement toward both decentralized processing and increased use of networks. The net result of these developments, according to the study, has been to make access to corporate data easier and control of that data more difficult.

Source: Ernst & Whinney, Chicago, 1986.

Types of Computer Crime

The types of computer crime are varied. Over half are fraud and money theft. For example, a programmer in an East Coast bank stole $200,000 by using Superzap. In Los Angeles, a computer consultant walked into the Fed Wire room at Security Pacific National Bank, read a money transfer code taped to a wall, and took the bank for $10 million. A man from Liberia, using nothing but a telephone and a few telegrams, was able to penetrate the banking industry's supposedly impenetrable electronic security system and drained millions of dollars from Swiss banks, money they thought was being lent to California banks. Then, in a double deception, the man convinced the California banks that the arriving funds were really loans to him from his family's fortune stored in Switzerland.

Theft of information and programs makes up probably 10 to 20 percent of computer abuse. For example, one customer of a service bureau in Texas, which served a number of oil companies, always requested a "scratch" tape to be mounted when a "read" light came on before a "write" light. He had worked out a clever scheme to "browse" through competitors' files and steal their seismographic data.

Software vendors can legitimately argue that the theft, copying, and distribution of their copyrighted programs is a major crime. At any rate, companies that purchase these programs should control their personnel from making unauthorized copies.

Illegal interception of data, unauthorized access to alter programs and data, destruction of data, sabotage, and malicious acts make up the remaining types of computer crime. Hackers, for example, use autodial modems to try thousands of random combinations of numbers and password schemes to log illegally into a computer system.

After gaining access to a computerized dispatch program of a major railroad company, a crime syndicate was able to arrange the "disappearance" of over 200 boxcars. A large department store in San Francisco was cheated out of more than $250,000 in merchandise by an employee who tapped into its computer to create phony credit card accounts. The infamous 414 Gang of Milwaukee, a big-time hacker group, has marauded freely through more than 70 major computer systems including Los Alamos Science Laboratories and Sloan Kettering Cancer Center.

The Enemy from Within

Enemy number one of the information system, however, is not hackers, saboteurs, terrorists, organized crime, or natural disasters, but the disgruntled, incompetent, careless, or dishonest employee. The effectiveness of the controls building block is ultimately dependent on the activities and attitude of responsible personnel and a strong control policy set by top management.

According to the American Bar Association, the greatest threat to the computer-based information system by far comes from individuals who work in the information system. The most frequently cited groups are executives, computer operations supervisors, computer operators, and application programmers. Also, over 10 percent of computer misuse is commited by executives and managers who are not involved directly with computers.

At Volkswagen AG, a group of insiders working with others outside VW, manipulated the automakers accounting records to cover up $259 million worth of trading losses on foreign currency transactions. Of the eight people arrested in connection with the VW caper, six were company employees.

A secretary for a manufacturer created phony vendors and then authorized payment of over $80,000 to them (her). A salesman for a chemical company was able to change a program to pay double commissions. A commodities broker skimmed $1.5 million off his trading pool. A programmer used the New York Board of Education's computer to keep track of his racing bets. A computer operator who felt his boss asked him to work too hard evened the score by destroying $2 million worth of the company's computer billing records.

Clearly, computers magnify the consequences of human error and increase the potential for fraud and manipulation of sensitive data. With access given to everyone from file clerks to top executives, the system is vulnerable to all kinds of misuse. In the accounting realm, for example, the potential for fraudulent financial reporting involving top management is increasing. Internal and independent auditors and audit committees need to become involved early on in information systems development to help to ensure that an adequate system of controls is built and maintained and to recognize when one does not exist and be prepared to "blow the whistle."

The first big case that involved internal computer fraud was the Equity Funding case. The courts found that those involved included the chief executive, a number of officers, and independent auditors. The computer aided in perpetrating a $200 million fraud based on the processing and updating of 64,000 fictitious insurance policies.

Stockholders and potential investors were deceived by another company that reported inflated earnings over several years, but suddenly filed for protection under the bankruptcy code. At the time of the bankruptcy filing, the inventory amount on the balance sheet was overstated by nearly $70 million. A computer program was written to maintain and process fictitious inventory quantities and prices. A $21 million fraud at Wells Fargo Bank worked because of weaknesses in Wells Fargo's computerized interbranch transaction processing system.

These million-dollar computer scams are dramatic and easy to quantify. The cost of errors of omission or commission, improper deletions, incorrect entry, erroneous alteration, lost files, and computer downtime is much more difficult to quantify. Most experts, however, agree that this cost is even greater than losses attributable to internal fraud, various crimes, and other abuses.

Management's Responsibility

Unfortunately, controls generally follow rather than precede disasters. That is, management starts thinking about controls and their implementation *after* something bad has happened. They want to shut the barn door after the horse is gone. Clearly, controls should be analyzed and established *before* these things happen. Moreover, once a system is developed and implemented, it is difficult, if not impossible, to retrofit controls.

The aim of management should be to build an overall framework of administrative, procedural, and physical controls that is cost-effective. Management should not throw a lot of controls at a system, build forts and bureaucracies that stifle efficiency, and spend money excessively in one area while leaving another area vulnerable. A fine balance must be struck in which controls are adequate to protect a peak-performing system. Controls should augment productivity and help get the job done no matter what happens. With a strong controls policy set by top management (discussed in the next section), systems analysts can proceed to build a system of controls that will be complied with and supported by both insiders and stakeholders.

14.3 BASIC COMPUTER SYSTEM CONTROLS

The controls presented in this section are basic to any kind of computer-based information system, large or small, sophisticated or simple. They include administrative, disaster recovery, input, processing, data base, output, documentation, hardware, operating system and utility programs, and computer operations controls.

Administrative Controls

Systems analysts are the ones who actually design and implement controls, but it is top management who provides the leadership and sets the tone and policy necessary for controls to work. Without full support of a system of controls from top executives, employees will generally circumvent controls.

In addition to establishing an environment favorable to controls, managers must become involved in functions, such as effecting a controls policy, selecting and assigning personnel, delineating responsibilities, preparing job descriptions, setting standards, supervising, preparing a strategic information systems plan, and acquiring adequate insurance.

Controls Policy

Studies indicate that where top executives understand the computer abuses that can occur, the system of controls is better and more effective. These top managers prepare, distribute, and present a controls policy that stipulates explicitly what the company regards as computer crime, abuse, and unethical conduct. It further states that computer facilities, software, documentation, and data are to be used only for appropriate business purposes. Also, it makes clear that any offender will be prosecuted to the fullest extent of the law.

A contact person, such as a security director or internal auditor, is typically designated so employees have someone to talk to if they suspect crime or abuse. All employees are required to sign a formal code of conduct stipulating key elements of top management's controls policy.

The internal audit staff, at least once a year, runs compliance tests to make sure that the controls are in place and working as planned. For new systems development, auditors become involved in the installation of controls from the first day systems work begins.

Personnel Control

Good personnel control begins with hiring the right people initially. These employees should have the technical ability, character, and past performance records necessary to contribute to the organization.

When hiring, management should make sure they are getting what they think they are. Many personnel specialists state that over 25 percent (some state more than 50 percent) of prospective employees falsify information on their resumes. It is therefore a good policy to run a background check on anyone who is coming on staff. For those who will work in sensitive areas, a more thorough investigation is recommended.

A new employee should never be thrust into an organization without some form of orientation and training. Management should establish a program not only to train new employees but also to update the expertise of all employees.

Once personnel are hired and trained, they must be supervised properly. Proper control of a computer system, for example, is a function of the proper supervision of computer employees. Not only should standards be established, but a system should be in place to report to management any significant deviation from standards. Measurement bases for standards are procedures, quality, quantity, time, and money. These standard measurements relate to personnel, hardware, software, and the data base.

Strategic Information Systems Plan

The overall benefit of a strategic information systems plan (discussed in Chapter 15) is organizational goal congruency. Such a plan provides a general roadmap that gives all employees and departments a sense of direction and sets a foundation for systems development.

Specifically, a strategic information systems plan unifies and coordinates systems and end-user personnel. It establishes benchmarks and gives a means of controlling activities and projects. It also reduces the number of isolated, noncompatible subsystems that might otherwise be developed.

Insurance Protection

Despite a sound disaster recovery plan, if a disaster occurs, it can cause financial problems as well as operational problems. Adequate insurance coverage should be purchased to provide ready cash for such emergencies.

Special electronic data processing insurance policies provide loss from theft, vandalism, fire, flood, earthquakes, and other disasters. These insurance policies should be written for the full replacement cost of the computer equipment, and also for software and other supplies and materials. Also, executives should acquire business disruption insurance that compensates the company for increased costs of operating while the system is down.

Disaster Recovery Plan

The development and design of a disaster recovery plan, in addition to safeguarding the business and producing efficiencies, is required by insurance companies. It is a "help me now, help me later" plan. In developing the plan, tasks are identified that could be performed better and tasks that should not be performed at all. That's the "help me now" part. Quick and full recovery from a disaster is the "help me later" part, which all concerned hope never takes place.

Fire, explosion, flood, earthquakes, and other disasters can produce a long-term computer failure. If this happens, most organizations would simply go out of business. Without a viable disaster recovery plan to support vital business functions, survival is impossible. The primary goal of a disaster recovery plan is to keep the *business* running. Clearly, such a plan includes those controls necessary to keep the computer-based information system itself running.

Components of the Disaster Recovery Plan

Components of the disaster recovery plan (or disaster recovery plan library) are (1) prevention plan, (2) contention plan, (3) recovery plan, and (4) contingency plan.

1. *Prevention Plan.* This plan stems from analysis and design of various controls discussed in this chapter. A number of systems analysts prepare a "Controls Evaluation and Justification Report" detailing each control and its justification. In essence, this is a prevention plan. This plan details how "to protect it."

SURVIVAL IS THE NAME OF THE GAME Data corruption rarely shows mercy: It doesn't matter if the disaster is an act of God or an act of a hack programmer. If it is missing or damaged, data can be gone without a hope of getting it back. Most acts that sap data integrity result in taking the system down.

A fault slipped, registering 5.9 on the Richter scale, and the information system at California Federal "went down inelegantly." To make matters worse, the third quarter's notes were due at the Securities and Exchange Commission (SEC) branch office. "It was the worst possible time for the quake to occur, says Frank Piluso, senior vice-president of computing and communications for Cal Fed. "I knew it was going to be a helluva day."

Within the first hours after the earth shook, Cal Fed employees under Piluso's direction began to get things under control.

"We saved everything but one CBX panel," Piluso says. The library was spared because the tapes were hung in prebuilt, cross-braced cabinets designed to withstand seismic shocks.

One hour later the contingency plan was activated. The Los Angeles headquarters was used as a command center to handle business and anxious inquiries. Furthermore, drinking water, portable toilets, walkie-talkies, food and cash were supplied to the 450 recovery workers, including vendors, technicians, laborers, and electricians, through 29 nonstop hours of work. It was back to business as usual—until Saturday night. A second shock hit the system.

Cal Fed's contingency plan also included a Sunguard hot site in Rancho Bernardo, California, and a disaster recovery service in Phoenix. Employees were sent to both sites to await the recovery outcome. The second recovery took nine hours.

Piluso, who also does quarterly simulated tests, reemphasizes one of his main points: "A lot of data processing types think it won't happen to them. But I wasn't singled out by God." He adds, "It's a moral responsibility to have a plan."

Excerpted from Helen Pike, "Survival Planning for Data Disaster," *Computerworld*, April 6, 1988, pp. FOCUS 27–29.

2. *Contention Plan.* This plan identifies and describes how personnel are to react while a disaster is occurring. This plan details how to "deal with what happened to it."

3. *Recovery Plan.* This plan details reestablishing and restoring the system to normal operations. This plan details how to "restore it."

4. *Contingency Plan.* This plan identifies and describes how the company

will operate and conduct business while recovery efforts are taking place. This plan details how to "keep the business running and solvent until the system is restored." This is the plan that is described in the following material.

Determining Vital and Necessary Functions

The first step in designing a contingency plan is to identify functions necessary to keep the company running. A classification scheme is vital, necessary, desirable, or trivial.

Certain applications are vital to keep the business running. Typically, these are transaction and order processing, accounts receivable, accounts payable, inventory control, pricing and billing, and payroll. Copies of all these applications including programs, data, and documentation should be stored in a secure place off-site.

Many factors determine criticality of functions. The length of time a department or operation can run without the function is examined. The company also may be exposed to regulations. For example, a large mail-order firm became embroiled in a lengthy and costly lawsuit with the Federal Trade Commission (FTC) when its system went down for an extended period preventing the mail-order firm from meeting the 30-day delivery rule and other FTC regulations. Various other legal penalties may also result such as union contract stipulations that penalize the company for missing a payroll. The analyst should also examine interdependencies to see if a failure in one area affects another area. Can a function that works on the computer fallback to manual methods? If not, this calls for more computer backup. Intangibles such as image and morale are important and should be quantified. For example, how much business would a bank lose if its computer system went down for several days? How would prospective and present customers view such a situation?

The analyst should estimate costs of not performing the vital and necessary functions. These costs are based on the preceding material.

Alternative Contingency Strategies

Next, the analyst investigates alternative contingency strategies for each critical function. One simple strategy is fallback to manual methods. Or the function may be performed by an outside service. For example, the company may hire a payroll processing service company to produce payrolls during the contingency and recovery period. Other alternative strategies, such as shells, service bureaus, mutual agreements, consortia, hot site, mobile data processing facilities, and company-owned backup facilities, are analyzed to determine the ones (or one) that are best for the company.

1. *Company-Owned Backup Facility.* The total system is replicated somewhere distant from the present system. This option is low risk and high cost. For example, Sears has an IBM 3090 mainframe in a Chicago suburb dedicated to running the Sears nationwide network. A mirror-image site in Dallas is also in place, prepared to take over command of the network

in the event of power failure or if any catastrophe hits the Chicago center. The system in Dallas is just like the one in Chicago, but it sits idle waiting to be put online in an emergency. It is tested each week in a mock trial.

2. *Reciprocal Agreement.* This option entails an arrangement or contract made between two companies with compatible computer systems to service each other in case of a disaster. This sounds like a viable option, but it generally does not work for two reasons. First, most systems do not have enough time for all their own processing needs, never mind the processing of another organization. Second, over time, because of changes at one or both companies, the computer systems become incompatible, and no one may be aware of this situation until it is too late.

   Computer vendors may be able to help in locating other companies who use the same equipment to form a users' group. This way, a particular company has several "buddies" to depend on for interim processing. If one drops out, changes computers, or cannot meet emergency needs, others can. In any event, once a reciprocal agreement is consummated, it should be reviewed and tested at least once a year.

3. *Hot Site.* This is a backup facility offered by a vendor on a fee basis to users of a particular family of computers. In the event of a disaster, subscribers can use the hot site within 24 hours and for up to three months. But if the disaster is widespread, the hot site may not be able to service all subscribers completely. This option is low risk if the disaster is not widespread and is offered at a reasonable cost.

4. *Consortium.* With this option, several companies get together and build their own backup facility. This option includes characteristics of the first three options.

5. *Commercial Service Bureau.* Contracting for emergency processing with a commercial service bureau is a workable option under certain circumstances. The system must be compatible, and it must be available when needed. Most service bureaus, however, run their systems at maximum capacity. Risk, cost, and effectiveness are moderate for this option.

6. *Shell.* A shell is a building with all the necessary outlets and connections but without the computer equipment. They are, however, immediately available to occupy and to accept equipment. Shells can be built by the organization for its own use or subscribed to from a commercial shell owner. For this option, risk is moderately high, costs are low, and effectiveness is low to moderate.

7. *Mobile Data Center.* A mobile data center, a unique approach to disaster recovery planning developed by the Borden Dairy Group, stands ready to serve any of Borden's far-flung systems installations. The system on wheels is housed in a semitrailer. The front section is for meetings and living quarters in case long-term use is required. The middle section of the unit has built-in workstations and supplies. The back section is the computer room, prewired for installation of a computer. The system remains on alert around the clock in a central, secure location.

Contention and Contingency Plans

In some organizations, both contention and contingency elements are combined in one plan. In any event, these plans, separately or together, should contain emergency procedures and contingency elements.

The objectives of emergency procedures are to handle emergencies in an orderly and calm manner, minimize damage to personnel and assets, and establish an environment for reconstruction and recovery to normalcy. Emergency procedures are organize for emergency; summon key personnel; evacuate; assess damage; notify management, fire department, and police, if necessary; initiate legal action; file insurance claim; contain damage; and declare end of emergency when appropriate.

Specific elements include the following:

1. Guidelines for emergency shutdown of the computer system and all auxiliary devices to prevent damage and lost data.
2. Location of emergency exits.
3. Location of fire extinguishers and instructions on how to use them.
4. Location of emergency power switches.
5. List of items that employees should take with them if they are forced to leave the building and what to do just before leaving, such as placing plastic coverings over equipment to prevent water damage.
6. Location of the interim processing facilities and telephone numbers of persons to contact to commence processing.
7. List of additional persons or services to contact and their telephone numbers, such as fire department, police, ambulance, equipment repair, managers, insurance agents, attorney, and temporary help.
8. List of vital applications and instructions on how to begin processing at alternate facilities.

Now, after the emergency phase, contingency operations begin. These operations require the disaster recovery team to make available evidence of damage by photos, film, or VCR; determine operating status and inventory of damaged facilities; activate backup strategies; and alert the off-site storage facility to prepare for retrieval of files and other materials.

Maintaining a Viable Contingency Plan

After designing the contingency plan in accordance with the preceding material, it should be maintained on a continuous basis to represent the most current conditions. Testing of the plan's design should be done periodically. Passive testing approaches include observation, inspection, review of checklist, and walk-through. Active testing includes physical tests that can be simulated such as drills and rehearsals or live tests that consist of tiger teams and break-the-glass procedures. Moreover, *all* personnel responsible for contingency plan activation and operation should be trained and updated on a regular basis to ensure the latest personnel are fully knowledgeable of the latest contingency plan edition.

Input Controls

Input controls consist of the following items:

1. *Transaction Codes.* Before any transaction can be input into the system, a specific code should be assigned to it. This aids in its authorization and identification.

2. *Forms.* A source document or screen form should be used to input data, and such forms should be designed in accordance with the design rules presented in Chapter 6.

3. *Verification.* Source documents prepared by one clerk can be verified or proofread by another clerk to improve accuracy. In a data conversion operation such as keying, each document can be key verified by a second operator. The verifying operator goes through the same keying operation as the original operator; the machine compares logically his or her keying efforts with the previous entries. A discrepancy in the data entered by the first and second operators is indicated by lights on the machine. Verification is a duplication operation and, therefore, doubles the cost of data conversion. To reduce this cost, it may be possible to (1) verify only critical data fields, such as dollar amounts and account numbers, while ignoring such fields as addresses and names; (2) key only variable fields and prepunch, machine duplicate, or establish constant tables; and (3) use programming logic to provide verification.

4. *Control Totals.* To make sure that data have not been lost and transactions have been processed accurately, control totals are prepared for specific batches of data. For example, a batch of invoices is sent to a control clerk in accounting where a control tape is prepared. This tape includes a total of the invoice numbers (a *hash* total) and a dollar total. These invoices are then transferred to a data entry unit, where they are prepared for entry in the data base's accounts payable file. Before they are posted to this file the computer also computes totals of the invoice numbers and dollar totals. Then these totals are transmitted to accounting, where they are compared. All of the invoices have been entered correctly. A mismatch indicates an error or errors that need to be investigated and reconciled.

This mainstay control can also be used in online systems in which terminals are scattered throughout the system. If the online system is operated in batch mode, then the process is pretty much the same as described previously. The VDT operator who is inputting sales transactions, for example, takes 25 forms and runs a total on the account number and quantities ordered. Then, he or she keys in these 25 transactions. But they are not posted to the data base; instead the system displays the total number of transactions entered, the sum of the account numbers, and the sum of quantities on the screen. With a match, the operator hits an update key for posting. Otherwise, the error or errors are detected and corrected.

What does one do, however, if the transactions are input online as they occur, as in a reservation system or with Fed Wire transfers? Basically, the same approach is used. After every 25 or so transactions, the system prompts the operator to input certain control totals that the operator has been logging. If these control totals match the system's, then no problem exists. If an error or errors exist, then adjusting debits or credits or other entries are made to correct them.

5. *Check Digit.*   These self-checking digits, discussed in Chapter 6, are used for important codes, such as customer account numbers to ensure that the proper number has been transcribed correctly and is valid.

6. *Labels.*   Labels containing data, such as file name, date created, date updated, and retention period, help to ensure that the right file is mounted for processing.

7. *Character and Field Checking.*   Characters are checked for proper mode: numeric, alphabetic, or alphanumeric. Fields are checked to see if they are filled in properly.

Processing Controls

Input and processing controls are intertwined and are difficult to discuss separately. Generally, though, input controls are the first line of defense to help prevent errors from entering processing activities. Once data get into the system, controls are embedded in various computer programs to help detect not only input errors but also processing errors. These controls are as follows:

1. *Limit or Reasonableness Check.*   This control is used to identify data having a value higher or lower than a predetermined amount. These standard high/low limits are ascertained and established from research performed by the systems analyst. This control technique detects only those data elements that fall outside the limits. Examples of how this technique can be used are as follows:

   a. If the highest account number in a customer file is 6000, but CUSTOMER–NUMBER 7018 is read, then CUSTOMER–NUMBER of this particular record is in error.

   b. If the minimum/maximum hourly rate for employees is $7.50/$10.50, any rate that falls outside this range is in error.

   c. All authorized B-coded purchase orders cannot exceed $100.

   d. An exception notice is printed or displayed if a customer order exceeds twice the customer's average order.

2. *Arithmetic Proof.*   Various computation routines can be designed to validate the result of other computations or the value of selected data fields. One method of arithmetic proof is *crossfooting*, which entails adding or subtracting two or more fields and zero balancing the result against the original result. This control method is applicable where total debits, total credits, and a balance forward amount are maintained for each account. For example, in the cash account, if the debits equal $5,000 and the total credits equal $4,000, then the balance of cash should equal $1,000.

   Another example uses approximation techniques. If fairly homogeneous items such as steel or grain are shipped to a customer, the billable amount can be checked for approximate accuracy. The average price for all steel stock may be $0.08 per pound. This rate is multiplied by the total weight of the shipment to derive an approximated billable amount. If this amount is not within 4 percent of the billed amount, then a message is displayed for subsequent investigation to determine if the billed amount is actually in error. As a final example, net pay for employees is determined by subtracting certain deductions from gross pay. In a separate routine, the deductions could be added back to the derived net pay. Then the resulting gross pay could be checked against the original gross pay to see if it matches.

3. *Identification.* Various identification techniques can be designed to determine if the data being processed are valid. This can be done by comparing data fields from transaction files to master files, or to constant tables, stored either internally to the program or on a peripheral device. Some examples of this technique are as follows:

   a. A chart of accounts may designate current assets with a number range of 100 to 199, where Cash is 100. If the cash register is being processed, then all cash credits or debits must contain the identifier 100.

   b. The warehouse that handles steel stock and pipe is coded with a 1. If issue and receipt transactions of steel and pipe inventory do not have the warehouse code of 1, then the transaction has either been entered in the wrong location or a keying error has been made.

   c. Each customer number entered in the order transaction file is compared with the customer master file. If a customer master record is not found, then the order transaction record is rejected.

4. *Sequence Check.* Files are often arranged in ascending or descending sequence by employee number, account number, part number, and so forth. Instructions written in the processing program compare the sequenced field of the preceding record or transaction. With this technique, any out-of-sequence error can be detected and the file can be prevented from being processed incorrectly. Typical reasons for an occurrence of an out-of-sequence error are use of an incorrect file, failure to perform (correctly) a required sorting operation, hardware malfunctions, and incorrect merge operation.

5. *Error Log.* A vital control technique used during processing is the maintenance of an error log. This log contains a record of all identified errors and exceptions noted during processing. As the errors are identified, they are written onto a special file, thus enabling the processing of that particular step to continue uninterrupted. At the completion of that processing step the error log can be checked, either by the computer or by the operator, and a decision made whether or not to continue processing.

   The error log is then forwarded to either the department or group who prepared the original input or to a specially designated control group within the information system where the entries are corrected, reconciled, and resubmitted for processing.

6. *Transaction Log.* A transaction log provides the basic *audit trail*. For audit and control purposes, the transaction log should indicate where the trans-

action originated, at what terminal, when, and the user number. For example, in an insurance company the transaction log supports all entries to the general ledger accounts. An entry into the general ledger that debits accounts receivable and credits written premiums is simultaneously recorded in the transaction log and contains the following detail support: user, terminal, and user identification numbers; time of day; day of the week; policy number; premium; and other identifying data. At any time the auditor can have the system produce a hard-copy listing of the transaction log for manual review or have the software print specific audit information. Moreover, if the transaction is recorded and the result of the transaction is recorded, then the transaction log can be used for recovery and backup in the event of a mishap.

Data Base Controls

The lifeblood of the organization is in the files and data base of the information system. Therefore, great care should be exercised to ensure its accuracy and safety. The following controls provide this insurance.

Physical Controls

To withstand stress and disasters (e.g., fire), a strongly constructed storage vault should be available to store files and documents that are not in use. In addition, all backup files, programs, and other important documents should be stored in secure off-site facilities. Fire, flood, theft, disgruntled employees, riot, vermin, or even nuclear attack represent hazards to an organization's vital records. Their secure storage is of utmost importance for the continued operation of any business. Several sites are available to management that guarantee safekeeping of records. Some of these storage centers are in mountains. One is in a 500-acre limestone cave that is 175 feet underground. This installation provides a dirt-free environment with a year-round temperature of 70°F and relative humidity of 35 percent. In addition to secure storage, many off-site installations provide services such as microfilming, telecopier long-line transmission of stored paper documents, copying and shipment of stored paper records, and 24-hour emergency shipment of stored documents. Records may be sent to an installation by truck, express, courier service, or U.S. Postal Service.

File protection devices (e.g., *file protect rings* for magnetic tape) should be used to prevent accidental erasure. All storage devices, especially magnetic tape and disk, should be kept free of air pollutants. Temperature and humidity conditions should be strictly controlled.

Librarian Control

Again, all files should be stored in the library (sensitive files in a vault) when not in use. The *librarian's* function should be independent and segregated from other functions (e.g., programmers and computer operators). The librarian should inventory all files and documents, listing the person to whom they are assigned, their status, and when they are due back. All files should contain external labels for identification. These labels, however, should be coded and understandable only to authorized personnel. For example, it would be unwise to label a file as CUSTOMER–ACCOUNTS–RECEIVABLE; a code like 14927 is preferable.

The librarian should ensure that all backup copies are properly maintained off premises. Unusable magnetic tapes and disks should be segregated from those that are usable until they can be cleaned, repaired, or replaced. This maintenance procedure, done on a regular basis, minimizes read/write errors and ensures an adequate supply of usable storage media. It should be noted that in many computer installations procedural controls that are adequate for the first shift are reduced for the second shift, and quite often cease to exist during the third shift.

Backup Procedures for Magnetic Tape Files

A simple, yet important file reconstruction procedure that is recommended for important sequential files contained on magnetic tape is illustrated in Figure 14.1. This backup system is usually referred to as the *grandfather-father-son* file

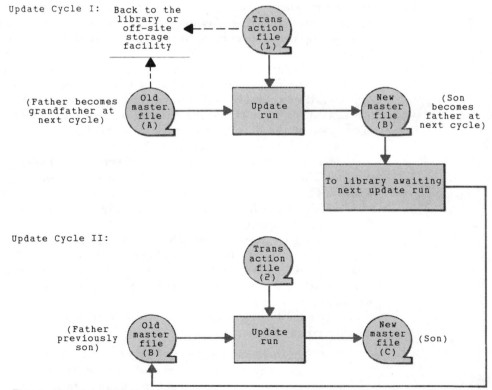

Figure 14.1 A grandfather-father-son file reconstruction for sequential files. If one file is lost or destroyed, enough data are available to reconstruct it.

reconstruction procedure. With this procedure, three versions of a file are available at any time. File A (father) in Update Cycle I produces File B (son). Update Cycle II, File B (now a father) produces File C (son of B). During this cycle, File A becomes the grandfather. Three generations of the master file and the previous and current versions of the transaction file are stored at *different sites*. Recreating a lost file simply involves redoing the update run.

The advantage of this control procedure is that recovery is always possible. For example, if File C contains errors or is damaged during processing, then the job could be repeated using File B with transaction data from transaction File 2. If both File B and File C are damaged or destroyed, File A (stored off premises) is still available along with transaction File 1 to create File B, which, in turn, can be used to create File C.

Backup Procedures for Magnetic Disk Files

In many systems, the "backup window" exists between the daily interactive and nightly batch processing cycles. With the growth in disk capacity and the implementation of more applications, the backup window is growing smaller and smaller. A case in point is the backup window found in systems operating 24 hours a day, especially when it takes 40 or more minutes to dump a large magnetic disk volume such as IBM's 3380. Some of these systems have gone from backing up disks once or twice a day to once a week, or less frequently. Consequently, such backup procedures open the system to added risks, especially with sensitive data.

In an online real-time system, backup strategies involve keeping a prior version of the data base plus a log of transactions. Recovery procedures are rollforward or rollback. Rollforward uses a prior dump of the data base and a transaction log to re-create the current state of the data base if it is lost. If a prior state of the data base must be restored because the data base's current state is invalid, then a rollback procedure must be used.

Several strategies of backup and recovery are available for online real time systems. The differences in these strategies are based on frequency of dumping versus logging. More frequent dumping enables fast recovery of the data base whereas logging is less expensive. The trade-off, therefore, is always between dumping and logging.

Logging by itself is generally not recommended, because if only a log is available for recovery, the possibility exists of having to rollback to the time the data base was first created. Periodic dumps eliminate this problem by making it unnecessary to roll back the log prior to the dump. But full dumps are costly and time consuming. Thus, like many components of systems designs, we have another trade-off riddle without precise answers. Some partial answers, however, are offered as follows:

1. *Complete Dumping and Logging Input Transactions.* This backup and recovery strategy includes copying the whole data base (or large portions of it) onto a backup medium such as magnetic tape. Every input transaction, containing time and date indicators, program and file or entity identifiers,

and various change parameters, that also comprise the accounting audit trail, are logged on a medium such as magnetic tape.

Figure 14.2 presents an example of this file recovery strategy. In this example, assume that the online direct access file (master file) is destroyed sometime during Period II. With Backup File A, which is a copy of the online master file as of the end of Period I, and Log 2, which recorded all before- and after-images of master file records changed by transactions, a new online master disk file can be rolled forward or reconstructed. First, all master file data from Backup File A are written on the new master disk file. Then, all after-images from Log 2 are recorded, thus bringing the master file to a correct present state.

2. *Residual Dumping and Logging Snapshots.*   This strategy is an alternative to taking periodic full dumps of the data base. Its main purpose is to reduce the time and cost of that strategy. Residual dumping involves copying all records that have not changed since the last residual dump to a residual dump file. The transaction log takes a "snapshot" of updated records before and after the transaction is made. In rollforward recovery, the system goes back to, but not including, the second-to-last residual dump taken. The data base is filled with after-images from the transaction snapshot file, which

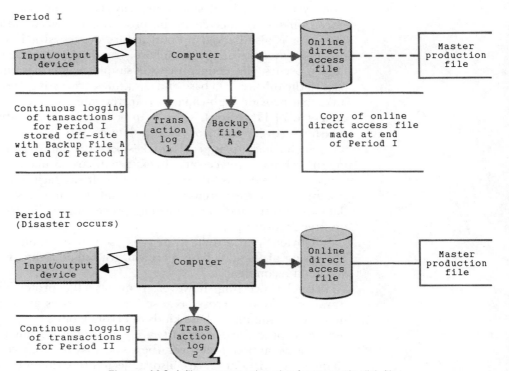

Figure 14.2 A file reconstruction plan for magnetic disk files.

reflects all changes made in the data base during the period. Empty slots still remaining represent records that have not changed during the period and, therefore, are filled with the last residual dump. With rollback recovery, the residual dump file is not relevant. Before-images from the transaction snapshot file are read backward up to the point where the data base becomes invalid and are used to replace the existing records on the data base.

3. *Differential File.* The differential file contains changes and updates to the main data base. The main data base is not changed. This differential file is stored on a separate, reliable, and high-speed medium. A different channel from the main data base channel is used. As the differential file grows, changes are made to the main data base. Frequent dumping of the differential file is quick and relatively inexpensive. Essentially, the main data base contains record before-images, so rollback is fairly easy, and the frequent dumping of the differential file facilitates rollforward. By building a differential-differential (D-D) file, reorganization and updating of the first differential and the main data base can occur simultaneously. The D-D file can be held in main storage while the reorganization and updating is taking place.

4. **Dual Backup and Recovery.** Dual backup and recovery involves online backup. This strategy provides two completely separate copies of the data base by updating both simultaneously. One copy is on-site; the other is stored off-site, connected to the processor by telecommunications. If the processor is also backed up and failure occurs, switches kick in the dual processor and the off-site data base. If a dual processor is not used and a failure occurs, the main processor simply switches from the on-site data base to the off-site data base and continues processing. Telecommunication links that provide high-capacity transfer rates, such as T-3 (44.736 Mbps) or T-4 (274.176 Mbps), serve as pipelines for transmitting vital data to disaster recovery vaults or backup data centers.

Such a backup approach makes periodic dumps or incremental copying of disk files unnecessary. Backup data are available online any time it is needed. If a disk is lost, data from the off-site facility is fed back into the system. If a disaster occurs and the total system is destroyed, the backup data are transmitted to an alternate processing site in accordance with the disaster recovery plan.

Obviously, this dual strategy is used in situations where continuous processing of the data base is critical. An online airline reservation system is a good example.

Dual processing, however, provides little protection against procedural or software errors because both data bases are corrupted simultaneously. To minimize these kinds of errors from ever happening, rigorous testing of procedures and software is done before conversion to the new system is permitted. Moreover, these systems are rarely changed. If systems changes are made, they are also subjected to stringent testing procedures before they are introduced into the system.

TELEVAULTING Although it sounds like an event from some future version of the Olympics, televaulting is a simple concept. When you sign up as a client of their service, Total Assets Protection, Incorporated of Arlington, Texas, set up a direct, high-speed T-3 data link via a fiber optic cable between your system and one of their secure installations.

Condensed from Michael Tucker, "Data Backup with a Twist," *Computerworld*, April 6, 1988, p. FOCUS 36.

Data Base Concurrency Controls

When data are shared among multiple users, concurrency controls must be established to ensure consistent updating and reading of the data base. It may appear that a clear solution to concurrent processes destroying data or updating values incorrectly is to lock out one user or process from the data base while it is being accessed by another user or process. In some processes of an online real time system, this lockout may cause the system to halt, a result some people refer to as the "deadly embrace."

A widely accepted control that helps to prevent concurrency and lockout problems is two-phase locking, which applies directly to transactions that are being processed. Before a transaction can read or write a data entity, it must possess a read-lock or write-lock on the data entity. Moreover, different transactions are not permitted to own conflicting locks concurrently. Two transactions can own read-locks on the same data entity but a read-lock and a write-lock or two write-locks are not permitted to occur concurrently. This rule prevents inconsistent results that may occur if two transactions concurrently read and write a data entity or two transactions concurrently write a data entity. Two or more transactions concurrently reading a data entity does not matter. A transaction should make data base changes before releasing its locks. Once the transaction releases a lock, it must release all locks.

Output Controls

Output controls are installed to ensure the accuracy, completeness, timeliness, and proper distribution of output, whether it is on screen, in printed form, or in magnetic media. The following control procedures relate to output:

1. An initial screening should be conducted to detect obvious errors.
2. Output should be immediately routed to a controlled area and distributed only by authorized persons to authorized persons.
3. Output control totals should be reconciled to input control totals to ensure that no data have been changed, lost, or added during processing or transmission. For example, the number of input records delivered for processing should equal the number of records processed.

4. All vital forms (e.g., paychecks, stockholder registry forms, passbooks) should be prenumbered and accounted for.

5. Any highly sensitive output that should not be seen by computer center personnel should be generated by an output device in a secure location away from the computer room.

6. When negotiable instruments are to be printed, dual-custody arrangements should be made between the system and the user departments to make sure that all instruments are accounted for and properly safeguarded.

7. Despite all the precautions taken, some errors will slip through. The major detection control point for detecting such errors is, of course, the user. Therefore, procedures should be established by the auditor to set up a channel between the user and the control group for the systematic reporting of occurrences of errors or improprieties. Such a systems design would employ a feedback loop in which users would report all errors to the control group, and the control group, in turn, would take action to correct any inaccuracies or inconsistencies that might be revealed.

Documentation Controls

The overall control feature of documentation is that it shows the manager, auditor, users, and others what the system is supposed to be and how it should perform. Besides improving overall operating, management, and auditing controls, documentation also serves the following purposes: (1) it improves communication; (2) it provides reference material for what has happened in the past; (3) it provides a guide for systems maintenance, modification, and recovery; (4) it serves as a valuable tool for training and educating personnel; and (5) it reduces the impact of key personnel turnover.

As many systems authorities have said the documentation area is really the "Achilles' heel" of information systems. Some of the consequences of not having appropriate documentation are (1) an increase in the "fog index," (2) creation of inefficient and uncoordinated operations, (3) an increase in redundant efforts, and (4) disillusioned systems personnel and users.

The documentation that directly relates to the computer-based information system and its operation consists of three types: general systems, procedural, and program.

General systems documentation provides guidance and operating rules for users when interfacing with the system. This part of documentation includes a *users' manual* that describes what the system is and how to receive services from it. It provides names and addresses of key personnel to contact, prices, and overall objectives. It also states the systems development method that was used and both the systems analyst's and users' responsibilities relating to it. The reports (e.g., General Systems Design Report) prepared during the development of the system provide for the overall documentation of the system itself.

The *procedures manual* introduces all operating, programming, and systems staff to the master plan of the system; computer operating standards, controls, and procedures; and programming standards and procedures. It is updated by the use of periodic guidelines.

Program documentation consists of all documents, diagrams, and layouts that explain aspects of the program supporting a particular systems design. The following constitutes a typical program documentation manual:

1. The program manual should start with a general narrative describing the system. Also, a general systems flowchart should be included. This material links the program manual to the systems manual.

2. Program flowcharts, showing the input/output areas, source and main flow of data, entrance and exit of subroutines and program modules, and sequence of program operations, should be clearly illustrated. Also, supporting notes, narratives, and decisions tables should be understandable and properly organized.

3. The job control language (JCL) used to interface the program with the computer operating system should be included, together with a complete explanation of the purpose of each job control statement. Without this explanation, many JCL statements are difficult to understand.

4. All programming aids used should be described (e.g., CASE).

5. Program listings of both the source program and the object program should be included.

6. Program testing procedures should be described.

7. Sample printouts of all reports generated by the program should be included.

8. All controls (explained in programming controls) written into the program should be clearly noted.

9. All operating instructions, operator console commands, and execution time parameter values should be defined. Computer operator instructions are contained in what is called a *console run book* (also called operators' manual, etc.). This book should contain (1) flowcharts and decision tables related to that part of the system to which the program applies, (2) identification of file media required for input/output, (3) all console switch settings, (4) a list of program halts and required action, (5) descriptions of any exceptions to standard routines and input of parameter values (e.g., current date, titles, constants), and (6) authorized disposition of output.

10. An approval and change sheet should be included and kept current. In addition, the names of persons who wrote, tested, and approved the program should be listed.

Because a number of programmers and systems analysts do not like to prepare documentation by conventional methods, many are videotaping their work to help others understand the system that is developed. They see videotaping as an excellent alternative to written documentation. Watching and listening to people explain their programs and systems and how they work has certain advantages over reading the material from a printed page. Moreover, the monotonous "talking head" can be alleviated by using a variety of presentation formats with voice-over explanations and graphical displays. Where printed material is absolutely necessary, supplementary manuals are provided.

Hardware Controls

Most computers have a variety of automatic control features to ensure proper operation. These controls come in the form of built-in hardware controls or vendor software controls. They are standard in most computers; where they are not, management should require that these control features be incorporated in the computer system by the vendor before installation.

1. *Built-in Hardware Controls.*   These controls are built into the circuitry for detection of errors that result from manipulation, calculation, or transmission of data by various components of the computer system. These equipment controls are required to ensure that only one electronic pulse is transmitted through a channel during any single phase, that data are encoded and decoded accurately, that specific devices are activated, and that data received in one location are the same as were transmitted from the sending location. Examples of some of these internal equipment control features follows.

   a. *Parity Checks.*   To ensure that the data initially read into the system have been transmitted correctly, an internal self-checking feature is incorporated in most computer systems. In addition to the set of bits (e.g., a byte) used to represent data, the computer uses one additional bit for each storage position. These are called parity bits, or check bits, and are used to detect errors in the circuitry when a bit is lost, added, or destroyed because of an equipment malfunction.

   b. *Validity Check.*   Numbers and characters are represented by specified combinations of binary digits. Representation of these data symbols is accomplished by various coding schemes handled by the circuitry of the computer system. In a single computer system several different coding schemes can be used to represent data at various stages of processing. For example, the Hollerith characters of an input card are converted to Extended Binary Coded Decimal Interchange Code (EBCDIC), or to American Standard Code for Information Interchange (ASCII). If output is written on a printer, for example, the data will have to be converted to yet another code. Therefore, a message being either transmitted or received goes through an automatic encoding and decoding operation that is acceptable to the sending or receiving device in question.

   c. *Duplication Check.*   This control check requires that two independent components perform the same operation and compare results. If any difference between the two operations is detected, an error condition is indicated. For example, punched cards being read by a card reader pass two read stations. If the two readings are unequal, an error is indicated. The same principle of duplication is used in nearly all computer system components. For example, much of the circuitry of the arithmetic logic unit of the CPU is duplicated. This requires calculations to be performed twice, thereby increasing the probabilities of accurate results.

   d. *Echo Check.*   This control feature authenticates the transmission of data to and from components of the computer system. The data transmission is verified by echoing back the signal received by the component and comparing it with source data for agreement. For example, the CPU transmits a message to a VDT to perform an operation. The VDT returns a message to the CPU that is automatically checked to see if the correct device has been activated.

e. *Miscellaneous Error Checks.*   In addition to the control checks discussed earlier, the computer system should contain controls to detect various invalid computer instructions, data overflows, lost signs, zero division, and defective components.

f. *Firmware Controls.*   Firmware or hardwiring implies the use of solid-state techniques to represent instructions. Unlike programming instructions, a hardwired instruction cannot be modified. New technology permits many hardwired instructions to be placed in ROM.

The concept of firmware is extremely important because it removes from the programmer the ability to alter programs, which includes the highly vulnerable operating system. Furthermore, because of the increased complexity and sophistication of computer systems, a requirement exists to place a greater reliance for internal control on the computer itself.

Unfortunately, not all computer equipment installed today has a total complement of built-in hardware controls. In making equipment selection, the individual charged with this responsibility must evaluate the completeness of the control features incorporated in a particular component. If equipment is selected with a limited number of these controls, the probability of errors occurring because of equipment malfunction is increased.

g. *Fault-Avoidance and Fault-Tolerant Design.*   Fault avoidance stems from well-designed, well-crafted machines made up of high-quality components. This design approach reduces the possibility of failure. But even with the best computers, failures do occur. With fault-tolerant design, internal redundant architecture is used to continue processing and neutralize the effects of failure. Approaches to fault-tolerant design are (1) tandem, in which the architecture includes dual processors, dual I/O controllers and channels, dual file drives, copied data, and redundant power systems; (2) pair and spare systems, in which major functions are replicated, and if they fail, the spare takes over; and (3) duplexed systems, in which processors and other components serve as a pool from which resources are drawn as needed to perform the tasks. Clearly, fault-tolerant systems are based on redundancy. Fault-avoidance design increases reliability; fault-tolerant design increases availability. Are they not the same? No, because a system can be reliable and still not be available to users. For example, during preventive maintenance, testing, and modular expansion, a conventionally designed computer system would not be available to general users.

A system that is 99.5 percent reliable may be unavailable for 4 to 6 hours a month if it operates 24 hours a day, seven days a week. Many systems, however, must be available around the clock. Examples of these systems are monitoring and control systems, commercial time-sharing, airline reservations, air traffic control, power plant control, military command, fund-transfer applications, teleshopping, and even traditional functions, such as online order entry, inventory control, and billing. Both fault-avoidance and fault-tolerant designed computers are, indeed, important for such applications.

FAULT-TOLER-ANT MACHINE EARNING ITS KEEP

The data processing department at Inland Power and Light has found a way to get more out of a fault-tolerant processor than redundancy.

Running in fault-tolerant mode, the second application processor and data storage processor back up the first processors. But when nighttime batch processing runs over to the next business day, Inland can run batch jobs on one of the processors while running online systems on the other. Similarly, the utility can split production and development between the two processors.

Excerpted from Ellen Muraskin, "Double-Duty Fault Tolerance," *Computer & Communications Decisions*, August 1987, p. 32.

---

2. *Vendor Software Controls.* These controls are designed into the operating system and, to a great extent, deal with the routine input/output operations of the system. These controls are as follows:
   a. *Read or Write Error.* In the event of a read/write error, the machine will halt the program and allow the operator to investigate the error. For example, the system will stop if a writing operation is attempted to defective tape or if the printer runs out of paper.
   b. *Record Length Checks.* In some instances, blocks of records are defined that are too long for the input buffer area of the computer. This control feature, therefore, ensures that data records read into the computer from tape or disk are the correct length (no longer than permissible).
   c. *Label Checking Routines.* Header and trailer are two kinds of labels. At a minimum, the *header* label should contain file serial number, reel serial number, file name, creation date, and retention date. The *trailer* label should contain the block count, record count, control totals, and end-of-volume or end-of-file condition. For input files the header label is used to check that the file is the one specified by the program. The trailer label is used to determine if all data on the file were processed and whether physical or logical file is at end. For output files, the header label is used to check whether the file may be written on or destroyed (e.g., today's date is after the file expiration date).
   d. *Access Control.* An error condition occurs when reference is made to a storage device that is not in a "ready" status.
   e. *Address Compare Control.* An error condition occurs when a storage

address referenced by one component does not compare properly with the component's address that is referenced. For example, the core storage address does not agree with the address referenced by a disk drive.

Control of the Operating System and Utility Programs

As we state in Chapter 11, an operating system is a set of programs that directs the computer to perform a number of basic tasks, such as compile application programs, schedule and supervise the processing of programs, and control various devices. Also, most computer systems have regularly used programs called utility programs that manipulate and copy files, perform various maintenance chores, and modify other programs. In addition, computer vendors are installing remote diagnostic and recovery utilities. From remote locations, vendors' systems engineers can get access to the system and manipulate data and programs in an attempt to solve local hardware and software problems. Needless to say, operating systems and utilities are required to carry on operations. But they also create a serious control problem because these programs can manipulate any data in the data base, erase data, and override passwords and other controls.

Admittedly, the system is vulnerable to these programs, and no real control solution exists. Most vendors, however, provide a program that produces an audit trail of any jobs processed by the operating system and utilities. An example is IBM's system management facility (SMF). The system console log combined with data from SMF tells the auditor what files were accessed, when, and for what reason. It also discloses what utilities are used, when and why, and what application programs and files they accessed. For further control, certain high-risk utility programs should be removed from the standard utility library and placed in a restricted utility program library, subject to strong access control based on authorized users' personal characteristics, such as fingerprints, hand geometry, or voice.

Computer Operations Controls

All computer center staff, especially operators, should be under direct supervision. Supervisors should establish job priorities and run schedules for every working day, and all computer operators should be required to sign the computer operating log at the beginning and end of their shifts.

Supervisors should require equipment utilization reports and maintain accurate job cost records of all computer time, including production, program listing, rerun, idle, and down time. On a periodic basis, the auditor should review these reports.

No business transactions should be initiated by any computer center staff. Only computer operators should operate the computer, but operator intervention to processing should be limited. Access of computer operators to sensitive tapes, disks, programs, and documentation should be tightly controlled.

Access to computer room facilities should be restricted to authorized personnel only. For example, many programmers request "hands-on" testing. Any hands-on use of the computer by programmers should be limited and closely supervised.

Good housekeeping procedures are fundamental to any system, especially a computer system. Floors should be cleaned on a daily basis, and underfloor cleaning should be done on a yearly basis. Printer ribbons should be changed periodically. A maintenance schedule should be followed for tape and disk drives, tape and disk media, the computer and other peripherals, and air conditioning. Fire-suppression systems should be checked periodically. All clutter, trash, idle equipment, and unused furniture should be removed from computer areas.

Basic to preventive maintenance is an inventory of spare parts. (It would be foolish to halt operations of a million-dollar system for want of a one-dollar part.) All service of equipment should be performed by qualified and authorized service engineers.

The console terminal, either typewriter or CRT, and the switches and buttons on the console control panel, enable the computer operator to enter messages or commands into and receive information directly from the storage unit of the CPU. Using keys, switches, audible tone signals, and display lights on the console unit, the computer operator can (1) start, stop, or change the operation of all or part of the computer system; (2) manually enter and display data from internal storage; (3) determine the status of internal electronic switches; (4) determine the contents of certain internal registers; (5) alter the mode of operation so that when an unusual condition or malfunction occurs the computer will either stop or indicate the condition (e.g., a jam in the card reader or the wrong tape file mounted) and proceed after the condition or malfunction has been corrected; (6) change the selection of input/output devices; (7) load programs and various routines; and (8) alter the data content of specific storage locations.

The operating log (also called the console log) can be in the form of a continuous paper printout from the console typewriter or, in some large installations, from a printer dedicated to printing the operating log. This latter alternative is preferable when the console typewriter is not fast enough to handle high-volume output. In some installations the operating log may be written out on magnetic media, especially if a CRT is used instead of a console typewriter. In any case, the operating log is a valuable control document because it gives a running account of all the messages generated by the computer and of all the instructions and entries made by the computer operator. In addition, it can indicate the beginning or end of various stages of processing and intermediate or final results of processing.

14.4 SECURITY CONTROLS

Ordinarily, security controls do not affect the proper and accurate processing of transactions as much as the controls discussed earlier. Conceptually, a secure system is one that is penetration-proof from potential hazards. Security controls help to ensure high systems standards and performance by protecting against hardware, software, and human failure. Absence of security controls can increase the probability of such things happening as (1) degraded operations, (2) compromised system, (3) loss of services, (4) loss of assets, and (5) unauthorized disclosure of sensitive information.

Security controls, as well as all of the controls discussed so far, apply to both small and large computer centers and to in-house and outside computer services. Security controls are a key ingredient in the system of controls and cannot be neglected.

Security Hazards

What follows are the classic security hazards of a computer-based information system, arranged by their probability of occurrence and their impact on the system. The rationale for this hierarchy is, in part, based on research, intuition, and generalizations. It cannot be proved or disproved. Therefore, not only is it a subject for debate, but in any particular system the arrangement of these hazards may be quite different.

1. *Malfunctions.*   People, software, and hardware error or malfunction cause the biggest problems. In this area humans are frequently the culprits by acts of omission, neglect, and incompetence. Some authorities have said that simple human error causes more damage than all other errors combined. We read of one incident in which a disk pack was warped from being dropped; the warped pack was mounted on a disk drive and damaged the access mechanism. The same pack was then moved to another drive, and a different pack was mounted on the first drive, and so on, resulting in several damaged drives and unusable disk packs.

2. *Fraud and Unauthorized Access.*   This hazard or threat is the attainment of something through dishonesty, cheating, or deceit. This hazard can occur through (1) infiltration and industrial espionage, (2) tapping data communication lines, (3) emanation pickup from parabolic receivers (the computer and its peripherals are transmitters), (4) unauthorized browsing through files by online terminals, (5) masquerading as an authorized user, (6) physical confiscation of files and other sensitive documents, and (7) installation of Trojan horses (those things that are not what they appear to be).

3. *Power and Communication Failures.*   In some locations this hazard may occur with greater frequency than other hazards. To a great extent, the availability and reliability of power and communication facilities is a function of location. In heavily populated areas brownouts occur frequently, especially during the summer. Conversely, there have been instances in which power surges have occurred, burning out sensitive computer components. This particular hazard can be easily controlled with a power regulator. Also, during each working day, communication channels are sometimes busy or noisy.

4. *Fires.*   Fires occur with greater frequency than many people realize, and they are one of the worst disasters.

5. *Sabotage and Riot.*   Components of computer centers have been destroyed by disgruntled employees and damage has occurred to computer centers installed in or near decaying urban areas that later become scenes of riots.

6. *Natural Disasters.*   Relatively speaking, natural disasters (so-called acts of

God) do not occur often, but when they do the results can be devastating. These disasters include earthquakes, tornadoes, floods, and lightning. Pre-planning can help to reduce their impact. For example, one organization installed its computer complex in a quite suburban center only to find later that the center was constructed on a lot beneath the flood plain—something that should have been ascertained prior to installation.

7. *General Hazards.*   This category covers a number of random hazards that are difficult to define and anticipate. Normally, general safeguards will lessen the probability of their occurrence. For example, one Sunday morning, a vice-president arrived at his office to find a fully loaded gasoline truck, with its brakes on fire, parked next to the computer center. Better isolation of the computer site from this type of traffic could have prevented this incident from occurring.

Goals of Security Controls Against Hazards

Goals of security controls against hazards can be viewed as levels of controls. That is, if one level fails, another control level takes over, and so forth.

1. *Deter.*   At this level, the goal is to prevent any loss or disaster from occurring.

2. *Detect.*   Complete deterrence often cannot be achieved. Therefore, the goal at this level is to establish methods to monitor hazard potential and to report this to people and equipment for corrective action.

3. *Minimize Impact of Disaster and Loss.*   If an accident or mishap occurs, procedures and facilities should be established to help reduce the loss. For example, a backup master file would help mitigate the destruction of a master file.

4. *Investigate.*   If a loss does occur, an investigation should be started immediately to determine what happened. This investigation will provide study facts that can be used for future security planning.

5. *Recovery.*   As mentioned earlier a plan of action to recover from the loss and return operations to normal as soon as possible should exist. For example, if the data processing operation for a bank could not operate for a week or two, financial failure would likely result. Recovery procedures can range from backup facilities to insurance coverage.

Physical Security Techniques

Physical security techniques include devices and physical placement of computer facilities that help guard against hazards. Some of these techniques are (1) physical controlled access, (2) physical location, and (3) physical protection devices.

1. *Physical Controlled Access.*   Access control protection is basic to a security system. If a potential penetrator cannot gain entry to the computer facilities, then the chance for harm is reduced considerably. The following items help to control access.

   a. *Guards and Special Escorts.*   Guards should be placed at strategic entry points of the computer facility. All visitors who are given permission to tour the computer center should be accompanied by a designated escort.

b. ***Sign-in/Sign-out Registers.*** All persons should be required to sign a register indicating time of sign-in, purpose, and time of departure. An improvement on the standard signature register incorporates devices that analyze signatures as a function of time and pressure. Thus, a counterfeiter may be able to duplicate the outward appearances of a signature, but take more time and apply less pressure during the signing.

c. ***Badges.*** Color-coded (e.g., red for programmers, blue for systems analysts) badges, with the badgeholder's picture when possible, can be used to identify authorized personnel and visitors readily.

d. ***Cards.*** Card control entry equipment, used alone or in conjunction with other measures, is probably the most popular access control device. Doors can be opened by either optical or magnetic coded cards. Authorization for entry can be dynamically controlled by individual doors, time of day, day of week, and security classification of individuals to whom the card is issued. Authorizations can be added or deleted easily, and entry activity logs and reports can be prepared and displayed to a control officer. Open or closed status of all doors can be monitored, and attempts at unauthorized entry can be detected immediately and an alarm sounded.

Smart cards (also called memory cards or chip cards) are the same size and shape as credit cards, and are of three types: monochip, multichip, and optical stripe. Primary applications of smart cards are electronic funds transfer (EFT), videotex access and teleshopping, applications requiring personal identification, such as passports, driver's license, ski-lift passes, hotel door keys, and input for computer processing. These cards are multifunctional. For example, memory cards can serve as a credit card, savings passbook, checkbook, and automatic teller access card. The cards have advantages over conventional cards in that they are easy to track if lost or stolen and they are difficult to counterfeit.

e. ***Closed-Circuit Monitors.*** Devices such as closed-circuit television monitors, cameras, and intercom systems, connected to a control panel staffed by security guards, are becoming increasingly popular. These devices are very effective in controlling a large area rather than concentrating on entry and exit points only.

f. ***Paper Shredders.*** Sensitive reports should never be disposed of by simply being thrown in waste containers. Numerous cases have been reported of penetrators being able to steal confidential information by gaining access to waste disposal facilities. Any sensitive reports should be shredded before being thrown away. A disintegration system that converts an end product into unclassified waste or microconfetti that cannot be reconstructed, works even better than a shredder. These machines will disintegrate bound manuals, computer printouts, carbons, microfilms, microfiches, EDP cards, plastic binders, printer circuits, and mylar computer tape.

COMPUTER ON A CARD Many analysts, consultants and manufacturers believe "smart cards"—credit-sized cards embedded with memory and, often, microprocessors—will exact change from nearly every sphere of the business world.

Such cards have the potential to link directly millions of people into computer and telecommunications networks while maintaining a high level of security that prevents access privileges from being abused. The possible uses of smart cards are as varied as the uses to which computers are put today since the cards are, in essence, tiny portable computers.

"It's like having a PC in your pocket, and you can do with it whatever you would with a computer," said Richard L. Dunham, president and CEO of Micro Card Technologies, Inc., of Dallas, a large smart-card manufacturer.

The cards' memory and processor are dedicated to specific tasks such as security control, financial transactions or manufacturing, and are designed to work with card readers that hook the card into a computer network. Often, a PC attached to the card reader relays information between a network and the card.

Excerpted from Preston Gralla, "'Smart Cards' Seen as Changing the Way Businesses Operate," *PC Week*, January 5, 1988, pp. C1 and C9.

g. *One-way Emergency Doors.* These doors are for exit only and are to be used in case of emergency situations such as a fire.

h. *Combination of Control Devices.* The above devices can be combined with other safeguards that we will be discussing in following sections to increase security even further. Card systems can be combined with a hand geometry identifier. In another example, entry through one door, equipped with a card reader, leads to a "man-trap" area that is sealed from the computer system by bulletproof glass. To get through the second door leading to the computer room, a valid card has to be used, plus identification over a combination intercom and television monitoring system.

2. *Physical Location.* Location of the computer system is an important consideration in security planning. Note the following guidelines:

a. *Remote Location.* The computer site should be away from airports, electrical equipment (e.g., radar and microwave), decaying urban areas, heavy traffic, steam boilers, and so forth. The more removed the computer system is from these kinds of hazards, the better. If the site cannot be as distant as desirable, then some remoteness can be achieved by clearing a 200- to 300-foot radius around the site, and installing floodlights and a perimeter fence.

b. *Separate Building.* Many security specialists recommend that the computer system be housed in a separate building. The advantage of doing this is that access control is easier and there is less risk from general hazards. For example, there would be less risk from fire caused by flammable products used by other building occupants. A disadvantage is that deliberate attack on the power source, the communication lines, and the air intake, could be easier because of specific identification. If the computer system is not housed in a separate building, then it should be centered in the building, away from the outside walls, and not located on the top floor, on the street floor in view of passersby, or in the basement. It should not be displayed as a showcase.

c. *Identification.*   The computer site should not contain any signs that identify it to outsiders.

d. *Carrier Control.*   Power and communication lines should be underground. Air intake devices, compressors, and cooling towers should be protected by fences and placed at heights that cannot be reached easily. Manhole covers should be locked.

e. *Backup Facilities Location.*   Backup plays a major role in many areas of a total system of control. Backup is the key element to recovery. As far as location is concerned, a backup facility should be far enough away from the main facility that it is not subject to the same hazards but close enough to provide quick recovery. When possible, the backup facility should be located in a place that uses a different power source. The location of the backup facility should be kept confidential.

3. *Physical Protection.*   Additional protective devices should be considered in an overall protection plan. These items are as follows:

a. *Drains and Pumps.*   Sometimes water pipes burst or water enters the site from a fire or flood. To help reduce these mishaps, drains and pumps should be installed.

b. *Emergency Power.*   Again, backup plays an important part in control. Uninterruptible power systems (UPSs) should be installed for power backup to provide continuous processing. The decision to install a UPS depends on the frequency and nature of the power disturbances and the effect they have on the computer system. Power failure or disturbance can range anywhere from transients of a few milliseconds' duration to long-term power outages. These power fluctuations can result in loss of data, processing errors, downtime, and equipment malfunction and damage. One major stock brokerage firm estimated that a power outage during trading would cost it $4 million an hour.

Minor fluctuations in the power source that might cause a light to flicker can crash a computer and destroy data. Experts blame more than 80 percent of all computer malfunctions on electrical problems, ranging from voltage surges and sags to full-blown outages. To make matters worse, computers will become even more sensitive in the future.

A UPS generally consists of a rectifier/charger, a battery, and an inverter. The rectifier/charger normally converts alternating current (AC) utility power to direct current (DC), and maintains a full charge on the battery. Should utility power fail, the battery provides DC to the inverter, which converts the DC power into clean and continuous AC power. Transfer of the critical load from the utility power source to the battery and back is generally accomplished with a static bypass switch. A static switch is electronic (unlike a mechanical switch) and therefore permits critical load transfer within the acceptable tolerances required by most mainframes and peripherals (4 msec). The power support time available from the UPS's batteries is a function of the number and size of batteries available. The recommended support time to shut down a system gracefully, versus a hard crash, is around 5 minutes. If a system cannot tolerate any stoppage in processing, such as in a hospital or air traffic control, then an alternative power source is required complete with a diesel engine and turbine.

A TOTAL UPS APPROACH   What many people fail to recognize, until it's too late, is that the UPS solution offered by a single vendor is not, by itself, the same thing as a truly effective UPS "system." What is needed is a total protection network that starts at the local utility's power grid, passes through several transformers, switch gear, conditioning, and control steps. It is supplemented by batteries and engine generators, and it continues all the way to the input power lugs on the computer itself. Anything that plays a role in this power path is part of the total UPS system, and any implementation must provide not just for the appropriate equipment, but also for operator training, on-going maintenance, testing, and emergency repairs.

Excerpted from Kenneth Brill, "Reliable Power: Beyond the Big Box," *InformationWEEK*, March 14, 1988, p. 40.

---

c. *Environmental Control.*   Adequate and separate air conditioner, de-humidification, and humidification systems should be installed. Regardless of what vendors say, computer systems still need a great deal of air conditioning to operate properly. Large mainframes also require chilled water systems to cool their densely packed circuitry. Although manufacturers often suggest that their equipment will operate in a temperature range of 50 to 95°F, a stricter guideline of 72°F $\pm$ 2° is advised to avoid malfunctions due to temperature fluctuations. Similarly, with respect to relative humidity (RH), manufacturers cite the range of 20 to 90 percent RH. A much safer guide is 50 percent RH $\pm$ 5 percent. Semiconductor life in a computer's logic and memory unit is very sensitive to temperature fluctuations. High RH levels (e.g., 80 percent and above) can cause problems in computer systems in various ways, including the corrosion of electrical contacts or the expansion of paper.

The latter effect can cause printers and card readers (or any equipment that uses paper) to malfunction. Low RH, on the other hand, can result in a buildup of static electricity causing paper to stick and jam.

d. *Coverings*.   All equipment should be covered with plastic covers when not in use. In several cases water damage to computer equipment was reduced during a fire because some alert individual covered the equipment.

e. *Fire Control*.   Basically, there are three kinds of fire: Class A—cellulosis, Class B—flammable liquid, and Class C—electrical. Consultation with fire department personnel and fire control equipment vendors should be made to determine the appropriate fire and smoke detectors and extinguishing methods. Normally, methods recommended will be a combination of (1) portable fire extinguishers, (2) fluoride gas, (3) Halon (causes no permanent damage to office material and equipment), (4) carbon dioxide (CO_2, good for extinguishing electrical fires but dangerous in that it can suffocate personnel), (5) water sprinklers, and (6) smoke exhaust systems. Smoke exhaust systems are a necessary element of fire control methods because smoke, in many instances, is the biggest problem, especially where there is a preponderance of vinyl and other plastic material.

Insurance companies report that more insurance claims are made for water and flooding damage from putting out fires than are made for damage caused by fires themselves. This situation reinforces the need for drains, pumps, and coverings.

When various detection and extinguishing systems are used, it is important that the detectors not release a fire extinguishing agent immediately. To do so is wasteful, and in the case of CO_2, it can be hazardous to personnel in the area. The detectors should trigger audible and visible alarms locally and at appropriate fire or guard stations. A control panel should be available to indicate which detector(s) triggered the alarm. By zeroing in on the fire, some designated individuals (no one should be sent alone) can go directly to the source of trouble, determine the extent of the fire, and put it out with a portable fire extinguisher if it is small and localized.

Most fire-prevention specialists prefer Halon 1301 and CO_2 to conventional water-sprinkler systems, because neither conducts electricity. Many do not recommend CO_2 because it can cause death by asphyxiation. These gases are less likely to damage valuable electrical equipment or leave much residue inside the equipment after a fire. In most cases, to satisfy insurance carriers, users, however, must install Halon 1301 and water-sprinkler systems. If the fire is throughout the building, Halon 1301 by itself will not be effective. To stop a fire, Halon 1301 must completely flood a room or space, an impossible task unless the room is completely sealed. Moreover, Halon 1301 systems are usually set up to dump once, which is often insufficient to stop a large, smouldering fire.

f. *General Building Safeguards*.   Walls of the building should be constructed from slab. Walls and ceilings should have at least a one-hour fire rating. The number of doors should be limited. The building should not have windows, and air ducts should be filtered and contain fire dampers.

Humidity-spawned static electricity can cause computers to "forget" and produce erroneous and funny-looking output. A person can generate more than 40,000 volts just walking across a carpet and transfer that charge to a computer or terminal. In addition to implementation of a humidity-controlling system, antistatic devices like sprays, floor and desk mats, and specially treated carpet should be installed.

One cannot install too many filters. Clean air can extend the life span of computers, peripherals, and air-conditioning equipment. To be sure, with information technology becoming more and more sensitive, an almost surgically clean environment is necessary.

g. *Emanation Protection.* With the right equipment, a spy can sit outside a building in an ordinary van and literally read the data and text being processed and transmitted inside. Computers emanate radio waves that can easily be picked up more than 100 yards away. Unprotected, computers can leak vital, sensitive information like a sieve.

Federal agencies and some commercial organizations take this leakage problem seriously. Together, billions of dollars are being spent to shield computers, word processors, printers, and even rooms to stop the emanations from being intercepted by spies.

The name given to the government's emanation-protection specifications is Tempest. Two methods are used by vendors to meet Tempest's specifications. One is containment, which involves the enclosing of equipment and rooms with leakproof materials that trap radio frequencies. The other is source suppression, which involves procedures that make circuit boards and wiring inside the computers leakproof. Tempest-based machines usually cost 20 to 30 percent more than standard ones.

Procedural Security Techniques

Whereas physical security techniques deal with a number of hazards, including fire, and natural disaster, procedural security techniques deal almost exclusively with access control. In some cases, a procedural technique will require the application of a physical technique.

Our discussion on procedural security techniques covers six concepts: integrity, isolation, identification, authorization, authentication, and monitoring.

1. *Integrity.* As a concept within the context of security controls, integrity is basically the assurance that the system is functionally correct and complete. Otherwise, the absence of integrity will make implementation of all the other concepts ineffective.

If a user is authorized to retrieve item A from a file, then the system must be depended on to provide item A, and only item A, to the user. Analogous to this idea of integrity is a case in which an authorized user is given a key intended to unlock door A but not doors B, C, and D. Therefore, the locking mechanism system should guarantee that the key does in fact unlock only door A. As another example, if a user is supposed to be in read only mode, the system should guarantee that the user cannot do something else (e.g., write).

Integrity procedures also apply during simultaneous job processing. The system should function in such a way that after one authorized job is completed, information from that job is sanitized (e.g., erased, scrubbed) so that unauthorized penetrators cannot read it by browsing. Without sanitizing procedures, confidential information would be exposed to unauthorized access at various points during processing.

2. *Isolation.*   In any system in which a high level of security is to be maintained, no individual or part of the organization should be in a position to put together all the components or subsystems to make a whole system. This isolation is sometimes referred to as *interface isolation* or *compartmentalization,* and is a concept used in the design and construction of secret weapons. In computer-based information systems, this isolation should be maintained between users and information as well as between hardware and software resources and processes. Several procedures that effect isolation are:

    a. *Disconnection and Separation.*   One form of isolation is achieved by geographical or logical distribution, in which certain elements of the system are not connected. For example, terminal 1 is not connected to computer A. This procedure employs total isolation, in which two or more elements are disconnected.

        In most situations some connection or interface among elements has to exist to make the total system operative. Several examples of key interface points that require logical separation procedures and tight control are (1) computer operator/console, (2) computer operator/programs, (3) computer operator/data base library, (4) programmer/computer, (5) systems analyst/programs, and (6) user/terminal.

        As in internal controls in traditional accounting, separation procedures, for example, mean that no single individual should have access to computer programs and operation of the computer and to the design of the system. Also, this means that those individuals who input transactions into the system should not also have access to programs.

    b. *Least Privileged Access.*   To make a system operative, certain privileged states and instruction sets must be assigned to appropriate users. This assigned privilege should be the minimum access authority necessary to perform the required process. For example, an order clerk may be given the privilege to access only quantity on hand and price of items in an inventory file. The clerk would not be able to access cost, vendor, vendor performance, and so forth. Another example of least privileged access is where programmers are required to use compiler languages such as COBOL, which automatically isolates them from the computer equipment and operating system.

    c. *Location of Terminal.*   Based on location, terminals are given different classifications and levels of security. For example, a terminal located in a warehouse easily accessible by a variety of personnel may be given few access privileges and permitted to perform only low-level tasks. A major problem with this kind of identification is that if terminals later need to be switched, authorization changes must be made. Consequently, it may be better to rely primarily on one or a combination of the other identification methods discussed.

d. *Encryption.* This procedure involves confusing, obscuring, or hiding a message where an unauthorized person cannot read it. An example of hiding is to not list the telephone number of the computer system in the building directory, or even the system's location. A more pervasive and complex problem, however, involves the protection of data once they are transmitted over the public airwaves, bouncing off satellites and from one earth station to another. Literally anyone with the right kind of receiving equipment can read the data. This is where an encryption method is employed for sensitive data.

Encryption techniques scramble data into secret form so that the original meaning is not understood by anyone but the intended receiver. Cryptographic techniques involve using a key, or more than one key, together with an algorithm, to encrypt and decrypt data. The algorithm used in most commercial applications in the United States is the Data Encryption Standard (DES), developed by IBM in 1977 and adopted by the National Bureau of Standards. The National Security Agency (NSA) has been involved in on-again, off-again certification of DES-based systems.

The DES can be implemented in a computer system through either a hardware addition or purchase of encryption software. Hardware implementation provides a higher level of security because software-based implementation is susceptible to penetration by programmers or others who understand the language used. Hardware-based encryption, in addition to being highly secure, is convenient and relatively inexpensive. Cryptoboxes, as hardware encryption devices are often called, can be purchased for less than $1,000 and can be used for both local and online encryption.

Figure 14.3 portrays the encryption/decryption process of the DES. The DES starts with 64 bits (8 bytes) of readable or understandable data called *cleartext*. The cleartext is put into an electronic "meat grinder," where it is tossed, tumbled, and jumbled. Injected during these mixing operations is a 64-bit *key*. It, too, gets mixed up in the encryption process. Finally, after cleartext has been sufficiently scrambled, out falls a 64-bit segment of meaningless data called *ciphertext*.

The ciphertext is decrypted or changed back to the 64 bits of cleartext by reversing all the encryption operations. Notice that the same 64-bit encryption key is used to decrypt the data. If different keys were used to encrypt and decrypt the data, the decryped data would be as meaningless as the ciphertext.

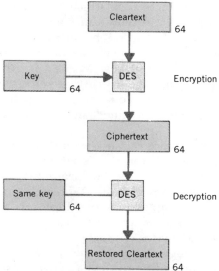

Figure 14.3 The encryption/decryption process of the DES.

Because 2^{56} combinations (8 bits are parity bits) of the keying variable are possible, the DES algorithm is considered highly secure. It, however, could be broken by experts who have at their disposal a powerful computer. Moreover, the DES is only as good as the security of the key.

The DES algorithm has been controversial since its adoption. The original project called for a 128-bit key, but was shortened to 64 bits. Critics claim that the shortened key weakened the DES algorithm. The official position of IBM, the American Banking Association, many other financial groups, and the National Bureau of Standards is that the DES is strong and adequate. No one yet has proven that the DES algorithm has ever been compromised or could be broken with anything less than a full commitment of supercomputer resources.

Although the National Security Agency still certifies DES-based equipment, it will, more than likely, cease certification within the next several years. NSA supports a plan to use a large number of algorithms from which users can choose. NSA, consequently, embraces a public key system. Unlike the DES, the public key system uses two different but mathematically complementary keys, one for encryption and the other for decryption. The encryption key is made public so anyone having it can transmit an encrypted message. The decryption key remains a secret, so only authorized users can decrypt the message.

Assume that A wishes to send a message to B using the public key system. A encrypts the data using B's published key. The only one who can decrypt the message is B using his or her secret key.

Spoofing is the main area in which the public key system is vulnerable. For example, C can send a message to B and call himself A. The message appears authentic to B because it is encrypted by B's public key and decrypted by B's secret key. The spoofer, however, can be shut out by using a combination of keys to ensure authentication. For example, A encrypts the message with A's secret key and B's public key. B then decrypts the message with B's secret key and A's public key. This way, the sender is uniquely identified, and B is assured that the message was originated by A.

Generally, organizations do not want their computer-based information systems talking to strangers. Therefore, encryption is increasingly catching on in business and financial markets as companies seek to expand their operations globally. Wholesale encryption, however, wastes computer and employee time. Moreover, a problem with file encryption is that if the key is lost, the data are lost. Consequently, sound and strict key management is critical.

Before introducing encryption, the systems analyst should classify data and programs according to their relative sensitivity. *Top secret* information and programs are to be seen and used by a few select people and should be encrypted when stored on file media and when transmitted from node to node in the network. Access should be controlled by biometric devices, such as fingerprint readers and retina scanners. *Confidential* information is files and programs restricted to selected employees or departments and should be encrypted or controlled by access devices, such as security cards or passwords. *Restricted* files and programs are available to all employees but not the general public. This area can be secured with data compression programs that effectively prevent employees from copying magnetic disks or tapes to take off-site.

3. *Identification.* If a system incorporates isolation procedures, then the system must also have the ability to identify authorized and proper interfaces. The system must be able to distinguish between those users to whom access is permissible and those to whom it is not. Based on the level of security required, the person, the terminal, the file, or the program must be identified so that the right to use the system can be verified and the user can be held accountable. Methods to effect identification are the following:

a. *Something the User Has.*   A user is identified by something in his or her possession. Identification items can consist of (1) codes (also called passwords, keywords, or lockwords), (2) keys to locks, (3) badges, (4) magnetic striped or optical cards, (5) phone numbers, (6) terminal ID numbers, or (7) encryption keys. The main disadvantage of these items is that the probability is relatively high that they could be obtained and used by others.

b. *Something the User Knows.*   Here, a user is identified on the basis of something he or she knows (the identification item is not physical). Examples of such items are personalized codes that are changed regularly and sequences in which the user answers a prearranged set of questions (e.g., previous address, birthplace, family member birthday, color of spouse's eyes). The effectiveness of this identification item is related directly to how often it is changed; the more often an item is changed (e.g., password, prearranged question), the less likely that it will be appropriated by others.

c. *The User's Characteristics.*   The user is identified on the basis of some physical characteristic uniquely his or her own. These characteristics can be divided into two categories, neuromuscular, such as dynamic signatures and handwriting, and genetic. The genetic category covers (1) body geometry (e.g., hand shape identification is being used to a limited extent), (2) fingerprints, (3) voice response patterns, (4) facial appearance (primary use is on badges), (5) eye iris and retina, (6) lip prints, and (7) brain wave patterns.

READING PALMS   Many products have been designed to prevent unauthorized entry into computer rooms, but a new device from Mitsubishi really deserves a big hand.

The company's Palm Recognition System requires users to give a high-five before gaining admission to secured facilities.

Individuals seeking entry to a sealed room must type a private seven-digit number into the machine and then place their hand on an illuminated screen.

The system stores up to 200 different palm prints, and will not permit access through the doors it protects without "seeing" one of those prints. According to its maker, the device is accurate to within 0.0001 percent, meaning that just one out of 1,000,000 people might sneak into a secret place without permission.

This is an improvement over keys and cards, which, unlike palm prints, can get into anyone's hands.

The only biometric security device that is more accurate, according to officials at Mitsubishi Electric Sales America, Inc., which is marketing the palm reader, is a machine that examines an individual's retina.

Excerpted from Don Steinberg, "Security System Reads Palms to Guard Computer Rooms," *PC Week*, June 16, 1987, p. C5.

A good example of how users are uniquely identified is a fingerprint system in which an employee approaches a small machine at an entrance to the computer facilities. He or she punches in a three-digit identification number and then inserts a finger into a small lighted opening. In a few seconds the door unlocks. When the employee inputs his or her identification number, the computer retrieves a copy of the person's filed digitized fingerprints and scans for the match. Because fingerprints, unlike cards, keys, or passwords, cannot be stolen or counterfeited, the fingerprint method represents a virtually foolproof access control method.

A microcomputer-based access control device is available that scans the retina of an individual's eye. Experts testify that each of us has a unique and unalterable retina structure. A quick glance into a small device, an infrared check of the blood vessel pattern on the retina, and an employee is clocked in for the day. It takes about as long as turning a door key or using a password. The chance of error in identification with this kind of scanning device is reputed to be as low as one in a million.

Some companies use voice identification to control access to sensitive areas or files, or to clock-in. A person speaks into a telephone-type device that breaks voice data into millisecond intervals. These data are transmitted to the computer, which matches them with previously stored voice patterns.

These James Bond–like access control devices are growing at a faster rate than many previously thought. Some experts are now predicting that within the next five years more than one-half of the companies will be using some kind of a biometric access control device. Clearly, fail-safe identification is their main appeal, but do they appeal to users?

Human behavior may be more significant in slowing down or preventing the commercial application of this kind of identification than the advance of technology. People normally resist an invasion of personal privacy. If this kind of identification technology is viewed as a personal invasion, then people will resist. Stories are told about an unauthorized user "kissing" a computer terminal and a clamp attaching his lips to the terminal until a security officer arrives, or about users having to stick their finger through a tiny guillotine for fingerprint identification—unauthorized user? Goodbye finger!

4. *Authorization.* Once a person has been identified as a valid user, the question becomes, what authority does this person have? That is, what does he or she have the right to do? For instance, in the security of a data base, procedures must be set up to determine who has access to what files, who has the right to make additions and deletions, and who is responsible for administration of the data base. The following items help to deal with the concept of authorization.

   a. *Categorize Authorization.* This step determines the specific authority of users, programs, and hardware; that is, each category is limited in what it can and cannot do. Classes of authority can include user to documentation, user to equipment, user to program, user to file, terminal to program, program to file, and program to program. Those activities that must be designated in conjunction with classes of authority are read, write, add, change, delete, copy, create, append, and display. For example, Joe Clerk may be given the right to use program 1 to read (entirely or a specific part of) file A.

b. *Use of Codes.*   Codes are linked to the authority table and the authority table is, in turn, linked to an identification table. That is, the validity of the user (or terminal) is first identified, then it is determined what the valid user can do. For example, Joe Clerk may be permitted to read only parts of file A. Therefore, codes may have to be assigned not only to files but to a category of records within files, or even to individual fields within records.

c. *Security Program.*   The computer system itself must be programmed not only to identify valid users but to ensure that proper authority is granted. To do so requires installation of a security program. What follows is a general, hypothetical example of the type of instructions contained in a security program.

User/Relation:

```
DEFINE RELATION (INVENTORY)
AUTHORIZE USER (JONES) RELATION (INVENTORY)
FOR (READ, CHANGE)
```

User/Program:

```
AUTHORIZE USER (JONES) PROGRAM (UPDATE)
FOR (READ, CHANGE = QUANTITY-ON-HAND DOMAIN)
```

In addition, the security program should have the ability to change readily the identifications and authorizations, as well as the security requirements based on time of day, day of week, weekends, and holidays. For example, certain users would lose their authority over weekends, vacations, or holidays. Included in the program should also be a routine to report immediately the source of any attempted violations.

IBM's RACF (resource access control facility) is a control software product that provides the ability to limit user access to information and system resources based on ownership of data and the need to know. Also, such software products monitor user activity and report on security violations for follow-up.

IBM's DB2's, a major data base management system, security philosophy is, "If the object was defined in DB2, then DB2 will control the access to it. Any activity involving a DB2 object, resource, or function is a privilege requiring authorization." The creator of any DB2 object is considered to be the owner of that object and can do anything to that object. Privileges to use other objects, resources, or data requires specific authorization.

For example, authority in IBM's DB2 is assigned in one of three ways: (1) implicitly through the *create* command, (2) explicitly through *grant* or *revoke* commands, and (3) by assigning *administrative authorities*.

Implicit authorization means that users can do anything to objects they create. The general grant command is GRANT "privileges" ON "resources" TO "user." The user is identified by an ID such as a number or password. Administrative authorities allow users a list of privileges to groups of objects and resources established by the GRANT command. Any privilege that can be GRANTed can be taken away using the REVOKE command, such as REVOKE "privileges" ON "resources" FROM "user." Also special privileges can be granted to certain users who are authorized to view data but not change it.

Another area of authorization is menus. Menu programs that list all applications tempt users, authorized or not. In highly sensitive applications, the systems analyst should probably design the user/system interface in a way in which the user must specify the desired application rather than select it from a menu. Only application supervisors would have access to a full-function screen.

5. *Authentication.*   Authentication is an action intended to determine whether something is valid or genuine. Someone or some facility may be identified appropriately and be given authority to access information or perform some activity. The system cannot be assured that the user is valid, however, especially if the user is identified on the basis of "what he has" (e.g., magnetic card) or "what he knows" (e.g., code or password). Periodically, especially for usage of sensitive files (as well as other resources), the user should be confirmed. This confirmation may include some or all of the following authentication procedures: (1) physical observation (e.g., sending someone to confirm the identity of the user), (2) periodic disconnects and callback procedures (e.g., a terminal is disconnected and called back to see if the appropriate terminal responds), and (3) periodic requests for further information or reverification from the user.

Clearly, then, the key problem in controlling remote access is to authenticate the user. This problem has been complicated by the introduction of large numbers of personal computers in the telecommunications network. In many installations, the mainframe has no way of knowing whether it is connected to a dumb terminal or a device that can download the data base and program library.

By using the callback method, the receiving device asks for the identification of the user, then disconnects. If the user's phone number matches an authorized phone number in the system's user directory, the receiving system will call back the originating system using this prearranged number. The assumption is that communication only occurs between a device located at an authorized phone number and the callback device. This scheme is appropriate if used by executives who always call from home or certain offices.

The effectiveness and feasibility of the callback method is, however, questionable in many instances. The callback system assumes that users will always call from the same phone number. But field personnel call in from different hotels or sites without a consistent callback number. Moreover, these users will often be calling from operator-interrupted phone systems such as office or hotel switchboards. It should also be noted that long-distance callbacks can cause phone bills to skyrocket.

Encryption, as stated earlier, can be used as an effective method for authentication. When the message is encrypted by both the receiver's public key and the sender's secret key, the receiver can feel secure that the sender is authentic. Encryption can also be combined with the callback method in some applications to provide the highest possible level of data security.

6. *Monitoring.*   Monitoring is the act of watching over, checking, or guarding something. This activity recognizes that eventually, either accidentally or intentionally, controls will be neutralized or broken. Some specific systems capabilities to support the monitoring concept procedure are the following:

  a. *Detection of Security Violations.*   A security system should be installed to detect any security violation as soon as it occurs. Examples of violations are mismatch of user or terminal identification code and unauthorized request for a file.

  If codes or passwords do not match, a "security break in progress" message should be transmitted to a monitor at the company's security station. If the goal is to apprehend violators, then the system should continue to operate to keep the violators busy until security guards arrive.

  b. *Locking of System.*   If certain security violations are serious, then controls should be set up to lock the system automatically from further use. For example, a terminal would be locked automatically after N unauthorized attempts.

  c. *Exception Reporting.*   All exceptional conditions should be reported to the internal auditor for review. Auditors should be skeptical if they receive no reports. The absence of any attempted violations may indicate that users are subverting controls.

  d. *Trend Reporting.*   The system should collect data concerning all user access. Typical data in this report would indicate (1) user, terminal, and so on; (2) type of processing (demonstration, training, testing, normal operations); (3) date; (4) time of day; and (5) items accessed (e.g., name of file). These reports should be reviewed systematically by auditors and security officers.

14.5 CONTROLS IN THE PC ENVIRONMENT

Generally, PCs play three roles in computer-based information systems. The PC itself serves as a stand-alone technology base for the information system of a small organization, such as a local retailer, health food store, law office, medical clinic, pharmacy, printing shop, and the like. Some of these small organizations with stand-alone PC-based information systems cannot survive if their microcomputer and data base are wiped out, just as in a large organization with a mainframe-based information system.

Another role in which PCs are used is in either wide area (WANs) or local area networks (LANs) where they are treated as one of a variety of nodes in the network. A third role is in large organizations, where PCs are scattered around on people's desks, unconnected and loosely managed, if at all. In this environment, bits and pieces of corporate data and applications are dispersed among end users, many of whom are "doing their own thing."

PC As information that was once kept on sacrosanct mainframes trickles onto the
SECURITY PC, these desktop machines are open game for the gamut of data offenders. Many PCs have slipped through the cracks in corporate security.

Excerpted from Robin Raskin, "As PC Technology Matures, Users Discover Need for a Security Blanket," *PC Week*, March 10, 1987, pp. 35–41.

Controls Common to Computer-Based Information Systems

One could reasonably state that the controls presented in all the preceding sections apply to PCs, and leave it at that, because many if not most, of the controls applicable to large mainframe-based information systems are also applicable to PC-based information systems. As a matter of fact, if PCs act as terminals in a network, controls for this aspect of PCs have already been covered. But what about controls where PCs act as stand-alone technology building blocks for small businesses, or as "personal" microcomputers scattered throughout the company? Most of the controls that are applicable to these PC-based information systems as well as mainframe-based or midrange information systems are briefly summarized in this section. Those control problems that are particularly applicable to PC-based systems are discussed in the following section.

Certain administrative controls are applicable in most instances, especially training. The typical PC user, more notably in a scattered and loosely managed environment, is untrained and unconcerned about computer controls. Every person who uses PCs should attend training sessions on general operating and backup procedures. Employees should be made aware of copyright laws and the illegal copying and distribution of software.

A disaster recovery plan for scattered PCs may be nothing more than buying a new PC if the old one is lost. In a stand-alone setting, the owner may buy two PCs of the same kind and store one off-site, ready for operation if the first one is lost or stolen or malfunctions.

Input controls, such as transaction codes, forms, verification, hash totals, check digits, labels, and character and field checking, are all applicable to PCs. Processing controls, such as limit or reasonableness checks, arithmetic proof, identification, error logs, and transaction logs are also appropriate for PCs.

The same can be said about output controls and documentation. All application programs should be tested and fully documented before implementation. This documentation should be kept current with changes in the program. The documentation should also be prepared so that other employees can understand it. A simple test for clarity is to see if a new user can run the application with no prior knowledge of it.

An inventory of all hardware, software, and documentation including serial numbers should be maintained. Certain kinds of physical protection may be even more important for PCs than mainframes. Clearly, stealing the entire computer is impractical when it fills a room, but easy when the computer can be hauled off in its own carrying case. In high-risk areas, PCs should be bolted to tables. Also, antistatic protection should be installed. Smoking, drinking, and eating near microcomputers should be prohibited.

For fire protection and other disasters, common sense control procedures apply to PCs as they do to mainframes or any resource. Good housekeeping, fire-detection devices, and fire extinguishers are applicable. Plastic coverings to protect the computer against water damage should be handy. In fact, all microcomputers and other sensitive equipment should be routinely covered after normal working hours.

Control Problems Particularly Applicable to PCs

PCs and PC-based information systems not only differ in size from mainframe- or midrange systems, but, in some instances, they differ in other areas as well. The most salient of these differences are control problems discussed as follows.

1. *Access Control.*   Obviously, all the access control methods discussed in this chapter can be used by PCs. But data stored on PCs are usually not given the same level of security and quality control that mainframe data have traditionally been given. Indeed, the general exposure of sensitive information is a significant problem in PC-based systems. Often, PCs can be accessed by anyone who has a key to the office. Floppies are left lying around for easy access and copying. Many employees even leave sensitive information on display when they go on breaks or perform other duties.

    The work-at-home phenomenon is also a part of the PC control problem. The paradox is that PCs are supposed to be *personal* and provide end-user processing power, user-friendliness, and open access, whereas controls focus on access control and data base protection. It is difficult to reconcile such a paradox. As one executive quipped, "There's enough information in those spreadsheets scattered around the company to start up hundreds of competitive businesses, not to mention the information diskettes sitting around people's dens next to their home computers. And worse, we don't know who has what. Our people have to work at home, so what can we do?"

    No easy solutions exist in this context, except to make employees control sensitive and try to get them to protect their systems by passwords, or other access control schemes, and encryption. Often where everyone is in charge of one's own control as exists in a scattered information system, no one really is in control. For the stand-alone PC-based information system, access control can be handled in ways similar to large systems.

2. *Segregation of Duties.*   The keystone of accounting control is segregation of duties, which means that no individual employee is allowed to handle all aspects of a transaction. That is, the custody, execution, and recording aspects of transactions are each handled by individual employees. In large and midsize computer-based information systems, the segregation of duties scheme is implemented by segregating various functions, such as systems development, programming, computer operations, data base control, data entry, and, sometimes, a security group. Such a segregation is based on the idea that if systems analysts and application programmers were permitted to operate the computer or get access to the data, or enter transactions, many of the designed processing controls could be circumvented. Similarly, if computer operators had access to program documentation, they might be able to alter the processing logic.

In a stand-alone PC-based information system, the same person may perform *all* these functions and pinch hit as a sales clerk. In small businesses, it is simply not technically, economically, or operationally feasible for the owner-manager to hire individuals for each function. Other things, therefore, must be done to compensate for the absence of segregation of duties. For example, the owner-manager must become actively involved in the processing of transactions (in some instances, the owner-manager may also run the information system) to serve as an overall controlling influence. Other controls such as using firmware or canned application programs, transaction codes, lables, limit or reasonableness checks, and transaction logs serve as compensating controls.

3. *Backup.*   Probably the greatest security problem in PC-based systems is loss of vital data because of inadequate backup procedures. The key to this problem is the internal hard disk and users' attitude. The internal hard disk is out of sight and out of mind, and many users do not worry about backing it up until it is too late. Most end users in a scattered system and some owner-managers in a stand-alone system simply do not take backup seriously.

Backup of the internal hard disks is imperative because they do fail. In other words, it is not a matter of *if* it fails, but *when* it fails. Moreover, when a hard disk fails and needs repair, part or all of the data on it are lost.

Copying the data on the internal hard disk to floppies can be a time-consuming and frustrating task sometimes requiring hundreds of floppy disks. Usually a better backup alternative is either streaming tape or external removable hard disk.

The owner-manager or each end user must decide what data and programs must be backed up and how long the backup must be saved. Files containing data and programs should be categorized based on sensitivity and value, leading to (a) no backup required, (b) periodic on-site backup, and (c) on-site and off-site backup. In addition, extremely sensitive files should be encrypted.

Vital programs such as order entry and data files such as patient records may require four backups. One is near the computer, another is on-site in a fire-resistant cabinet under lock and key or vault away from the computer, one is off-site (a small business can get by with a bank safe deposit box or a fire-resistant safe at the owner-manager's home), and still another one is an archival or master file. All files should be stored away from extreme temperatures, humidity, magnets, telephones, and radios.

A common backup procedure for vital files involves daily backup using four files. To get started, three backup copies of the master file are made and labeled internally and externally. Then the master file is returned to its off-site storage. A master file is never used as a working file, only its copy.

Work begins using file-1 as the working copy. At the end of the day, file-1 is copied onto file-2. The second day's operations use file-2 as the working file. At the end of the second day, file-2 is copied onto file-3. The next day file-3 is used as the working file, and it is copied onto file-1. These files continue this rotation for the week. If, for example, file-2 and file-3 are lost, file-1 is available from the previous day. Only one day's data are lost.

At the end of the week, the last disk in rotation is copied onto a fourth file. File-4 is stored off-site with the master file. Once a week, file-4 and the master file are brought from off-site storage to be backed up. In addition, it is recommended that vital data and programs be printed on hard copy to provide paper, human-readable backups.

CASE OF THE ATTORNEY'S LOST PRACTICE An attorney in Tennessee kept his client data and billings on a hard-disk microcomputer. He dutifully made backup copies of all his files on floppy diskettes and stored them in his desk drawer. A thief broke into the attorney's office one night and stole his computer and all contents in his desk drawers.

The next morning, the attorney realized how vulnerable he was. His entire practice had vanished overnight. All his notes, confidential client information, case histories, and financial information were gone without a trace.

It took him over three months to piece together and re-create most of the lost information. Besides recovery costs and lost productivity, the attorney's credibility was shot, his professional stature tarnished, and client relationships damaged.

---

4. *Power Control.* Some random access memory (RAM) is volatile, which means that electrical surges or sags and other power interferences can destroy the data stored on RAM. Nonvolatile RAM is complementary metal oxide semiconductor (CMOS), which is more expensive than regular RAM. The extra expense for CMOS, however, may be cost effective in most cases.

CMOS requires extremely small doses of energy. High-quality lithium batteries allow the chips to retain data and programs for several months or more.

For additional safety, installation of a power manager is recommended. The microcomputer operator can turn all components on or off with the flick of a single switch. Also included is a surge suppression component, which prevents random electrical spikes and line interference from causing damage and zapping RAM.

In some critical and extensive PC applications, a UPS may be cost-effective. Users should consider the loss a single malfunction could cause and then decide whether they can afford the risk.

Clearly, the first step in the power-problem area is to make a power analysis to determine the exact nature of power problems indigenous to the PC's environment so money will not be wasted on devices that are not needed or are not appropriate for those specific power problems. Weather conditions have a lot to do with appropriate power control. For example, thunderstorms are common in southern Florida, but rare in southern California. Also, a number of power problems have occurred on sites in which the building and electrical system were not properly grounded. A detailed power-protection analysis therefore ensures that PCs will not be under- or overprotected.

Simply protecting microcomputers against occasional surges and spikes could cost as little as $10 to $15 for simple surge suppressors. Line conditioners that smooth out power may cost from $100 to $1,000 or $2,000. UPSs that can keep the microcomputer running for some time period during power outages, while at the same time, feeding clean power to the PC, range from several hundred to several thousand dollars, depending on the duration of full protection required.

Again, the owner-manager or end user must clarify what they are trying to protect against: voltage transients or long-term power failures. Moreover, a stand-alone system for a small business may require a UPS because the entire business depends totally on the system's continuous operation, just like a big business depends on its mainframe-based system. On the other hand, certain PCs that serve as nodes for a loosely connected network may require surge suppressors, but the file server, which stores most of the data, would require a UPS. Clearly, not every microcomputer in the organization has to have the same level of protection.

After protective devices are installed, the job of protecting PCs is not complete. For example, as effective as surge suppressors are in dissipating large electrical jolts, they have short lives. These devices therefore should be monitored to see if they still work after handling high voltage. In some instances, after controlling several large power surges, they can cause as many problems as they are supposed to cure.

14.6 TRADITIONAL RECORDS AND ACCOUNTING CONTROLS

Even in the most sophisticated computer-based information systems, the systems analyst, to some degree, must still deal with ways to handle paper records and implement traditional accounting controls. A brief description of both areas is presented in the paragraphs that follow.

Record-Keeping Controls

One of the first steps in the development of a record-keeping system is the classification of records according to those to be retained permanently; those to be retained for a period of time, perhaps microfilmed, and then destroyed; and those to be preserved for some time and then destroyed. Each type of record should be considered with respect to such probable future reference needs as the following: (1) supports title to property, (2) supports payments made to others, (3) supports claims against outside parties, (4) supports record requirements by governmental agencies, (5) provides protection against future tax claims, and (6) provides essential operating statistics.

Means of classifying records include (1) vital or essential, (2) valuable, (3) important, (4) useful, and (5) nonessential or temporary. *Essential* records are irreplaceable or are not replaceable immediately and are needed for the business's survival. Examples are deeds and leases, powers of attorney, minutes of shareholder and director meetings, accounting records, blueprints and drawings, copyrights, patents, trademark authorizations, laboratory notebooks, and capital stock records. *Valuable* records are those necessary to prevent financial loss or to recover money or property. Some examples are accounts receivable ledgers, inventory records, insurance policies, securities, and audit reports. *Important* records are administrative tools that might be obtained after considerable effort or delay and that would not adversely affect essential operations to any serious degree. A few examples are cost reports, projections, shipping reports, manuals, and credit reports. *Useful* records are those that are not needed for current operations but are helpful for reference and similar purposes. Such records ordinarily would be destroyed when current usefulness ceases. The *nonessential* records are those that are available for destruction relatively soon and do not have long-term value.

Traditional Accounting Controls

The purpose of accounting controls in general is to safeguard assets from waste, fraud, and inefficient use; to promote accuracy and reliability in the accounting records and data base; to encourage and measure compliance with company policies; to promote and evaluate efficiency of operations; and to ensure that transactions are authorized and recorded properly.

Every transaction should involve the steps of authorization, initiation, approval, execution, and recording. No one person or department should handle all aspects of a transaction from beginning to end. Accounting control will, indeed, be enhanced if each of the steps is handled by relatively independent employees or departments. For example, top management *authorizes* credit policy and terms, customers *initiate* orders through the sales department, credit sales are *approved* by the credit department, shipments are *executed* by the shipping department, and the transactions are *recorded* by the accounting department. The probability of missed shipments, several different shipments going to the same customer, missed collections, stealing of merchandise, and collusion, are reduced because of the separation of duties. Furthermore, this specialization of labor contributes to the overall efficiency of operations.

The need for the classical internal accounting control procedures just presented is beginning to disappear as more fully integrated information systems are developed. Many of the transactional steps that people used to perform are now handled in the innards of the computer. For example, authorized users are recognized by certain access control schemes, authority is given or denied by a set of parameters in control software. Access privileges are controlled by authorization tables. Authentication of authorized users is performed by a variety of methods. Approval of credit may be performed by an algorithm residing in the computer. Instructions to execute certain functions may be communicated directly to robots or automated carts by a terminal located in a warehouse and online to the information system. Most, if not all, of the preparation of documents, such as invoices, bills of lading, and picking and packing lists, and the updating of inventory and accounts receivable files are done automatically by the computer.

The classical segregation of duties in computer-based information systems is now applied to the functional areas. For example, systems analysts usually do not write programs, and programmers do not operate the computer or enter transactions. Computer operators do not write programs, or enter transactions. Terminals are segregated and designated as to what functions they are permitted to perform. This "new" form of segregation of duties is based on the "checks and balances" concept of the "old" segregation of duties technique and is in complete compliance with the conventional purpose of accounting controls as stated in the first paragraph of this section.

14.7 A METHODOLOGY TO DETERMINE AN OPTIMUM MIX OF CONTROLS

Installing a controls building block in a computer-based information system is a delicate balancing between providing protection and degrading productivity. Too many controls or the wrong kind stifle productivity and waste money. Controls installed to keep intruders out should not restrict employees from doing their jobs efficiently. Not enough controls create sloppy procedures, cause inefficiencies, and invite abuse and disaster. And not paying any attention to controls is irresponsible.

Applying a formal methodology to implement the best framework of controls for the money spent involves understanding available controls, what they are used for, and their level of effectiveness; setting a value for the information system and its related components; determining the information system's exposure to hazards; and selecting and implementing a cost-effective, optimum mix of controls.

Hazards and Controls Matrix

Figure 14.4 presents a hazards and controls matrix that lists the major hazards to which most information systems are exposed and the controls that help to

Controls \ Hazards	Fragmentation, Missteps, and Inefficiencies	Bottle-necks	Errors and Omissions	Misunder-standing	Lost Data and Documents	Unauthorized Changes of Programs	Mal-functions	Processing Wrong Files	Logic Bombs and Trojan Horses	Computer Failure	Power Failure	Eavesdropping and Wiretapping	Unauthorized Access	Natural Disaster	Fire	Crime and Fraud	Sabotage
Records management			●	●	●									●	●		
Accounting controls	●	●	●	●	●											●	
Systems plan	●	●		●													
Contingency plan										●				●	●		●
Personnel controls	●	●	●	●					●							●	
Input controls		●	●		●			●					●			●	
Processing controls		●	●		●			●	●							●	
Data base controls					●			●						●	●		●
Output controls		●	●		●								●			●	
Documentation controls	●		●	●	●	●			●					●			●
Hardware controls						●	●		●	●						●	
Operating system and utility programs controls						●		●	●				●				●
Operations controls	●	●	●	●			●			●			●	●			●
Physical controlled access						●						●	●			●	●
Physical location										●			●		●		●
Physical protection							●			●	●		●	●	●		●
Procedural security techniques						●						●	●			●	●

Figure 14.4 Hazards and controls matrix.

safeguard the information system against these hazards. Understanding the content of this matrix provides sufficient background to move to the next steps in performing hazard assessment and establishing an optimum mix of controls.[1]

Exposures to Hazards and Expected Loss Analysis

Hazard and loss analysis involves determining how exposed the system is to various hazards and the expected loss from each hazard. This analysis may be conducted with management and staff members of the information system using interviews and questionnaires. Management and staff should be asked questions such as "What would you do if so and so happened? What is the probability that this hazard would occur? What would your loss be if it did occur?" In this way, a priority of exposures to hazards can be established by evaluating the probability of occurrence in conjunction with the magnitude of expected loss of each hazard.

Assume that the value of the information system is $3 million. That is, in the event of a disaster causing total or nearly total destruction, it is estimated that the loss would amount to $3 million when the costs of all physical assets, recreation of files, replacement of personnel, and so forth were included.

A sample of how the probability of exposures to hazards and expected losses may be quantified is shown in Figure 14.5. For example, the exposure to fire hazard is determined by consulting with the fire department and/or insurance company for the probability of a fire occurring at this particular site. Assume that the probability is set at .70 percent. In the "Probability That Hazard Will Occur" column, the .70 percent probability is entered. This percentage represents the probability of the occurrence of a fire in a one-year period.

The next column shows the range of loss in thousands of dollars. It is estimated that if a fire occurs, the loss may range from $10,000 to total destruction, or $3 million. The last column represents the results of multiplying the probability of occurrence by the high and low estimated losses and then dividing by 2 for an approximate average expected loss. Similar estimates of probability of occurrence and ranges of loss are made for additional exposures to hazards. Some of these estimates may be nothing more than hunches. Others, such as malfunctions and human error, may be based on actual experience and thus provide fairly precise results.

Even if some of the estimated figures represent hunches, the use of probabilities formalizes these hunches and intuitive judgments of management and staff. If management is going to take a "calculated risk," then some calculations ought to be involved. Moreover, this approach forces all personnel to come to grips quantitatively with what they know and what they think they know. They have to put their estimates down on paper. Also, by formalizing the measurement and decision-making process, the combined wisdom and expertise of appropriate personnel can come into play. By participating in this process, they can understand the system better and become more aware of the purpose of controls.

In many cases, maximum losses from hazards such as fire or natural dis-

---

[1]Hazard assessment material condensed from John G. Burch, and Joseph L. Sardinas, *Computer Control and Audit: A Total Systems Approach* (New York: John Wiley, 1978), Chapter 8.

Exposure to Hazards	Probability (%) that Hazard will Occur (Level of Exposure)	Loss Range ($000)	Weighted Values ($)	
			Low	High
Malfunctions and Human Errors				
• Equipment	5.00	1–250	50	12,500
• Software	10.00	10–100	1,000	10,000
• Programmers	70.00	1–20	700	14,000
• Computer operators	60.00	1–10	600	6,000
• Maintenance	90.00	1–10	900	9,000
• Users	90.00	1–15	900	13,500
• General personnel	50.00	1–20	500	10,000
		Subtotal average	4,650 39,825	75,000
Fraud*				
• Embezzlement	5.00	10–100	500	5,000
• Confiscation of files	10.00	10–100	1,000	10,000
• Tapping	5.00	10–100	500	5,000
• Program changes	20.00	5–25	1,000	5,000
		Subtotal average	3,000 14,000	25,000
Power and Communication Failures				
• Brownouts and failures	50.00	1–10	500	5,000
• Surges	30.00	1–50	300	15,000
• Busy	20.00	1–20	200	4,000
		Subtotal average	1,000 12,500	24,000
Fire	.70	10–3000	70	21,000
		Subtotal average	70 10,535	21,000
Sabotage and Riot				
• Internal	.20	10–3000	20	6,000
• External	.40	10–3000	40	12,000
		Subtotal average	60 9,030	18,000
Natural Disasters				
• Earthquake	.01	500–3000	50	300
• Tornado	.20	500–3000	1,000	6,000
• Flood	.10	500–3000	500	3,000
• Lightning	.01	10–1000	1	100
		Subtotal average	1,551 5,475	9,400
General Hazards	1.00	1–500	10	5,000
		Subtotal average	10 2,505	5,000
		Grand total average	10,341 93,870	177,400

*Losses in this category are estimated for direct losses relative to the information system, if any, plus losses of assets that are controlled by the information system, such as embezzlement of funds.

Figure 14.5 Hazard and loss analysis table.

asters receive more attention than they deserve in comparison with losses from hazards such as malfunction and human errors, fraud, and power and communication failures. Using probabilities that hazards will occur and calculating an average expected loss give a more accurate picture of reality.

Measurement of exposures to hazards and expected losses therefrom is imprecise. Moreover, results will vary from one organization to another and even between computer systems in the same organization. Nevertheless, such an analysis provides a means of ordering the relative importance of various hazards and justifying the need for expenditures for controls to counteract the exposures to these hazards.

Of course, the main purpose of the hazard and loss analysis is to provide management with a basis for making budgetary decisions. The total weighted values in Figure 14.5, include a low value of $10,341 and a high value of $177,400, or an average total of approximately $93,870 per year. This figure gives management a benchmark; that is, management can reasonably assume that an annual outlay of $93,870 could be justified for a system of controls.

Optimum Mix of Controls

Now, as the analysis in Figure 14.5 indicates, management can justify an expenditure up to approximately $93,870 for a system of controls. This money will not be spent wisely if controls are acquired indiscriminately, however. The question that must be answered is, "How can an expenditure of $93,870 (or less) be made to gain an optimum mix of controls?"

To find this mix where the total expected cost line is at its lowest point (zero slope), the following formula is used:

$$TEC(K) = S(K) + L(K)$$

where

$TEC(K)$ = total expected cost (dollars/year) in using control system K

$S(K)$ = cost (dollars/year) to install and operate controls comprising system K

$L(K)$ = average expected loss (dollars/year) due to exposures to hazards if control fails

The total expected cost of a system of controls has three major components: (1) average expected loss associated with exposures to hazards (determined in Figure 14.5), (2) cost of installing and operating controls that are available to combat exposures, and (3) probability that various controls will fail.

The exposures to hazards and expected losses therefrom are listed in Figure 14.6. These entries represent the average losses taken from Figure 14.5.

In Figure 14.7, the controls selected to protect exposures to hazards are shown with their probability of failure. This is an abbreviated list of controls. In practice, the table would include many more specific controls (e.g., badge system, encryption devices). The concept and method are the same, however, whether the table is in detail form or not.

Each set of controls requires an expenditure of time and money. The costs to install and operate these controls are listed in Figure 14.8.

Exposures to Hazards	Average Expected Loss per Year ($)
E1 Malfunctions and Human Errors	$39,825
E2 Fraud	14,000
E3 Power and Communication Failures	12,500
E4 Fire	10,535
E5 Sabotage and Riot	9,030
E6 Natural Disasters	5,475
E7 General Hazards	2,505
Total average expected loss	$93,870

Figure 14.6 Exposures to hazards and expected losses.

To determine the optimum system of controls, the total expected cost for each combination of controls [system (K)] must be calculated. This cost summary is presented in Figure 14.9.

Notice that, in Figure 14.9, the organization will suffer an average expected loss of $93,870 without any system of controls. With the implementation of all controls C1, C2, C3, and C4 (System 15), the total expected cost of the system is $62,805. That is, without any control system, the organization is out $93,870; with System 15, the organization is out $62,805, or a cost savings of $31,065. Is this the best system of controls? No, because when the total expected cost of all combinations of controls is calculated, System 11 represents the best combination of controls, with a cost savings of $93,870 less $40,614, or $53,256. Therefore, the implementation of additional controls will not always prove to be cost-effec-

Controls	Exposures Protected	Description of Controls	Probability (%) Control Fails
C1	E1, E2	Administrative, Operational, Documentation	1.00
C2	E3	Backup	2.00
C3	E4	Fire Detection and Extinguishing System	3.00
C4	E5, E6, E7	Various Security Controls	1.00

Figure 14.7 Controls that protect exposures to hazards.

Controls	Cost to Implement ($)	Costs per Year to Operate ($)
C1	10,000	3,000
C2	6,000	500
C3	2,000	1,000
C4	22,000	15,500

Figure 14.8 Control costs.

Control System (K)	Control Comprising (K)	SI (K)	SO (K)	S (K)	L (K)	TEC (K)
No. System	No. System	$ 0	$ 0	$ 0	$93,870	$ 93,870
1	C1	10,000	3,000	13,000	40,583	53,583
2	C2	6,000	500	6,500	81,620	88,120
3	C3	2,000	1,000	3,000	83,651	86,651
4	C4	22,000	15,500	37,500	78,561	116,061
5	C1, C2	16,000	3,500	19,500	28,333	47,833
6	C1, C3	12,000	4,000	16,000	30,364	46,364
7	C1, C4	32,000	18,500	50,500	25,274	75,774
8	C2, C3	8,000	1,500	9,500	71,401	80,901
9	C2, C4	28,000	16,000	44,000	66,311	110,311
10	C3, C4	24,000	16,500	40,500	68,342	108,842
11	C1, C2, C3	18,000	4,500	22,500	18,114	40,614
12	C1, C2, C4	38,000	19,000	57,000	13,124	70,124
13	C1, C3, C4	34,000	19,500	53,500	15,055	68,555
14	C2, C3, C4	30,000	17,000	47,000	56,092	113,092
15	C1, C2, C3, C4	40,000	20,000	60,000	2,805	62,805

EXPLANATION OF SYMBOLS:

$SI(K)$ = Cost to implement Kth control

$SO(K)$ = Cost to operate Kth control per year

$S(K)$ = $SI(K)$ + $SO(K)$

$L(K)$ = The sum of all losses from exposures to hazards and the probability that the control will fail

$TEC(K)$ = $S(K)$ + $L(K)$

Figure 14.9 Cost summary.

System 1 ($):

$\quad$ S (1) = 10,000 + 3,000

$\qquad$ = 13,000

$\quad$ L (1) = 39,825 (1.00) + 14,000 (1.00) + 12,500 (100.00) +

$\qquad$ 10,535 (100.00) + 9,030 (100.00) + 5,475 (100.00) +

$\qquad$ 2,505 (100.00)

$\quad$ L (1) = 398 + 140 + 12,500 + 10,535 + 9,030 + 5,475 +

$\qquad$ 2,505

$\qquad$ = 40,583

$\quad$ TEC (1) = 13,000 + 40,583

$\qquad$ = 53,583

Explanation: Without controls, the probability is 100.00 percent that exposures to hazards E1 and E2 will result in an average expected loss of $39,825 and $14,000, respectively. System 1 is the application of controls C1 which protects these two exposures to hazards with a probability of failure of 1.00 percent. Average expected loss of E1 and E2 are both multiplied by this probability, reducing the average expected loss of $398 and $140, respectively. The other average expected losses, E3, E4, E5, E6, and E7, are multiplied by 100.00 percent probability because it has been determined that without controls average expected losses of $12,500; $10,535; $9,030; $5,475; and $2,505 will occur.

System 11 ($):

$\quad$ S (11) = 18,000 + 4,500

$\qquad$ = 22,500

$\quad$ L (11) = 39,825 (1.00) + 14,000 (1.00) + 12,500 (2.00) +

$\qquad$ 10,535 (3.00) + 9,030 (100.00) + 5,475 (100.00) +

$\qquad$ 2,505 (100.00)

$\quad$ L (11) = 398 + 140 + 250 + 316 + 9,030 + 5,475 + 2,505

$\qquad$ = 18,114

$\quad$ TEC (11) = 22,500 + 18,114

$\qquad$ = 40,614

System 15 ($):

$\quad$ S (15) = 40,000 + 20,000

$\qquad$ = 60,000

$\quad$ L (15) = 39,825 (1.00) + 14,000 (1.00) + 12,500 (2.00) +

$\qquad$ 10,535 (3.00) + 9,030 (1.00) + 5,475 (1.00) + 2,505

$\qquad$ (1.00)

$\quad$ L (15) = 398 + 140 + 250 + 316 + 903 + 548 + 250

$\qquad$ = 2,805

$\quad$ TEC (15) = 60,000 + 2,805

$\qquad$ = 62,805

Figure 14.10 Sample calculations for systems 1, 11, and 15.

tive. In other words, purchasing more controls, C4, as indicated in System 15, does not reduce expected loss from hazards enough to justify the additional cost. Sample calculations for Systems 1, 11, and 15 are presented in Figure 14.10.

In conclusion, any attempt at determining the cost-effectiveness of a system of controls is imprecise at best. The methods that we have presented allow management to (1) select an optimum system based on financial terms, (2) objectively compose various alternatives, (3) weed out redundant alternatives, and (4) stay within budget. Conversely, this analysis ignores a long-range plan (e.g., a five-year plan), but this could be an advantage, because the system of controls should be reevaluated at least once a year to see if some controls could be eliminated and others added, all on a cost-effective basis. Furthermore, this analysis ignores the time value of money and competing projects for limited funds. These two aspects could easily be added, but they are beyond the scope of this text.

SUMMARY

Information systems operate in hazardous environments. Information systems are vulnerable to a variety of threats and abuses from people both inside and outside the organization, from natural disasters, from undependable and faulty services, and from everyday incompetencies and inefficiencies. While ease of end-user access is a main goal of a well-designed information system, the greater the access, the greater the vulnerability of the information system.

Properly selected and applied controls ensure protection of the information system from these hazards, and effective and efficient operation in its environment. Each information system, however, and the environment in which it operates are different. For example, PC-based information systems have somewhat unique control problems in the area of access control, segregation of duties, backup procedures, and power supply. Consequently, the systems analyst must determine specifically what hazards the system is exposed to and develop a cost-effective optimum mix of controls that precisely fits the control needs of that particular information system. Hazards and controls must be viewed in a total context. Too much emphasis on controls for security hazards, such as natural disasters, sabotage, and fires, and neglect of records management, traditional accounting controls, and basic computer controls can result in a lopsided controls building block, and vice versa.

IMPORTANT TERMS

access control

accounting
control

address compare
control

administrative
controls

approximation
technique

arithmetic proof

audit trail

authentication

authorization

backup and
recovery
procedures

backup facility

badges

built-in hardware
controls

business disruption insurance

callback method

check digit

ciphertext

cleartext

closed-circuit monitors

concurrency control

console run book

consortium

contention plan

contingency plan

control total

cross-footing

data encryption standard (DES)

deadly embrace

differential file

disaster recovery plan

dumping and logging input transactions

duplication check

echo check

emanation protection

encryption

error log

fault-avoidance/ fault-tolerant designs

firmware controls

fraud

general systems documentation

grandfather-father-son

halon

hash total

header/trailer labels

hot site

identification

job control language (JCL)

least privileged access

librarian

limit or reasonableness check

lockout

logic bomb

malfunctions

mobile data center

natural disasters

paper shredders

parity check

power and communications failures

procedures manual

program documentation

read/write error

reciprocal agreement

record length check

residual dumping and logging snapshots

rollback/ rollforward recovery

segregation of duties

sequence check

service bureau

shell

sign-in/sign-out registers

smart cards

strategic information systems plan (SISP)

superzap

tempest

transaction code

transaction log

trojan horse

unauthorized access

uninterruptible power system (UPS)

users' manual

validity check

virus

⇨ *Assignment*

REVIEW QUESTIONS

14.1 What is the down side to achievement of the goal of well-designed information systems?

14.2 From the standpoint of a threat to an information system, what is a Trojan horse? What is a logic bomb? What is a superzap?

14.3 Define the responsibility of management with respect to controls for the information system.

14.4 Administrative controls are important in maintaining the organizational environment preferred by management. Four of the major administrative controls include a controls policy, personnel controls, a strategic information systems plan, a disaster recovery plan, and insurance protection. Define these controls and present a complete discussion on the components of each.

14.5 List the seven contingent interim processing options that may be built into a disaster recovery plan.

14.6 Enumerate and briefly describe seven input controls necessary to maintain the integrity of input data.

14.7 Once data are entered into the processing system, they are monitored and checked by edit routines embedded within the various computer programs. These programs not only detect input errors, they also help detect processing errors. List the six processing controls enumerated in the text, and briefly describe each.

14.8 What are the two main divisions of data base controls? Briefly describe each. Explain the grandfather-father-son file reconstruction procedure.

14.9 The end product of information systems is quality output. Several procedures and controls exist to provide reasonable assurance that output will be free from errors. Discuss seven such controls.

14.10 Weak documentation has historically been one of the greatest deficiencies of information systems. Good systems documentation is indispensable when the system must be modified or debugged. To maintain good documentation practices consistently, controls should be implemented and enforced. One major control area relates to program documentation. List 10 controls that comprise a typical program documentation manual.

14.11 List seven examples of built-in hardware controls.

14.12 Explain the five types of controls designed into the operating system.

14.13 How can operating systems and utility programs be misused to affect the information system? Can this misuse be controlled?

14.14 What procedures can be followed to strengthen control over computer operations?

14.15 Discuss seven common security hazards that potentially threaten the operation of the information system.

14.16 One of the most significant areas of control relating to computer-based information systems is physical security. Physical security control techniques can be divided into three major categories: physical controlled access, physical location, and physical protection devices. Give five examples of each of these major categories.

14.17 Outline the six concepts of procedural security techniques, explaining their application to access control.

14.18 PCs and PC-based information systems not only differ in size from mainframe systems, but, in some instances, they differ in other areas as well. List four differences that cause control problems and discuss what can be done to minimize each of the control problems.

14.19 What is causing the disappearance of the need for classical internal accounting control procedures in fully integrated information systems?

QUESTIONS FOR DISCUSSION

14.20 Very often the implementation of controls is an after-the-fact activity—after the disaster has occurred. Many managers see the probability of a major computer-related disaster as so slim they conclude it will never strike their company. Other managers are aware of the benefits implementing controls offers but simply cannot justify diverting any resources to that end. Finally, procrastinating managers realize the necessity of implementing adequate controls, and they have sufficient resources to do so; however, they always have more important things to do. Discuss a variety of ways in which these managers could be convinced of the urgency and necessity of protecting a completely exposed computer-based information system from hazards and abuse.

14.21 Discuss the importance of absolute support by top-level managers for any control system. How can this supportive attitude be communicated to and, indeed, internalized by information workers at the operations level?

14.22 Many of the controls presented in the text relate to a comprehensive control environment usually found in larger companies placing complete reliance on their information system. Do these same controls apply to the small business that has 12 employees and uses a microcomputer to run payroll and keep track of receivables? Discuss how you might implement separation of duties in a six-person insurance office, for example.

14.23 Computer control systems often conjure up images of sophisticated, top-security clearance procedures, expensive, state-of-the-art alarm systems, and complicated, built-in computer security programs. Other individuals often perceive control systems as a strangulating and antiproductive mass of incoherent policies and procedures that management designed for the torture of otherwise happy employees. Outline a sound system of general controls that could be implemented at little or no cost in a small to medium-sized business. Discuss what control areas should receive priority and what criteria must be met before a particular control procedure is accepted for implementation. How would you justify *not* accepting some control measures for a specific application?

14.24 Advances in satellite communication and microwave transmission technology have prompted many international firms to link their multinational offices through these telecommunication systems. Text, voice, and data transmissions, sometimes highly confidential, are routinely exchanged between offices in New York, Los Angeles, London, and Paris, for example. At some point in the transmission route, these messages take the form of radio waves being bounced off communications satellites in space. Discuss the security problems inherent in this process and suggest appropriate controls. Some persons have suggested that because these communications are transmitted over public air space, they lose their proprietary nature and are thus subject to interception by anyone willing to acquire the necessary equipment. Do you agree? Why? Why not?

14.25 Discuss ways in which a company's control system can be an important concern to individuals external to the firm. such as customers, governmental agencies, stockholders, creditors, suppliers, auditors, and insurance companies.

14.26 "Striving for a 'fail-safe' system is an exercise in futility." Comment.

14.27 Many systems personnel give "lip service" to the advisability of proper and complete documentation, and yet a review of their manuals, programs, and maintenance routines reveals a pervasive disregard for adequate documentation techniques. Programmers complain that by the time they finish documenting the program, it has already been changed, so they just do not bother. Operators claim that their job is so routine, anyone could master it in a few hours and, therefore, no operating procedures are necessary. Librarians argue that they are so busy locating and putting away tapes and disks they just do not have time to update many of the file labels. Anyway they know what each tape or disk contains. Discuss the potential problems arising from poor or nonexistent systems documentation. What steps could be applied to change the apathetic attitude of the systems personnel just described? Does a possibility of over documentation ever exist?

14.28 Frequently, the implementation of a new system is performed under conditions of stress and tension as the implementation crew works feverishly around the clock to stay within the demanding time schedule. In this atmosphere, it would be easy for the systems task force to cut corners on documentation and programmed controls. At what point can overrunning the time schedule be justified to implement the planned control procedures? Who should make this decision? What arguments would you present to prevent any cutting of corners in the controls area?

14.29 Discuss some of the controls unique to multisite installations (as opposed to a single-site office). What unique control problems would be experienced by a multinational firm with computer installations in foreign countries? What types of controls would be applicable?

EXERCISES AND PROBLEMS

14.30 As the new office manager at Herbicott Manufacturing Company, you decide to take a brief tour to review the operating procedures in the company. Your first stop is at Henry's desk in the mailroom. Henry opens incoming mail and prepares a list of receipts of payments on account, which he then forwards to the accounts receivable clerk. Because the office is currently understaffed, Henry was recently given the additional assignment of endorsing checks and preparing the bank deposits.

Moving along, you arrive at Jodi's desk. Jodi, you observe, receives invoices from suppliers, files them by due date, and writes checks to pay the invoices on the due date. Juan, who sits next to Jodi, is responsible for the timekeeping function and, each week, supplies a record of hours worked by each factory employee to Missy. Missy then prepares the paychecks and gives them to Juan for distribution to the employees. Juan also maintains the personnel records for all the employees. On your way out of the work area, Henry remembers to tell you only one bank account is used by the company and bank reconciliations have not been prepared since the bookkeeper was fired two years ago.

Required: Prepare a report to your supervisor outlining the change you recommend to strengthen the accounting control system. In a different paragraph, discuss which of the current employees could be embezzling funds from the company and how.

14.31 Following is a list of scenarios in which errors or fraudulent activities took place. For each scenario, suggest controls that would prevent or at least reduce the likelihood of the situation recurring.

1. A customer payment was enclosed along with the remittance advice showing $28.50 but was entered into the computer system using punched cards as $2,850.00.

2. The accounts receivable master file was incorrectly loaded on a drive that was supposed to hold the payroll master file. When the payroll program was run, it destroyed the accounts receivable file.

3. A payroll check issued to an hourly employee was based on 98 hours for a week's work instead of 40.

4. A chemical salesperson entered a customer's order from a portable terminal using a valid but incorrect product number, which resulted in a delivery of 16 drums of floor wax instead of insecticide.

5. A bank customer transaction was coded with an invalid customer account number and was not detected until the customer received the monthly statement, which did not show the transaction.

6. In the processing of payroll checks, the computer somehow omitted four of the total

3,052 checks that should have been processed. The omission was not discovered until the checks were distributed by each department.

7. A fire destroyed the inventory master file and a complete inventory had to be taken to set up a replacement file.

14.32 Describe the reasonableness checks that could be embedded in the programs processing the type of information that follows. Also, indicate what information would be necessary for these checks to be accomplished.

1. Public utilities—production of monthly bills with meters read once a month.

2. Automotive parts distributor—an online order-entry system that generates all supporting invoices, shipping documents, and packing slips.

3. Health insurance company—policyholders' application for maternity benefits.

4. Large university—textbook ordering.

5. State government—motor vehicle registration.

6. International airline—a system that consists of terminals placed in travel agents' offices. The system generates a ticket after processing a few key data inputs.

7. Internal revenue service—processing of personal income tax returns.

14.33 A young man opened an account at a large bank in the Midwest. A week or two later, after an electronic communication from a California bank authorized a payment of $2.5 million into his account, the young man absconded with the money. When the bank went to collect from its West Coast correspondent, it found that there had been no authorization for such a payment.

The security manager for the California bank's computer manufacturer was called in to investigate. His first question was, "Who's recently left your data processing department?" The reply was, "Oh, only Jenny who's going to be married next week."

The security manager went to see Jenny immediately, and found her waiting for her young man to take her to Mexico for their honeymoon. When shown a photograph of the absconder, Jenny said that it was her fiancé. She was asked if her fiancé had told her to do anything in particular with the computer console she operated. "Yes," she replied, "he told me he had a buddy in some Midwest bank and asked me to please type in some funny little numbers so they could say hello to each other."

So Jenny typed in those funny little numbers and the bank was $2.5 million the loser.

List the controls that would reduce the probability that this kind of problem could happen again.

14.34 A methodology for hazard assessment and optimum mix of controls is presented in the text. Using this methodology and the following tables, calculate the best combination of controls based on total expected cost.

VALUE VERSUS EXPECTED LOSS

Exposure Point or Route to Hazards	Value of Resource ($)	Average Number of Attempted Exposures per Year	Expected Loss ($)
E1	100,000	0.5	50,000
E2	50,000	0.2	10,000
E3	20,000	1.5	30,000
E4	700,000	0.1	70,000
E5	900,000	0.2	180,000

EXPOSURE TO HAZARDS PROTECTED BY CONTROLS

Controls	Exposure Points Protected	Description of Controls	Probability Control Fails
C1	E2, E3	Encryptoboxes	0.01
C2	E1	Badge system	0.02
C3	E4	Fire control	0.03
C4	E5	Emergency doors	0.01

CONTROL COSTS

Controls	Description	Cost to Implement ($)	Cost to Operate ($)
C1	Encryptoboxes	10,000	3,000
C2	Badge system	5,000	12,000
C3	Fire control	80,000	4,000
C4	Emergency doors	15,000	1,000

14.35 From the following data, compute TEC(K) for a system with no controls, a system with control C_1 only, a system with control C_2 only, and a system with controls C_1 and C_3 only. Which system has the lowest total expected cost (TEC)? Because controls cost money, wouldn't it be less expensive not to acquire controls? Why? Why not?

Exposures to Hazards	Average Expected Loss
E_1 Malfunctions and human errors	$50,000
E_2 Fraud	15,000
E_3 Power failure	10,000
E_4 Fire	15,000
Total expected loss	$90,000

Controls for Exposures	Description	Cost to Install	Cost per Year to Operate
C_1 for E_1, E_2	Administrative, documentation, security	$10,000	$ 8,000
C_2 for E_3	UPS	20,000	1,000
C_3 for E_4	Fire suppression	10,000	1,000
Total cost to install and operate		$40,000	$10,000

Controls for Exposures	Probability of Failure
C_1	.05
C_2	.01
C_3	.02

14.36 Questionnaires are frequently used to analyze and evaluate the control systems of computer installations. The questionnaires help detect weaknesses in the control structure before they become a serious threat to the integrity of the system. Following is a list of questions typically found on a control questionnaire. Study the list and indicate the objective of each question. Anticipate the errors or weaknesses that might exist if any of the questions are answered "no."

1. Does the systems manager review and approve all new systems design work? Are user departments allowed any input in the design?
2. Have emergency and backup procedures been fully documented? Is a list of key personnel with their phone numbers easily accessible?
3. Is an updated organization chart of the systems department available?
4. Are all systems personnel required to take vacations?
5. Are internal file labels tested by each computer program to validate set-up?
6. Are check digits used with key entries?
7. Are nonroutine changes to major files properly authorized?
8. Are output reports received by user departments for general reasonableness and quality?

14.37 The advent of PCs in the workplace has made many information systems managers nervous. They sense the almost dictatorial control they have enjoyed for years slowly slipping away as PC users access the mainframe computer to generate reports that better meet their information needs. Experts agree that the increased use of PCs will present new, but solvable, problems. For instance, one firm placed a PC in its stores department because turnaround time from the management information system was not rapid enough to make efficient stores control possible. The employee that operates the PC is responsible for receiving stores requisitions, reviewing them for reasonableness and appropriate approvals, disbursing the requested items and entering the transaction into the PC. The PC is used exclusively for this function, and only this employee knows how to operate it. Because the PC is out of the formal jurisdiction of the management information system, no system of controls has been developed for its use. The department manager feels his employee is more than qualified to operate the machine without a lot of interfering controls.

Required: What problems can you see with the manager's reasoning? List and fully describe five types of controls that would apply to this PC application.

14.38 Administrative controls play a key role in establishing a comprehensive control structure that will allow the firm to operate in a free but closely monitored environment. One of the most important administrative controls deals with the hiring practices of a firm. Because most controls are not fail-safe, employees have the responsibility of abiding by the control dictates of management. The first step toward this end is implementing sound hiring practices. Study the following case, then prepare a report outlining changes you recommend to strengthen the hiring controls of this firm.

Techno-Systems, Inc., is always in the market for talented, honest, hard-working employees. Because Techno-Systems is involved in high-tech support systems, it prefers to hire college graduates with a degree in either business or computer science. All hiring is done by the personnel director. She places advertisements of job openings in all major trade journals as well as local employment agencies. The director interviews all applicants for all job openings and selects those she believes will fit the job description best. Newly hired employees do not generally meet their immediate supervisor until the first day on the job.

In choosing who she will hire, the director relies exclusively on the application filled out by the prospective employee in the personnel office. The application does not ask for references because the director never has time to call them anyway. The director has never questioned any claims made on the application forms and has never verified academic or work credentials listed. She figures if the new employees lie they will not be able to do the job and will be fired. She describes this as her "self-policing" strategy.

The personnel director used to perform background checks on employees for felony convictions or other irregularities in their past. The frustration of trying to get a "straight answer" from police clerks, however, caused her to abandon the policy. Without this background search, Techno-Systems' bonding company refused to bond any new employees.

At a recent company picnic, officers of the company were surprised when they were introduced to a total of 12 employees who were related to the personnel director. What made the situation even stranger was that most of the related employees had less than two years with the firm although the personnel director had issued a memo 20 months ago stating that a hiring freeze would go into effect immediately.

14.39 Many banks do a large percentage of their transactions in raw dollar amounts over electronic funds transfer systems (EFTS). Sometimes these systems employ terminals strategically placed in retail outlets to increase their customer base. Modern automated teller machines allow for deposits, withdrawals, loan payments, and mortgage payments to be transferred via EFTS. Your assignment is to research some of these EFTS applications and prepare a list of security considerations that should be incorporated into the system. Consider the entire system—customers, retail outlets, terminals, interbank transfers, and any other component of EFTS.

14.40 A bank in Pittsburgh must relocate its data processing facilities within the next two years because of anticipated growth and the concomitant need for more physical space. Four possible sites for the new computer center are being evaluated: (1) the ground floor of the main office in the center of town, which recently has been renovated with exterior walls of plate glass; (2) the basement of the same building cited in alternative 1; (3) the twelfth floor of the same building described in alternative 1; and (4) an old, converted warehouse about two miles from the main office at the edge of the business district.

Considering the criteria of (1) sabotage—internal, (2) sabotage—external, (3) fire—explosion, (4) flood—water, (5) transmission, and (6) electrical interference, evaluate each alternative described and rank them in order of most to least desirable. If a criterion applies equally over all alternatives, it may be omitted. Support your conclusions.

14.41 A steel products fabricator in the Midwest is in the process of installing a computer-based order-entry system. Upon receipt, customers' orders will be coded and batched for processing on an hourly basis. The order information will be maintained on a magnetic tape, where it will provide the means for producing shipping papers, invoices, and, later, sales statistics. Because of this significant impact on all stages of the company's operations, the analyst has designed an extensive validation process early in the processing of customer orders. A customer master file exists on magnetic tape, which contains a customer code, name and address, salesperson identification, credit limit, and special shipping instructions for all approved customers. Similarly, a product master file exists on magnetic disk that contains the product number, market price, cost, unit of measure, current inventory amount, and miscellaneous information concerning weight, size, volume, and so on for all approved products.

Required:

1. With a customer master file and a product master file online, identify the minimum data that would comprise a customer order.

2. In conjunction with manual control procedures, what program control procedures should be implemented?

14.42 What physical and procedural security techniques would be effective in preventing incidents of the following type:

1. A teenager in Atlanta used a long-distance telephone call to tap the lines of a time-sharing firm in Macon, Georgia, extracting data from its ledgers as well as records of its customers.

2. An employee of a popular weekly magazine was able to walk off with a tape containing a subscriber list. Subsequently, he used a service bureau to duplicate the list for sale.

3. The data processing manager was able to steal $81,000 from a brokerage house by making program changes that caused fraudulent payments to be made to her account.

4. A 300-watt bulb overheated a fire-resistant ceiling and touched off a blaze that engulfed both the tape library and the adjacent computer room.

5. It was reported that several reels of magnetic tape were erased by energy emitted from the radar equipment of a nearby Air Force base.

6. War protesters invaded Dow Chemical's unmanned computer center in Michigan. A thousand tapes were damaged and cards and manuals were ransacked. Damage was estimated at $100,000.

14.43 One of the most common reports generated by the computer system is an error log. These logs identify errors as the data are being processed by the computer. As the errors are identified, they are written to a file that is printed on completion of the processing run. The error log is then distributed to the preparers of the input data or the systems analyst to isolate and correct the problem. Following is a schedule showing the checks performed by the computer on each data entry. If the condition (data check) is violated, that data entry is not processed, and the appropriate error message is written to the error report.

Field Name	Character Position	Data Check	Error Message
ID code	0–3	Numeric only	Nonnumeric character in numeric-only field
ID name	4–7	Alphabetic only	Nonalphabetic character in alpha-only field
Period	8	Period only	Nonperiod character not allowed
Slash, hyphen	9–10	/ or -	Only / or - allowed
Amount	11–16	Out of range	Amount > 200,000 invalid
		Numeric only	Nonnumeric character not allowed
Space	17		Space only field
ID suffix	18–20	Numeric	Nonnumeric character not allowed
		Positive integer	Negative not allowed

Required: Design an error report with appropriate titles and headings. Use the following columnar headings on your report:

Entry No.	Data Entry	Error Field Name	Error Message
21	1123BR3.//010300 543	ID name	Nonalphabetic character in alpha-only field

Evaluate the following data entries for violation of the above listed checks and write any invalid entries to the error report as in the example. (Ø = zero.)

Entry No.	Character Position																				
	Ø	1	2	3	4	5	6	7	8	9	10	11	12	13	14	15	16	17	18	19	2Ø
1	1	7	8	9	A	R	T	H	.	/	/	Ø	2	3	5	2	1		4	3	2
2	2	3	5	2	B	L	U	E	.	-	-	3	4	6	1	7	2		7	1	8
3	7	6	2	1	J	I	M	M	.	/	-	Ø	1	Ø	Ø	1	Ø		2	Y	5
4	8	2	A	4	K	A	Y	2	.	-	/	2	Ø	Ø	Ø	Ø	Ø	*	-	2	8
5	4	3	9	Ø	L	A	R	R	.	/	/	1	Ø	9	8	Y	2		6	2	4
6	*	2	6	3	C	L	A	R	*	-	+	2	Ø	Ø	Ø	Ø	1		5	3	B
7	2	-	2	Ø	G	E	O	R	.	/	/	9	1	5	1	9	6		2	4	1
8	Ø	Ø	Ø	Ø	O	O	O	O	.	-	/	Ø	Ø	Ø	Ø	Ø	Ø		Ø	Ø	Ø
9	7	Q	Z	Q	P	E	T	E	/	/	/	1	1	9	9	2	1		1	8	2
10		3	5	Ø	S	A	M	I	.	/	*	1	Y	3	2	7	1	+	6	2	9

14.44 The state commissioner for revenue is concerned about potential exposures her state income tax processing system may have. She sums up her feeling as follows:

"First, I am concerned that someone who knows a valid taxpayer ID or a corporation's federal identification number will use it to gather unauthorized data about that taxpayer. Second, I want to guard against the possibility of other state employees outside the Revenue Department searching through the files. Third, I believe it's essential to make sure only authorized Revenue Department employees enter tax return data."

The state's new income tax system was installed 17 months ago under a large consulting contract awarded a "Big Eight" CPA firm. It handles returns of individuals and corporations and features direct tax return input and inquiry capabilities. Data for the system are input directly from tax returns through terminals located in the main processing facility of the department. Processing of the returns entails checking the mathematical accuracy of the data, testing the reasonableness of deductions, identifying returns that might be considered for audit by the state auditors, and issuing refund checks to taxpayers.

Inquiry service is provided taxpayers through online Revenue Department terminals located in nine regional offices throughout the state. Taxpayers can determine the status of their returns or obtain information about their last two years' returns by calling or visiting one of these regional offices.

Required: Recommend controls for each of the problems expressed by the state commissioner for revenue.

14.45 Burgers N' Stuff is a fast-food restaurant located in the Washington, D.C., area. It has recently installed a PC-based system connected to four terminals at the order counter. The owner-manager of Burgers N' Stuff wants the system to compute the amount of a customer's order, tell the order taker the amount of change to give the customer, and accumulate sales totals by the 69 different food items.

Required: What controls and security measures are appropriate for the simple PC-based system of Burgers N' Stuff?

BIBLIOGRAPHY

AIKENS, WILLIAM. "Jesse James at the Terminal." *Harvard Business Review*, July–August 1985.

ALBERT, DOUGLAS J. "Combatting Software Piracy by Encryption and Key Management." *Computer,* April 1984.

BEAVER, JENNIFER E. "Shielding Computers from Power Mishaps." *Computer Decisions,* March 1984.

BRIDGES, LINDA. "Software, Hardware 'Vaccines' Stem Threat of Deadly Computer Viruses." *PC Week,* March 8, 1988.

BRILL, KENNETH. "Reliable Power: Beyond the Big Box." *InformationWEEK,* March 14, 1988.

BURCH, JOHN G., and JOSEPH L. SARDINAS. *Computer Control and Audit: A Total Systems Approach.* New York: John Wiley, 1978.

CANNING, RICHARD C. "Information Security and Privacy." *EDP Analyzer,* February 1986.

CERULLO, M. J. "General Controls in Computer Systems." *Computers and Security,* 1985.

CRUS, R. A. "Data Recovery in IBM Database 2." *IBM Systems Journal,* Summer 1984.

CUSHING, BARRY E., and MARSHALL B. ROMNEY. *Accounting Information Systems and Business Organizations,* 4th ed. Reading, Mass.: Addison-Wesley, 1987.

DAVIS, G. B., and R. WEBER. "The Impact of Advanced Computer Systems on Controls and Audit Procedures." *Auditing: A Journal of Theory and Practice,* Spring 1986.

ERNST & WHINNEY, Chicago, 1986.

FISHER, ROYAL P. *Information Systems Security.* Englewood Cliffs, N.J.: Prentice Hall, 1984.

GALLEGOS, FREDRICK, DANA R. RICHARDSON, and A. FAYE BORTHICK. *Audit and Control of Information Systems.* Cincinnati: South-Western, 1987.

GIBSON, STEVE. "Computer Viruses Express Themselves in Many Ways." *InfoWorld,* April 18, 1988.

GRALLA, PRESTON. " 'Smart Cards' Seen as Changing the Way Businesses Operate." *PC Week,* January 5, 1988.

HORWITT, ELISABETH. "Protecting Your Network Data." *Business Computer Systems,* July 1985.

MOSCOVE, STEPHEN A., and MARK A. SIMKIN. *Accounting Information Systems,* 3rd ed. New York: John Wiley, 1987.

MURASKIN, ELLEN. "Double-Duty Fault Tolerance." *Computer & Communications Decisions,* August 1987.

PIKE, HELEN. "Survival Planning for Data Disaster." *Computerworld,* April 6, 1988.

PORTER, W., and WILLIAM E. PERRY. *EDP Controls and Auditing,* 4th ed. Boston: Kent, 1985.

PRIEST, GEORGE E. *The DP Executive's Guide to Microcomputer Management and Control.* Wellesley, Mass.: QED Information Sciences, 1984.

RAHMAN, MAWDUDUR, and MAURICE HALLADAY. *Accounting Information Systems.* Englewood Cliffs, N.J.: Prentice Hall, 1988.

RASKIN, ROBIN. "As PC Technology Matures, Users Discover Need for a Security Blanket." *PC Week,* March 10, 1987.

ROMNEY, MARSHALL B., and JAMES V. HANSEN. *An Introduction to Microcomputers and Their Controls.* Altamonte Springs, Fla.: The Institute of Internal Auditors, 1985.

ROMNEY, MARSHALL B., and KEVIN D. STOCKS. "Microcomputer Controls." *Internal Auditor,* June 1985.

STEINBERG, DON. "Security System Reads Palms to Guard Computer Rooms." *PC Week,* June 16, 1987.

STREHLO, CHRISTINE. "The Well-Protected Network." *Personal Computing,* January 1988.

Swartz, Michael. "Making Sense of DES." *Computerworld,* June 7, 1982.

Troy, Gene. "Thwarting the Hackers." *Datamation,* July 1, 1984.

Tucker, Michael. "Data Backup with a Twist." *Computerworld.* April 6, 1988.

Tyler, Michael A. "Hard Facts on Hardware Reliability?" *Datamation,* October 1, 1984.

Wilkinson, Joseph W. *Accounting and Information Systems,* 2nd ed. New York: John Wiley, 1986.

PART 4

INFORMATION SYSTEMS

STRATEGIC PLANNING, DEVELOPMENT, AND MANAGEMENT

Having attained an understanding of the basic building blocks of information systems and the design forces that impact these building blocks, our attention will turn to the process of developing strategically viable, user-oriented information systems. This process, called the systems development methodology, is illustrated in the accompanying window. It is based on an organizational-wide, information systems policy and a strategic information systems plan—topics that are addressed in Chapter 15.

The systems development methodology is what systems analysts follow in doing their systems work. Its major phases are systems analysis, general systems design, systems evaluation, detailed systems design, and systems implementation. The first four of these major phases, contained in Chapters 16–19, are directed toward providing specific values for the building blocks. The last phase of the systems development methodology, described in Chapter 20, deals with the activities of making the building blocks operational.

The systems analysis phase produces two documented deliverables. Each of the other four phases produces one. These six documented deliverables demonstrate what kind and how much progress is being made. They keep a clear communication channel open between systems professionals and end users, thus making sure that the system's project stays on track as it evolves. And when the information system has been built and implemented, the documented deliverables provide complete documentation of its history, development, and current status.

Information systems in organizations represent significant investments in time and money and often play critical roles in determining their existence and success. This text is concluded by presenting in Chapter 21 several important areas that help to ensure better management of this valuable resource.

15

STRATEGIC INFORMATION SYSTEMS PLANNING

15.1 INTRODUCTION

To this point, we have analyzed information systems in terms of information as a valuable resource, information systems that produce it, different dimensions and structures of information systems, the basic building blocks of information systems, and design forces that impact these building blocks. Now we turn our attention to performing strategic information systems planning (SISP), the first major step on the long road to building strategically viable, user-oriented, and goals-based information systems. Specifically, the objectives of this chapter are:

1. To provide an overview of different systems philosophies.
2. To discuss the proactive systems philosophy.
3. To show the relationship of SISP to the company's business plan and goals and the systems development methodology (SDM).
4. To demonstrate the three steps required to prepare a strategic information systems plan.
5. To present the NSU Tigers Event Center Strategic Information Systems Plan.

15.2 OVERVIEW OF INFORMATION SYSTEMS POLICY AND PLANNING

A companywide information systems policy provides a unified outlook and springboard for the information systems planning process. In turn, the information systems plan incorporates the policy and sets the baseline for beginning the systems development methodology. The way these activities, including information systems management, work together is illustrated in Figure 15.1. The way not to do it kicks off this section.

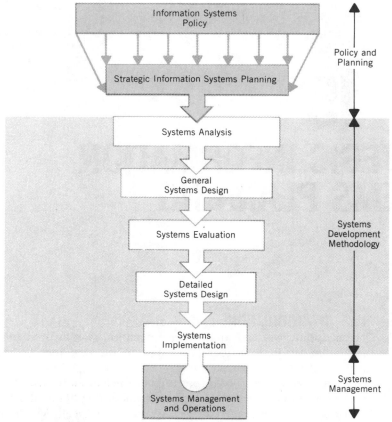

Figure 15.1 The information systems policy-setting, planning, development, and management process.

The Way Not to do Systems Work

We will start with the way not to do systems work by including the following lament from a user.

> When you want to get something done, you have to submit a written request. Then they reject the request after sitting on it for a month. At that point, you find out the request does not say what they want it to say, so you have to rewrite it. Then they tell you it cannot get done for six months because of other priorities. Or maybe they cannot do it for a year because it involves some crazy technical problem. Finally, I'm given a target date that is never met. What really upsets me is that after all that aggravation, their program does not do what it's supposed to do. And I am no further ahead than when I started.[1]

[1]Fred Kirchgraber, "Users and Information Systems: The Odd Couple," *Best's Review,* February 1987, p. 83.

This user, and probably thousands of others, feel they are met with an unreasonable amount of information systems red tape and delays. But the systems analysts have their own tale to tell, documented in the following quote.

> We get virtually no user support. User requests are poorly documented, and they have no sense of what is needed for us to begin a project. Users are so busy with their day-to-day activities that we practically have to drag them into their own projects. They resist ongoing involvement and object to their required participation in final testing and sign-off. Users want everything done yesterday, and they are constantly changing project priorities. Their starting and stopping of projects is killing us.[2]

Clearly, these comments indicate lack of a sound systems policy from top management and use of strategic information systems planning that involves key users throughout the user community. What follows in this chapter is an attempt to present the "right way" to give direction to both users and information systems personnel and alleviate the gap between these two groups so both can work toward the achievement of mutual goals.

Different Philosophies

Generally two philosophies can be used in the way information systems are developed and deployed in organizations. One philosophy accepts the information system as a tactical and operational defensive weapon to meet basic data processing requirements and various reporting obligations, to help the company stay on track, and to help the company survive. Information system projects are developed based on reactions to the environment and set by a budget. The basic question to all systems work is, "How much can we save?" Such an information systems philosophy is reactive, bottom-line oriented.

A different information systems philosophy views the information system as a strategic offensive weapon which can give the company a competitive edge. This philosophy holds to the viewpoint that information systems can be developed not only to help reduce costs but also increase revenue. This philosophy is proactive, bottom- and top-line oriented. The basic question asked is, "How can we deploy our information system to support the strategic goals of our business?" Once this question is answered, a budget is set that meets the needs of the information system to carry out its mission.

With either philosophy, information systems plans are required. When viewed as a defensive weapon, the information systems planning horizon is usually year-to-year and narrow in scope. Alternatively, when the information system is viewed as a strategic offensive weapon, the strategic information systems plan's scope covers the entire company, and its time frame is typically three or more years. This philosophy, stressed in this chapter, incorporates top management's policies and input, aligns information system goals with business goals, anticipates future information requirements, and uses emerging information

---

[2]Ibid.

technologies to assist the company in carrying out its business plan. A policy that adopts this philosophy is presented next.

Proactive Information Systems Policy

Proactive information systems policy cuts across departments, staff, and line functions and eliminates disparate and redundant islands of information that work on a task-by-task, day-by-day basis. Top management lets it be known, loud and clear, that the information system is just as important to the organization as land, buildings, and production equipment. And, of course, such advocacy must be backed up with sufficient funds to support development of the information system desired and planned for.

Proactive systems policy recognizes the development and convergence of information technology, such as telecommunications, computers, and multifunctional workstations; the combination of voice, text, numbers, and graphics; and applications such as computer-integrated manufacturing, teleshopping, electronic mail, and teleconferencing. Such policy stresses the unequivocal support for a total system of controls to safeguard the information system. Sound proactive systems policy advocates conformance with design forces, such as integration, user/system interface, information quality and usability, systems requirements, data processing requirements, organizational factors, cost-effectiveness requirements, human factors, and feasibility requirements. Moreover, good proactive systems policy encourages the corporate culture to accept and support information systems development.

PROACTIVE INFORMATION SYSTEMS STRATEGY

According to William A. Roberts, vice-president of information systems at Pacific Mutual Life Insurance Company, one of the major activities of information systems is strategic planning. Each year, prior to the beginning of the budget planning cycle, information systems people meet with each business unit to discuss the unit's plan for the coming year. At the same meeting, information systems personnel review systems opportunities that may impact the unit and ask the unit if it wants information systems to adopt any particular technologies or techniques to help it meet its objectives.

Like many other MIS departments, Roberts and his colleagues in information systems are taking an increasingly proactive part in the development of strategic systems that contribute directly to the success of the business enterprise.

Excerpted from John Kirkley, "The Restructuring of MIS: Business Strategies Take Hold," *Computerworld,* March 21, 1988, pp. 79–93.

Top management should realize that the information system must be developed and managed by professionals and highly skilled personnel. Whether the system follows a star, ring, or some other network topology to mesh and match the organization, it still must be developed and unified under a single command, such as a chief information officer (CIO), who is also a member of the top management team. But the principal developers and designers of information systems are systems analysts, who must be given free rein to transcend departmental lines to perform their work thoroughly and professionally.

Certainly, one of the key motivators for setting proactive systems policy is to identify opportunities and make a strong commitment to use information systems to increase managements' effectiveness, improve productivity, and augment product-service differentiation. For example, a number of years ago, top management at McKesson made a strong policy commitment to establish systems plans and to develop a fully integrated information system that would provide management with sufficient information, increase the productivity of employees, and provide customers with unmatched service.

Today, McKesson is the world's largest drug distributor. Top management, employees, and customers alike give most of the credit for McKesson's success to its information system. Among other things, it provides druggists with hand-held scanning devices that allow quick and easy inventory taking and order entry. The druggists simply scan the inventory items they want to reorder and key in the quantity; the system does the rest. Order data are transmitted to one of McKesson's distribution centers where picking, packing, and loading instructions and shipping papers are prepared automatically. Within 24 hours or less, druggists receive their orders. The best that most of the competition can do is three- to four-day turnaround. But the key point to remember is that the system started with a clear and cogent systems policy from top management.

Strategic Information Systems Planning in Perspective

In 1881 William Winchester, son of the famous rifle manufacturer, died leaving $20 million to his widow, Sara. During her mourning, she consulted a fortune-teller. The seer revealed that Sara's own survival depended on the construction of a house: as long as work on the house continued, Sara would live and prosper. Workers continued to add new wings and rooms until Sara's death 36 years later.

The still unfinished house has 160 rooms and covers six acres in San Jose, California. It has blind chimneys, doors that open into blank walls, stairways that lead to ceilings, windows blocked by later construction, and countless oddities that suppress any sense of the unity normally associated with the notion of a house. It's an interesting phenomenon, a freak, an example of on-the-fly design. The materials and workmanship of each room are the best that money could buy. But, built without an architectural plan, it cannot function as a house.[3]

Without proper strategic information system planning, systems projects are often built piecemeal, resulting in incompatible, redundant, and inflexible infor-

---

[3]Quoted from William R. Synnott, *The Information Weapon* (New York: John Wiley, 1987), p. 225.

mation systems that begin to take on some of the characteristics of the Winchester house. Too often, managements make blind stabs at quick-fix solutions and try to fit jobs to technology without proper planning and figuring out what is really needed. In many instances, for example, a new computer is not needed, just some good old-fashioned systems work to get the information system back on track. Throwing technology at problems without proper planning always ends in failure.

**PLAN,
PLAN, PLAN**   In a nice, orderly, predictable business world, the processing of information can run as smoothly as a Swiss watch. But, of course, business doesn't work like that. Orders come in ebbs and flows—even tidal waves for businesses such as retailing. And if volume isn't jumping up and down, something else is playing havoc with the MIS department: a sudden crush of demands for new applications, an outbreak of faulty software, the inopportune absence of key people.

In a big distribution company, the marketing department decided to double the number of product lines a few months before the busy Christmas season. Orders flooded in, and MIS couldn't keep up. Data entry of orders backed up and then was dropped on an outside service bureau, which proceeded to inject a rash of processing errors. All this resulted in angry customers, lost business, and product returns.

Excerpted from "How MIS Rides Out Business Cycles," *InformationWEEK*, June 20, 1987, p. 14.

The best way to avoid such problems is for top management to prepare a proactive systems policy and to adopt a formal strategic information systems planning (SISP) methodology. This methodology is a predetermined process by which top executives and user departments supply much of the input that can be used to translate organization strategies and goals into a strategic information systems plan for achieving these goals.

An ideal planning group includes the chief executive officer (CEO), the chief financial officer (CFO), the chief information officer (CIO), all senior vice-presidents, and support staff. This SISP team defines business goals and draws upon multiple perspectives and varied experiences within the organization.

SISP is elevated to the same level as planning for such things as plant expansion, product development, mergers, and long-term financing. It is just as important to have a clear roadmap indicating the direction that the information system will take and systems projects it will develop as it is to have a business plan and a schedule of major investments.

The most important facet of SISP is that it determines the best system projects to develop from the perspective of both users and systems personnel. The systems projects are prioritized, mission critical, goal congruent, and success directed. For example, the strategic information systems plan gives top priority to the development of an inventory management and distribution systems project if the organization's lifeblood is getting finished goods from manufacturer to retailer. Or, if the organization's business goal emphasizes product differentiation, the systems plan will include system projects that link with and support this goal.

SELLING STRATEGIC IS PLANNING An IBM consulting program that focuses on the client's strategic goals is the controversial Information Services Investment Strategies (ISIS) program. IBM client corporations provide IBM with an array of operating and financial information. In return, IBM consultants provide free strategic analysis and advice. The aim of ISIS, in addition to bolstering IBM's marketing strategy, helps executives understand how IS can better meet corporate goals.

Putting It All Together
SISP is a cyclic process, producing actions that cause results, and then learning from results and making adjustments. This phenomenon is illustrated in Figure 15.2.

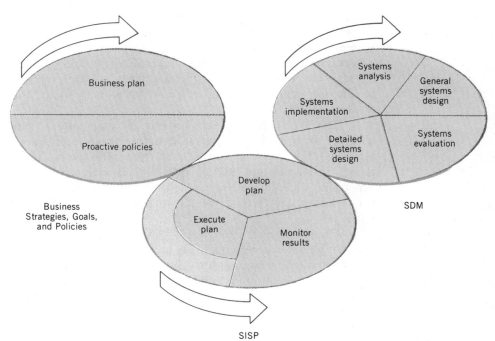

Figure 15.2 Interrelationship of business plans and policies, SISP, and SDM.

The business plan's strategies and goals and top management's system policies are linked to and drive SISP. After the strategic information systems plan is completed, its execution triggers the systems development methodology. The SDM, in turn, is applied to design and implement specific systems projects. The results are monitored to measure actual performance against goals of the systems plan. Progress on projects is monitored and postimplementation reviews are made to see if completed projects are on time, within budget, and meet users' needs. Specific components of the plan are revised as current conditions and new information warrant. In essence, the business plan and systems plan are supposed to select the right things to do and set direction; the SDM is supposed to do the things right and deal with specifics.

Planning, Development, and Systems Life Cycles

As already stated, systems work is cyclical. Overall systems work starts with systems policies and plans, then the SDM is employed to develop the new system, then during implementation the new system is turned over to operations where it is managed and maintained, then because of changing conditions and requirements, the process starts all over again.

Figure 15.3 demonstrates this cyclical phenomenon of systems work. The figure shows that efforts and resources are deployed to plan, develop, and operate and maintain the information system. The information system, in turn, provides benefits to the organization.

Not only do SISP and SDM have life cycles but the information system itself has a life cycle similar to the life cycles of products, equipment, fashions, and people. The information system is given birth by the SISP process and SDM. If well designed (or its "genetics" are good), the newly implemented information system is accepted by users and quickly grows to maturity where it operates for a relatively long time. But after several years of maximum service the system begins to become technically, economically, and operationally obsolete ceasing to function as effectively and efficiently as it once did and gradually deteriorates to eventual death.

Usually, the information systems life span ranges from three to six years, although information systems in dynamic organizations and various subsystems may have life cycles significantly shorter. Moreover, using top-down modular design principles and abiding by design forces, such as systems requirements, especially reliability, growth potential, and maintainability; organizational factors; and human factors; will all work together to help extend the system's life span.

The cost curves in Figure 15.3A show all the costs of systems work. The operating and maintenance costs begin before final implementation because in many instances certain modules, such as transaction processing, are implemented before the total system is converted. Also some of the operations personnel are trained during implementation. And in some installations, both the old system and new system run parallel before finally converting the old system to the new system. See, for example, where system I is converted to system II.

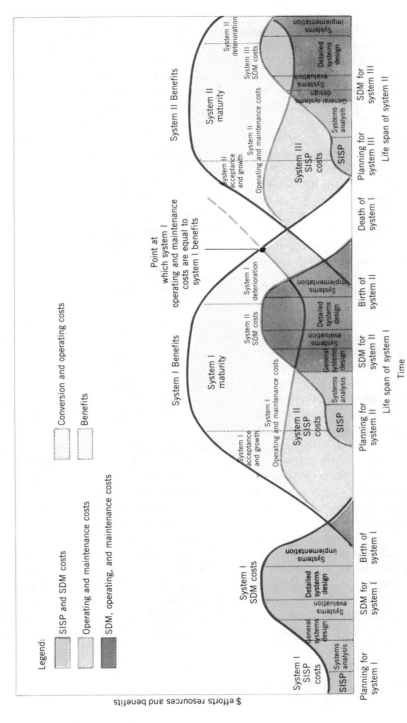

Figure 15.3 Planning, development, and systems life cycles related to costs and benefits over time.

539

Operating and maintenance costs will rise after implementation because of the learning curve effect and also because the new system may require fine-tuning and minor modifications. Of course, the more effort that is put into design, training, and testing before conversion, the less the operating and maintenance cost line will increase during this initial period.

Systems benefits increase sharply as the users accept system I and learn how to operate and work with it effectively and efficiently. Users begin to enjoy the full-service potential of the system. Benefits will begin to stabilize and operating and maintenance costs will begin to decrease slightly and also begin to stabilize. But after a time, when the information system begins to reach full maturity, operating and maintenance costs will begin to rise as inefficiencies creep in; as more maintenance, repairs, and "patchwork" are required; and as technical and operational obsolescence begin. Also during this time, changes are occurring. The organization's goals are being revamped, business plans are being revised, and the organization may be moving to a more centralized or decentralized form of management.

In some instances (not shown in the figure), major modifications can be made and additional resources acquired during a system's life cycle that can reduce costs and increase benefits, or both, and therefore extend the system's life for several years beyond normal maturity. As a matter of fact, an information systems plan often includes one or two stages for acquiring additional resources over the total life of the system. Eventually, however, the system will deteriorate to a point where a new system is required.

Obviously, the level of systems benefits also begin to decline after maturing. Although this decline is often gradual, it is critical that SISP and SDM for system II begin well before the point where the benefits and the operating and maintenance costs lines intersect.

Often, SISP and SDM must begin one or two years in advance while the present information system is robust and at its peak in providing benefits to the organization. Behaviorally, it is very difficult for one to start planning and developing a new system when the present one is working so well. But it is logical to do so, and indeed it must be done to ensure continuous and smooth operations. It is therefore necessary for top managers, other users, and systems personnel to work together to determine about when the benefits and costs will be equal for system I and an approximate idea of the size and scope of system II. Then time measurements are forecast to ensure that system II begins operation just before or when benefits and costs of system I are equal. For example, if it is estimated that the costs will be equal to benefits in system I two years hence and it will take three months for system II SISP process and 17 months for the system II SDM cycles, then the organization has four months before SISP for system II commences.

15.3 STEPS IN STRATEGIC INFORMATION SYSTEMS PLANNING

Three steps are required to develop a systems plan: (1) establishing information system goals, (2) eliciting and prioritizing information system project requests, and (3) assessing information system resources and capacity. These steps are presented next.

STEP 1: Establishing Information System Goals

This step involves the review of the organization's scope of operations, system policies, and business plan. The aim is to define the organization's goals and link the goals of the information system with them. From this process, systems project ideas begin to emerge that support the goals. The SISP team gathers input from each team member. Also, other people who may contribute to the planning process are brought in such as outside consultants and auditors.

IS OPPORTUNITIES The IS planning process should align IS activities with business strategy, focusing the portfolio of systems projects on a company's strategic goals and identifying the areas in which high-payoff opportunities are likely to be found. This planning process is business driven.

Excerpted from N. Dean Meyer, "A Strategic Tree in the Forest of IS Opportunity," *Information Strategy: The Executive's Journal,* Spring 1988, pp. 24–27.

The review of additional documentation can also be helpful in this first step. This kind of documentation includes previous systems plans, postimplementation reviews and periodic system evaluation reports, important directives and memos, organization charts and job descriptions, internal and external auditors' reports, and systems documentation and procedures manuals.

From this investigative process, general information system goals are formulated. These goals may be stated as (1) to design and implement system projects that support organizational goals, (2) to exploit business opportunities provided by new information technologies, and (3) to follow a systems development methodology that interacts with users and provides the status and progress on all new systems projects.

STEP 2: Eliciting and Prioritizing Information System Project Requests

During step 1, a great deal of interaction between users and systems personnel takes place. From this interaction, very broad information systems project requests begin to materialize. Some of the ideas for these projects may come from users, others may come from systems personnel. In any event, systems project requests are elicited and given in a free exchange of ideas.

But no company or its information system has enough resources to meet all systems project requests, nor are all the requests necessarily good ones. Therefore, a method must be applied that prioritizes systems project requests based on strategic and feasibility factors. This method entails filling out a systems project request form, illustrated in Figure 15.4; preparing a systems project request priority worksheet, shown in Figure 15.5; and plotting a systems project request priority grid, displayed in Figure 15.6.

The weights range from 0 to 10 for both strategic and feasibility factors. All members of the planning team provide weights on how well a particular project request is linked to the company's strategic goals of increasing productivity, enhancing product and service differentiation, and improving management decision making. The same is done for the feasibility factors: technical, economic, legal, operations, and schedule. Typically, one of the experienced systems analysts, working with the CIO, will provide these weights.

Both sets of weights are simply averaged to give a strategic factor's score and a feasibility factor's score. These scores are then plotted on the project request priority grid. The point on the grid indicates each project request's level of priority. A project that scores a 10 is the best project to undertake. On the other hand, a project that scores less than 5 indicates an extremely poor project to undertake because it is not congruent with the company's strategic goals and will be difficult to design and implement because of weak feasibility factors.

In the systems project request priority worksheet, 10 projects are given points based on how well they contribute to strategic factors and the feasibility of implementing them within a reasonable time economically and making them operational. These data are taken from the systems project request forms. Each project's grades are plotted on the systems project request priority grid, which is divided into four quadrants.

Projects C, D, F, and J are in quadrant 1, which means they are strongly linked to strategic factors of the business plan and will therefore support the company's business goals. Also, they are highly feasible for succeeding as information system applications. Therefore, these project requests are high-priority projects.

Project H is moderately strong in feasibility factors, but only moderate in strategic factors. One would assume that PERT would increase productivity. The general view of the planning group was, however, that its implementation would not add significantly to productivity because the type of work in the company is not very project oriented, nor would it help materially in product differentiation. They did agree, however, that if sufficient funds are made available, it would be a project worth pursuing.

Projects A, B, and I are rejected outright because of low scores in both strategic and feasibility factors. Projects E and G fall into quadrant 4 and show good strength for meeting strategic goals. They both, however, have questionable feasibility. For example, a great deal of doubt exists as to whether implementation of computer-to-computer ordering system E would cause restraint of trade legal problems. Others in the group questioned if computer-to-computer ordering was really technically and operationally feasible with many of their customers. Others thought it would take too long to implement project E and therefore may take resources away from more feasible projects. Project G is a borderline case, which could easily be treated as a high-priority project if it could be shown that it would become operational and not become bogged down in development.

REQUEST FOR SYSTEMS WORK

PART 1 *(to be completed by requestor)*

DATE SUBMITTED: _____MM/DD/YY_____   REQUEST FOR: ☐ Modification of System

                                                                  ☐ Redesign of System

                                                                  ☒ New System

SUBMITTED BY: _____Bob Hopeful_____   _____Marketing_____
                                      (Name)   *(Department)*

NATURE OF REQUEST: Develop an integrated, online order entry, invoicing, and shipping system to supplant the batch system.

REASONS FOR MAKING REQUEST: The company has developed a reputation for poor customer service, late deliveries, and inability to determine the status of in-process orders. The new system should help to alleviate this problem.

SUPPORTING DOCUMENTS ATTACHED: A compilation of the customer complaint file and statements from all of our company sales representatives are combined in the report attached to this form.

PART 2 *(to be completed by the CIO or a systems analyst)*

MODIFICATIONS APPEAR TO BE: ☐ MINOR ☒ MAJOR ☐ EXTENSIVE

IMPLEMENTATION MAY REQUIRE ADDITIONAL:
  ☒ SOFTWARE ☐ HARDWARE ☐ PERSONNEL

COMMITMENT OF RESOURCES WOULD BE:
  ☐ MINOR ☒ MAJOR ☐ EXTENSIVE

FEASIBILITY FACTORS SCORE: T $\underline{8}$ E $\underline{8}$ L $\underline{9}$ O $\underline{9}$ S $\underline{8}$. SCORE __8.4__

PRELIMINARY INVESTIGATION COMPLETED BY: _____Wanda Candu_____
                                                                          (Name)

PROJECT ID _____C_____   _____MM/DD/YY_____
                                                                (Date)

PART 3 *(to be completed by the systems planning committee)*

STRATEGIC FACTORS SCORE: P $\underline{9}$ D $\underline{9}$ M $\underline{6}$. SCORE __8.0__

PRIORITY ASSIGNED: _____High_____

  ☒ START SYSTEMS WORK APPROVED. STARTING DATE: _____MM/DD/YY_____
  ☐ TENTATIVE APPROVAL DEPENDING ON FURTHER ANALYSIS
  ☐ REJECTED

Figure 15.4 A systems project request form.

Project Request Priority Worksheet

Project Name	Strategic Factors Productivity	Strategic Factors Differentiation	Management	Strategic Factors Score	Technical	Economic	Feasibility Factors Legal	Operational	Schedule	Feasibility Factors Score
Ⓐ Computer production scheduling	9	1	2	4.0	5	2	9	4	1	4.2
Ⓑ Teleconferencing	4	1	3	2.7	3	1	6	3	2	3.0
Ⓒ Online order entry	9	9	6	8.0	8	8	9	9	8	8.4
Ⓓ Cash management	4	4	8	5.3	8	7	9	8	8	8.0
Ⓔ Computer-to-computer ordering	8	8	5	7.0	4	5	1	3	3	3.2
Ⓕ Inventory control	8	9	9	8.7	8	8	8	7	6	7.4
Ⓖ Forecasting and market modeling	5	9	9	7.7	5	6	7	3	3	4.8
Ⓗ Application of PERT	3	3	8	4.7	6	5	8	6	5	6.0
Ⓘ Application of expert system	2	2	8	4.0	4	4	7	2	2	3.8
Ⓙ Standard costing system	9	8	8	8.3	7	8	7	9	8	7.8

Figure 15.5 A systems project request priority worksheet.

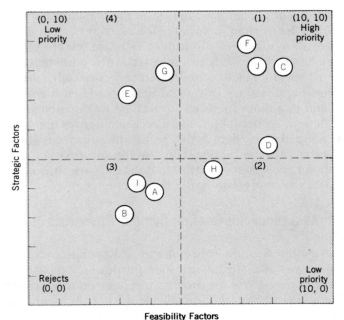

Figure 15.6 A systems project request priority grid.

The project request priority grid provides a logical base from which top management can select projects. Those in the high-priority area are clear choices. Borderline cases that approach quadrant 1 are tentatively approved contingent on new evidence that may increase (or decrease) their scores or on a substantial increase in information system resources.

Clearly, this planning procedure ferrets out and rejects projects that possibly "sound good" but if undertaken would suck up valuable resources and waste months of systems work. Furthermore, this procedure helps to establish an information systems budget and sets an agenda of projects to be worked on over a particular planning horizon rather than tackling information system projects willy-nilly.

The only deviation from this procedure would be the development of mandatory projects required to meet legal or contractual obligations. Information system resources for new development would be allocated first to all mandatory projects and then to projects with the highest priorities next.

Other techniques that aid the project prioritizing and selecting process can be added at the planning group's discretion. For example, a profitability index (PI) facilitates ranking systems projects based on relative economic benefits. PI is calculated by dividing the total present value of the anticipated net cash inflows from a project by the present value of the project's cost. The larger a PI is for a project proposal, the greater is its chance for being selected for design and implementation. A project with a PI less than 1.0 is considered an undesirable investment of information system resources.

The discount factor used in computing present values is typically provided by the controller or chief financial officer. At this stage in the systems work, costs and benefits are extremely difficult to estimate, except on a gut-feel basis. On the other hand, if they can be estimated with some degree of reasonableness, then by all means the PI should be used. Typically, the PI and other cost-effectiveness analysis are calculated in a broad-brush manner during systems analysis and in a more specific and detailed way immediately following general systems design. At that point, more accurate figures are available.

As alluded to earlier, at this point, the organization is trying to establish general goals, a sense of direction for the information system, and a logical starting point for systems analysts to do their work. It is during the application of the SDM that more nitty-gritty details emerge.

STEP 3: Assessing Information System Resources and Capacity

The information system's key resources and operating capacity are represented by its personnel and technology. The purpose of step 3 is to determine what impact the planned systems projects will have on these resources and to make sure that sufficient capacity is available during the planning cycle to not only support present operating needs but to accommodate new projects.

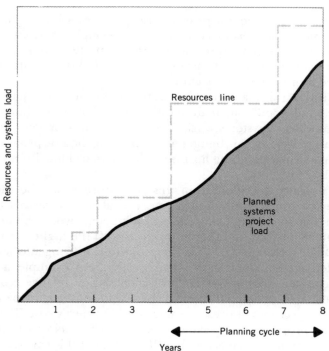

Figure 15.7 A load-line graph and resources upgrades.

Changes in information system capacity typically follows a step function, whereas the growth in capacity needs is somewhat steady and continuous. This relationship is portrayed in Figure 15.7. This graph illustrates how technology upgrades, including software, mainframes, auxiliary storage, channels, peripherals, telecommunication networks, and systems personnel must be made to handle growth and satisfy capacity requirements over time. At the point where the dashed line is about to intersect with the load line, maximum capacity has been reached. Upgrades are necessary prior to this point to prevent the degradation of service to users.

Top management begins to allocate sizable additional funds to the information systems budget when the graph begins to warn of an impending overload. This process may be necessary several times during the five years covered by the plan. In the example, two large infusions of additional funds are required in year 1 and year 3 of the planning cycle.

At this stage of systems planning, not enough information is available to make concrete decisions on personnel and technology. Only general estimates

Year Needed \ Resources	Technology	Personnel
Year 1	Telecommunications backbone 2 Mainframes 4 Minicomputers 20 Microcomputers 30 Gbytes of auxiliary storage 1 DBMS Various software packages Estimated cost: $12M	14 Systems analysts 24 Application programmers 14 Operators 40 Support staff Estimated cost: $3M per year
Year 3	1 Mainframe 4 Midrange processors 30 Workstations 2 PABXs 12 Laser printers Estimated cost: $3M	6 Shift supervisors 6 Operators 5 Systems analysts 4 Security guards Estimated cost: $900K per year

Figure 15.8 A resources requirements matrix.

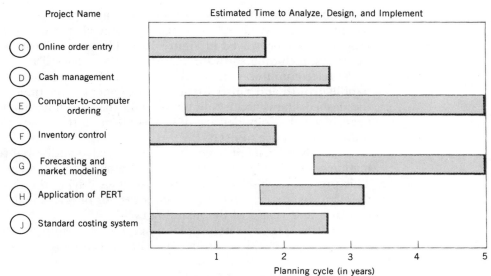

Figure 15.9 Schedule of approved systems requests.

are given. Specifics and detail come from application of the SDM. A resource requirements matrix giving general estimates is displayed in Figure 15.8. A schedule of planned system projects is shown in Figure 15.9, assuming top management gives final approval to project requests C, D, E, F, G, H, and J.

15.4 SHORT CASE

American Express's main business goal is unequaled customer service. Management's policy is to use information technology to exploit opportunities and support this goal.

In the latter part of the 1970s, top management at American Express established a systems policy to automate its operations area for instant customer service so that it could differentiate its service from the competition. During strategic information systems planning, a wide-ranging project was proposed that came to be known as "Modernization." A key component of Modernization was automation of clerical work, such as maintaining accounts, writing letters, and making financial adjustments. The mandate from the strategic information systems plan was to provide an online application to edit, process, and report on all adjustments to card member accounts. Further, the system would have to be available 7 days a week, 24 hours a day.

A systems project team was formed and the systems analysis phase of the SDM began to establish specific business requirements. As is typically the case, it soon became apparent that the application was not as straightforward and simple as it seemed during planning.

The systems analysis phase finally produced specific business requirements. Interaction between users and systems analysts continued until a point was reached where users were willing to sign off on the business requirements. A problem, however, arose in which users were producing new, additional requirements. At some point, the systems analysts put a freeze on these new requirements in order to begin and finalize the general systems design phase. Requests that could not be included were documented for inclusion in future developments.

During general systems design, logical design models were presented to

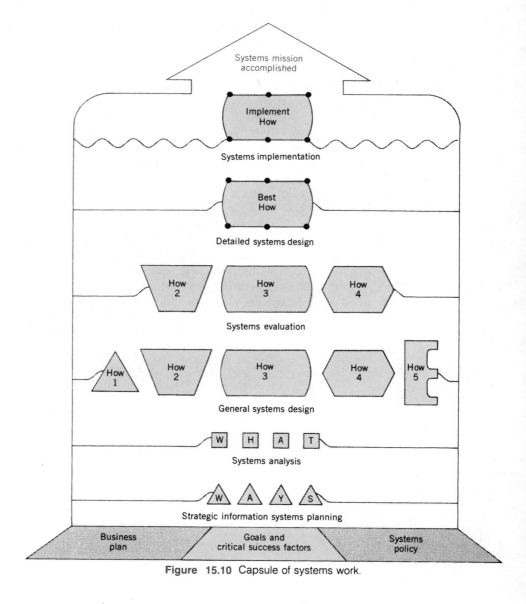

Figure 15.10 Capsule of systems work.

the user community. These logical design models were adjusted, refined, and evaluated. Then detailed design began.

The detailed systems design was coded, tested by a user-testing team, and eventually released to production. During this implementation phase, work flow changes were made, and a self-paced audiovisual training package was developed and administered. Within a two- to three-month period, all centers had completed their training and were using approximately 90 percent of the new system. The system was fully implemented by 1982.

Today, users have forgotten about the old paper-based system of processing account adjustments. Moreover, American Express revenue has more than tripled since the late 1970s. A great deal of credit for the growth at American Express is given to its "Modernization" project.

15.5 TOTAL SYSTEMS WORK IN A CAPSULE

Figure 15.10 portrays systems work in a capsule. This depiction helps to summarize this chapter and gives a preview of subsequent chapters.

The organization's business plan, goals and critical success factors (also called key variables, key performance areas, and key pulse points), and systems policy provide the power and general direction of the total systems mission. The SISP stage spells out the general systems mission and supplies specific systems projects to develop over a certain time period. During this stage, budgets are also established to boost and give *ways* to accomplish the systems mission.

The systems analysis phase defines *what* should be done before entering the general systems design phase. This general systems design stage of the systems journey produces general systems design alternatives that effectively show *how*, in broad terms, particular systems projects can be effected. The systems evaluation phase chooses the best alternative for detailed systems design. The detailed systems design phase produces a finished system that is ready to be launched from the systems development orbit to the operations orbit. The systems implementation phase launches the system and the systems mission is accomplished.

THE NSU TIGERS EVENT CENTER
Strategic Information Systems Planning

THE ENVIRONMENT

John Ball, the campus event center director, sits at his desk wondering how to develop solutions to the problems facing the event center. Since the expansion of the facility was completed six months ago, the number of events booked has doubled as promoters capitalize on the additional facilities available.

The information needs were easily satisfied before the expansion when the event center hosted only basketball games, an occasional club meeting, and three to four pep rallies a year. Additional building space and seating has attracted the promoters of rock concerts, conventions, and professional boxing matches to the center.

Several events have almost ended in disasters because of coordination problems. On one occasion the advertising department learned only a few days before an event that a show program to be sold at the door had not been produced. Although the printing was completed on time, the event lost money because the rush delivery charges levied by the printers were large, and the advertising department was unable to solicit the required number of advertisers.

For every event, the facilities planning department complains about problems encountered preparing the facility for an event. Requirements for the event, such as the seating arrangement and the number of chairs and tables needed, often are not communicated in a timely fashion. The facilities planning department has found itself short of chairs, tables, and other resources because two events are scheduled in different parts of the center at the same time, each competing for the same resources. Personnel has had difficulty scheduling ushers, parking attendants, and ticket takers. To prepare properly they feel that they should be notified as soon as the event is booked by the activities office. The lack of information about the resources available has caused the activities office to take up to a week to inform all offices of the requirements for a given event. Even the accounting office has had problems paying the promoters because of delays in receiving information concerning ticket revenue and expenses.

The worst problems seem to be in the ticket office. The ticket office handled only general admission tickets before the expansion. Now, the office provides tickets for reserved seating, festival seating, and general seating for different kinds of events that have varied seating plans.

TAKING ACTION

Mr. Ball knows he has to address these problems. The Board of Trustees of the college approved the expansion of the facilities assuming that the center would host more events, increase the variety of events, and show a profit. At present, the center is losing money and credibility with the promoters of events. Staff members are unhappy because they feel that the problems are a direct result of their performance. Mr. Ball, indeed, recognizes that the only way to solve this growing problem is to take action to meet the increased information requirements of the center.

STRATEGIC INFORMATION SYSTEMS PLANNING

Mr. Ball realizes that the business plan goal of increasing the operations of the event center has been met since expanding the facilities. They could meet the goals set forth by the Board of Trustees much more efficiently, however, if they could achieve better communication between the various departments in the center. An information system that integrates all the departments of the event center would provide the communication necessary to meet this need.

Mr. Ball sends a memo to all his department heads asking them to meet with him and Tyronne Topps, the chief information systems officer (CISO), next Monday for a strategic-level conference about the development of a new information system. He also requires each department head to bring systems project request forms (attached to his memo) filled out, ready for presentation and prioritization.

On Monday, with aid and direction from Tyronne Topps and several assistants, the department heads and Ball hammer out a systems plan after some heated discussions. See Figure SISP 1.1 for the request. Priority documentation includes the systems project worksheet, shown in Figure SISP 1.2, and the systems project request priority grid, disclosed in Figure SISP 1.3.

From work put into preparing the plan, a consensus is reached that the highest-priority projects will solve immediate critical problems. The others of lower priority will fulfill long-term management goals.

THE STRATEGIC INFORMATION SYSTEMS PLAN

Mission

To develop an information system that will increase the effectiveness and efficiency of the planning and controlling functions of the event center

PRIORITIZATION OF INFORMATION SYSTEMS PROJECTS

A. SCHEDULE OF EVENTS AND TICKETS SYSTEM
1. Integrate the activities and ticketing functions.
2. Provide the activities office with a system for setup and management for each event.
3. Provide the ticket office with a system for issuing tickets and provide the activities office status of sales on demand for each event.

B. FACILITIES MANAGEMENT AND SEATING LAYOUT SYSTEM
1. Provide information to the facilities department necessary to prepare the center for each event.
2. Provide feedback to the activities office about availability of resources and progress reports on facility setup for upcoming events.

C. ADVERTISING AND PRINTING CONTROL SYSTEM
1. Provide information about printing and advertising needs to the advertising department to prepare for each event.
2. Provide feedback to the activities office on the status of advertising and printing efforts.

D. PERSONNEL MANAGEMENT AND SCHEDULING SYSTEM
1. Provide information about required staffing for each event to the personnel department to schedule staff.
2. Provide feedback to the activities office on staffing and scheduling status.

E. PROMOTERS/BOOKING AGENT TRACKING SYSTEM
1. Provide the activities office with the information necessary to contact representatives for events scheduled.
2. Provide the activities office with the information necessary to manage current bookings at the center.

F. ACCOUNTING CONTROL AND TRACKING SYSTEM
1. Provide accounting information to all levels of management in a timely manner.
2. Provide accurate reporting for all financial data to central university financial management division.

G. POTENTIAL EVENTS CATALOG
1. Provide master catalog of types, booking criteria, and other information for all events which may potentially be booked in the future.
2. Provide cost information for all potential future events.

Figure SISP 1.1 The strategic information systems plan for the event center.

by providing more timely, relevant, and accurate information to managers and their staff.

Systems Goals
1. Better communication between the various departments
2. Adequate reporting to each department
3. Central strategic management reporting and decision support

PROJECT REQUEST PRIORITY WORKSHEET

PROJECT NAME	STRATEGIC FACTORS				FEASIBILITY FACTORS					FEASIBILITY FACTORS SCORE
	PROFITS	SERVICE	DECISION MAKING	STRATEGIC FACTORS SCORE	TECHNICAL	ECONOMIC	LEGAL	OPERATIONAL	SCHEDULE	
A Schedule of Events and Tickets System	9	8	7	8	8	8	9	7	9	8.2
B Facilities Management and Seating Layout System	5	6	7	6	6	3	9	7	5	6
C Advertising and Printing Control System	7	4	3	4.7	8	4	6	7	5	6
D Personnel Management and Scheduling System	2	2	2	2	8	8	7	7	9	7.8
E Promoters/ Booking Agent Tracking System	4	5	7	5.3	7	3	9	3	1	4.6
F Accounting Control and Tracking System	8	4	6	6	2	1	7	3	4	3.2
G Potential Events Catalog	1	5	3	3	2	3	2	4	9	4

Profits: Increase Revenue and Decrease Expenses
Service: Provide Organized and Problem-Free Events
Decision Making: Coordination Between Departments

Figure SISP 1.2 The systems project request priority worksheet

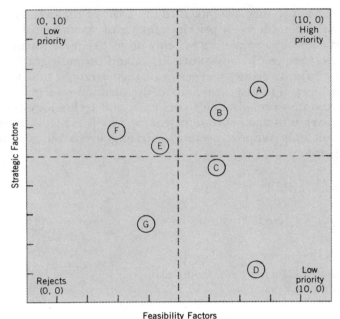

Figure SISP 1.3 The systems project request priority grid for the event center.

4. Accurate and timely control of events
5. Timely reporting of accounting activity
6. Efficient and controlled ticket handling
7. Cost-effective system

SUMMARY

An information systems policy provides a unified outlook and springboard for the information systems planning process. If the philosophy behind the policy is proactive, information systems will be viewed as strategic offensive weapons that give organizations a competitive edge. A proactive systems policy encourages the corporate culture to embrace and nurture the development of information systems that are mission critical, goal congruent, and success directed.

A formal strategic information systems planning methodology is the linchpin in ensuring the development of those systems projects that best reflect the philosophy of the systems policy. SISP is driven by the strategies and goals of the business plan and, in turn, triggers the execution of the systems development methodology for an information systems project. Because information systems have a limited life span, this process of systems planning and development is cyclical.

The first step in SISP is to establish the goals of the information system, making sure they are linked to the goals of the organization. The second step in SISP is to derive a priority ranking of systems project requests. This step is facilitated by completing systems project request forms, by preparing systems project request priority worksheets, and through graphically representing systems priority requests in terms of their strategic and feasibility factors. SISP's third step is to assess the impact the planned information systems projects will have on an organization's personnel and technology resources. The intent of this step is to make sure sufficient capacity is available during the planning cycle to not only support present operating needs but also to accommodate new projects.

IMPORTANT TERMS

critical success factors
proactive systems policy
project request priority grid
strategic information systems planning (SISP)

systems development methodology (SDM)
systems plan
systems project request priority worksheet

Assignment

REVIEW QUESTIONS

15.1 On the one hand, information systems can be developed based on reactions to the environment and set by a budget. What is this systems philosophy called and what is the basic question asked of all systems work? On the other hand, information systems can be developed based on not only their prospects for helping reduce costs, but also because they hold the promise of increasing revenue. What is this systems philosophy called and what is the basic question asked this time of all systems work?

15.2 Explain the relationship that exists among an organization's business plan and policies, its strategic information systems planning process, and the systems development methodology it uses.

15.3 How long is the normal life span of an information system? What design principles and forces can be applied to extend the life span of an information system?

15.4 Three steps are required to develop a strategic information systems plan. List the steps and define each step's goal or purpose.

15.5 What does each dimension of a systems project request priority grid comprise?

15.6 How is a profitability index used in SISP?

15.7 What are the two outputs of the third step of SISP? What does each output show?

QUESTIONS FOR DISCUSSION

15.8 Discuss the importance of a systems plan to any organization.

15.9 Discuss the importance of human resources in developing a systems plan.

15.10 Do you see any conflict in the fact that systems work must be creative and adaptive and at the same time must function through prescribed orderly procedures? Can creative people be systematic?

15.11 Discuss the objectives and priorities of the three-step SISP methodology described in this chapter.

15.12 How can a computer department avoid having to make frequent requests for additional computer capacity? What are the dangers in this strategy? How does the development of a plan for information systems activities affect this problem?

15.13 The approach to information systems planning described in this chapter is evident for large organizations that have substantial investments in information systems technology and people. Discuss whether the same approach to information systems planning is valid and appropriate for small organizations, which have, for example, an investment in technology of less than a million dollars and an information systems staff of less than 20 people?

15.14 Discuss the process by which external strategic information about markets and competitors is incorporated into, and what affects this information might have on the information systems plan.

EXERCISES AND PROBLEMS

15.15 Designing information systems poses a number of difficulties because of basic assumptions that are often built into such systems. Here is a list of assumptions concerning the implementation of management information systems. Critique each statement.

1. *Assumption:* The critical deficiency under which most managers operate is the lack of relevant information.

2. *Assumption:* The manager is the only one who can determine what information is required for decision making.

3. *Assumption:* A manager does not have to understand how the information system works, only how to use it.

15.16 Policies in most companies are simply documents that grant authority or assign responsibility. They must be implemented through documented procedures, which establish in some detail the methods used to implement the policy and specifically assign responsibility within the organizations affected. List some procedures for management information systems.

15.17 A computer-based human resources information system (HRIS) is being proposed for Black Bear Telephone of Oaktree County, Maine. At present all functions of the proposed system are being performed manually. These functions include the processes to identify, hire, and maintain human resource requirements; to evaluate and reward employees; and to enhance professional development. The manual system also supplies payroll data to the financial management information system.

Senior management of Black Bear have dictated the HRIS system must be implemented in segments or subsystems because of the shortage of technical personnel and financial resources within the company. As a planning aid, especially with respect to establishing priorities of segment development, senior management has stated HRIS fits best into the overall goals and objectives of Black Bear Telephone if it achieves the following benefits:

1. Provides management with decision support capabilities to control and manage proactively the human resource assets within their control.

2. Enhances quality and timeliness of employee information, such as attendance and sick leave statistics, for management control.

3. Enables Black Bear Telephone to identify candidates with proper skills and experience levels to fill vacant positions as they arise.

Step 2 of SISP has compartmentalized the processes of HRIS into the following subsystems (projects):

- **Career Planning, Training, and Education.** This subsystem would include the processes of training, educating, and developing skills of job advancement requirements for Black Bear employees. The subsystem's information would be available to all employees for career planning and identify available self-study, inhouse, or outside education to assist in skills enhancement.
- **Compensation and Benefit Planning.** This subsystem would include the processes of evaluating compensation and benefit plans to determine the impact on the organization.
- **Employee Administration.** This subsystem would include collecting and maintaining employee information. This information would include job history, performance history, skills, education, salary history, absences, on-the-job accidents, injuries, and illnesses. Also included in the data base would be the information required by EEOC and Black Bear's labor unions.
- **Payroll.** This subsystem would include the processes of keeping track of hours worked and calculating and distributing payroll checks. These processes involve the accounting for salary and wages, and absences and vacations for the employees.
- **Recruiting.** This subsystem would include the processes necessary for identifying personnel needs and recruiting people from inside and outside Black Bear Telephone. These processes include the ability to develop candidate lists from existing employees and applicants by skills, locations, and availability and to enhance management's capability to fill vacancies and newly created jobs with the person best suited for the position.

> *Required:* Assume each of the benefits stated by senior management has equal importance in terms of evaluating the priority to be attached to the subsystems of HRIS. Construct a project request priority worksheet for these subsystems and prepare a brief narrative that summarizes the reasons for arriving at your overall priority rankings.

BIBLIOGRAPHY

BARRETT, STEPHANIE S. "Strategic Alternatives and Interorganizational System Implementations: An Overview." *Journal of Management Information Systems,* Winter 1986–1987.

CURTICE, ROBERT M. *Strategic Value Analysis.* Englewood Cliffs, N.J.: Prentice Hall, 1987.

DOLL, WILLIAM J. "Avenues for Top Management Involvement in Successful MIS Development." *MIS Quarterly,* March 1985.

EASTLAKE, J. J. *A Structured Approach to Computer Strategy.* New York: John Wiley, 1987.

HENDERSON, JOHN C., JOHN F. ROCKART, and JOHN F. SIFONIS. "Management Support Systems in Strategic IS Planning." *Journal of Management Information Systems,* Summer 1987.

"How MIS Rides Out Business Cycles." *InformationWEEK,* June 20, 1987.

JENSTER, PER V. "Firm Performance and Monitoring of Critical Success Factors in Different Strategic Contexts." *Journal of Management Information Systems,* Winter 1986–1987.

KIRCHGRABER, FRED. "Users and Information Systems: The Odd Couple." *Best's Review,* February 1987.

KIRKLEY, JOHN. "The Restructuring of MIS: Business Strategies Take Hold." *Computerworld,* March 21, 1988.

LONG, LARRY E. *Design and Strategy for Corporate Information Services: MIS Long-Range Planning.* Englewood Cliffs, N.J.: Prentice Hall, 1982.

MEYER, N. DEAN. "A Strategic Tree in the Forest of IS Opportunity." *Information Strategy: The Executive's Journal,* Spring 1988.

PORTER, MICHAEL E., and VICTOR E. MILLAR. "How Information Gives You Competitive Advantage." *Harvard Business Review,* July–August 1985.

SULLIVAN, CORNELIUS H., JR. "Systems Planning in the Information Age." *Sloan Management Review,* Winter 1985.

SYNNOTT, WILLIAM R. *The Information Weapon.* New York: John Wiley, 1987.

VEHKATRAMAN, N. "Research on MIS Planning: Some Guidelines from Strategic Planning Research." *Journal of Management Information Systems,* Winter 1985–1986.

16

SYSTEMS ANALYSIS

16.1 INTRODUCTION

The development of an information system, no matter what its size and complexity, requires many coordinated activities and the use of a variety of tools and models. The systems development methodology (SDM) is a standard way to organize and coordinate these activities. Systems analysts can apply the SDM in any kind of organization regardless of their expertise with respect to the organization's operations.

As discussed in the previous chapter, strategic information systems planning (SISP) should take place first to give the systems analyst direction. During SISP, "W"-questions of "where?" and "ways?" are answered. During systems analysis, the first phase of the SDM, more specific answers to W-questions of "why?" "where?" "who?" "when?" and especially "what?" are ascertained. The evaluation phase answers the other W-question, "which one?" During the general systems design and detailed systems design phases the "H"-question "how?" is answered.

Systems analysis gets at the root of the problem or need and defines users' requirements. Often what users think they need or what the problem appears to be at the outset turns out to be something quite different after a thorough analysis is performed. When the systems analyst gets with the users and both start digging, new and sometimes different requirements will emerge that were not necessarily evident early on. And, as often as not, additional system opportunities become obvious.

How much time should be spent on systems analysis? Some say as little as 10 percent of the total SDM time. Others say as much as 40 percent or more. Still others believe that "too much time" spent on systems analysis results in "analysis paralysis" in which the victim cannot move from the systems analysis

FOLLOWING THE SDM FOR SUCCESS

The first and foremost consequence of development without methodology is failure. It may come at once: The project may miss its deadline, overrun its budget and destroy the careers of its participants. But it may also come slowly, lying dormant in the nerve centers of an application and then inexorably eating away at it.

Second, these systems tend to neglect the human interface. In the absence of a methodology, design is left to analysts and programmers who, understandably, tend to equate a system with its collection of jobs, programs and files.

Furthermore, without a methodological framework, even the automated side of a system is often not viewed as an organic whole. Any documentation above the program level is either perfunctory or nonexistent. The overall impact of changes to one piece of the system cannot be assessed or communicated clearly. The risk here is that the next ostensibly isolated last-minute, must-have modification will result in collapse of the application.

Methodologies also possess a good logical inventory of proven work steps, described in terms of phases, activities and tasks. In a methodology, we know what to do. And if we are late, at least we can retrace our steps to determine why.

All in all, a methodology provides a positive, even somewhat instructive, step away from anarchy. It reduces the risk of project failure by virtue of its work breakdown structure, required documentation and management checkpoints and reviews. Through its discipline, a methodology improves the chances of a system being implemented correctly the first time and surviving any changes. Many systems projects would be a lot better off under the direction of a successful Broadway choreographer than a methodless, confused DP designer.

Excerpted from Fred Viskovich, "From Anarchy to Architecture," *Computerworld*, April 25, 1988, pp. 73–77.

phase into the other SDM phases because of uncertainty. But certainty is a luxury that systems analysts can seldom afford. In any move from one phase to another, some degree of uncertainty will always be present.

All systems professionals agree that the other phases rest on what is established in the systems analysis phase. It helps ensure that the information system that is built is the right system. Therefore, one could say that systems analysis is the most important phase. In any event, the basis for an information system that users will be happy with is good, complete systems analysis.

The specific objectives of this chapter are:

1. To discuss preliminary systems analysis.

2. To present the NSU Tigers Event Center Proposal to Conduct Systems Analysis Report.
3. To explain the sources of study facts for systems analysis.
4. To describe techniques for gathering study facts.
5. To inquire into the concluding of systems analysis.
6. To illustrate the NSU Tigers Events Center Systems Analysis Completion Report.

16.2 PRELIMINARY SYSTEMS ANALYSIS

After a systems project is initiated, the systems analyst tries to define its scope and to develop a keen focus on user requirements. The documented deliverable from this preliminary analysis is the Proposal to Conduct Systems Analysis Report. This document demonstrates that a meeting of the minds between the systems analyst and users has been achieved.

Reasons for Initiating Systems Analysis

Systems analysts must have an understanding of why systems work is to be done in the first place. The basic reasons for initiating systems analysis are as follows:

1. *Strategic Information Systems Improvement.* Ideally, new systems work is started to develop a strategic information system that not only performs transaction processing and other operations but also fits the organization's strategy and supports the organization's goals. Strategic information systems improvement entails increased productivity, enhanced product and service differentiation, improved management performance, cost reduction, and faster and more complete reporting. The initiator of strategic information systems improvement is the systems plan. The main component of the systems plan is a portfolio of priority systems projects to be developed over the planning horizon as explained in the previous chapter.

2. *New Requirement.* A new requirement or regulation means that systems work has to be done to meet such requirements. Examples may include new tax laws, accounting procedures, and payroll provisions.

3. *Implementation of New Idea or Technology.* The systems analyst may perform systems work to determine if a new way of doing things or a new piece of technology can enhance performance or reduce costs. For example, the systems analyst may investigate the use of bar codes for inventory control.

4. *Unplanned Problem Solving and Maintenance.* In companies that do not use SISP, systems work starts with a need to be fulfilled, a malfunction that needs correcting, or a problem that needs solving. Usually, a high degree of urgency is connected to all these endeavors because information systems plans are not developed that would anticipate and help coordinate systems projects. In such an environment, maintenance takes a large part of the systems budget as more and more new projects are backlogged.

Requesting Systems Analysis

The systems plan contains a portfolio of systems project requests. These requests are very general and are used primarily to establish systems project priorities and give general direction for the information systems effort over a planning horizon of three to five years.

What the systems analyst needs at the beginning of systems analysis, however, is something a little more specific. Therefore, no matter what the reason for initiating systems analysis is, all systems projects should start with an information systems service request form similar to the one illustrated in Figure 16.1.

This request form not only gives information about the systems project and its objectives but also anticipated benefits. It also serves as something of a

INFORMATION SYSTEMS SERVICE REQUEST

SYSTEMS NAME: _____ ☐ NEW   REQUESTED DATE: _____
                                ☐ REVISED   REQUIRED DATE: _____

ANTICIPATED BENEFITS: _____

_____

_____

            OUTPUT   **INPUT**

REQUESTED BY: _____ DEPARTMENT: _____ TITLE: _____

 APPROVED BY: _____ DEPARTMENT: _____ TITLE: _____

☐ APPROVED

☐ APPROVED ON CONDITION. REASON: _____

☐ REJECTED. REASON: _____

SIGNATURE: _____ DEPARTMENT: _____

                          TITLE: _____

                          DATE: _____

COMMENTS: _____

_____

Figure 16.1 An information systems service request form.

contract or agreement between the prospective user and the systems analyst. Also, it establishes a base for user participation throughout the SDM cycle.

In many instances, users and systems analysts work together to complete the information systems service request form. Typically, the user has fairly definite ideas about the output required, the necessary inputs, and possibly a general notion of controls needed. The systems analyst can interact with the user to refine, add to, and synthesize these ideas. It is not expected, however, that all details of the systems project are answered at this point. Clearly, gaps are closed, and some changes occur during systems analysis. Indeed, in some instances, changes occur well into the general systems design phase or beyond. Moreover, anticipated benefits may never materialize or benefits may prove to be greater than those anticipated earlier. Nevertheless, the information systems service request form provides a clear starting point, thus eliminating several false starts, which is the main thing to avoid at this stage.

Incidentally, the systems project should be given a short, catchy name or acronym. A name personalizes the project and makes reference to it easier. Moreover, it has been found that if prospective users name the systems project it then becomes their system. For example, a new standard costing system may be called SCATS (standard cost accounting transaction system). COPS may stand for computer organizer and production scheduler.

Defining the Scope of Systems Analysis

Just what should be the scope of the new systems project? A systems analyst who apparently has a lot of experience trying to answer this question, made the following observation.

> Building a system is a lot like carving the statue of an elephant. You get a big block of marble and cut away everything that doesn't look like an elephant. The problem with most systems is that people want to put a howdah on the elephant's back and a maharajah in it and before you know it eighty percent of the effort is going into designing the rings on the maharajah's left hand.[1]

The activities and events comprising systems analysis are for the most part directed toward answering the question: "What is the new system to include?" In many cases this question can be more accurately phrased as: "What more is the existing system to include?" In answering these general questions, the analyst must address many specific questions. What information is needed? by whom? when? where? in what form? where does it originate? when? and how can it be collected?

Moreover, the scope of sytems analysis can vary widely in terms of duration, complexity, and expense. Consequently, the scope must be defined somewhat arbitrarily at times to meet constraints such as time and cost. The primary problem for both the novice analyst and the skilled professional is converting unconsciously an instruction such as "I want to know what yesterday's sales were by 8:00 A.M. today," into "Develop a new sales reporting system."

---

[1]Quoted from John Boddie, *Crunch Mode* (Englewood Cliffs, N.J.: Prentice Hall, 1987), p. 15.

Often, in practice, an analyst who fails to define the scope of systems analysis properly either fails to achieve objectives or achieves them at a great loss of both time and money. It must be understood, however, that the presence of limiting objectives (or constraints) on the scope of the analysis, limits the potential solutions or the recommendations that result from the analysis. As a rule, the initial definition of purpose and scope, as well as any given objectives and constraints, are subject to redefinition at a later date, based on findings in the analysis.

Focus of Systems Analysis

One of the most damaging temptations involved in systems analysis is to think in terms of computers and to emphasize the technology building block first. The primary focus during systems analysis should be on business operations, users' requirements, and the input, output, data base, and controls building blocks— not on computers, not on magnetic tape or disk, not on telecommunications, and not on software. One of the biggest mistakes repeated over and over again in "systems work" is capsulized as follows: "Let's get the computer; then we'll see if some software exists to run it on; and after that, we'll see how we're going to use it." It's putting socks over shoes and it seems ludicrous, but some organizations do it all the time. A large government installation, for example, purchases new equipment every three years. Their system, however, seems to be getting less productive and has a new development backlog measured in years. Time as measured in three-year intervals becomes the controlling factor.

RANGE OF USERS' REQUIREMENTS In the early stage of development, the cost of meeting a specification cannot be estimated with great accuracy. Furthermore, users—who presumably should play the dominant role in setting functional specifications—generally harbor only a vague notion of how much it costs to satisfy a specification; their forte is to deal with the *value* side of the equation. Users should therefore provide a *range* of needs, along with some indication of the relative value of meeting them.

One method of eliciting such information is to invite users to specify each of their needs in terms of three categories:

- ***Must Do.*** A rock-bottom need required to carry out the essential functions of the business.
- ***Should Do.*** A need that the user judges both desirable and feasible, but is willing to negotiate in striking the best balance between the value and cost.
- ***Nice to Do.*** A "frill" that the user regards as desirable from a business standpoint, but not necessarily justifiable in terms of the cost of attaining it.

Condensed from James C. Emery, *Management Information Systems: The Critical Strategic Resource* (New York: Oxford University Press, 1987), p. 145.

The aim of both users and systems analysts during systems analysis is a meeting of the minds to establish what is really needed to do the work and what the system can give them. Clearly, an architect would not design a bridge or building before thoroughly understanding the requirements of those who will use them and before conducting a thorough study of the environment in which they will operate and the laws and regulations with which they must comply.

Concluding Preliminary Systems Analysis

Once the systems analyst completes the initial interviews and determines that systems analysis should be conducted, an understanding of what must be accomplished and the general approach toward this goal must be communicated formally to both the requestor and the systems analyst's own management. This communication is termed the Proposal to Conduct Systems Analysis Report. It provides a checkpoint at which the requestor can evaluate whether or not the analyst clearly understands what is desired, and it gives the analyst's management an opportunity to evaluate the approach and amount of resources to be used during the analysis.

The report should facilitate an initial in-depth understanding, as well as provide reference points that can be accessed when actual performance of the analysis can be periodically reported. It should include the following:

1. A clear, concise definition of the reasons for conducting the analysis.
2. A specific statement concerning the performance requirements of the proposed system.
3. A definition of the scope of the analysis.
4. An identification of the facts that will likely need to be collected during the analysis.
5. An identification of the potential sources where the facts can be obtained.
6. A schedule listing the major events or milestones of the analysis.

THE NSU TIGERS EVENT CENTER
Preparing the Proposal to Conduct Systems Analysis Report

PROCEEDING TO SYSTEMS DEVELOPMENT

The accounting staff, with guidance from Ball and Topps, prepared a cost estimate of $800,000 to support the strategic information systems plan. John Ball then requested this amount to support the total systems effort. Knowing the urgency of this request, the Board of Trustees immediately allocated $650,000, less than what was requested, but possibly enough to complete some of the higher-priority projects over the next year.

John Ball was elated, and quickly contacted his department heads and Topps to tell them the good news. The budget of $650,000 makes a good portion of the plan economically feasible.

Then Mr. Ball gave a general directive for systems work to begin immediately starting with the schedule of events and ticket system, and within two weeks, projects B, C, and D. Mr. Ball also had a meeting with Ms. Trixy Stub, scheduling and ticket department head. She was told to "start getting your people together with the systems people beginning first thing in the morning."

REQUESTING SYSTEMS ANALYSIS

Ms. Trixy Stub called Tyronne Topps and told him, "Well, it looks like we're ready to get started on my scheduling and ticketing system."

"Yes, I heard," Tyronne said. "What I'm going to do is have you get with Sally Forth, our chief systems analyst. She'll be able to get us off to a good start. Why don't I transfer you to her office?"

"OK, thanks."

"Hello, Sally Forth speaking."

"Oh, yes. Hi, I'm Trixy Stub, head of scheduling and ticket sales at the event center. Mr. Topps told me that you are going to do our systems work. Happy to have you aboard."

"Thanks. I'm looking forward to working with you," Sally responded. "Actually, Tommy Tune, one of our systems analysts is prepared to get with you this morning and prepare an information systems service request."

"Oh, I've already filled out one of those forms," said Trixy. "You know, the one we did for planning."

"No, that's a systems project request form that you guys use for your own strategic planning and for budgeting," responded Sally. "The information systems service request form that you fill out for us is just that, a request from you for our service. It's a little more specific than what you did earlier, and it gives us a starting point and serves as an agreement, if you will, between our users and the information systems group. It's a 'meeting of the minds,' so to speak."

"Another form?" complained Trixy. "I don't know anything about it or how to fill it out. And we just started using the systems project request form."

"Well, you know us, we couldn't operate without forms," laughed Sally. "Don't worry, Tommy Tune will help you fill it out. Then we can get started."

"Thanks, that will help me a lot," sighed Trixy, relieved that she was going to receive help.

"By the way," Sally said, "As soon as my staff and I go over your information systems service request, we will start mapping out our work. One thing we will need to do at the start, I'm sure, will involve a great deal of interviewing of you and your people. Will you please make them available to us starting Tuesday at 8:00?"

"We're ready," exclaimed Trixy.

"Fine. I'll see you Tuesday morning," Sally responded.

"Good-bye."

"Bye."

PREPARATION OF THE INFORMATION SYSTEMS
SERVICE REQUEST FORM

Shortly after 10:30 that morning, Tommy picked up his briefcase and went to Trixy's office.

"Hi, I'm Tommy Tune, one of the systems analysts from Administrative Computing. I guess Sally Forth told you that I was coming to see you," said Tommy.

"Oh yes, pleased to meet you," said Trixy. "I was on the phone with Sally a little earlier this morning, and she told me that you were coming."

"Great!" replied Tommy. "If you're ready, we'll get started."

"Well," responded Trixy, "I've never been involved in a complete information systems overhaul as we're doing here. Where do I begin?"

"What would be helpful," Tommy explained, "is if you could start by telling me some of your basic and common problems."

"To begin with," Trixy stated, "we are having trouble with our seating system. There are times when the same seat is sold to at least two different people. All of us in this department feel that once is once too often, and we try to do our best to keep the public happy. But this is now a common problem."

"So, you are having a ticket sales problem," said Tommy.

"A problem?" exclaimed Trixy. "It's becoming a catastrophe! Some of our ushers came back with reports from several people recently that this was the worst event center they had ever been to. Another thing, I've had five people in the last month personally call me up and tell me that they were sold tickets for the wrong event! I looked into the matter, and sure enough, they were sold tickets for the wrong event."

"Oh wow!" remarked Tommy. "I can see exactly what you mean. That would be enough to make practically anyone want to throw in the towel. You *are* having big problems with your scheduling of events and ticket system. Why don't we call the first project Schedule of Events and Ticketing System (SEATS)."

"Sounds good to me," said Trixy. "SEATS . . . I like it."

"Why don't we get started on the information systems service request form?" prodded Tommy.

"OK, I'm ready. What do you need to know first?"

Tommy and Trixy spent over an hour filling out the information systems service request form. It is displayed in Figure SEATS–SA 1.1.

PREPARATION AND PRESENTATION OF THE PROPOSAL TO CONDUCT SYSTEMS ANALYSIS REPORT

After going over the information systems service request form prepared by Trixy and Tommy, Sally talked with Trixy and some of her staff to get a better feel for the problems, reasons for the request, and scope of the project. She and Tommy worked together to define the systems project scope, to determine the study facts they would need to collect, and the sources of these facts. A schedule of major events was also prepared.

Sally and Tommy worked late to prepare the Proposal to Conduct Systems Analysis Report. Sally knew from earlier bad experiences that typically one type of prospective systems users don't know exactly what they need, and the other type expects everything to be computerized on a personal computer immediately.

Sally knew that if you try to leapfrog several phases of the SDM, you nearly always wind up with a system nobody wants or needs. As a matter of fact, following the lead of typical users, and in essence letting them guide systems development, is similar to a doctor allowing a patient to guide surgical procedures or prescribe medicine.

So, to make sure that everybody is still "on the same page" and wavelength, the Proposal to Conduct Systems Analysis Report, the first major documented deliverable of the SDM, was presented both orally and by a written document. Everyone pretty much agreed that the systems work was still on track.

INFORMATION SYSTEMS SERVICE REQUEST

SYSTEM NAME: Schedule of events and ___X___ NEW
            ticketing system (SEATS) ___ REVISED

REQUESTED DATE: MM/DD/YY
REQUIRED DATE: MM/DD/YY

ANTICIPATED BENEFITS:
- Schedule with more accuracy and control ticketing for events for center
- Control the issuing and reserving of tickets
- Account for and control ticket revenue

OUTPUT

1. TITLE: Event Schedule Report
   FREQUENCY: Weekly Quantity: 4 Copies
   COMMENT: Lists name of event, cost, date, and duration ticketing status. Also ability to make online inquires about the same items should be provided.

2. TITLE: Reservation Status and Ticket Control Report
   FREQUENCY: Weekly Quantity: 4 Copies
   COMMENT: Lists reservation by name and event, tickets logged by number, tickets issued, and receipts. Online inquires about same items should be provided.

3. TITLE: Profit and Loss Report
   FREQUENCY: Weekly Quantity: 4 Copies
   COMMENT: Lists revenue or expense item by event, data, and type of revenue or expense incurred.

4. TITLE: Resources Inventory Listing
   FREQUENCY: Weekly Quantity: 4 Copies
   COMMENT: Lists available resources such as chairs, tables, lighting, staging products.

INPUT

1. TITLE: Event Input
   FREQUENCY: Random Quantity: 200 per year
   COMMENT: Includes seating requirements for event, beginning date, ending date, and special accommodations.

2. TITLE: Ticket Sales
   FREQUENCY: Random Quantity: Thousands per week
   COMMENT: Reservation form should include name of patron, number of reservations, event name, and date. Ticket transaction log should contain ticket number, date, and price.

3. TITLE: Event Revenue and Expense Input
   FREQUENCY: Random Quantity: 200 per year
   COMMENT: Includes all expenses incurred for event, date for expense, and amount and type of expense.

4. TITLE: Resources Add/ Change/ Delete
   FREQUENCY: Random Quantity: As needed
   COMMENT: Input all equipment in stock at the center including tables, chairs, lighting and staging products for inventory.

REQUESTED BY: John Ball   DEPARTMENT: Event Center   TITLE: Director
APPROVED BY: Paul Smith   DEPARTMENT: Administration   TITLE: VP of Affairs

___X___ APPROVED

___ APPROVED ON CONDITION. REASON: _____

___ REJECTED. REASON: _____

___ SIGNATURE: _____   DEPARTMENT: Information Systems
                                                  TITLE: Chief Information Systems Officer
                                                  DATE: DD/MM/YY

COMMENTS: Sally Forth is the chief systems analyst and her assistant is Tommy Tune. Systems analysis begins next Monday. The systems analysis phase will take approximately two weeks. Please notify employees at the event center to make themselves available for Sally and Tommy to interview. Full cooperation will expedite the systems analysts work and help to ensure a successful systems project.

Figure SEATS–SA 1.1 Information systems service request form for SEATS.

PROPOSAL TO CONDUCT SYSTEMS ANALYSIS REPORT

March 10, 19xx

TO: All Department Heads
FROM: Sally Forth, Chief Systems Analyst
SUBJECT: Schedule of Events and Ticketing System (SEATS)
COPIES: John Ball, Event Center Director and Tyronne Topps, CISO

Reasons for the Analysis

The recent expansion of the event center has increased the frequency of events, which has, in turn, added to the complexity of hosting them. The current manual information system is not meeting the information needs of those responsible for implementing the event center's business plan.

Performance Requirements of the System

The strategic information systems plan previously completed provides the basis for establishing the following users' requirements for the information system:

1. To increase organization integration.
2. To improve organization communication.
3. To provide more timely reporting.
4. To improve the quality of service to the community.
5. To reduce expenses.
6. To increase revenues.

Scope of Systems Analysis

The sytems analysis work will determine the feasibility and direction(s) of the information needs as outlined in the systems plan and the information systems service request form. The findings of systems analysis will be included in the Systems Analysis Completion Report. We will be responsible for the delivery of this report within two weeks from beginning of the analysis. Responsibility for general systems design will be determined at the end of this systems analysis phase. We solicit your support for this effort because it is critical to undertake such a development if we are to improve our current management situation.

Facts to Be Collected

To develop a complete picture of the proposed system, several details must be investigated further:

1. The sequence of steps and time required for each step in the process of hosting an event (Gantt or PERT chart).

2. Identify potential bottlenecks and a critical path for each type of event.
3. Determine the feasibility of integration of information between departments.
4. Determine the type of reports needed by each department and management for each type of event.
5. Identify problems that exist in the current system.
6. Collect possible solutions from users.
7. Determine the feasibility of computerization as the solution.
8. Determine the opportunities and problems associated with each alternative system.
9. Determine the feasibility of in-house development.
10. Determine the impact on the event center's culture.
11. Determine the timetable for development and implementation.

Potential Sources of the Facts

The current organization should be investigated first to provide baseline information necessary for identifying any proposed enhancements. This falls into several specific categories:

1. **The Present Information System** The event center currently has separate systems within each department. All are manual systems with the exception of accounting. We propose to evaluate the effectiveness of the present system to determine whether a new system should be developed or whether the current system should be modified. An analysis of the old system will provide a starting point for any new development and provide design ideas. Understanding the current system enables us to evaluate the resources necessary for modifying the current system or developing a new one. Familiarity with the current system will help in planning for the conversion to a new system.

2. **Management and Employees of the Event Center** The use of questionnaires, interviews, and informal discussions with the stakeholders of the event center allows us to develop an understanding of the needs of the users and how the current system operates.

3. **Current Paper Documentation** Accounting procedure manuals, financial statements, management policies, organizational charts, job descriptions, and other forms of paper evidence will be reviewed to determine how the organization is operating and how it plans to operate. Current paper documentation will be used to reinforce the definition of relationships between the various departments of the event center, interdepartmental functions, and people within the departments.

4. Contact with Other Event Centers Event centers with similar characteristics will be contacted to determine the type of system they use. This will allow us to document the types of problems which might be encountered with alternative systems. It will also enable us to gain an understanding of alternative solutions available.

Schedule of Major Events or Milestones

The systems analysis will be undertaken as a series of tasks, each of which will have a specific scope and completion date:

1. Review of the current system, interviews with people and review of documentation will take approximately one person two weeks to complete and will be performed by Sally Forth. (80 person-hours)
2. Contacting other event centers will take approximately one person one week to complete and will be performed by Tommy Tune (40 person-hours) concurrent with task 1.
3. Analysis of facts, determination of feasibility, definition of user requirements and direction will take two people approximately two weeks to complete and be performed by both analysts (80 person-hours) after completion of tasks 1 and 2.
4. Study facts synthesis and the Systems Analysis Completion Report will take two weeks to complete by both analysts (80 person-hours) after completion of task 3.

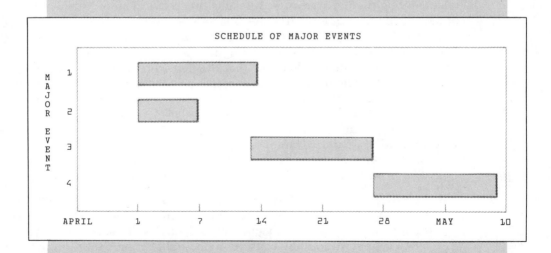

Based on our discussions in the past few weeks, I feel that we must give serious consideration to beginning this analysis for SEATS as soon as possible. Ideally, we should begin our analysis within the next two weeks so that we can have answers to the requirements issues prior to our next fiscal budgeting session, which will start in early May.

16.3 SOURCES OF STUDY FACTS FOR SYSTEMS ANALYSIS

In this section we discuss the various sources of study facts in and around the organization that are available to the analyst during systems analysis. Three categories of study facts are (1) the existing system, (2) other internal sources, and (3) external sources.

Studying the Existing System

It is rare indeed when an analyst is provided with an opportunity to develop an information system where one did not exist before. In most cases a system or subsystem exists that serves the organization. As a result, the analyst is confronted with decisions such as: What role does the old system have with respect to the new system? Should I analyze the old system? If so, what subsystems in the old system should I analyze?

Often a great deal of time and money is spent investigating, analyzing, and documenting the old system, with results that seem to be of little benefit in the design of the new system. It is not uncommon to have experienced managers comment, "We spent $20,000 studying the old system only to have them tell us that we were correct in asking for a new system." At the other end of the spectrum, some state emphatically that the first step in all systems studies is to analyze the old system. Again, many managers who have experienced new systems conversions comment, "I will never consent to implementing another new system before I have analyzed thoroughly my present system."

Although it may be impossible to reconcile fully these two extreme positions, an examination of the advantages and disadvantages will shed some light on when and to what extent the old system should be studied.

The primary advantages of analyzing the old system are as follows:

1. *Effectiveness of Present System.*   Studying the old sytem provides an opportunity to determine whether that system is satisfactory, is in need of minor repair, requires a major overhaul, or should be replaced. To design a new system without this consideration might be comparable to purchasing a new car without knowing if your present car may only be out of gas.

2. *Design Ideas.*   Analyzing the old system can provide the analyst with an immediate source of design ideas. These ideas include what is presently being done and how, as well as what additional needs or capabilities have

been requested over the years. The analyst is able to gain insight into how the present information system serves the decision-making function as well as to ascertain key relationships.

3. *Resource Recognition.*   Examining the present system allows the analyst to identify the resources available for the new system or subsystem. These resources might include the management talent, the clerical talent, and the equipment currently owned and operational.

4. *Conversion Knowledge.*   When the new system is implemented, the analyst is responsible for having previously identified what tasks and activities will be nescessary to phase out the old system and begin operating the new system. To identify these conversion requirements, the analyst must know not only what activities will be performed, but also what activities were performed. Studying the present system gives the analyst the "what was" answer.

5. *Common Starting Point.*   When communicating with management, the systems analyst is an agent of change. As such, the analyst will often be confronted with resistance to new techniques, ideas, and methods, lack of understanding of new concepts, procrastination in obtaining decisions, lack of commitment to making the new system work, and other similar manifestations of people being asked to change familiar activities. To minimize these reactions, the analyst can compare and contrast the new system with the old system and demonstrate that it is not entirely new.

The primary disadvantages of analyzing the old system are as follows:

1. *Expense.*   Studying the old system requires time, and in all organizations time can be converted to money. As one executive asked, "Why spend months analyzing and modeling the system that's going to be thrown away?"

2. *Unnecessary Barriers.*   An extensive analysis of an existing system can result in unnecessary barriers or artificial constraints being included in the design of the new system. For example, in the existing system, in a given department, there may be a document flow and a series of actions taken with that document. The analyst can become so involved with improving those actions that the involvment of the department in the first place is left unquestioned. The more familiar an analyst becomes with a given system, the more likely it is that some perspective or objectivity concerning it will be lost. One may argue logically that an *ideal systems concept* should be used in performing systems work. That is, the analyst formulates an ideal system and then proceeds with his or her systems work using this ideal systems framework.

Internal Sources

The single most important source of study facts available to the analyst is *people*. This includes not only the formal management, but the clerical and production workers as well. Information requirements can best be stated by users of the information. The analyst, however, can help users define their requirements by

Documents Describing How the Organization Is Organized	Documents Describing What the Organization Plans to Do	Documents Describing What the Organization Does
Policy statements	Statement of goals and objectives	Financial statements
Methods and procedure manuals	Budgets	Performance reports
Organization charts	Schedules	Staff studies
Job descriptions	Forecasts	Historical reports
Performance standards	Plans (long and short range)	Transaction files
Delegations of authority	Corporate minutes	(including: purchase orders, customer orders, invoices, time sheets, expense records, customer correspondence)
Chart of accounts		Legal papers
(All other coding structure references)		(including: copyrights, patents, franchises, trademarks, judgments)
		Master reference files
		(including: customers, employees, products, vendors)

Figure 16.2 The various types of documents available to the analyst in an organization from which information may be obtained pertaining to systems analysis.

explaining to them what can be provided. It is important to note that most individuals are guided in formulating their needs by arbitrary and often antiquated notions of what they "think" can be provided. The analyst's function, then, is to remove or expand these attitudes so that the real information requirements can be obtained.

A secondary source of study facts for the analyst comes from the existing *paperwork* within the organization. The paperwork in most organizations can be classified as that which describes how the organization is structured, what the organization is or has been doing, and what the organization plans to do. In Figure 16.2 a partial list, by types, has been provided of some of the documents found in organizations.

A word of caution is in order when organizational documents are used as sources of study facts in systems analysis. The documents identified as describing how an organization is structured, and what it plans to do, *do not* necessarily reflect reality. At best, these documents serve to give the analyst an understanding

	New Products	New Markets	Training	Salary and Commission
President	A			A
Vice-President Marketing	A	A		A
General Manager Sales	C	A	A	AP
Regional Manager Sales	C	P	AP	C
Manager Product Planning	PC	P		
Vice-President Personnel				A
Manager Supply and Transportation	O	O		
Manager Product Engineering	APC			
Manager Manufacturing	O			
Salespeople	O	O	PO	
Manager Research and Development	P			
Controller				PC
Manager Information Systems	O	O	O	PO

Figure 16.3 A linear organization chart of some of the marketing functions.
Legend: A = approval, C = control, P = planning, O = operation.

of what management considered its structure and direction to be at one point. It is not uncommon for organizations and plans to change while their documentation remains unchanged.

A third source of study facts important to the analyst can be termed *relationships*. Defining the relationships between people, departments, or functions can provide the analyst with information and insights not formerly known or documented anywhere within the organization.

To depict aspects of shared responsibility or interfunctional relationships, the analyst can develop what is termed a linear organization chart (LOC). Figure 16.3 illustrates a linear organization chart reflecting various marketing functions in a medium-sized corporation.

In our example, the activity pertaining to the development and usage of a new product line is a multifunctional responsibility. The president, the vice-president of marketing, and the manager of production engineering, all share in the approval process. Planning is the responsibility of the manager of research and development, the manager of product planning, and the manager of product engineering. Control is exercised by the general manager of sales, the manager of product planning, and the various regional sales managers. Operations responsibility is shared by various levels of marketing personnel in addition to supply and transportation, and manufacturing.

External Sources

The systems analyst's work can take him or her outside the boundaries of the segment of the organization for which the analysis is being conducted. Exploring other information subsystems within the organization can be a useful source of data collection, data processing, or information reporting ideas and techniques. Moreover, reviewing other systems provides an opportunity to identify potential interface points when the analyst is involved in a limited or subsystem analysis.

Just as meaningful, though often overlooked, is a review of similar information systems in other organizations. Not only can this be a source of new ideas but it can provide the analyst with an opportunity to actually see systems, subsystems, concepts, techniques, and mechanisms in operation. Many organizations zealously guard manufacturing and marketing techniques, but information processing exchanges are common. In fact, many societies and organizations exist whose sole purpose is the exchange of information and data processing experiences, both good and bad.

If systems analysts do not have a deep understanding of the company's operations and "folklore" of the users, then systems analysts can probably relate what they do understand about the present systems project to another familiar application. Really, the range of systems applications is not quite as broad as some people might think. Building a reservation system for a hotel has similarities to a reservation system for an airline or a patient accounting system for a hospital. Handling bets at a racetrack is not entirely unlike using automatic teller machines. Inventory control works pretty much the same whether one is talking about items on shelves, houses on streets, or rooms in a building. To realtors, the houses and property they have for sale is their inventory. To hostelers, rooms in hotels are their inventory. If analysts relate differences and similarities of a system they do know to one that they do not know very well, they will increase significantly their ability to figure out what is really required.

Textbooks and professional journals provide still another source of study facts for the analyst. Studying this material may entail reviewing known theory and practice or searching for new ideas, theories, and proposals. Similarly, the analyst can profit from attendance at professional seminars, workshops, and conferences held throughout the country.

Sales brochures from equipment and computer software vendors are an excellent source of concepts and ideas. When we consider that products and services are developed and marketed to satisfy needs, it follows that the brochures and proposals of the vendors offering the products define the needs they propose to satisfy.

The sources of study facts available to an analyst during systems analysis are varied and plentiful. What sources are exploited will differ from analysis to analysis as time and cost constraints are considered. The size and complexity of the system or subsystem under study will also help to determine which sources are utilized. Common sense is often the most compelling factor determining what sources of study facts the analyst actually selects. It is important, however, to recognize what the overall choice of sources can be.

16.4 TECHNIQUES FOR GATHERING STUDY FACTS

In the analysis phase of the information system's development process the systems analyst relies on specific techniques for gathering study facts. Like any good craftsperson, some analysts rely more heavily on one technique to serve them. In most systems endeavors, however, the systems analyst requires many forms of assistance.

The techniques presented in this section do not represent an exhaustive list of what is available or what is used. This section does, however, identify the major techniques used by systems analysts.

The Interview

In many instances, the best way to obtain critical study facts is to conduct a series of interviews. In general, questions such as "Does this report give you what you need?" and "How could this be done better?" allow respondents to contribute to the analysis. Other questions that elicit the basis for further systems work are "What is your job?" or "What is the objective of your job?" or "What information are you getting now to help you meet these objectives?" or "What additional information do you need?"

It is important that the systems analyst make sure that each respondent understands the ultimate objective of systems work is to make the new system more useful. Eliciting meaningful and helpful facts from respondents is a function of a positive attitude by all participants. It is also important that systems analysts actively *listen* to respondents. Subtle overtones and nuances by respondents can be as significant as their direct responses to questions. Ultimately, because the final system developed will, to a great extent, rest on facts supplied by people, it will be no better than the facts on which it was based.

SYSTEMS WORK MUST BE PEOPLE-ORIENTED

By identifying the desired "deskside manner" by successful information systems analysts, efforts may be taken to improve their performance. People-oriented skills, combined with personal practices and technical competencies, must be employed.

Ten people-oriented characteristics identified in order of importance were:

1. Works well with others
2. Compromises
3. Communicates well with others
4. Thinks, reasons and creates order
5. Functions with objectivity
6. Is considered technically competent
7. Possesses high personal ethical standards
8. Views a situation as a system
9. Motivates and develops others
10. Manifests patience

Summarized from Paul D. Maxwell, "Developing a Successful 'Deskside' Manner for Systems Analysts." *Journal of Systems Management*, April 1988, pp. 6–9.

Within an organization, interviewing is the most significant and productive fact-finding technique available to the analyst. Simply stated, the interview is a face-to-face exchange of information. It is a communication channel between the analyst and the organization. Interviewing is used to gain information concerning what is required and how these requirements can be met. The interview can be used to gain support or understanding from the user for a new idea or method. Moreover, the interview provides an excellent opportunity for the analyst to establish rapport with user personnel.

Interviewing is conducted at all levels within the organization, from the president or chief operating officer to the mail clerk or the maintenance engineer. Consequently, the interview proceedings can vary from highly formal to somewhat casual. Even the location where interviewing is conducted is subject to wide variation (e.g., the plant operating floor or an executive suite). Interviewing success is dependent on how well the analyst is able to adjust to these environmental variables.

Preparing to Interview

Before beginning the interview, the systems analyst should confer with and obtain cooperation from all department managers to be included in the systems project. The analyst should fully explain to the department managers the scope and nature of the analysis and stress that its scope may be subject to change upon further investigation.

We believe that several of the following points are helpful in preparing an interview and obtaining the necessary cooperation and support:

1. Arrange for an appointment ahead of time. Do not just "drop in."
2. Identify the interviewee's position within the organization and job responsibilities and activities. Set up the interview at a time that is convenient to the interviewee and when he or she will not be distracted by interruptions.
3. The primary aim of the interview is to gather study facts. Therefore, prepare an outline of the forthcoming interview, along with pertinent questions. If appropriate, forward a copy of the questions to the interviewee. Do not go into an interview and try to "play it by ear." Figure 16.4 illustrates an example of an interview form.

INTERVIEW FORM

Person interviewed: _____Clifton Shultz_____ Title: _____Sales Manager_____

Topic: _____Customer Service System (CUSS)_____

Interviewed by: _____Jennifer Masters_____ Title: _____Systems Analyst_____

Date: DD/MM/YY Start Time: 9:30 AM Time allocated: 1 hour Place: Room 204

1. How many customer complaints are processed per week?

2. Procedures now used to record, track, evaluate, and respond to complaints?

3. What tasks do you now perform?

4. What tasks will you perform after the new system is installed?

5. What information do you need to perform these tasks?

6. Why is the present system inadequate?

Figure 16.4 An interview form.

Conducting the Interview

In conducting the interview, the systems analyst should behave in a manner, and ask questions, that will get the required study facts in as little time as possible. The analyst should not take the position of a "know-it-all" or an interrogator. Before going into the interview, the analyst should have a fair understanding of the duties and responsibilities of the interviewee, along with the individual's working and personal relationships with others in the organization. Additionally, the analyst should have some awareness of the kinds of answers the analyst is looking for and will probably receive. Much of this information comes from other interviews with higher-level management, which assumes a top-down approach.

Some points that will be helpful in conducting an interview are as follows:

1. Explain who you are, what the purpose of the interview is, what the systems project is about, and what contribution the interviewee will make in the development of a new system. A typical question for clarification subsequent to this introduction is, "At this point, would you like to know anything more concerning the systems project?"

2. Make sure that you have a correct understanding of the interviewee's job responsibilities and duties. A typical question is, "It is my understanding that your job is . . . (a brief job description). Is this correct?"

3. It is important to attempt to ascertain the interviewee's decision-making model (i.e., what decisions are made and how the interviewee makes them). Typical questions are, "It is my understanding that, as a cost accountant, to prepare a monthly cost-analysis summary you need to decide how telephone costs are allocated between departments. Can you decide how this is to be done with the information you are now receiving? If not, what precisely is the information you need and how many days before closing do you need it?"

4. As much as possible, try to ask specific questions that allow for quantitative responses. A typical question is, "How many telephones do you now have in this department?"

5. Avoid buzz words, meaningless jargon, and broad generalizations. Typical statements to avoid are, "We will probably interface a CRT with an XYZ front-end, multiplexed in a conversational mode online to a DASD using synchronous broadband channels connected to our 369 Mod 1000 Number Cruncher, which has 100 megabytes of virtual storage."

6. Develop an awareness of the feeling of the person being interviewed. Learn to listen well. Guard against anticipating answers before the interviewee has had sufficient time to respond.

7. Maintain control of the interview by using tact and discrimination to end ramblings and extraneous comments. A typical response: "Now back to that problem of cost allocation we were talking abour earlier; do you propose that we use toll-call usage as an allocation base?"

8. Vague answers to questions should be pursued for full clarification. A

typical statement is, "Please bear with me, but I do not quite understand how you propose to handle this."

9. Determine if the interviewee has any additional ideas or suggestions that have possibly been missed. A typical question is, "Do you have any additional suggestions or recommendations concerning the method used to calculate budget variances?" Also, find out if the interviewee wants credit for any suggestions or recommendations. It is very important for the systems analyst to give credit where credit is due. A typical question is, "Do you want your supervisor or others to know of your suggestion?"

10. At the end of the interview, summarize the main points of the session, thank the interviewee, and indicate you will return if you have any further questions.

Taking notes is a traditional and sometimes accepted method for the analyst to use during the interview to record various points, observations, and answers to questions. As when taking notes during a lecture in school, the analyst must guard against excessive note taking, thus losing the ideas and responses being presented. Using voice recorders instead of taking notes is becoming a common practice. Although this eliminates the problems associated with taking notes, the presence of a voice recorder may make the interviewee nervous and overcautious in answering questions. Common sense is usually the best guide to the systems analyst when choosing among fact-recording techniques.

Pitfalls of the Interview

Interviewing is an art and, accordingly, does not always proceed as planned. Normally, people react to an interview in different ways, some favorable and some unfavorable. The following table includes a spectrum of reactions the systems analyst is likely to encounter, along with some suggested stopgap activities to offset them.[2]

Behavior of Interviewee	StopGap Activity
Appears to guess at answers rather than admit ignorance.	After the interview, validate answers that are suspect.
Attempts to tell the analyst what the analyst presumably wants to hear instead of the correct facts.	Avoid putting questions in a form that implies the answer. Validate answers that are suspect.
Gives the analyst a great deal of irrelevant information or tells stories.	In a friendly but persistent fashion, bring the discussion back into the desired focus.
Stops talking if the analyst begins to take notes.	Put the notebook away and confine questions to those that are most important. If necessary, come back later for details.

[2]Material adapted from Ronald J. DeMasi, *An Introduction to Business Systems Analysis* (Reading, Mass.: Addison-Wesley, 1969), pp. 38–39.

Behavior of Interviewee	StopGap Activity
Attempts to rush through the interview.	Suggest coming back later.
Expresses satisfaction with the way things are done now and wants no change.	Encourage the interviewee to elaborate on the present situation and its virtues. Take careful notes and ask questions about details.
Shows obvious resentment toward the analyst, answers questions guardedly, or appears to be withholding data.	Try to get the interviewee talking about some self-interest, or his or her previous experience with analysts.
Sabotages the interview with noncooperation. In effect, refuses to give information.	Ask the interviewee, "If I get this information from someone else, would you mind checking it for me?" Then proceed on that plan.
Gripes about his or her job, associates, supervisors, and unfair treatment.	Listen sympathetically and note anything that might be a real clue. Do not interrupt until the list of gripes is complete. Then, make friendly but noncommittal statements, such as "You sure have plenty of troubles. Perhaps the study can help with some of them." This approach should bridge the gap to asking about the desired facts. Later, make enough of a check on the gripes to determine whether or not there is any foundation for them. In this way you neither pass over a good lead nor leave yourself open to being unduly influenced by groundless talk or personal prejudice.
Acts as eager beaver, is enthusiastic about new ideas, gadgets, techniques.	Listen for desired facts and valuable leads. Do not become involved emotionally or enlist in the interviewee's campaign.

Group Analysis Method

The following kinds of systems projects are likely to benefit the most from the group method: (1) a system that affects several user groups that are involved in different activities and have varied interests; (2) a system that will change established relationships of people, machines, and methods; and (3) a system that will serve a new business function for which no previous experience exists.

Ford Motor Company, for example, used a group analysis method to develop requirements for a system to track about 50,000 company-owned vehicles used for business transportation, materials movement, testing, and other purposes. The new system covered a number of departments including high-level executives. The following quote gives some high points of how the group method worked at Ford.

> In one session, part of the discussion centered on how much detail about vehicle options the system should include. Knowing whether a particular car has air conditioning, for example, would be useful in several business areas: It would help those assigning a car as an employee vehicle to decide whether to send it to Alaska or Florida; it would let the finance department

place a more accurate value on the car; and it would help those in charge of selling the used cars fill orders. In contrast, knowing the color of the interior would not be important to as many people.

This process was repeated for several proposed system features. The group would initially consider rich functionality and then try to whittle down to essentials. "We're talking about a vehicle tracking system, not a system for sending something to the moon," one participant argued at one point.[3]

The Questionnaire

A questionnaire can be used at various times by the systems analyst in the systems development process. It can be used in systems work to obtain a consensus, to identify a direction or area for in-depth study, to do a postimplementation audit, and to identify specific but varying requirements.

Use of the Questionnaire

For fact-finding, the questionnaire is a somewhat restricted channel of communication and should be employed with great care. Analysts must identify what it is they desire to know, structure the questions that will result in the answers to these needs, and prepare and submit the questionnaire to the individual who is to complete it. Unlike in the interview, the analyst has no immediate opportunity to readdress comments that are vague or unclear in a questionnaire. Moreover, the analyst cannot follow up tangent comments that might well lead to additional facts or ideas.

The questionnaire can be used best as a fact-finding tool when the recipient is physically removed from the analyst and travel is prohibited for either person, where there are many potential recipients (e.g., a sales force), and when the information is intended to verify similar information gathered from other sources.

Limitation of the Questionnaire

The reasons for recommending a limited use of the questionnaire in systems analysis are numerous. First, it is extremely difficult to structure meaningful questions without anticipating a certain response. Second, the inability for immediate follow-up tends to limit the real value of this type of communication. Finally, it appears that blanket-style documents, especially questionnaires, are assigned low priority and importance by most people.

Guidelines for Constructing a Questionnaire

When the analyst decides to use a questionnaire, a few, but important, guidelines should be followed:

1. Explain the purpose, use, security, and disposition of the responses.

---

[3]David Kull, "Software Development: The Consensus Approach," *Computer & Communications Decisions,* August 1987, p. 66.

2. Provide detailed instructions on how you want the questions completed.

3. Give a time limit or deadline for return of the questionnaire.

4. Ask pointed and concise questions.

5. Format questions so that responses can be tabulated mechanically or manually.

6. Provide sufficient space for a complete response.

7. Phrase questions clearly. For example, the question, "Has your processor stopped malfunctioning?" can be frustrating to answer for the respondent whose processor has never malfunctioned.

8. If a question cannot be responded to objectively, provide an opportunity for the respondent to add a clarifying comment.

9. Identify each questionnaire by respondent's name, job title, department, and so on.

10. Include a section where respondents can state their opinions and criticisms.

Question Formats

Figure 16.5 illustrates several formats that can be used to prepare questions for a questionnaire. Note that the content of the sample questions is only illustrative.

Observation

Another technique available to the analyst during fact-finding is to observe people in the act of executing their job. Observation as a fact-finding technique has widespread acceptance by scientists. Sociologists, psychologists, and industrial engineers use this technique extensively for studying people in groups and organizational activities. Auditors observe a number of things such as inventory. Items covered in dust or rust, or prior-year inventory tags may indicate excess, slow-moving, or unsalable inventory. The purpose of observation is multifold. It allows the analyst to determine what is being done, how it is being done, who does it, when it is done, how long it takes, where it is done, and why it is done.

The systems analyst can observe in the following manner. First, the analyst may make a walkthrough and take note of people, things, and activities at random. Second, the analyst may observe a person or activity without awareness by the observee and without any interaction with the analyst. Unobtrusive observation is probably of little importance in systems analysis as it is nearly impossible to achieve the necessary conditions. Third, the analyst can observe an operation without any interactions but with the person being observed fully aware of the analyst's observation. Last, the analyst can observe and interact with the persons being observed. This interaction can be simply questioning a specific task, asking for an explanation, and so forth.

Observation can be used to verify what was revealed in an interview or as a preliminary to the interview. Observation is also a valuable technique for gathering facts representing relationships. Observation tends to be more meaningful at the technical level of data processing where tasks can be more easily quantified. Technical activities include tasks related to data collection, accumulation, and transformation. Decision-making activities do not lend themselves

1. **Check-off Questions.** These kinds of questions are structured to enable the respondent merely to check an appropriate response(s). Examples are as follows:

   a. Which vendor is the supplier of your CPU?

   _____ CDC _____ DEC _____ IBM

   _____ CRAY _____ Honeywell _____ UNISYS

   Other _____

   b. What access do the application programmers have to the computer center? (check one)

   _____ Unrestricted access

   _____ Restricted access (e.g., by password, magnetic card)

   _____ Controlled access by permission of data processing manager

   _____ Other

   c. The data base system can be best described as (check one)*

   _____ A relational structure

   _____ A tree structure

   _____ A network structure

   *You may phrase a similar question and specify in parenthesis, "check all that apply."

In addition to the above formats, a simple checklist such as the following can also be used:

Fire Protection Checklist
(*Partial*)

☐ 1. Smoke and heat detectors are placed at strategic locations.

☐ 2. Excess combustible materials are removed on a regular basis from the data processing center.

☐ 3. Portable fire extinguishers are placed at points for ready access.

☐ 4. All emergency telephone numbers are posted for ready access.

☐ 5. Emergency exit doors are checked daily for obstructions.

☐ 6. Fire drills are conducted monthly.

2. **Yes/No Questions.** This kind of question format is quite popular and is used extensively not only by systems analysts but by auditors as well. Examples are as follows:

	Answer		Answer based on		
	Yes	No	Inquiry	Obser-vation	Test
a. Are all out-of-balance or error conditions brought to the attention of the accountant?	_____	_____	_____	_____	_____

Figure 16.5 Question formats for questionnaire preparation.

b. Is the EDP department independent of all depart-
ments for which it
processes data? _____ _____ _____ _____ _____

A simple yes/no question, with an explanation, is illustrated as follows:

	Yes	No	Not applicable

c. We use 24-hour service
on our communications
equipment. _____ _____   _____

If not applicable, please explain: _____

_____

All yes/no questions should be phrased in such a way that responses run
in a predetermined direction. For example:

	Yes	No

d. Do you prepare telephone budgets? __x__ _____

e. Do you pay toll bills without verification? __x__ _____

There are two "yes" responses. If the preparer of these questions wanted
a preponderance of "yes" answers to indicate good accounting controls,
then he or she has failed because the answer to the second question is
also "yes." The second question should be rephrased:

	Yes	No

f. Do you verify toll bills before payment? _____ __x__

3. *Opinion or Choice Questions.* These questions are phrased to allow the respondent to give an opinion or make a choice, but in a very specific area.
Examples are as follows:

a. If your operating system is modified, note the relative importance of each
of the following goals in your design process (scale them from 1 through
10, where 1 is least important and 10 is most important).

_____ Improve throughput or service level

_____ Maximize number of concurrent processes

_____ Interface to special equipment

_____ Protect operating system from user processes

_____ Increase reliability

_____ Provide special accounting or billing

_____ Protect system files

_____ Protect user files

_____ Simplify command language

_____ Simplify file access or sharing

Figure 16.5 Question formats for questionnaire preparation (cont'd).

b. You are presently receiving enough information to help control the toll calls made from your department. (circle one)

Strongly   Strongly
disagree   1 2 3 4 5 6 7 8 9 10   agree

c. Rate on a scale of 1 to 10 the awareness of those who control the cost of telephone usage. (circle one)

Not   Very
concerned 1 2 3 4 5 6 7 8 9 10   concerned

d. Circle one of the five numbers to indicate your disagreement or agreement with the following statement.

1 = strongly disagree   4 = agree
2 = disagree   5 = strongly agree
3 = neither agree nor disagree

Departments, for which records are maintained on the tabulation of toll calls, maintenance, expense allocation, and equipment costs, should have the following rights:

1 2 3 4 5   To be informed of the existence of such records
1 2 3 4 5   The right to review, on demand by department managers, the records' contents
1 2 3 4 5   To be furnished monthly reports of budgeted toll calls and expenses, as compared with actual expenses incurred for that month

How would you rate your switchboard workload?

☐ Too heavy for adequate service   ☐ Average workload
☐ Heavy, but not impossible   ☐ Light
☐ Heavy to average

4. **Fill-in-the-Blank Questions.** This type of question is structured to provide the respondent with the ability to give an unconstrained response or a short, qualitative answer. Examples are as follows:

a. In what states does your organization operate?

_____

b. What percentage of the operating budget is allocated to production?
_____ %

5. **Combination Questions.** The following is an example of how two formats, check-off and fill-in-the-blank, can be combined into one format.

a. Please check the tasks for which you are responsible, and insert in the blank spaces to the right of each checked task, the percentage of time in your workday you devote to each task.

Figure 16.5 Question formats for questionnaire preparation (cont'd).

☐ Preparing flowcharts ____ %   ☐ Testing ____ %

☐ Coding ____ %   ☐ Implementing ____ %

6. **Short Questionnaire.** The following is an example of a short questionnaire:

TITLE   Report Analysis—Batch EVR   PAGE NUMBER ____

CODE NUMBER 1274-Batch-Per

PURPOSE   To determine the usefulness of the Expense Variance Report

1. Do you wish to receive the Expense Variance Report?
   ☐ Yes   If yes, answer all remaining questions.
   ☐ No   If no, do not answer the remaining questions, and skip to the bottom.

2. How often would you like to receive the Expense Variance Report?
   ☐ Daily   ☐ Monthly   ☐ Semiannually
   ☐ Weekly   ☐ Quarterly   ☐ Yearly

3. What do you do with this report after you receive it?
   ☐ Use it for budget planning   ☐ Read it for general information only

   ☐ Use it to control expenses   ☐ Other ____

4. How do you rank this report in relation to other reports you receive?
   ☐ Superior   ☐ Equal   ☐ Inferior

5. Is this report suitable in its present form?
   ☐ Yes   ☐ No
   or should additional information be provided, such as:
   ☐ Ratios   ☐ Trends   ☐ Prior-period figures
   ☐ Other ____

6. Please list any other comments or suggestions as to form, content, or method of preparation.

   _____

   _____

Thank you for your participation

Signed _____ Title _____

Department _____ Date _____

Figure 16.5 Question formats for questionnaire preparation (cont'd).

to observation as easily. Decision-making activities can best be understood through the process of interviewing and use of decision-level analysis discussed earlier in this chapter.

To maximize the results obtainable from observation, a number of guidelines should be followed by the analyst.

Preparing for Observation

Before observation begins, the analyst should (1) identify and define what is going to be observed, (2) estimate the length of time this observation will require, (3) secure proper management approval to conduct the observation, and (4) explain to the parties being observed what will be done and why.

Conducting the Observation

Observation can be conducted most effectively by the analyst following a few simple rules. First, the analyst should become familiar with the physical surroundings and components in the immediate area of the observation. Second, while observing, the analyst should periodically note the time. Third, the analyst should note what is observed as specifically as possible. Generalities and vague descriptions should be avoided. Fourth, if the analyst is interacting with the persons being observed, then he or she should refrain from making qualitative or value judgment comments. A final rule that should be followed when conducting the observation is to show proper courtesy and heed safety regulations.

Following Up the Observation

Following the period of observation, the analyst's notes and impressions should be formally documented and organized. The analyst's findings and conclusions should be reviewed with the person observed, his or her immediate supervisor, and, perhaps, another systems analyst.

The benefits to be derived from skillful observation are many. As analysts gain experience, however, they become more selective as to what and when they observe. Observation is often quite time consuming and thus expensive. Moreover, people in general do not like to be observed. We strongly recommend that when observation is used, it should be used in conjunction with other fact-finding techniques to maximize its effectiveness, particularly with less experienced analysts.

Sampling and Document Gathering

Two additional techniques available to the analyst, particularly during fact-finding endeavors, are sampling and document gathering. Both these techniques are oriented to paperwork stored throughout the organization. Both techniques provide a source of information unavailable by any other fact-finding approach.

Sampling

Sampling is directed to collecting and accumulating data on problems that are either unmeasurable or entail a tremendous amount of detail work to obtain a given piece of data. For example, if an analyst wants to find out how long it takes to process 10,000 customer orders in the shipping room, he or she might measure the time required to process a sample of 40 customer orders, and based on this sample, extrapolate the expected time to process 10,000 orders.

40 orders require T time

$$\frac{T}{40} = \text{time per order}$$

$$10,000 \times \frac{T}{40} = \text{time for 10,000 orders}$$

Another practical instance of sampling is illustrated in the following example.

"How many purchase orders required a vice-president's signature of approval last year?" asked the manager of purchasing of Grace Dee, systems analyst. "Well," replied Grace, "the policy states that any P.O. greater than $10,000 requires V.P. approval. I checked the P.O. 'dead' file for last year, and found that we have 13 drawers filled with P.O.'s. I asked Bob, the file clerk, if he kept any records concerning approvals or dollar amounts on P.O.'s and he said he did not. He said there was no particular organization to the 'dead' file. I knew you needed some idea of how many V.P. approvals there were, so I took a sample."

"I measured the drawers and found that the file space was about 2 feet in length. That told me I had 26 feet of P.O.'s and 30 minutes to figure out how many had V.P. stamps. I took about 4 inches of paper out of one of the drawers and fingered through the documents. I noted seven 'big' ones. I figured that if there was no special handling involved with V.P.P.O.'s, that would be about 21 to a foot; 21 times 26 feet is about 540–550 purchase orders with vice-presidential signatures."

The purchasing manager thanked Grace for her help and proceeded to call the president. "Jim, we don't keep records concerning executive signatures required on P.O.'s. A sampling the systems people made on the closed file indicates about 600 a year are required."

This example is, of course, hypothetical and may raise a number of questions concerning its mathematical validity. Large transaction files, however, do exist in most organizations. And, surprisingly, in this day and age, statistics similar to that requested by the purchasing manager are not available. Although Grace might have used more scientific methods to obtain her number (certainly we can question the size and representation of the sample), systems analysts often use rules of thumb to arrive at this type of information. But whether you use rules of thumb or classic algorithms, the technique of sampling can provide valuable facts and insights during the systems analysis phase. Sampling is also an effective technique for projecting resource requirements. It is, again, not unusual for an analyst to measure a certain activity on a limited basis and then project the resources required to perform this function for a complete system.

16.5 CONCLUDING SYSTEMS ANALYSIS

Throughout the systems analysis phase, the analyst should maintain extensive communications with the requestor, users, management, and other project personnel. This communication begins with the Proposal to Conduct Systems Analysis Report described previously. On a continuing basis this communication effort includes feedback to persons interviewed, or observed, as to what the analyst understands; verification with user personnel as to the findings in other, related functions or activities that the analyst identifies; and periodic status meetings to inform management and other project personnel about progress, status, and adherence to schedule.

Preparing the Systems Analysis Completion Report

Perhaps the most important communication of all, however, is the *Systems Analysis Completion Report,* which describes findings of the systems analysis. The format and content of this report include the following:

1. A restatement of the reason for and scope of the analysis.
2. A list of the major problems identified.
3. A statement of all users' requirements.
4. A statement of any critical assumptions made by the analyst during the analysis.
5. A projection of the resources required and the expected costs involved in designing any new system or modification to the present system. This projection includes the feasibility of continuing further systems work.
6. Any recommendations concerning the proposed system or its requirements.

In general, the Systems Analysis Completion Report is directed to two different recipients. First, the analyst's management uses the report to determine if the analyst has done a competent job in identifying users' requirements and ascertaining how these requirements fit into any overall or master plan for systems development in the organization. Second, the report provides general and user managements with an opportunity to determine whether or not the analyst has considered all of the organization's requirements.

To provide a meaningful report to both of these interested parties, the analyst should strive to be concise but thorough in preparing the report. Requirements should be quantified and explained specifically. The analyst should avoid technical jargon and acronyms in the report. Exhibits and supporting working papers used in the systems analysis should be attached.

Oral Presentation Methods

Simply handing out your systems reports is not sufficient. An oral presentation is necessary for clear communication of your work. Four methods of orally delivering your systems reports are memorization, off-the-cuff, reading, and extemporaneous. Each has its place, but generally the extemporaneous method is the most effective.

A memorized presentation is somewhat effective and gives you a feeling of security, but it sacrifices freedom and freshness. Even with a memorized presentation, you need an outline in case you become lost.

The off-the-cuff method is an unrehearsed presentation and is absolutely not recommended for presenting your systems reports. Because you are the author of these reports, you may feel you do not need to review them; but if you do not, you will forget major points and tend to ramble.

Reading from your reports can be described in two words—ho and hum; it is a sleeping pill. It has all the drawbacks of memorization plus the inability to maintain eye contact.

The extemporaneous method is the best way to present your reports. If you have done your homework and know your reports inside out, then this is the most versatile and expressive method of delivery. You are spontaneous and energetic. You can readily adapt to topics and situations for which you had not planned. This method gives you the best opportunity to maintain eye contact and establish rapport. Master your material thoroughly, develop an outline, and go from there. With this method, you have strong organization on one side and flexibility and energy on the other.

The use of diagrams, flowcharts, matrices, and decision tables should become an integral part of your presentation and help to support it. If well prepared, they increase the listeners' understanding and make you more credible. Other visual aids that may be effective are pictures, blackboards and flip charts, films, audio aids, videotapes, prototypes, full-scale models, and samples. Also, people can be used as the most effective visual aid of all, especially to demonstrate a procedure or how a task is to be done. Visual aids, indeed, can sometimes achieve what words alone cannot.

Final Results of Systems Analysis

The following are five alternative outcomes for any particular systems analysis:

1. *Stop Work.*   This outcome means that no further work is to be performed and that systems work and resources should be directed toward other projects. This outcome might result because a proposal(s) does not meet TELOS feasibility considerations, because of a change in management's or the requestor's decisions or a reshuffling of systems priorities, which results in the present project being scrapped.

2. *Wait State.*   This outcome is quite common and usually results from a lack of funds or a conservative attitude of management.

3. *Modify.*   This outcome means that management decides some aspects of the proposal must either be changed or combined with another subsystem.

4. *Conditional Proceed.*   This outcome means that systems work will proceed as proposed but that the final design proposal before implementation will have to be justified on a TELOS feasibility basis.

5. *Unconditional Proceed.*   Many system or subsystem proposals are authorized by management with full knowledge that costs will exceed measurable benefits. For example, severe constraints imposed on the organization by

legislative and judicial action might require the development of a system regardless of cost. Or it may be that broader organizational objectives dictate the development of a system that is not cost-effective. For example, management may be planning to expand in a market area that will not be profitable for a number of years. A subsystem to support this venture would not be cost-effective for some time.

THE NSU TIGERS EVENT CENTER
Preparing the Systems Analysis
Completion Report

INTERVIEWING

Sally did most of the interviewing. Some of the study facts derived from these interviews are disclosed in Figure SEATS–SA 1.2 which was her interview with Susie Ticketaker.

Interviewee: Susie Ticketaker
Interviewer: Sally Forth
    Duties: Head Cashier, Ticket Sales
     Date: April 10, 19xx

As cashier at the ticket window, she sees that several obvious problems exist:

- often difficult to determine from the charts how many seats are in a group (for call-in reservations for a block of seats), customers tend to get angry when it takes a few minutes to figure out what's available, in fact more than once customers have become angry and left without purchasing any tickets

- encountered numerous problems with having several people selling tickets concurrently, it's tough to keep two people from selling the same seat at the same time

- the time delays are especially difficult with a group of young kids who get fussy at having to wait while their parents get tickets (especially when the Sesame Street puppeteers were in town)

- getting an accurate accounting of the money collected for each event only once a day is inefficient; management needs a more timely report but there just isn't staff to do it

- if they could only have a picture on a screen of the layout of the center with a seating chart for a given event which all of the cashiers could see simultaneously, it would make it a lot easier to give the customers tickets for good seats as fast as they want them

- returned tickets create a real problem because you have to chase around to all of the cardboard charts and correct the blocked out seats

- ticket takers are frustrated from being bounced around and yelled at by mad customers, impatient management and nosy accounting staffs who need the results of what we do faster, faster, faster . . .

Figure SEATS–SA 1.2 Sally's interview notes.

QUESTIONNAIRE

A questionnaire for patrons of the event center was sent out to a random sample of local residents. Sally wanted to determine the nature of complaints and gather additional study facts to design the system better. Figure SEATS–SA 1.3 illustrates this questionnaire.

NSU TIGERS EVENT CENTER
SCHEDULING AND TICKETING QUESTIONNAIRE

Dear Patron:

As you know, we have enjoyed major expansion in the event center recently. To serve you better, we need your help by answering the following questions.

1. You have been able to buy tickets without having to wait
Strongly   Strongly
Disagree   1   2   3   4   5   6   7   8   9   10   Agree

2. You learn of coming events in time to plan to attend
Strongly   Strongly
Disagree   1   2   3   4   5   6   7   8   9   10   Agree

3. You always get your assigned seat
Strongly   Strongly
Disagree   1   2   3   4   5   6   7   8   9   10   Agree

4. You can reserve seats easily
Strongly   Strongly
Disagree   1   2   3   4   5   6   7   8   9   10   Agree

5. When you enter the center for a particular event, your ticket is checked and verified properly
Strongly   Strongly
Disagree   1   2   3   4   5   6   7   8   9   10   Agree

6. You are directed to your seat efficiently and without hassle
Strongly   Strongly
Disagree   1   2   3   4   5   6   7   8   9   10   Agree

Comments:

Figure SEATS–SA 1.3 Patron questionnaire.

GATHERING AND ANALYZING ADDITIONAL STUDY FACTS

One of Tommy's first tasks was to determine how the information flowed, or at least how it was supposed to flow in the present system. This general flow is represented in Figure SEATS–SA 1.4.

After some further analysis, Tommy prepared the HIPO visual table of contents (VTOC), illustrated in Figure SEATS–SA 1.5. Tommy also included a seating chart and physical layout of the event center which is shown in Figure SEATS–SA 1.6. An organization chart for the event

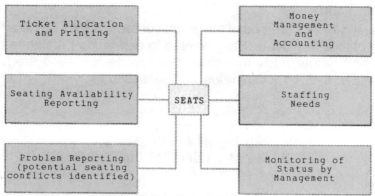

Figure SEATS–SA 1.4 Flow of information in system.

center did not exist, so Tommy sketched the one illustrated in Figure SEATS–SA 1.7.

DETERMINING RELATIONSHIPS IN THE TICKETING FUNCTION

Tommy and Sally spent a great deal of time trying to determine and put together relationships in the total ticketing process. After a great deal of frustration and false starts, they finally came to the realization that tickets and ticketing was essentially an inventory control and marketing system. Once this assumption was made, they developed two entity-relationship (ER) diagrams that reflect this concept. Figure SEATS–SA 1.8 illustrates an ER diagram that models a ticket transaction from a selling viewpoint. Figure SEATS–SA 1.9 demonstrates an ER diagram from an accounting and control viewpoint.

PREPARING THE SYSTEMS ANALYSIS COMPLETION REPORT

Sally conducted most of the interviews and handled the questionnaire. Tommy performed the data processing and flow analysis. Both combined their study facts and, after several meetings, hammered out the Systems Analysis Completion Report.

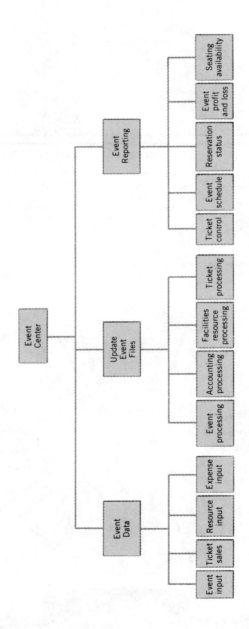

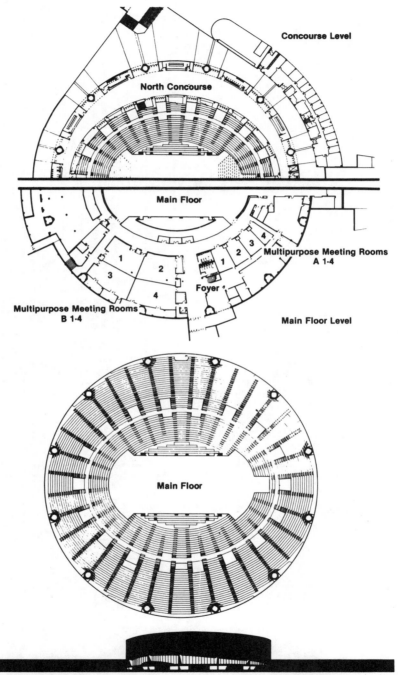

Figure SEATS–SA 1.6 Event center seating chart and physical layout.

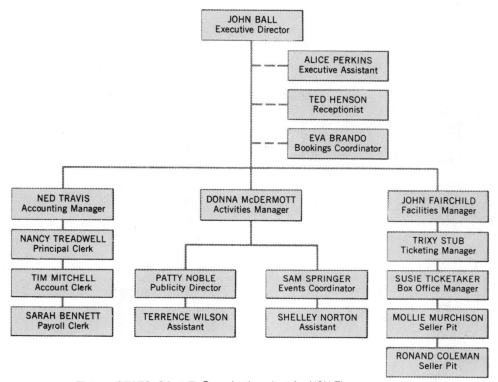

Figure SEATS–SA 1.7 Organization chart for NSU Tigers event center.

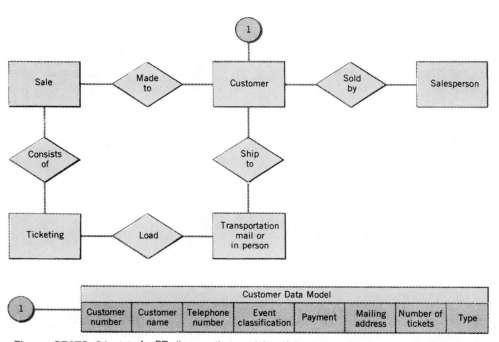

Figure SEATS–SA 1.8 An ER diagram that models a ticket transaction from a selling viewpoint.

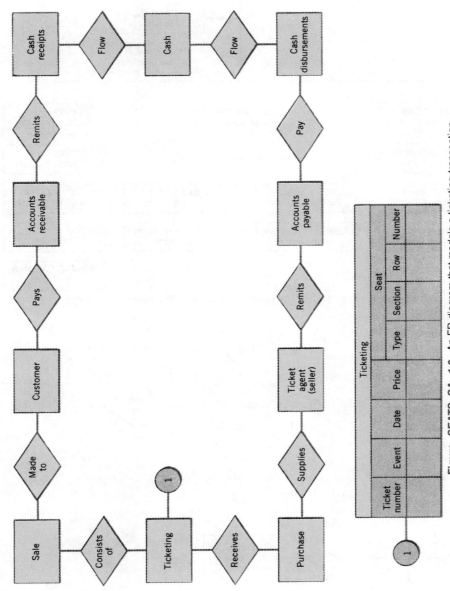

Figure SEATS–SA 1.9 An ER diagram that models a ticketing transaction from an accounting and control viewpoint.

SYSTEMS ANALYSIS COMPLETION REPORT

May 10, 19xx

TO: All Department Heads

FROM: Sally Forth, Chief Systems Analyst

SUBJECT: Schedule of Events and Ticketing System (SEATS)

COPIES: John Ball, Event Center Director and Tyronne Topps, CISO

Reasons and Scope

The systems analysis was conducted to determine the feasibility and direction of SEATS. This report contains the findings of the systems analysis.

Major Problems Identified

Several major problems routinely experienced by the event center staff:

1. Lack of coordination between departments.
2. Lack of information on the status of resources.
3. Lack of information on scheduling required resources.
4. Lack of sales and expense status information for events.
5. Poor internal control of cash and tickets.

Specific Problems Identified

Consider some specific examples of how these problems have affected the ability of the event center staff to meet their commitments:

1. The activities office is unable to communicate in a timely fashion the special accommodations required for special events such as boxing, concerts, and conventions. For example, for concerts and conventions, more communication is required because they are often not informed of special requirements such as room set-ups or planning for a vendor fair until much too late to plan properly for and notify the relevant departments of the extra needs for the event. On the other hand, university basketball games require little coordination and the current level of communication is still adequate.

2. The current system of booking events has failed on several occasions, resulting in double bookings of events. The lack of a central system for tracking the status of negotiation has led to different representatives of the event center promising and booking two conflicting types of events in the same time period, which were extremely difficult to service.

3. The activities office is often unable to determine the status of specific resources available at the center for a certain date. The result is the inability to meet commitments to promoters and staff on a timely basis because staff was not scheduled early enough.

4. The inefficiencies relating to scheduling and the underestimating of the resources available in the center have led to a policy of allowing slack time between events to maintain quality of service. By computerizing we will be able to increase the number of events and schedule them more closely together. This will allow us to increase the facility usage from the current 30 percent rate.

5. The activities office is not able to determine the status of ticket sales to date on a timely and cost-effective basis. This information is required by the staff at the scheduling office to determine whether to cancel an event before the contracted drop date.

6. The ticket office is unable to control ticket sales between the sales staff in the ticket office. Control can only be attained by cutting staff or centralizing the information. Reducing staff is not feasible considering the volume of ticket sales. The only alternative is centralization of information.

7. The inability to account for credit card sales results in the slow processing and collection of credit card payments.

8. The reconciliation of cash is time consuming. We never know what we should have in receipts because ticket dispensing is not controlled.

9. Poor control of ticket sales for assigned seating has resulted in the same seat being sold twice or more. Concurrently, some seats remain empty. This situation contributes to lost revenue and unhappy clientele.

Statement of All User Requirements

During the interviews and from other research we identified the following specific requirements:

1. Timely and efficient communication of event requirements to all departments.
2. Efficient and accurate production and distribution of tickets.
3. Timely information on the status of ticket sales and expenses incurred for each event.
4. A system to ensure proper internal control of ticket sales and cash within the ticket office.
5. A simple and efficient system to reconcile cash.
6. A system to manage credit card sales.

Statement of Critical Assumptions

All possible future constraints cannot be determined in the systems analysis phase. Future development is based on several critical assumptions.

1. After a period of parallel conversion from the current system the old system will be eliminated and the only system to be used will be the one developed as a result of this proposed project.

2. The final system developed will require that personnel be trained as required, and the funding and support for the training will be committed.

3. The hardware and software required can be installed. No physical limitations of facilities will preclude implementation.

Resources Required

If the commitment to systems development is made, the event center must identify additional resources that do not currently exist or recommit staff time from current commitments. These resource requirements include:

1. The development phase will require additional personnel to form a development team. We anticipate the need for two system designers. They should have experience in systems design and programming experience in one language.

2. If the development is done in-house, acquisition of hardware and software as specified in the systems design is required. If programs are acquired from an outside vendor, a similar acquisition is anticipated to support the product obtained. At this time it is anticipated that two personal computers with word processing and programming development software will be required.

3. The general systems design phase will require 1400 person-hours to complete at a cost of approximately $28,000.

4. Management support is required for success.

Recommendations

The discussions with department heads and other personnel indicate that the centralization of information would enable the organization to function more efficiently. It was universally felt that a computerized system that linked all the departments together would improve coordination by improving communication through the use of centrally accessible specialized reports.

The systems development should be started as soon as possible. Problems experienced with the current information system have caused lost revenues and additional nonmonetary costs. A General Systems Design Proposal Report will be produced in a few weeks that will provide feasible information systems design alternatives.

SUMMARY

The basic reasons for initiating systems analysis are to make a strategic information systems improvement, meet a new requirement, take advantage of a new idea or technology, or correct an unsolved problem. Although the plan produced by the SISP process contains a portfolio of systems project requests, the systems analyst needs something more specific to begin systems analysis. Therefore, no matter what the reason for initiating systems analysis is, all projects should start with an information systems service request form. Based on the service request form, the systems analyst will then conduct a preliminary systems analysis. After completing the initial interviews and determining that systems analysis should be conducted, the systems analyst will communicate his or her understanding of what must be accomplished and the general approach to be followed in a document called the Proposal to Conduct Systems Analysis Report.

The study facts come from three major sources: (1) the existing system; (2) internal sources, which include people, documents, and relationships; and (3) external sources, which include other interface points outside the present system, user groups, societies to which the organization belongs, textbooks and periodicals, seminars, and vendors. Techniques for gathering study facts include interviews, group analysis, questionnaires, observations, and sampling and document gathering.

After the study facts have been gathered and analyzed, the systems analyst is ready to prepare a Systems Analysis Completion Report. This report and others are prepared in a professional manner and copies are given to all interested users and managers. These reports are also delivered orally to these people, normally in a formal meeting. The systems analyst should use the extemporaneous method of oral presentation and visual aids where appropriate. The final results of systems analysis include five alternatives: stop work, wait, modify, conditional proceed, or unconditional proceed.

IMPORTANT TERMS

document gathering

group analysis method

interview

observation

paperwork

proposal to conduct systems analysis report

questionnaire

sampling

strategic information systems planning (SISP)

systems analysis completion report

systems development methodology (SDM)

systems plan

▷Assignment

REVIEW QUESTIONS

16.1 What is the name of the documented deliverable from preliminary systems analysis?

16.2 List the four basic reasons for initiating systems analysis.

16.3 Describe the primary purpose of the information systems service request form and list other purposes it may serve.

16.4 The Proposal to Conduct Systems Analysis Report is the systems analyst's vehicle for communicating formally to the requestor his or her understanding of what must be accomplished during systems analysis. List six topical areas it should cover.

16.5 One possible source of study facts during systems analysis is the existing system. List five advantages and two disadvantages of studying the existing system.

16.6 What is the single most important source of study facts available to the systems analyst? What are two other important internal sources of study facts?

16.7 What is an interview? How does it differ from a questionnaire? Explain.

16.8 List three kinds of systems projects that are likely to benefit most from the group analysis method.

16.9 Describe the format and content of the Systems Analysis Completion Report.

16.10 Discuss the four methods of orally delivering the systems analyst's reports.

QUESTIONS FOR DISCUSSION

16.11 It usually takes 5 to 10 percent of the total effort just to define systems objectives and 25 to 40 percent to complete the systems analysis phase. Justify the need for this heavy investment.

16.12 Discuss the details of a Proposal to Conduct Systems Analysis Report.

16.13 Managers have complained about not really having a choice when it comes to approving a new system based on a feasibility study. Instead, the managers say that they are presented with one very encompassing system to approve; the only alternative is to do nothing. How does the approach to the preliminary systems analysis help solve this problem? What new problems does it introduce?

16.14 The systems analyst of a manufacturing concern contacts the supervisor of the production department. She briefs him on the survey that she has taken. She asks the supervisor to help her get answers to some questions. The following dialogue takes place:

Analyst: What is the job of your department?

Supervisor: We ship to customers once the radios have been assembled.

Analyst: How many people work here?

Supervisor: Why do you want to know that?

Analyst: It could be that you have too many people.

Supervisor: Maybe I should be the judge of that.

Analyst: What's that girl doing there? She hasn't done a thing since I walked in here.

Supervisor: She verifies the shipping orders. It could be that she hasn't received any yet.

Analyst: Why do you need to check these orders when they have already been checked out at the inspection department?

Supervisor: We've had occasions when the items sent over were not those called for in the shipping order.

Analyst: Could I talk to that girl?

Supervisor: I guess you can.

The manager walks with the systems analyst to the clerk's desk. She is idle. The manager introduces the analyst to her.

Analyst: What work do you do, Miss Wilson?

Clerk: I verify the goods we receive against the shipping orders.

Analyst: How do you know that the goods are correct?

Clerk: I read the information on the carton and compare it with the information on the shipping order.

Analyst: What makes you think that the information on the carton represents what is inside the carton?

Clerk: I don't know. I assume that this step has been verified by the inspection department.

Analyst: Aren't you wasting your time doing this?

Clerk: You'll have to ask Mr. Kolb (the supervisor) that.

The supervisor, standing by, is beginning to look irritated. The analyst now talks to the supervisor.

Analyst: That's all I wanted to find out from this area. What are those other girls doing there?

Supervisor: They're preparing bills of lading.

Analyst: I'd like to walk over and talk to them for a minute.

Supervisor: They're pretty busy right now. If you're after the procedure they follow, we have it all documented. I'd be glad to give you a copy.

Analyst: No, I'd rather hear it from them. I'm not sure your documentation is up to date, anyway.

The supervisor walks with the analyst to the west corner of the department where several people are typing bills of lading. He introduces the analyst to the head typist.

Analyst: How many bills of lading does your average typist prepare a day?

Head typist: Around 60.

Analyst: You have five typists in this area and your total output is only 300 bills a day? What else do they do?

Head typist: They do follow-up filing and correspondence. Occasionally, they contact customers to verify the units that are being shipped.

Analyst: This is fine, but there must be other jobs they do.

Head typist: Well, we keep track of the bills of lading that go to the dock and make sure they're signed by the driver.

Analyst: Don't you think that this running around is a waste of time?

Head typist: (no answer)

Questions:

a. How do you rate the interview? Explain.

b. Should the analyst have asked all respondents the questions in the same sequence? Why?

c. Critique the analyst's questions in terms of (1) question content, (2) question wording, and (3) question format.

d. If you were the systems analyst, illustrate how you would have conducted the interview.

16.15 Under which circumstances or for what purposes would a systems analyst use an interview over other fact-gathering methods? Explain.

16.16 What sources of error affect the reliability of data from respondents? Elaborate.

16.17 What is the advantage of modeling techniques such as HIPO in specifying the structure of a program?

EXERCISES AND PROBLEMS

16.18 The order-entry system in most commercial organizations provides for shipping products on a delayed-payment basis, assuming that the customer has a proven credit record. In many instances, however, a new customer is subject to credit approval. Consequently, most order-entry systems are designed to contain a credit-checking operation as a standard procedure. The Tricor Company is no exception.

The centralized order-entry system is computerized. A customer master file is used to process all orders. This file contains a record for each approved Tricor customer. Among the many fields of data in each customer record is a customer code, a trade class, a credit limit field, a current accounts receivable dollar field, a past-due accounts receivable dollar field, and a credit referral field. Currently, all orders must pass through the credit manager before they can be processed by the computer. A sampling has shown that fewer than 5 percent of all orders are held by the credit manager. You have suggested that the credit check might be performed by the computer and only problem orders forwarded to the credit manager before shipment. This would eliminate the credit manager having to handle all the orders, as well as decrease the overall order processing time. The credit manager has agreed to try this approach.

The following narrative represents the credit manager's thoughts on how the credit checking procedure should operate in Tricor.

All orders received at Tricor will have a credit check performed. All orders received from new customers must be forwarded to the credit manager. All orders exceeding $1,000 must be forwarded to the credit manager. If the dollar amount of an order plus the present accounts receivable balance for that customer exceeds the credit limit assigned to the customer, then the order must be sent to the credit manager. All orders from customers with past-due accounts receivable balances must be forwarded to the credit manager. All orders from customers on "credit referral" are forwarded to the credit manager. Orders from customers coded to class of trade 100 are not sent to the credit manager unless the account is on "credit referral" or the order exceeds $10,000, or the present accounts receivable balance is greater than $50,000. Orders that pass the credit check are sent directly to the shipping department.

As the systems analyst you have three concerns with the above narrative:

1. You must understand fully what is required.
2. You want to ensure that the credit manager has not forgotten or misrepresented any concern.
3. You want to communicate this credit-checking logic to the programmer as clearly as possible.

Required: Develop a decision table to satisfy these requirements.

16.19 List at least five different sources of facts for each of the following assignments:

1. Payroll system.
2. Accounts receivable.
3. Inventory management.
4. Sales forecasting.
5. Employee skill bank.

16.20 Choose an individual responsible for a large number of decision-making activities in an organization, and conduct an interview for the purpose of identifying the types of information presently received by this person as well as any additional information this person might require to perform his or her duties better. In preparing for your interview, sketch a rough outline of the questions you will ask. When you complete the interview, prepare a completion report that summarizes the proceedings. Last, write a brief summary comparing and contrasting what you anticipated in the interview with what actually was said and done.

> *Note:* The person whom you interview may be part of the administration of your school (e.g., registrar, a dean or department head, student housing director). Additional ideas for interviewing include a management person in the organization where you are employed, or someone in a local business establishment or government agency. Employed friends and associates provide a third choice for interviewing, although this alternative should be used as a last resort only.

16.21 Select an individual in an organization whose prime responsibility is to process data and observe his or her activities. Briefly outline what you plan to observe. Take notes as you observe, and prepare a report summarizing what you have observed. Last, prepare a brief recommendation for any improvements or alternatives concerning the activity you observed.

16.22 Outline in broad terms the approach you would take to conduct a systems analysis in the following situations:

1. Customer complaints concerning poor-quality merchandise.
2. Inability of the shipping department to meet shipping schedules.
3. Inaccurate invoices being sent to customers.
4. High level of obsolescence in raw materials.
5. Excessive amount of returned goods from customers.

16.23 Define the HIPO function to determine the gross earnings of an employee. Assume that regular and overtime pay rates are available from a master employee record and that regular and overtime hours are available from an employee time card record.

16.24 Based on facts in the following letter, prepare a Proposal to Conduct Systems Analysis Report.

Barbara D. Student
Systems Analyst
Southwest Oil Co.

Dear Barbara,

I enjoyed talking with you yesterday and am looking forward to seeing you again next week. I cannot tell you how pleased I am to hear that you are the analyst who will conduct the investigation for developing a forecasting system to assist in operating our lines. I thought I might take this time to provide you with some background on our needs.

As you are aware, we operate 3,600 miles of pipeline throughout the South. We are a contract carrier for petroleum products for 10 major oil companies in addition to Southwest, our parent firm.

Petroleum products enter our lines from 5 different refineries, from 40 different storage tanks, and from 4 pipeline interface points in batches (we call them tenders). We deliver these products to 174 different bulk stations in addition to the above-mentioned storage tanks and interface points.

Currently we employ over a thousand delivery people whose sole responsibility is to open a valve to withdraw or input a product and close it when the proper amount of a product has been transferred. In a significant number of instances a delivery person will not have any activity during a shift.

It is our opinion that if we could better forecast when products will be available at a given valve, we could reduce the number of delivery people required by consolidating assignments.

A few years ago we installed about 300 meters in strategic locations throughout the lines which measure the product flow and report this information back to our central dispatching station via teletypewriter on demand. Perhaps we could feed this information into one of those computers you have and predict arrivals at our tenders at selected valves.

I know you will need more facts than this before you decide what we need, but I do hope I have given you some insight into what we want.

If I can be of any further help, please call on me.

Until next week,

R. G. Sherman
Director,
Southwest Pipeline Co.

16.25 The selling and exchanging of mailing lists has become a profitable undertaking for many firms, particularly those firms that have computer-accessible lists. The data processing service bureau that you work for has decided to construct a generalized mailing list for the metropolitan areas of Pittsburgh, Pennsylvania; Akron, Ohio; and Cleveland, Ohio.

The potential customers for this list will be small- to medium-sized retail establishments as well as local direct-mail companies. Your president feels the opportunity to market this mailing list will improve if potential customers can select the type of individual they wish to reach on personal criteria other than solely geographical.

Your assignment is to conduct an investigation to determine what data will be included in this generalized mailing list and submit your findings and recommendations to the president. Based on the foregoing facts and any assumptions you deem necessary, prepare a Systems Analysis Completion Report.

16.26 Scheduling the work for professional, semiprofessional, and clerical workers is a modern management practice gaining wide acceptance in government and industry. This technique is usually called work measurement or work scheduling. The basic idea behind this mechanism is the establishment of standard times for performing specific tasks and measuring actual performance against these standards.

One approach to using this technique is to assign persons some measurable quantity of work and periodically check (e.g., every two hours) their progress. Another approach is simply to assign daily or routine tasks on a longer time period basis (such as weekly or monthly), and check progress at some interval.

The key factor that makes this technique attractive to many managements is that a task can be estimated and, depending on the expected volume and time constraints, an approximate staffing level can be projected. Whether or not a person progresses on schedule, the supervisor can evaluate the impact of their progress according to the plan. Where work standards are proven to be loose, they can be tightened, and vice versa. Additional advantages, such as following individual performance trends, evaluating fluctuating volumes, and costing specific activities regardless of who performs them, increase the attractiveness of this technique.

A significant disadvantage is that a seemingly high degree of clerical support is required to calculate performance ratios for each time period, to perform maintenance according to schedules of work standards, and to provide periodic summary reporting for middle and upper management.

You are a systems consultant who has been requested to install a work scheduling system in a mail-order firm that employs 270 persons merely to open correspondence and forward it to the shipping or production departments. This firm has access to a computer that supports online terminals. Based on the foregoing facts, prepare a Proposal to Conduct Systems Analysis Report.

16.27 A systems analyst for a West Coast cosmetic manufacturer called a meeting of the various functional managers to solicit their ideas, experiences, and information requirements, as she was about to initiate a systems investigation project related to sales statistics. The participants of the meeting included the following: manager, accounting; manager, credit; manager, customer service; vice-president, sales; manager, market research; manager, budgets; manager, manufacturing; and manager, new product development.

The following notes were recorded by the analyst:

Manager, accounting—Sales statistics provide the financial entry each month (dollar figure for all sales); basis for paying monthly commissions; basis for paying quarterly bonuses; input to selected analysis and profitability studies; basis for paying state sales taxes.

Manager, customer service—Sales statistics used to resolve disputed shipping problems and/or invoicing problems; to assist customers in understanding what was purchased and when; to provide special analyses for salespeople, customers, and sales management.

Manager, credit—Sales statistics are not directly essential; however, accounts receivable and current and past due balances are important; customer payment history provides analytical insight.

Vice-president, sales—Historical record of customer purchases for each product; basis for developing future quotas; routine summary reports of different dimensions of performance (i.e., product by customer, total product class, product within territory, actual versus budget, this year versus last year).

Manager, new product development—Provides favorable/unfavorable trends; orders placed for new products; test market results of specific products, advertisements, promotions, etc.

Manager, budgets—Historical sales provide part of input for preparing new budget, as well as measuring old budget, both at the salesperson level and product level.

Manager, manufacturing—A history of orders and shipments provides a comparison of supply and demand; potential inventory problems; provides an input to production forecast; reflects prior periods' performance.

Manager, market research—Provides a measurement to evaluate competitor sales as reported in journals, studies, and so on.

Required: Analyze these facts and prepare a Systems Analysis Completion Report.

16.28 Charting, Inc., your new client, processes its sales and cash receipts in the following manner:

1. ***Payment on Account.*** The mail is opened each morning by a mail clerk in the sales department. The mail clerk prepares remittance advices (showing customer and amount paid) for customers who fail to include a remittance with their payment. The checks and remittance advices are then forwarded to the sales department supervisor, who reviews each check and forwards the checks and remittance advices to the accounting department supervisor.

The accounting department supervisor, who also functions as a credit manager in approving new credit and all credit limits, reviews all checks for payments on past-due accounts, and then forwards the checks and remittance advices to the accounts receivable clerk, who arranges the advices in alphabetical order. The remittance advices are posted directly to the accounts receivable ledger cards. The checks are endorsed by stamp and totaled, and the total is posted in the cash receipts journal. The remittance advices are filed chronologically.

After receiving the cash from the previous day's cash sales, the accounts receivable clerk prepares the daily deposit slip in triplicate. The original and second copy accompany the bank deposit; the third copy of the deposit slip is filed by date.

2. **Sales.** Sales clerks prepare sales invoices in triplicate. The original and second copy are presented to the cashier; the third copy is retained by the sales clerk in the sales book. When the sale is for cash, the customer pays the sales clerk, who presents the money to the cashier with the invoice copies.

A credit sale is approved by the cashier from an approved credit list after the sales clerk prepares the three-part invoice. After receiving the cash or approving the invoice, the cashier validates the original copy of the sales invoice and gives it to the customer. At the end of each day the cashier recaps the sales and cash received and forwards the cash and the second copy of all sales invoices to the accounts receivable clerk.

The accounts receivable clerk balances the cash received with cash sales invoices and prepares a daily sales summary. The credit sales invoices are posted to the accounts receivable ledger, and all the invoices are sent to the inventory control clerk in the sales department for posting on the inventory control cards. After posting, the inventory control clerk files all invoices numerically. The accounts receivable clerk posts the daily sales summary in the cash receipts and sales journals and files the sales summaries by date. The cash from cash sales is combined with the cash received on account to comprise the daily bank deposit.

3. **Bank Deposits.** The bank validates the deposit slip and returns the second copy to the accounting department where it is filed by date by the accounts receivable clerk. Monthly bank statements are reconciled promptly by the accounting department supervisor and filed by date.

Required: You recognize the weaknesses are in the existing system and believe a data flow diagram would be of assistance in evaluating your client's needs. Accordingly, prepare a data flow diagram for sales and cash receipts within the accounting and sales departments of Charting, Inc.

16.29 For each of the following situations, identify the most appropriate technique for gathering study facts, and explain why you believe the systems analyst should use this technique:

1. Defining the procedure followed by the accounts payable clerk in performing the bank reconciliation.

2. Determining the extent of coding errors in classifying oil field royalties in a oil and gas holding company.

3. Ascertaining the opinions of professors at a local college about the quality of their benefits package.

4. Determining the productivity of a section of data entry workers.

5. Determining the information needs of a portfolio manager of a $100 million mutual fund.

6. Determining the average number of purchase orders issued each month by a major automobile parts supplier.

BIBLIOGRAPHY

AIKTAS, A. ZIYA. *Structured Analysis and Design of Information Systems.* Englewood Cliffs, N.J.: Prentice Hall, 1987.

BODDIE, JOHN. *Crunch Mode.* Englewood Cliffs, N.J.: Prentice Hall, 1987.

CLARKE, RAYMOND T., and CHARLES A. PRINS. *Contemporary Systems Analysis and Design.* Belmont, Calif.: Wadsworth, 1986.

DAVIS, GORDON B., and MARGRETHE H. OLSON. *Management Information Systems,* 2nd ed. New York: McGraw-Hill, 1985.

DeMASI, RONALD J. *An Introduction to Business Systems Analysis.* Reading, Mass.: Addison-Wesley, 1969.

EISNER, HOWARD. *Computer-Aided Systems Engineering.* Englewood Cliffs, N.J.: Prentice Hall, 1988.

EMERY, JAMES C. *Management Information Systems: The Critical Strategic Resource.* New York: Oxford University Press, 1987.

KEEN, JEFFREY. *Managing Systems Development,* 2nd ed. New York: John Wiley, 1987.

KIRKLEY, JOHN. "The Restructuring of MIS: Business Strategies Take Hold." *Computerworld,* March 21, 1988.

KULL, DAVID. "Software Development: The Consensus Approach." *Computer & Communications Decisions,* August 1987.

LESLIE, ROBERT E. *Systems Analysis and Design.* Englewood Cliffs, N.J.: Prentice Hall, 1986.

MARSHALL, GEORGE R. *Systems Analysis and Design: Alternative Structured Approaches.* Englewood Cliffs, N.J.: Prentice Hall, 1986.

MARTIN, CHARLES F. *User-Centered Requirements Analysis.* Englewood Cliffs, N.J.: Prentice Hall, 1988.

MAXWELL, PAUL D. "Developing A Successful 'Deskside' Manner for Systems Analysts." *Journal of Systems Management,* April 1988.

MILLS, HARLAN D., RICHARD C. LINGER, and ALAN R. HEVNER. *Principles of Information Systems Analysis & Design.* Orlando, Fla.: Academic Press, 1986.

PETERS, LAWRENCE J. *Advanced Structured Analysis and Design.* Englewood Cliffs, N.J.: Prentice Hall, 1988.

STEWARD, DONALD V. *Software Engineering with Systems Analysis and Design.* Monterey, Calif.: Brooks/Cole, 1987.

VISKOVICH, FRED. "From Anarchy to Architecture." *Computerworld,* April 25, 1988.

17
GENERAL SYSTEMS DESIGN

17.1 INTRODUCTION

After the systems analysis phase, it becomes fairly clear in many cases *what* must be done. The time has come, therefore, to create general systems designs that show *how*.

Any or all of the analysis techniques presented in the previous chapter and modeling techniques presented in Chapter 7 are also used to represent design models. What we, however, stress in this chapter are additional design techniques that help systems analysts deal with situations in which users' requirements are difficult to define or the systems being developed are oriented to a specific problem or decision that relies on the availability of expert individual knowledge.

Also stressed in this chapter is the use of a designers' workbench that coordinates and automates systems development. The last part of the chapter examines systems design, make or buy, and operational options.

The objectives of this chapter are:

1. To present an overview of general systems design and to establish an insight as to its role in developing information systems.
2. To analyze the general systems design process, stressing the value of presenting design alternatives, and discuss the General Systems Design Proposal Report, the third documented deliverable of the SDM.
3. To discuss and illustrate the use of sketching and prototyping.
4. To outline the role that designers' workbenches play in systems development.
5. To consider a user/system interface design hierarchy.
6. To examine systems options.
7. To illustrate some general systems design examples.

8. To demonstrate the NSU Tigers Event Center General Systems Design Proposal Report.

17.2 GENERAL SYSTEMS DESIGN OVERVIEW

Many systems analysts view the general systems design phase as the fun part of systems work. For others, it can be the most frustrating part. The following material defines this phase and provides some insight into its role in the systems development methodology (SDM).

Design Levels

Just as factories must be modernized, new buildings erected or old ones renovated, or ships refitted, so too must information systems be modified or built from scratch to meet changing conditions and needs. New products and services are being developed routinely, old production facilities are replaced by new ones, competitive forces press for more efficient operations, managements change, cultures change, systems become ineffective or outdated, the organization wants to convert from a manual-based to a computer-based system, good accounting procedures and controls need to be installed, inventory and other resources are not being managed efficiently, the organization lacks an integrated communications network, or the organization is isolated from its customers and other stakeholders.

Because of these and other similar situations, systems analysts become involved in anything from the redesign of a small systems component or subsystem to the creation and design of a total information system. Figure 17.1 shows the levels of information systems design. No matter what the level is, systems analysts

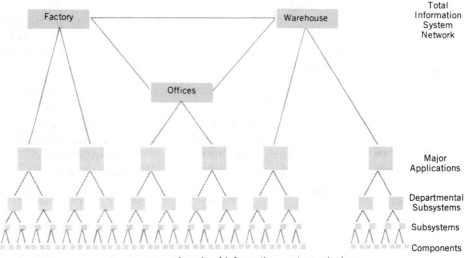

Figure 17.1 Levels of information systems design.

must search for alternative "design solutions" to meet the needs as established during the systems analysis phase. Although systems work at the component level is much less complicated with fewer people involved than at the total systems level, systems work is basically the same.

Design Definition

General systems design can be defined as the drawing, planning, sketching, or arranging of many separate elements into a viable, unified whole. Whereas the systems analysis phase answers the questions of what the system is doing and what it should be doing to meet user requirements, the general systems design phase is concerned with how the system is developed to meet these requirements.

The general systems design phase is technically oriented to the extent analysts must answer the question, "How do we do it?" On the other hand, design is an art, and creatively oriented, to the extent systems analysts continually ask, "what if?" and "why not?" questions.

The Designing Mind

In their work, systems analysts possess and use three minds: the analyzing mind, the designing mind, and the evaluating mind. But these minds are not compartmentalized as such. They merge and mix, and where appropriate, one is more focused and active than the other two.

As study facts are being analyzed and the findings reviewed, broad design concepts begin to crystallize in the designing mind. By adding doses of imagination and by relating study facts and users' requirements to other similar and familiar applications, the designing mind begins to generate design ideas. The systems analyst formulates and converts these design ideas to design models using some of the modeling techniques, such as data flow diagrams, entity relationship diagrams, and structure charts.

On paper or screen, these models are visualized, evaluated, and redrawn until they appear appropriate and feasible. Design alternatives are juggled mentally and evaluated further until several begin to stand out from the others.

Noncritical details are put aside for resolution during the detailed systems design phase. Some of the more pertinent design ideas generated from brainstorming and group interviews may also be accessed and used at this time and mixed and mingled with design models.

In some instances, the designing mind will not do its job and provide the systems analyst with clearly defined design ideas. If this occurs, the systems analyst should focus on the study facts and users' requirements to a point of exhaustion, then stop and do something else like watch a movie, hike, or go fishing.

But the systems analyst should bring a notebook along and keep it handy because design ideas often illuminate in the designing mind and spring forth at the most improbable times. When this happens, the systems analyst should quickly sketch and document these ideas into tangible models in the notebook because such ideas are often fleeting and once lost cannot be easily recaptured.

The systems analyst should perform the exhaustion-to-illumination procedure several times while employing users' requirements as guiding lights. When repeated, new and better design concepts will often emerge that are increasingly closer in alignment with the systems plan, users' requirements, and design forces.

Design Evolution

Figure 17.2 shows that the SDM is an evolving process from top-level generalities to low-level specifics. Users and systems analysts work together to move the systems project from defining users' requirements in systems analysis to general systems design and eventually to a full-blown operating system.

First-cut general systems design alternatives are used to detect misunderstandings, inconsistencies, and omissions. Systems work will not proceed until appropriate changes have been made. Evaluation of several viable general systems design alternatives will produce the best one, which is designed in detail, programmed, and cutover to operations.

A Design Analogy

A better understanding of general design can be gained by using architects and their work as an analogy. Similar to systems analysts, architects are involved in

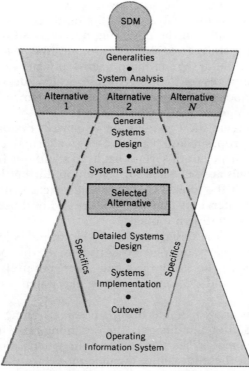

Figure 17.2 A view of systems design evolution.

designing anything from the addition of a small room, to major renovation of an old building, to the creation of a new building complex.

Let us assume that an architect is commissioned to design a new university building. A meeting with university officials is scheduled. The architect interviews them to determine their needs and goals. Questions are asked such as, "How many classrooms are needed?" "What are the minimum and maximum size classes?" "What is the expected enrollment over the next 10 years?" "What is the enrollment-to-faculty ratio?" "What is the faculty-to-staff ratio?" "What special rooms and facilities are needed?" "For what purposes?" "How much money has been allocated for this building?"

Next, the architect does extensive research and analysis. Other buildings are observed and a preliminary visit is made to the proposed site. What the architect is trying to determine is the scope of the project and any constraints that might be imposed on the work to be done. Some assumptions must be made at this point because a final answer on several issues may be pending. After interviewing, researching, and observing, many study facts have been gathered. These facts are analyzed thoroughly to define clear measurable objectives and performance requirements.

After completing the analysis phase, the architect's findings are presented to officials of the university so that any misunderstandings or differences can be resolved. It is important for the architect to test the analysis and to receive feedback from all parties concerned so that a "Taj Mahal" is not designed when a functional structure is all that is wanted. The process of testing and feedback is carried out to see how architectural design forces—such as aesthetics, integration with other buildings, efficient use of land, cost-effectiveness, safety, comfort, energy conservation, zoning, freedom of movement for all including the handicapped, and ventilation—impact on the building blocks of space, materials, light, and style.

With the successful completion of the analysis phase, work at the drawing board begins. General design alternatives are created that meet the requirements of the users and the design forces and remain within the scope of the systems project. The architect draws "plans" that show how the rooms on each floor of the building will be arranged. A sketch is made of how the inside of the building will look and how it will appear from the outside. Even a three-dimensional model of each alternative plan may be constructed. The general systems design alternatives are presented to university officials so that they may select the "best" designs or require the architect to "go back to the drawing board" to develop better designs.

Finally, after careful consideration, university officials approve several design alternatives, some of which may represent composites of other alternatives, for further evaluation to determine the optimum one. This selected alternative is designed in detail. In these detailed plans, the architect shows the size of each room; where desks are located; the lighting, heating, plumbing, and air-conditioning systems; and even where telephone jacks are to be installed. Specifications are prepared that describe the sizes, kinds, and quantities of materials to be used. The architect prepares documents that stipulate the rights and duties of the university, of the architect, and of the building contractor. The architect sees to it that the building is constructed in accordance with the detailed design.

17.3 GENERAL SYSTEMS DESIGN PROCESS AND PRESENTATION OF DESIGN ALTERNATIVES

A basketball coach once said, "It's what you learn after you know it all that counts." This wise statement has a lot to do with systems work and is particularly applicable in general systems design and the development of design alternatives.

Further insight and greater understanding is achieved by the systems analyst while considering and developing general systems design alternatives. The same thing is also achieved by users while reviewing and assessing these alternatives. Both learn how each design alternative may be improved by comparing and contrasting one with the other and, in some instances, how the best aspects of several alternatives can be combined into one alternative that is much improved over any single alternative.

Design Process and Presentation of Alternative Designs

The general systems design process is illustrated in Figure 17.3. The systems analyst knows the users' requirements, the systems scope, and the resources available. Design forces are considered and weighted to determine their impact

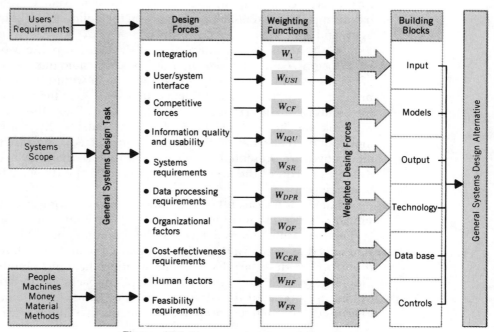

Figure 17.3 The general systems design process.

on the building blocks and eventual systems designs. Different design alternatives are created to take into account different weighting functions. For example, in one alternative a great deal of weight may be given integration, user/system interface, competitive forces, and human factors. In another alternative, more weight may be given to systems requirements and cost-effectiveness requirements.

Based on design forces, a number of alternative designs can be created for users' consideration. For example, one alternative may be based on a star network topology, whereas another may be based on a ring. One alternative may extend into the environment, such as in customers' systems, and another may handle orders in a traditional manner. One may offer a great deal of filtering, monitoring, and interacting capabilities; another may offer little. One design alternative may include a technology building block consisting of many recent advances, whereas another includes only established technology. Or design alternatives may stem from leasing versus purchasing equipment, or developing software packages versus buying them from software vendors.

The point is that the systems analyst is a professional and presents users with a number of design alternatives from which several can be selected for further evaluation. The systems analyst tries to cover all contingencies by giving users an opportunity to look at different ways to meet their requirements. Presenting alternatives increases the probability that the right design will eventually be implemented, because in many instances, users do not really know what they want until they are shown!

Example of Dealing with Design Alternatives

The goals of an accounts payable system can be stated as (1) efficiently maintaining an accurate and timely account of monies owed by the organization to its vendors; (2) providing internal control mechanisms that will ensure the reliability of systems performance; and (3) producing a variety of technical, tactical, and strategic information to support the organization's overall objectives and operations.

By definition, the goal of the accounts payable system is not subject to change. The content and format of each specific input, output, and processing requirement, however, is subject to change as organizational needs change. Let us examine briefly the various alternatives the analyst might consider when designing the specific building blocks required to support the system's goals.

The basic inputs to the accounts payable system are identified in Figure 17.4 as the purchase order, the receiving report, and the vendor's invoice. Purchase order data can be input to the system directly from a computer-based purchase order system, or it can be input by means of a hard copy of the purchase order. The receiving report can be input by means of a hard-copy document or from an online terminal at the receiving depot. Finally, the vendor's invoice can also be input either online or offline. The specific data content can also vary in two different ways. First, the purchase order could contain all the descriptive input data, while the receiving report and invoice contain only variable data, such as the actual quantity received and dollars owed. Second, the quantity of descriptive data associated with the payables function could vary from that re-

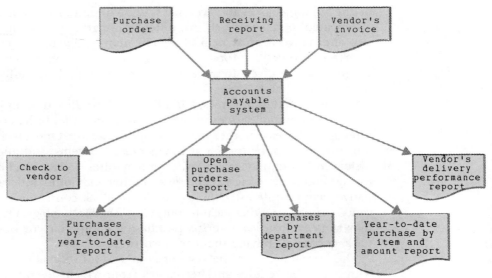

Figure 17.4 A conceptual design model of an accounts payable system.

quired to satisfy basic technical requirements to that used to produce related tactical and strategic information.

The basic technical information produced by the system includes the check to the vendor and the accounts payable financial entry for the balance sheet. The number and composition of control reports (e.g., input registers, error reports) depends on both the stated needs of the users and the type of data processing logic included in the system. Finally, tactical and strategic information outputs (e.g., vendor performance, departmental usage) will vary continuously with the operating environment and demands of the organization as a whole.

Figure 17.4 represents a conceptual model of an accounts payable system that is universal among organizations. Constructing this conceptual model of the payables function does not necessarily demand that the analyst review any specific organizational requirements. When the analyst begins to consider the design forces and present different alternatives, however, the design must be somewhat more detailed, as illustrated in Figure 17.5.

Preparing the General Systems Design Proposal Report

The General Systems Design Proposal Report is prepared to communicate to management and users in the organization how, at a broad level, the designed system will satisfy their information systems and data processing requirements. The following guidelines are offered for assistance to the analyst in preparing the General Systems Design Proposal Report:

1. Restate the reason(s) for initiating systems work, including specific objectives. Relate all original user requirements and objectives to the present systems design proposal.

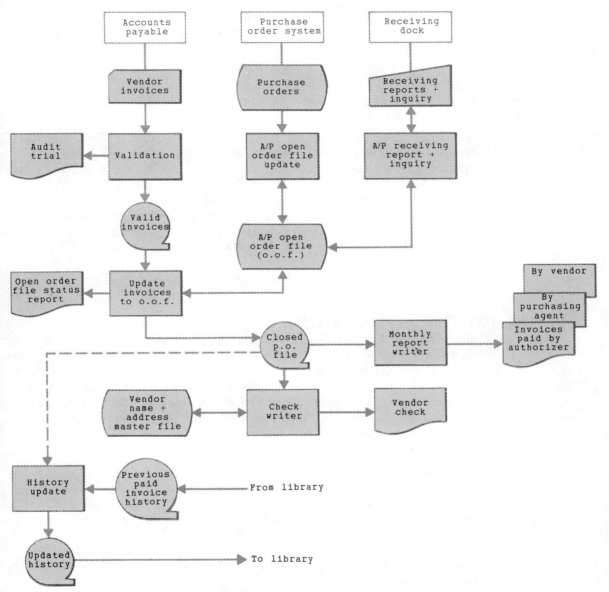

Figure 17.5 A more detailed design alternative of an accounts payable system.

2. Prepare a concise but thorough model of the proposed systems design. Always try to include design alternatives from which management can make choices, rather than presenting only one approach. Not only does the presentation of alternatives allow management to choose, but often it can be shown that a different alternative will have a significantly different impact on the organization. For example, design proposal B may meet 90 percent

of the requirements of design proposal A, but B may cost only 40 percent of A. The analyst should never get into a situation in which he or she must choose between one particular design and nothing.

3. Show all of the resources required to implement and maintain each alternative.

4. Identify any critical assumptions or unresolved problems that may affect the final systems design.

Certainly, the format of the General Systems Design Proposal Report is subject to wide variation from organization to organization. The main thing to keep in mind when preparing a design proposal, however, is that the person(s) who must authorize the development of one of the alternatives or a combination thereof must have sufficient facts on which to base a decision.

In effect, the systems analyst is inviting criticism and suggestions from users when the General Systems Design Proposal Report is presented. It is certainly not "engraved in stone" because typically the probability is high that the general systems design alternatives will have to be changed several times before users finally accept those they feel meet their requirements fully.

17.4 SKETCHING AND PROTOTYPING

Unless the kind of systems project being developed is traditional, such as a basic accounting system, users may not always be able to define their requirements adequately and precisely. Like art critics who know a good painting when they see it, users know what they want and need *after* they see it. They simply cannot prespecifiy their requirements. They have to discover them. Three analysis and design techniques that help in this serendipitous process are building block sketching, blank paper sketching, and prototyping.

Building Block Sketching

Bringing all the building blocks together on one sheet of paper, as shown in Figure 17.6, or screen for each design alternative gives a rough sketch and overview of the total system. Alternatives can be sketched for users to react to and give valuable feedback to the systems analysts. These imitative representations of functioning systems increase understanding by both systems analysts and end users, help to detect missing elements, and generate additional design ideas. Each final design candidate is contained on one building block sheet. These sheets become a main part of the General Systems Design Proposal Report.

Blank Paper Sketching

Blank paper sketching is a design technique that has its roots in prototyping, simulation, and brainstorming. Prospective users are simply given a blank page or screen and asked to sketch what they want as output. Users, with minimal prompting and guidance from systems analysts, sketch elements such as tables and charts and the content of the desired output. The first-cut sketches may be

BUILDING BLOCK DESIGN SHEET

COMPANY: Shadow Mountain Clinic
SYSTEM: Patient Reporting and
Control

SYSTEMS ANALYST: T. Rivera
DATE: DD/MM/YY

Input
- Patient form
- Patient code
- Payments
- Medicare codes
- Treatment code
- Physician code
- X-ray charges
- Test codes
- Function keys and menus

Output
- Bank reconciliation report
- Monthly cash receipt report by physician and department
- Patient treatment report
- Medicare cost reports
- Aging of accounts receivable

Models
- Bank reconciliation procedure
- Physician code + patient code + cash received per month
- Patient code + treatment code + physician code
- Medicare costing procedures
- 0–30/31–60/61–90/day aging of accounts receivable by patient code
- Word processing function

Technology
- CRTs for departments and each physician
- Multitask/multiuser CPU
- Magnetic disks, both hard and floppy
- Magnetic tape
- Computer to output microfilm
- Dot-matrix and daisywheel printers

Data Base
- Patient master file
- Subsidiary ledgers for lab and X-ray
- COM/CAR system for archival patient file
- Logical files based on relational structures

Controls
- Separation of duties of cash collection, deposit, reconciliation, payment, and posting
- General accounting controls
- Control totals
- Passwords
- Backup on magnetic tape

Figure 17.6 A building block design sheet.

primitive and incomplete. But through each sketching, iterative learning takes place. Indeed, a fairly complex design process can begin with sketches and progress into representations that have greater detail and meaning. Eventually, a level of detail is reached from which the final sketch can be implemented. And most important of all, systems analysts can be somewhat assured that systems they implement will be ones users want and need.

Prototyping

One of the worst things that can happen to a systems analyst is to design and implement a system users do not want or need. All the techniques and concepts presented thus far in this book help to prevent this problem from occurring. During SISP, systems analysts are given direction and specific systems' missions. In systems analysis study facts are gathered from a number of sources. These study facts are analyzed and pored over intently. Presentations of analysis proposal and completion reports are made to all users for their criticism and evaluation. Differences are resolved and agreements are reached. Systems analysts, with an even clearer vision and more specifics in hand, begin the general systems design phase and develop several design alternatives based on what has been learned to that point. Users again have a chance to accept, reject, or mix these design alternatives.

Isn't all this systems work enough to avoid implementing a bad system? Not necessarily. Why? Because experienced systems analysts know that in some instances, "What users ask for is not what they want, what they want is not really what they need." Indeed, some users simply don't know what they need until they see it in physical terms and work with it. That's where prototyping comes into play. It is more advanced than building block and blank paper sketching in that the user actually works with a mock-up of the system that will be implemented.

As was discussed at length in Chapter 7, the use of prototypes or functional models enables users to not only see what they are going to get but also gives them a chance to "test drive it." If the users don't like it, another model is built for testing and evaluation. Applied in this manner, prototyping is essentially building systems by learning and discovery.

Generally, prototyping is not applicable for standard function-specific systems such as accounting, but it is particularly useful for developing unique or innovative systems projects that entail a large number of qualitative benefits or in designing small, parochial subsystems to meet the special reporting and decision-making needs of one or a few users. Prototyping can also be used effectively for fine-tuning and upgrading parts of the existing system.

Typically, systems analysts develop prototypes by focusing on the output building block, data entities and attributes, and user/system interfaces while only secondarily considering other things such as controls and technology. Systems analysts, working hand-in-hand with users, create different screen output or reports using query languages or report generators. Systems analysts discuss with users their needs and then develop prototypes on the terminal with users. If the needs are complex, analysts may take a week or so to produce a specimen. In any event, prototypes are demonstrated. Users see how they work and use them. Then, frequently, users request changes such as the addition of subtotals or categories or more information. Systems analysts create more prototypes showing different forms of output, such as tables and charts. Through each iteration, the prototypes are improved until they precisely meet the users' requirements.

A number of prototypes can be created at a terminal. Because of online interaction with relational data bases and query languages, easy-to-use modeling languages, function keys, menus, and a variety of screen forms, the need for classic computer programming is minimized. Therefore, creating prototypes while sitting at a CRT will become easier and quicker.

Clearly, the life cycle of prototyping is much shorter than is the SDM's life cycle. The methodology of prototyping is usually not as formal as the SDM, but it nevertheless follows a methodology. Actually, prototyping is a microcosm of the SDM except that prototyping produces a working physical model of proposed designs whereas the SDM's proposed general systems designs are normally more conceptual and broader in scope. How prototyping works with the SDM is illustrated in Figure 17.7.

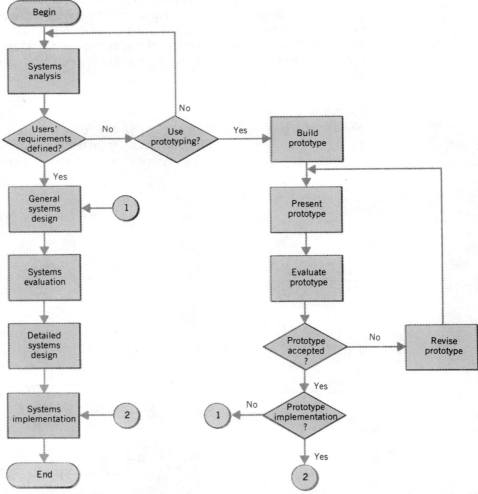

Figure 17.7 Flowchart of how prototyping is used to aid in defining users' requirements and designing systems.

If the accepted prototype is part of a larger system, then it is integrated into general systems design and developed according to the remaining phases of the SDM. It serves as a basis for a set of complete and validated users' requirements, and the SDM keeps the systems project advancing. If, on the other hand, the accepted prototype is a unique or stand-alone system that is implementable, then the systems analyst performs the necessary tasks to convert the new prototype directly to full operation.

17.5 DESIGNERS' WORKBENCH

The designers' workbench, depicted in Figure 17.8, is another name for systems development workstations or computer-aided software engineering (CASE) systems. The reasons for using a designers' workbench are the same as those for computer-aided design (CAD) and computer-aided manufacturing (CAM) systems used by engineers. CASE systems increase systems analysts' efficiency and productivity, reduce paper and pencil busy work, shorten development life cycles, and provide a top-down structured approach for working on large, complex projects. CASE systems are as great a boon to systems analysts as word processors are to writers.

Overview

The designers' workbench integrates all the tools required to analyze, design, evaluate, document, and implement any information system or subsystem into one unified, automated work environment. Everything systems analysts need to

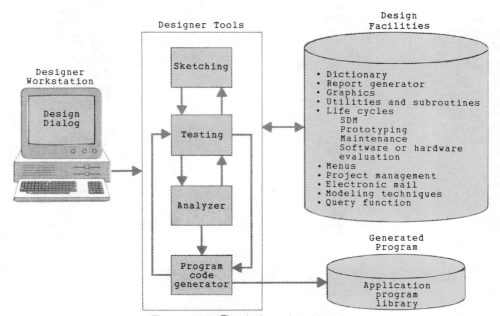

Figure 17.8 The designers' workbench.

perform their work is at their fingertips. Moreover, CASE systems provide tutorials and menus that lead junior systems analysts through a particular life cycle.

Large high-resolution screens display diagrams, tables, matrices, documents, and data structures exactly as they will appear on a printed page. Systems analysts can build, store, and review systems specifications quickly and accurately. After design and evaluation are complete, the CASE system generates application program code in accordance with the design specifications.

AUTOMATING THE ENTIRE DEVELOPMENT LIFE CYCLE Arthur Andersen & Company has developed what it characterizes as a fully integrated computer-aided software engineering (CASE) package. Arthur Andersen's CASE tool kit, named Foundation, automates the entire application development life cycle and includes a code-generation facility and data dictionary.

Alan Alper, "Accountant Takes CASE," *Computerworld*, April 11, 1988, pp. 23–25.

Networking of systems development workstations is particularly important and effective in large, complex systems projects because such environments typically require multiuser and team-oriented development. Or a systems analyst can work alone on small systems projects. In either case, the development of information systems or subsystems is virtually automated.

Design Facilities

The dictionary contains all the information about the systems project in one place. It includes copies of documented deliverables, data structures, status reports, process logic, and various design models. By using the dictionary, systems analysts can quickly review and update systems documentation, list any item on the screen, create additional entries, or update any of the items stored in the dictionary. As the systems project evolves, specification changes can be made electronically to keep documents up to date. The system automatically tracks these changes and produces reports on them at any time.

The dictionary permits systems analysts to share information. This feature promotes communication and coordination of many systems analysts on large projects. Access privileges can be established to control access to files and to monitor which team members add or modify project elements.

Reports can be generated that verify the accuracy, completeness, and consistency of design. Preformatted documented deliverables, such as the General Systems Design Proposal Report and others can be easily produced and distributed to all users for feedback. Any changes can be made electronically. Each version is logged and maintained to keep track of design changes and effort.

Graphics facilities of a designers' workbench enable systems analysts to create and extract various diagrams, record layouts, input forms, and output graphs. They can be easily integrated into reports or used as stand-alone presentations. The graphics facility not only enhances the design of input and output, but also supports and makes easier prototyping sessions.

Utilities provide a set of functions for backing up and restoring files and changing user passwords and access privileges for the entire system and individual projects. Also, generalized subroutines that have universal application, such as statistical packages, capital budgeting routines, and forecasting algorithms are available on call.

The designers' workbench can accommodate several life cycles, such as the SDM, prototyping, maintenance, and even a life cycle for evaluating hardware and software packages. The life cycles can be used at whatever design level the systems analyst chooses and customized to fit specific development needs.

Online sessions, tutorials, and menus lead team members through the systems development process. Task menus identify the work to be done at a particular point in the life cycle, such as determining project scope, conducting interviews, modeling the current system, and defining users' requirements. The workbench specifies documented deliverables needed at the completion of each phase. The workbench also continually reflects the most recent work completed at any given time during the development life cycle.

Project management routines provide project bar charts or PERT-like (review Chapter 7) networks for scheduling phases and tasks. Each task in the development life cycle is visible, and its impact on cost and schedules is readily evident. Updates to schedules are made instantly, so changes and status are available at all times. Also, what-if scheduling can be done easily.

The use of the electronic mail and message facility improves communication between team members. This facility enables team members to exchange memos, messages, or documents with other team members who may be in remote locations.

The modeling techniques facility permits systems analysts to prepare any of a number of analysis and design models, such as data flow diagrams, entity relationship diagrams, structure charts, HIPO charts, and Warnier-Orr diagrams. This facility increases significantly the efficiency and productivity of systems analysts. Developing and changing these modeling techniques using pencil and paper is an onerous task, but drawing and redrawing them electronically on the workbench makes the mechanics of this task almost trivial. With the mechanical burden lifted, systems analysts can concentrate on the model's logic rather than worrying about drawing, erasing, and redrawing by hand.

As already stated, the workbench dictionary contains all the pertinent, up-to-date information about the systems project. The query function facility provides convenient access to any element in the dictionary.

17.6 USER/SYSTEM INTERFACE DESIGN HIERARCHY

The user/system interface is one of the strongest design forces from the viewpoint of users and their specific requirements. The user/system interface design hierarchy, illustrated in Figure 17.9, shows the range of these interfaces.

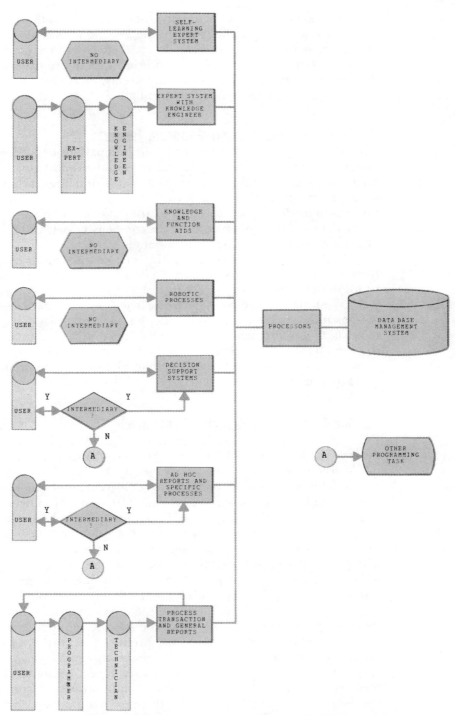

Figure 17.9 The user/system interface design hierarchy.

As one moves up the hierarchy, users' requirements are more information oriented where design objectives are decreasing intermediaries between users, improving management performance, and effecting product and service differentiation. Lower-level user/system interfaces are more process oriented where design objectives are efficiency of operations, increased productivity, and also improved product and service differentiation.

Process Transactions and Generate Reports

The design at this level deals with conventional business transactions, such as buying, selling, and paying; generating periodic reports, such as cost of goods manufactured, schedules, financial statements, and budgets; and producing various documents and business forms, such as payroll checks, remittances, and invoices. The design objective of this user/system interface is to process transaction data and maintain records of the company's assets and liabilities to support operations and make things run smoother.

End users are components in the total process, and their interaction with the information system is task oriented. This interaction is usually effected by COBOL programmers and various technicians like data entry clerks.

The tasks performed in the process are fairly standard and decisions made are generally routine. Therefore, the design effort is straightforward in which most users' requirements are somewhat universal. Thus, many applications at this level have been predesigned in the form of canned software packages. The systems analyst uses these packages along with some customization work to meet users' requirements.

Ad Hoc Reports and Specific Processes

Processing at this level may be periodic or random. The reports may be predetermined and static, or they may be spur-of-the-moment, requiring several quick prototypes before final acceptance by the user.

Often, the design emphasis is more focused and fashioned with individual users' specific and immediate requirements in mind. Moreover, this user/system interface provides flexibility in the design process by adapting easily to changing processing and reporting requirements. For example, a sales manager needs to process some data to generate a sales performance report by region, by product, and by salesperson for a sales meeting Friday morning. A construction superintendent needs percentage-of-completion and bid-item costs on project A by tomorrow morning to take with him on a flight to Detroit.

In the design process, the systems analyst may use a number of prototypes, models, and sketches to determine the specific requirements and then use a fourth-generation language (4GL) to produce a report. Originally, 4GLs were intended to reduce end users' dependency on application programmers, thus resulting in a user/system interface that is direct without the need for intermediaries. Indeed, 4GLs are simple and straightforward, with powerful macro instructions. Nevertheless, many end users have not taken the time or shown the inclination to learn commands, verbs, and syntax of these programmer-efficient languages. In these cases, an intermediary such as an applications programmer is needed.

Decision Support Systems

Although experts differ on the precise definition of decision support systems (DSS), most agree that these systems support users by providing them with models and data to make decisions in relatively unstructured environments. With DSS, users can initiate a series of commands in a high-level or natural language to make use of a data and model base in ways that need not be prespecified or anticipated.

The key to effective DSS is flexible access. Workstations connected together in local area and wide area networks are more important than large-scale processing facilities to the attainment of flexible DSS. Moreover, because DSS are structurally "free form," the number or level of variables in their models can be altered easily. For example, an energy company constructed a decision support system using a Monte Carlo risk analysis model to evaluate a proposed joint venture. The initial output from the system projected a very favorable economic result for the proposed joint project. Because of the reaction of an executive vice-president who felt uneasy over the accuracy of the initial analysis, an additional half-hour's worth of modeling was performed. This time the decision support system projected considerable downside risk and the proposal for a joint venture was abandoned.

Robotic Processes

Robots, guided by automatic controls, perform functions in a humanlike manner. End users generally observe or monitor the robots to see if processes are performed correctly. If changes or adjustments are required, the end user makes them to fit the new need.

Knowledge and Function Aids

Users have long sought aids that help them do their work more efficiently and make better decisions. Today, aids or programs are available that do just that by enhancing knowledge and functions performed by persons in particular trades or professions.

Accountants have their spreadsheets, writers their word processors, lawyers their library-search routines, and design engineers their high-resolution graphics. Even some artists are interacting with the computer to compose and play music. In fact, this entire user/system interface is ripe for creatively designed applications.

Expert Systems with Knowledge Engineer

This expert systems design interface is comprised of the expert and a knowledge engineer who elicits and structures the expert's knowledge for the expert systems shell. Working together, they design an expert system that is used by other people to solve problems and perform tasks the same way the expert would do them. Expert systems are also embedded in robots to mimic the expert.

The expert system simulates the expert based on a number of if-then rules. By tapping into this expert system, end users can leverage their minds significantly, in some ways analogous to how big machines leverage muscles of people to build hydroelectric dams and move tons of freight thousands of miles in hours.

Expert Systems without Knowledge Engineer

The expert systems shell contains an interview module that dynamically manages the interaction with the human expert during knowledge acquisition. The expert/system interface is comprised of communication and dialogue aids, such as windows, pop-up menus, fill-in-the-blank prompters, tutorials, and voice response. The expert is guided through comparison scenarios (e.g., "Of the three—COBOL, FORTRAN, and PRINTER—which one is most unlike the other two?") to provide definition to concepts and attributes and to determine the structure of the expert's thoughts.

Knowledge acquisition and expertise transfer represent the major bottleneck in designing expert systems. The future of expert systems and their role in information systems will depend largely on how well the expert/systems interface is designed. If well designed, the number and kind of expert systems applications are limitless.

For an example, import and export laws, duties, and tariffs are extremely complicated and entangled even more by the latest political whim. The typical customs employee or bureaucrat cannot be expected to keep current and understand such a boiler of spaghetti regulations. To deal with this problem, a top import-export attorney could be retained to interact with an interview module in the expert systems shell and build specific rule-based expert systems that are put online for the bureaucrats. An example of a particular rule on importing automobiles may look something like this:

```
IF origin of automobile =
    Europe or Japan
AND catalytic converter = yes
AND code X motor block = yes
AND air bags or level-3
    restraining devices = yes
AND hydraulic-controlled
    bumpers = yes
AND MPG rating greater than 20 = yes
THEN automobile can enter with Type-1 tariff.
```

Self-learning Expert Systems

A self-learning expert system is designed to analyze and interpret data in a way that helps end users to understand the data better. The inference engine performs both deductive and inductive reasoning to reveal patterns and relationships and provide unexpected information.

Today, for the first time in history, many companies have more pure data processing power than they need for current applications. In some companies, computers are idle 8, 16, and sometimes 24 hours per day. The self-learning expert system supported by these voracious data manipulators is turned loose to roam freely through the data base, gobbling up and digesting data and thereby becoming one of the most robust design approaches in the user/system interface design hierarchy.

The self-learning expert system can distill oceans of data during off-hours or while human users are attending to other tasks. The design objectives are to filter out unwanted data based on user-supplied parameters and tell users what queries are relevant to make in structured query language (SQL). In other situations, relationships that no one else has thought of are discovered in the data base by the self-learning expert systems, which may read something like these:

> For the last five years, when Acme and Zyno purchased over 60 tons of number 2 aggregate within a 30-day period, total sales for number 2 aggregate rose an average of 20 percent per month for the next three months and cement sales increased 30 percent for the next two quarters.
>
> or
>
> Over 80 percent of the customers who buy products A, C, and E and who reside in Parkland Place and who are between the ages of 30 and 40 buy 90 percent of S-coded items.

The first relationships found by a self-learning expert system indicate that Acme and Zyno are leading indicators that help the purchasing agent to make better stocking plans for a building supply company. The second relationships provide some possibly unexpected information that can be used to determine where to locate a branch store specializing in S-coded sporting goods. Parkland Place and the surrounding areas may be consumer hotbeds for a sporting goods store.

Critical success factors or key variables may be discovered that help ensure a successful marketing campaign (hypothetical) such as

> The critical success factors in selling hamburgers in the Soviet Union are:
> *Logo* = sports-related symbols widely accepted by Soviet culture
> *Unacceptable logos* = certain kinds of arches represent dark, satanic symbols, faces with red dots represent smallpox
> *Acceptable colors* = red-gold (.90), red-yellow (.85), red-blue (.75)
> *Unacceptable colors* = green-white (.95), brown-yellow (.90), blue-white (.70)
> *Unacceptable terms:* whopper = Russian slang that means a threat or profanity, big mac = nickname of a revered revolutionist
> *Meat type* = coarse ground, rare, and thick
> *Produce* = radioactive, must import
> *Combinations* = favorite produce with meat are softly boiled cabbage and fried onions, not lettuce and raw onions.

Dining habits = sitting at a table with four to six people is ideal, standing or eating in a car is totally against Soviet's mores.

SMART MACHINES   In a machine learning system, the program discovers relevant questions by performing an intelligent data analysis. Often, this analysis points out unexpected relationships that may be pursued. Thus, machine learning may be viewed as a layer on top of the data base query system.

Based on advances in expert system technology and machine learning, such a goal is completely feasible and has been implemented in a number of systems. Examples include the RX system at Stanford University, which analyzes ARAMIS, the data base of the American Rheumatology Association, and AT&T Bell Laboratories' Rex, a front end to a regression analysis system.

The payoffs from machine learning are likely to be significant. Even if we manage to provide a fraction of data base users with hidden knowledge from their data bases, we will increase productivity substantially within society as a whole.

Excerpted from Kamran Parsaye, "Machine Learning: The Next Step," *Computerworld,* November 23, 1987, p. S16.

17.7 SYSTEMS OPTIONS

Three kinds of systems options are available to analysts. These systems, which entail design, make-or-buy, and operational options, are discussed in this section and illustrated in Figure 17.10.

Design Options

At least three basic design options are available to systems analysts each time a set of users' requirements is evaluated. The analyst can recommend that nothing be done, that an existing system be modified, or that a new system be designed.

1. *Do Nothing.* In every systems decision as to how to satisfy users' information requirements or requests for systems improvements, the analyst has an opportunity to recommend that no action be taken at this time. The reasons for choosing this option include (a) poor identification and definition of requirements or needs, (b) a determination that it is not feasible to develop a meaningful system or solution to users' needs, (c) other systems requests having higher priorities and developmental resources are fully allocated, or (d) users' needs as stated are not real needs.

2. *Modify an Existing System.* The majority of all systems investigations conducted in organizations include some consideration of existing systems and subsystems. To satisfy new or revised user requirements, the analyst often

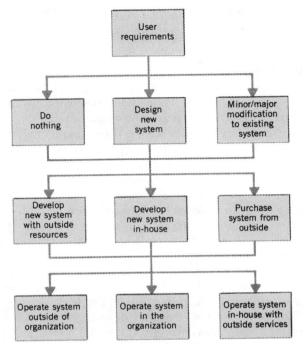

Figure 17.10 A chart showing the major design options available to the analyst.

recommends modifying existing systems rather than designing new ones. Depending on the size of the organization and the particular subsystem being evaluated, systems modifications can have a larger impact on an organization than the development of an entirely new subsystem. This impact can result from either the size of the systems effort expended or from the change resulting in the organization.

When systems support is applied to solving an organizational problem, the emphasis is on immediate results. Thus, changes are often implemented to existing systems until a new system can be defined and developed. In addition, the level of information systems development that exists today in many medium-to-large organizations has reached a point at which new user demands often require relatively small changes to data collection and storage elements, and the emphasis is placed on accessing available data in a new format or on a more timely basis.

3. Design a New System. The final option available for the analyst to recommend is to design a new system to satisfy users' requirements. This alternative is obviously the most complex and difficult solution to implement. This option can be viewed as a combination of two further choices of action. When an analyst recommends that a new system be implemented, a decision must be made whether this system is to be developed from the very beginning or an acceptable system is to be purchased from other sources. Traditionally, this is termed the "make-or-buy" decision.

Make-or-Buy Options

Make-or-buy options are not new to the management process. Manufacturing management continually reviews their operations to determine if a certain product or assembly can be manufactured as efficiently as it can be purchased. In the area of information systems, however, the make-or-buy decision is becoming increasingly important. The development of computer-based information systems is an expensive proposition in any organization when weighed against the resources available to that organization. Until recently, only very large organizations could afford extensive computer-based systems development. As a result, many consulting firms and service bureaus have been established to provide data processing systems for implementation in an organization. In many cases these firms actually assume responsibility for operating a selected portion of an organization's data processing requirements.

But over time, as the manufacturers of data processing equipment, particularly computers, were able to reduce the initial cost of equipment greatly, many smaller organizations acquired the equipment necessary to process their own data. The cost of redoing the payroll or accounts payable applications in every organization (i.e., "reinventing the wheel"), however, became even more expensive. Consequently, organizations began to purchase their basic data processing systems from consultants, computer manufacturers, and software houses, whose primary function is to design, develop, and operate data processing systems for universal application.

The make-or-buy decision is less important in large organizations or where an information requirement is somewhat unique or unusual. In most medium- to small-sized organizations, however, the choice between making or buying, for at least the basic data processing system, represents a very important decision.

The advantages and disadvantages of purchasing and of building a specific system or subsystem are illustrated in Figure 17.11.

Operational Options

A system can be operated outside an organization, such as from a service bureau or from a bank that provides major processing services for some of its customers. It can also be operated within the organization in a traditional manner. Or a system can be internal to the organization but operated by a facilities management firm whose job it is to manage and develop systems.

Service Bureau

A service bureau is a company that provides computer processing services and charges its customers at an hourly rate. Generally, smaller companies use service bureaus, or banks who are in the service bureau business, to process routine and standard applications, such as accounts receivables, payables, and payroll.

In-House Development		System Purchase	
Advantages	Disadvantages	Advantages	Disadvantages
1. System tailored to requirements. 2. High degree of design integration possible. 3. Optimum use of organizational resources possible. 4. Advanced state of the art techniques utilized.	1. Lengthy developmental time. 2. Costs and benefits uncertain. 3. Developmental talents are scarce and not always available. 4. Debugging and other problems occur long after implementation. 5. Usually more expensive.	1. System tested and proven. 2. Implementation time reduced. 3. Advantages/ disadvantages known. 4. Developmental resources freed for other efforts. 5. Usually less cost.	1. Does not meet all requirements. 2. Inefficient use of resources. 3. Maintenance and modification are a greater problem. 4. Less integration with other systems. 5. Demoralizing to developmental staff. 6. Generally, not latest state of the art.

Figure 17.11 Advantages and disadvantages related to the system's make-or-buy decision.

Some service bureaus provide only data processing; others provide a full range of services including systems development and programming. Some organizations that have their own systems use a service bureau for backup facilities or to handle temporary data preparation and processing overloads. The major disadvantages of service bureaus are lack of control and security, and questions of file and program ownership.

Some service bureaus offer time-sharing services that provide users with access to computer and storage devices through a terminal located at the user's organization. The computer and storage devices are physically located at the service bureau. The disadvantage of time-sharing is that it is limited to small jobs with small amounts of input and output; its advantage is fast turnaround.

In-House Staff
Probably the ideal operational option is a fully competent, dependable in-house staff who can develop and manage an information system. It is very difficult, however, to recruit and retain a full staff of qualified systems personnel. The demand simply outstrips the supply. In many organizations a small in-house staff is maintained with additional work performed by consultants, software firms, and systems houses that provide turnkey services for a fee.

Facilities Management

Facilities management firms specialize in managing, staffing, and operating computer-based information systems for a number of organizations. Generally, organizations own or lease the hardware installed at their sites, and the facilities management firm operates the hardware based on an agreement with the organization. This option is certainly feasible especially for those organizations installing their first computers. Also, the facilities management option is used in industries in which processing needs are standardized, such as hospitals and insurance companies. A facilities management firm offers the new user expertise and competent personnel. The obvious disadvantage is that outsiders manage a significant and, in many instances, a sensitive part of the organization's resources.

17.8 GENERAL SYSTEMS DESIGN EXAMPLES

Throughout this chapter guidelines and techniques have been presented to provide a better understanding of how to perform systems design. In this section, we provide two design examples, one dealing with specific areas of the building blocks, the other describing all the building blocks.

Accounts Receivable/Credit System—an Overview

From a financial viewpoint, the accounts receivable system is designed to maintain a permanent record of monies owed the organization by its customers. The credit function may or may not be performed in conjunction with the accounts receivable operation. The purpose of the credit function is to control the issuance of credit to customers as well as to follow up the collection of monies owed. As a rule, the credit function is the primary user of technical and tactical information produced from the data accumulated by accounts receivable.

Many organizations use the cash flow analysis concept for the development of both short- and long-range planning. This strategic information can, at least in part, be obtained from an accounts receivable/credit system.

Accounts Receivable/Credit—Data Collection

The two primary inputs to the accounts receivable/credit system are the customer payments for goods and the organization's invoices to its customers. Figure 17.12 illustrates how these data are collected and input to the system.

Customer payments are entered to the accounts receivable open item file through online keyboard devices. At this time the operator enters the account number, payment amount, and the document number of the item being paid. If a problem occurs, such as input with an invalid account number, then an error message is produced and the transaction is voided. The operator can verify the account number or place the payment document in a manually maintained file of problem payments. A second level of reconciliation would have to occur before that payment could be entered into the system.

At the completion of inputting specified payment batches, the operator

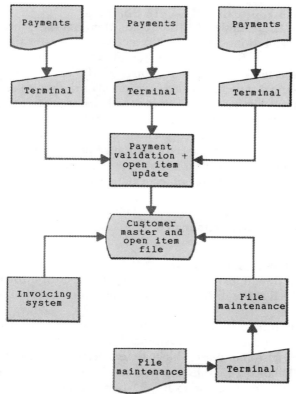

Figure 17.12 The accounts receivable data collection operation.

requests a control total from the system and to this total adds any error documents. This combined total must equal the batch control total given to the operator by another function (e.g., accounting).

The second primary input to the system is the organization's invoice. In our systems design, note that this input is a direct update to the accounts receivable open item file from the billing system. In other words, as an invoice is produced for the customer, the invoice data required for accounts receivable processing are produced and updated simultaneously. This integration of data flow eliminates the need to produce an additional copy of the invoice for internal use and a subsequent reentering of these data into the computer portion of the accounts receivable system. Absolute financial control is maintained by a daily comparison of the total dollar and quantity amounts of invoices produced in the billing system to the total dollar and quantity amounts of invoices that have updated the accounts receivable system.

A secondary input to the system is file maintenance. In our design, this is shown as an online operation; however, it could as easily be performed as an offline batch operation. This input allows any file discrepancies caused by erroneous input to be corrected.

Accounts Receivable/Credit—Data Base

As Figures 17.12 through 17.14 illustrate, the data base contains (1) an open-item file, (2) a closed-item file, and (3) a customer master file.

The open-item file is designed for direct updating and access. All three figures show this file as being resident on a DASD. The closed-item file, however, is shown as being a tape file, which is primarily oriented to sequential or offline batch processing. Figure 17.14 shows the ability to interrogate the closed-item file from a remote terminal. The difference is reflected in the fact that the open-item file is used for technical requirements, whereas the closed-item file is used to produce tactical or strategic information requirements, or both, as needed.

The customer master file is a source of reference data for our system. Thus, it is shown here only as a source of information with no updating or maintenance requirements. Again, this systems design demonstrates that an integration of systems is desirable, because duplicate data processing operations pertaining to customer data have been eliminated.

Accounts Receivable/Credit—Output

In our systems design, examples of the various types of information that can be produced, as well as the different ways in which it can be represented, have been provided.

Technical information is provided to the order processing system (Figure 17.13) in various ways. When a customer order is entered, the order processing system uses the customer master file to determine the customer's account balance. The account balance, in conjunction with a preestablished credit limit field on the customer master file, for example, permits automatic credit checking on every order processed. In addition, the credit manager has the capability of

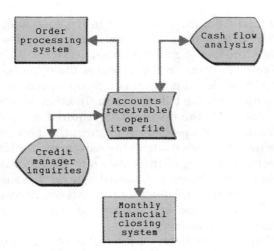

Figure 17.13 The online status of the accounts receivable open item file. This file provides management with significant tactical information for short-term planning and control.

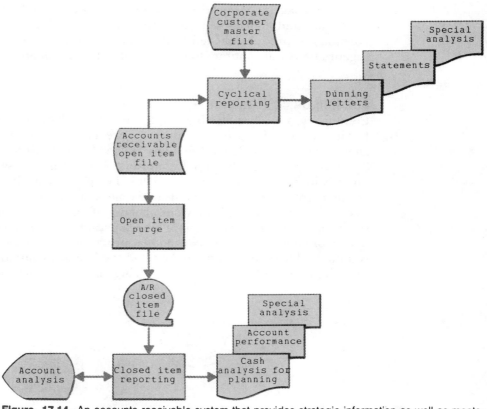

Figure 17.14 An accounts receivable system that provides strategic information as well as meets technical requirements.

interrogating open items for an in-depth analysis of one or more customer accounts. Routine technical requirements such as dunning letters and customer statements are also produced by the system. In these latter cases, however, the processing is accomplished offline.

Tactical and strategic information, representing cash flow and payment performance, is also produced both offline and online for management's use. For example, sales management can see what effect the establishment of a service charge would have on cash flow. Another example might be to assess the effect of a special marketing promotion for smaller accounts. The payment performance of small accounts might adversely affect the short-term cash flow, in which case management might have to look to another source of short-term financing.

Accounts Receivable/Credit—Summary

The accounts receivable system, traditionally viewed by management as a necessary bookkeeping evil, can become the key element supporting technical, tactical, and strategic information requirements. Unless the systems analyst is able to show management how the use of new technology can be profitable, not only from the standpoint of reducing operating cost, but also in providing an opportunity to produce needed tactical and strategic information systems, many organizations will continue to operate without this valuable resource.

Building Block Example

Compuserv, a local service bureau, has installed a large time-sharing computer facility available for use by families. Figure 17.15 illustrates one of the design alternatives from a General Systems Design Proposal Report prepared by Joe Seemore, systems analyst for Compuserv. Each family leases a personal computer, which is connected to this facility. Lease payments by a family are based on the personal computer, mainframe time, storage costs, and consultation services. The system provides various analyses of expenses versus budget, a worksheet for income tax preparation, other operating information, and a complete library of video games and educational programs. In addition, the total system is connected to other systems in the retail and banking community. This network provides users with teleshopping, banking, and other financial services.

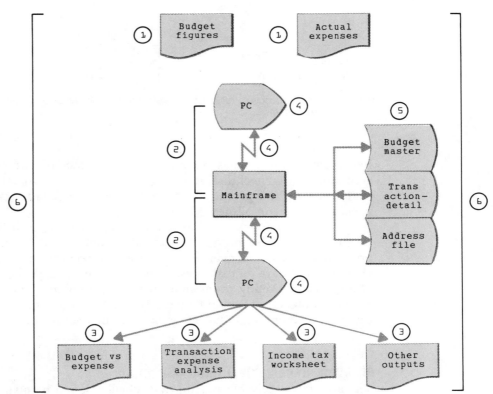

Figure 17.15 A general systems design proposal for a family budget system.

① INPUT

A. Each family enters its budget forecasts by account numbers at least monthly. Data entries required include the following:

- Account number
- Account name
- Dollars per month (maximum 12 months)

The system automatically updates forecasted expenses each month as they are entered and tracks year-to-date expenses.

B. Actual expenses are entered as incurred. Update may occur immediately, daily, weekly, or monthly. In some instances, these expenses may be recorded automatically by the system (see other output).

C. Personal codes and passwords give users the authority to access infomercials from member retailers and make purchases. Also financial information, such as stock quotes, and NYSE, AMEX, and NASDAQ reports are available online and in real time. Users can purchase or trade stocks over their personal computers without the aid of a broker.

② MODELS

A. Each user is trained to use the system. Thirty minutes of training is sufficient.

B. A background form appears on the screen. All a user has to do is "fill in the blanks."

C. Budget models and programming are handled by the staff of the computer service company.

D. A variety of menus are available.

E. Financial analysis models are available for computing price trends of specific stocks.

③ OUTPUT

A. A variance report is produced by comparing budgeted with actual expenses. Output is produced either by direct inquiry from the family personal computer or as the result of the system monitoring expenses related to budget and automatically notifying the user of significant variances.

B. In the event a user wants to see a projection of expenses to budget estimates for the remaining part of the year, a request is made of various simulated expense projections. The system can also be queried to provide a detailed account of transactions affecting a given account.

C. The accumulation of expenses reported in a calendar year permits the system to produce a simulated detail income tax return. Output is achieved by relating the expense account codes in the budget master file to an income tax schedule coding system, updated and maintained by the service company management.

D. Other optional features include such things as automatic check writing. Certain family obligations that are constant from month to month (e.g., utilities, insurance payments, loan obligations, rent, or mortgage payments) are paid automatically by the system. The family is billed by the system for the total value of checks it issued, plus a service charge. Expenses are updated to each account as they occur, thus eliminating the need for reentry of each expense item by the family.

E. A complete list of all purchases is provided along with gains and losses of stock transactions and a current portfolio.

④ TECHNOLOGY

Each family is required to lease a personal computer for stand-alone processing and input/output purposes. A large computer mainframe with telecommunication capabilities is furnished by the service company. A multiplexer or front-end processor handles communication and switching requirements. The service bureau's mainframe handles the bulk of financial and teleshopping processing.

⑤ DATA BASE

A. Physical files are stored on DASDs.

B. Each family is furnished the following three logical files:
1. The budget master file contains the annual budget data as well as the actual expenses (summarized) incurred by account. This file is organized indexed sequentially to support both sequential and direct access. The records in this file are owners of the records in the transaction detail file.
2. The transaction detail file contains all individual transaction and expense records either input to the system or generated by the system. This file is organized randomly.
3. The address file is accessed by the budget master file and contains the address for all the expense detail records that support a given budget master record.

⑥ CONTROLS

A. System controls include the following:
1. A highly trained, professional staff.
2. A set of contingency plans in case of systems failure.
3. Various input controls.
4. Programming controls, such as limit checks and arithmetic proof.
5. Data base controls, which include copies of all the files stored in an underground storage facility. Moreover, all logical files have a lockout system to prevent unauthorized access.
6. The central computer facility is housed in an environmentally secure location.

B. Access control is achieved by issuing all users personal identification numbers and passwords.

THE NSU TIGERS EVENT CENTER
Preparing the General Systems Design Proposal Report

DESIGN LEVELS
To get a little better perspective on the SEATS project, Sally and Tommy prepared a functional diagram, depicted in Figure SEATS–GSD 1.1. This diagram, combined with a thorough review of their study facts gathered during systems analysis phase, began to merge together, helping to form building blocks. Indeed, design ideas began to blossom.

DESIGN FORCES
Sally had told Tommy on several occasions, "The right hand doesn't know what the left hand is doing over at the event center. Moreover, results of the patron questionnaire were extremely negative. They need a system that will integrate their activities. Otherwise they're down the tube."

"Yeah, I know," Tommy responded. "They're trying, but they don't have much to work with."

"Also, we've got to think about users' level of expertise. Most of them will be unskilled. Therefore the user/system interface must be carefully planned."

"They better start getting serious," said Tommy. "The city is putting in its own convention center, so competition may get a little rough before too much longer."

"They're getting some information now, if you want to call it that, but it's not usable. It's too late, so it's no better than zero information. The timeliness for information seems to me to be a vital consideration in design. And if they don't start getting some pretty soon, they won't be able to compete," said Sally.

"I'm sure we'll be able to meet the systems requirements. The idea of building channel systems to other businesses for ticket sales is a good one, but I believe it's a little premature at this stage of the game," said Tommy.

"Yeah. First things first," Sally agreed, "but we can direct our designs toward enabling this kind of hookup if they want to go that way in the future."

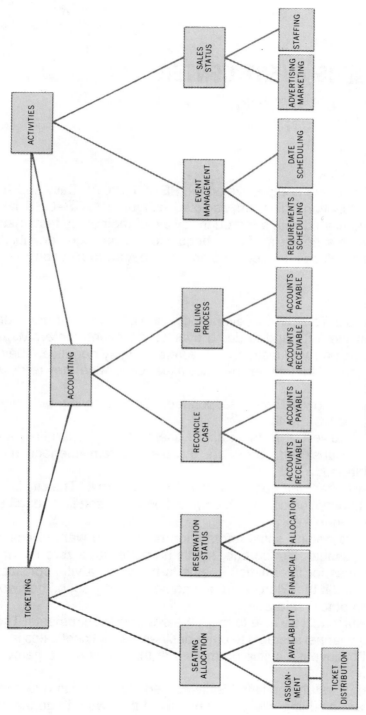

Figure SEATS–GSD 1.1 SEATS design levels.

"If they approve the kind of systems design I have in mind, data processing requirements will be a piece of cake," said Tommy.

"Yeah. No problem," Sally responded.

"You know, I've been thinking," said Sally, "the event center is just like any business that services a lot of people. Sometimes, I tend to look at systems differently if they're on campus, but in reality all systems can pretty much be described in the flow of people, materials, and data. The event center is organized along divisional lines and decentralized management because Ball lets them run their own areas."

"That's true. It's just a typical business organization."

"Something else that's really going to impact us is cost-effectiveness. All the top people, and especially the Board of Trustees, are coming down hard on cost-effectiveness. I overheard Mr. Ball tell Tyronne that the board allocated the money in the budget, but they're not going to approve anything unless it's cost-effective."

"Most of the time they just look at costs. That is, if it costs less then they're saving money, and that's not always true. Sometimes, cutting costs is the worst decision."

"You bet," agreed Sally. "Just look at what they've done over at the event center. They haven't spent any money, and look where they are—hanging by a thread."

"Something that's not quite as tangible as dollars but may produce big dollars is from the human side," Tommy offered.

"I totally agree," Sally said. "They're really down over there. A few people told me they were quitting. They just can't take the hassling and confusion any more."

"We may look like real heroes when this is over," Tommy said enthusiastically.

"If they can keep the right kind of people on staff, I agree. We can do some good things for them, but we're getting ahead of ourselves. First, we've got to come up with some viable designs for them to look at, and go from there. And what will make them viable is to consider and be aware of the design forces we've been discussing."

Sally and Tommy continued to weigh the impact of design forces on their design conceptualizations. From what they had learned so far, it indicated to them some design forces should be weighed heavily in the design process. Their design forces weighting schema is disclosed in Figure SEATS–GSD 1.2.

PREPARING A GENERAL DATA FLOW DIAGRAM

Sally had prepared a data flow diagram (DFD) of the present system. It is displayed in Figure SEATS–GSD 1.3. From this model, she and Tommy

DESIGN FORCES
WEIGHTING SCHEMA FOR
EVENT CENTER

DESIGN FORCE	DESCRIPTION	WEIGHTING FACTORS (total 100)
Integration	• Needed among accounting, activities, and ticketing • Users need ready access to system	15
User/system interface	• Many users are novices • Need ease-of-use and limited training • Automatic monitoring and reporting	15
Competitive forces	• Pooled and sharing of resources • Concurrent ticketing for several events • Need for immediate access to ticketing information • Patron mailing list for promotion • Service to promoters • Extend reach into northern part of bordering state	10
Information quality and usability	• Timely and accurate seating availability • Timely and accurate ticket disbursement • Timely and accurate details for tickets disbursed	10
Systems requirements	• Reliability goal is 100 percent in scheduling events and ticket sales • Availability goal is 100 percent to all users • Flexibility goal is to extend ticket selling into selected businesses in a tristate region • Installation schedule is targeted at the end of next quarter • Life expectancy is set for five years with 100 percent growth potential • Maintainability is ensured by use of structured design standards, documentation, and modular programming	10
Data processing requirements	• Volume is over 2 million separate transactions per year with projections on nearly 4 million within five years • Complexity involves scheduling of events and matching resources to support each event • Time constraints, for maximum productivity, require online real-time processing • Computational demands are relatively low	5

Figure SEATS–GSD 1.2 Design forces weighting schema. (*Continued next page*)

DESIGN FORCE	DESCRIPTION	WEIGHTING FACTORS (total 100)
Organizational factors	• Nature of the event center's business makes proper scheduling and ticket selling an integral part of its operation • Type is divisional or departmental which facilitates reporting requirements • Size of the event center is one of the largest in the country that can accommodate a wide variety of performances • Structure is a stand-alone operation with limited ties directly to NSU, so for all intents and purposes the event center is to be run like any other profit-making business • Management style is decentralized	5
Cost-effectiveness	• More efficient ticket disbursement with fewer staff • Must be developed for current staff • Management and trustees require a formal cost-effectiveness report • An audit is conducted 6 and 12 months after implementation to verify cost-effectiveness analysis	10
Human factors	• Ease-of-use • Users have feeling they're in control • Reduce frustration in dealing with angry patrons • Raise morale	15
Feasibility requirements	• Technical feasibility is not a problem • Economic pressures are to stay within budget • Legal impact means safeguarding patron and promoter data • Operational means the present staff and future personnel with limited expertise must be able to use the system with limited training	5

Figure SEATS–GSD 1.2 Design forces weighting schema.

developed a number of models on a CASE-based workstation. The one they finally settled on is illustrated in Figure SEATS–GSD 1.4. Then Sally and Tommy developed three general systems design alternatives disclosed in the following General Systems Design Proposal Report.

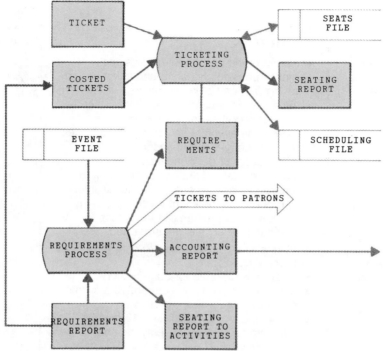

Figure SEATS–GSD 1.3 Data flow diagram of the present ticketing process.

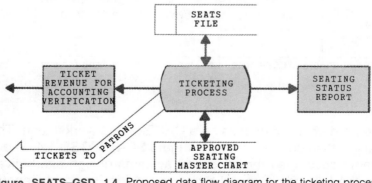

Figure SEATS–GSD 1.4 Proposed data flow diagram for the ticketing process.

GENERAL SYSTEMS DESIGN PROPOSAL REPORT

May 25, 19XX

       To: All Department Heads
     From: Sally Forth, Chief Systems Analyst
  Subject: Scheduling of Events and Ticketing System (SEATS)
   Copies: John Ball, Event Center Director and Tyronne Topps, CISO

Reasons for the Design

The present system does not meet the information and accounting control needs of the event center. Present operations are confusing and inefficient from all users' and stakeholders' viewpoints. For business continuity and to support a major expansion, it is imperative that new, viable systems be considered for further evaluation, design, and implementation.

Alternative General Systems Design Models

We have prepared three general models for your consideration. We do not recommend one over the other. They all are viable based on our work to this point. The one or ones you select, or a combination thereof, will be evaluated further as to the best technology platform available to support the designs. Once we have defined precisely all the resources necessary to implement the systems being considered, we will perform a thorough cost-effectiveness analysis to determine the one that yields the best effectiveness-to-cost ratio.

The three general systems design alternatives can be classified as (1) stand-alone batch alternative, (2) network-based alternative, and (3) centralized alternative. The building blocks of each system are described in the following material.

I. THE STAND-ALONE BATCH ALTERNATIVE

Building Block Design Sheet

COMPANY: Event Center
  SYSTEM: SEATS

INPUT:
- Event Input Sheet
- Ticket Sales Recap Sheet
- Resources Available Input Sheet
- Ticket Sales Revenue Log
- Event Expenses
- Ticket Deposit Slip

MODELS:
- Matching of Event Requirements Against Resources Available
- Profit and Loss for Each Event (Income = Revenue − Expenses)

DATA BASE:
- Resources Master File
- Ticket Master File
- Event Master File
- Accounting File

OUTPUT:
- Ticket Control Report
- Event Schedule Report
- Reservation Status Report
- Seat Availability Report
- Event Profit and Loss
- Resources Inventory Listing

TECHNOLOGY:
- Manual Systems in Ticket Office
- Personal Computer in Accounting
- Personal Computer in Activities Office
- Batch Processing of Input Sheets Between Departments

CONTROLS:
- Preprinted Tickets
- Tickets Equal Seats
- Backup on Floppies
- Seating Chart Marked as Seats are Sold

(1) **INPUT**

A. The activities office fills out an event input sheet when an event is booked. The data sheet contains the following information:

- An event ID number (accounting number)
- Name of the event or performer
- Estimated cost of the event
- Date of the event
- Duration of the event
- Resource requirements (i.e., staging, lighting, seating)
- Selection of resources configuration layout

The data sheets are batched and entered into the activity office PC on a daily basis.

B. As preprinted tickets are sold, they are entered on a ticket sales revenue log sheet by the ticket office. The data sheets are sent to the activities office on a daily basis and entered in the PC.

Ticket deposit slips (bank deposit slip) and the ticket sales recap sheet are sent to the accounting office on a daily basis. The accounting office batches and posts these data sheets as part of the normal accounting cycle. The data sheets contain the following information:

- Log sheet line number
- Name of the patron (if phone order)
- Number of reservations (ticket numbers)
- Event, event name, performer name
- Date purchased
- Purchase price
- Amount deposited

C. As resources become available or the availability changes, the facilities department fills out a resources available input sheet. This data sheet is sent to the activities office and entered on the PC. An expense sheet

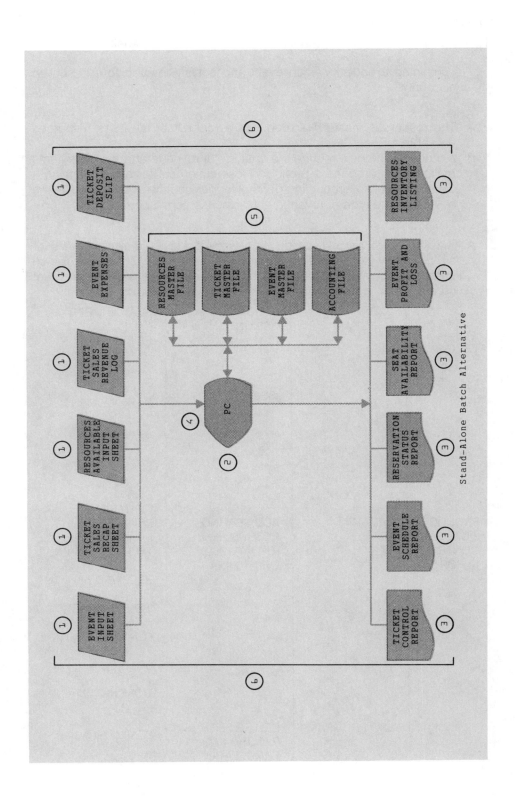

Stand—Alone Batch Alternative

containing a code for each event and costs allocated to it is sent to accounting.

② MODELS

A. The resources master file produces a report that identifies resources available for each event.

B. Accounting models require the analysis of revenue and expense items per event to produce a profit and loss statement for each event on a weekly basis. An accounting general ledger code is used to identify the event and the type of revenue and expense item incurred.

③ OUTPUT

A. A ticket control report is produced to show tickets sold against seats for a match. Any variances or duplicates are highlighted. This report is also used by accounting to verify cash deposited. Processing of the ticket control report is illustrated in the following W-O diagram.

PRODUCE TICKET CONTROL REPORT	BEGIN PROGRAM	ID SEAT ASSIGNMENT (0,1)	SEAT NUMBER (1) PRINT TICKET (1)
		ISSUE TICKET	SEAT NUMBER(S) (1) POST PAYMENT (1)
	UPDATE SEATS FILE	ADD SEATING RECORD (0,1) (UPDATE MASTER EVENT FILE)	SEAT NUMBER (1) SEAT DESCRIPTION (1) COST (1) PRICE (1) TYPE OF PAYMENT (1) RECEIVED PAYMENT (1) ISSUED TICKET (1) QUANTITY ON HAND (1) SOLD OUT (1) TICKETS REMAINING (1)
	END PROGRAM	DELETE SEATING RECORD (0,1) CANCELATION	SEAT AVAILABILITY (1)

B. An event schedule report is produced by listing the names of all events, performers, cost of events/performers, date of the event, and duration. The report can be printed and distributed weekly by the activities office or more often if needed. Online inquiry will only be available at the activities office.

C. Reservation status report is produced analyzing the status of ticket sales in the ticket master file and the event master file. A separate report is produced for each event. Each report contains a list of reservations by ID/name, tickets inventory logged by number, and tickets issued.

D. A seating availability report is produced using the ticket master file. The report indicates the seats and tickets that are still available for each event.

E. The event profit and loss statement is produced using the accounting files. The report contains ticket receipts to date and expenses incurred to date.

F. A resources inventory listing is produced from the resources master file. This report contains a listing of available staging, lighting, seating, and concession facilities available in the event center.

④ TECHNOLOGY

A. The ticket office works on a manual system. Tickets are preprinted and the results of daily sales are entered on data sheets. The data sheets are sent to the activites office for processing on their personal computer.

B. The facilities department is supplied with input, change, and delete forms that they submit to the activities office to maintain accuracy of the resources master file.

C. The activities office processes the forms from the ticket office and the facilities department on their personal computer. Forms generated from their own department are also processed. The appropriate menu-driven software will be available to maintain the files and produce the reports. Batch processing of data sheets is also performed.

D. The accounting department uses a personal computer to maintain the accounting file used to produce the event profit and loss statements.

⑤ DATA BASE

A. The resources master file contains all the resources available in the event center. The items are classified and coded by asset type such as staging, seating, or concession.

B. The ticket master file contains the ticket inventory for each event, the price of each ticket, and the seat assigned if applicable.

C. The event master file contains the name and ID of the event or performer, estimated cost of the event, date of the event, duration of the event, and resource requirements.

D. The accounting file contains information on revenue and expenses incurred for each event.

⑥ **CONTROLS**

A. System controls are as follows:

1. Batch processing control totals of ticket office activities.
2. Preprinted tickets accounted for and under tight access control.
3. Seating chart is marked as tickets are sold.
4. Tickets sold equals the number of seats marked.
5. Files are backed up on magnetic tape.

B. Access control is achieved by issuing keys to rooms that have computers.

II. NETWORK-BASED ALTERNATIVE

Building Block Design Sheet

COMPANY: Event Center
SYSTEM: SEATS

INPUT:
- Online Ticket Deposit Slip
- Online Event Input
- Online Ticket Sales
- Online Resources Input
- Online Event Expenses Input

OUTPUT:
- Online Ticket Control Report
- Online Event Schedule Report
- Online Reservation Status Report
- Online Event Profit and Loss Report
- Online Seat Availability Report
- Online Resources Inventory Listing
- Online Ticket Sales Recap Report

MODELS:

(Same as Alternative I)

TECHNOLOGY:
- Local Area Network Connecting Departments
- Personal Computer in Accounting
- Personal Computer in Ticket Office
- Personal Computer in Facilities
- Real-Time Processing of Events and Ticketing
- Batch Processing in Accounting

DATA BASE:

CONTROLS:
- Preprinted Tickets
- Central Backup on Magnetic Tape

(Same as Alternative I)

- Tickets Equal Seats
- Seating Chart Marked as Tickets are Sold
- Passwords

① INPUT

A. The activities office inputs directly into their PC event data when an event is booked. The input screen contains the following information:

- An event ID number (accounting number)
- Name of the event or performer
- Estimated cost of the event
- Date of the event
- Duration of the event
- Resource requirements (i.e., staging, lighting, seating)
- Selection of resources configuration layout

B. As preprinted tickets are sold, they are entered directly into a PC in the ticket office. Ticket deposit slips and the ticket sales recap sheet are sent to the accounting office on a daily basis. The accounting office batches and posts these data sheets as part of the normal accounting cycle. The input screen contains the following information:

- Log sheet line number
- Name of the patron (if phone order)
- Number of reservations (ticket numbers)
- Event name or performer name
- Date purchased
- Purchase price
- Amount deposited

C. As resources become available or the availability changes, the facilities department enters add, change, or delete information directly into its PC.

② MODELS

A. The resources master file produces a report that identifies resources available for each event.

B. Accounting models produce a profit and loss statement for each event on a weekly basis. An accounting general ledger code is used to identify the event and type of revenue or expense item incurred.

(Note: The same data flow diagram presented earlier depicts this model.)

③ OUTPUT

A. A ticket control report is produced to show tickets sold against seats. Any variances or duplications are highlighted. This report is also used by accounting to verify cash deposited.

B. An events schedule report is produced by listing the names of all events, performers, cost of events/performers, date of the event, and duration. Online inquiry or report output is available at all offices.

C. A reservation status report is produced analyzing the status of ticket sales in the ticket master file and the event master file. A separate report is produced for each event. Each report contains a list of reservations by ID, name, tickets inventory logged by number, and tickets issued. Online inquiry or report output is available at all offices. (Note: The same W-O diagram presented earlier models this alternative.)

D. The event profit and loss statement is produced using the accounting file. The report contains ticket receipts to date and expenses incurred to date. This report is available only through the accounting office.

E. A seat availability report is produced using the ticket master file. The report indicates the seats and tickets that are still available for each event. Online inquiry or report output is available at all offices.

F. A resources inventory listing is produced from the resources master file. This report contains a listing of the available staging, lighting, seating, and concession resources available in the event center. Online inquiry or report output is available at all offices.

G. A ticket sales recap sheet and deposit slip is produced and used for accounting input and control.

④ **TECHNOLOGY**

A. The accounting department, the activities office, the ticket office, and facilities department are linked together by a local area network system. These departments enter information directly into a personal computer in their department or office. The information is shared by the other departments.

B. The ticket office preprints tickets.

C. Information from the activities office and the ticket office is provided in real time.

D. Information produced in the accounting department is restricted for inquiry in the other departments or offices. The accounting department processes transactions in batch processing mode.

⑤ **DATA BASE**

A. The resources master file contains all resources available in the event center. The items are classified and coded by asset type such as staging, seating, or concession.

B. The ticket master file contains the ticket inventory for each event, price of each ticket, and seat assigned if applicable.

C. The event master file contains name and ID of the event or performer, estimated cost of the event, date of the event, duration of the event, and resource requirements.

D. The accounting master file contains information on revenue and expenses incurred for each event and other financial data.

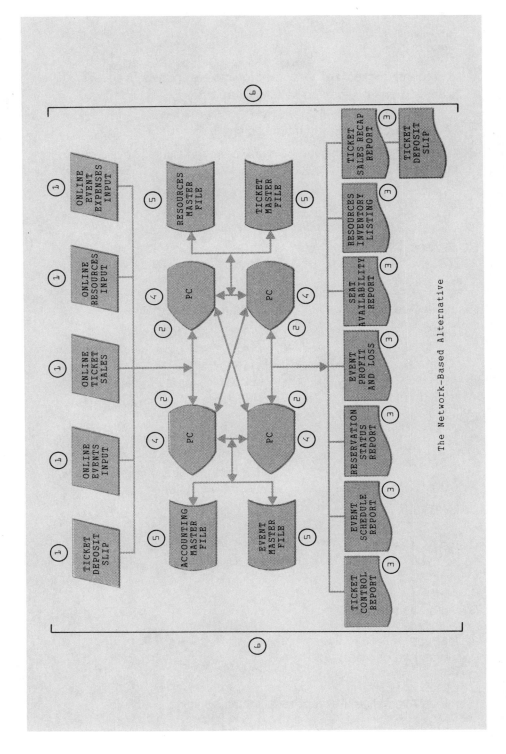

The Network-Based Alternative

⑥ **CONTROLS**

A. System controls are as follows:

   1. Preprinted tickets are accounted for and are under tight access control.
   2. Seating chart is marked as tickets are sold.
   3. Tickets sold equals the number of seats marked.
   4. Files are backed up on magnetic medium.

B. Access control is achieved by passwords and issuing keys to the rooms containing computers.

III. CENTRALIZED ALTERNATIVE

Building Block Design Sheet

COMPANY: Event Center
 SYSTEM: SEATS

INPUT:
(Same as Alternative II)

OUTPUT:
(Same as Alternative II)

MODELS:

TECHNOLOGY:
- Multitasking, Multiuser Operating System
- Mini Central Processing Unit
- CRT's for All Departments and Offices

(Same as Alternative II)

- Real-time Processing of Events, Ticketing, and Accounting
- Dialup Access from Downtown Ticket Station

DATA BASE:

CONTROLS:
- Automatic Ticket Printing

(Same as Alternative II)

- Central Backup
- Passwords

① **INPUT**
(Same as Alternative II)

② **MODELS**
(Same as Alternative II)

③ **OUTPUT**
(Same as Alternative II except for automatic printing of tickets)

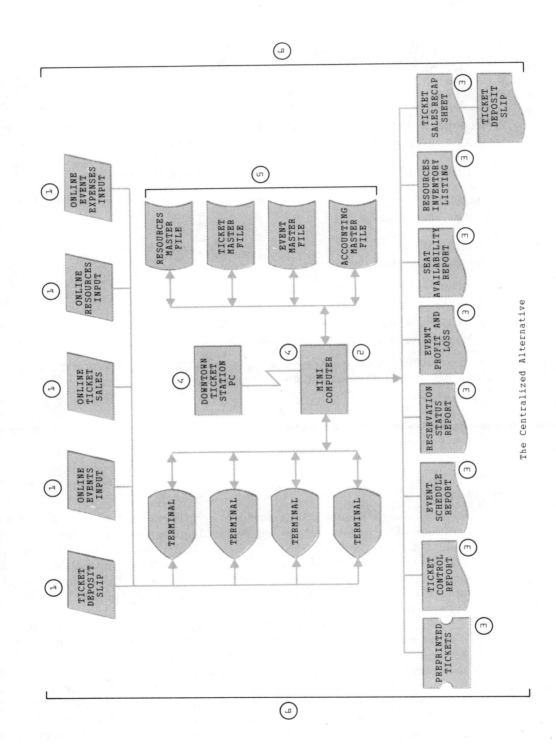

The Centralized Alternative

④ **TECHNOLOGY**
A. All departments and offices enter data by online terminals.
B. The system has its own ticket-printing device.
C. Information from the activities office and the ticket office is provided in real time.
D. Information produced in the accounting department is restricted. The accounting department operates in a real-time processing mode.
E. Access to the ticket reservation system is provided to the downtown ticket station. This is expected to improve public access to events.

⑤ **DATA BASE**
(Same as Alternative II)

⑥ **CONTROLS**
A. System controls are as follows:

1. Tickets are not printed until sold.
2. Electronic seating chart is marked as tickets are sold.
3. Tickets sold equals the number of seats marked.
4. Files are backed up on magnetic medium.

B. Access control is achieved by issuing keys to the rooms containing terminals or the computer and by issuing passwords.

SUMMARY

General systems design is the phase that gives meaning to the building blocks and shows how they can be put together and used in several feasible alternative systems designs. Not only do these design alternatives have to meet users' requirements and stay within the systems scope, but they also must abide by the design forces. This holds true whether the systems analyst is working at a component or total systems level. The major result of this phase is the General Systems Design Proposal Report.

The user/system interface, one of the strongest design forces, can be thought of as a hierarchy of user requirements. At its bottom level, user/system interfaces are process oriented, geared to efficiency. At the higher levels of the user/system hierarchy where the requirements are information oriented, the systems analyst has the opportunity to weave into the fabric of the design alternatives ideas from decision support systems, knowledge and function aids, and expert systems.

To help specify user requirements, the systems analyst can employ the analysis and design techniques of building block sketching, blank paper sketching, and prototyping. Here, the analyst's productivity can be improved by using a designers' workbench or computer-aided software engineering system.

Generally, systems analysts have a number of systems options. First, the design option means they can do nothing, design a new system, or modify an existing system. Second, the development option means that they can develop a new system with outside resources, develop a new system in-house, or purchase a system from outside. Third, the implemented system can be operated outside the organization, operated in the organization, or be operated in the organization by a facilities management firm.

IMPORTANT TERMS

ad hoc report
blank paper sketching
building block sketching
computer-aided software
  engineering (CASE)
decision support systems (DSS)
designers' workbench
dictionary
expert systems
facilities management

General Systems Design Proposal
  Report
knowledge engineer
make or buy
prototyping
robots
self-learning expert systems
service bureau
sketching
utilities

Assignment

REVIEW QUESTIONS

17.1 If the systems analysis phase answers the questions of what the system is doing and what it should be doing to meet user requirements, what question should be answered in the systems design phase?

17.2 In systems work, systems analysts possess and use three minds. What are these three minds and how is each used in systems work?

17.3 Define the content of the General Systems Design Proposal Report from the standpoint of its general format.

17.4 Define what is meant by the analysis and design techniques of building block sketching, blank paper sketching, and prototyping.

17.5 What kind of system projects lend themselves to prototyping? What kind do not?

17.6 How can CASE systems improve a systems analyst's productivity and efficiency?

17.7 List six design facilities and specify how each can help the analyst in the design process.

17.8 Given that a user/system design hierarchy exists, what is the character of its lower-level interfaces? its upper-level interfaces?

17.9 Define what is meant by the term decision support system? robotic processes? knowledge and function aids?

17.10 Describe how an expert system can be developed without the participation of a knowledge engineer.

17.11 Explain how expert systems "learn."

17.12 Describe the three basic design options available to the systems analyst each time a set of users' requirements is evaluated.

17.13 What economies are achieved with in-house time-sharing versus an external commercial service? What benefits can the service provide?

17.14 Review and explain the general systems design examples given in the chapter. How are they related to the General Systems Design Proposal Report?

QUESTIONS FOR DISCUSSION

17.15 Summarize the prerequisites for systems design. What is their purpose?

17.16 How critical do you feel the requirements of a new system are? Could the analyst compromise one or more of these requirements without effecting the functioning of the new system? Discuss.

17.17 The accounts receivable department of the company you work for discovers that a mail-order customer has never been billed for a shipment. This information turned up when a customer's secretary telephoned the department and requested the bill.

1. What went wrong in the billing system?
2. Design a control procedure to ensure billing after the merchandise has been shipped and shipping tickets invoiced to the customer.

17.18 Consider the following chart depicting the major steps in systems design. Discuss each step in detail.

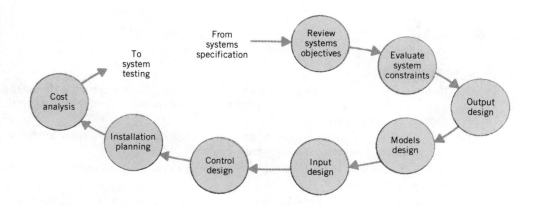

17.19 Make a list and discuss at least four places in the process of systems design in which standards are most important.

EXERCISES AND PROBLEMS

17.20 In conducting systems design, several questions have to be considered. List 10 questions that must be asked during the systems design phase.

17.21 Construct an illustration of an inventory control data collection operation.

17.22 Illustrate the input/processing/output of a system to grade student tests and post grades to student records.

17.23 Prepare a conceptual design model showing the relationships among an inventory control system, a purchasing system, and an accounts payable system in a manufacturing organization.

17.24 You have been hired by a large country club to design an information system for its golfing activities. This system is to accept golf scores from members and their guests and automatically update the members' handicaps. In addition, the system is to have the capability of providing members with a complete analysis of all matches they participated in for a given year showing their strokes per hole. Finally, the club's management would like to have the ability to analyze activity on the course by day.

You are given the following information: The course has a CRT tied into a large time-sharing computer system. The CRT is operable from 6 A.M. to 10 P.M. The course uses a handicap system that assigns a golfer a handicap equal to 80 percent of the difference between actual scores and par based on the last 10 rounds played. Prepare a General Systems Design Proposal Report for your proposed system.

17.25 In many small- and medium-sized organizations, telephone expenses are a significant part of the total business expense. Although the telephone company provides a detailed list of charges each month, these data as presented on the bill are not readily adaptable for controlling individual telephone users. In many organizations a company telephone operator places all long distance calls and accepts all incoming collect calls. In each case the operator is able to log which extension-user in the company placed or received the call.

The telephone bill each month shows the total cost of all installed equipment (e.g., extension phones, switchboard, multiple lines on phones). A separate inventory list provides monthly equipment costs. Long-distance, collect, third-party calls, and credit card charges are shown in detail on the monthly bill. Often these charges, however, are a month or two late in being billed. Credit card numbers are issued by the telephone company and are usually logged by a clerk in the accounting department. The monthly telephone bill shows detail fields for each line item as follows: (1) date the call is placed or received, (2) number called or number called from, (3) code for type of call, (4) city called or called from, (5) credit card number, if applicable, (6) length of call, and (7) charge for call. Analyze these facts and provide the following:

1. A general design of an information system that collects, processes, and reports telephone expenses. Assume the organization has a computer that operates in batch processing mode utilizing punched cards, magnetic tape, and magnetic disk.
2. The forms and procedures required to collect input data.
3. The records and files to be contained in the data base.
4. Your recommendations for the information outputs to be received by each department manager and the company controller.

17.26 A Midwestern state plans to experiment with a new way of dispensing drugs required by doctors' prescriptions. In general, each hospital, doctor's office, and pharmacy will be required to purchase or lease a small terminal capable of accessing a large, centralized computer. Rather than write prescriptions in the traditional sense, the doctor will enter the prescription into the terminal and forward the data to the computer. A data base maintained at the central computer will contain inventory records for each pharmacy in the state. Patients can request that the prescription be filled at a pharmacy of their choice, or at one of the several pharmacies in a specified geographical area based on some criteria such as price, availability, and so on.

The goals of this system are to reduce the mishandling and misinterpretation of patients' prescriptions, reduce the costs related to obtaining prescriptions, and provide a method for exercising control over illegal drug dispensing.

Prepare a General Systems Design Proposal Report for this system as you visualize it operating. Prepare a two- or three-page report discussing the advantages and disadvantages of this type of information system.

17.27 A food manufacturer has traditionally relied on "money-back coupons" for promoting its products. This means that when consumers purchase a manufacturer's product, they simply return the label from the product with their name and address to the manufacturer who, in turn, refunds part (25 to 50 cents) of the purchase price to the consumer. As business has grown, however, the vice-president of marketing has had two concerns: (1) this type of promotion is not very successful in many parts of the country, and (2) the cost of operating the promotion is nearing $1,000,000 annually.

The cost includes approximately $150,000 for manually processing refunds and $850,000 in payments. The firm has a large computer with online processing capabilities through CRTs. The vice-president believes processing costs can be reduced by 50 percent if the computer were used to replace the manual processing.

Analyze the above facts and make any assumptions you deem necessary; then prepare a General Systems Design Proposal Report. Your design should include not only the processing of consumer claims but considerations for informing management as to the success or failure of the promotion through specific analytical reports.

17.28 Fix-It-Rite repairs exhaust systems, transmissions, and brakes in its 10 shops scattered throughout the Tampa Bay area. On a busy day it services about 300 car owners, about 50 percent more owners than on an average day. Each shop maintains a standard inventory of approximately 1,000 different exhaust, transmission, and brake parts. A supervisor and an average of four mechanics staff each shop. All shop supervisors report to a shop operations manager.

Based on the bottlenecks occurring with the existing manual system, which was implemented six years ago when the business started, a new PC-based system is being considered. It would need to handle the various transactions for shop work, parts issue, and time reporting at the 10 shops, and must prepare such outputs as shop orders for the mechanics, itemized receipts of shop work done for Fix-It-Rite's customers, and a daily analysis of shop work for supervisors. Moreover, the new system should foster data control and security and enable supervisors to access specific shop orders within fifteen seconds. It should be capable of operating from 8 A.M. to 6 P.M., six days a week.

Required: Illustrate a PC-based design alternative of the proposed system for Fix-It-Rite.

17.29 For each of the following situations describe in broad terms how decision support systems might be profitably used:

1. Brokers for a national real estate company must attend a three-week training seminar within the first two months of their employment. The manager in charge of scheduling this school is required to produce a schedule of start dates. Factors that must be considered when producing the schedule are current staffing and salary levels of the instructors, estimated attrition rates for new brokers (which is extremely high), forecasted demand (which is cyclical and seasonal), costs of opening and running the school for each class, and complex rules about consecutive start dates and school administration.

2. A large chemical company's yearly budgeting process must bring together a hierarchy of mining sites, production facilities, inventory depots, and sales locations. One of its

fundamental budgeting problems is to develop plans and budgets that reflect the best interests of the company as a whole, while at the same time also providing appropriate incentives to the managers at each level in the organization.

3. An international shipping organization operates a fleet of 34 freighters. Management's basic problem is knowing what to bid (charge) for carrying shipments from their port of origin to their destination because of the variation in the characteristics of the ships and of the voyages.

4. Division comptrollers in a New York bank meet monthly with cost center managers to discuss the reason for budget variances. The managers must come to each meeting armed with detailed printouts of budgeted to actual expenses in categories ranging from employee overtime to the purchase of staplers. Both the comptrollers and the managers are frustrated by the length of time spent meeting and the general lack of focus at these meetings.

5. One of the 10 largest life and casualty insurance companies needs to evaluate and adjust rates periodically on group (e.g., airline pilots, underground miners, college professors) insurance policies. This evaluation is based on the historical relationship between the premiums this group pays and the claims its members make against their policies. Presently, underwriters calculate renewal rates by hand and in a relatively undisciplined manner. This results in a large clerical burden being placed on these professionals, and the inability of the company's senior managers to ensure that rate calculations are consistent and accurate.

17.30 J. B. Sharp recently joined Colonial Home Furnishing of Durham, North Carolina. J. B.'s title is systems analyst, a position for which he is qualified by virtue of receiving a degree in business information systems from the University of North Carolina. In his first few assignments, J. B. performed exceedingly well, and on this basis, his supervisor, Mary Hardgrove, felt confident in assigning him late Thursday afternoon to interview the manager of inventory, Colin Blount.[1]

At four in the afternoon Mary told J. B., "Your task has two dimensions. First, I would like you to uncover facts to aid in correcting problems that have been traced to the inventory management function. Second, it's essential to get Blount's cooperation in an analysis and redesign of the inventory management system."

J. B.'s enthusiasm for the tasks showed itself when he appeared at 8:30 Friday morning at Blount's office. After explaining that his business was urgent, Blount canceled his scheduled staff meeting to talk with J. B.

J. B. opened the interview by telling Mr. Blount that top management is "concerned about serious problems in the inventory management function." He continued by explaining he was here to help correct these problems.

"In fact," he said, "our systems group can completely redesign your inventory procedures without bothering you at all. All we need is your story concerning the problems, and we can get started. We'll even keep a tight lid on what we are doing during our study so your people won't know what's going on. In that way they won't be distracted in their work and worried about possible layoffs when the new system is installed."

J. B. continued by offering suggestions about several small problems pertaining to inventories that he had noted while walking through the inventory area before the interview. He also explained the working of scientific inventory order models he had read about in a production class, including their ability to "minimize the array of inventory

---

[1]Adapted from Joseph W. Wilkinson, *Accounting and Information Systems,* 2nd ed. (New York: John Wiley, 1986), pp. 849–850.

expenditures and optimize return on investment." J. B. felt that this showed Blount he "knew his stuff."

After J. B. finished this exposition, he asked Blount if he was willing to cooperate. "After all," explained J. B., "it's to your benefit to clear up these problems before more are uncovered."

Blount replied, as J. B. turned on his tape recorder, that he will have to discuss the matter with his boss, the production superintendent.

J. B. felt this reply was a rebuff to his efforts. Therefore he stated that he had another meeting to attend, got up, and left Blount's office. When he saw Mary later that morning, he repeated what Blount had said and shrieked, "I don't think Blount wants to cooperate. He certainly didn't offer any facts, and he seemed to be stalling when I put the question to him!"

Required: Critique the interviewing approach of J. B. Sharp.

BIBLIOGRAPHY

ALPER, ALAN, "Accountant Takes CASE." *Computerworld,* April 11, 1988.

CLARKE, RAYMOND T., and CHARLES A. PRINS. *Contemporary Systems Analysis and Design.* Belmont, Calif.; Wadsworth, 1986.

DAVIS, GORDON B., and MARGRETHE H. OLSON. *Management Information Systems,* 2nd ed. New York: McGraw-Hill, 1985.

EISNER, HOWARD. *Computer-Aided Systems Engineering.* Englewood Cliffs, N.J.: Prentice Hall, 1988.

LIANG, TING-PENG, and CHRISTOPHER V. JONES. "Design of a Self-evolving Decision Support System." *Journal of Management Information Systems,* Summer 1987.

MARCA, DAVID A., and CLEMENT L. MCGOWAN. *Structured Analysis and Design Technique.* New York: McGraw-Hill, 1988.

PARSAYE, KAMRAN. "Machine Learning: The Next Step." *Computerworld,* November 23, 1987.

PETERS, LAWRENCE J. *Advanced Structured Analysis and Design.* Englewood Cliffs, N.J.: Prentice Hall, 1988.

RAUCH-HINDIN, WENDY B. *A Guide to Commercial Artificial Intelligence: Fundamentals and Real-World Applications.* Englewood Cliffs, N.J.: Prentice Hall, 1988.

SHNEIDERMAN, BEN. *Designing the Human Interface.* Reading, Mass.: Addison-Wesley, 1987.

SPRAGUE, R. H. JR., and E. D. CARLSON. *Building Effective Decision Support Systems.* Englewood Cliffs, N.J.: Prentice Hall, 1982.

STEARD, DONALD V. *Software Engineering with Systems Analysis and Design.* Monterey, Calif.: Brooks/Cole, 1987.

THIERAUF, ROBERT J. *User-Oriented Decision Support Systems: Accent on Problem Finding.* Englewood Cliffs, N.J.: Prentice Hall, 1988.

WILKINSON, JOSEPH W. *Accounting and Information Systems,* 2nd ed. New York: John Wiley, 1986.

18
SYSTEMS EVALUATION

18.1 INTRODUCTION

General systems design alternatives have been·prepared, critiqued by users, possibly redesigned, and reviewed by users again, and the systems analyst is finally given the go-ahead to proceed to the evaluation phase. Although some form of evaluation goes on continuously throughout systems work, it is in the systems evaluation phase where structure is applied to this key process.

Heretofore, the systems analyst has been on a creative path asking a lot of what-if and formal questions, brainstorming, prototyping, zooming into the clouds, changing course by buffeting design forces, sketching and resketching, diagramming, trying to find out "what" users really need and want to do their job, and developing alternative "ways" to meet these requirements.

Along this path, the analyst did not let technology get in the way of conceptual design. Technology was not necessarily ignored, it just wasn't the main driving and influencing factor. Output, models, input, data entities and attributes, and ·controls, along with design forces were. Therefore, the technology building block has not been precisely defined yet.

Now, the systems analyst needs to determine the technology that will best serve as a building block or platform for the other building blocks inculcated in the general systems design alternatives. To do this, the systems analyst performs a controlled and strict evaluation process that leads to the appropriate technology. Then, the general systems design alternatives, including now well-defined technology building blocks with precise cost data, are subjected to cost-effectiveness analysis to. discover the best design alternative for detailed design. The results of all this work are codified and arranged in the fourth documented deliverable, the Final General Systems Design Report. This report is presented to management to make an informed, final selection of the design alternative that will proceed to the next phase—detailed systems design, the subject of the next chapter. The objectives of this chapter are:

1. To explain the reasons for preparing a request for proposal.
2. To show how to prepare an RFP and make a general review of vendors' proposals.
3. To demonstrate the eight-screen evaluation process.
4. To discuss and illustrate the Final General Systems Design Report.

18.2 REQUEST FOR PROPOSAL

After sufficient analysis and design work has been performed, the systems analyst is ready to obtain proposals from vendors to provide software, hardware, and services—the technology building blocks or platforms—that will support the general systems design alternatives. To obtain these vendor proposals, the systems analyst prepares a formal document called a request for proposal (RFP).

When the proposals are received, they are reviewed for completeness and their ability to meet the requirements of the general systems design alternatives. The systems analyst is trying to penetrate vendors' images and get at specific operations and performance, not hype. The systems analyst is also trying to learn *before* selecting a vendor what that vendor will be like *after* the system is implemented. Three approaches to obtaining vendor proposals are discussed next.

Proposal from One Vendor

An approach sometimes used by systems analysts who are weak in the computer and information technology area or who, for whatever reason, want to deal with only one vendor, is to pick a vendor and provide that vendor with the systems design alternatives. The vendor then responds with a proposal to meet these design alternatives based on the vendor's available technology.

The advantage to this approach is that the systems analyst spends little time and effort in preparing a formal RFP and in evaluating different vendors and their proposals; thus, he or she can concentrate on other activities. The obvious disadvantage is that a particular vendor will seldom (never?) recommend adopting better products from other vendors. Moreover, the systems analyst is at the mercy of the vendor and thus has little negotiating leverage. Because of these disadvantages, this approach is not recommended.

Proposal for a Specific System

With this approach, the analyst specifies the computer configuration, software packages, and services, and requests that various vendors submit proposals based on these particular specifications. This approach has been likened to a request for quotation (RFQ). One advantage of this approach is that it tends to reduce the complexity of evaluating different vendors' proposals. Second, it reduces the time period required by vendors to prepare a proposal. Also, unlike the first approach, it brings competition between vendors into the evaluation process.

The primary disadvantage is that this approach generally rules out a vendor offering new or different technology not known to the analyst.

Proposal for Systems Performance Objectives

With this approach, the systems analyst translates the general systems design alternatives into performance objectives and submits them to several qualified vendors, requesting proposals for technology that satisfies these systems performance objectives. For example, instead of stipulating that a computer must be able to support six online terminals, the analyst indicates that online information is required by six departments. Other stipulations may include multitask processors, types of access and security controls, I/O volume, output forms, methods of input, and so forth. If the RFP will contain sensitive, proprietary information, vendors should sign a nondisclosure agreement before receiving the RFP. Also, before the RFP is declared complete and sent out to vendors, top managment and a lawyer should review and approve it.

18.3 CONTENT OF THE RFP AND VENDORS' PROPOSAL EVALUATION

Where possible, a preliminary and broad-brush evaluation should be made to eliminate vendors who obviously do not meet the needs of the company and who should not even receive an RFP in the first place. Actually, some of the elements in the RFP should be applied during this preliminary evaluation, such as analyzing vendors' financial condition and checking with some of their customers to gather performance information. If a preponderance of negative evidence at this level exists on certain vendors, then they clearly should not receive an RFP.

This section presents the elements that make up an RFP, especially one oriented to soliciting proposals based on systems performance objectives. Also included in this section are general comments on the evaluation of vendors' proposals. This evaluation pertains only to the level of responsiveness by vendors and a broad review of the content of their proposals. Actual vendor and technology evaluation is performed only after obviously poor proposals have been weeded out and qualified proposals are in hand, ready to be evaluated further.

Elements of a RFP Based on Systems Performance Objectives

The elements of the RFP presented here invite vendors to submit proposals that clearly satisfy the company's stated systems performance requirements and the general systems design alternatives, among many other important considerations. The general objectives of this kind of RFP, and presumably RFPs based on other vendor proposal approaches, are to spell out what is expected of the vendors who receive the RFP and to leave nothing to chance in making the final vendor(s) selection. The elements of such a RFP are as follows:

1. *Introduction.* The introductory section of the RFP indicates its purpose,

including a general description of the company, its business purpose, operations, and environment. Also, the company should state up front that it may select one or a combination of vendors and that it reserves the right to accept or reject any or all proposals. The RFP should also stipulate that the company has the right to amend the RFP at any time before final selection or to cancel the acquisition process before executing a written contract.

2. *Imperatives and Desirables.*   Requirements are either *imperative* or *desirable*. The imperatives are essential to the implementation and operation of the new system and, no matter how one changes the overall systems design, are always present and must be adhered to. For example, an imperative might be that the system must process X number of payroll checks, produce a payroll register, and update all employee files, by noon each Friday. Or, an imperative may call for a fiber optic local area network (LAN) for broadband signaling. Or the central processing unit (CPU) must have a disk operating system (DOS) and a COBOL 85 compiler.

Desirables, on the other hand, aid and enhance the system but are not absolutely necessary for the system to become operative. For example, although it might be desirable to enter data by voice input devices, it may be determined that, because of a variety of circumstances, data must be prepared and entered by keyboard-to-storage devices.

If a vendor cannot meet the imperatives, then it doesn't have to waste time with the remaining RFP elements. This vendor, therefore, eliminates itself from further evaluation by not submitting a proposal.

3. *Proposal Preparation Guidelines.*   This element provides information for vendors on how to prepare their proposals, including instructions on format and due date. Also, the proposal should contain the time period that the proposal is valid. In some cases, the systems analyst may choose to structure some of the elements, especially data processing and systems requirements, in the form of a questionnaire that the vendors can complete with yes or no, or short answers. By doing it this way, the systems analyst gets precise answers on specific questions that are applicable to the company's operations.

4. *Vendor Performance and Financial Condition.*   This element requires information about the vendor's performance history, growth, financial strength, and general evidence of its ability to meet RFP requirements over the long haul.

If a proposal for services is being sought, a biographical sketch on each person involved in the installation and support of the proposed technology should be requested. This biographical sketch should include work experience related directly to the technology and number of years associated with the vendor. Also, a list of responsibilities and tasks related to customer support should be provided.

Names and addresses of the vendor's customers who have acquired the same or similar technology should be included in the proposal. A list of 10 to 15 customers should be enough to interview to ascertain their satisfaction or dissatisfaction with the technology's and vendor's performance. The aim is to discover weaknesses and problems. Among the questions to ask these customers are "What don't you like about the vendor and its hardware and software?" "Who else do you know has acquired technology from the same vendor?" These other customers of the vendor should also be interviewed along with those on the list. Their responses may be more informative than the ones received from those on the vendor's list.

Request copies of the vendor's documentation. This material presents a tangible view of and insight into the vendors' technology, especially the software. Ask for a copy of the vendors' system release documentation that accompanied the last three or four hardware and software releases.

Demand a copy of the vendors' policies and procedures for hardware and software testing. Are the people who test the technology a different group from the ones who develop it? Also, ask for beta test results.

Because most vendors are public corporations, their last three or four years of audited financial statements should be provided. If the technology that the company plans to acquire is critical, then it is not too much to ask for audited financial statements of the vendor even if it is a closely held corporation. The ability of the vendor to remain a going concern over the life of the system is a paramount consideration in the evaluation and selection process. Therefore, an in-depth financial analysis of the vendor should be made. Also, the auditor's opinion of the financial statements should be noted. Obviously, an unqualified opinion is sought. The reasons for a qualified, adverse statement, or disclaimer of an auditor's opinion should be thoroughly investigated and resolved; otherwise, a vendor receiving such an opinion should be deleted from further evaluation.

5. *Legal and Business Procedures.* Vendors should be required to submit copies of their purchase contracts, service and maintenance plans and agreements, and other pertinent legal documents so they can be examined by the company's attorney. Business procedures include discounts, payment schedules, and cancelation policies.

6. *General Systems Design Proposals.* Copies of the General Systems Design Proposal Report, or relevant portions thereof, should be included in the RFP. This document provides vendors with excellent information on users' requirements, building blocks, and the system's working environment to guide them in preparing their proposals.

7. *Data Processing Requirements.* This is a design force discussed in earlier parts of this book that the vendor must respond to. Typically, these requirements can be defined and set up in hardware and software criteria comparison matrices, possibly listing the criteria, such as million instructions per second (MIPS) and disk capacity, in rank order. If the company plans to use benchmarks to test some of these criteria, this should also be included in the RFP. A questionnaire requiring short, objective answers may also be applicable here.

8. *Systems Requirements.* Systems requirements represent another design force discussed earlier in this book. It is not the same thing as users' requirements.

Systems requirements are those items that contribute to a better functioning system and, therefore, help to effect good systems design that, in turn, supports users' requirements. Moreover, systems requirements make a substantial impact on selection and application of hardware and software, or the technology building block. The vendor must therefore specify its technology's performance based on such things as reliability and availability measured by mean time between failure (MTBF), modularity, compatibility, installation schedule, ease of use, maintainability measured in terms of mean time to repair (MTTR), and vendor support. A questionnaire prepared to reflect the status of these systems requirements may be helpful to vendors and thereby speed up completion of proposals.

9. *Full Description of Technology Building Blocks.*   The vendor should present a full description of the technology building blocks they recommend for each of the general systems design alternatives, even if some parts of this description are repeated between each technology building block and elsewhere, such as in the questions from elements 7 and 8. Clear statements should be made about network topologies, architectures, model number, operating systems, primary storage capacity, front-end and back-end processors, language processors, security and control features, application program packages, and peripherals.

Each technology building block description should also contain statements about maintenance and service offered for that particular recommendation. The level of training, testing, and implementation support should also be disclosed.

10. *Price and Financing Plans.*   Full prices of the recommended technology building blocks should be provided in detail along with financing arrangements and alternative acquisition methods, such as purchase, rent, lease, or license.

11. *Evaluation Methodology.*   The company may wish to outline how it plans to evaluate the vendor's proposal and technology, and when the vendor can expect a response from the company. Of course, from the elements in the RFP, vendors should understand how they and their proposal and, specifically, their technology will be evaluated. But beyond this, if the systems analyst plans to benchmark or run simulations, vendors should understand what their responsibilities are and how these evaluation methods will be applied. Also, if the company intends to question the vendor's customers about what they think of the vendor's technology and its performance, then this too should be disclosed.

The advantages of preparing a RFP based on the preceding material are that (1) it helps to reduce the bits, bytes, and acronym syndrome; (2) vendors have to put their most competent personnel on this kind of RFP because it forces vendors to fit the technology building block recommendations to the systems designs and requirements; (3) all vendors are placed on a "level playing field," making evaluation fair and comparable; (4) because they are actively competing for business, vendors must prepare their best offer; and (5) this kind of RFP forces vendors to put specific commitments in writing.

General Review of Vendors' Proposals

At this level of evaluation, all the systems analyst is trying to do is identify a few vendors who have complied with all or nearly all the elements set forth in the RFP. The systems analyst is not trying to select the "best" vendor at this point, but is reviewing the proposals to weed out vendors who have inferior proposals and who fall short, and is putting together vendors' proposals worthy of more stringent evaluation. Vendors who are responsive to the RFP stay in the hunt. Vendors who do not respond, or whose proposals come up short, are eliminated from further evaluation.

Some vendor proposals may include a number of vague, hazy, and open-ended words or phrases that seem impressive on first reading but are subject to a variety of interpretations. Some examples are "We will do everything in our power to respond to your needs." "We meet service requests promptly." "We have an outstanding history of meeting our obligations." "We will assist you in every way we can." Taking into account that all vendors are entitled to some puffery, vendors who submit proposals that are unduly foggy without clear, substantive commitments should also be eliminated from further consideration. The same applies to vendors who submit proposals that include a number of promises about future products, services, and enhancements. Unless the vendor is prepared to document fully and back up such promises, they should be ignored. Promises have a way of not being kept.

SYSTEMS EVALUATION WORDS OF WISDOM

You are going to be bombarded by proposals from a wide spectrum of vendors, all guaranteeing success for your project if only their hardware or software is chosen. How to respond? Well, if you really intend to succeed, you'll do well to observe the following six guidelines:

- Develop a well-conceived evaluation plan;
- Don't delegate technical data processing evaluation to anyone but qualified professional staff;
- Check vendors' references religiously;
- Go to the top of your organization and get the time, staff, and financial resources to do a proper benchmark;
- Analyze the continuing vendors' financial viability;
- Evaluate vendors' post-sales support.

Excerpted from Robert Tasker, "How to Avoid Fumbling When Handling Vendor Proposals," *InformationWEEK*, September 7, 1987, p. 64.

Preparing for the Evaluation Screen Process

At this point, the systems analyst is ready to perform a rigorous and disciplined evaluation process. To do this, candidate vendors are pushed through the next

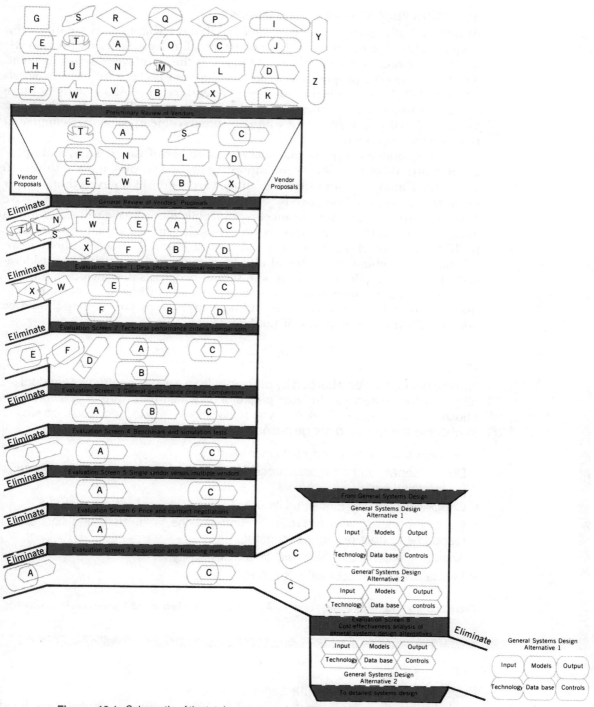

Figure 18.1 Schematic of the total systems evaluation process with emphasis on the eight evaluation screens.

eight evaluation screens to ascertain the best vendor. Figure 18.1 displays a schematic of this process.

As stated earlier and as the figure indicates, a preliminary investigation is made to determine a list of seemingly capable vendors to whom RFPs are sent. Proposals received are reviewed for general responsiveness. Then the evaluation screen process begins.

Proposals are desk checked in detail, technical performance criteria comparisons are made, general performance criteria are tested against each vendor, benchmark and simulation tests are run, single-vendor approach versus multiple-vendor approach are analyzed, price and contract terms are negotiated, acquisition and financing methods are examined, and finally general systems design alternatives along with the technology building block that supports them are evaluated based on benefits and costs to determine the one that is most cost-effective. By using the evaluation screens, the systems analyst is assured of picking the absolute best one.

18.4 EVALUATION SCREEN NUMBER ONE: DESK-CHECKING PROPOSAL ELEMENTS

Now the remaining qualified vendors are ready to be "pushed through" the first evaluation screen to determine those that qualify for the second evaluation screen. At this first level, the objective is to focus on vendors and their ability to meet commitments and their record of performance. If they pass through this screen, then how good and fast their "boxes" and software are will be evaluated next.

Vendors' Personnel

Possibly more important than hardware and software performance is the skill and dependability of vendors' personnel who will serve as liaison between the vendor and user company and who will be involved in installing and maintaining the technology building block. Skills required to perform these tasks should be analyzed thoroughly. Skills should not, however, be limited to technical proficiencies but should include management, business, and human-relation skills.

Another important consideration is the length of time the liaison personnel have worked for the vendor and their intention of staying with the vendor for at least the next several years. Also, try to determine if they are 9-to-5ers and play telephone tag or if they are easy to reach and are willing to come in at night and weekends to keep the system running. If the unspoken message seems to be that the system must operate to fit their schedule and at their convenience, then it's probably better in the long run to eliminate such vendors now.

Interviewing Vendors' Customers

Valuable information about technology and vendors' support can be gathered by interviewing vendors' customers. With this approach, the company is really simulating their association with a particular vendor and the use of its technology.

Typical questions put to vendors' customers are "How often has your system malfunctioned?" "How long does it take the vendor to respond to and fix the problem?" "What level of training and installation support did you get?" "Do users like to work with the system?" "Did you have any hidden or unexpected costs?" "Does your vendor meet its contractual obligations?" "Does your hardware and software fit and support your systems design?" "On a scale of 1 to 10, rate your vendor's support and the technology's performance." "If you were starting over, what would you do differently?" "What are the names of other vendor customers?"

Reviewing Vendors' Documentation

Does the vendors' hardware and software documentation meet the three Cs? That is, the documentation should be clear, current, and complete. A great deal of time should be devoted to reading vendors' documentation to see if it is easy to follow, free of computerese, and informative. Also, it should be checked to determine if it matches the last systems release. Outdated documentation is often worse than no documentation at all.

Determine if the systems release documentation is clear, detailed, and instructive. Does its contents represent true enhancements or merely bug fixes? While interviewing customers, they should be asked if the vendor informs them quickly and directly about bugs and how to fix them. Vendors who put the customer first notify all appropriate customers about a bug and how to fix it as soon as it's detected.

Vendors' Testing Procedures and Policies

A test group should be separate and independent of the development group. Such defined responsibility and independence ensures complete and rigorous testing of vendors' technology. Also, if the technology was at beta test sites before it was put into full production and widely marketed, find out who hosted the beta tests. These people should be interviewed to discover how much effort and discipline was put into developing and running the beta tests and what they thought of the test results.

Vendors' Financial Condition

Financial condition is a very important element that tells whether vendors are able to provide customer support and meet long-term obligations. Vendors whose financial condition is weak are likely to skimp on services and are less likely to provide hardware and software enhancements. Also, availability of maintenance personnel and spare parts is likely to become a problem. If the vendor is forced into bankruptcy, all source code and original documentation for software packages may be lost unless put into escrow.

General preliminary investigation was performed to weed out vendors who were obviously not good candidates to receive a RFP. But now, vendors who submitted proposals are put to a much tougher and detailed test to ascertain their financial worthiness. Three areas of investigation can help make this determination.

First, credit rating agencies and vendors' bankers can provide information on the general business practices and performance in meeting obligations. Also, courthouse records should be examined for liens and pending litigation. Further investigations should be conducted to discover contingencies and unasserted claims.

Second, the independent auditor's report on vendors' financial statements should be examined. If the auditor rendered an unqualified report, then this means the financial statements are presented fairly and can be relied on for further analysis. If, however, the auditor's report states that the financial statements do not present fairly the financial position and results of operations, or substantial doubt exists as to the vendor's ability to continue as a going concern, then such a vendor should be eliminated from further consideration.

Third, if the financial statements are fairly presented, then work should be performed on them using horizontal and vertical comparative analysis over a three- or four-year period to establish trends. Also, key solvency, asset management, and profitability ratios should be computed to highlight trouble spots, if any.

Vendors' General Legal and Business Procedures

All specimen contracts, such as sales agreements, service and maintenance, licenses, and other legal documents should be examined thoroughly by the company's attorney. Pricing schemes, financial plans, acquisition methods, and tax ramifications should be scrutinized by an accountant.

At this level, it is normally not worthwhile to try to negotiate better financial and contractual terms. Such negotiations should occur later in the evaluation process when the population of competing vendors has been reduced to two or three. The kind of terms that can be struck between the company and these last few qualified vendors is often the final deciding factor as to which vendor is selected.

18.5 EVALUATION SCREEN NUMBER TWO: TECHNICAL PERFORMANCE CRITERIA COMPARISONS

The vendors who successfully pass through the first evaluation screen are ready to have their products evaluated based on software and hardware technical performance criteria to find out how well their products form appropriate technology building blocks, to determine their technical feasibility, and to see if they meet the data processing requirements design force.

This second evaluation screen requires that each vendor's software technical performance criteria be placed side-by-side in a matrix to compare and contrast one vendor with the other and determine how well the software meets design requirements. Then each vendor's hardware technical performance criteria are evaluated in the same manner to find out how well the hardware fits the software and supports the data processing requirements. Not all possible technical performance criteria are listed and evaluated, but enough are listed in the following examples to demonstrate how such comparisons are made.

SELECTING THE RIGHT PACKAGE FOR THE JOB

The detail of each company's search for software reflects its own needs. Do you want an in-house system or a time-share service, a customized or pre-packaged system?

But when the time comes to pick one particular piece of software over all the rest that are on the market, your shopping list must be redrawn in minute detail. The criteria used by Peat Marwick Mitchell (PMM) to select a freight management system for Western Digital were drawn up from an extensive questionnaire compiled by the shipper, which forced potential vendors to describe their systems strictly in terms of Western's goals.

Some of the variables given the most weight in PMM's analysis were degree of customization, proven track record among current users, expandability, completeness of documentation, suitability to a network environment, and service and support.

When PMM crunched all the numbers, considered all the customer testimonials, and narrowed the field of vendors down to one, the system that was left was marketed by Vocam System, Inc.

During implementation, the reasons for PMM's heavy weighting became clear. During the actual implementation of the system at Western, Vocam in effect took over from PMM as Western's consultant. Vocam also trained all users at Western.

Condensed from Bruce Heydt, "The Computer Challenge: A Strategy for Software Selection," *Distribution*, April 1987, pp. 26–30.

Software Technical Performance Criteria Comparison

As discussed in Chapter 11, two general groups of software are: (1) computer operations oriented, such as operating systems, network management systems, and various utilities, and (2) user applications oriented, such as payroll, accounts receivable, inventory control, spreadsheets, and expert systems. Typically, the computer hardware vendor furnishes the computer operations software and possibly some or all of the applications-oriented packages required in a particular systems design. The more likely scenario is that the company acquires the hardware and computer operations software from a computer manufacturer and either develops its own applications-oriented packages using a programming language such as COBOL or acquires canned application packages from a software vendor or user group.

In any event, the software must match and support the general systems design alternatives. As a general rule, software is much more important than hardware because software is really what makes the information systems design work properly and meets users' requirements. Roughly, a company spends more per second for a manager's salary than it costs to process millions of instruction by the latest CPUs within that same second. Is it any wonder that systems design is directed to users first, then software, and finally hardware? Moreover, hardware costs are often less than 10 to 20 percent of total software costs.

In the software technical performance criteria comparison matrix displayed in Figure 18.2, we assume that the company is planning to develop in-house some of its applications and acquire order-entry and scheduling packages from a vendor. We also assume that all the vendors are striving to become turnkey vendors. The entries in the matrix are furnished by the vendors' proposals and some further investigation by the systems analyst. Please note that the entries in the matrix are hypothetical and do not necessarily represent any real-world vendor.

From the software technical performance criteria comparison matrix, systems analysts can focus on the technical performance criteria they deem most important. If, for example, the operating system of choice is Unix, then only vendors A and D would remain in the hunt. If a back-end controller that interacts with the data base and stages data for processing is a key technical performance criterion, then vendor E would be eliminated. Vendor E would also be deleted if a LAN file server, a COBOL compiler, and a relational or network data base management system (DBMS) are required. Similar decisions are made throughout the process of examining the criteria.

Note that vendor F does not offer an order-entry and scheduling software packages. This may or may not eliminate vendor F from further evaluation. The company may decide that vendor F compares so favorably in other technical performance criteria that a decision would be made to leave vendor F in the race and acquire the order-entry and scheduling packages from another vendor, assuming that vendor F is the final choice. In the future, as more and more major computer hardware vendors get into the applications software business, the more they will be evaluated as turnkey vendors.

In our example, it is assumed that vendors E and F are removed at this point from the evaluation process. The systems policy of the company is to go with turnkey vendors as much as possible, which eliminates vendor F. Vendor E is deleted because it does not meet some of the software technical performance criteria requirements and is therefore not technically feasible. It also appears to have a weak order-entry package. Its lack of point-of-sale (POS) entry limits its ability to achieve integration throughout the company. The absence of a spreadsheet interface limits its ability to meet the user/system interface design force. Lack of fill-in prompting forms and window inquiry make it weak in the human factors area.

Hardware Technical Performance Criteria Comparisons

Figure 18.3 illustrates the hardware technical performance criteria for hypothetical vendors A, B, C, and D. The purchase prices are for a turnkey system, which include the software.

The results of comparing hardware technical performance criteria between vendors seem to be fairly even, except for vendor D. For example, vendor D's

Software Technical Performance Criteria \ Vendors	A	B	C	D	E	F
Operating system for mainframe	MS/DOS DOS, UNIX	VM, MVS DOS, OS/2	VMS, UNIX OS/2, DOS	VMS UNIX	CPM DOS	VSE DOS
Front-end controller	Yes	Yes	Yes	Yes	Yes	Yes
Back-end controller	Yes	Yes	Yes	Yes	No	Yes
LAN file server	Yes	Yes	Yes	Yes	No	Yes
Spooling package	Yes	Yes	Yes	Yes	Yes	Yes
Programming languages	COBOL, FORTRAN	COBOL, C, FORTRAN	COBOL, C, RPG	COBOL, ADA	FORTRAN, BASIC	COBOL, C, FORTRAN
DBMS	Relation Tree	Relation	Relation Tree	Relation	Tree	Network
Query language	SQL	SQL	SQL	QBE SQL	SQL	SQL
Operating system for server	MS/DOS UNIX	VM, MVS DOS, OS/2	VMS, UNIX OS/2	DOS UNIX	DOS	DOS UNIX
Main storage required	512 KB	600 KB	512 KB	700 KB	600 KB	512 KB
Disk storage required	30 MB	20 MB	30 MB	40 MB	30 MB	30 MB
Access control	Password	Password	Password	Password	Retina scan	Card and password
Telecommunication protocols	TOP/MAP X.25	TCP/IP SNA	SNA, TCP/IP NETVIEW	DECNET	OVERVIEW	TOP/MAP OSI
LAN topology	Star	Ring	Ring	Bus	Loop	Ring
Access schemes	PABX	Token	Token	CSMA-CD	Token	Token
Encryption scheme	DES	DES	Public key	DES	DES	Public key
Order-entry package	Yes	Yes	Yes	Yes	Yes	No
Point of sale	Yes	Yes	Yes	Yes	No	—
Bar code entry	Yes	Yes	Yes	Yes	No	—
Forms fill-in prompting	Yes	Yes	Yes	No	No	—
Backorder processing	Yes	Yes	Yes	Yes	Yes	—
Window inquiry	Yes	Yes	Yes	Yes	No	—
Quantity discount levels	4	5	6	5	3	—
Order tracking	Yes	Yes	Yes	Yes	Yes	—
Spreadsheet interface	Yes	Yes	Yes	Yes	No	—
Item number	45 AN char	20 AN char	40 AN char	40 AN char	30 AN char	—
Scheduling package	Yes	Yes	Yes	Yes	Yes	—
Documentation media	Manuals	Manuals	Video and manuals	Manuals	Manuals	—
Documentation quality	B	B-	A-	B-	C	—
Operating system required	MS/DOS UNIX	MVS DOS	VMS, UNIX OS/2	VMS UNIX	CPM DOS	—
Main storage required	256 KB	300 KB	350 KB	256 KB	400 KB	—
Hard disk required	30 MB	20 MB	30 MB	40 MB	30 MB	—

Figure 18.2 A software technical performance criteria comparison matrix.

Hardware Technical Performance Criteria \ Vendors	A	B	C	D
Purchase price	$1.5M	$1.9M	$1.8M	$2.1M
CPU instructions per second	100 MIPS	120 MIPS	115 MIPS	100 MIPS
Main storage	1.0 GB	1.2 GB	1.3 GB	.9 GB
Extended main storage	.5 GB	.5 GB	.6 GB	.4 GB
Large hard disk	6.0 GB	6.0 GB	6.4 GB	5.0 GB
Winchester disk	500.0 MB $5\frac{1}{4}''$	1.0 GB $5\frac{1}{4}''$	1.0 GB $3\frac{1}{2}''$	1.0 GB $3\frac{1}{2}''$
Multifunctional workstations	500 ports	400 ports	400 ports	100 in LAN
High-resolution graphics	Yes	Yes	Yes	Yes
Page printers (pages per minute)	150	110	140	70
Resolution (pixels per inch)	300 × 300	240 × 240	260 × 260	200 × 300
Print medium	Paper	Fanfold	Sheet	Sheet
Print modes	Letter quality	Draft	Letter quality	Draft
Laser printer	Yes	Yes	Yes	Yes
Fonts in library	78	48	52	60
Line printer (lines per minute)	2000	1200	1500	1200
Monochrome display	Amber Gold	Green	Green	Green

Figure 18.3 A hardware technical performance criteria comparison matrix.

cost is out of line and not economically feasible. The other vendors' purchase price is about $150,000 per million instructions per second (MIPS), whereas vendor D's purchase price is over $200,000 per MIPS. Moreover, vendor D's main and extended storage and hard-disk capacities are significantly less than that of the other vendors. The ratio of large hard-disk storage capacity to main storage capacity is about 6 to 1 for all vendors, which is pretty much on target.

If the company's general systems design alternatives require online distribution of over 300 multifunctional workstations throughout the planned network, then vendor D is not even close to meeting data processing requirements, integration, technical feasibility, and other design forces. Therefore, vendor is eliminated from further evaluation.

In some cases, certain features of several vendors can be comb produce the best possible hardware configuration. For example, the printer facilities of vendor A could be used with vendor B's CPU and other devices to produce a better configuration than either one using a full complement of their hardware. Combining multivendor hardware, however, will not work unless the devices are compatible and can "talk to each other."

18.6 EVALUATION SCREEN NUMBER THREE: GENERAL PERFORMANCE CRITERIA COMPARISONS

Now that vendors A, B, and C still remain as viable candidates in the evaluation process, the systems analyst is ready to see how they stack up against general performance criteria of compatibility, modularity, maintainability, reliability, life expectancy, installation schedule, and vendor support. These criteria determine how well the vendors' products meet the systems requirements design force.

Compatibility

Compatibility ensures that all building blocks of a systems design come together to operate in harmony, without disruption and major alteration, and that these building blocks form a totally congruent information system during its life cycle. Compatibility is a generic performance criterion that is somewhat synonymous with and supportive of terms, such as flexibility, independence, migration, portability, and universality. Compatibility therefore is an umbrella criterion that covers all these subcriteria.

Flexible software and hardware are designed for a variety of purposes and can support a number of applications with equal facility. Modularity, covered in the next subsection, also increases flexibility.

Independence means that the technology does not have to rely on other facilities to operate and is free of technical constraints. Unix, for example, is a generic operating system, whereas many of the other operating systems are proprietary. Therefore, Unix is machine independent and also gives the systems analyst a rich supply of application programs.

Portability of software and hardware means that either can be moved to another environment and continue to operate without alteration. Application program A, for example, can run on computer X, Y, or Z.

Migration is path oriented in that the technology can move from one level or stage to another and another without revision. Can the vendor make advances in its operating system and hardware without customers being left out in the cold? The aim of systems analysts is not to be shut out in the cold by selecting a vendor with a single, cohesive software and hardware strategy that provides a well-defined migration path.

Universality means that the technology is widespread. Particular software and hardware are accepted, understood, and supported by a large number of users. For example, COBOL could be called a universal programming language.

IBM's systems application architecture (SAA) strives to provide users' applications with independence from IBM's different hardware products and operating systems. That is, practically any user application and canned software package are compatible with any IBM computer because the SAA isolates these applications from the different operating systems, as depicted in Figure 18.4.

The very different operating systems, VM, MVS, 3X, and OS/2, will look virtually identical to application programmers, DBMSs, structured query language (SQL), and software vendors. The underlying operating systems and hardware platforms are really made irrelevant to anyone who is writing or installing a software package because the SAA masks the differences in IBM multiple operating systems by providing common services and compatible interfaces. For example, a programmer may write an accounting package in C or COBOL for a Personal System/2 (PS/2) and later run it on 3X or 370 hardware platforms.

Users can migrate from one IBM family of products to another and thereby leverage investment in applications software. Also, it helps IBM because otherwise they would have to write one software application package, such as an office automation, banking, or inventory control package for four or five operating systems environments. Obviously, this costs IBM money and time. Moreover, software vendors like Lotus, Ashton-Tate, McCormack & Dodge, and Cullinet can market essentially the same application packages to all IBM customers.

Software vendors and application programmers cannot, however, write below SAA to the operating systems level, which typically means giving up hardware performance. In other words, it is a trade-off between hardware performance on one side and application compatibility and portability on the other side. With the price/performance ratio in hardware improving at a 20 percent or more rate per year, this trade-off becomes less and less significant.

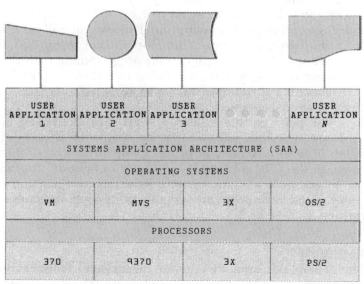

Figure 18.4 Isolation of users' applications from internal operations to effect compatibility across disparate technology.

The key to selecting a particular programming language or software package is its universality. COBOL, for example, continues to be the programming language of choice for the vast majority of information systems applications. And FORTRAN is to scientists and engineers what COBOL is to businesspeople. Some believe that Ada, the programming language developed by the U.S. government and mandated as the standard for military and federal government software, is the language of the future and is taking aim at COBOL and FORTRAN. Ada is a language that is easily ported to different hardware platforms and easily maintained.

For strict hardware performance, the ultimate is assembler language, but assembler is poor in terms of programmer productivity. COBOL is at the opposite extreme in that it gives good programmer productivity but does not yield good program performance. But again this trade-off for better hardware performance is not as important as it once was. Moreover, if a company writes thousands of lines in assembler code for its applications and later has to install hardware that is not compatible with the assembler language, then a major conversion will be required.

Furthermore, not many skilled programmers are available who can write in assembler languages. Also, IBM's SAA project excludes assembler languages. It, on the other hand, sanctions C, COBOL, and FORTRAN. IBM has also "embraced" Ada in its third-party software programs.

The C language is often referred to as a "programmer's language" because it has strong commands and is compatible on a variety of machines. C does not excel in either hardware performance or programmer productivity, but it is strong in both areas. C is, therefore, a fairly good fit between assembler and high-level lenguages, such as COBOL and FORTRAN. C works well in a micro, mini, midrange, or mainframe environment.

Some believe that C, because of its "techie look," will do well in scientific and engineering programming installations, but will be shunned by business application programmers and therefore will never approach COBOL's universal acceptance. Indeed, the applications programming path is scattered with programming languages that have failed to dislodge COBOL from the business environment. For example, PL/1 was heralded for years as COBOL's replacement. It never happened.

The point to this is: always select a programming language as well as hardware and other software that are compatible across different systems and widely accepted. A number of cases exist in which an obscure programming language was used to develop thousands of lines of programming code. Then the programmer who knew how to write this code left, and replacements could not be found to maintain the program or develop new ones or to use it on other machines.

Modularity

This general performance criterion means that hardware components and software modules can be added or changed easily. Moreover, the technology building block can grow and change to meet needs of a growing and changing information system. The organization, for example, can start with a basic computer system and then increase the capacity of main storage and power of the mainframe and add peripherals as needs arise. Modularity therefore aids flexibility and growth potential of systems.

It is wasteful to buy software and hardware that are more advanced or complex than what the systems design alternatives call for. If systems are designed properly, they optimally meet both current and future requirements. Modularity of software and hardware enables the system to do this by meeting present requirements and also accommodating downstream requirements. Or instances may occur in which the company does not want to implement a full-blown system but rather wants to install it module-by-module. Obviously, modularity gives the flexibility to do this also.

Many software vendors offer software packages that consist of a secure, unmodifiable core (also called kernel, nexus, or base). The core provides basic services and capabilities. It is supplemented by a set of features and functions that can be tailored within broad limits to the application environment. These modules provide a broad array of reports and query capabilities to help meet different users' specific output requirements. Moreover, certain procedures may change in the future, such as a change from first-in, first-out (FIFO) to last-in, first-out (LIFO) inventory accounting or from straight-line to sum-of-the-years'-digits method of depreciation. Options are available in most packages that allow these changes to be made easily. Online tutorials guide users through the installation of a new module, and help keys enable them to refresh their memory about how a previous module was installed.

Maintainability

Mean time to repair is the basic measure of maintainability. The MTTR consists of the time required to accomplish the following: detect the nature of the failure, isolate the malfunctioning element, remove the malfunctioning element, obtain a replacement for it, replace it, verify its operability, initialize the replacement, and proceed to an operable state. The accomplishment of these actions is influenced by the physical construction, the level at which replacements can be made, the training of the maintenance technicians, the ability to detect and isolate malfunctions, the extent and quality of diagnostic tools, the built-in test and diagnostic facilities of the system, and the repair facilities of the complex.

Probably the biggest pitfall in application software packages is maintenance. Difficult-to-maintain packages may work just fine as long as the applications they process remain static, but as new users' requirements evolve, software packages must also be modified. To facilitate this maintenance, good, clear documentation; complete user training; high-quality source code; modular design; and an array of optional features and functions are especially important in these packages. Therefore, the systems analyst should investigate thoroughly vendors' software maintainability. Some application packages are designed for easy maintenance while others are a bear to maintain.

A large construction company bought a "complete" software package for estimating, job costing, and billing. A major new contract required that job costing and billings be handled in a way that the package could not accommodate. A totally new package had to be developed. Another corporation signed a new union contract that called for a new, complicated method for calculating benefits and wages. Suddenly, the payroll package could not process the payroll. Modifications were so cumbersome and difficult that a new payroll package had to be written.

Some software packages are designed without any hooks (or interfaces) for user-oriented code to run ad hoc applications. Difficult-to-maintain packages may not even provide source code or it may be written in a low-level language that no one understands. Or for some users who are planning on maintenance support and enhancements from their vendors, the final blow is struck if these software vendors go out of business. If users insist that the source code be clearly documented and held in escrow, then this may ease some of the pain of the software vendor's disappearance.

Reliability

Reliability means that users can depend on the software and hardware working as planned. Two factors that increase technology's reliability are fault avoidance and fault tolerance.

Fault avoidance (or fault intolerance) is a concept that uses procedures to reduce the probability that the system will fail. Fault-avoidance procedures include skilled design techniques, independent design reviews, breadboard and prototype testing, use of high-reliability components, precise production techniques, and quality control and rigorous product testing.

Fault tolerance uses redundant software and hardware components and fault-detection techniques to discover and to bypass the effects of a failure and recover back into a working system. The term fault-tolerant computing is defined as the ability to recover and perform processing tasks in the presence of component failures.

Mean time between failure is the quantitative measure of reliability. MTBF is regarded as the average time technology may be expected to operate before it fails.

Both reliability (MTBF) and maintainability (MTTR) are combined in the concept of availability. An increase in MTBF and a decrease in MTTR increases the technology's availability to users. Clearly, the objective is to select a vendor whose technology's MTBF is measured in years and MTTR is measured in minutes or seconds. Obviously, the ideal to shoot for is a fault-avoidance system. This is an ideal that may be approached but probably never attained.

The three classes of recovery in a fault-tolerant system procedures are full recovery, degraded recovery, and safe shutdown. Full recovery in a real-time environment provides continuous and complete operations even in a faulty environment. Degraded recovery enables selected applications to operate fully, or the total system operates with performance characteristics below standard until repairs are made. Safe shutdown permits a graceful shutdown of the system to avoid damaging components, such as head crashes, to terminate operations in an orderly manner, and to deliver appropriate messages and diagnostics to users and maintenance personnel.

Life Expectancy

Two aspects of life expectancy are product standardization and product life cycle. If a computer is not part of the vendor's standard product line, it is considered a "dead-end" system. It is not compatible with standard peripherals and operating systems and is often not modularly designed, which decreases its flexibility and growth potential. When the information system "tops out" on a dead-end computer, there is no place to go. The closer the technology is to its top capacity when installed to support the information system, the shorter its life expectancy and the sooner it dies. The information system will then have to be redesigned completely and new programs written or acquired before conversion can be made to another technology building block.

As far as the technology's life cycle is concerned, the systems analyst must consider both capacity and acquisition methods. Typically, the analyst should not acquire technology late in its life cycle because the company ends up either being stuck with it or unable to acquire new technology because of the financing arrangement of the current technology.

The more the technology is at the early stages in its life cycle, the greater its residual value. The objective is to acquire technology with a useful life and residual value at a level that minimizes budget impact and maximizes flexibility to react to opportunities. This objective is a function of how long the current capacity will hold out, what management's systems policy is for staying technologically current, and how quickly the vendor will introduce new technology. Generally, the systems analyst should project useful life and residual value of technology where the residual value falls to roughly 30 to 40 percent of the total cost around the time the vendor is expected to introduce its next system.

If technology is late in its life cycle, it might be better to buy, lease, or rent used technology to tide the company over rather than to make a large commitment at the tail end of a particular technology's life cycle. Also, it is always a good idea to stay away from acquisition methods and financial arrangements that prevent the company from moving to new technology when it becomes available.

Another very important aspect of the product's life cycle is the continuing level of support and enhancements offered by the vendor. For example, it is generally unwise to acquire a product line that has become "functionally stabilized" by the vendor. This term is just an euphemism that means development, enhancements, and support of this product line has ceased.

Installation Schedule

In some companies, systems development backlogs are measured in years. In-house software projects may take months or years to develop and the final development cost may far exceed the budget. Worse than this, in-house development may never produce a completed software package or one that is bug free.

Generally, it is better to purchase or license a software package than it is to build it from scratch, assuming that it is cost-effective, well designed, and documented; meets users' requirements; and, of course, can be installed within the system development methodology's (SDM's) projected time period. Generally, software packages can be installed within hours or days at a known fixed cost. Also, if the software package is widely used, it is probably bug free because it has been tested numerous times.

On the other hand, if the systems design is unique or the company's operations are "we don't do it like anybody else," then the system will probably require customized software. Before going this route, however, the systems analyst may be able to make only some minor design adjustments to fit a canned software package. If not, consideration should be given to contracting with a programming specialist to write the program in a high-level language such as COBOL on a turnkey basis with a firm completion date. This alternative assumes that the company does not have the necessary in-house programming skills, or if it does, these skills are already committed to other projects. Also, the use of fourth-generation languages (4GLs), computer-aided software engineering (CASE) systems, and data base management systems (DBMSs) should be considered as ways to decrease installation schedule time.

On the hardware side, installation schedules can sometimes present a problem. The vendor may promise delivery of a particular product at a certain time, and the analyst schedules other systems work with the promised date as a key milestone. But because of unforeseen circumstances, the vendor cannot meet the deadline, so the total systems project is in limbo waiting for the vendor.

In other similar instances, a vendor makes an announcement of a new product along with its delivery date. Enough specifications are published for some companies to tie their new information systems designs to the announced product, but the product is six months late, a year late, and in some instances is never delivered. This unfortunate situation is termed vaporware.

Vendor Support

Support from the vendor is one of the most critical criteria in the evaluation process. The general advice is to make vendors prove their support claims and to "get it in writing" because in the long run, software and hardware are no better than their support from the vendor. This support includes such things as (1) availability of training facilities; (2) installation support; (3) systems development, conversion, and testing assistance; (4) experience level and competency of vendor's personnel; (5) duration of time any support is available after installation; (6) availability of a user group; and (7) availability of specialized software systems, such as data base management systems.

An important vendor support issue revolves around bundling and unbundling. If a computer vendor offers a bundled product line, this means that the price of the computer system includes the hardware, operating system, language processors, programs for specific applications, educational services, installation support, and a systems engineer for X hours. An unbundled product line price means that the price is for the hardware only. Most vendors have moved to something of a semibundled approach in which they bundle the hardware, operating system, language processors, and some level of installation support, but unbundle other services and application software packages. Some leading computer manufacturers are, for example, becoming deeply involved in developing application software packages and marketing them aggressively to run on their hardware or competitors' hardware. Such packages are priced as stand-alone product lines.

Although software and especially hardware reliability, compatibility, modularity, and life expectancy may be virtually equivalent between vendors, a failure or problem with one vendor's product line may cost considerably more than with other vendors because of differences in levels of support after the technology has been installed. Some vendors may have the attitude that once they sell it, it's yours for better or worse, or if customers want help they will have to pay for it. As one information systems executive remarked, "If you have to scream and yell, raise hell and put a chunk under it to get service, it's not worth it."

The systems analyst should check if the vendors under consideration communicate directly with their customers to inform them about problems, potential failures, and bugs and give support for making fixes. Another indicator of a strained and rocky relationship between vendor and customer is the number of separate divisions the vendor maintains. In some instances, if product lines are separated and hardware development is separate from software development, it could be that the "left hand doesn't know what the right hand is doing," which generally equates to a "passing-the-buck" trap and poor service. This passing-the-buck routine can also occur in multiple-vendor environments in which one vendor will say that their device doesn't work properly because it is connected to a competitor's device, which is obviously causing all the problems.

The final key thing that the systems analyst looks for is the vendor's support methodology used after the technology has been installed. Figure 18.5 illustrates by a flowchart a support methodology that should work well in most circumstances. The illustration should be self-explanatory as to how support is given by the vendor to resolve customer problems.

General Performance Criteria Comparisons

Whereas the technical performance criteria are more quantitative and objective, the general performance criteria are qualitative and subjective. Nonetheless, the general performance criteria represent a significant component of the evaluation process and therefore deserve to be researched, scrutinized, and measured by the systems analyst. Figure 18.6 reveals a method by which the general performance criteria can be measured and comparisons made between vendors.

To prepare the general performance criteria comparison matrix, the systems analyst first determines the relative weight of each criterion using a base of 100. Next, based on the best information about the criteria applicable to each vendor, the analyst assigns a value to each criterion. The weights are then multiplied by the criteria values. Each resulting score is finally summed to give a total score for each vendor. In our example, vendor C has the highest score, but the scores are too close to make a final selection although some concern is justified about vendor A's reliability, life expectancy, installation schedule, and vendor support. On a scale of 0 to 10, these general performance criteria are only average. Because reliability is inversely related to maintainability, vendor A's high maintainability helps to compensate a little for its average performance in reliability.

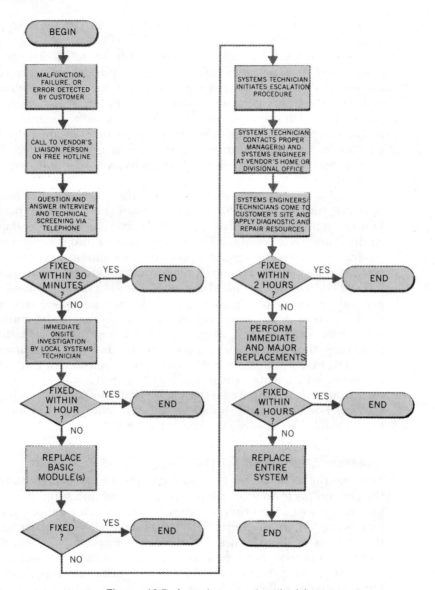

Figure 18.5 A vendor support methodology.

Evaluations from Professional Service Companies

Professional service companies[1] are in business to gather a wealth of information about all the computer manufacturers and their equipment. They, in turn, sell this information to subscribers. The history and a management summary of each

---

[1]Datapro Research Corporation, Delran, N.J.

General Performance Criteria	Weight	Vendor A		Vendor B		Vendor C	
		Value	Score	Value	Score	Value	Score
Compatibility	10	6	60	7	70	5	50
Modularity	10	7	70	7	70	5	50
Maintainability	20	8	160	6	120	7	140
Reliability	20	6	120	7	140	9	180
Life expectancy	10	5	50	6	60	8	80
Installation schedule	10	4	40	5	50	6	60
Vendor support	20	5	100	6	120	6	120
Total	100		600		630		680

Figure 18.6 A general performance criteria comparison matrix.

manufacturer are provided. Other information consists of main storage capacity and cycle time, control storage, registers, instruction repertoire, instruction timing, and input/output control. Also, peripheral devices are described and their speed is given. The operating system software is described, along with available utilities and application program languages. Support provided by the manufacturer, such as training, installation, and maintenance, is covered together with

Performance Criteria	Ratings of Users				
	Excellent	Good	Fair	Poor	WA
Ease of operation	7	5	2	0	3.4
Reliability of mainframe	7	5	2	0	3.4
Reliability of peripherals	4	8	1	1	3.1
Maintenance service:					
Responsiveness	4	7	1	2	2.9
Effectiveness	2	7	5	0	2.8
Technical support	4	5	4	0	3.0
Manufacturer's software:					
Operating system	3	6	4	1	2.8
Compilers	3	6	5	0	2.9
Application programs	2	5	4	1	2.7
Ease of programming	4	6	3	0	3.1
Ease of conversion	4	3	5	0	2.9
Overall satisfaction	4	6	4	0	3.0

Figure 18.7 Fourteen user responses to a survey about a particular computer manufacturer (conducted by Datapro Research Corporation). (Weighted average on a scale of 4.0 for excellent.)

items that are bundled/unbundled. A complete price list of all equipment is supplied. Responses are compiled from surveys of customers who use the equipment (i.e., "ask the person who owns one"). An example of results from these surveys is shown in Figure 18.7. In some surveys, technical support, responses to troubleshooting, education, and documentation are included. This information, plus the information already presented, assists the prospective computer user in making an informed decision.

18.7 EVALUATION SCREEN NUMBER FOUR: BENCHMARK AND SIMULATION TESTS

Reviewing and desk-checking vendors' proposals, querying them about their technology, researching their product lines, and comparing various technical and general performance criteria eliminate those vendors who do not measure up. The vendors left in the running at this point appear to be reasonably close to each other in what they are offering. But which one actually performs the best under operating or near-operating conditions? Two methods that can be used to determine this status are benchmarks and simulation.

Benchmark Method

Test problems are prepared and run on the equipment configuration proposed by the vendor. Overall, the benchmark programs test (1) anticipated work load, (2) compilers, (3) operating system, and (4) application and utility packages. To apply benchmark programs, the systems analyst can obtain an agreement with the vendor to run the programs at the vendor's location, run the programs on some other user's computer system (assuming it is the same as the one proposed), or hire a consulting firm to perform the benchmark testing.

Unfortunately, in a number of independent benchmark cases, the results have drawn fire from some vendors who believe that the benchmarks are conducted unfairly. Charges and countercharges are made without much help and enlightenment for users. For example, a major DBMS vendor claimed that its system achieved 65 transactions per second in an automated teller machine (ATM) application. Another benchmark test conducted by an independent company showed the same DBMS processed only 20 transactions per second in an order-entry application compared to 40 transactions per second by a competing DBMS.

Generally, if the technological stakes are high and the software applications run on the new hardware platform are critical, then the benchmarks should be run on the same kind of technology that the analyst is evaluating. If, on the other hand, the new software and hardware are not exceedingly critical and the stakes are not that high, then the analyst can use benchmarks and simulations run by independent testing companies or an association of computer users using generalized transactions and program applications. If a software package is the only piece of the technology building block that will be acquired, then the package should be run on the company's hardware for at least a 30-day trial period.

The benchmark test problems should represent the kinds of applications

USE FULL-STRESS BENCHMARKING

Published DBMS benchmarks can be particularly misleading when they extrapolate results from low-volume tests, according to consultant Carl Longnecker of Arthur Andersen & Company. DBMSs have internal software bottlenecks that limit the number of concurrent users regardless of the available resources. These bottlenecks may not show up until the system is actually "stressed," that is, presented with a number of concurrent queries or transactions that at least equal the number it will have to handle in production. Longnecker says benchmarks should include a representative number of data update operations, because updates require more processing than queries. This implies that benchmarks that test queries only will usually be misleading.

George Schussel, a counsultant with Digital Consulting, points out that the performance of a DBMS depends to a large extent on how well the operators understand its workings. A vendor, therefore, can make the product run much more efficiently than its potential customers. Schussel gives this guideline for evaluating vendor-supplied results: "Discount them by at least 100 percent."

Excerpted from David Kull, "Beware the Benchmark," *Computer Decisions,* February 9, 1987, pp. 48–51.

that will run in the new system. In general, the two types of applications are input/output bound and process bound. Some technology handles process-bound problems such as complex mathematical algorithms very efficiently, but may be weak in input/output-bound problems such as a large payroll application. It is therefore imperative that the applications tested be very close to or duplicate the actual applications' work loads and data processing requirements of the systems design alternatives. For payroll, how fast can the system prepare checks, update files, and generate reports? For interaction with the data base, how fast can the DBMS access and display a variety of records? For a sophisticated model, how long does it take to derive the results? For a large volume of input/output, are channels capable of handling the workload? Often, a user acquires a computer system without benchmarking it, installs it, and converts to the actual workload, only to bring the system to its knees because it cannot handle the I/O load.

Benchmarking should be a cooperative effort between user and vendor, not an adversarial one. If possible, the systems analyst should benchmark a similar up-and-running system in another user's organization with the same kind of network, terminals, processor, files, and applications. The key is total performance measurements, not sleight-of-hand functional measurements like generating random numbers, calculating prime numbers, or playing chess. Also, if the vendor runs the benchmarks, the systems analyst should be in attendance to make sure that the computer system benchmarked is the same as the one that will be delivered, not one with a special optimizing code or a special configuration.

Figure 18.8 demonstrates the benchmark results of vendors A, B, and C.

> **THE COMPUTERS COULDN'T KEEP UP**
>
> Accoring to the General Accounting Office (GAO), the stock exchange computer systems were unable to handle the volume of transactions attempted during the stock market crash of October 1987.
>
> The bottleneck resulted from a control device through which all orders are transmitted to the printers. The controller has a capacity of 68 messages per second, which was exceeded by peak volume of 72 messages per second on October 19 when the Dow Jones industrial average fell 508 points. The deals meant that market orders were executed at prices significantly different from those in effect when the orders were entered.

Applications which are representative of the systems design alternatives were run on the vendors' proposed configurations. The results reveal that vendors A and C are close in actual timed performance, whereas vendor B's benchmark performance rates are a poor third. Also, it was found that vendor B's peripherals did not perform very well. The disk system malfunctioned twice, and the printer speed was considerably less than what was indicated in the technical performance criteria matrix. Also, the printer did not stack the paper straight

Applications \ Vendors	Vendor A	Vendor B	Vendor C
Order-entry and accounts receivable update	45.0 minutes	57.4 minutes	39.3 minutes
Backup of disk to tape	24.1 minutes	43.7 minutes	22.9 minutes
Output of accounts receivable aging report	3.4 minutes	9.3 minutes	3.1 minutes
Processing of 1000 order-entry transactions	23 per second	10 per second	24 per second
Query data base for order status	2.4 seconds response time	12.4 seconds response time	2.9 seconds response time
Processing 3-D images	9.7 per second average	11.7 per second average	9.1 per second average

Figure 18.8 Results of an applications benchmark test for vendors A, B, and C.

and the feeder caused the paper to jam twice while generating the accounts receivable aging report. Moreover, the query response time for vendor B was excrutiatingly slow.

Simulation Method

Simulation packages are available to simulate the performance of a variety of computer systems. These packages incorporate mathematical models that accept measurements, such as sizes and structures of files, frequency of access to files, I/O volumes, and workload descriptions. These models are then run on computers to predict time considerations such as turnaround time, clock time, and response time. In addition, simulation models help to predict systems capacity (used and unused) and to define optimal equipment configurations. Simulation packages can be purchased or leased from various suppliers of software.

18.8 EVALUATION SCREEN NUMBER FIVE: SINGLE VENDOR VERSUS MULTIPLE VENDORS

The company must decide if it is going to use one vendor for its total hardware and software platform or acquire a processor from one vendor, telecommunications front-ends and cabling from another, peripherals from another, and software from yet another. Both approaches have advantages and disadvantages, which should be studied carefully before selecting either strategy.

Single Vendor

A responsible turnkey vendor can provide hardware and software; training, testing, and conversion; offer supplies and communication services; and perform maintenance. With a single vendor, the advantages are (1) the ability to deal and negotiate with only one vendor; (2) fewer complexities and provisions in the contract; (3) easier enhancements, changes, and trade-ins; and (4) better support. The disadvantages of selecting a single vendor are (1) usually a higher price, unless the company uses the evaluation process discussed in this chapter that stresses competitive bidding among vendors; (2) less negotiating leverage, unless competitive evaluation methods are used; and (3) a weaker user/vendor relationship if the user is viewed as a captured customer.

In some cases, however, the customer can negotiate a better package deal by bargaining with one vendor rather than trying to nail together bits and pieces of the system from several vendors. Some managers feel that a potpourri of equipment is just one more thing to worry about. Also, little glitches in the interfaces can occur that can cause all kinds of headaches. The rationale of the people who choose the single-vendor approach is that it's safer and that they have more clout by dealing with one vendor. Their recommendation is to evaluate several vendors similar to the process in this chapter and narrow the field to two or three that are somewhat equal, negotiate with each one, and go with the one who gives the best contract and financial arrangement.

Multiple Vendors

With multiple vendors, the advantages are (1) the user can generally acquire the total system at a lower cost, (2) a better performing, more efficient system may result due to putting together a configuration that combines the best features of each vendor, and (3) competition among vendors is increased and thus negotiating leverage is improved. The disadvantages of selecting multiple vendors are (1) more work and time is involved in reviewing proposals and putting the total system together, (2) compatibility problems may result, (3) total vendor commitment may be reduced, and (4) enhancements, changes, and trade-ins are more difficult.

18.9 EVALUATION SCREEN NUMBER SIX: PRICE AND CONTRACT NEGOTIATIONS

At this stage, only a few vendors remain in the running. In our example, only vendors A and C remain. It is now time to negotiate with these vendors to determine which one gives the "best deal" based on price and contract provisions. The "asking price" is already known. Negotiations set the "selling price." The major objective of an adroitly negotiated contract from the company's viewpoint is a high level of confidence that the technology is usable and maintainable over its expected life and the technology selected gives the best price/performance ratio.

Contract Negotiations Overview

A wise old adage is "Get it in writing." Taking precautions to avoid problems before acquisition is indeed much more sensible and easier than is trying to find a solution afterward. But what should the company get in writing? In most cases, the vendor's standard contract is one-sided, prepared in favor of the vendor. Therefore, this contract should serve as the starting point in the negotiations process to bring the terms more in line with what is reasonable and equitable to both parties.

The final contract should contain key elements of the original vendor proposals that were submitted in accordance with the RFP. Especially important is to include the price and detailed specifications of software and hardware to disclose exactly what is to be delivered and a guarantee that the technology will perform according to these specifications. Also acquisition price and financing arrangements, discussed in the next major section, should be specified in detail.

Delivery Date and Acceptance Test

Two important points to include in every contract are a delivery date and an acceptance test. Delivery dates should be stated for all components, including a "time is of essence" covenant with the delivery dates.

Some 60 to 90 days prior to the delivery date, the analyst should furnish the vendor with the acceptance test required by the contract. It is in the vendor's

GET IT IN WRITING Disputes between buyers and sellers of computer systems are almost never the result of bad faith but of bad contracts.

The simple truth about contracts is that the more that gets out on the table and written down—and the sooner in the acquisition process that occurs—the greater the probability of a successful installation. And while it is true that hammering out a detailed contract has caused more than one deal to fall through, it is better to part company at an early stage than after the waiting disaster has occurred. Nobody ever lost out by getting a lurking misunderstanding out in the open.

In the request for proposal, the buyer should state clearly that the vendor will be expected to commit to a specific level of performance as part of the agreement. This puts all bidders on notice that a response-time guarantee is expected, so they are all on equal footing when they propose.

Without an objective definition of acceptable throughput, neither party has any clear recourse in the event of a dispute involving failure of the system to perform adequately.

If there is a throughput guarantee but no specified remedies, that is as good as no guarantee at all. The odds are that the issue will be wrestled in court, which essentially kills any chance of coming to a satisfactory and reasonable business solution.

Tips for writing a no-fault systems contract include: Outline from the start prominent realistic characteristics of your prospective automated environment. Solicit a guarantee of online performance from the vendor regarding such features as systems throughput and response time. Work with the vendor to develop a fair test situation that will accurately predict the system's performance at your probable peak processing burden. Agree to specified remedies if performance guarantees are not met.

Excerpted from Lee Gruenfeld, "Avoiding Contract Disaster," *Computerworld*, July 13, 1987, pp. 83 and 88.

interest to see that the computer configuration and software pass the test before it is shipped.

Before choosing a date, the analyst must consider what his or her organization has to do to accept delivery in a meaningful and systematic fashion. While awaiting delivery, the analyst must make sure that all interface equipment is ready for connection. Test programs and data must also be prepared for use when the technology is delivered.

The on-site acceptance test should be run during the implementation phase (see Chapter 20) and for some specified period thereafter. If the technology is unacceptable, the contract should permit its return to the vendor without charge. Payments, if any, should be refunded immediately. A better approach would be to defer most, if not all, of the payment for software and hardware until the total system is implemented and operating satisfactorily.

Warranties and Other Provisions

Earlier in this chapter, we discussed several aspects of maintainability. This general performance criterion is assured further by including a warranty, warranty period, and remedies for breach of contract. Typically, the remedy for a breach of contract is repair or replacement by the vendor within a specified time period at the vendor's expense. An added remedy requires the vendor to compensate the company for downtime. For purchased technology, the warranty period may run from 30 days to a year after acceptance. For leased or rented technology the warranty should be in effect throughout the time it is leased or rented and on the company site.

From a legal viewpoint, customized software is different from off-the-shelf software from the local computer store. The enclosed contract for off-the-shelf software covers only licensing, sometimes referred to as "shrink-wrap licenses." The user buys the package without a warranty, or caveat emptor. Some vendors, however, provide a warranty that the program performs in accordance with the published specifications, documentation, and advertisements. A number of user groups are lobbying for warranties to be part of all off-the-shelf packages.

The buyer enters into a binding contract the moment the plastic wrapping is broken. The only right that the buyer has is to use the package. The vendor retains title to the software in perpetuity. It is illegal for the buyer to make copies and sell or rent them.

For customized software, special application packages, and utilities, the company should be able to use the package throughout the organization, including subsidiaries and affiliates. The company should be able to integrate it with other subsystems, back it up, and disclose the documentation to others who need to know how it works.

If possible, a copy of the source code and all documentation, including data flow diagrams, record layouts, and comments to the source code, and a list of updates should be provided. If this is not feasible, then a source code escrow provision should be included so users will have access to it if the vendor goes out of business.

If it is a customized package written by an external programmer, the contract should state that the company owns it, not the vendor. The independent programmer may understandably want to retain ownership rights and sell the package to other companies. Also, if applicable, nondisclosure provisions should be included to protect the company's trade secrets and special knowledge.

Maintenance and Service Contracts

During the warranty period that may range from 30 days to one year, the vendor performs virtually all maintenance free of charge. When the warranty expires, the company can get service protection in the form of renewable one-year agreements from the vendor, vendor-authorized service centers, or third-party maintenance companies. Charges may run from 10 to 15 percent of the purchase price per year for carry-in service contracts and 15 to 20 percent of the technology's purchase price annually for an on-site, or "house-call," service contract.

Provisions for maintenance and service contracts should include MTTR. In this case, MTTR stands for mean time to respond. For example, "The vendor will provide a one-hour response time between 8 A.M. and 6 P.M., Monday through Friday, excluding specified holidays. Level 1 service is for routine repairs and module replacement. Level 2 service involves the solution of complicated problems provided by our regional service center. Response time for level 2 service is 24 hours or less." The other MTTR (mean time to repair) would be an even stronger provision.

A provision should be included to send bug status reports and methods used to correct such errors to the company as soon as they are encountered. Also, the company should be given access to new releases and updated documentation. Minimum qualifications of support personnel and their continued availability should also be stipulated.

A final comment is in order. In preparing the contract, avoid meaningless phrases, such as, "We will try to . . . ," "We'll stand behind our product . . . ," and the like. A contract is a written, binding agreement that can be used to define the terms, functions, quality, and support. The more explicit, the better; because well-written, clear contracts decrease the probability of disputes and protracted litigation that cost time, money, and opportunity for both parties.

18.10 EVALUATION SCREEN NUMBER SEVEN: ACQUISITION AND FINANCING METHODS

Four methods used to acquire and finance the technology are (1) rent, (2) lease, (3) purchase, and (4) installment purchase. Typically these methods are negotiated and decided on during contract negotiations. In other instances, a particular acquisition and financing method may have been established early in the strategic information systems planning cycle and therefore is an imperative. For example, top-management policy might be that all computer equipment must be leased.

In our presentation in this chapter we, however, have assumed that all the vendors being evaluated can sell, rent, or lease any or all of their technology and that the user company is trying to achieve the best deal from the standpoint of price, performance, and financing. Also, by presenting a separate section on acquisition and financing methods, we can provide a sharper focus on this very important evaluation factor rather than mixing it in with other material.

Rent

Usually, rental is on a month-to-month basis, sometimes with a minimum of a one-year contract. The rental rates are such that the basic purchase cost of the computer is recovered by the vendor within 45 to 60 months. The user can also receive purchase credits that range from 10 percent to as much as 50 percent of rental payments, depending on the vendor.

Vendors typically offer either an unlimited use rental contract or a prime shift rental contract. The first type provides for a fixed monthly price regardless of the number of computer hours used. The prime shift rental contract establishes a fixed monthly rental for one predetermined eight-hour period each day. The rental is proportionately increased by the number of additional eight-hour shifts used during the month. For example, the prime shift (first eight-hour shift) may be charged at $100 per hour; additional hours of usage beyond the prime shift may be charged at $10 per hour.

Advantages of Renting

The advantages of renting are as follows:

1. It is helpful to the users who are uncertain about the proper equipment application.
2. In some cases, it is psychologically more acceptable to management.
3. Offers high flexibility.
4. If an organization does not have past experience with computers, this may be the safest method.
5. Maintenance charges are included in rental payments.
6. Allows a favorable working relationship with the vendor.
7. No long-term commitment is made.
8. Avoids technological obsolescence.
9. Usually offers state-of-the-art technology.

Disadvantages of Renting

The disadvantages of renting are as follows:

1. Over approximately five years, this is the most expensive method.
2. Rental payments increase by some factor less than one if usage exceeds a specified number of hours per month, assuming prime shift contract.
3. New computer or programs may not be proven or fully debugged.
4. Generally offers no residual value unless purchase option provisions are exercised.

Lease

A computer lease is a contractual agreement conveying the right to use the computer for a stated period of time. The two parties to the lease contract are the lessor and the lessee. The lessor is the party who legally owns the computer and who conveys the rights to use the computer to the lessee.

This presentation on leasing is primarily concerned with hardware; however, some lessors are into leasing software separately or as part of the technology package. Therefore, many of the following points will also apply to software.

Type of Lease

The typical computer equipment lease is an operating lease, not a capital lease as some may think. The IRS's equivalent of an operating lease is what tax authorities call a "true lease."

The lessor views the lease as a cash outflow to acquire the computer and a stream of cash inflows represented by the rental payments and residual value, that is, the estimated value of the computer at termination of the lease.

The estimation of residual value is critical to the pricing of the lease. In an operating lease, lessors base their rates on retrieving 70 to 80 percent of their investment in equipment from a first lease and making additional money on the residual value when the computer equipment is sold or leased again.

The systems analyst should try to estimate the residual value of the technology that the company plans to acquire. This figure should indicate approximately the lease rates bid by lessors. The higher the residual value at the end of the lease term, the lower the lease rate and the greater the service and support that should be negotiated into the lease contract.

Some lease agreements may require a guaranteed residual value by the lessee to eliminate the lessor's downside risk by shifting the residual value risk to the lessee. Or, similarly, the lessee could be penalized if the residual value of the equipment at the end of a lease is less than the lessor had expected.

These kinds of guarantees or penalties are called indemnification clauses that may be written into the lease agreement by the lessor. Therefore, it is important to the lessee to go over the lease with a "fine-tooth comb" to uncover such stipulations and, if so, negotiate them out of the lease agreement. If, on the other hand, the lessee is willing to either participate in or bear the total residual value risk, then much lower rates and greater services should be negotiated into the agreement. Moreover, from a tax standpoint, if the lessee effectively purchases the machine at the end of the lease period, the IRS will most likely consider it not a "true lease" and the lessee will lose the tax advantages of an operating lease.

If the lessor is affiliated with the computer manufacturer by ownership or some other arrangement, the lessor is more likely to accept a higher risk and higher estimate of residual value than other lessors.

Tax Ramifications of Leasing

Because of changes in the tax laws, the lease-versus-buy decision is in favor of leasing for most lessees. The repeal of the investment tax credit and the inclusion of some rather complicated tax rules relating to owning and depreciating equipment have combined to eliminate a major incentive to purchasing equipment. Therefore, leasing has grown due in part to lessees taking advantage of tax planning alternatives.

Strength and Stability of Lessor

If the method of acquiring and financing the technology block is leasing, then a key consideration is the assurance that the lessor (vendor) is able to stay in business and be there for the company if additional upgrades or services are needed, or for "box swaps" if a major increase in hardware capacity is required.

As we recommended early in this chapter, the systems analyst should research the lessor's or vendor's history, track record, and financial condition. The ability to build a good working relationship with a strong, ongoing lessor is a critical part of the evaluation process. Securing the lowest lease rate bid may not be the most cost-effective decision in the long run if the lessor who submitted the lowest bid is not going to be around to fulfill contractual obligations.

Also, lessees should develop a relationship with a lessor who is strong in marketing and adept at re-leasing. The better the lessor is in this area, the more flexibility the lessees will ultimately enjoy.

Flexibility and Other Advantages of Leasing

During the past couple of decades, the used computer market and computer leasing have become big business. This marketing and financing phenomenon is fueled by changing tax laws, shortening computer equipment life cycles, widening computer markets, and spiraling sales increases.

Today, a large number of lessors are in the business to buy, sell, and lease new or used mainframes, midrange processors, peripherals, personal computers, and software. Some of these lessors are indeed turnkey vendors who can meet all the technology needs of many companies.

Early on, computer equipment lessors looked to leased rates and residual value only. Today, many lessors look beyond these items and offer a variety of service options, technical assistance, and flexibility in contract negotiation. On the lessee side, many lessees are willing to pay a little higher rate if a good working relationship with the lessor can be established. These lessees believe that a long-term, solid working relationship with the lessor is much more important than the immediate transaction. Their key objective is price *and* performance.

Many lessees, both large and small, believe they get a better financing arrangement by leasing all or most of their technology needs. These lessees do not have to put up any upfront capital, which frees up funds to support operating needs or make additional investments.

Leasing provides the flexibility to lease old, used equipment or the latest up-to-the-minute technology. If a lessee's goal is to maintain a state-of-the-art position, leasing will help them do that. Leasing is indeed an excellent way to avoid technological obsolescence and perform better asset management.

Lessees can "swap boxes" in the middle of a lease with minor increases in lease payments, and, in some instances, even enjoy a sizable reduction in cost. Some lessees, for example, have gone from a 10-MIPS machine to a 50-MIPS machine at one-half the lease payments of the less powerful machine.

Lessors go through all the machinations of buying and disposing of computer equipment. Therefore, lessees don't have to hire or assign personnel to perform this rather specialized task. This intrinsic service generally results in better computer equipment management and frees up lessees to concentrate on things that they do best.

If the general systems design alternatives call for just raw computer power, a box to crunch numbers, the best deal for the lessee may be to acquire a machine that is at the end of its life cycle and is in its second lease. The lessor has already recovered 70 to 80 percent of its investment, so the lessee should be able to negotiate extremely attractive lease terms.

If the lease contract is properly negotiated, a lessee can get hands-on proof of performance. If the technology isn't everything it's supposed to be, the lessee can get out of the lease or get another, more suitable hardware platform. To do this with a purchase may be difficult or impossible.

Top-notch leasing companies are proficient at handling upgrades and new product announcements. They usually know ahead of time when an upgrade will be needed and have planned for it before the lessee even knows about it. This situation is generally true even if the user company had purchased the technology. Lessors can also help lessees understand the impact of new announcements. Essentially, in the long run, reputable lessors help lessees with proper timing and matching technology to capacity needs.

Purchase

With the purchase method, the company buys the technology, takes title to it, and depreciates it over its useful life. Usually, a purchaser wants to acquire the computer equipment when it is first released, keep it over its entire life cycle, and have total control over it.

If the technology is early in its life cycle, and if the company is cash rich without a sufficient number of investment alternatives to use this cash, then it may be to the company's advantage to buy instead of renting or leasing the technology. Also, if the company is low growth, it can keep the equipment for a long time without the fear of running out of capacity.

A few companies are quite adept at buying and selling their own computer equipment. A company, for example, might buy a computer at the beginning of its life cycle and sell to another user or possibly to a leasing company in two or three years or just before a major upgrade. The theory behind this approach is to achieve upgrades by buying the latest product line rather than going through a major upgrade on the present computer, which can be time consuming and costly. Moreover, if timed correctly, the company may even make a profit by buying and selling their computer equipment. Also, it may be important for a company that acquires their computer equipment this way to develop a good relationship with two or three leasing companies who are more likely to know if user companies are in the market for the old machine and be willing to broker the deal.

At the other end of the purchase method are user companies that buy two computer systems no longer being manufactured at a bargain-basement price and cannibalize one for parts. The key factor with this method is to have a technical person available who knows how to do the cannibalization.

Installment Purchase

With the installment purchase, the user makes a down payment and agrees to pay the remainder of the acquisition price in specified amounts at stated intervals over a period of time. The vendor may retain technical title to the computer system or may take other means to make repossession easier in the event that the user defaults on the payments.

Advantages of Installment Purchase

The advantages of installment purchase are as follows:

> It offers advantages of both straight purchase and lease or rental.
>
> Users own the computer system after all payments are made.
>
> Generally involves fewer legal restrictions than leasing.

Disadvantages of Installment Purchase

The disadvantages of installment purchase are as follows:

1. It involves more restrictions than an outright purchase.
2. The cost of financing may be more than with other acquisition methods.
3. It may not enjoy enhancements and upgrades.
4. It is less flexible than renting or leasing.

Three-Tier Acquisition System

Some information system managers use a three-tier acquisition system, as shown in Figure 18.9. At the base of the pyramid is equipment purchased and owned outright by the organization, or purchased using the installment method. This level represents the basic equipment required to operate the information system (e.g., the CPU, line printers).

The second level of the pyramid is for systems growth potential, in terms of both capacity and capability. The planning horizon is from two to three years. Once the basic system is established, this level allows the addition of more or a different mix of equipment as the long-term need arises.

The third level of the pyramid is for a crisis situation, in which the level

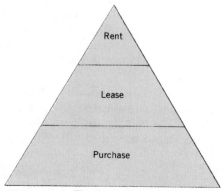

Figure 18.9 Three-level system of acquisition of computer equipment.

of operations of a particular area or function has been grossly underestimated. This level of acquisition allows the short-term rental of additional equipment. It lasts from 6 to 12 months and gives management room to maneuver and time to reassess their total acquisition pyramid and system needs.

18.11 EVALUATION SCREEN NUMBER EIGHT: COST-EFFECTIVENESS ANALYSIS OF GENERAL SYSTEMS DESIGN ALTERNATIVES

This screen is the last one in the evaluation process. The systems analyst is prepared to compare benefit dollars against cost dollars to determine which general systems design alternative comes out on top.

At this point, the technology building blocks that are required to support the general systems design alternatives have been defined, and the vendor (or vendors) who gave the company the best deal on price, performance, and financial arrangements is selected. All the legal terms, conditions, and specifications have been negotiated and settled. The systems analyst has in hand confirmed price quotes of the technology. So, now costs are a certainty whereas before, in the early phases of the SDM, they were general estimates.

Nothing, however, has been signed to consummate the deal with the selected vendor. Why? Because the systems analyst needs to push all the general systems design alternatives along with their technology-block costs through this final evaluation screen. The best one that pops out of this screen will be designed in detail.

Costs

The costs that typically apply to the development, implementation, and operations of an information system are systems development and implementation, site facilities, technology, programming development, operations, and maintenance costs. These costs should be gathered and classified for further analysis.

Technology Costs

At this point, the technology costs are known because of bids submitted by vendors, such as manufacturers, lessors, or dealers. In fact, much of the systems evaluation work is directed to not only determining the best vendor but also to deriving accurate cost figures contained in firm bids.

Site Facilities Costs

The site costs should be fairly easy to determine. Site facilities for the new system may be nothing more than cleaning one's desk off or rearranging office furniture to make room for the new technology (in which case the site cost would be nil). Or site preparation may require renting several rooms in an office building or even the construction of a large information systems center which may cost several million dollars.

Costs for a full-blown information systems center include all aspects involved in preparing the site not only for the equipment, but for offices, storage space, and conference rooms. The efforts in preparing this site can range anywhere from the minor renovation of an existing site to the construction of a new building. In addition to the site itself, other features are needed such as the following:

1. *Power Requirements.* Different system configurations require different power requirements. The power parameters for any system, however, are measured in kilovoltamps (KVAs). For an approximate cost for power, the total average KVA per month would be computed, based on the number of hours of use per day.

2. *Air Conditioning.* Newer computer systems have reduced to some extent the total need for air conditioning, but even with the newer generation of equipment, air conditioning is still a major consideration. Not only does air conditioning ensure proper functioning of equipment, but it provides comfortable working conditions for operating personnel.

3. *Furniture and Fixtures.* Proper furnishings must be provided for the personnel operating the system.

4. *Miscellaneous Features.* Other features that may be included in the environment costs are false flooring, special lighting, fire-prevention equipment, access control systems, lead-lined walls, uninterruptible power systems, and off-premises storage.

Systems Implementation Costs

Systems implementation is a phase in the SDM that requires equipment installation, programming, training, testing, and conversion costs. If the programming is customized, this cost is usually separated from systems implementation as another cost category. If, on the other hand, the software is bought or leased from a vendor, it may be lumped in with systems implementation costs. It's really a function of how fine the analyst wants to classify and categorize costs, such as:

1. *Equipment Installation.* In some cases the physical installation of equipment may present problems that require the use of special equipment such as cranes. Installing a system on the tenth floor of a building is not an easy task, but the cost is often overlooked until actual installation. Another charge not considered in some cost estimates is freight. It should be determined whether or not the vendor prepays freight. The freight charges for even very small systems, which are frequently sent by air, can run as high as $1,500.

2. *Programming.* This cost category is generally for customized application programs written by an in-house or an independent programmer. The cost estimate is based on hours required to write the program times the programmer's rate per hour plus overhead. If the programs are canned packages, the purchase or lease price plus installation fees represent the costs for this category.

3. *Training.* The training costs are incurred to prepare all users for the new system. Training procedures may range from brief overviews to intensive on-the-job training sessions.

4. *Testing.* A variety of tests are run on all the building blocks before converting to the new information system. This task requires a great deal of planning and preparation of effective test data.

5. *Conversion.* The cost of conversion depends on the degree of conversion, which, in turn, depends on how many applications in the first system are to be changed and how many are to be handled as in the past. Several factors need to be included in the estimate of cost of conversion:
   a. Preparing and editing records for completeness and accuracy as, for example, when they are converted from manual media to magnetic disk.
   b. Setting up file library procedures.
   c. Preparing and running parallel operations.

Operations and Maintenance Costs

Operations and maintenance costs include all factors necessary to keep the information system working. These factors are:

1. *Staff Costs.* These costs include the payroll for all employees in the information system and for occasional consulting fees. This staff consists of the information systems manager, systems analysts, accountants, programmers, systems engineers, computer operators, data preparers, data base administrators, security officers, and general clerks.

2. *Cost of Supplies.* As the system operates, it consumes supplies. These supplies are in the form of printer paper, ribbons, magnetic tape, magnetic disk, and an array of general office supplies. These items are drawn from inventory and should be subject to management control procedures.

3. *Equipment Maintenance.* Maintenance of a system may be performed by the company's own engineers and technicians, by the vendor's personnel, or by a combination of the two. In any event, maintenance is a recurring expense.

4. *Systems Maintenance.* These costs are incurred in debugging the system, adapting the system to meet new requirements, improving the system on the behalf of users, and enhancing the system for operations.

5. *Power and Light.* After the initial electrical equipment for servicing the system is installed, there is a recurring charge, based on use, for power and light.

6. *Insurance.* For purchased equipment, it is sound policy to obtain insurance for fire, extended coverage, and vandalism. For equipment rented, determine whether or not to obtain similar insurance while the equipment is in the company's possession. To safeguard against disgruntled employees who might be inclined to do injury to the system, it is advisable to obtain a DDD (disappearance, dishonesty, destruction) bond.

Benefits

All proposed general systems design alternatives possess both tangible and intangible benefits. These benefits represent the value or performance side of the cost-versus-effectiveness ratio. Analysts often call this area of evaluation, cost-effectiveness, cost-benefit, or price-performance analysis. Whatever the name, the analyst attempts to match rather hard, well-defined cost dollars against somewhat soft benefits. Therefore, the key to a reasonable evaluation is fairly accurate benefit estimates, typically plus or minus 10 percent for tangible benefits and no more than plus or minus 20 percent for intangible benefits. This range in benefit estimates may seem rather large, but most authorities believe that if benefits prove to be within 10 to possibly as much as 30 or 40 percent of estimates and actual costs within 10 to 30 percent, then the benefits-to-cost analysis is a success. Moreover, the more unique and innovative the systems design, the greater the gap between what actually takes place and what was originally estimated.

Tangible Benefits

Tangible benefits are realized from cost savings or profit generation. Cost savings can result from increased productivity. For example, in the present system, it may cost $2.00 to process a transaction whereas the proposed system will process the same transaction for $1.50. Or an order-entry clerk may be able to enter twice as many sales orders with the new system. Or, because of better control and processing of accounts receivable, the organization's cash balance may increase. Or sales and profit may increase from connecting the information system to customers' ordering systems. Or errors may be reduced by 30 percent, resulting in a significant cost savings.

Intangible Benefits

Many benefits are intangible and cannot be easily traced to the system. An attempt should be made, however, to express in quantitative terms those that can be identified. For example, an analysis of customer sales might show that the organization is losing 5 percent of its gross sales annually because of inventory stockouts. The present system has an 85 percent customer service level, which means that, on the average, 85 percent of all customer requests for stock items can be met by inventory on hand. The proposed system will achieve a 95 percent customer service level because of new inventory control models and a better data base. It is estimated that this expected increase in customer service will increase annual sales by 5 percent, resulting in a net profit increase of $10,000.

What about intangible benefits related to an improvement in human factors? For example, the proposed system may be ergonomically designed with more pleasant working conditions. What is the payoff? Presumably, employee absenteeism and turnover will decrease, which will result in less training cost and fewer job disruptions. With the implementation of point-of-sale devices in a retail organization, average checkout time is reduced by three minutes. What is it worth to the organization to reduce checkout time by three minutes? The benefits may be both tangible and intangible. Additional clerks may not have to be hired, a cost-avoidance benefit. Sales may also increase because customers like the quicker service and are thereby attracted to this store.

JUSTIFYING FUNDS FOR SYSTEMS PROJECTS

Estimating PC-related expenses clearly is a difficult and inexact process. Ken Ross, president of Atrium Information Group, believes the continuing cost of a new PC is three or four times the cost of hardware and software.

John Crockett, supervisor of office automation for Pharmaceutical Card System (PCS), stresses that you're not running your business very well if you don't look at the cost of a systems project in its entirety. Along with cost estimates, users of PCs must also estimate benefits. These include "quantifiable" benefits, such as savings in salaries and "intangible" benefits, such as better service to the firm's clients. Costs and benefits are tracked after the system is implemented to see how accurate the estimates were.

Condensed from Jim Leeke, "Budget Ahead for the Continuing Cost of PCs," *PC Week*, September 15, 1987, p. 55.

Estimating

One technique used to formalize hard-to-quantify estimates is shown in Figure 18.10. Values are estimated by participants based on optimistic, pessimistic, and most likely categories.

Each participant gives his or her own estimate. These estimates can be gathered and calculated by a designated person. During the estimation process, participants should not be allowed to review others' estimations. Such a constraint guards against any individual exerting undue influence on the other members of the group. You might liken this step to part of the Delphi procedure.

Direct Benefit Estimates	Strength of Subjective Categories	Odds for Occurring	Amount
$10,000	Optimistic	3/10	$3,000
4,000	Pessimistic	1/10	400
6,000	Most likely	6/10	3,600
		Expected value =	$7,000

Figure 18.10 General example of calculating an expected value using optimistic, pessimistic, and most likely categories.

Benefits and Costs Example

Vendor C was chosen as supplier of the technology building block for the two general systems design alternatives still under consideration. Originally, using the best from both vendor A and vendor C was examined, but management decided to stick with one vendor so as to obtain a better working relationship. Moreover, vendor C gave slightly better leasing terms and was also willing to share the risk of some innovative applications of system 2 if this system proves more cost-effective than system 1. For system 2, vendor C will assign an ergonomics engineer to develop several prototype kiosks containing some of the latest computer-aided design (CAD) technology. Also computer-to-computer ordering will be beta tested at three customers' sites.

Management is also pleased with the evaluation process used to choose the best vendor or vendors. It feels that from every perspective, vendor C is indeed the best vendor with which to do business.

Now, the systems analyst is ready to bring all the costs and benefits of system 1 and system 2 together for comparison to determine the one chosen for detailed systems design. At this point, many of the key costs are known and firm. In the early stages of strategic information systems planning (SISP) and on into general systems design, many of the cost and benefit estimates were more or less seat-of-the-pants estimates and extrapolations of historical figures. Even now, however, some of the benefits are soft dollars, but they are the best measurements with which the systems analyst has to work. As a matter of fact, some intangible benefits won't be known until after the information system has been implemented, and even then they won't be known with certainty. Figure 18.11 illustrates both the benefits and costs of system 1 and system 2.

System 1 Overview

The company designs and manufactures innovative mining and drilling equipment. Large labor savings will be realized by converting from hand-drafting design specifications to the use of CAD workstations. Also, a payroll software system, online badge readers, and time clocks will reduce the need for a number of timekeepers and payroll clerks.

Increased revenue will be produced by a faster turnaround on special-design jobs for drillers in the North Sea and other remote and hazardous regions. Nearly every manufacturing job is unique because of the variety of equipment designs. Therefore, better scheduling and layout of these jobs help to increase productivity.

At present, because of the diversity of equipment the company manufactures and significant delays in design and production, management is kept busy with one crisis after another. Once the new system is implemented and smoother operations are realized, management will not only have current and accurate information for planning and coordinating but will also have more time to devote to these important activities.

Improved customer relations will come about by quicker order entry, job bidding, and better tracking and status information on when the customers' equipment will be completed. Some drilling contracts have penalty clauses that

Benefits and Costs of System 1		Year 1	Year 2	Year 3	Year 4	Year 5	Benefits and Costs of System 2		Year 1	Year 2	Year 3	Year 4	Year 5
TANGIBLE BENEFITS	Labor savings	$ 500	$ 700	$ 800	$ 700	$ 400	TANGIBLE BENEFITS	Labor savings	$ 500	$ 700	$ 800	$ 600	$ 400
	Increased revenue	400	600	700	400	300		Increased revenue	600	700	800	500	250
INTANGIBLE BENEFITS	Better scheduling	200	300	300	200	100	INTANGIBLE BENEFITS	Better scheduling	100	100	100	100	50
	Better decision making	100	200	300	100	50		Better decision making	100	200	300	100	50
	Improved customer relations	100	200	200	100	50		Improved customer relations	100	300	400	100	50
	Total benefits	$1300	$2000	$2300	$1500	$ 900		Total benefits	$1400	$2000	$2400	$1400	$ 800
COSTS	Systems development and implementation	$ 600					COSTS	Systems development and implementation	$ 500				
	Site facilities	100	$ 100	$ 100	$ 100	$ 100		Site facilities	100	$ 100	$ 100	$ 100	$ 100
	Technology	400	400	400	400	400		Technology	800	400	400	500	800
	Programming development	800	100					Programming development	200				
	Maintenance			100	200	350		Maintenance				300	400
	Operations	100	100	100	100	150		Operations	200	100	100	100	100
	Total costs	$2000	$ 700	$ 700	$ 800	$1000		Total costs	$1800	$ 600	$ 600	$1000	$1400
Net cash inflow		⟨$ 700⟩	$1300	$1600	$ 700	⟨$ 100⟩	Net cash inflow		⟨$ 400⟩	$1400	$1800	$ 400	⟨$ 600⟩

Figure 18.11 Benefits, costs, and net cash inflow of general systems design alternatives 1 and 2 (000 omitted).

amount to thousands of dollars per day if the driller does not begin drilling by a certain date. Missing completion dates have caused the company to lose a number of profitable mining and drilling customers.

A design package that a group of FORTRAN programmers are working on will help field engineers model what-if designs at customers' offices by using portable workstations online to the central mainframe. Sophisticated what-if design scenarios can be shown in the prospective customers' office or conference room.

About $300,000 has already been spent in systems work for system 1 to reach this point. These are sunk costs and are, therefore, irrelevant to the decision at hand, but they are included in the example to account fully for all costs. An additional $300,000 is required for detailed design and implementation. A lease will be signed with the owner of a "smart" office building for the system's site. One of the features of the building is an installed fiber optic backbone. As a matter of fact, the company is planning to move all its administrative and engineering personnel to this new location within the next six months.

The technology building block for system 1 will lease for $400,000 per year for five years. The hardware platform consists of a large mainframe, back-end and front-end processors, large disk systems, four midrange processors, 450 multifunctional workstations, and a fiber optic LAN with a variety of peripherals. Vendor C also will provide a number of software packages consisting of a generic operating system, utilities, and an order-entry package.

System 1 features a sophisticated PERT-time and PERT-cost scheduling and planning software package and an expert system that will manage a large cutting machine to lay out and cut forms with more precision and a reduction in scrap. These applications will be developed the first year by an independent software vendor, a division of vendor C. These scheduling and expert systems packages will be tailor-made for the company. All rights will be retained by the company because it plans to market this software to other companies; however, the revenue from such sales is not included in the analysis because it's just too iffy. Indeed, it's not certain that the packages will even work for the company; therefore, stringent benchmark tests will be run on them before their acceptance.

Maintenance in system 1 will start in the third year because it is estimated that changes and enhancements will have to be made as the system begins to move out of the mature stage and into the decline stage of its life cycle. Maintenance for the hardware platform will continue to be handled by vendor C. Cost of operations is projected at $100,000 per year.

System 2 Overview

Even though a great deal of effort and money will be spent to build workstation kiosks that feature human factors engineering and greater symbiosis at the engineer/user interface, no labor savings are projected based on these design force objectives. Labor savings will be brought about by reduction in draftsmen, the same as in system 1. In fact, the labor savings are estimated to tail off a little quicker in system 2 in case the design engineering test group becomes tired of the experiment and it backfires because of the slightly insular culture exhibited by many engineers. It is hoped by management, however, that the experiment will succeed and the labor savings estimate will prove to be far too conservative.

Increased revenue in system 2 is greater than that estimated in system 1 because of the installation of a computer-to-computer ordering system. The beta test sites will be at three customers who have agreed to run the tests. Their systems will be connected to the new system via satellite, and they will have access to design algorithms and the spare parts and equipment data base. They will also be able to track their jobs through the manufacturing process. This featured component of system 2 is expected to produce more revenue than system 1. Indeed, two of the beta test companies have not done any business with the company in several years. Managements of these two companies said they would be happy to purchase some special equipment and replacement parts if the application proves to be viable.

Scheduling in system 2 is not as sophisticated as in system 1. Vendor C has offered to throw in for "free" a simple Gantt-type package that it thinks might work fairly well. A few of the personnel in the shop think that it may work even better than the "fancy system" proposed in system 1.

The decision-making benefit is projected to be about the same in both systems. It is expected, however, that system 2 will produce better customer relations from the computer-to-computer ordering system because of the way it will differentiate the company's service from its competitors.

It is estimated that about $100,000 in systems development and imple-mentation costs will be shifted to vendor C because of more turnkey aspects of implementing the special workstation kiosks and more involvement in the order-entry and tracking applications. Site facilities will rent for $100,000 per year, the same as in system 1.

Vendor C believes, and rightfully so, that the workstation kiosks and the computer-to-computer ordering applications contain significant technological risks. Some of the technology will be tailored to meet the specific needs of the company and the unique ways it does business. Therefore, none of the tech-nology for these applications will be easily sold or re-leased at the end of system 2's life cycle. In fact, vendor C has projected residual value of this technology to be close to its scrap value.

Vendor C also estimates that these applications will cost them more than system 1. Its technology lease for system 2, consequently, is priced at $900,000 more in total than the price quoted for system 1.

Programming development in system 2 involves writing programs that will interface with the Gantt scheduling and order-entry applications. Also, a major COBOL program will have to be written for a new accounts receivable and billing application to accommodate the computer-to-computer ordering appli-cation. These programming development costs are expected to run about $200,000 and will be completed in about three months.

Maintenance costs for changes and upgrades begin in the fourth year of system 2's life cycle. Vendor C is responsible for all the maintenance of the customized applications. The operations learning curve is a little steeper in system 2 because of the innovations in ordering and workstation design. An extra $100,000 is therefore included in the first year to account for the added

Year	General Systems Design Alternative 1 (000 omitted)			General Systems Design Alternative 2 (000 omitted)		
	Net Cash Inflow	Present Value Factor at 20%	Present Value of Net Cash Inflow	Net Cash Inflow	Present Value Factor at 20%	Present Value of Net Cash Inflow
1	⟨$ 700⟩	.833	⟨$ 583⟩	⟨$ 400⟩	.833	⟨$ 333⟩
2	1300	.694	902	1400	.694	972
3	1600	.579	926	1800	.579	1042
4	700	.482	337	400	.482	193
5	⟨ 100⟩	.402	⟨ 40⟩	⟨ 600⟩	.402	⟨ 241⟩
	$2800		$1542	$2600		$1633

Figure 18.12 The net present value method used to evaluate system 1 and system 2.

complexity of operations. It is assumed that operations will become routine and costs will level off beginning in the second year.

Benefits and Costs Evaluation
The analyst can use several techniques to evaluate the benefits and costs of each system for comparative purposes. The benefit-cost ratio for system 1 is $8000:$5200, or 1.54. The benefit-cost ratio for system 2 is $8000:$5400, or 1.48. It therefore appears that system 1 is the more cost-effective.

But the benefit-cost ratio attaches the same value of net cash inflow that will be realized in year 5 as it does to net cash inflow that will be realized in year 1. No allowances are made for difference in timing of these net cash inflows. Obviously, this is unsound reasoning because a dollar received today has more value than does a dollar collected five years from now. Moreover, the benefit-cost ratio simply averages the total benefits and costs over the life of both systems. The annual amounts of these flows are significantly different in each system. Also, this technique does not consider the company's internal rate of return, which is 20 percent.

Figure 18.12 illustrates the net present value method used to evaluate system 1 and system 2. Recognizing irregular net cash inflows and the time value of money, this method of evaluation indicates that system 2 is the better one by $91,000 ($1,633,000 − $1,542,000).

Therefore, system 2 will be the one designed in detail and implemented unless management overrides this quantitative analysis and selects system 1 for qualitative reasons. For example, very conservative managers may believe that too many operations and development risks are present in system 2, and they are simply not willing to take those risks.

Preparation of the Final General Systems Design Report

The Final General Systems Design Report, the fourth documented deliverable, includes results of all the material explained in this chapter, such as RFPs, vendor proposals, evaluation methods used, acquisition considerations and their advantages and disadvantages, costs and benefits, and complete cost-effectiveness analysis.

Based on this report, top management will make the final determination as to which of the general systems design alternatives will be designed in detail and implemented. As mentioned earlier, management's decision may be different from the one indicated in the report.

THE NSU TIGERS EVENT CENTER
Preparing the Final General Systems Design Report

THE EVALUATION PROCESS

Once the three general systems design alternatives were finalized, Sally asked Trixy Stub to schedule a meeting of the project team to review them. Because the final choice of a systems alternative would have a major impact on the function of the event center, it was critical that the project team be involved in the review. Sally felt that by making a formal presentation, she and Tommy would be forced to take a critical look at the work completed to date.

After Sally presented the findings, Mr. Ball opened up the session for general discussion. The three alternatives identified were significantly different in the capabilities provided for the next three to five years. The meeting was long, and often heated. A brief synopsis of the comments is included here.

The stand-alone batch alternative automates the current manual system. Sally and Tommy estimated that at best it would provide a 20 percent increase in efficiency. Although they felt this increase would adequately solve the problems in the event center, they were concerned that this alternative revolved around manual handling of ticket dissemination for a given event. Most events require using three to four ticket salespeople concurrently and only one centralized preprinted batch of tickets for an event. Either the ticket sales staff would be bumping into each other or they would have to break up the tickets into smaller batches and allow each sales person to sell for only one section of the center. They would also have to share one seating chart or face difficulties in not duplicating seats offered to customers. The computer system portion of this alternative seemed extremely inexpensive to implement and administer. Costs of maintaining portions of the current manual system were yet to be determined. The question Sally asked was, "Is this the best alternative when total costs are compared to total benefits?"

The project group felt the network-based alternative provided a means for each department to share information. A 50 to 60 percent improvement in efficiency was anticipated. This coordination and efficiency improvement would allow the event center to operate at near capacity.

The centralized alternative, although most enticing to all concerned, was clearly going to be the most expensive one. Because the NSU budget had been historically low, they felt that requesting the funding for such an elite system might not be politically sound. As a professional, however, Sally was compelled to present the centralized alternative because benefits were projected to far exceed the costs, thus resulting in a better benefits-to-cost ratio than the other two alternatives. Early on, Sally realized that investing dollars in systems rather than saving dollars was generally a wiser course of action.

By the end of the meeting the committee concluded that they could not reach a decision on the general systems design alternatives until vendor proposals were evaluated and facts concerning the specifics on each technology platform were gathered and a cost-effectiveness analysis was performed.

Before developing the request for proposal (RFP), Sally felt that one enhancement should be made. For each ticket disbursement by a given sales agent, a summary statement should be printed that would serve as a receipt for the transaction. This statement would include the number of tickets, type of tickets, type of payment, amount of payment, and so forth, and would serve as input to the accounting system. Then, if the customer needed further service, a record of the prior service could be obtained.

Sally and Tommy prepared an RFP and sent it to 15 vendors. After vendor responses to the RFP were received, Sally and Tommy subjected them to a stringent evaluation process to determine the best vendor proposals. Then, the selected technology platforms along with the general systems design alternatives they support were evaluated to determine the one with the best effectiveness-to-cost ratio. The result of this work is shown in the following Final General Systems Design Report.

FINAL GENERAL SYSTEMS DESIGN REPORT

September 17, 19XX

       To: All Departments Heads
     From: Sally Forth, Chief Systems Analyst
  Subject: Scheduling of Events and Ticketing System (SEATS)
   Copies: John Ball, Events Center Director and Tyronne Topps, CISO

General Evaluation Strategy

This report includes a copy of the request for proposal sent to 15 vendors. It is a systems performance-based RFP versus an equipment-based RFP. Therefore, a copy of the General Systems Design Proposal Report was included with each RFP. Vendors who submitted acceptable proposals were subjected to a seven-screen evaluation process to select the best vendors with the best technology platforms. The eighth evaluation screen subjected each systems design alternative with its technology platform to a cost-effectiveness analysis. The one with the best effectiveness-to-cost ratio will be designed in detail for implementation.

Request for Proposal

Introduction
The NSU Event Center requests proposals for a Seating and Ticketing System (SEATS) to be provided on or before October 31, 19XX. This system should enhance current administrative and accounting support for the ticketing function of the center for all types of events currently scheduled. These events are of three types: (1) school athletic events for which open seating is required, (2) events such as concerts for which designated categories of tickets and set-up are required, and (3) academic events such as professional conferences that have specialized requirements for ticketing and seating. The system provided should enhance the ability of the event center to maintain a mix of types and numbers of events on a tight schedule, properly maintaining accounting and other requisite record keeping for the center on a timely basis. The proposals should address the mandatory requirements in full. The agency welcomes suggestions for enhancements and options within the spending guidelines.

Imperatives
The following issues must be addressed for the RFP to be considered:

Centrally accessible data—Ability to share data and printed reports among the activities office, the ticket office, and the resources department.

Menu driven—User friendly, menu-based system for commonly used capabilities.

Expandibility and upgradability—As the event center expands, the system must be expandable to meet the increased need.

Desirables
Addressing the following items will improve the consideration for the proposed solution:

User report generation—Independence in production of reports necessary for each departmental user of the system.

Online help—Access to information on software use from all workstations at all times.

Proposal Preparation Guidelines
Vendors should prepare and deliver proposals to the NSU Purchasing De-

partment Office to meet the specific needs designated in the attachments on or before October 31, 19XX.

Vendor Performance and Financial Condition

Proof of the vendor performance history, growth, and financial strength is required. An audited financial statement is also required.

A biographical sketch (resume) for all persons who will be involved in installation and support is required. Also, a list of the responsibilities and tasks assigned to each participant is required.

A list of customers (10–15) who have acquired the same technology being proposed is required.

Systems Documentation

Samples of documentation for systems similar to the ones being proposed must be included. Complete review of the available online and offline documentation must be provided on request by vendors who make the final candidate review list.

Vendors Policies and Procedures

Relevant policy information for hardware and software testing and beta test results should be described.

Legal and Business Procedures

Submit copies of your purchase contract and service and maintenance agreements. Include information on discounts, payment schedules, and cancelation policies.

General Systems Design Proposal Report

A copy of the General Systems Design Proposal Report developed by the NSU staff is included. This document will provide information on user requirements, building blocks, and the systems working environment for use in preparing proposals.

Data Processing Requirements

Provide definition of hardware and software set-up criteria. Include responses to the following questions:

- Disk capacity?
- Disk speed?
- Disk access requirements?

Note: Benchmarks are planned to evaluate technology platform proposals.

Systems Requirements

Items that contribute to a better functioning system and effect good systems design should be recommended as needed, including:

- Reliability measured by MTBF
- Ease of use

- Modularity
- Compatibility
- Installation schedule

- Maintainability measured by MTTR
- Vendor support

Full Description of Technology Building Blocks

A full description of each recommended technology platform is required, including:

- Network topology
- Architecture
- Model number
- Operating system
- Primary storage capacity

- Front-end and back-end processor(s)
- Language processors
- Security and control features
- Application program packages
- Peripherals

Price and Financing Plans

Include full pricing, financing, and acquisition methods.

Evaluation Methodology

Simulations and benchmark tests may be scheduled during evaluation as required. Customers will be contacted about their experiences with the proposed technology, its performance, and ease of use.

Response from Requests for Proposals

The RFP and the General Systems Design Proposal Report were sent to 15 vendors. Three of the vendors were computer manufacturers, seven general computer systems vendors, and five were OEMs (original equipment manufacturers) specializing in theater/event center ticketing and control systems.

One general computer systems vendor did not respond and another general computer systems vendor was eliminated in the general review of the proposal because of unclear substantive commitments. One computer manufacturer proposal was eliminated because it contained only hardware specifications without software. Twelve vendors remained after the general review and a seven-step screening process was begun to consider the proposals of two computer manufacturers, five general computer system vendors, and five OEMs. The following is a list of the vendors and the alternatives to which they responded. Alternative 1 is the stand-alone batch general systems design. Alternative 2 is the network-based general systems design. Alternative 3 is the centralized general systems design.

Vendors	Technology Block for General Systems Design
Computer Manufacturer	
VENDOR 1 —ICL Business Machines	Alternative 3
VENDOR 2 —Digit Computers	Alternative 3
General Computer Systems	
VENDOR 3 —The Computer Place	Alternatives 1, 2
VENDOR 4 —Enter Computer Stores	Alternative 1
VENDOR 5 —21st Century Systems	Alternatives 1, 2
VENDOR 6 —Data Control Services	Alternative 2
VENDOR 7 —National General System (NGS)	Alternative 1
Original Equipment Manufacturers	
VENDOR 8 —Central Information Associates	Alternatives 2, 3
VENDOR 9 —Orbcam Data Processing	Alternative 2
VENDOR 10—Tickets Systems	Alternative 3
VENDOR 11—Online Reservations	Alternative 2
VENDOR 12—Amusement Services	Alternative 3

Evaluation Screen One: Desk-Checking Proposal Elements

The following criteria were used to screen vendors in the first evaluation.

A. Vendor personnel

B. Vendor customers

C. Vendor documentation

D. Vendor testing procedures and policies

E. Vendor financial condition

F. Vendor general, legal, and business procedures

Based on this evaluation, Xs were placed in appropriate cells of the following grid when unacceptable:

Vendor Number

	1	2	3	4	5	6	7	8	9	10	11	12
A.	*	*	*	*	*	X	*	*	*	*	*	*
B.	*	*	X	*	*	*	*	*	*	*	*	*
C.	*	*	*	*	*	X	X	*	*	*	*	*
D.	*	*	*	*	*	*	*	*	*	X	*	*
E.	*	*	X	*	*	*	*	*	*	*	*	*
F.	*	*	*	*	*	*	X	*	*	*	*	*

Vendor 3 was eliminated based on phone calls made to this vendor's customers. They complained about training and installation support and unexpected costs that were incurred. Vendor 3 also presented an audited financial statement that contained a disclaimer concerning meeting generally accepted accounting principles. Vendor 6 is a well-known vendor with a reputation for rapid turnover of personnel and was therefore eliminated. The documentation for vendor 6 was also unclear and difficult to follow. Vendor 7 was eliminated because the contract included a license agreement that called for a large yearly payment for a minimum of 10 years without the possibility of ownership. Vendor 7 was also eliminated for unclear and incomplete documentation. Vendor 10 did not provide evidence that testing procedures were conducted by a test group that was separate and independent from the development group.

Based on the outcome of this screening, vendors 1, 2, 4, 5, 8, 9, 11, and 12 remained in the running.

**Evaluation Screen Two: Technical
Performance Criteria Comparisons**
This section contains:

- Hardware technical performance criteria comparisons
- Software technical performance criteria comparisons

Hardware Technical Performance Criteria \ Vendors	Technology Platform for Stand-alone Batch System (Alternative 1)	
	4	5
Purchase price	$5,000	$10,000
CPU	80386	80386
CPU speed	18 Mhz	18 Mhz
Main storage	1 Mbytes	1 Mbytes
Hard disk provided	40 Mbytes	30 Mbytes
Hard disk access time	60 Mls	40 Mls
MTBF rating	40,000 hours	30,000 hours
Display provided	EGA color	Monochrome
Display resolution	640X400 PPI	1000X800 PPI
Display graphics	Yes	Yes
Backup system	Floppies	Mag tape
Network upgradable	Yes	Yes
Printer provided	24-pin dot matrix	Laser
Expansion slots	8	7

Software Technical Performance Criteria \ Vendors	Technology Platform for Stand-alone Batch System (Alternative 1)	
	4	5
Operating system	MS-DOS	PC-DOS
Programming languages provided	BASIC C	BASIC SQL/DB
Programming language used	C	SQL/DB
Source code provided	No	Yes
Main storage required	640K	512K
Disk storage required	20 Mbytes	30 Mbytes
Menu driven	Yes	Yes
Network upgradable	No	Yes
Access control	None	Passwords
Backup program	Yes	No
Structured design	No	Yes
Integrated	Yes	Yes
Documentation quality	Fair	Good
Modules:		
Seating allocation	No	No
Reservation status	No	No
Reconcile cash	No	Yes
Billing process	Yes	Yes
Event management	Yes	Yes
Sales status	Yes	Yes

After reviewing the two proposals, vendor 5 was chosen as having the best proposal for alternative 1 because of the ability to upgrade to a LAN system. We then compared vendors 5, 8, 9, and 11 for alternative 2.

Hardware Technical Performance Criteria \ Vendors	Technology Platform for Network-Based System (Alternative 2)			
	5	8	9	11
Price	$18,000	$25,000	$30,000	$20,000
Workstations	Equal 1 plus	IBL at 339	IBL Model 45	NEK ProMate
CPU speed	18 Mhz	25 Mhz	25 Mhz	20 Mhz
Main storage	640K	512K	1 Mbytes	640K
Network cards	Enable/LAN	Ethernet	Net II	G-Net
Hard disk	20 Mbytes	30 Mbytes	30 Mbytes	40 Mbytes
Hard disk speed	60 Mls	45 Mls	45 Mls	40 Mls
MTBF rating	40,000 hours	30,000 hours	Unavailable	Unavailable
Display	CGA color	VGA color	Monochrome	EGA color

(continued next page)

Hardware Technical Performance Criteria \ Vendors	Technology Platform for Network-Based System (Alternative 2)			
	5	8	9	11
Display resolution	320X200 PPI	640X200 PPI	640X200 PPI	720X400 PPI
Display graphics	Yes	Yes	No	Yes
LAN system	3-Com	IBM ring	IBM PC Net	MS-Net
Server	Equal III+	IBL model 6	IBL model 8	NEK
Server speed	25 Mhz	25 Mhz	25 Mhz	25 Mhz
Hard disk	80 Mbytes	60 Mbytes	Bernoulli 20 + 20	115 Mbytes
Backup system	60 Mbytes Tape	40 Mbytes Tape	None	60 Mbytes Tape
Data transfer	10 Mbps	15 Mbps	12 Mbps	9 Mbps

Software Technical Performance Criteria \ Vendors	Technology Platform for Network-Based System (Alternative 2)			
	5	8*	9	11
Price	$15,000	$14,000	$20,000	$12,000
LAN system	Adv. Netware	Adv. Netware	PC-Net	MS-Net
Programming language provided	SQL/DB	Pascal BASIC	SQL/DDL C	SQL/FTP
Programming language used	SQL/DB	Pascal BASIC	SQL/DDL C	SQL/FTP
Main memory required	500K	460K	320K	1 Mbyte
Main storage required	20 Mbytes	12 Mbytes	10 Mbytes	27 Mbytes
File locking	Yes	No	Yes	Yes
Passwords	Yes	Yes	Yes	Yes
Menu driven	Yes	Yes	Yes	Yes
Report generators	Yes	No	No	Yes
Documentation	Excellent	Poor	Good	Fair
Service rates	$60/hr	$300/mo	$50/hr	$4,000/yr

*Eliminated vendor 8 because of poor documentation.

Hardware Technical Performance Criteria \ Vendors	Technology Platform for Centralized System (Alternative 3)			
	1	2	8	12
Price	$89,500	$135,655	$94,850	$110,640
CPU	Supreme 3020	DEQ Vac II	IBL RC	IBL 9480
CPU speed	16.7 Mhz	25 Mhz	25 Mhz	20 Mhz

(continued next page)

Hardware Technical Performance Criteria \ Vendors	Technology Platform for Centralized System (Alternative 3)			
	1	2	8	12
Main storage	12 Mbytes	10 Mbytes	10 Mbytes	12 Mbytes
Hard disk	344 Mbytes	145 Mbytes	70 Mbytes	260 Mbytes
Hard disk speed	25 Mls	30 Mls	40 Mls	30 Mls
MTBF rating	100,000 hr	70,000 hr	40,000 hr	95,000 hr
Backup system	Mag Tape	Mag Tape	Mag Tape	Disk
Backup power	None	15 minutes	30 minutes	Auto Save
Input devices	Mouse	Lightpen	Touch screen	Mouse
Terminals	Wyze 50	Dynac Pac	IBL 3164	DEQ VT 10
Terminal resolution	720X512 PPI	1000X480 PPI	860X600 PPI	640X480 PPI

Software Technical Performance Criteria \ Vendors	Technology Platform for Centralized System (Alternative 3)			
	1*	2	8	12*
Price	Included	Included	Included	Included
Operating system	Pick	VMS 2.0	Unix System 1	CSCI
Programming language provided	COBOL	COBOL FOCUS	C and REXHUS	C and FOCAL
Programming language used	COBOL	SQL/DA	ORICAL	SQL/DP
Main storage required	15 Mbytes	25 Mbytes	35 Mbytes	30 Mbytes
Disk storage required	56 Mbytes	79 Mbytes	60 Mbytes	44 Mbytes
File locking	No	Yes	Yes	Yes
Menu driven	Yes	Yes	Yes	Yes
Passwords	Yes	Yes	No	Yes
Documentation	Fair	Good	Good	Excellent
Report generators	No	Yes	Yes	No
Online help	No	Yes	Yes	No
Monthly service	$900	$1,335	$1,050	$1,675

*Eliminated vendor 1 because it does not provide a 4GL. Vendor 12 was eliminated because its proposed system did not contain online help.

Evaluation Screen Three: General Performance Criteria Comparisons

Because vendor 5 was the only one remaining for alternative 1, it becomes the vendor of choice for alternative 1. Vendor 8 was eliminated from alternative 2 because the documentation was poor. Vendor 1 was eliminated from alternative 3 because programming in a fourth-generation language is preferred over COBOL. Vendor 12 was eliminated from alternative 3 because it was deemed inadequate without a report generator or online help. Screening for alternative 2 and alternative 3 remain based on the following general performance criteria:

- Compatibility—Flexible, independent, portable, and universal
- Modularity—Segments merged readily and modules changed easily
- Maintainability—Changes in the program are made easily and low MTTR
- Reliability—Safe shutdowns, high MTBF
- Life expectancy—Newer technology and support system over its life
- Installation schedule—Time to install
- Vendor support—Quality and cost of support when needed

General Performance Criteria	Weight	Network-Based System (Alternative 2)						
		Vendor 5*		Vendor 9		Vendor 11*	
		Value	Score	Value	Score	Value	Score
Compatibility	20	7	140	5	100	8	160
Modularity	20	9	180	8	160	9	180
Maintainability	10	4	40	2	20	1	10
Reliability	10	8	80	9	90	10	100
Life expectancy	5	9	45	7	35	4	20
Installation schedule	5	10	50	8	40	5	25
Vendor support	30	6	180	10	300	4	120
Total			715		745		615

*Eliminated: Although vendors 5 and 11 received higher marks for compatibility and modularity, vendor 9 prevailed because of a very high mark for vendor support. Vendor 9 offered a five-year support contract included in the price of the system. Vendor 9 received favorable comments from customers concerning their level of support and a users group has been formed. Vendor 9 also provides training facilities with experienced personnel.

General Performance Criteria	Weight	Centralized System (Alternative 3)			
		Vendor 2		Vendor 8*	
		Value	Score	Value	Score
Compatibility	10	6	60	5	50
Modularity	10	9	90	8	80
Maintainability	5	1	5	2	10
Reliability	10	9	90	7	70
Life expectancy	20	9	180	7	140
Installation schedule	5	7	35	9	45
Vendor support	40	8	320	6	240
Total			780		635

*Eliminated: Although vendor 8 provided higher-performing hardware, it was felt compatibility, modularity, maintainability, and vendor support were more important. For these reasons vendor 2 prevailed.

Evaluation Screen Four: Benchmark and Simulation Tests

The vendors left in the running up to this point are reasonably close to each other in what they are offering. The question now becomes which one actually performs the best under operating or near operating conditions.

At this point, vendor 5 supports alternative 1, vendor 9 supports alternative 2, and vendor 2 supports alternative 3.

Benchmark tests are based on:

- Anticipated work load
- Compilers
- Operating system
- Application and utility packages
- Input-bound and process-bound speed

Applications	Vendor 5 Alternative 1	Vendor 9 Alternative 2	Vendor 2 Alternative 3
Ticket entry	NA	NA	30 sec
Backup of disk	30 min	10 min	45 sec
Print event listing	10 min	9 min	4 min
Process 20 events	2 min	1 min	20 sec
Query data base	NA	5 sec	3 sec
Process a ticket request	5 sec	4 sec	1 sec

Simulation tests considered were:

- Turnaround time
- Clock time
- Systems capacity
- Define optimum equipment configuration

Note: Simulation tests were not performed because of the unavailability of appropriate programs and personnel.

Vendor 2 performed better based on the benchmark tests over vendors 5 and 9. Similarly, vendor 9 performed better than vendor 5. This difference in the performance is not cause to eliminate any of the three at this point because of the price and configuration differences.

Evaluation Screen Five: Single Vendor Versus Multiple Vendor

The evaluation team decided that dealing with a single vendor is advantageous. A single vendor involves fewer complexities and better support. Upgrades and changes are easier to obtain. It is also difficult to combine software packages from different vendors.

Evaluation Screen Six: Price and Contract Negotiations

After negotiations with the remaining vendors, we determined the actual selling price. The terms of the bids are now in writing and the price and financial arrangements are specified in detail. Delivery dates are mutually agreed upon and specified and acceptance criteria have been outlined. The specifics of all warranties have been spelled out and approved by legal counsel and purchasing.

Contract terms	Vendor 5 Alternative 1	Vendor 9 Alternative 2	Vendor 2 Alternative 3
Selling price	$10,000	$45,000	$125,000
Delivery date	11/15/X9	12/30/X9	2/15/X0
Financing available	Purchase or rent	Purchase or installment purchase	Operating lease or finance lease
Warranties	1 year	1 year	5 years
Service contract	$385/year Level 1	$1,200/year Level 2	$6,500/year Level 2
Acceptance criteria	Letter of approval within 30 days	Letter of approval within 90 days	Acceptance test

Evaluation Screen Seven: Acquisition and Financing Methods

Before determining costs versus benefits of the three alternatives, it is necessary to determine the best acquisition and financing method.

Based on our analysis, it is best to purchase the technology block for alternative 1, to use the installment purchase method for the technology platform for alternative 2, and lease using the operating method for the technology block for alternative 3. A summary of the financial details are as follows:

Contract terms	Vendor 5 Alternative 1	Vendor 9 Alternative 2	Vendor 2 Alternative 3
Financing method	Purchase	Installment purchase	Operating lease
Cost	$10,000	$780.88/mo	$1,208.33/mo
Term	NA	7 years	10 years
Depreciation	$2,000/yr for 5 years	$9,000/yr for 5 years	NA
Salvage value	zero	zero	NA
Residual	NA	NA	$50,000

Evaluation Screen Eight: Cost-effectiveness Analysis of General Systems Design Alternatives

We use the present value (PV) of cash flows method to determine which alternative over a period of ten years will provide the best financial benefit to the event center. Our analysis is based on the following costs and benefits:

Benefits
1. Tangible
   a. Labor savings from more efficient scheduling and coordination
   b. Revenue from additional event bookings
   c. Cost savings from improved scheduling
   d. Efficient and controlled ticket handling
   e. Increased revenue from the ability to sell tickets downtown (for Alternative 3 only)
2. Intangible
   a. Customer goodwill from efficient and controlled ticket handling

Costs
1. Systems implementation costs
   a. Equipment installation
   b. Programming
   c. Training
   d. Testing
   e. Conversion
2. Technology costs
   a. Cost to acquire the initial system with finance charges
   b. Cost of additional programming and hardware if required
3. Cost to operate the computer facility
   a. Power requirements
   b. Air conditioning
   c. Furniture and fixtures
   d. Supplies
   e. Staffing
   f. Maintenance contract fees
   g. Insurance

| | STAND-ALONE BATCH ALTERNATIVE 1 | | | | | | | | | |
	1	2	3	4	5	6	7	8	9	10
Labor savings	3000	4000	4000	5000	5000	6000	8000	11000	15000	25000
Revenue	40000	60000	80000	80000	80000	80000	90000	90000	90000	100000
Cost savings	6000	6000	8000	8000	10000	10000	15000	15000	18000	20000
Ticketing	0	0	1000	1000	2000	1500	1500	1000	1000	0
Benefits	49000	70000	93000	94000	97000	97500	114500	117000	124000	145000
Implementation	2500									
Hardware	0	0	0	4000	0	0	0	6000	0	0
Price	10000									
Programming	3500	0	0	0	5000	0	0	0	5000	0
Maintenance	500	500	500	500	500	500	500	500	500	500
Operations	15000	15000	15000	16000	16000	16000	18000	18000	18000	20000
Costs	31500	15500	15500	20500	21500	16500	18500	24500	23500	20500
Net cash	17500	54500	77500	73500	75500	81000	96000	92500	100500	124500
Factor @ 20%	0.833	0.694	0.579	0.482	0.402	0.335	0.279	0.233	0.194	0.162
PV	14578	37823	44873	35427	30351	27135	26784	21553	19497	20169
Total PV	278188									

NETWORK-BASED ALTERNATIVE 2

	1	2	3	4	5	6	7	8	9	10
Labor savings	4000	5000	7000	8000	10000	11000	12000	14000	14000	15000
Revenue	110000	110000	115000	120000	120000	130000	130000	130000	130000	130000
Cost savings	6000	6000	8000	8000	10000	10000	15000	15000	18000	20000
Ticketing	4000	4000	5000	5000	6000	6000	6000	6000	6000	6000
Benefits	124000	125000	135000	141000	146000	157000	163000	165000	168000	171000
Implementation	7500	0	0	0	0	0	0	0	0	0
Hardware	0	0	0	13000	0	0	0	15000	0	0
Installments	9370.5	9370.5	9370.5	9370.5	9370.5	9370.5	9370.5	0	0	0
Programming	1000	1000	1000	1000	5000	1000	1000	1000	5000	1000
Maintenance	2200	2200	2200	2200	2200	2200	2200	2200	2200	2200
Operations	18000	18000	18000	21000	21000	21000	21000	21000	21000	20000
Costs	38070	30570	30570	46570	37570	33570	33570	39200	28200	23200
Net cash	85929	94429	104429	94429	108429	123429	129429	125800	139800	147800
Factor @ 20%	0.833	0.694	0.579	0.482	0.402	0.335	0.279	0.233	0.194	0.162
PV	71579	65534	60465	45515	43589	41349	36111	29311	27121	23944
Total PV	444517									

CENTRALIZED ALTERNATIVE 3

	1	2	3	4	5	6	7	8	9	10
Labor savings	5000	7000	8000	9000	11000	13000	13000	13000	13000	13000
Revenue	120000	12000	140000	140000	150000	150000	160000	160000	180000	180000
Cost savings	9000	12000	15000	18000	18000	18000	18000	18000	18000	18000
Ticketing	6000	10000	10000	10000	15000	10000	10000	10000	10000	10000
Downtown	24000	24000	28000	28000	30000	30000	32000	32000	36000	36000
Benefits	164000	65000	201000	205000	224000	221000	233000	233000	257000	257000
Implementation	10500									
Hardware	0	0	0	14000	0	0	0	16000	0	0
Lease	14500	14500	14500	14500	14500	14500	14500	14500	14500	64500
Programming	10000	3000	3000	3000	15000	3000	3000	3000	20000	3000
Maintenance	8500	8500	8500	8500	8500	8500	8500	8500	8500	8500
Operations	20000	20000	20000	25000	25000	25000	28000	28000	28000	28000
Costs	63500	46000	46000	65000	63000	51000	54000	70000	71000	10400
Net cash	100500	19000	155000	140000	161000	170000	179000	163000	186000	153000
Factor @ 20%	0.833	0.694	0.579	0.482	0.402	0.335	0.279	0.233	0.194	0.162
PV	83717	13186	89745	67480	64722	56950	49941	37979	36084	24786
Total PV	524589									

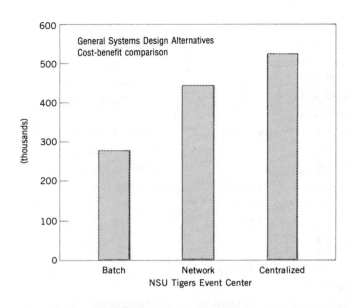

General Systems Design Alternatives
Cost-benefit comparison

NSU Tigers Event Center

SUMMARY

The objective of the systems evaluation phase is to determine the technology that will best serve as a platform for the other building blocks defined by the general systems design alternatives. To accomplish this objective, the systems analyst follows a controlled and strict evaluation process. The steps in this process consist of preparing a request for proposal, "pushing" vendor responses to the RFP through eight evaluation screens, and documenting the results of the systems evaluation phase with deliverable number four, the Final General Systems Design Report.

IMPORTANT TERMS

acceptance test
benchmark
building blocks
compatibility
data processing requirements
degraded performance
estimating
evaluation-screen process
fault tolerance

Final General Systems
   Design Report
full recovery
imperative and desirable
   requirements
independence
installation schedule
installment purchase
intangible benefits

life expectancy	residual value
maintainability	safe shutdown
maintenance and service contract	simulation method
	site facilities cost
migration	systems application architecture (SAA)
modularity	
performance objective	systems requirements
portability	universality
reliability	vendor support
request for proposal (RFP)	warranties
request for quotation (RFQ)	

Assignment

REVIEW QUESTIONS

18.1 Describe the three approaches to obtaining proposals from vendors for software, hardware, and services and the advantages and disadvantages of each approach.

18.2 List the 11 elements that make up a request for proposal based on systems performance objectives.

18.3 What is the difference between an imperative and a desirable requirement?

18.4 List five types of evidence that can indicate a vendor's ability to meet RFP requirements over the long haul.

18.5 What is the purpose of performing a general review of vendors' proposals?

18.6 What is the objective of evaluation screen number one, desk-checking proposal elements? What six key aspects of a vendor's proposal are evaluated by this screen?

18.7 Describe the major components examined and method used in the second evaluation screen.

18.8 List the seven general performance criteria used in evaluation screen three to determine how well the vendors' products meet the systems requirements design forces.

18.9 Support from a vendor is one of the most critical aspects of the evaluation process. List seven questions that might be asked to determine vendor support.

18.10 Give examples of the type of information supplied by professional service companies and the role this information plays in the evaluation process.

18.11 What do benchmark test problems represent? Identify the four components of a vendor's proposed system that can be tested by benchmark programs.

18.12 List the advantages and disadvantages of using a single vendor for both hardware and software; of using multiple vendors.

18.13 Why is it necessary to have a source code escrow provision in the contract for customized software?

18.14 Define what is meant by an unlimited use rental contract; by a prime shift rental contract.

18.15 List several advantages and disadvantages of renting computer equipment.

18.16 Identify the tax ramifications of leasing computer equipment.

18.17 List three advantages afforded lessors by leasing computer equipment.

18.19 List three advantages and disadvantages of the installment purchase method of acquiring computer equipment.

18.20 What is the systems analyst trying to ascertain by applying evaluation screen number eight?

18.21 List and define the five categories of systems implementation costs; the six categories of operations and maintenance costs.

18.22 Give two examples of tangible and intangible benefits.

QUESTIONS FOR DISCUSSION

18.23 Although some costs are difficult to estimate, certain costs can be estimated readily. While many of these figures will only be approximations, the costs usually can be estimated to such a degree of accuracy that a valid economic analysis can be made of a proposed system. The first type of costs to be considered are the one-time costs that occur during systems development. The other type of costs that are important in estimating the expense of operating the system are recurring costs. Make a list of costs that fall into each category and discuss why you placed the cost in that category.

18.24 Discuss the types of errors that can be made in evaluating proposals from vendors.

18.25 Organizations often develop questionnaires to gather information from vendors. Prepare a list of questions that might appear on this type of questionnaire and discuss the reasons you believe the questions should be included.

18.26 The economics of computer systems probably do not vary significantly from the economics of other types of equipment and systems acquisition that organizations employ. The following four principles are necessary considerations in analyzing economics of computers. Discuss each statement.

1. Lowest cost is not always the best.

2. Accomplishment is more important than cost.

3. Most decisions are trade-offs.

4. When in doubt, use historical or industry guidelines.

18.27 Construct a rating scale listing the following nine major technical attributes in vendor selection. Assign a value to each characteristic and discuss the reason behind the assignment.

1. Hardware.
2. Software.
3. Modularity.
4. Support.
5. Reliability.
6. Maintainability.
7. Installation schedule.
8. Compatibility.
9. Life expectancy.

EXERCISES AND PROBLEMS

18.28 Classify each of the following cost items by behavior (variable or fixed) and function (development, operational, or maintenance).

1. Rental charges for the computer mainframe based on $150/CPU hour.

2. Rental charges of $1,000/month for a line printer.

3. Cost of installation of one-way emergency doors.

4. Delivery charges on the computer mainframe.

5. Wages of a special instructor to train a class of programmers in the new virtual storage operating system.

6. Programming charges of $36,000 for conversion of accounts receivable application package from an IBM 1401 to an IBM 3032.

7. Analyst costs of $3,500 for preparing a Proposal to Conduct Systems Analysis Report on a sales analysis package.

8. Operator payroll fringe benefit charges of $1,900.

9. Charges for repairing three broken keypunch machines this month.

18.29 Barry Bright, systems analyst for Graphics, Inc., has just completed his systems design proposal report. Included in this report is some information concerning the acquisition of a computer configuration. This information is listed as follows:

1. The purchase price of the computer is $1,200,000. Maintenance expenses are expected to run $60,000 per year. If the computer is rented, the yearly rental price will be $370,000, based on an unlimited use rental contract with free maintenance.

2. Mr. Bright believes it will be necessary to replace the configuration at the end of five years. It is estimated that the computer will have a resale value of $120,000 at the end of the five years.

3. The estimated gross annual savings derived from this particular alternative computer configuration are $450,000 for the first year, $500,000 the second, and $550,000 each of the third, fourth, and fifth years. The estimated annual expense of operation is $190,000, in addition to the expenses mentioned earlier. Additional nonrecurring costs are $70,000.

4. If Graphics decides to rent the computer instead of buying, the $1,200,000 could be invested at a 25 percent rate of return. The present value of $1.00 at the end of each of five years, discounted at 25 percent is

End of Year	Present Value
1	$.800
2	.640
3	.512
4	.410
5	.328

Required: Based on the foregoing financial considerations alone, ignoring the tax impact, which method of acquisition do you recommend?

18.30 The following are results of benchmark problems run on configurations A, B, and C. The benchmark problems run on each configuration are representative sample workloads, which test for both I/O and internal processing capabilities of each configuration. The monthly rental, based on projected usage of at least 176 hours per month, is $30,000 for configuration A, $34,000 for configuration B, and $32,000 for configuration C.

BENCHMARK RESULTS: CPU TIMES (IN SECONDS) FOR COMPILATION AND EXECUTION OF DIFFERENT PROGRAMS

Type of Problem / Vendor	Process-Bound Problem	Input/Output- Bound Problem	Hybrid Problem
A	400.5	640	247.5
B	104.9	320	260.3
C	175.4	325	296.8

Required: Which configuration should be selected? Why?

18.31 A company proposes to acquire a computer system. Three alternate designs are being considered: A, B, and C. The firm wishes to use cost-effectiveness analysis to analyze the three alternatives. Julie Goodrich, a financial analyst for the firm, estimates these costs:

	A	B	C
Initial cost	$ 500,000	$ 300,000	$ 500,000
Operating costs for five years	800,000	1,000,000	600,000
Costs for software	150,000	—	50,000
Total costs	$1,450,000	$1,300,000	$1,150,000

Computer, Inc., a local computer consulting firm, estimates the equivalent dollar benefits from each system: $B_i = 100,000X_1 + 50,000X_2 + 10,000X_3$, where

	X_1	X_2	X_3
A	1.0	1.0	1.0
B	.6	.9	1.0
C	.1	2.8	2.8

Which project offers the largest difference between costs and benefits?

18.32 Clayborn Mines is contemplating installing a computer system that will save them an estimated $96,000 per year in operating costs. Clayborn estimates that the useful life of the system will be four years and that it will have no residual value. The computer system may be purchased from Honeywell for $260,000, or it may be leased from a third party for $80,000 payable at the end of each year. The noncancellable lease would run for four years.

Clayborn Mines is a fast-growing corporation and requires that all capital investments earn a rate of return of at least 26 percent. Through a favorable agreement with a large Chicago bank they are able to borrow funds for capital investment projects at 20 percent.

Required: Ignoring tax effects, what should Clayborn do? (Note: The present value of a $1.00 annuity for four years is $2.588 and $2.300 at rates of 20 and 26 percent, respectively.)

18.33 A computer center has four jobs whose processing times are directly related to the speed of the input/output components and the volume of data being processed. The input medium is cards and the card reader has a rated speed of 1,000 cards per minute. On the output side, the printer is rated at 1,100 lines per minute, and the card punch has a rated speed of 600 cards per minute.

Since these devices share a single multiplexer channel, simultaneous operation of the components results in interference, and, consequently, degrades each component's level of efficiency (rated speed).

	Level of Efficiency (in Percent) of Components with			
Components	Card Reader	Card Punch	Printer	Both Other Components
Card reader	100	90	85	70
Card punch	90	100	87	70
Printer	85	87	100	70

The volumes of the four jobs are as follows:

Job	Input Cards	Output Cards	Output Lines
(1)	3,000	400	4,000
(2)	50,000	1,000	1,000
(3)	5,000	300	10,000
(4)	50	800	800

Required: Assuming that output is not dependent on input, determine the shortest processing time for each of the four jobs.

18.34 The Wing Commander of a tactical fighter wing has requested the implementation of a formal information system to assist him in evaluating the quality of aircrew members. Although many factors are related to determining an individual's quality level, it has been recommended that one source of objective data is from the testing process administered by the Standardization/Evaluation Section in the fighter wing. Each flight crew member is tested periodically either by an instrument check or by a tactical/proficiency check to detect violations of standardized operating procedures or errors in judgment. The result of a test is either pass or fail and discrepancies such as single-engine landing, dangerous pass, incorrect holding pattern, and so forth are noted where applicable. A general feeling exists in the Standardization/Evaluation Section that if these reports were prepared and disseminated in a timely fashion, the Wing Commander could take swift corrective action to prevent a hazardous practice or critical weakness from causing a decline in mission performance or even an accident from occurring. Further analysis indicates that such a report can be prepared daily, five days a week throughout the year, at a cost of $14.10 per day per report. This time period for reporting is judged acceptable by the Standardization/Evaluation Section.

While many benefits are anticipated from implementing such a system, the Wing Commander has requested that all new information systems be justified initially on economic grounds alone. As the systems analyst assigned to this project, you have decided to take the approach that the proposed system will help change the probability of a major accident per flight from .00002 (without the report) to .000015 (with the report). From your investigation you have gathered the following statistics concerning major accidents:

COSTS OF A MAJOR ACCIDENT

Certain costs

Aircraft	$1,600,000
Accident investigation	6,000
Property damage (impact point)	2,000
Total	$1,608,000

Possible costs (both crew members are lost)

Invested training in crew members 2 @ $25,000	$ 50,000
Survivors benefits and mortuary costs 2 @ $50,000	$ 100,000
Total	$ 150,000

Probability of crew loss .25

Required: Can the proposed system be economically justified using this approach? (Hint: It may be helpful to calculate the number of flights that would have to be made each year by the wing to cover the cost of generating the report.) Identify other economic factors not considered in this problem.

18.35 A large fabricator and marketer of customized aluminum products has a sales force of 400 people throughout the continental United States and Canada. A traditional problem in the company has been the delay of entering orders (via mail) from each of these salespeople to a centralized data processing center in St. Louis, Missouri. In addition, the salespeople are unable to respond to a customer's inquiry concerning the status of an in-process order in less than two days. A marketing study has estimated that delays in order-entry costs the company $200,000 in lost sales annually. Moreover, customer frustration with late shipments resulted in a loss of $300,000 from canceled orders in each of the last two years. The average profit margin for the company is 30 percent.

A recently completed systems analysis has revealed the following facts:

1. Each salesperson can be assigned a small portable terminal to access the corporate computers directly at an initial cost of $500 per terminal.
2. Special communication networks to permit toll free calls can be installed at a cost of $20,000 initially and $3,500 per month.
3. Maintenance for all the terminals is estimated at $10,000 annually.
4. System development and implementation costs are estimated at $250,000.
5. To operate the system with the centralized computer is estimated at $20,000 annually.
6. Corporate guidelines require new projects to pay back within five years or less.

Required: Analyze the above facts and prepare a report describing the economic feasibility of implementing the new system.

18.36 Tidex Manufacturing is planning to acquire a computer system. The costs for the undertaking have been projected over a five-year period. Year 0, the first year, is prior to the computer installation, while the remaining four years represent the life of the system. The costs and savings have been estimated as follows:

	0	1	2	3	4
1. Initial systems and programming	74,000				
2. Environment preparation	7,000				
3. Conversion	15,000	14,000	3,000		
4. Parallel operations		9,000	6,000	1,000	
5. Equipment rental		75,000	81,000	85,000	115,000
6. Systems and programming		70,000	70,000	70,000	70,000
7. Operations		60,000	64,000	70,000	72,000
8. Reduction in service bureau costs		65,000	95,000	125,000	130,000
9. Reduction in clerical costs		12,000	18,000	24,000	55,000
10. Reduction in inventory costs		35,000	150,000	160,000	160,000
11. Reduction in rental of old equipment		10,000	15,000	20,000	25,000

(continued next page)

	0	1	2	3	4
12. Reduction in over-time			6,000	30,000	40,000
13. Increased customer service level		6,000	58,000	95,000	100,000
14. Improved management planning		8,000	45,000	50,000	50,000
15. Improved management control		9,000	50,000	50,000	50,000

Required: Analyze these costs and benefits and indicate when total benefits exceed total costs, and where total direct benefits exceed total costs.

18.37 All of the basic transaction processing of Heartland Feed and Grain of Iowa City, Iowa, is done by a service bureau located in Des Moines. The owner of Heartland, Jack Crawford, has asked his accounting manager, Greg Gantt, to undertake the project of replacing the service bureau's processing of Heartland's payroll, accounts receivable, and accounts payable transactions with an in-house, computer-based system. With the assistance of Heartland's local CPA, Gantt prepared a request for proposal and sent it to five vendors in the Iowa City area. The proposal was made up of three sections and contained the following information:

1. An introductory section contained a general description of Heartland Feed and Grain, its basic business purpose and short-term goals, and a fairly lengthy description of its operations.

2. The second section of the RFP contained all accumulated documentation of the service bureau's processing of payroll, accounts receivable, and accounts payable transactions. Unfortunately, the documentation was over three years old because Gantt's predecessor, Thelma Crawford, "trashed" more recent documentation received from the service bureau because she didn't understand it.

3. The last section of the RFP asked each prospective vendor to specify the technical characteristics of the processor, disk storage, and printer they were recommending. Vendors were also asked to identify the programming languages available for the recommended configuration, and the availability of alternative software packages most suitable for handling each of the three transaction types.

Accompanying the RFP was a cover letter signed by Gantt asking that prospective vendors respond in writing within two weeks and to call him if they had any questions about the RFP.

Required: Evaluate the contents of Heartland's RFP.

18.38 As the head of your school's academic computing evaluation committee, you have narrowed the choice for a replacement processing configuration down to three prospective vendors, Alpha, Beta, and Omega. At this point in the evaluation process, you want to see how the candidate systems stack up against the general performance criteria of evaluation screen number three.

One month later your committee has evaluated the three proposed processing configurations and produced the following scores on a scale of 0–9:

1. Compatibility: Alpha, 6; Beta, 7; Omega, 5.
2. Modularity: Alpha, 7; Beta, 7; Omega, 5.
3. Maintainability: Alpha, 8; Beta, 6; Omega, 7.
4. Reliability: Alpha, 7; Beta, 7; Omega, 9.

5. Life expectancy: Alpha, 5; Beta, 6; Omega, 8.
6. Installation schedule: Alpha, 4; Beta, 4; Omega, 5.
7. Vendor support: Alpha, 8; Beta, 4; Omega, 6.

This past summer your committee conducted a survey of the major users of the present academic processing configuration to determine the weights to be placed on the general performance criteria. Based on this survey, your committee assigned the following weights: compatibility, 30; modularity, 20; maintainability, 50; reliability, 50; life expectancy, 30; installation schedule, 20; and vendor support, 50.

Last Friday you received a call from the director of Academic Computing. During the course of your conversation with her, she expressed concern over the evaluation process in general and the weights placed on the general performance criteria in particular.

"We have made great strides in the last three months with respect to hiring some top-notch technical support people. I expect with our increased level of funding to be able to attract at least five new technical support persons in the next six months. I hope the weight you place on this evaluation criterion reflects these facts. I also want you to know that in the last two weeks I have received a number of inquiries from departments that you normally don't think of as users of computing. I believe the universality of the new system has to be greater than first anticipated if these departments' computing needs are close to being realistic."

> ***Required:*** Prepare a general performance criteria matrix based on the weights initially decided upon based on the user survey. Also prepare a second general performance criteria matrix that reflects your recent conversation with the director of Academic Computing. This time, assign the weights of 50 to compatibility and 20 to vendor support. What conclusions can you draw as a result of this analysis?

BIBLIOGRAPHY

AUER, JOSEPH, and CHARLES EDISON HARRIS. *Major Equipment Procurement.* New York: Van Nostrand Reinhold, 1983.

BUSS, MARTIN D. "How to Rank Computer Projects." *Harvard Business Review,* January–February 1983.

CROSS, EDWARD M. *How to Buy a Business Computer and Get It Right the First Time.* Reston, Va.: Reston, 1983.

GORDON, MARK L., and STEVEN B. STARR. "Computer Maintenance Contracts." *Infosystems,* March 1984.

GRUENFELD, LEE. "Avoiding Contract Disaster." *Computerworld,* July 13, 1987.

HEYDT, BRUCE. "The Computer Challenge: A Strategy for Software Selection." *Distribution,* April 1987.

HUMPHREY, SCOTT R. "The Quest for Performance." *Data Management,* July 1985.

KULL, DAVID. "Beware the Benchmark." *Computer Decisions,* February 9, 1987.

LEEKE, JIM. "Budget Ahead for the Continuing Cost of PCs." *PC Week,* September, 15, 1987.

LEVIN, HENRY M. *Cost-effectiveness: A Primer.* Beverly Hills, Calif.: Sage, 1983.

MILLS, HARLAN D., RICHARD C. LINGER, and ALAN R. HEVNER. *Principles of Information Systems Analysis & Design.* Orlando, Fla.: Academic Press, 1986.

PETERSON, ROBERT D. *Managing the Systems Development Function.* New York: Van Nostrand Reinhold, 1987.

ROBINSON, DAVID G. "Synchronizing with Business Values." *Datamation,* June 15, 1984.

ROWLAND, CHARLES A. "Figuring the Bill for MIS Services." *Infosystems,* July 1984.

STEWART, RODNEY D. *Cost Estimating.* New York: John Wiley, 1982.

TASKER, ROBERT. "How to Avoid Fumbling When Handling Vendor Proposals." *InformationWEEK,* September 7, 1987.

VANECEK, MICHAEL. "Computer System Acquisition Planning." *Journal of Systems Management,* May 1984.

WHIELDON, DAVID. "May the Best System Win." *Computer Decisions,* May 1984.

WIENER, HESH. "Lessors on Leasing." *Datamation,* May 15, 1984.

19
DETAILED SYSTEMS DESIGN

19.1 INTRODUCTION

During the detailed systems design phase, the precise format and content of output is determined. Prior to this phase, output might have been a sales report containing specific information that the sales manager needs. But now headings are developed and the number of spaces between output and the number of lines advanced are specified along with exact editing. Precise formatting of screens including windows, instructions, prompts, and menus is achieved. Generally, the starting point is output because it dictates the input and data base requirements.

Input formats are designed in a like manner to produce the output. Forms are defined zone by zone.

Appropriate models are refined and are made ready to implement and receive input. Detailed specifications are developed for models to be programmed.

Data entities are described in accordance with data attributes, attribute values, and data representations. Relations, networks, or hierarchies are defined if a data base approach is used. Sequential, direct, or indexed sequential files are defined if a file approach is used.

In addition to specifying a number of processing controls, the analyst designs and specifies administrative, input, data base, output, documentation, hardware, and security controls. Also, traditional records and accounting controls are examined and updated if necessary.

The technology, especially computer, peripherals, and telecommunications have, in many cases, already been defined and may be in place ready to accept and run the other building blocks after they have been designed in detail. If the software has to be customized and written, design specifications prepared for the programmer will typically include output and input layouts; various models such as HIPO, data flow diagrams, and Warnier-Orr; and structured English or pseudocode. Ideally, the software specification package follows structured, modular design procedures. Moreover, detailed procedures are written for personnel.

The general purpose of this chapter is to portray by examples and discussion the role of detailed systems design in the systems development methodology (SDM). Indeed, it is in this phase where all the T's are crossed and the I's are dotted, so to speak. The objectives of this chapter are:

1. To present a perspective on the evolution of systems development up to and including the detailed systems design phase.
2. To examine modular design principles, a key part of well-designed systems.
3. To consider customized versus off-the-shelf designs.
4. To analyze interactive detailed design methods and show how they support and conform to the user/system interface and human factors design forces.
5. To describe detailed output design.
6. To explain detailed input design.
7. To demonstrate by a small case detailed data base design.
8. To inquire into detailed controls design.
9. To give examples of detailed program and personnel procedures design.
10. To offer a method of detailed program design with an emphasis on modularity.
11. To illustrate several detailed hardware design configurations.
12. To outline the Final Detailed Systems Design Report, the SDM's fifth documented deliverable.
13. To demonstrate the NSU Tigers Event Center Final Detailed Systems Design Report.

19.2 EVOLUTION TO DETAILED SYSTEMS DESIGN

Figure 19.1 illustrates the evolution from strategic information systems planning (SISP) to detailed systems design. It also portrays the roles end users, systems analysts, and programmers play in this evolution.

End users (later we will provide more precise categories of users) are concerned with business tasks, transactions, processes, and various information. They possess semantic knowledge that pertains to their specific tasks and is technology independent.

Programmers and other technicians are occupied with technology and its application. These players possess a high level of syntactic knowledge that is technology dependent. Their prime objective is to apply technology to the detailed systems design.

Systems analysts, through the SDM, move from definitions of business tasks, processes, and information that are semantic oriented to definitions of technology processes that are syntactic oriented. Now, for the first time, systems analysts must bring the two knowledge domains together in a viable mix and design their elements precisely, the goal of detailed systems design.

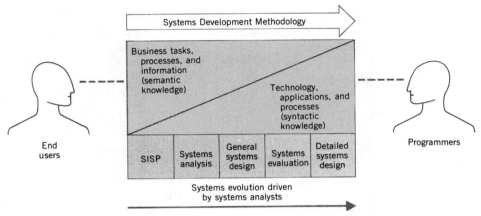

Figure 19.1 Evolution of systems work from SISP to detailed systems design.

In the Semantic Phase

Scarlotti Distributors sells a variety of furniture and office supplies in a three-state area. Joe Scarlotti is the sales manager, Ellen Sullivan is a systems analyst, and Thai Woo is a COBOL programmer.

During a recent interview, Joe told Ellen that he was "losing control of sales" and he had to "get a better grip on what's happening out in the field." She took that as her cue to design a sales report that would help Joe manage sales better.

During general systems design, one of the alternatives presented to Joe is illustrated in Figure 19.2. This was the design alternative that was selected from evaluation as the best one for detailed systems design and implementation.

During detailed systems design, Ellen prepared a visual table of contents (VTOC) displayed in Figure 19.3. The top box in the VTOC is the boss module. It and a few other pieces of documentation evolved out of systems analysis. Then in general systems design, it, along with some prototyping and blank paper sketching, helped to provide viable general systems design alternatives. This documentation, along with other subsystem documentation, formed the total general systems design alternatives Ellen pushed through the evaluation process.

In the Syntactic Phase

Ellen used the numbering system of 000 for the boss module, 100, 200, and 300 for the next-level modules, and so forth, because it's compatible with COBOL programming. COBOL paragraph names cannot contain a decimal, such as 1.0, 2.0, 3.0, 1.1.1, and 2.1.1.

Each module becomes one COBOL paragraph. The connecting lines show which paragraphs PERFORM other paragraphs. The shaded corner identifies a module that is called or PERFORMed by more than one module. Module 110 is called by modules 100, 250, and 300. Module 270 is also called by modules 250 and 300. Modules 110 and 270 appear only once in the COBOL program.

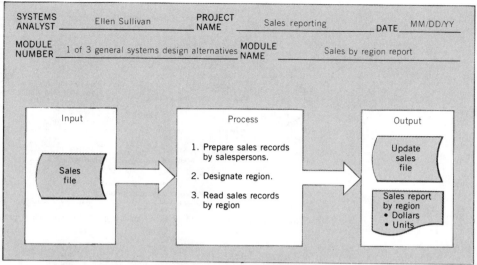

| SYSTEMS ANALYST | Ellen Sullivan | PROJECT NAME | Sales reporting | DATE | MM/DD/YY |
| MODULE NUMBER | 1 of 3 general systems design alternatives | MODULE NAME | Sales by region report | | |

Figure 19.2 A HIPO diagram used in the general systems design phase.

Having produced a blueprint for the COBOL program in the form of a VTOC, the next step performed by Ellen was detailed logic design of each module. This detailed logic can be done by structured English or pseudocode, structure charts, Nassi-Shneiderman charts, or Warnier-Orr charts. In the example, we show Ellen's application of pseudocode to module 200.

A single detailed HIPO diagram, shown in Figure 19.4, represents one

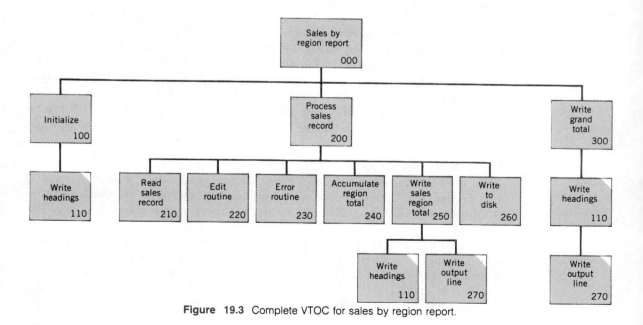

Figure 19.3 Complete VTOC for sales by region report.

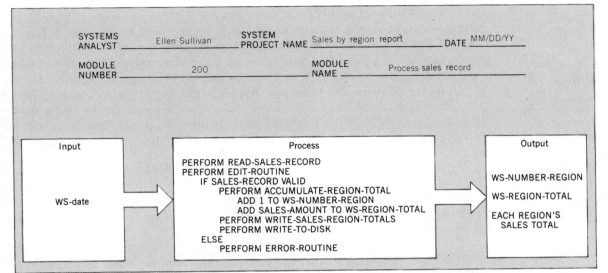

Figure 19.4 A detailed HIPO diagram and pseudocode for module 200

COBOL module (or paragraph). In our example, the HIPO diagram provides specifications for module 200. All the modules together, designed in this manner, will give sufficient detailed design specifications for Thai Woo, who has sufficient syntactic knowledge to code the complete SALES BY REGION REPORT program.

Before turning the detailed specifications over to Thai, Ellen "played computer" and desk checked the detailed design to catch omissions or errors in logic. Ellen believes that finding errors at this stage is much more cost-effective than discovering them when Thai is well into coding, or worse, after the COBOL program has been implemented.

19.3 MODULAR DESIGN

People deal better with things that are modular than with those that are unorganized, cluttered, or monolithic. The key to structured design and decomposition of complex systems to simple, manageable systems is modularity, one of the strongest design procedures analysts use.

Modular Design Objectives

Modularity increases systems flexibility as discussed in Chapter 18. Modular systems are more easily changed, expanded, or contracted than are monolithic systems designs. Most users find modular systems designs easier to understand.

Clearly, modularity is a basic rule of good design. Well-designed interfaces allow each module to be implemented independently of the other modules with which it communicates.

Modular Design Postulates

Modules should be low in coupling and high in cohesion, as depicted in Figure 19.5. Coupling refers to the number of connections between a calling and a called module as well as the complexity of these connections. Cohesion means how tightly bound together the instructions are within a module. So our concern is the degree of variability between (coupling) and within (cohesion) modules.

Each instruction should contribute directly to carrying out the single function of that module. If the module performs more than one discrete function, however, the instructions in that module are not bound very closely together, and it is said that this module has weak cohesion.

Strong cohesion in modules is desirable because concentrating related functions together makes the system simpler and easier to understand. This concentration of related functions together within modules reduces unnecessary intermodule references. Furthermore, modules that perform complete, well-defined functions can be reused in other systems.

If a module contains a number of calls to a number of other modules, coupling becomes complex. In this situation, the module is considered to have high coupling.

The fan-out from a module is the number of different modules it calls directly. Module fan-out should be kept below eight to avoid confusion. If a module has a fan-out of eight or more, such a module should be factored into two or more modules. A module with a fan-out of one or two, however, is probably the result of needlessly creating modules.

Fan-in to a module is the number of different modules that reference it directly, which is the number of immediately superior modules in a HIPO or structure chart. In most instances, high fan-in is desirable because it reduces the amount of program code required to implement a system, but the analyst must be alert to overdoing it. If a module with high fan-in executes an independent function in an online, real-time system, other calling modules may have to wait for it to perform a function for them, which degrades the overall performance of the system. Moreover, some analysts may make changes in a module to increase its fan-in capacity, which will generally impair cohesion. These undesirable situations should be avoided even at the expense of designing more modules in the system.

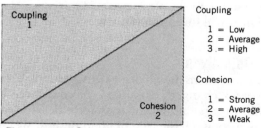

Figure 19.5 Schematic of an ideal module design.

Cohesion goes hand-in-hand with coupling. Typically, a design with strong cohesion within modules exhibits good and logical coupling between modules.

Modular Design Rules

The following basic rules should be used when developing and designing modules:

- A module should be considered to be a cohesive, bounded, or self-contained group of structures; it should be given a name by which it can be referenced.
- An initialization module should be written to establish key values for a program.
- Each module should solve one clearly defined part of a program such as input, edit, process A, process B, . . . , process W, or output. Besides making sure modules obey a single purpose, they should also have single entry and exit points.
- Modules should receive data, perform one operation or a logical group of operations on the data, and return output data. An attempt should be made to minimize the amount of data any module can reference. This means that instead of receiving entire records or relations, modules ought to receive only the necessary fields or domains. The less data passed the less chance of error!
- A program's external input and output operations should be isolated in as few modules as possible. If this is done, a change from one data structure to another can be accommodated with relative ease.

Application of HIPO Modular Design to COBOL Programming

The objective of modular design is to have one module equal one function. In modularly designed COBOL, it's one module equals one paragraph.

Once the VTOC is completed, detailed logic is constructed for each module. Sometimes one module becomes too complex and difficult to understand. By dividing such a module into two or more modules, the program code is easier to develop. Also, excessive nesting can be avoided.

The boss or executive module typically calls a level 1 module repeatedly comprising the main program loop. In COBOL, this loop is usually in the form of PERFORM UNTIL END OF FILE.

Generally, one READ module is used per input file and one WRITE module per output file. The READ and WRITE modules are called by any module in which an input/output operation is required. If output, however, requires both headings and detail amounts, which is generally the case, each should have its own WRITE module.

Do not set up excessive calls. If, for example, a module is trivial and does not receive repeated calls, then it should be eliminated and its instructions placed in the module that calls it.

A module should contain no more than 50 lines of COBOL code, which is equal to one page of source code. Any module larger than one page should be evaluated to see whether some operations should be moved into lower-level modules. Also, modules should call only those modules that are below their level.

Summary of Modular Design Benefits

Good detailed modular design results in simplified program coding and debugging. Coding is straightforward because each module is precisely defined for simple conversion to programming syntax.

As we shall also see in the next chapter, modular design simplifies testing because each module has already been reviewed a number of times to remove errors and inconsistencies. Furthermore, testing can begin while coding is being done rather than having to wait and test the whole monolithic program at one time.

Good detailed modular design simplifies and supports maintenance because documentation is straightforward and uncluttered. Modular structure facilitates change because small, well-defined modules are easy to understand. Low interdependence among modules makes it easier to isolate problems because problems are likely to be contained within a module rather than at the interface of, or coexisting within two or more modules.

And, finally, a number of modules may contain functions that have more than one application. If the development of new systems can use some of these modules, development time and programming costs can be saved, especially when one considers that a good COBOL programmer produces only about 10 to 30 implementable instructions per day and that a 10,000-line program can cost from $60,000 to $150,000 just for the coding.

19.4 CUSTOMIZED VERSUS OFF-THE-SHELF DESIGNS

One extreme of systems design is a fully customized system designed from scratch. At the other extreme, the total system is supported by a canned package, off-the-shelf system purchased or leased from vendors. To find either of these extremes supporting a total information system is somewhat rare.

Level of Detailed Design Effort

The amount of work that must be done during the detailed systems design phase depends on what came out of the systems evaluation phase. If a small, simple system is being developed that will consist primarily of an off-the-shelf canned software package or a well-defined prototype, most of the detailed work has already been done and the systems analyst can therefore go directly to the implementation phase. If, on the other hand, the system being worked on is complex and broad in scope and interfaces with a variety of users, then detailed systems design becomes a major phase in the SDM.

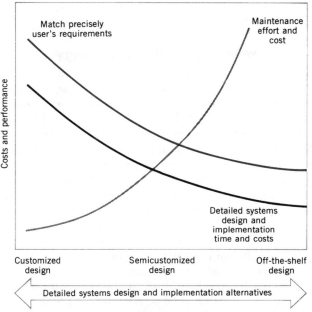

Figure 19.6 Trade-offs among detailed systems design and systems implementation alternatives.

Trade-offs Between Customized Design and Off-the-Shelf Design

Figure 19.6 shows cost and performance trade-offs among these detailed systems design and systems implementation alternatives. Clearly, a customized system should match users' requirements perfectly, whereas off-the-shelf systems rarely meet all users' requirements. Normally, compromises and changes by users have to be made before the canned system can be implemented.

Detailed systems design costs are generally high for customized design but almost nil for an off-the-shelf package. Moreover, implementation for canned packages generally requires less time and effort.

If the systems analyst follows good, structured, modular design procedures in developing and designing a customized system, then maintenance efforts and costs should be fairly low. On the other hand, changing an off-the-shelf package to adapt to changing users' requirements often presents a real problem for analysts and application programmers. In some cases, an off-the-shelf package cannot be changed.

19.5 INTERACTIVE DESIGN METHODS

Clearly, one major goal of detailed systems design is precise specifications for systems implementation, as we learned in the earlier HIPO-COBOL example.

But another goal, just as important, is to design a system that users have confidence in and with which they feel comfortable working.

The Benefits of Good Interactive Design Methods

A user-centered design goal demands systems designs that reduce the time required to learn how to use the system, increase user productivity, decrease errors, and increase systems knowledge retention time, especially for occasional users. It appears, therefore, that the main design forces impacting on this phase of the SDM are user/system interface and human factors.

In addition to satisfying programmers with precise specifications and users with application of good design methods, another benefit of design effectiveness is cost savings. For example, if our design methods produce a 20 percent decrease in the time required to perform tasks, then this, in turn, produces a 20 percent decrease in the costs for operators and technicians, and a 20 percent reduction in hardware costs.

If you work for a company that processes 2,000,000 transactions per year through terminals and you can, through your input screen design, reduce the time required to process each transaction by 30 seconds, then you can reduce the number of hours by nearly 17,000. If the company pays $12 per hour for this work, then you have reduced labor costs by over $200,000. Some banks and insurance companies process well over 10 million transactions per year, so cost savings produced by slight changes in screen design could result in million-dollar savings.

What are good design methods that are particularly applicable at the user/system interface? These are (1) user categorization, (2) message formulation, (3) directing users' attention, (4) menu design, (5) forms fill-in, (6) command language, (7) natural language, and (8) direct visual manipulation.

Know Thy Users

When designing the user/system interface, systems analysts must understand fully users and their tasks. We already know from earlier material that some users like graphs better than lists of numbers, have different tasks to perform, and operate at different levels and in different environments. In essence, knowing more about users leads to better designs. One way to "get a handle on users" is to categorize users as novice, occasional knowledgeable, frequent light, and frequent power users.

Semantic and Syntactic Knowledge

Users also have different semantic and syntactic knowledge. Semantic knowledge, as we know from an earlier discussion, is computer independent and is meaningful for the user's task. Syntactic knowledge is computer dependent, often arbitrary, and unstructured, and is acquired by rote memorization. Without continuous use, syntactic knowledge is soon forgotten, whereas semantic knowledge is more permanent.

A user can be a syntactic expert and a semantic novice, and vice versa. For example, an accountant is knowledgeable in performing accounting tasks, but may be a novice in computer syntax. A technician, on the other hand, may be a syntactic expert, but know nothing about accounting procedures.

Frequent light and power users generally possess a high level of syntactic knowledge. Novices and occasional users are often frustrated and constrained by syntactic "meaninglessness." Much of the design effort is, therefore, directed toward reducing the need for syntactic knowledge especially by novice and occasional users.

Designing for Novice Users

Novice users have no syntactic knowledge and typically only a smattering of semantic knowledge. Designing for these users presents a significant challenge.

The development of simple reference manuals, video demonstrations, step-by-step tutorials that evolve from basic to more difficult tasks, informative feedback, meaningful error messages, menus, pop-up instructions, and prompts together help overcome design limitations posed by novice users.

Occasional Knowledgeable Users

Occasional knowledgeable users have the semantic knowledge and can retrieve it quickly from their long-term memory even if they have not used it for weeks or months. These users, however, have difficulty in retaining syntactic knowledge.

The use of natural and some command languages, menus, macros, graphics, and mnemonics can help mitigate this design problem. Logical sequencing, meaningful messages, and timely prompts also help. Well-organized reference manuals and "cheat sheet" windows including key syntactic components are often useful.

Frequent Light Users

Frequent light users' work is generally narrow in scope and highly repetitious. Therefore, these users maintain a high level of semantic and syntactic knowledge that pertains specifically to their work domain.

Application of ergonomics and pleasing surroundings are especially applicable for these users. Also, because of the repetitive and often boring nature of frequent light users' work, strong processing controls should be designed into the system to cross-check and verify input and processing.

Frequent Power Users

Frequent power users possess high levels of semantic and syntactic knowledge. Generally, their demands are efficiency oriented, such as for faster response time, shortcuts, macro commands, and abbreviations. Ergonomics is also a serious design consideration for power users.

Trying to design one interactive interface for all these users is a significant design challenge. The solution is to integrate into the interface all the effective designs applicable to all users, but permit users to zero in on those features appropriate for them and ignore or leapfrog irrelevant ones.

Message Formulation

Messages from the system to users should indicate that users are in control. The messages should be courteous, have a positive tone, and be nonintimidating. Don't use imperatives, such as ERROR, INVALID, ENTER DATA, ILLEGAL, and ABORT. Instead, use subservient and helpful messages, such as READY FOR YOUR COMMANDS or ABC COULD NOT INTERPRET DIRECTORY CODE, WHICH IS SUPPOSED TO BE A CODE WITH 4 CHARACTERS SUCH AS WKFI.

Error messages should be friendly and informative. What do CATA-STROPHIC ERROR, SYNTAX, ILLEGAL, BAD COMMAND, or FQX mean? Such messages are virtually worthless to most users, especially to novice and occasional users. Moreover, such messages are discouraging and intimidating.

Suggestions that computers can think, know, feel, or understand should be reduced, if not abandoned entirely. Everyone knows it's a deception, and after several encounters it begins to wear thin. For example, things begin to get a little annoying after three or four sessions with "Hi. I'm Dr. Tom, the computer. I will ask you to touch each entry in the following list that applies to you. OK, let's get started and have a nice day."

Substitute "We will begin as soon as you enter your name and press RE-TURN" with "You can begin the program by typing your name and pressing RETURN." Design less chatty messages and avoid superficial value judgments, such as "You're doing great. Keep up the good work."

Directing Users' Attention

In cases that are time dependent, drawing the attention of users to particular tasks can improve performance. Multiple attention-getting techniques are intensifying at several levels; marking by underlining, enclosing in a box, or using bullets and asterisks; including several character sizes and fonts; blinking; applying color codes; and installing tones or voices for certain feedback.

Using too many of these attention-getting techniques can diminish their effectiveness and create "schlocky" screens. Novices need simple instructions, logically organized that guide their actions. With knowledgeable and power users, subtle highlights and logical positioning are generally sufficient.

Another aspect to attention getting is error message displays. First, the error message should get the user's attention. Second, it should give instructions for error correction. Don't just report the problem with a negative TRY AGAIN, SYNTAX ERROR, or ILLEGAL. Rather, design informative and positive messages, such as YOUR RANGE OF CHOICES IS 1 THROUGH 5, USE MM/DD/YY FORMAT, or UNMATCHED LEFT PARENTHESIS FOUND.

Menu Design

The lead to follow in menu design is a restaurant's menu that separates breakfast, lunch, and dinner with appropriate listing of food items, such as appetizers, soups, entrees, drinks, and desserts. Like patrons in a restaurant, systems users select from a list of items the one most appropriate for the task at hand, initiate it, and observe the results.

Menus reduce the need for training and syntactic memorization and increase the semantic knowledge relevant to users' tasks. Generally, menus are not for power users unless these users are put on a fast track and can jump to specific tasks they want performed.

Common selection methods are keyboard, pointing, touch screen, and voice. Classification of the following menu designs are single, serial, tree, network, and embedded.

Single Menu

Single menus present two or more choices. Typically, they require one screen and are often the pop-up or pull-down type. Figure 19.7 illustrates a single menu.

Serial Menu

A serial menu design provides several interdependent menus that guide users through a series of choices. Each menu follows naturally from its predecessor menu. Figure 19.8 shows a serial menu design.

Tree Menu

Tree-structured or hierarchical menus make available a large number of options. Users are presented a number of screens and instructions to select the desired category on each screen. See Figure 19.9 for an example of a tree menu.

Generally, each menu should contain eight or fewer options. The total tree should be four levels or less. Anything more than this often confuses and frustrates users because as the level of the tree menu grows, users tend to get lost in the branches. To lessen this problem, furnish users with a tree diagram or map of the total menu package.

Network Menu

Network menu packages are generally more complex than trees, but networks offer alternate paths. Figure 19.10 demonstrates a network menu.

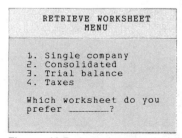

Figure 19.7 A single menu design.

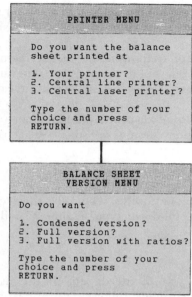

Figure 19.8 A serial menu design.

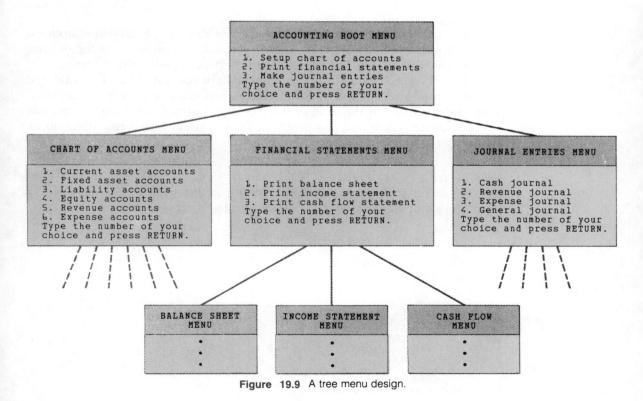

Figure 19.9 A tree menu design.

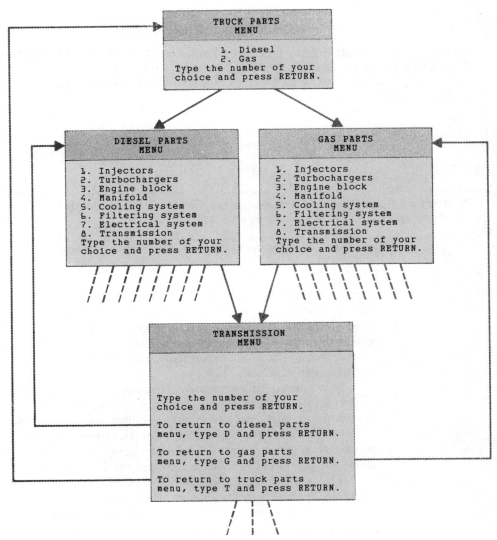

Figure 19.10 A network menu design.

Embedded Menus

Embedded menus permit users to retrieve detailed information by selecting a name in context. Names are selected by moving a selector box or cursor to the highlighted reference and then retrieved by pressing RETURN. A mouse version enables selection by pointing at the name and clicking the mouse; a touch-screen version enables selection by merely touching the highlighted reference.

Figure 19.11 depicts an embedded menu. By selecting the uppercase items, users get a display that demonstrates what flowcharts and questionnaires are, how they look, and how they are applied in the audit program.

ABC AUDIT DOCUMENTATION

The audit routine first establishes a CASH INTERNAL CONTROL
FLOWCHART and a CONTROL QUESTIONNAIRE that are used by
auditors during their preliminary audit of the client
company. Before these . . .

•

•

•

To access highlighted items: move selector box over the first
word of your selection and press RETURN.

Figure 19.11 Embedded menus in an audit documentation package.

Providing Quick Access to Menus

As response times lengthen and display rates increase, frequent menu users
need shortcuts to access a certain menu quickly. By assigning names, single
letters, or mnemonics to every menu in the tree or network, and providing direct
access, frequent users can leapfrog anywhere in the total menu package to
perform a specific task.

In an accounting tree menu, the adjusting journal routine may be three
or four levels removed from the main menu. Rather than having to traverse the
intervening menus, prompts, and messages, the accountant merely types AJE
to access directly the adjusting journal entries routine and performs the necessary
adjustments. Furthermore, this leapfrogging ability designed into the system
allows novice users to evolve to knowledgeable users easily.

This same design approach is used to put power users on a fast track.
Additionally, a design option can be provided to permit these users to assign
their own macro commands. When the macro is invoked, the traversal is executed
automatically. With this approach, individual users can tailor the menu networks
or trees to fit their specific needs.

Forms Fill-in

Menus are excellent ways to permit users to select items from a list, but some
tasks such as data entry are not handled very well by menus. Generally, keyboard
typing and forms fill-in provide the best design methods. A typical forms fill-in
example is shown in Figure 19.12.

With forms fill-in design (also called fill-in-the-blanks), all the data are visible
to the user, providing a sense of user control. Familiar zone captions should be
used, and users must understand permissible zone contents. Therefore, some
training is required.

Fewer input actions improve productivity and decrease the chance for

---

PROGRAM DOCUMENTATION FORM

Type in the information below, pressing TAB to move the
cursor, and press ENTER when done.

Program Name: _____   Language Used: _____

Job Number: _____   Date: _____

Programmer: _____   Phone: (____) - _____

Revisions by	Date (MM/DD/YY)	Authorized by	Reason for Revision
_____	_____	_____	_____
_____	_____	_____	_____
_____	_____	_____	_____
_____	_____	_____	_____

Figure 19.12 A screen forms fill-in design.

error. Therefore, where possible, design a fill-in form that includes simple menus in which the user can make a single keystroke, lightpen touch, or finger-press selection. Figure 19.13 illustrates this design procedure. Generally, it is not a good idea to use automatic completion when the last zone is filled, because users may wish to go back and review or alter entries.

Command Language

For power users, command languages provide high user control. Power users know the syntax and can use it to express complex algorithms without having to read a number of distracting prompts and superfluous messages.

Command languages are used to effect a particular and immediate result on some object of interest. Once this is done, that command may not be used again. Many of these commands, therefore, may be transient.

Menus initiate and provide leading instructions and prompts. Users of command languages do the initiating. Often command languages are characterized by complex syntax. For example, @ DSUM (A2..D200, 3, F1..G2) creates a table that shows sales totals by salesperson and by month.

A simple command list includes entries such as H (go to home position), L (go to last line), W (forward one word), and CTRL-F (go forward one screen). These are just a few examples of 40 or more commands for cursor control. Clearly, such a list of commands is overwhelming to novice and occasional users.

Such commands as COPY, RETRIEVE, PRINT, EDIT, and MOVE are followed by one or more arguments, such as FILEA, FILEB, AND FILEC. Commands and arguments read this way: COPY FILEA, FILEC, which means

CUSTOMER CHANGE FORM

Ⓝ New customer. Fill in all sections of this form.

Ⓓ Delete customer. Fill in customer's number and name.

Ⓒ Change data in existing record. Enter the customer's number
   and name as well as the data for the fields that must be
   changed.

```
_____                          _____
CUSTOMER NUMBER                       CUSTOMER NAME
```

Ship-to address: Bill-to address: If same as
                                   ship-to address, type S.

Street _____   _____

PO Box _____   _____

City _____   _____

State _____   _____

ZIP _____ ____   _____ ____

	Credit Code		Category		Discount
①	$10,000 credit limit	①	Wholesale	①	2 percent
②	$20,000 credit limit	②	Jobber	②	5 percent
③	$50,000 credit limit	③	Government	③	10 percent
④	Unlimited credit	④	Retail	④	15 percent

Date created: M M/D D/Y Y   Change authorized by: _____

Figure 19.13 A forms fill-in with embedded menus.

copy the contents from file A and write it on file C. Or a little less obvious command that does the same thing may read COPY A:*.* C:.

Commands with arguments and options read like this: PRINT/3, AD FILEC. This command produces three copies of file C on the accounting department's printer.

As the number of arguments and options grow, the complexity becomes overwhelming, even with rigorous training. Certain persons are, however, motivated to learn a great body of this syntactic knowledge. In doing so, they become wizards of sorts who speak in unknown tongues, similar to tax gurus.

A tree menu can be designed to organize and provide structure to powerful command languages and thereby increase their access by a greater number of users. This structure facilitates learning and retention. Figure 19.14 shows an abridged version of such a command language menu.

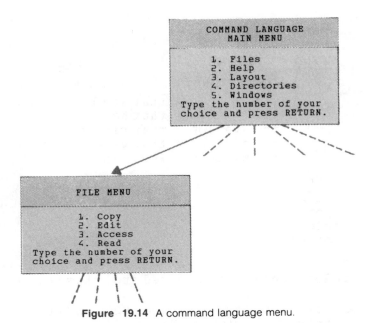

Figure 19.14 A command language menu.

Natural Language

The design aim has always been to design an interface that makes the computer respond to natural language, spoken or typed. Users, therefore, would not have to gain any, or very little, syntactic knowledge. Their language would be natural, such as "Display all monthly telephone bills since September."

Natural language, for the most part, are still in research and development. Some limited commercial applications are available, however.

The major research efforts are directed toward voice systems. Substantial effort is required to establish the lexicon for the natural language interface. Users must define all possible words they may use. Minor deviations are not tolerated. The main natural language designs that are achievable are simple applications that can accept and process formal and abbreviated commands.

Intellect from Artificial Intelligence Corporation of Cambridge, Massachusetts, is a program that enables occasional users with high semantic knowledge but with limited syntactic knowledge, such as executives, salespeople, and various managers, to search data bases and retrieve ad hoc reports. Expert systems presented earlier in this book also represent important attempts to provide natural language interfaces.

NaturalLink, distributed by Texas Instruments, is a blend of natural language and menus. Users specify natural language queries formed in a command window by phrases from a set of menus. Users see the full range of possible queries, which ensures that each query is semantically and syntactically correct. A condensed version of NaturalLink is displayed in Figure 19.15.

```
                        NATURALLINK MENU
COMMANDS:           FIND    FIND THE           FIND ALL

FEATURES:                   CONNECTORS:     QUALIFIERS:
birthdate                   and             that are listed on
date hired                  or              that have
name                        the average     that request
operation number            the maximum     that were turned in for
department                  the minimum     who have

COMPARISONS:       NOUNS:
between            job card
    =              operation
    >              order
    <              worked


Example of natural language command formed from this set of
menus:
Find all employee operation numbers between 6000 and 8000 who
have date hired between March 19X1 and March 19X2.
```

Figure 19.15 A natural language menu package.

Direct Visual Manipulation

The proof of good interface design is in users' quick mastery of the system, full competence in performing their tasks, and enjoyment in using the system. A stride forward in achieving these goals is the replacement of syntactic-intensive command language with direct visual manipulation.

This user/system interface design permits users to manipulate objects of interest directly by pointing at icons, graphics, or metaphors of objects and tasks. Such manipulation appeals to many users from novices to frequent power users.

Take a simple illustration of driving a car, something we take for granted. This user/system interface is visual and direct. We see the signs that tell us where to go, we pass cars, we stop for pedestrians, we turn corners, we speed up, we slow down, all to get us to our destination. Now, let's slip an intermediary interface or layer between us and our cars that requires command languages for us to drive our cars. Imagine trying to feed in TR90MS30MPH, which may be translated as turn right 90 degrees and maintain speed at 30 miles per hour. This command example is issued just to turn a corner. How many commands do you think would be required to drive down to the local pizza parlor?

Using full-page display editors is an example of moving a little closer to looking at the information system's world from a "windshield." The advantages of full-page display editors include the following: the document displayed on the screen is as it will be printed. This style is called WYSIWYG ("what you see is what you get" or some people say it is really "what you see is what you have"). A blinking arrow, underline, or box on the screen gives the operator a clear sense of where to focus attention and apply action. Arrow keys or cursor motion devices, such as a trackball, joystick, pen pad, graphic tablet, or mouse provide physical mechanisms that provide natural manipulation for users.

Permanent menu selection keys labeled CENTER, UNDERLINE, BOLD, LOCATE, INSERT, and DELETE remind users of functions available and eliminate the need to learn complex command language syntax. When an action occurs, results are displayed on the screen immediately.

High display rates combined with short response time invokes a feeling of user mastery. By coupling this speed with spatial and pattern representations, such as graphics, metaphors, icons, pop-up and pull-down menus, windows, relations, systems analysis and design models, text editing, and complete visual representations of an office or plan or inventory system, we have the ability to provide direct visual manipulation that begins to mimic our car-driving analogy.

Maybe better analogies than driving cars are video games and computer-aided design. In any case, application of the direct visual manipulation design method provides capacity at users' fingertips to manipulate objects of interest directly, see results immediately, and generate multiple alternatives quickly.

Electronic spreadsheets display a visual image of a spreadsheet and its cell values. Cell values can be changed by using a mouse to move the cursor to the cell to be changed and then keying in the new value.

Desktop publishing systems provide palettes of icons, such as in-basket, out-basket, trash basket, files, and so forth. A number of forms and output is designed and produced by the what-you-see-is-what-you-get (WYSIWYG) method. Another excellent example is the computer-assisted software engineering (CASE) and computer-aided design packages.

Interface libraries exploit the metaphor of pieces of paper on a desktop. Users can build an application the same way that a role of transparent acetate, stencils, scissors, glue, paint, and brushes help an artist create an animation. The artist cuts sheets of acetate to any size, draws images and patterns on them, and positions them with respect to each other.

Modern paper mills, oil refineries, power plants, and some railways are large complexes managed by one or two people via an interactive interface that displays colored-coded schematics of all operations. By pressing buttons, managers can decompose these schematics to their lowest levels of detail and press other function buttons or flick switches that open or close values, switch tracks, increase or decrease temperatures, and mix ingredients automatically. These analogs interface with the information system to provide operating information and various reports.

The downside to direct visual manipulation designs is that users must learn rules of representation and other syntax. Moreover, graphics, icons, and other spatial representations are not always superior to textual displays and numbers, especially for left-brain users who thrive on numbers and tend not to think metaphorically.

Often patterns are cluttered, which leads to confusion rather than clarity.

MANIPULATING METAPHORS

The user/system interface—the place where the human mind meets the computer processor—is the industry's most concentrated and important area of energy, and eventual change. Using metaphors at the interface is growing. The dominance of visual metaphors in human thought is the common phrase indicating understanding: "I see."

"The idea of metaphors is to try to make the computer work like something the user already knows," says Brad A. Myers, a scientist in the computer science department at Carnegie Mellon. "The users coming in off the street may not know about computers, but they know about something, such as offices, menus in restaurants, or recipes."

One of the most literal PC metaphors is the desktop, or office, metaphor used in the Apple Macintosh. It is a system that attempts to draw users into the sustained illusion of an electronic desk where small pictures of common objects. called icons, represent their real-life counterparts. In the Macintosh office, for example, files are "stored" in folders that are opened in the desktop, read and disposed of by a mouse-directed flick into a picture of a trash can. The Macintosh also allows a user to dig through the trash can to retrieve discarded data. The interaction between user and computer is icon-driven rather than command-driven.

Visual metaphors have long been used on PC software. A spreadsheet, for example, is a metaphor in which the spatial relationships of individual cells, rows, and columns represent mathematical relationships.

But some believe metaphors are overdone. "Metaphors are just one of the tools in my toolbox when I'm designing a product," says John Page, vice-president of research and development for Software Publishing Corporation. "But dogmatic adherence to them is wrong."

Other interfaces, according to Page and others, such as menus of available command words, are just as easily operated. Mr. Page adds, "Most users, in my experience, have a lot of trouble dealing with icons."

Paul Heckel, president of Quickview Systems, divides software metaphors into two categories, which he calls shallow and deep metaphors. An example of a shallow metaphor is Macintosh's icon-based desktop metaphor.

A deep metaphor distinguishes itself by acting as a flexible tool to manipulate information, such as spreadsheets. The card-stack metaphor called Hypercard is another deep metaphor in which "stacks" of cards that contain text, graphics, or sound can be linked to each other, or to cards in other stacks.

Condensed from Paul Karon, "Software Metaphor: Where the Mind Meets the Power of the PC," *PC Week,* September 15, 1987, pp. 58 and 64.

General interpretation may be a problem. An icon may mean one thing to the designer and something entirely different to the user. And in some applications, keyboarding may actually be faster and easier to use than manipulation devices such as a mouse or joystick. Generally, though, direct visual manipulation is a design method that can be used effectively in a number of interactive interfaces.

19.6 DETAILED OUTPUT DESIGN

The objective of detailed output design is to define the content and format of all printed documents, reports, and screens that will be produced by the system. Output is the boss building block because all the other building blocks are designed in a way to produce the desired output.

Printed Documents and Reports

When designing a printed document or report, systems analysts begin with a rough sketch of the document or report format, what will be contained in the document or report, and who will receive the output. Printer layout forms, as illustrated in Figure 19.16, are then filled in by the systems analyst. As you can see, each horizontal line of rectangles represents one printed line, and each column corresponds to one print position on a line. The standard printer layout form allows for up to 60 lines to the page and up to 132 print positions per line.

When documenting output ideas on printer layout forms, many systems analysts also use the following special notations to indicate facts or characteristics about the fields that will appear on a document or report:

1. Preprinted information, such as an organization's logo, is drawn in on the form.
2. X's indicate placement of alphanumeric characters.
3. 9's indicate where numeric data are placed.
4. Commas and a decimal point (period) indicate editing characteristics of numeric fields.
5. Z's indicate replacement of leading zeroes in numeric fields with spaces (zero suppression).
6. $'s indicate replacement of leading zeroes in numeric fields with spaces up to the zero just to the left of the nonzero portion of the numeric field. This zero is replaced by a dollar sign, and thus the dollar sign appears to "float" up to the nonzero portion of the numeric field (e.g., the field 009.77 is edited to b$9.77).

Besides defining fields and specifying their format, the systems analyst must consider the following characteristics about each report and document:

1. The sequence or order of the data for certain fields. For example, the information on a sales report might be ordered by the value of products sold.

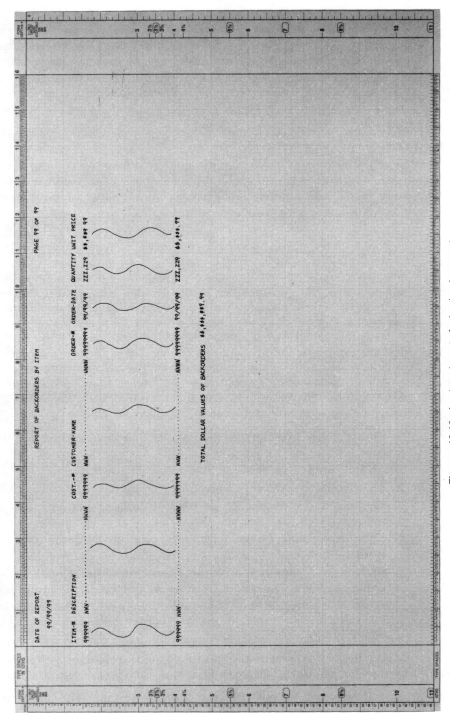

Figure 19.16 A printer layout of a backorder report.

2. Control breaks based on totals or subtotals. For example, a product analysis report might show subtotals of sales by product classes.

3. Paper type (weight and bond of paper) and approximate number of sheets required for a particular (report) output.

4. Requirements for producing multiple copies of the output.

5. The output's distribution, security, and the means and timing of disposal.

Having completed the form, the proposed output is sent to the user for review to ensure that all important fields have been included, enough space has been allowed for each field, and, for numeric fields, the editing is appropriate. If the proposed output is approved, the systems analyst and user will sign the form. If the output is in any way incomplete or unsatisfactory, the form is returned to the systems analyst for redesign or modification and for resubmission for review by the user.

Report Writer

The objective is to generate a report to display some data from the data base in a meaningful manner. For example, a fourth-generation language (4GL) may be used, as demonstrated in Figure 19.17, to generate a sales report by region and by quarter.

```
Data Base Definition

Attributes in data base entity:
 • quarter
 • region
 • amount


Report Definition
LIST BY region ACROSS quarter
  SUM ROWTOT


Sample Report
```

Region	Q1	Q2	Q3	Q4	Total
East	$5000	$6000	$4000	$7000	$22,000
South	4000	6000	7000	6000	23,000
Midwest	2000	4000	5000	3000	14,000
West	6000	7000	8000	4000	25,000

Figure 19.17 A report designed by a 4GL.

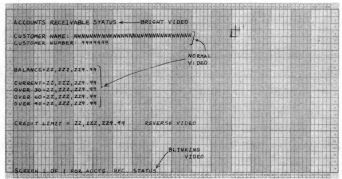

Figure 19.18 Screen output form for display of accounts receivable status.

Screen Output

The procedure for designing screen output parallels that for designing printer output. The screen display layout form of Figure 19.18 looks like a printer spacing chart except that its dimensions are normally 24 lines to a screen and 80 characters to a screen line. Because a screen has certain highlighting capabilities (e.g., reverse, blinking, and bright video), a notation is placed beside each field on the screen spacing form indicating their use.

Screen output also allows the imposition of a form on the data. For example, the systems analyst may impose data in bright video on an invoice form that is displayed in normal brightness.

With the additional format options available to the systems analyst for screen design, the tendency is to put too much data on one screen. Rather than try to squeeze all the data on one screen, the systems analyst ought to consider using two screens, with a status indicator at the bottom of each screen notifying users which screen they are seeing at a particular instant.

19.7 DETAILED INPUT DESIGN

Generally, input designs that require little keystroking, minimize error possibilities. Design devices that reduce the number of keystrokes are menus, badges, magnetic cards, lightpens, joysticks, and the mouse. Moreover, controls should be installed at the point of data entry to edit and weed out a piece of incorrect input before it has a chance to pollute the entire system.

Although output enables users to make intelligent decisions and provides evidence of the processing of transactions, its quality is only as good as the input that generates the reports and documents. Correct customer billings are the result of accurate and complete order entry; meaningful decisions on significant production variances are the product of timely and correct capture of data about the manufacturing process.

As is the case with detailed design of output, when the systems analyst prepares specifics about the content and format of input, attention must be paid to the people who will be collecting and entering the input, and consideration must be given to the existing methods of data entry in the organization. Moreover, because of the rapid advancement in data entry technology, the systems analyst must keep abreast of developing hardware, in terms of its application, features, and economic feasibility.

Batch Input

In file-oriented systems, batch processing is still one of the principal methods used to input data. This input method requires capturing the data on a source document, accumulating these documents for some period, converting source documents to machine-readable form, and entering the data for processing. The detailed design process for this input method is illustrated in Figure 19.19.

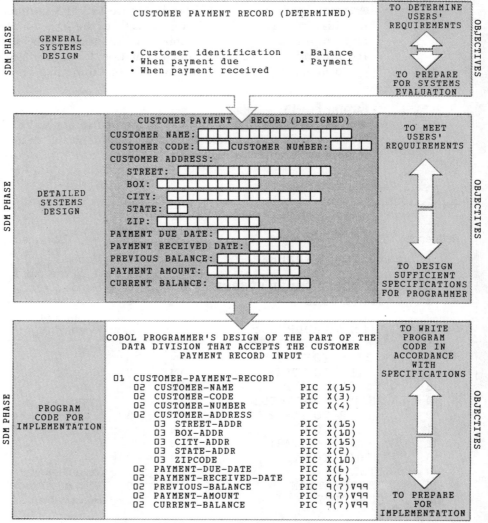

Figure 19.19 The design process for batch input.

Input Documentation

When entities (data base approach) or records (file approach) are designed, attributes or fields should be documented with their values. An abbreviated version of an input data dictionary is demonstrated in Figure 19.20.

Screen Input

Whether a systems analyst works unaided or uses a special software package for screen design, the resulting product should depict the exact appearance of the input. The screen design should specify the name and title of the screen, the list of all entries required to be input by the terminal operator, the locations on the screen where the data will be entered, the location and contents of all error messages, and particulars on how data collection for the screen will terminate. A screen layout form is depicted in Figure 19.21. A number of analysts do not use this screen layout form but go directly to the screen and design their layout or form interactively. In a number of instances, this layout form is, however, recommended for hard-copy documentation, if not for design. Another method of documenting screen input may look something like Figure 19.22.

Forms Fill-In

We have discussed forms fill-in as an interactive method earlier in this chapter. Now, we treat this method from a development and design viewpoint by presenting an example in Figure 19.23.

Data Dictionary for Customer File				
Reference	Field Name	Type	Size	Edit Checks
1	CUSTOMER NUMBER	N	10	Modulus 11, arithmetic progression
2	CUSTOMER ORDER NUMBER	AN	8	Mandatory
3	ORDER DATE	N	6	All numeric, MMDDYY
4	BILL–TO ADDRESS:			Mandatory
5	BILL–TO STREET	AN	15	
6	BILL–TO CITY	AN	15	
7	BILL–TO STATE	AN	2	
8	BILL–TO ZIP	AN	9	
9	SHIP–TO ADDRESS:			Mandatory
10	SHIP–TO STREET	AN	15	
11	SHIP–TO CITY	AN	15	
12	SHIP–TO STATE	AN	2	
13	SHIP–TO ZIP	AN	9	
14	ITEM–NO	N	7	Valid number
15	DESCRIPTION	AN	20	Valid description
16	QUANTITY	N	10	Reasonableness

Figure 19.20 Input documentation for a customer file data dictionary.

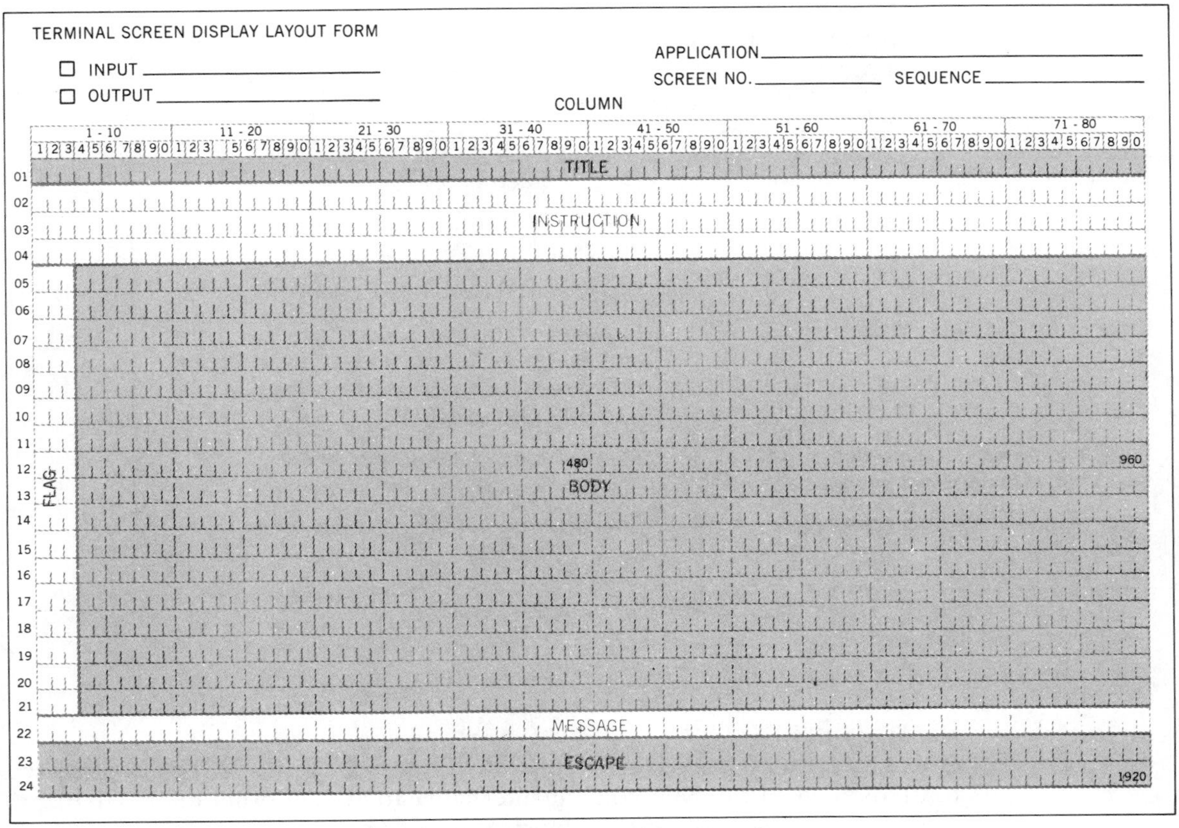

Figure 19.21 A screen display layout form.

The requisition form provides a blinking instruction to tell the user to enter data at all captions but costs. Costs are automatically generated and completed by the system. Moreover, not shown on the screen but designed into the application, is the use of two intensities. Low-intensity display gives directions for data entry. High-intensity display shows actual data being entered. If the data being entered pass validation, their intensity of display is lowered. If the data being entered fail validation, they remain bright and begin to flash off and on to signal that an error has occurred and a pop-up window appears to provide a message on how the error may be corrected. Once corrected, the form continues to guide the user through the entry process.

Textual Specification

Textual specification uses a language to define forms' zones and captions. Screen COBOL language, for example, uses a textual specification for screen forms design and implementation.

In Figure 19.24 the upper part is the form's design. The lower part is the necessary code in Screen COBOL to implement the form.

SYSTEM NAME: Order entry	
TRANSACTION: Enter order for old customer	
MODE: Forms fill-in and menu	
USER INPUT	SYSTEM RESPONSE
Press function key 1	Display order form
Select menu O for old customer	Display "Ready to accept order for old customer"
Enter customer number	Display customer name for verification
Enter order number and details	Display item number, description, price, and availability of inventory. If an item does not have sufficient quantity on hand, a backorder is indicated
Enter Y to process backorder or N for customer who does not want a backorder	Acknowledge of backorder status
Enter menu C for forms completion	Acknowledge of forms completion and order in process

Figure 19.22 Screen documentation design.

Query by Forms

Query By Forms (QBFs) is an adaptation of Query By Example (QBE), discussed in Chapter 11. It can be used as an alternative to SQL or other query languages in some situations. The interesting feature of QBF is that the commands are simply mapped into a form similar to entering transactions and updating in traditional forms.

One way of designing QBF is shown in Figure 19.25. The specified query retrieves purchase orders for customers in Michigan who have ordered over $10,000 worth of item 24D, square-pointed shovels.

IBM's DBEDIT is a Query By Example package. Oracle, RTI, and Tandem offer Query By Forms systems.

Question and Answer Dialogues

Question and answer (QA) dialogues are designed to elicit input from users. The system asks a question about the value of some item and the user provides this value. In some instances, instructions may also be provided along with data values. A typical QA dialogue design is presented in Figure 19.26.

Other Forms Design Methods

Another approach to designing forms is to engage the analyst in a question and answer session that defines the form. Oracle Corporation offers such a form's design package called interactive application generator (IAG) that asks the an-

Requisition Form

INSTRUCTIONS: ENTER DATA FOR ALL ITEMS EXCEPT COST < BLINKING >

JOB NUMBER: XXXXX–X   DATE OF REQUISITION: MM/DD/YY

DEPARTMENT NUMBER: XXX   DELIVERY DATE: MM/DD/YY

ITEM NO	DESCRIPTION	QUANTITY	COST	TOTAL COST
XXXX	AAAAAAAAA	XXX	99999.99	9999999.99
XXXX	AAAAAAAAA	XXX	99999.99	9999999.99
XXXX	AAAAAAAAA	XXX	99999.99	9999999.99
XXXX	AAAAAAAAA	XXX	99999.99	9999999.99

POP–UP ERROR
MESSAGE WINDOW   TOTAL CHARGE   999999999.99

MESSAGE WINDOW
- TRANSMIT TO STORES BY PRESSING F3
- PRODUCE HARD COPY BY PRESSING F4
- DEPARTMENT WILL RECEIVE ACKNOWLEDGEMENT WITHIN 30 MINUTES
- IF ACKNOWLEDGEMENT IS NOT RECEIVED WITHIN 30 MINUTES, CALL 1473
TO EXIT: TYPE QUIT

Figure 19.23 A screen form.

alyst about each zone and then generates a textual language description that is compiled.

The WYSIWYG method for forms design uses an editor that enables the analyst to edit the form's design while it is displayed on the screen. With this method, the analyst immediately sees the effect of changing the design of the form, such as moving or expanding zones, changing captions, locating messages, or adding features.

The WYSIWYG method is a very efficient method for designing forms. ADR/Ideal, ADS/Online, and Ingres/ABF provide WYSIWYG forms design packages.

19.8 DETAILED DATA BASE DESIGN

Jon Devereaux recently joined the information systems staff at Stanislaus University. His specialty is data base design.

(a) Form's design

Student Information

Name: _____

Department: _____

Major: _____

FUNCTION KEYS:
F1 Enter data
F2 Clear input
F3 Exit screen

(b) Form's Screen COBOL definition

Screen Section

```
01 EXAMPLE-FORM SCREEN 24,80.
    02 FILLER        AT 1,30      VALUE ''Student
                                  Information''.
    02 FILLER        AT 4,2       VALUE ''Name:''.
    02 NAME          AT 4,7       PIC A(20) LENGTH 1 THRU 20
                                  TO NAME-IN OF ENTRY, FILL
                                  '____'.
    02 FILLER        AT 6,2       VALUE ''Department:''.
    02 DEPARTMENT    AT 6,13      PIC X(20) LENGTH 1 THRU 20
                                  TO DEPARTMENT-IN OF
                                  ENTRY, FILL '____'.
    02 FILLER        AT 8,2       VALUE ''Major:''.
    02 MAJOR         AT 8,8       PIC A(20) LENGTH 1 THRU 20
                                  TO MAJOR-IN OF ENTRY, FILL
                                  '____'.
    02 FILLER        AT 12,1      VALUE ''Function Keys:''.
    02 FILLER        AT 13,2      VALUE ''F1 Enter data''.
    02 FILLER        AT 14,2      VALUE ''F2 Clear input''.
    02 FILLER        AT 15,2      VALUE ''F3 Exit screen''.
```

Figure 19.24 Form's design using Screen COBOL.

(a) Query specification

Customer Purchase Order

Customer Name: _____ P.O.: _____

Street: _____

City: _____ State: ____MI____ Zip: _____

Item No.	Description	Quantity	Cost	Total
24D	Square-pointed shovels	_____	____	_____
_____	_____	_____	____	_____
_____	_____	_____	____	_____

Grand total = __>$10,000__

(b) Displayed response

Customer Purchase Order

Customer Name: ___Tri-State Hardware___ P.O.: ___7457-T___

Street: _____258 Brownstone_____

City: _____Lansing_____ State: ____MI____ Zip: __48924__

Item No.	Description	Quantity	Cost	Total
24D	Square-pointed shovels	775	$20	$15,500.00
_____	_____	_____	____	_____
_____	_____	_____	____	_____

Grand total = __$15,500.00__

Figure 19.25 QBF.

Initial Meeting

At a meeting last week of the information systems steering committee, Tamra Armondo, vice-president of operations, quizzed Jon about data base design.

"Jon, really, what is a data base?" she queried. "I keep reading about them, and I see things about ANSI and relations and all the other stuff. When you boil it all down, it's just a bunch of files, right?"

```
                      Capital Budgeting
                          Analysis
Which budget evaluation methods?
  Present value method
  Present value index

Discount rate?
  12

Number of periods?
  15
```

Figure 19.26 A QA dialogue design.

"Not quite," Jon responded. "The main contribution of ANSI/SPARC model, which is what I'm sure you're referring to, is the accommodation of a multilevel architecture that employs different data models in a single data base."

"What are data models?" Tamra asked.

"The three principal data models are hierarchical, as it's sometimes called, a tree, network, and relational. All three can be used to capitalize on their particular strengths."

"What are these strengths?" asked Tamra.

"Essentially, data models are mechanisms for representing data and relationships. The three models are almost equivalent in data representation. Sometimes, however, you run into situations where people are calling the same thing different names."

"Like what," chimed in Anunzio Baker, superintendent of maintenance.

"Well, some people use the terms 'entities' and 'attributes.' Others call entities and attributes 'records' and 'fields.' Many other examples exist in systems, but as far as data representation is concerned, we're all trying to develop surrogates that adequately represent objects and people. Whether we call them entities or records is not terribly important."

"But let's get back to the strengths," Tamra demanded.

"OK, as I said, all models do a good job in representing data. We can build a single student file that includes attributes about almost anything. We can do the same for anything on campus, such as buildings, faculty, and automobiles. The challenge is to establish relations between files and develop a way to navigate easily through them. That's where the difference between data models comes into play. If you want to process payroll for faculty and that's all you want to do, then I would build you a file with the records defined by fields, set it up hierarchically, sequence the records by faculty number, and probably store it on a tape file. This way, you would have the most efficient way to process a payroll. But if you want to know the names of professors who teach 101 Computer Science, then the design of a hierarchical data model presents a problem because at most one relationship, direct or indirect, can exist between any two entities."

"Yes, but we want you to tell us what data model we need," prompted Kathy Peterson, dean of arts and sciences.

"Theoretically, if you process a lot of data at one time, the hierarchical data model stored on a sequential file is the way to go. If you want to establish a lot of relationships between entities, then the network or relational data model should be your choice."

"Jon, I hate to interrupt, but we've gone a few minutes over, and we've all got other meetings to attend," said Kathy. "Really, what we're trying to accomplish sounds like a relationship kind of data base, or whatever you call it, from which our people can retrieve information about students, faculty, who is taking what, and who is teaching what. You know, that sort of stuff. Could you come back next week and bring us up to date and show us how we might go about meeting our needs?"

"Sure. How about this same time?"

"Is this time good for everybody?" Kathy asked.

A chorus of "OK," "sure," and "fine" set the meeting time for next week.

Detailed Design Presentation

Kathy called everyone to order at the next meeting and turned it over to Jon. Figure 19.27 shows what Jon displayed to the steering committee to help him explain data base design to the members. Since the last meeting, Jon had spent a lot of time interviewing and gathering study facts. He felt fairly comfortable that he had the problem solved.

Tamra said, "I really like that presentation, Jon. Things are beginning to clear up a little, but I still don't see how we're going to get from what you're showing us to anything practical."

"Let's take a look at a hierarchy data model I designed," said Jon.

Jon placed on the projector a transparency of his hierarchy data model, displayed in Figure 19.28.

"Hey, Jon, you really did your homework," Anunzio responded.

"Yeah, that's it. That's exactly what we want," echoed Tamra.

"Whoa, wait a minute," said Jon. "The simplistic design of the hierarchical data model appears attractive, but in practice, especially based on what you told me you wanted to do last week in relating a lot of things together, this design may be cumbersome and restrictive. Moreover, no ANSI or CODASYL (COnference on DAta SYstems Languages) committees are working on drafting specifications or standards for hierarchical data definition language (DDL) and data manipulation language (DML)."

"Jon, do we really care what those people are doing?" asked Kathy.

"Maybe not directly, but their work gives us a good indication of what direction data bases are taking and what will be commercially available and supported in the future. And, as I said before, if we don't require extensive collections of complex relationships, the hierarchical data model provides sufficient power and generality. But allow me to proceed."

"Yeah, go ahead Jon," they all responded.

Jon then displayed, in Figure 19.29, an entity relationship (ER) diagram

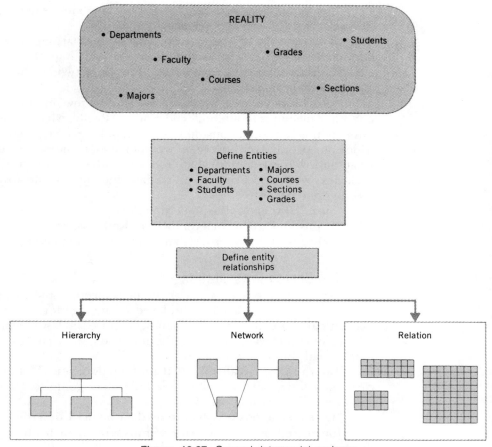

Figure 19.27 General data model designs.

that reflected his understanding of the relationships required by frequent power and occasional users he had interviewed earlier.

"Hey, that's even better," Anunzio offered.

"Looks confusing to me, " said Kathy. "What are you going to do with it, Jon?"

"Well, I could easily convert it to a network data model because the network model is more robust than the hierarchical model and can accommodate the relationships shown in the ER diagram. The network data model can handle one-to-one, one-to-many, and many-to-many relationships. A number of top software vendors have implemented the network data model in their data base management systems that we refer to as DBMSs. It's basically the same data model developed by the Data Base Task Group (DBTG) years ago. In fact, some people still call it the DBTG model. Furthermore, ANSI and CODASYL continue to support its development and work to establish design standards."

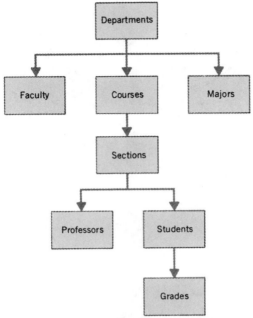

Figure 19.28 Hierarchical data model design.

"Here we go again with those acronyms," Kathy interjected.

"I charge nothing extra for this information," kidded Jon.

"But what are we at SU going to do?" Kathy fretted.

"OK, but remember you're the ones who wanted an explanation of the three data models, and we still have one to go."

"This stuff is so new to me," Kathy forced a laugh. "Go ahead, Jon. I'm sorry. You'll just have to be patient with me."

Jon then flashed a transparency on the screen that showed entities and attributes of the relations indicated in the ER diagram. These relations are disclosed in Figure 19.30.

"Here are the entities and attributes in relational form," Jon said.

"Looks simple enough," said Tamra.

"Yes, I agree," said Jon. "The relational data model is heralded for its ease of use, precise definition, simplicity of data structure, generality, and absence of detail and clutter."

"It looks easy to use," said Kathy, "but just how do we use it?"

"I'm glad you asked," said Jon. "I took the liberty to go ahead and set up a data base using the relational schema I just displayed. Would you like to see how I created these relations in the data base?"

"Sure," exclaimed everyone.

Jon then showed, in Figure 19.31, how each relation was created.

"Looks a little complicated," said Anunzio.

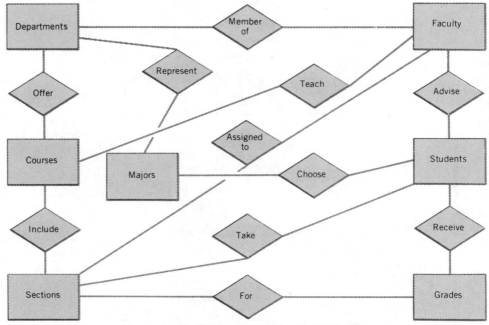

Figure 19.29 ER diagram of proposed data base.

"Well, a little maybe," said Jon. "But we're ready to do some work. In fact, I brought with me a terminal that we can use, as soon as I plug it in, to show you how it works."

"Oh, great!" exclaimed Kathy. "I can't wait."

After Jon had everything set up and ready to go, everyone crowded around the terminal. He typed in the first query:

```
SELECT    NAME
FROM      FACULTY
```

```
DEPARTMENT: (DEPT-NO, NAME, SCHOOL)
FACULTY: (SSN, NAME, RANK)
STUDENT: (SSN, NAME, GPA, ADVISOR)
MAJOR: (SSN, DEPT-NO)
COURSE: (COURSE-NO, DEPT-NO, NAME, SSN)
SECTION: (SECT-NO, CREDITS, DEPT-NO, ROOM, TIME, SSN)
GRADE: (SECT-NO, SSN, GRADE)
```

Figure 19.30 A relational schema for the university data base.

```
CREATE TABLE DEPARTMENT              CREATE TABLE COURSE
  (DEPT-NO    (CHAR (5),               (COURSE-NO      (CHAR (4),
              NONULL),                                 NONULL),
  (NAME       (CHAR (20)),             (DEPT-NO        (CHAR (5),
  (SCHOOL     (CHAR(20))                                NONULL),
                                       (NAME           (CHAR (10)),
CREATE TABLE FACULTY                   (SSN            (CHAR (11))
  (SSN        (CHAR (11),
              NONULL),               CREATE TABLE SECTION
  (NAME       (CHAR (20)),             (SECT-NO        (CHAR (3),
  (RANK       (CHAR (5))                               NONULL),
                                       (CREDITS        (CHAR (1)),
CREATE TABLE STUDENT                   (DEPT-NO        (CHAR (5)),
  (SSN        (CHAR (11),              (ROOM           (CHAR (4)),
              NONULL),                 (TIME           (CHAR (5)),
  (NAME       (CHAR (20)),             (SSN            (CHAR (11))
  (GPA        (CHAR (3)),
  (ADVISOR    (CHAR (20))            CREATE TABLE GRADE
                                       (SECT-NO        (CHAR (3),
CREATE TABLE MAJOR                                     NONULL),
  (SSN        (CHAR (11),              (SSN            (CHAR (11),
              NONULL),                                 NONULL),
  (DEPT-NO    (CHAR (5),               (GRADE          (CHAR (3,)
              NONULL))
```

Figure 19.31 Creation of the university relations.

The terminal displayed the names of all faculty members.

"That's pretty good," Tamra said. "Couldn't we have done that just as well with the hierarchical data model?"

"Oh, yes," Jon said. "For that particular query, a hierarchical data model may have produced the list of faculty names even more efficiently. But how about this one?"

Jon typed in the following query:

```
SELECT NAME
FROM FACULTY
WHERE SSN IN
    SELECT SSN
    FROM COURSE
    WHERE NAME = "INFORMATION SYSTEMS"
```

Three names of professors who teach information systems courses appeared instantly on the terminal screen.

"How long would it take to get that information from a COBOL program?" asked Anunzio.

"It's not so much how long it will take. If we knew ahead of time that this was the specific inquiry that was going to be made, we could write a program to do it. But that's just it, we never know exactly what kind of queries users will make. That's why we create a number of general relations that enable users to make a vast number of specific inquiries."

"You've convinced us," said Kathy. "Folks, it looks like we've got us a data base."

"Amen," said Anunzio.

Everyone at the meeting soon left for their offices, except Tamra and Jon. As Jon was collecting all his material, Tamra approached him and said, "You know, I'm kind of interested in this area. As I said at the other meeting, I've read some material about it."

"It gets pretty hard to keep up with everything that's going on in this area," said Jon.

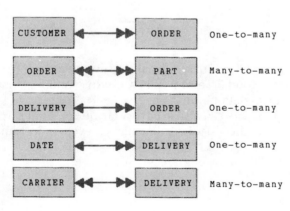

Entities:

    CUSTOMER
    ORDER
    PART
    DELIVERY
    DATE
    CARRIER

Relationships:

CUSTOMER	◄──►►	ORDER	One-to-many
ORDER	◄◄──►►	PART	Many-to-many
DELIVERY	◄──►►	ORDER	One-to-many
DATE	◄──►►	DELIVERY	One-to-many
CARRIER	◄◄──►►	DELIVERY	Many-to-many

Attributes:

CUSTNUMBER	DATE
CUSTNAME	DELIVNUMBER
CUSTADDRESS	DELIVDATE
CUSTCREDIT	DELIVQTY
ORDERNUMBER	DELIVWEIGHT
PARTNUMBER	DELIVADDRESS
PARTNAME	CARRIERNUM
PARTLOCATION	CARRIERNAME
PARTPRICE	CARRIERTERRITORY

Figure 19.32 Presentation of a data base design alternative.

"I'm sure," Tamra responded. "I was just thinking about that ER diagram you showed us. It looks a little complicated. Can't we demonstrate data base designs using a simpler method?"

"I don't know about a simpler method, but many alternative ways can be used to demonstrate the same thing," Jon said. "Here, let me sketch a design on the board for you. This time we'll use a business example."

Jon quickly sketched a data base design to demonstrate to Tamra that an alternative method can be used to design a data base. The results of Jon's sketch are illustrated in Figure 19.32.

"Yes, I like this one better," said Tamra. "I guess I have trouble with flowcharts and symbols. Anyway, thanks a lot. You've done a great job, and we really thank you for everything."

19.9 DETAILED CONTROLS DESIGN

A vast number of information systems controls are available to systems analysts. These controls were discussed in Chapter 14. Figure 19.33 brings all these controls together and provides a controls design perspective for this section. Selected controls from this figure are designed in detail in the following subsections for illustrative purposes.

Input Controls

The systems analyst should specify controls to keep erroneous input out of the information system. For critical fields, control of input entails verification or rekeying. If a field is critical to the identification of an input and subject to transcription or tranposition errors, such as an account number or an employee identification number, the analyst might also elect to append a check digit to it. Therefore, a particular check digit algorithm must be decided on and documented.

Depending on the type of data entry method used, various reasonableness tests may need to be performed on the input. The systems analyst must identify the fields to be validated and their validation rules. If input is batched, then the systems analyst must prepare batch control procedures. This effort encompasses designing a batch control cover document and a batch register and earmarking the fields for which various control totals will be prepared.

Typical controls to check the validity of input are listed in Figure 19.34. These input controls are applied at four levels: (1) fields, (2) records, (3) batches, and (4) files. Online entry can also use the same kind of controls. If errors occur in an online environment, a buzzer or bell is sounded, or the cursor is made to flash to show the data item in error with appropriate pop-up windows to display the nature of the error and how to correct it.

Processing Controls

Even though the systems analyst might propose an extensive set of input controls for the system being developed, some input errors will always elude detection, and additional errors may be created during processing. Operating under the

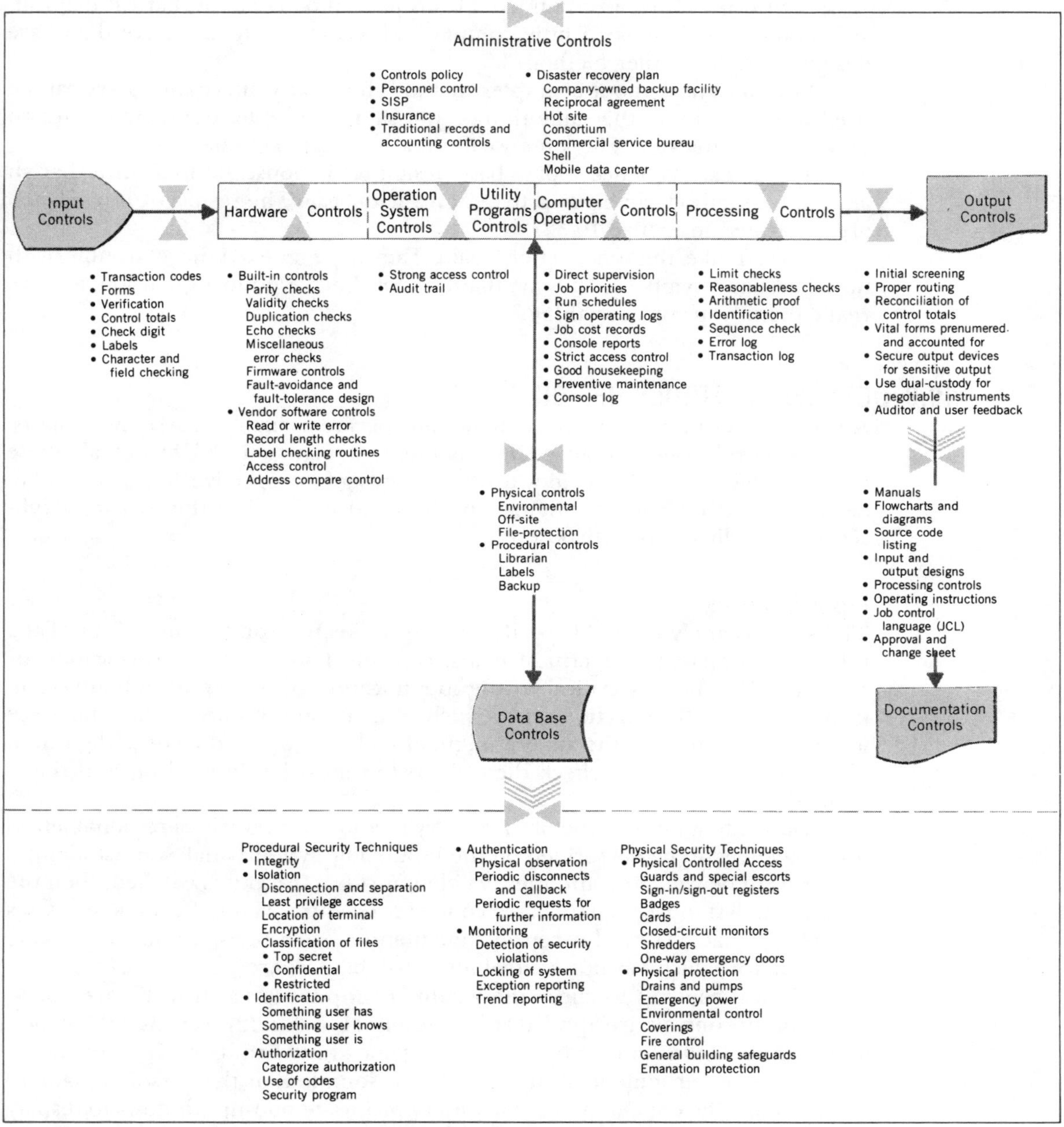

Figure 19.33 Information systems controls.

INPUT CONTROLS	
Field Checks	**Design**
CUSTNUM	This field should contain all numerics.
Range	Numbers range from 01000 to 79999.

Check digit	Use modulus 11 with
	1212 weighting:
	    5 1 2 8 4
	    X X X X X
	    1 2 1 2 1
	$5 + 2 + 2 + 16 + 4 = 29; 29 \div 11 = 2$
	with remainder of 7; $11 - 7 = 4$
	The check digit 4 is added to CUSTNUM 512844.

Record Checks	**Design**
Reasonableness	Structural steel is ordered in 20-foot lengths. Orders are generally in 50,000-pound multiples. Display "Recheck steel order" if orders fall outside these parameters.
Valid sign	No field contains a negative sign.
Batch Checks	**Design**
Control totals	Invoice totals should be summed and printed without a label on the last page of the printout. This value is transmitted to the control section for reconciliation.
Transaction code	The transaction code displayed on the console must agree with the transaction code on the batch header.
Hash total	The last three digits of the CUSTNUM are summed and displayed without label on the last page of the printout. This value is transmitted to the control section for reconciliation.
File Checks	**Design**
Internal label	The internal label should read "Customer Master File."
Retention date	The date is nine months subsequent to the end of the fiscal period.
Record count	The end of file contains the number of records within the file.

Figure 19.34 Input controls.

assumption that no information system is completely error proof, the systems analyst embeds certain input-like controls into the processing programs.

Reasonableness Check

Reasonableness checks are specified for coding into programs that are downstream from the basic input validation routines. For example, suppose a proposed procurement system is authorized to generate purchase orders automatically for material requisitioned by production. The systems analyst might wisely decide to include a processing control based on a reasonableness test in this part of the system. The processing control would identify and hold for purchasing agent approval any system-generated purchase order for an amount in excess of $100,000.

Transaction Log

Transaction logs are used for backup, recovery, and accounting audit trails. For all these purposes, the transaction log should include information about where, when, and from what terminal transactions originated plus the user number. For example, in an insurance company, the transaction log supports all entries to the general ledger accounts. An entry into the general ledger that debits accounts receivable and credits written premiums, is simultaneously recorded in the transaction log, and contains the following detailed support: initiator, terminal, and user identification numbers; time of day; day of week; policy number; premium; and other identifying data. At any time, the auditor can have the system produce for him or her a hard-copy listing of the transaction log for manual review.

In a system with a transaction log, transactions can be traced from the original source, to the point of entry to the computer system, and finally to a printout (if desired) of transactions processed by the computer. Moving in a reverse direction, the current status of any master record updated by transactions can be reconstructed. A common example of doing this is to provide for a "date of last transaction" on the status printout and a "date of last transaction" on each entry on the transaction log.

Any transactions that fail to pass the edit controls should be entered on a transaction error listing. These transactions should be corrected and reentered for processing. Control of errors is concerned with quality of the procedure for identifying and recording errors in the system. A proper system of controls ensures that edit checks are designed into the system to recognize error conditions.

Normally, one person is given the responsibility for controlling the error listings. When a correcting transaction is prepared, a notation is made on the error listing indicating date of correction, person making the correction, and transaction number of the correction. The individual responsible for error control reviews the listing on a regular basis to ensure that all errors have been corrected.

Transaction logs should be recorded and maintained in a secure location with controlled access. No access should be granted to systems analysts, programmers, and computer operators. Moreover, none of these people should have access to terminals that can originate transactions. Periodically, all transactions should be balanced against independent records of transactions maintained in user departments.

An ideal situation would be one in which the internal auditors have a separate terminal in their department under their control. They could select certain transactions for testing and follow-up, just as selected items are tested in a quality control system.

The transaction log, however, is not only for the use of the auditor. The results of transactions draw a large number of inquiries from other sources such as customers, employees, vendors, and government officials. There must, therefore, be a means by which the initiation and authorization of the transaction and its effect upon accounts can be traced. Furthermore, the Internal Revenue Service specifically requires that taxpayers with computer-based information systems be able to answer such inquiries.

The IRS regulation, which has become a generally accepted standard, applies equally to nonprofit organizations. Following are excerpts from Internal Revenue Procedure 64-12.

1. "The audit trail should be designed so that details underlying the summary accounting data, such as invoices and vouchers, may be identified and made available to the Internal Revenue Service upon request."

2. "The records must provide the opportunity to trace any transaction back to original source and forward to a final total. If printouts are not made of transactions at the time they are processed, then the system must have the ability to reconstruct those transactions."

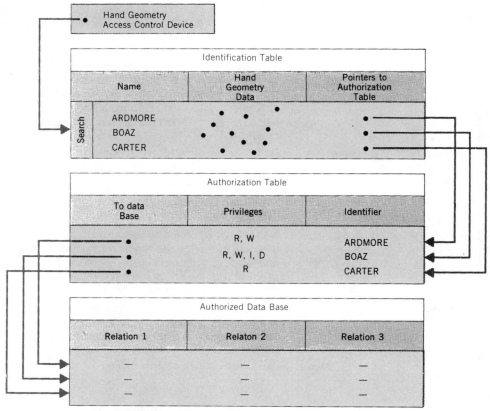

Figure 19.35 Access control of the data base.

Threat	Control Design
	GENERAL BATCH REPORTS
• Undetected removal of pages	• Install page numbering and end-of-job labels.
• Unauthorized access	• Prepare a distribution list and routing and designate authorized courier.
• Loose and casual procedures	• Classify level of security as top secret, secret, and internal use only.
• Inadvertent destruction	• Include retention date and method of destruction.
• Confusion	• Include report name, time and date of production, processing period covered, program producing report, and perform initial screening.
• Inaccuracy	• Reconcile control totals on report with totals prepared in control section.
• Unauthorized changes	• Install tight access controls to spooling and printing software.
• Unauthorized copying	• Destroy printer ribbons and extra copies and burn or shred immediately after retention period.
• Unauthorized browsing	• Top-secret reports are printed from a remote printer under control of a security officer. Secret reports are printed at the computer center. Three covering pages are printed first to enable operators to perform printer housekeeping and adjustments before the contents of the report are printed. Top-secret multipart documents contain a blacked-out or blind top copy. All financial reports to Advest Investment Banker are line-filled with characters. A template is furnished to Advest's merger officer to detect report characters from camouflage characters.
• Physical confiscation of printed report	• Do not accumulate reports in the computer room. Place in a locker and collect periodically. Have courier sign for reports and check them off as they are collected.
	ONLINE OUTPUT
• Interception of report	• Encrypt data.
• Unauthorized browsing	• Place terminals that display top-secret and secret information in separate rooms, use hoods on terminals, display output at low intensity, position terminals so users sit with their backs to the wall, and turn off screen while away from terminal.
• Unauthorized access	• Top secret terminals are physically locked while not in use and user access is by dynamic signature. Secret terminals are controlled by keyboard locks and password access.

Figure 19.36 Detailed output controls design.

Threat	Control Design
VITAL FORMS AND NEGOTIABLE INSTRUMENTS	
• Failure to keep track	• Maintain an inventory management system for all prenumbered documents.
• Unauthorized destruction or removal	• Store documents in a secure location and control access.
• Forgery	• Implement dual-custody and dual-signature and use preprinted documents.

Figure 19.36 (*Continued*)

Data Base Access Controls

Access controls include a large number of devices and procedures from locked doors and sign-in/sign-out procedures to biometric devices. Figure 19.35 demonstrates access control between users and the data base.

Based on a hand geometry access control device, authorized users are identified. Pointers connect authorized users to the authorization table, which specifies what each user can do once given access to certain relations or data sets in the data base.

Ardmore, Boaz, and Carter are permitted to access relations 1, 2, and 3. Ardmore is authorized to read and write. He is a data entry clerk. Boaz is authorized to read, write, insert, and delete entities, attributes, and attribute values. She is a data base administrator and therefore needs full authorization. Carter is a desk salesman and simply needs to query the data base.

Output Controls

Once the output is produced, certain controls should be in place to ensure that this output is not lost, corrupted, or stolen. Generally, the most extensive controls apply to batch output because a greater number of people are involved in producing and distributing its hard copy. Online output normally on screen requires fewer controls because of the direct user/system interface and tighter access controls. The detailed output controls design is illustrated in Figure 19.36.

19.10 DETAILED PROGRAM AND PERSONNEL PROCEDURES DESIGN

One of the major benefits of the SDM is the automatic generation of documentation and procedures as a by-product while performing systems work. By the time you've completed the detailed systems design phase, you have pretty much completed, among many other things, procedures both for application programs and personnel.

Structured English, data flow diagrams, and detailed design of output, input, data base, controls, and procedures provide sufficient specifications to enable programmers to write code. When the applications programmer finishes a program, additional detail, such as a program identification number, job control language (JCL), testing procedures, and a source listing are added to form a complete application program documentation package like the one outlined in Chapter 14.

Activities performed by personnel are also identified by systems analysts. Procedures are written to guide people in their tasks similar to procedures written for application programs. A sales order-entry example is presented to illustrate procedures written for application programmers, followed by cash discount procedures for sales and order-entry personnel.

Sales Order-Entry Procedures for the Programmer

An example of sales order-entry procedures for the applications programmer is outlined in Figure 19.37. Assume that the sales order-entry form and record layouts have already been designed in detail and are enclosed with these procedures.

System:	Sales order-entry processing	Programmer:	Al Kryzstofik
Program:	Sales order entry	Date:	MM/DD/YY
Analyst:	Matilda Matthews	Page:	1 of 1

1. Input
   When the customer account number is keyed in, the customer's identification data are automatically displayed on the screen for visual verification. After verification, the sales order-entry form is displayed to accept order data. Only item numbers and quantities are keyed in. Fixed data, such as item description and prices, are automatically retrieved by item number and extensions and totals are also automatically computed.

2. Processing Controls
   a. Inventory item numbers must be all numeric and fall within 10000 and 69999 range.
   b. Orders over $10,000 must be displayed on credit manager's terminal and written to an order-pending file. Release of these orders must be performed by the credit manager by inputting a release code in the 001 to 500 range.

3. Output Controls
   a. A count of invoices is made and transmitted to data entry control.
   b. The AMOUNT field is summed and this control total is transmitted to data entry control.

4. Output Produced
   a. Invoices are printed in accordance with the detailed design. When an item is backordered, the statement "Backordered" is printed on the invoice in the area normally reserved for unit price and extension.
   b. Inventory and customer accounts receivable files are updated.
   c. Backorder and pending files are appropriately updated.
   d. The transaction log includes every sales order entry in accordance with the layout design.
   e. A hard copy of all orders is printed for data entry control.

Figure 19.37 Sales order-entry procedures for programmers.

Cash Discount Procedures for Sales and Order-Entry Personnel

Written procedures are used for reference material and for a communications link between personnel. While the specific content of each procedure depends on the activity it describes, in general the procedure should supply the answers to the following questions:

What activity is being described?

Who must perform the activity?

Where is the activity performed?

When is the activity performed?

Why is the activity performed?

How is the activity performed?

Figure 19.38 illustrates one example of a written procedure. As can be seen, the format is directed to answering an individual's specific question or problem rather than to reading as a novel at one sitting. Each section of the procedures answers one or more of the preceding questions clearly but concisely.

Title Cash Discounts	Procedure Number 175
	Effective MM-DD-YY

Policy Statement: All customers are entitled to a cash discount of 2 percent on purchases as follows: a. The order exceeds $1,000, or   b. The order is paid in full within 10 days of shipment, or   c. The order is received as part of a special promotion which grants the cash discount as part of the promotion.
Locations Affected: All sales divisions.
Authorization: Vice-President, Marketing
Specific Instructions: *Salesperson*   1. Enter the words "Cash Discount Due" on all orders eligible for cash discount.   2. If only selected items are eligible for cash discount on an order, circle the line item number and place the letters "C.D.D." next to that line item.   *Order-Entry Clerk*   1. If an order contains the words "Cash Discount Due," enter an "X" in column 7 of the order total line.   2. If an order contains the letters "C.D.D." and the appropriate line item number is circled, enter an "X" in column 17 of the line item line.   3. All other orders are to be left blank in these columns.

Figure 19.38 Procedures for sales and order-entry personnel.

The terminology used is somewhat arbitrary. For example, the section labeled "Title" might also be labeled "Subject" or "Purpose."

19.11 DETAILED PROGRAM DESIGN

So far in the detailed design phase, the systems analyst has specified the inputs, outputs, data base, controls, and procedures for the new information system. If the new information system requires additional hardware or systems software, the systems analyst will have seen to it that the process of procurement of such resources is underway. The detailed design of programs requires concentrating the efforts of the systems analyst on defining the programs that will make up the information system, the detailed modules of each program, and the relationships between and among modules and programs.

Program Definition

The goal of program definition is the preparation of a description of every program in the information system. The systems analyst might start by grouping the outputs to be produced by the information system. Then, a program to generate each group of outputs might be designated. A similar grouping and designation process might be followed for inputs, considering such tasks as input validation and editing. If data need ordering, other utility programs might be defined.

This process of grouping inputs and outputs and then thinking through the transformations necessary to get from input to output, yields a list of programs. This list will contain the name, coded number, and a brief definition of each program in the information system.

Module Design

Whereas program definition is meant to give the overall nature of each program in the information system, module design entails dividing each program into small, cohesive parts or groups of actions with identifiable beginnings and ends. Making the modules a manageable size is important. If the programs for the information system will be written from terminals, then the standard size of a module should be what can be displayed on one screen, or up to 24 lines. If terminals will not be used to write programs, the standard module size should be limited to what can be placed on a single sheet of paper, or up to 50 or 60 lines.

19.12 DETAILED HARDWARE DESIGN

From the systems analyst's viewpoint, detailed hardware systems design involves selecting and putting together a hardware platform that supports the other building blocks. But not every project entails detailed hardware systems design.

Generally, four conditions exist from the perspective of systems work and hardware systems design. These conditions are:

1. The detailed systems design of the other five building blocks are implemented on existing hardware.
2. Part of systems development involves selecting and configuring some hardware components such as new terminals and hard disks or a laser printer.
3. Systems development entails a conversion from the old hardware configuration to a new one.
4. Systems development requires a major conversion from a manual-based system to one that is computer-based.

Much of the detailed hardware systems design in the preceding cases 3 and 4 comes from the material in Chapter 18. In many instances, the new hardware will already be ready for installation or may already be installed before detailed design of the other building blocks is completed. In other cases, technology is not ordered until the Final Detailed Systems Design Report is completed and reviewed in depth by all parties involved.

Hardware Overview

In the early 1980s, terminal-to-mainframe connections were pervasive. Today, many hardware configurations are host-to-host, host-to-mini, LAN-to-LAN, or LAN-to-WAN. The advent of new developments in telecommunications, such as the fiber optic standard, fiber distributed data interface (FDDI) and other

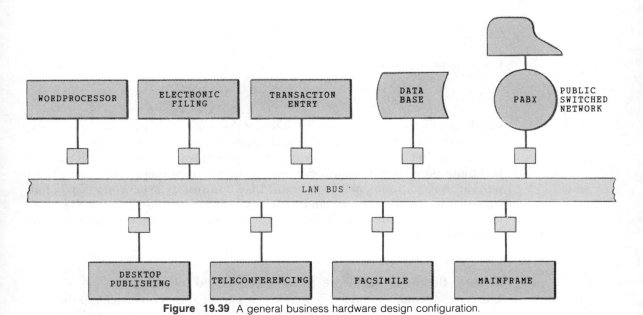

Figure 19.39 A general business hardware design configuration.

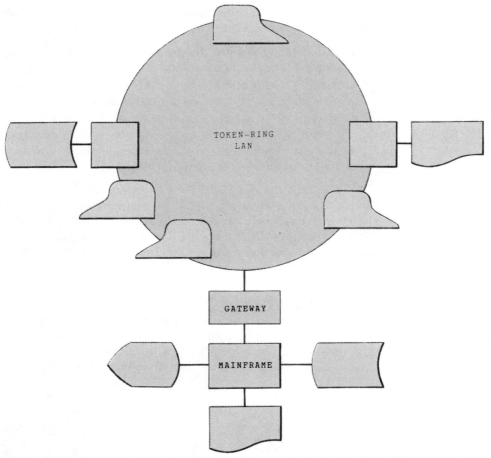

Figure 19.40 A hardware design configuration involving a twisted-pair ring LAN connected to a mainframe system.

standards discussed in Chapter 10, permits these new hardware configurations. Just about any configuration you can imagine is now technologically feasible.

In the following sections, we give examples of some configurations that are becoming popular in the businesss world. Absent from these configuration designs are specifications such as Netbios, LU6.2 transport, synchronous data link control (SDLC), and vendor names, such as IBM 3090 or PS/2, and DEC's VAX. Once you develop the design configuration you want, such details can be inserted in the symbols.

General Business Hardware System Connected by a Bus

The system demonstrated in Figure 19.39 is part of a LAN bus, such as Ethernet, which enables a great deal of resource sharing required in a general business environment. Resources connected to the bus are word processing, desktop publishing, electronic filing, teleconferencing, transaction entry and processing, facsimile, data base, and mainframe. The PABX is also connected to the bus and provides a gateway to other networks and also handles voice, data, and video traffic.

Token-Ring LAN

This hardware design, displayed in Figure 19.40, includes a twisted-pair channel that connects four PCs, one file server, hard-disk file, print server, and laser printer. This LAN's primary purpose is to process trust deeds and other financial

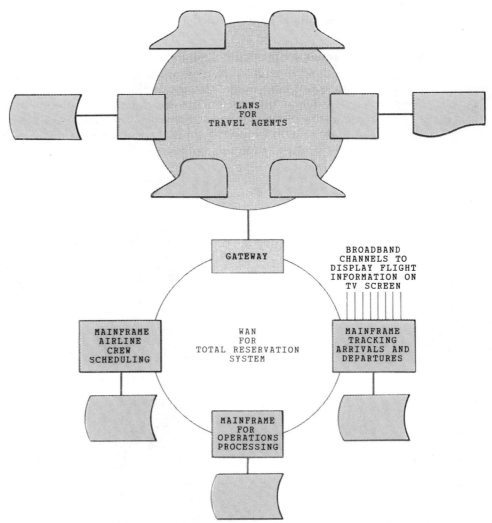

Figure 19.41 An airline's reservation hardware systems design.

and legal documents for the trust department of a bank. A gateway links this LAN to the bank's mainframe.

Wide Area Network with LANs

Consider Figure 19.41. This figure represents an airline reservation hardware design configuration. Three large mainframes are connected in a wide area network. Each mainframe is assigned a well-defined function, such as airline crew scheduling; tracking arrivals and departures; and operational processing for airplane maintenance, inventory control, payroll, and accounting.

The mainframe that tracks arrivals and departures also produces this information and transmits to TV screens scattered in airport terminals across the country. LANs are installed for all travel agents who service the flyer with ticket sales and other flight services.

Star Network Hardware System

Figure 19.42 portrays a star network for a casino with the mainframe as the central, controlling node. Electronic slots and other gaming devices are connected to the mainframe. Performance statistics, accounting, food services, hotel reservations, and general operations are supported by the mainframe. The minicomputer system, connected to the mainframe, is used primarily for cash and currency control, counting, and verification.

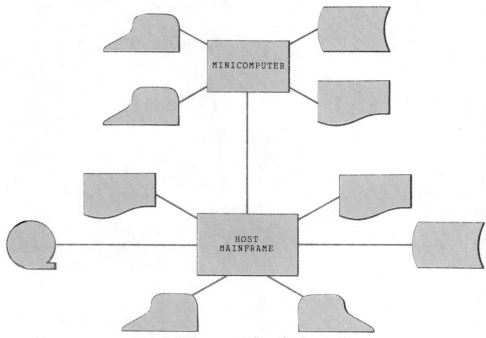

Figure 19.42 A star configuration for a casino.

19.13 COMMUNICATING THE DETAILED SYSTEMS DESIGN

The Final Detailed Systems Design Report brings together knowledge learned during general systems design and systems evaluation phases. It demonstrates the systems analyst's design adroitness. If well designed, this report provides comprehensive systems documentation and communicates precisely syntactic and semantic information to various recipients.

For many systems analysts, the Final Detailed Systems Design Report is the most enjoyable report to prepare because its focus is on one systems design. Analysts have a clear vision of what users require and can spend their talents on designing building blocks precisely to meet these requirements.

This fifth documented deliverable of the SDM contains program specifications, micro instructions, diagrams, and the six building blocks for the specific system to be implemented. Vendors and technology have been selected and committed to the system along with other resources. Budgets are approved. Most, if not all, of the pending and iffy questions are nailed down.

Report Presentation

Typically, this fifth documented deliverable is voluminous, containing a large number of forms, layouts, and diagrams. Therefore, some systems analysts prepare levels of the Final Detailed Systems Design Report. Level 1 is an abstract for executives and contains only a few pages. Level 2 is a condensed version of the total report and is intended for middle managers and supervisors who have a need for more detail than executives. Level 3 is the total detailed report and is prepared for personnel who are members of the implementation team. Also, subreports can be prepared that contain only elements of the report for people with a specific need to know about certain tasks, forms, or procedures.

Like all documented deliverables of the SDM, presentations are written and oral. This kind of presentation permits a thorough examination by all involved parties. Some design errors or omissions may be found and corrected before implementation begins. The chance, however, of outright rejection of the report or any part thereof at this stage in the SDM is highly unlikely.

Upon approval, the report becomes a trigger for the implementation phase and a variety of work, such as implementation plan development, site preparation, technology installation, programming, and personnel selection and training. The major elements of the Final Detailed Systems Design Report follow.

Old System

A concise description of the old system (if one existed) should be provided along with a list of its major problems. Some users and various managers need to be reminded why systems work was begun in the first place.

New System

A brief description of the new system is included and used to compare the new system with the old system and demonstrate the new system's benefits. In addition, a generalized model supported by flowcharts or other modeling techniques are used to give an overview of the new system and its subsystems. This systems design is followed by detailed design of each building block.

Input

Detailed input design involves where and how to create or capture input; design of source documents, forms, and codes; media selection; development of a transaction trail or log; and input verification. Source documents and screen formats are clearly defined by layout forms.

Transaction trails provide backup for the system and an audit trail for auditors. A variety of tables are designed to provide fixed input such as customers' names, prices, and pay rates.

Models

Some models are driven by application programs. Therefore, detailed logic and specifications, sufficient for application programmers to understand, are developed. Detailed specifications are presented using structured techniques, such as structured English or pseudocode, Nassi-Shneiderman charts, structure charts, Warnier-Orr diagrams, structured analysis and design technique (SADT), or HIPO techniques. Edit controls to be included in programs are also specified.

If, on one hand, program specifications are highly detailed, application programmers feel the challenge is removed from their work and only routine coding remains. On the other hand, if program specifications are too general, an inexperienced programmer may not be able to develop the program and include all the features required by the system. The systems analyst needs to ascertain where the balance point is and design program specifications accordingly.

Human procedures are designed using manuals, decision tables, data flow diagrams, icons, and structured English. The key to well-designed human procedures is understanding by the user.

Output

The precise format of output is determined and displayed in the report. Output requirements dictate input, file, and data base requirements. When detailed output layouts are reviewed by the systems project team members, users, or programmers, omissions and design errors may be detected. If so, changes in input, models, or output formats may be required. For interactive systems, a user interface design includes detailed procedures for entering, requesting output, and initiating other system functions.

Technology

The complete technology platform is presented in detail. All the "boxes," including their specifications, are connected by telecommunications and various connector boxes such as front-end processors to form a specific topology. Various software interfaces are specified.

Data Base and Files

A system may use the data base or file approach, or both. In any event, the systems analyst must describe all entities, records, attributes, and fields and their representations, relationships, and query language. Precise specifications for each field or attribute are displayed along with how and where data are stored.

Generally, a data dictionary is designed to help manage more complex data bases and data operations. Essentially, the data dictionary contains data about data, such as a list of all data items and their fields, records or entities, data base organization, transactions that use data items, where and how the data items originate, output produced by data items, and programs that access data items.

Controls

All the processing controls built in programs should be listed here and cross-referenced to program specifications. From the total array of controls, certain ones are selected and described. Detailed explanations indicate how they are to be implemented.

THE NSU TIGERS EVENT CENTER
Preparing the Final Detailed Systems Design Report

OVERVIEW

Sally and Tommy, along with representatives of Digit, spent several weeks working out the details and making modifications to ensure that the detailed systems design would meet precisely the building blocks of the centralized system alternative selected in the systems evaluation phase. The results of their work were documented and made ready to prepare the Final Detailed Systems Design Report.

Following is the Final Detailed Systems Design Report that Sally and Tommy prepared. It, first, presents the centralized design alternative for reference. Then, the report presents detailed design specifications of each building block. Only selected parts (those shown as three-dimensional) of each building block are demonstrated to save space and give a less cluttered representation. The items demonstrated, however, are in sufficient detail to provide specifications necessary for implementation.

Input and *output* in SEATS are handled by menus. Therefore, a menu tree is used to illustrate an overall view of all the menus, screens, and screen forms necessary to perform input and output tasks. Next, all the *models* in SEATS are procedural except the diagramming models used in systems analysis and general systems design. These models are described in narrative form and are coded during systems implementation. The *technology* platform is the one that was selected during systems evaluation and acquired from Digit Computers. A *data base* schema and data dictionary detail the data base building block. And, finally, a sampling of *controls* is presented. All this material prepares SEATS, IS staff, management, Digit representatives, and users for systems implementation, the next and final phase of the SDM.

FINAL DETAILED SYSTEMS DESIGN REPORT

March 21, 19xx

To: All Department Heads and IS Staff
From: Sally Forth, Chief Systems Analyst

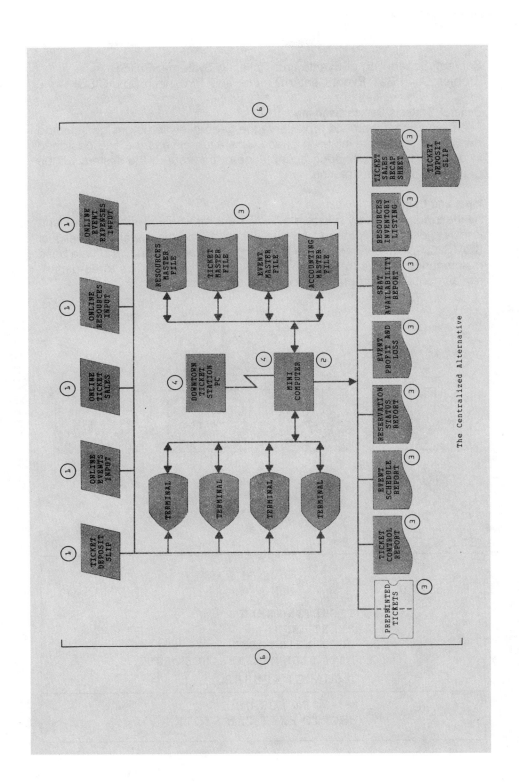

The Centralized Alternative

Subject: Scheduling of Events and Ticketing System (SEATS)
Copies: John Ball, Event Center Director and Tyronne Topps, CISO

General Systems Design Overview

The preceding schematic represents the general systems design selected during the systems evaluation phase. This alternative is the one designed in detail in this report. Upon acceptance of this report, the system will be prepared for implementation.

Input and Output

All the input necessary to operate SEATS and produce reports are in menu form. Following, is a menu tree that shows all the menus and screens of SEATS. Off-page connectors link ticketing, event, accounting, and data base maintenance menus to their supporting screens. (Note: The three-dimensional menus and screens are selected for demonstration.)

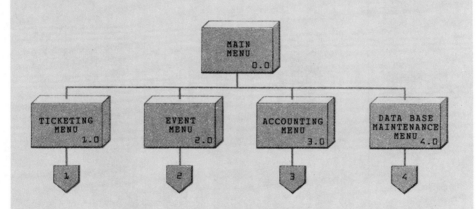

MENU SELECTION SCREEN   0.0

```
┌──────────────────────────────────────────────────────────────┐
│                   NSU TIGERS EVENT CENTER                      │
│  Release 1.0          MAIN MENU               MM/DD/YY          │
│                                                                │
│       1. TICKETING MENU                                        │
│       2. EVENT MENU                                            │
│       3. ACCOUNTING MENU                                       │
│       4. DATA BASE MAINTENANCE MENU                            │
│          SELECT NUMBER [    ]                                  │
├──────────────────────────────────────────────────────────────┤
│                      F1 FOR HELP                               │
│                (ESC) TO EXIT THE SYSTEM                        │
└──────────────────────────────────────────────────────────────┘
```

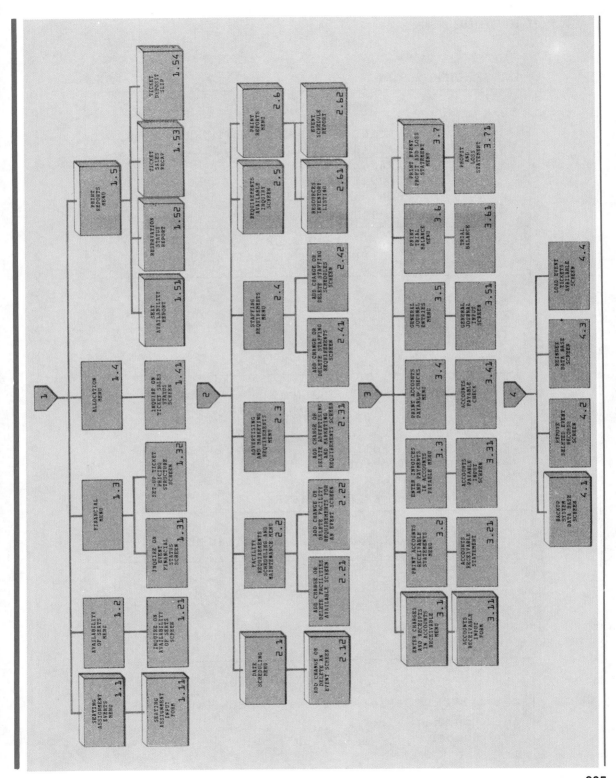

805

MENU SELECTION SCREEN   1.0

```
                    (SEATS) TICKETING MENU

            1.  SEATING ASSIGNMENT EVENT MENU
            2.  AVAILABILITY OF SEATS MENU
            3.  FINANCIAL MENU
            4.  ALLOCATION MENU
            5.  PRINT REPORTS MENU
                SELECT NUMBER [    ]
```

```
                    F1 FOR HELP
        (ESC) TO RETURN TO THE MAIN MENU
```

MENU SELECTION SCREEN   1.1

```
              (SEATS) SEATING ASSIGNMENT EVENT MENU
                    UPCOMING EVENTS
        EVENT                      DATE
        1.  Susie's Follies        Nov. 20-22 19xx
        2.  Globe Trotters         Dec.  2-12 19xx
        3.  Colloquium             Dec. 22-28 19xx
                SELECT NUMBER [    ]
```

```
                    F1 FOR HELP
        (ESC) TO RETURN TO THE TICKETING MENU
```

ENTRY SCREEN 1 OF 1   1.11

```
            (SEATS) SEATING ASSIGNMENT INPUT FORM

        EVENT: Susie's Follies Nov. 20-22, 19xx
        Log Sheet Line
        Number                  [            ]
```

```
Name of Patron            [                    ]
Phone Number              [    -    -    ]
Date of
Reservation               [MM/DD/YY] Number [ ]
Amount Paid               [$       .  ] Amount
                          Due      [$     .   ]
Date of
Purchase                  [MM/DD/YY]
Seats                     [    ][    ][    ][    ][    ]
                          [    ][    ][    ][    ][    ]
                          [    ][    ][    ][    ][    ]
                          [    ][    ][    ][    ][    ]
```

F1 FOR HELP
(ESC) TO RETURN TO THE SEATING ASSIGNMENT
EVENTS MENU

MENU SELECTION SCREEN   1.5

(SEATS) PRINT REPORTS MENU

1. SEAT AVAILABILITY REPORT
2. RESERVATION STATUS REPORT
3. TICKET SALES RECAP
4. TICKET DEPOSIT SLIP

SELECT NUMBER [   ]

F1 FOR HELP
(ESC) TO RETURN TO THE MAIN MENU

SEAT AVAILABILITY REPORT (1.51)
(North Concourse)

EVENT NUMBER: 87123
EVENT NAME: SUSIE'S FOLLIES
DATE: November 21, 19xx
TOTAL SEATS SOLD TO DATE: 3168
TOTAL SEATS STILL AVAILABLE: 1623

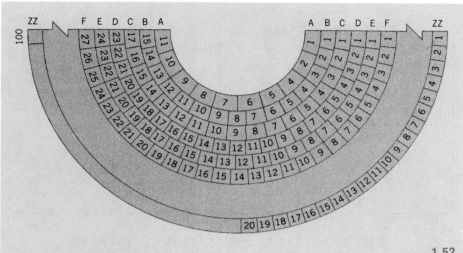

1.52

Page 1 of 1	RESERVATION STATUS REPORT		
Event: SUSIE'S FOLLIES			EVENT NO: 87123
Tickets Number	Name of Ticket Holder	Amount Paid	Amount Due
A 1–5	John Patterson	0.00	$ 62.50
B 6–7	Peter Lazarus	0.00	$ 25.00
B 1–3	Amy Smith	0.00	$ 37.50
C 7–8	Jeff Henry	0.00	$ 25.00
D 14–15	Mary Jones	0.00	$ 25.00
.	.	.	.
.	.	.	.
.	.	.	.

Total Number of Tickets Sold 99999		Total Receipts $ 99999.99	
Event: GLOBE TROTTERS			EVENT NO: 87124
Tickets Number	Name of Ticket Holder	Amount Paid	Amount Due
A 1–15	Sam Smith	$ 7.00	$ 0.00
F 1–4	Sue Peterson	$ 15.00	$ 0.00
.	.	.	.
.	.	.	.
.	.	.	.
.	.	.	.
.	.	.	.
.	.	.	.
.	.	.	.

Total Number of Tickets Sold 99999		Total Receipts $ 99999.99	
Event: COLLOQUIUM		EVENT NO: 87125	
Tickets Number	Name of Ticket Holder	Amount Paid	Amount Due
	Reservations handled by the con-ference committee.		
Total Number of Tickets Sold 99999		Total Receipts $ 99999.99	

1.53

TICKET SALES RECAP

EVENT	Ticket Price	Number Sales to Date	Dollar Sales to Date	Remaining Number to be Sold	Remaining Dollars to be Sold
Susie's	$12.50	1593	$19913	2947	$36838
Follies	$15.50	3684	$57102	854	$13237
	$18.50	4227	$78200	1068	$19758
Globe	$ 7.50	954	$ 7155	1546	$11595
Trotters	$ 9.50	1571	$14925	358	$ 3401
Colloquium	$ 3.50	153	$ 536	(unlimited)	

TICKET DEPOSIT SLIP
TRANSACTION RECORD

TRANSACTION DATE: MM/DD/YY
TELLER: E. Johnson

EVENT NO. 87123
EVENT NAME: Susie's Follies
SEATS ACCOUNT NUMBER: AE23S43-3422
CURRENCY AMOUNT: $2525.50
            CHECKS: $1525.00
    CREDIT CARDS: $1852.50
    TOTAL DEPOSIT: $5903.00

MENU SELECTION SCREEN   2.0

```
                    (SEATS) EVENT MENU

    1.  DATE SCHEDULING MENU
    2.  FACILITY REQUIREMENTS SCHEDULING AND MAIN-
        TENANCE MENU
    3.  ADVERTISING AND MARKETING REQUIREMENTS MENU
    4.  STAFFING REQUIREMENTS MENU
    5.  REQUIREMENTS AVAILABILITY INQUIRY SCREEN
    6.  PRINT REPORTS MENU
                    SELECT NUMBER [    ]

                    F1 FOR HELP
            (ESC) TO RETURN TO THE MAIN MENU
```

MENU SELECTION SCREEN   2.1

```
                (SEATS) DATE SCHEDULING MENU

    0.  ADD CHANGE OR DELETE AN EVENT      DATE

    1.  Susie's Follies                    Nov.  20-22 19xx
    2.  Globe Trotters                     Dec.   2-12 19xx
    3.  Colloquium                         Dec.  22-28 19xx
                SELECT EVENT NUMBER [    ]

        F1 FOR HELP (ESC) TO RETURN TO THE EVENTS MENU
```

ADD CHANGE OR DELETE SCREEN 1 OF 1   2.12

```
            (SEATS) ADD CHANGE OR DELETE AN EVENT

    Event Number [       ] Entry Date [ / / ]
    Event Name [                                              ]
    Performer(s)    [                                         ]
    Event Date(s) [ / / ][ / / ][ / / ][ / / ][ / / ]
                  [ / / ][ / / ][ / / ][ / / ][ / / ]
    Seating Code [ ] Financial Code [ ]
    Reservation Minimum [ ]
```

```
Contact Name [                                    ]
Title        [                                    ]
Phone        [     -    -    ]
Address      [                                    ]
City         [         State          Zip         ]
```

F1 FOR HELP	⟨Ctrl⟩ D Delete Event
⟨ESC⟩ RETURN TO DATE SCHEDULING MENU	⟨Ctrl⟩ U Undelete Event

INQUIRY SCREEN OF AS MANY AS NECESSARY   2.5

(SEATS) REQUIREMENTS AVAILABLE INQUIRY

Enter Date [MM/DD/YY]

Number of People Available by Position:	Ushers	Ticket Sales	Parking	Security
	2	5	4	1
	Concession	Supervisor		
	5	1		

Number of Facility Items by Group:	Chairs	Tables	Lighting	Sound	Stages
	72	22	4	5	1

Events Scheduled:
  87123   Susie's Follies   MM/DD/YY

F1 FOR HELP
⟨ESC⟩ TO RETURN TO THE EVENTS MENU

MENU SELECTION SCREEN   2.6

(SEATS) PRINT REPORTS MENU

1. RESOURCES INVENTORY LISTING
2. EVENT SCHEDULE REPORT

SELECT NUMBER [   ]

F1 FOR HELP
⟨ESC⟩ TO RETURN TO THE MAIN MENU

RESOURCES INVENTORY LISTING
Susie's Follies
November 20–22, 19xx

Staging Requirements
  1-#C6421B-100 × 50 stage backdrop, black
  1-#C6852A-100 × 100 × 4 modular steel stage

Lighting Requirements
  7-#L6481F-Small cluster group setting spots
  4-#L7865A-Master arena spots

Sound Requirements
  4-#S1268G-Standard floor monitors
  8-#S1275C-Hanging ceiling PA monitors

Concessions
  9-#B8642C-Beverage and beer stands
  6-#B9652F-Snack bars

Display Setups
  12-#V7421B-8 × 12 Vendor booths

Comments:
  Skating rink is to be setup 24 hours prior to November 20th by performer's crew chief and staff.

Page 1 of 1   EVENT SCHEDULE REPORT
                  Status as of MM/DD/YY

EVENT NO.   87123
EVENT NAME   Susie's Follies
COST $108,950
DURATION   November 20-22,
                               19xx

TICKETING STATUS
  AVAILABLE   4869
  SOLD TO DATE   9504

EVENT NO.   87124
EVENT NAME   Globe Trotters
COST $15,000
DURATION   December 2-12,
                               19xx

```
TICKETING STATUS
   AVAILABLE                        1904
   SOLD TO DATE                     2525

EVENT NO.                           87125
EVENT NAME                          Colloquium
COST                                $8,650
DURATION                            Dec. 22-28, 19xx
TICKETING STATUS
   AVAILABLE                        (Unlimited)
   SOLD TO DATE                     153
```

MENU SELECTION SCREEN   3.0

```
                (SEATS) ACCOUNTING MENU

1.  ENTER CHARGES AND RECEIPTS IN ACCOUNTS
    RECEIVABLE MENU
2.  PRINT ACCOUNTS RECEIVABLE STATEMENTS MENU
3.  ENTER INVOICES AND PAYMENTS IN ACCOUNTS
    PAYABLE MENU
4.  PRINT ACCOUNTS PAYABLE CHECKS MENU
5.  GENERAL JOURNAL ENTRIES MENU
6.  PRINT TRIAL BALANCE MENU
7.  PRINT EVENT PROFIT AND LOSS STATEMENT MENU
```

```
                     F1 FOR HELP
        (ESC) TO RETURN TO THE MAIN MENU
```

MENU SELECTION SCREEN   3.1

```
           (SEATS) ENTER CHARGES AND RECEIPTS
               IN ACCOUNTS RECEIVABLE MENU

1.  Susie's Follies              Nov. 20-22 19xx
2.  Globe Trotters               Dec.  2-12 19xx
3.  Colloquium                   Dec. 22-28 19xx
            SELECT EVENT NUMBER [    ]
```

```
                     F1 FOR HELP
       (ESC) TO RETURN TO THE ACCOUNTING MENU
```

ENTRY SCREEN 1 OF 1   3.11

(SEATS) ACCOUNTS RECEIVABLE INPUT FORM

Enter Event Number [   ]
Name of Event   [   ]
Balance Forward $99999.99

Amount Due	Date Due	Description
[$.]	[/ /]	[ ]
[$.]	[/ /]	[ ]
[$.]	[/ /]	[ ]
[$.]	[/ /]	[ ]
[$.]	[/ /]	[ ]
[$.]	[/ /]	[ ]

Enter Payment	Date Paid	Comments
[$.]	[/ /]	[ ]

New Balance Due $99999.99

F1 FOR HELP
(ESC) TO RETURN TO THE ACCOUNTING MENU

MENU SELECTION SCREEN   3.7

(SEATS) PRINT EVENT PROFIT AND LOSS STATEMENT MENU

Enter Event Number to Print [   ]

F1 FOR HELP
(ESC) TO RETURN TO THE ACCOUNTING MENU

                                                    3.71

PROFIT AND LOSS STATEMENT
Susie's Follies
as of MM/DD/YY

REVENUE:

TICKET SALES	$ 9999.99
ADVERTISING SALES	$ 9999.99
CONCESSION SALES	$ 9999.99
PARKING FEES	$ 9999.99
TOTAL REVENUE	$99999.99

```
EXPENSES:
KOSS RADIO                            $  9999.99
KNBA TV                               $  9999.99
ROE AND SONS BILLBOARDS               $  9999.99
EJ'S SOUND                            $  9999.99
JANIS PARKS                           $  9999.99
MIKE EVANS                            $  9999.99
IAN EMERSON                           $  9999.99
KARL MADISON                          $  9999.99
ACME FOOD DISTRIBUTORS                $  9999.99
NSU POLICE DEPARTMENT                 $  9999.99
YOU-HAUL TRUCKS RENTAL                $  9999.99

TOTAL EXPENSES                        $99999.99

PROFIT OR (LOSS)                      $99999.99

DISTRIBUTION TO THE EVENT CENTER      $99999.99
DISTRIBUTION TO THE PROMOTER          $99999.99
```

MENU SELECTION SCREEN   4.0

```
                (SEATS) DATA BASE FILE MAINTENANCE MENU

    1.  BACKUP SYSTEM DATA BASE SCREEN
    2.  REMOVE DELETED EVENT RECORDS SCREEN
    3.  REINDEX DATA BASE SCREEN
    4.  LOAD EVENT TICKETS AVAILABLE SCREEN
                        SELECT NUMBER [    ]

                            F1 FOR HELP
                 (ESC) TO RETURN TO THE MAIN MENU
```

PROMPT SCREEN 1 OF 1   4.1

```
                  (SEATS) BACKUP SYSTEM DATA BASE

    Is the backup tape mounted (Y)es or (N)o ?  [    ]
    Enter the primary tape number [    ]
    Enter the tape number for the overflow tape if appli-
    cable [    ]
    Enter Date [MM/DD/YY]

                            F1 FOR HELP
                 (ESC) TO RETURN TO THE MAIN MENU
```

MODELS

1. Ticketing Model

Menu option 1.11 (SEATING ASSIGNMENT INPUT FORM) will allow the user to input seating assignments. When a ticket is sold or a seat is reserved, the input screen form records information about the patron, the amount paid, the purchase date, and the seats assigned. The "available" relation will have to be updated to indicate a ticket is sold or a seat is reserved and therefore cannot be reissued. Only after this had been done will the ticket be printed.

2. Event Recording Model

Menu option 2.12 (ADD CHANGE OR DELETE AN EVENT) will allow the user to add, change, or delete an event. If the user chooses to add an event, then the system must sequentially assign a new event number to the event and store the number in the data base. The last event number recorded in the "events" relation will have to be incremented by 1 and assigned to the new event being booked.

3. Resources Planning Model

Menu option 2.22 (ADD CHANGE OR DELETE FACILITY REQUIREMENTS FOR AN EVENT) will allow the user to add, change, or delete facility requirements for an event. The key to planning for facility resources is the reporting on a daily basis the resource requirements for each event. When the user makes a request for a resource, the availability is checked against all other requests on the same date. If the resource is unavailable, the system will notify the user of this situation.

4. Accounting Model (Payable)

Menu option 3.4 (PRINT ACCOUNTS PAYABLE CHECKS) will be used to print accounts payable checks to vendors. The system will have to compute the check amount by totaling all the debit and credit entries in the "payables" relation. After the check is issued, the system will have to record the balance in the "vendors" relation.

5. Data Base Maintenance Model

Menu option 4.4 (LOAD EVENT TICKETS AVAILABLE) will be used to copy all the ticket numbers avilable for sale for an event into the "available" relation. Using the seating layout code assigned when a new event is booked, the system will load the tickets "available" relation from files containing master seating layouts based on the following seating layout codes:

CODE   CONFIGURATION
1.   Upper/Lower Concourse assigned seating only and no floor seating
2.   Upper/Lower Concourse and floor assigned seating
3.   Lower Concourse and floor assigned seating
4.   Upper/Lower Concourse (except behind stage) and floor assigned seating

5. Upper/Lower Concourse (except behind stage) assigned and floor unassigned
6. Entire arena unassigned

TECHNOLOGY

Digit will provide us with the following hardware:

1 DEQ VAC II minicomputer
25 Mhz CPU speed
10 Mbytes main storage

1 Hard disk
30 Mls disk speed
145 Mbytes disk storage

1 Magnetic tape backup system
60 Mbytes storage

1 Power supply backup
15-minute backup time

5 Dynac Pac terminals
1000 × 480 PPI resolution

2 Modems
9600-baud modem speed

5 Printers
24-pin letter quality
384-CPS draft print speed
80-CPS letter-quality print speed

Digit will provide all necessary cabling to connect the hardware configuration based on the following layout:

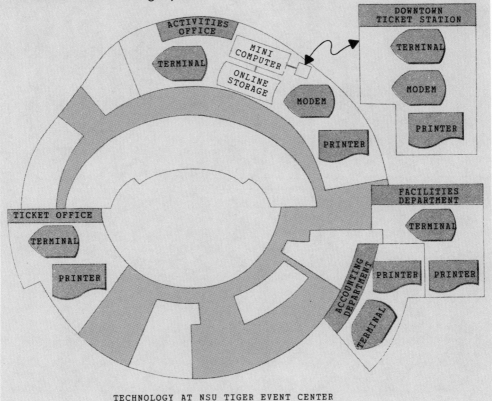

TECHNOLOGY AT NSU TIGER EVENT CENTER

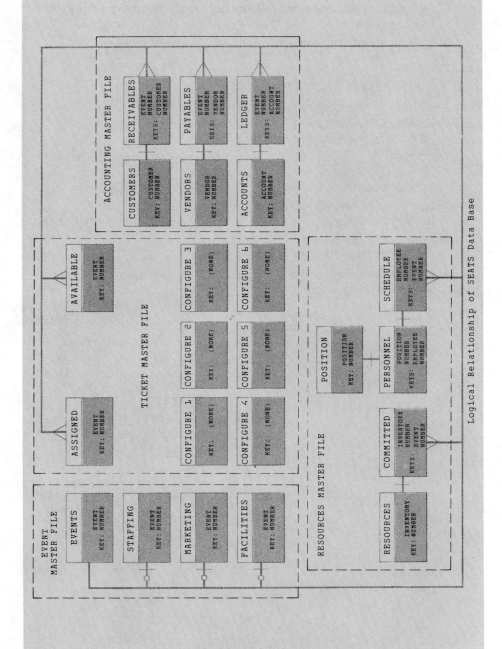

Logical Relationship of SEATS Data Base

DATA BASE

The preceding schematic shows the logical relationship of the four master files that comprise the SEATS data base. Following this schematic is each file's data dictionary.

EVENT MASTER FILE

ENTITY NAME: events
ENTITY DESCRIPTION: This relation stores the information captured when a new event is booked. It contains one record for every event booked.

ATTRIBUTE NUMBER	DATA ATTRIBUTE	DATA REPRESENTATION
KEY 1	EVENT_NUMBER	8 Numeric
2	EVENT_NAME	50 Character
3	FIRST_DATE	8 Date
4	SECOND_DATE	8 Date
5	THIRD_DATE	8 Date
6	FOURTH_DATE	8 Date
7	FIFTH_DATE	8 Date
8	SIXTH_DATE	8 Date
9	SEVENTH_DATE	8 Date
10	EIGHTH_DATE	8 Date
11	NINTH_DATE	8 Date
12	TENTH_DATE	8 Date
13	CONTACT_NAME	8 Character
14	CONTACT_TITLE	8 Character
15	CONTACT_ADDRESS	50 Character
16	SEATING_CODE	8 Character
17	FINANCIAL_CODE	8 Character
18	RESERVATION_MINIMUM	2 Numeric

ENTITY NAME: staffing
ENTITY DESCRIPTION: This relation stores the staffing requirements by date for each event. It contains one record for each event.

ATTRIBUTE NUMBER	DATA ATTRIBUTE	DATA REPRESENTATION
1	EVENT_NUMBER	8 Numeric
2	DATE	8 Date
3	USHERS	3 Numeric

4	TICKET_SALES_STAFF	3 Numeric
5	PARKING_STAFF	3 Numeric
6	SECURITY_STAFF	3 Numeric
7	CONCESSION_STAFF	3 Numeric
8	SUPERVISOR	3 Numeric
9	OTHER_CODE_1	3 Numeric
10	OTHER_CODE_2	3 Numeric
11	OTHER_CODE_3	3 Numeric

ENTITY NAME: marketing
ENTITY DESCRIPTION: This relation stores the marketing information needed by the advertising department by
date for each event. It contains one record for each
event.

ATTRIBUTE NUMBER	DATA ATTRIBUTE	DATA REPRESENTATION
KEY 1	EVENT_NUMBER	8 Numeric
2	DATE	8 Date
3	BROCHURE_NEEDED	1 Character
4	NEWSPAPER_NEEDED	1 Character
5	TV_NEEDED	1 Character
6	RADIO_NEEDED	1 Character
7	OTHER_NEEDED	25 Character
8	PRICING_SCHEME_CODE	2 Numeric
9	PRODUCT_REQUIRED	25 Character
10	FACILITY_REQUIRED	25 Character
11	MEMO_FIELD_1	80 Character
12	MEMO_FIELD_2	80 Character
13	MEMO_FIELD_3	80 Character
14	MEMO_FIELD_4	80 Character
15	MEMO_FIELD_5	80 Character

ENTITY NAME: facilities
ENTITY DESCRIPTION: This relation stores the facility
inventory requirements for each event by date. It contains one record for each event.

ATTRIBUTE NUMBER	DATA ATTRIBUTE	DATA REPRESENTATION
KEY 1	EVENT_NUMBER	8 Numeric
2	DATE	8 Date
3	GROUP_NUMBER	8 Numeric

TICKET MASTER FILE

ENTITY NAME: assigned

ENTITY DESCRIPTION: This relation contains information captured when a patron buys a ticket or makes a reservation for an event. It contains one record for each transaction with a patron.

ATTRIBUTE NUMBER		DATA ATTRIBUTE	DATA REPRESENTATION
KEY	1	EVENT_NUMBER	8 Numeric
	2	EVENT_NAME	50 Character
	3	LOG_NUMBER	8 Numeric
	4	PATRON	50 Character
	5	PHONE	12 Numeric
	6	RESERVATION_DATE	8 Date
	7	NUMBER_OF_RESERVATIONS	8 Numeric
	8	AMOUNT_PAID	8 Numeric
	9	AMOUNT_DUE	8 Date
	10	PURCHASE_DATE	8 Date
	11	SEAT_ASSIGNED_1	8 Character
	12	SEAT_ASSIGNED_2	8 Character
	13	SEAT_ASSIGNED_3	8 Character
	14	SEAT_ASSIGNED_4	8 Character
	15	SEAT_ASSIGNED_5	8 Character
	16	SEAT_ASSIGNED_6	8 Character
	17	SEAT_ASSIGNED_7	8 Character
	18	SEAT_ASSIGNED_8	8 Character
	19	SEAT_ASSIGNED_9	8 Character
	20	SEAT_ASSIGNED_10	8 Character
	21	SEAT_ASSIGNED_11	8 Character
	22	SEAT_ASSIGNED_12	8 Character
	23	SEAT_ASSIGNED_13	8 Character
	24	SEAT_ASSIGNED_14	8 Character
	25	SEAT_ASSIGNED_15	8 Character
	26	SEAT_ASSIGNED_16	8 Character
	27	SEAT_ASSIGNED_17	8 Character
	28	SEAT_ASSIGNED_18	8 Character
	29	SEAT_ASSIGNED_19	8 Character
	30	SEAT_ASSIGNED_20	8 Character

ENTITY NAME: available

ENTITY DESCRIPTION: This relation is built using an option in the file maintenance menu that copies all the

ticket numbers available for sale from one of the configured files based on the configuration option selected when an event is booked. It contains one
record for every ticket available for sale for all
upcoming events.

ATTRIBUTE NUMBER	DATA ATTRIBUTE	DATA REPRESENTATION
KEY 1	EVENT_NUMBER	8 Numeric
2	TICKET_NUMBER	8 Numeric
3	ISSUED(Y/N)	1 Character
4	PRICE	5.2 Numeric

ENTITY NAME: Configure1
ENTITY DESCRIPTION: This relation contains all the
ticket numbers available for configuration 1.

ATTRIBUTE NUMBER	DATA ATTRIBUTE	DATA REPRESENTATION
1	TICKET_NUMBER	8 Numeric

ENTITY NAME: Configure2
ENTITY DESCRIPTION: This relation contains all the
ticket numbers available for configuration 2.

ATTRIBUTE NUMBER	DATA ATTRIBUTE	DATA REPRESENTATION
1	TICKET_NUMBER	8 Numeric

ENTITY NAME: Configure3
ENTITY DESCRIPTION: This relation contains all the
ticket numbers available for configuration 3.

ATTRIBUTE NUMBER	DATA ATTRIBUTE	DATA REPRESENTATION
1	TICKET_NUMBER	8 Numeric

ENTITY NAME: Configure4
ENTITY DESCRIPTION: This relation contains all the
ticket numbers available for configuration 4.

ATTRIBUTE NUMBER	DATA ATTRIBUTE	DATA REPRESENTATION
1	TICKET_NUMBER	8 Numeric

ENTITY NAME: Configure5
ENTITY DESCRIPTION: This relation contains all the
ticket numbers available for configuration 5.

ATTRIBUTE NUMBER	DATA ATTRIBUTE	DATA REPRESENTATION
1	TICKET_NUMBER	8 Numeric

ENTITY NAME: Configure6
ENTITY DESCRIPTION: This relation contains all the ticket numbers available for configuration 6.

ATTRIBUTE NUMBER	DATA ATTRIBUTE	DATA REPRESENTATION
1	TICKET_NUMBER	8 Numeric

RESOURCES MASTER FILE

ENTITY NAME: resources
ENTITY DESCRIPTION: This relation contains every specific facility inventory resource available at the event center that can be used to support an event.

ATTRIBUTE NUMBER	DATA ATTRIBUTE	DATA REPRESENTATION
KEY 1	INVENTORY_NUMBER	8 Numeric
2	INVENTORY_NAME	50 Character
3	GROUP_NUMBER	8 Numeric

ENTITY NAME: committed
ENTITY DESCRIPTION: This relation contains all the facility inventory items that are committed to events.

ATTRIBUTE NUMBER	DATA ATTRIBUTE	DATA REPRESENTATION
KEY 1	INVENTORY_NUMBER	8 Numeric
KEY 2	EVENT_NUMBER	8 Numeric
KEY 3	DATE	8 Date
4	GROUP_NUMBER	8 Numeric

ENTITY NAME: personnel
ENTITY DESCRIPTION: This relation contains specific information on each employee.

ATTRIBUTE NUMBER	DATA ATTRIBUTE	DATA REPRESENTATION
KEY 1	EMPLOYEE_NUMBER	12 Numeric
2	EMPLOYEE_NAME	50 Character

3	POSITION_NUMBER	8 Numeric
4	POSITION_GROUP	8 Numeric

ENTITY NAME: position
ENTITY DESCRIPTION: This relation contains a description
of the responsibilities and title for every position at
the event center.

ATTRIBUTE NUMBER	DATA ATTRIBUTE	DATA REPRESENTATION
KEY 1	POSITION_NUMBER	8 Numeric
2	POSITION_TITLE	50 Character
3	RESPONSIBILITIES	80 Character

ENTITY NAME: schedule
ENTITY DESCRIPTION: This relation stores the staffing
schedules entered by the user for each event.

ATTRIBUTE NUMBER	DATA ATTRIBUTE	DATA REPRESENTATION
KEY 1	EVENT_NUMBER	8 Numeric
KEY 2	EMPLOYEE_NUMBER	12 Numeric
KEY 3	DATE	8 Date
4	START_TIME	8 Date
5	END_TIME	8 Date

ACCOUNTING MASTER FILE

ENTITY NAME: customers
ENTITY DESCRIPTION: This relation is used to store specific information on a receivable customer.

ATTRIBUTE NUMBER	DATA ATTRIBUTE	DATA REPRESENTATION
KEY 1	CUSTOMER_NUMBER	8 Numeric
2	CUSTOMER_NAME	50 Character
3	CUSTOMER_ADDRESS	50 Character
4	TERMS	20 Character
5	DATE	8 Date
6	BALANCE	5.2 Numeric

ENTITY NAME: receivables
ENTITY DESCRIPTION: This relation contains the entries for charges and payments of the customers.

ATTRIBUTE NUMBER	DATA ATTRIBUTE	DATA REPRESENTATION
KEY 1	EVENT_NUMBER	8 Numeric
KEY 2	CUSTOMER_NUMBER	8 Numeric
3	INVOICE_NUMBER	8 Character
4	DATE	8 Date
5	DEBIT_CREDIT	1 Character
6	AMOUNT	5.2 Numeric
7	DESCRIPTION	50 Numeric

ENTITY NAME: vendors
ENTITY DESCRIPTION: This relation contains specific information on accounts payable.

ATTRIBUTE NUMBER	DATA ATTRIBUTE	DATA REPRESENTATION
KEY 1	VENDOR_NUMBER	8 Numeric
2	VENDOR_NAME	50 Character
3	VENDOR_ADDRESS	50 Character
4	TERMS	20 Character
5	DATE	8 Date
6	BALANCE	5.2 Numeric

ENTITY NAME: payables
ENTITY DESCRIPTION: This relation contains entries for invoices from and payments to vendors.

ATTRIBUTE NUMBER	DATA ATTRIBUTE	DATA REPRESENTATION
KEY 1	EVENT_NUMBER	8 Numeric
KEY 2	VENDOR_NUMBER	8 Numeric
3	PO_NUMBER	3 Numeric
4	VENDOR_INVOICE_NO	12 Numeric
5	DATE	8 Date
6	DEBIT/CREDIT	1 Character
7	AMOUNT	5.2 Numeric
8	DESCRIPTION	3 Numeric

ENTITY NAME: accounts
ENTITY DESCRIPTION: This relation contains specific information on each account in the general ledger.

ATTRIBUTE NUMBER	DATA ATTRIBUTE	DATA REPRESENTATION
KEY 1	ACCOUNT_NUMBER	8 Numeric
2	ACCOUNT_NAME	50 Character
3	BALANCE_FORWARD	5.2 Numeric

```
ENTITY NAME: ledger
ENTITY DESCRIPTION: This relation contains all the gen-
eral ledger debit and credit entries.

ATTRIBUTE              DATA ATTRIBUTE              DATA
  NUMBER                                          REPRESENTATION
KEY 1                  EVENT_NUMBER               8 Numeric
KEY 2                  ACCOUNT_NUMBER             8 Numeric
    3                  DATE                       8 Date
    4                  DEBIT/CREDIT               1 Character
    5                  AMOUNT                     5.2 Numeric
    6                  REFERENCE                  3 Character
    7                  DESCRIPTION                50 Character
```

CONTROLS

The controls recommended by the vendor of choice are provided, and we have added some. A complete report includes administrative, procedural, and physical controls. A sampling of the details for each type of controls are presented in the following material.

Administrative

1. Staff certification of expertise will be required of all employees with access to financial programs. For ticket sales, students with prior experience in computer classes will work in pairs with individuals who have permanent part-time status.
2. Responsible parties will be bonded as a requirement for employment.
3. Access to the computer itself will be limited to computer center professionals who are responsible for maintaining the software and hardware.

Procedural

1. Input controls
   a. Passwords are unique to the functional requirements of the staff in the department where the terminal is located.
   b. Program screens include data verification upon entry.
   c. Protected fields guard against unreasonable entry of data into the data base.
   d. Event scheduling is matched against previously scheduled events on entry to avoid duplication in scheduling.
   e. Position numbers and event identification numbers are subject to automatic validation upon entry.
2. Data base controls
   a. Planned expenditures are matched against funds to ensure coverage.

b. Balanced debit and credit entries are required as with all standard accounting programs.
c. Minimal required accounting data are needed for all events.
d. Cash transactions, including cutting checks and ticket disbursement, are automatically screened for reasonableness.

3. Output controls
   a. Ticket disbursements are validated against available seating.
   b. Reports are available at specified locations as determined by electronic verification of terminal location.
   c. Exception reporting includes resource availability, vendor availability, and personnel scheduling conflicts.

4. Documentation controls
   a. Complete manuals are provided by the vendor.

SUMMARY

The goal of systems analysts in the detailed design phase is to bring together for the first time the semantic-oriented knowledge domain of business tasks, processes, and information with the syntactic-oriented technology processes. The key to the process of translating a general or conceptual design alternative into specifics is to decompose the proposed system into smaller parts called modules. A modular systems design simplifies changing, expanding, or contracting the system and increases user understanding of the system.

Most information systems involve portions of custom and off-the-shelf design. On one side of the coin, the systems analyst must determine the benefits of a customized system's ability to meet users' requirements against its high design cost. On the other side of the coin, the systems analyst must be aware of the problems in adapting a minimum cost, off-the-shelf package to the changing requirements of users.

Although one goal of the detailed systems design phase is to prepare precise specifications for the next phase of systems implementation, another major goal is to design a system with which users feel confident and comfortable working. This goal can be achieved by addressing the user/system interface and human factors through the application of the design methods of user categorization, message formulation, directing users' attention, menu design, forms fill-in, command language, natural language, and direct visual manipulation.

The objective of detailed design of output is to define the form and content of all printed reports and documents, as well as any screens produced by the information system. The quality of output, however, is only as good as the input that generates the reports, documents, and screens. Therefore, when the systems analyst prepares specifics about the content and format of input, attention must be paid to the people who will be collecting and entering the input. Here the systems analyst might find it appropriate to use the design methods of forms fill-in, textual specification, query by forms, and question and answer dialogues. The systems analyst must also give consideration to the existing methods of data entry in the organization in light of advancements in data entry technology.

A number of alternatives are available to the systems analyst when work begins on the detailed design of the data base block. After the systems analyst has mapped reality into entities and their attributes, and defined the relationship among the entities, a choice must be made among a hierarchical, network, or relational data model design.

Controls are an essential part of every information system. During the detailed systems design phase the systems analyst specifies input controls to keep erroneous data out of the system, processing controls to catch errors that elude detection at input or that are created during processing, and output controls to ensure that output is not lost, corrupted, or stolen. Additionally, data base access controls are designated.

After the composition of the procedures and processing programs for the system are formulated, the systems analyst may have to select and put together a hardware platform that supports the other building blocks. The systems analyst should give particular attention to alternatives, such as terminal-to-mainframe, host-to-host, host-to-mini, LAN-to-LAN, and LAN-to-WAN.

The culmination of the systems analyst's work in this phase is the completion of the Final Detailed Systems Design Report. This fifth documented deliverable of the systems development methodology contains program specifications, micro instructions, diagrams, and the specifics for the six building blocks of the system to be implemented.

IMPORTANT TERMS

audit trail

batch input

check digit

cohesion

command language

coupling

customized design

desktop publishing

direct visual manipulation

electronic spreadsheet

embedded menu

fan-out/fan-in

Final Detailed Systems Design Report

forms fill-in

frequent light user

frequent power user

interactive design

interface library

message formulation

modularity

natural language

network menu

novice user

occasional knowledgeable user

off-the-shelf design

printer layout form

procedure

query by form (QBF)

question and answer (QA) dialogue

reasonableness test

report writer

screen display layout form

screen input

semantic knowledge

serial menu

star network

strategic information systems planning (SISP)

syntactic knowledge

systems development methodology
(SDM)

textual specification

token-ring local area network (LAN)

transaction log

tree menu

what-you-see-is-what-you-get
(WYSIWYG)

wide area network (WAN)

ASSIGNMENT

REVIEW QUESTIONS

19.1 Define what is meant by the semantic and syntactic knowledge domains of systems development.

19.2 List five basic rules in developing and designing modules. What are the benefits of good
modular design?

19.3 Describe the trade-offs between a fully customized system designed from scratch, and a
total system supported by a canned, off-the-shelf package purchased or leased from
vendors.

19.4 One goal of detailed systems design is to design a system with which users feel confident
and comfortable working. What are the benefits of attaining a user-centered design goal
and what design methods are particularly applicable to the user/system interface?

19.5 When designing the user/system interface, systems analysts must understand users and
their tasks fully. List the various categories of users, and identify factors that would enter
into the design interface for each of these users.

19.6 List some "do's and don'ts" words to use in message formulation.

19.7 Assume menu selection can be made by keyboarding, pointing, touching the screen, and
by voice input. Describe five different classifications of menu design.

19.8 What are command languages? natural languages? What kind of users is each language
intended?

19.9 When documenting output on printer layout forms, many systems analysts use special
notations to indicate facts or characteristics about the fields that will appear on a document
or report. Describe what X, 9, Z, and $ mean.

19.10 How can the capabilities of a screen be used to highlight report data?

19.11 List the five logical sections of a screen display.

19.12 The systems analyst should specify controls to keep erroneous input out of the information system. List four levels on which input controls can be applied.

19.13 Explain how an authorization table is used to control access to the data base.

19.14 What is the purpose of writing procedures? List six general questions a procedure should
answer.

QUESTIONS FOR DISCUSSION

19.15 List some specifications to be considered in evaluating the system's inputs.

19.16 In what respect are rules, captions, and column headings related to forms design? Explain.

19.17 If you were asked to organize a forms control program for your organization, show how you would proceed in planning this activity.

19.18 List and discuss the types of reports that might be produced by a system.

19.19 All output from a system should be specified in writing, usually by the use of special forms such as record layouts, printer layouts, forms layouts, and specialized listings. Output to be produced usually depends on the following considerations:

1. The reason for it.
2. The data needed to produce it.
3. The format.
4. The volume.
5. The frequency.

Elaborate on each topic.

19.20 The user of computer output reports complains to the systems analyst that she cannot read or understand the report. The user makes the statement, "It is all Greek to me." What should have been done to avoid this situation?

19.21 What is the scope of input design? That is, where does it start and where does it end?

19.22 Structured English is an approach to programming that stresses modularity and a structured method of problem solving. What are the major reasons that such an approach is advantageous in programming?

19.23 Discuss the various controls outlined in the chapter and explain their role in systems design.

EXERCISES AND PROBLEMS

19.24 List and discuss several major requirements for good document design.

19.25 Transfer the items from the following source document into a record.

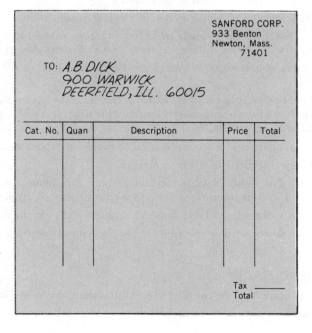

19.26 Construct an example of an output report used in any business.

19.27 The form shown here is an example of a poor layout. List all the errors you can discover in this form.

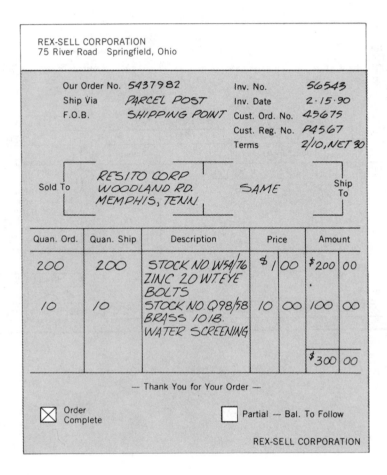

REX-SELL CORPORATION
75 River Road   Springfield, Ohio

Our Order No. *5437982*		Inv. No.	*56543*
Ship Via *PARCEL POST*		Inv. Date	*2·15·90*
F.O.B. *SHIPPING POINT*		Cust. Ord. No.	*45675*
		Cust. Reg. No.	*P4567*
		Terms	*2/10, NET 30*

Sold To *RESITO CORP WOODLAND RD. MEMPHIS, TENN.* *SAME* Ship To

Quan. Ord.	Quan. Ship	Description	Price	Amount
200	*200*	*STOCK NO. W54/76 ZINC 20 WT EYE BOLTS*	*$1 00*	*$200 00*
10	*10*	*STOCK NO. Q98/58 BRASS 1018. WATER SCREENING*	*10 00*	*100 00*
				$300 00

— Thank You for Your Order —

☒ Order Complete   ☐ Partial — Bal. To Follow

REX-SELL CORPORATION

19.28 Draw an example of a printer layout sheet for a trial balance format.

19.29 The following is an example of a finished business form. Show the design of the business form on a form layout sheet.

New England Business Service, Inc. Townsend, Mass. 01469
(617) 597-8711

| NEBS | BIM PUBLISHERS
P.O. Box 4101
Memphis, TN 38104 | INVOICE | PLEASE RETURN
THIS STUB WITH
YOUR PAYMENT. |

Invoice No.	Invoice Date	Date Shipped	Control No.	Code No.	Prepaid Amount	File Code
41249422-1	4·19·90	5·19·90	319910	62638	12.75	381048MPB

Quantity	Product	Product Description	Amount
500	78·6	P.S. MAILING LABELS
PARCEL POST 1.18	12.75 *

If you ordered products not listed on this invoice they will be billed and shipped separately. Write our invoice number(s) on checks and correspondence

Make checks payable to:

NEBS Inc.
Townsend,
MA
01469

Thank You!

*New prices effective 6/1/90.

| Terms: | F.O.B. TOWNSEND, MA   NET 7 DAYS | .00 |

INVOICE NO.
41249422-1

Pay Amount 7.00

19.30 The following is a hierarchical data structure of a payroll file. List the data definition of the hierarchical structure.

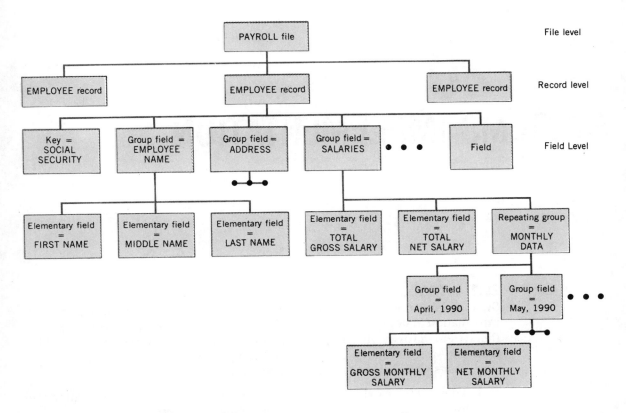

19.31 Construct a printer layout of a customer master list.

BIBLIOGRAPHY

CLARKE, RAYMOND T., and CHARLES A. PRINS. *Contemporary Systems Analysis and Design.* Belmont, Calif.: Wadsworth, 1986.

CROKER, ALBERT. "Improvements in Database Concurrency Control with Locking." *Journal of Management Information Systems,* Fall 1987.

DAVIS, GORDON B., and MARGRETHE H. OLSON. *Management Information Systems,* 2nd ed. New York: McGraw-Hill, 1985.

KARIMI, JAHANGIR. "Automated Software Design Methodology." *Journal of Management Information Systems,* Winter 1986–1987.

KARON, PAUL. "Software Metaphor: Where the Mind Meets the Power of the PC." *PC Week,* September 15, 1987.

KONSYNSKI, BENN R. "Advances in Information System Design." *Journal of Management Information Systems,* Winter 1984–1985.

PETERS, LAWRENCE J. *Advanced Structured Analysis and Design.* Englewood Cliffs, N.J.: Prentice Hall, 1988.

SHNEIDERMAN, BEN. *Designing the Human Interface.* Reading, Mass.: Addison-Wesley, 1987.

20
SYSTEMS IMPLEMENTATION

20.1 INTRODUCTION

Systems implementation requires several tasks be performed before the new information system "crosses the Rubicon." Once the tasks are performed and the system "crosses" the implementation "river," primary responsibility shifts from the systems analyst to end users and operations personnel.

The specific objectives of this chapter are:

1. To provide an overview of how to prepare for systems implementation and list the elements of the Final Implementation Report.
2. To discuss how to test technology.
3. To explain the training and educating task.
4. To show how the programming tasks should be carried out.
5. To present different ways to form programming organization structures.
6. To demonstrate program testing procedures.
7. To analyze ways to test input, output, data base, and controls.
8. To examine conversion methods.
9. To consider implementation follow-up.
10. To demonstrate the NSU Tigers Event Center Final Implementation Report.

20.2 PREPARING TO IMPLEMENT

Although a system may be well designed and properly developed, a major part of its success is contingent on how well systems implementation is planned and executed. A system that does not meet users' requirements and is full of errors creates a stigma that remains long after the problems have been resolved, if they ever are.

To avoid such a "credibility gap," a Final Implementation Report should be prepared. The key component of this documented deliverable is the implementation plan based on a program evaluation and review technique (PERT) diagram or Gantt chart.

The Last Documented Deliverable

The systems development methodology's (SDM's) last documented deliverable is the Final Implementation Report. If the new system is simple and narrow in scope, this report is also simple. If, however, the new system represents a major change from the old system, then the Final Implementation Report is usually quite involved.

This last report differs from the SDM's other documented deliverables because part of it must be prepared before the implementation phase begins and the remainder of the report is completed after the new system is implemented. Before implementation work begins, a detailed implementation plan is prepared. During implementation, documentation is prepared for procedures and programs, tests are conducted, and test results are logged, along with results of conversion, follow-up, and acceptance.

Implementation Plan

Generally, the implementation plan, a key part of the Final Implementation Report, is actually prepared several weeks or months in advance of the technology's arrival, depending on scope and complexity of the total systems project. For a very simple project such as installing a software package for a PC, actual implementation may require an hour or less. In this case, the Final Implementation Report may be a brief memo containing user instructions.

For a major systems project built from scratch, the implementation planning lead time is measured in months and entails the coordination and scheduling of a number of activities and tasks performed by an implementation team made up of systems analysts who designed the system, managers and various staff, vendor representatives, primary users, programmers, and a host of technicians. A typical big systems project implementation plan is illustrated in Figure 20.1. At this point, technology has already been evaluated and selected. Purchase orders are released to acquire the selected technology building block. Site preparation begins immediately, so it is ready to receive the technology platform from the vendor(s).

A programming team is formed and programmers begin review of the design specifications to ensure a clear understanding before coding starts. If certain personnel are needed, they are selected and hired. Training begins immediately for all personnel and users and continues until it is completed. When the technology arrives, its site is ready for installation.

The technology is subjected to a variety of tests to make sure it is operating efficiently and as intended. Programs are also subjected to various test cases to ensure a high level of program reliability. Test cases are also created and applied

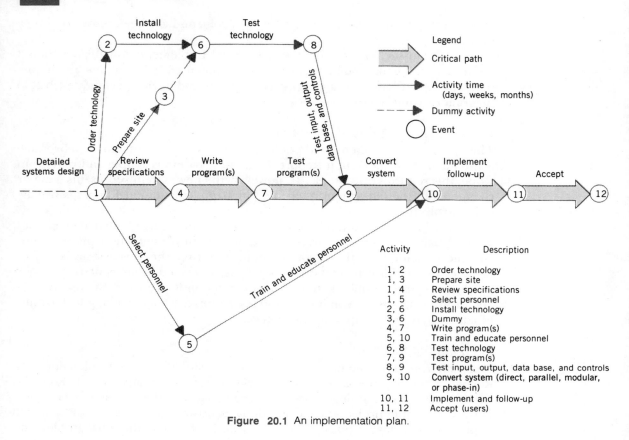

Figure 20.1 An implementation plan.

to input, output, data base, and controls to make sure that the total system is working as expected.

If test results are successful, the system goes through a conversion process, such as direct, parallel, modular, or phase-in. Usually, an implementation follow-up is performed to make sure the system is successfully converted and is operating as planned using live data. Fine-tuning may be appropriate to enhance the new system's performance.

During this time, users or their representatives have been running an acceptance test. If everything at this stage of the game is copacetic—smooth runs, correct results, clear and comprehensive documentation, trained personnel, and clear operating procedures—the system moves from development status to operational status. This "crossing of the Rubicon" indicates acceptance by users and operations personnel.

20.3 TECHNOLOGY TESTING

In Chapter 18, we presented ways to evaluate vendors and their technology. Before the technology is finally accepted, however, additional tests should be conducted. Tools used to perform a variety of technology tests include burn-in, job accounting system, hardware and software monitors, performance utilities, and ergonomics.

Burn-in Test and Site Preparation

Before a vendor delivers the technology, a diagnosis of the technology should be run at the vendor's site to simulate several weeks of continuous operation. This "burn-in test" checks for shorts in the electrical system, switches, connectors, and various components.

While burn-in tests are performed, site preparation for the technology should be near completion. Further, this site should meet environmental standards to ensure valid acceptance testing once the technology arrives from the vendor.

Adequate space should be provided for each piece of equipment and furniture. Appropriate wiring, cables, supplies, ventilation, and air conditioning should be installed to ensure a viable and clean environment. Antistatic comfort mats and carpets should be laid. Sufficient shelving, stands, tables, and disk and tape storage trays and cabinets should be made available. The human factors design force requires acoustic privacy panels, printer enclosures and acoustic printer cushions, and ergonomically designed furniture and workstations.

A properly prepared site ensures quick and easy installation when the technology arrives. Furthermore, on-site technology tests can begin with a high degree of assurance that if errors are detected or failures occur, they will not be caused by site inadequacies.

Job Accounting System

This system can be used to test design efficiency, help in capacity planning, and project growth patterns. IBM's system management facility (SMF) is an example. Among many things, it can be used to obtain large amounts of useful test information about a computer system's operating environment. It shows who used the system and how long they used it, along with the data files accessed. SMF indicates the amount of available space on direct access storage devices and gives basic error statistics for magnetic tape files. Other vendors provide similar software packages.

Hardware Monitor

A hardware monitor consists of sensors connected to the computer's innards. They measure CPU active, CPU wait, disk seek, disk data transfer, disk mount, tape active, tape rewind, and internal memory timings and utilization. The sensors are, in turn, connected to a small computer that records various signals. With sufficient utilization statistics, properly evaluated, the total computer equipment budget may be reduced by improving overall efficiency through changing the CPU, dropping channels, or reconfiguring tapes and disks. The broad purpose of using a hardware monitor is to match the "horsepower" of the computer to the demands of the information system.

Software Monitor

To evaluate overall system performance, a software monitor can be used in conjunction with a hardware monitor and a job accounting system. A software monitor is a program that resides in the computer system to be tested. Software components commonly measured are operating systems, support software, and application programs. Measurement of the operating system identifies inefficient sections of code. The existence of such sections could compel management to ask the vendor for improvement, or if this is not possible, other commercially available software might be considered as a replacement.

Support software falls in the gray area between user programs and the operating system. Although handled in the system much like user programs, support software is written by the vendor and appears to the ordinary user as part of the operating system. Compilers, communication programs, and utilities are examples of support systems. With compilers and communication programs, the user is not seeking to modify the code of such complex programs, but rather to know what they cost in terms of resources. The aim is to ask the vendor to improve the program or to investigate the feasibility of using alternative software.

Application or user programs are measured to determine resource utilization and code efficiency. These measurements record and report the amount of time a program used each resource, such as internal memory, disk, and tape. For example, a program may request eight tape drives, even though it would normally need only four. If the installation rations tape drives, the tester should ask the programmer to change the program.

Another important aspect of resource analysis is the determination of input/output activity and block sizes. Sometimes, for example, a program might require 10 more physical I/Os than necessary because records are improperly blocked.

A software monitor can isolate heavy paging areas in virtual storage systems. Heavy paging can occur when application programs access routines repeatedly, causing a "thrashing" of pages condition to occur. The CPU is forced to spend excess time accessing pages from and storing them on disk. With analysis and program rewrites, this program inefficiency can be reduced.

Performance Utilities

Data set reorganizers reduce wasted file storage on disk and improve throughput by reducing access time. Virtual storage code reorganizers reduce resources used in paging. Code optimizers reduce consumption of resources by eliminating unnecessary program statements. Schedulers help meet timing demands and balance job mix.

Ergonomics

Clearly, the health, well-being, and comfort of personnel who are going to operate and use the technology is a paramount consideration. These human factor goals, to a great extent, rest on how well the technology and its environment is designed ergonomically.

The best way to test ergonomics is to put the users and operating personnel in a real work environment and observe them in action and interview them periodically. Working for several hours at poorly designed workstations and around noisy printers, for example, causes eyestrain, backaches, headaches, fatigue, and nervous tension. If these are the results of the ergonomics test, redesign should be performed immediately to alleviate, if not prevent, these and other ill effects.

20.4 TRAINING AND EDUCATING PERSONNEL

People design, develop, operate, and maintain the system, and they use its output. If a new information system is to be implemented successfully, everyone who is affected by it must be made aware, first, of their individual system responsibilities and, second, of what the system provides them.

Ideally, training should be performed before the technology's installed. While this is not always feasible, as much preinstallation training as possible should be done. Otherwise, the system will sit idle while users and staff are being trained. Discussion of various training and educating methods follows.

Training and Educating Categories

Users of information and operating personnel represent two broad categories of people who must receive education and training.

Users of Information

This category of personnel includes general management staff, specialists, and personnel in various functional areas, including salespeople, accountants, and production schedulers. This category might also include customers, vendors, government officials, and other stakeholders of the organization. It is generally termed "education" when the users of the information are informed of what the system requires and provides. The educational process for many members of this group actually begins in the analysis phase when they identify their information requirements. The emphasis at this later point in development is directed toward explaining how these requirements are met by the system.

Operating Personnel

This category of personnel includes all individuals involved in preparing input, processing data, and operating and maintaining both the logical and physical components of the system. It also includes those persons responsible for direct control over the system. Generally, we call their educational process "training." Training operating personnel has two dimensions that must be considered by the analyst. First, operating personnel must be trained initially to run the new system. Second, training must be provided to this general category of personnel on a continuing basis as the system is modified, or as new personnel are hired. The importance of recognizing this second aspect of training will become clear as we discuss the various methods that might be used to provide acceptable training when the system is implemented initially.

Approaches to Educating and Training Personnel

Psychologists and educators have demonstrated that different educating and training objectives call for a variety of educating and training approaches. A lecture is appropriate to explain to a group of users generally how the new system operates, whereas a "learn-by-doing approach" might be used to train new operations personnel. Likewise, many people can perform any given job satisfactorily after they have performed that job once or a few times. Some approaches used by systems analysts include the following:

1. *Seminars and Group Instruction.* This approach allows the analyst to reach many people at one time. It is particularly useful when the analyst is presenting an overview of the system. Additionally, this approach is worthwhile in large organizations where many people perform the same tasks.

2. *Procedural Training.* This approach provides an individual with the written procedures describing his or her activities as the primary method of learning. Usually the individual has an opportunity to ask questions and pose problems concerning the procedure, either in a group session or individually. An extension of this technique is to provide a formal writeup of the system, particularly of the outputs, to each affected user.

3. *Tutorial Training.* As the term implies, this approach to training is more personal and, consequently, fairly expensive. In conjunction with other training approaches, however, this technique can eliminate any remaining void that prevents a satisfactory understanding of the system. In systems in which certain tasks are highly complex or particularly vital to successful operations, tutorial training may be necessary to achieve the desired results.

4. *Simulation.* An important training technique for operating personnel is the simulated work environment. This environment can be created relatively easily by reproducing data, procedures, and any required equipment and allowing the individual to perform the proposed activities until an acceptable level of performance is attained. Although simulation seems to be an expensive training method, fewer errors and less rework usually result when the individual is later placed in an operating environment.

5. *On-the-Job Training.* Perhaps the most widely used approach to training operating personnel is simply to put them to work. Usually the individual is assigned simple tasks and given specific instructions on what is to be done and how it is to be done. As these initial tasks are mastered, additional tasks are assigned. The learning curve in this approach can be quite lengthy and, in many cases, what appears to be immediate results or production can be very deceptive. Moreover, if a particular operation is highly complex and difficult to master, the individual designated to carry it out may become frustrated and request a transfer.

6. *Information Center.* As mentioned several times in this text, an information center is an effective approach to training and guiding users, fol-

lowing up, and providing ongoing support. The attitude of the information center staff should be, "What can we do to help?" They can develop a brief introductory course and an equipment or application demonstration, provide individualized training, help users apply a particular software package to a specific business problem, feature case studies that cover information systems problems and applications of a particular industry and company, and arrange workshops and seminars. The goal of the information center is to encourage users to expand and explore the information system's benefits and services and to show how users can solve their own problems.

The first step in determining training requirements and training approaches is to compile a list of all the tasks required by the new system and the skills needed to perform them. The next step is to prepare an inventory of skills already available. The difference between these lists indicates the number of skilled personnel to be trained (some may also be hired who are already trained). The amount of time spent in training relates to the levels of difficulty and complexity of each task.

General Considerations When Choosing Training Approaches

The analysts's primary objective during systems development is to provide training for existing personnel so that the new system can be implemented. Careful planning at this time, however, can result in a meaningful training mechanism that should reduce employee turnover and that can be used by the organization on a continuing basis. This consideration is important because employee turnover is expensive and affects all levels in the organization. When a training approach is developed that meets both objectives, the analyst should not hesitate to construct more expensive aids and programs for this initial requirement. For example, full-scale training sessions, simulated facilities, programmed instruction, computer-assisted instruction, and videotapes can rarely be justified for a one-time training effort. Their benefit rests on reuse on a continuing basis.

A second, corresponding consideration might be termed *direct* versus *indirect* training. Once a system is implemented, the systems analyst often is reassigned to an entirely new area of the organization. Consequently, the analyst is not available to assist with the day-to-day systems problems with either operating personnel or users. To ensure that these problems can be addressed satisfactorily and resolved, the analyst can take a more indirect role during initial training. In other words, a select group of supervisors might be trained in the areas of data preparation and operations and allowed to conduct individual training for both clerical workers and user personnel. With this approach the analyst is rapidly removed from all but the exceptional problems related to the system. In most organizations this approach is highly desirable.

20.5 PROGRAMMING

Programming is a process performed by programmers to write instructions (also called code) that are executed by computers. The code produced by programmers is based on specifications prepared by the systems analyst during the detailed systems design phase. These specifications are typically in the form of one or a combination of structured English or pseudocode, Nassi-Shneiderman diagrams, Warnier-Orr diagrams, structure charts, HIPO, decision tables, and the like.

Unless a large part of the new system uses off-the-shelf software, the writing of application programs is usually one of the largest single activities in the systems implementation phase. Because of the sheer magnitude of the programming effort, any productivity or code enhancement practices management of the information systems facility can adopt are likely to result in substantial economies. Described in this section are programming practices that have potential for producing such programming economies.

Eliminate Unstructured Programming

Some authorities estimate that over 80 billion lines of COBOL code are in operation today, representing a $2.5 trillion investment. Most of this COBOL code is unstructured, making it difficult, if not impossible, to maintain. Some say it's like Alexander the Great's Gordian Knot; others call it messy spaghetti. Some researchers have found that about one out of four changes to such unstructured code introduces a new bug.

To eliminate unstructured code from finding its way into new systems, programming managers should prevent the use of interparagraph GOTOs, ALTER statements, and "fall throughs." Moreover, a policy that requires structured programming for all application programs should be set and followed by all application programmers.

If an organization already has a great deal of spaghetti-like code, a restructuring program can be applied to reengineer the present software system. For example, a COBOL restructuring program sifts through the code and processes it into structured code, creating documentation along the way. This restructuring works like a comb pulled through the code to eliminate snags and dead code.

Making programs easy to read is one of the main benefits of restructuring code. These newly structured programs are better understood by maintenance programmers, thus increasing their productivity and reducing substantially the heavy maintenance backlog burden that exists in most organizations.

Program restructuring, however, doesn't work magic. Bad code is still bad code, now it's just structured bad code. Also, restructuring programs doesn't replace the need for good planning and documentation.

Restructuring programs available are COBOL/SF, from IBM; Superstructure, from Group Operations; Recoder, from Language Technology; and Structured Retrofit, from Peat Marwick Mitchell Catalyst Goup. Peat Marwick Mitchell Catalyst Group and Language Technology (LTI) offer restructuring as a service as well as selling restructuring packages directly to clients.

Structured Programming Techniques

Structured programming techniques require programmers to follow a particular discipline mainly characterized by the prohibition of the interparagraph GOTO statement. That is why some people refer to structured programming as GOTO-less programming. Application of modular techniques, discussed in Chapter 19, also plays a major role in building structured programs.

Hierarchy of Modules

A structured program is organized hierarchically, with one and only one root or boss module at the top as illustrated in Figure 20.2. Execution begins with the root module. From the root, control is passed down the structure level by level to other modules. Any module can pass control to a module at the next lower level. Program control enters a module at its entry point and must leave at its exit point. Control returns to the invoking module when the invoked module completes execution. When the program finishes execution, control returns to the root.

Each program module can be coded, tested, and executed as independent programs. The modules range from a few statements up to a page of code.

The adoption of a modular approach to program development has several benefits. First, programming productivity is improved by parceling out the more difficult modules to the more skilled programmers. Second, processing efficiency can be enhanced by focusing optimization efforts on the modules used most frequently. Third, programs are more maintainable because changes can be isolated to local modules rather than cause widespread change.

Structured Program Functions

Structured programming is based on the mathematically proven structure theorem, which states that any program task can be structured as a proper program module with one entry and one exit, using as logic structures only the following program functions:

1. *Sequence.* Statements are executed in a stated sequence. For example,

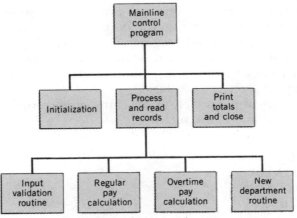

Figure 20.2 A structured program.

COBOL statements are executed in sequence as follows:

```
MOVE ZEROES TO AMOUNT-OUT
MULTIPLY HOURS-WORKED BY RATE GIVING GROSS-PAY
SUBTRACT DEDUCTIONS FROM GROSS-PAY GIVING NET-PAY
```

2. *Selection Based on Condition.*   A set of statements are executed only if a stated condition applies, based on an IF-THEN-ELSE construct. For example,

```
IF HOURS-WORKED GREATER THAN 40
    THEN COMPUTE GROSS-PAY WITH OVERTIME RATE
    ELSE COMPUTE GROSS-PAY WITH REGULAR RATE
ENDIF
```

3. *Repetition.*   A set of statements is repeated on the basis of a test. One type of repetition control is DOWHILE where the termination test is applied before the set of statements is executed. The other type is DOUNTIL where the termination test is applied after the set of statements is executed. For example,

```
PERFORM READ-MASTER UNTIL
    RECORD-TYPE EQUALS 999
PERFORM UPDATE-CUSTOMER WHILE
    CUST-NO IS VALID
```

Other Structured Programming Standards

In addition to improving the division of labor, testing, and maintenance, structured programs are designed to be readable through the use of self-documentation. Standards promote a consistent programming style within an organization, thereby making it easier for other people, especially maintenance programmers, to understand programs.

Programming standards demand consistency in file, table, record, variable, and module names. Comments are also used liberally to document functions of a module and explain complex logic.

Indentation of program logic structures on the printed page clearly shows logic flow and relationships, such as

```
IF a THEN
    b function
    c function
    IF p THEN
        IF s THEN
            g function
```

```
    ELSE
        DOWHILE h
            d function
        ENDDO
    ENDIF
    k function
    END function
ENDIF
```

Also, each sentence begins a new line, and subsequent lines belonging to a sentence are indented.

Programming Aids

Programming aids reduce the time and effort of writing code. They also often provide clearer documentation and improve the accuracy of coding. The following represent some of the more popular programming aids.

1. *Shorthand Aid.* This programming support tool provides abbreviations (P for PERFORM and M for MOVE) of required COBOL words and phrases, which can reduce the coding effort by as much as 40 percent, or more. For example, a programmer writes ED, CS, SC, IBM-370. OC, IBM-370. IOFC, SEL TRANSACTION TO UT-S-TRANS. The shorthand processor will output

```
ENVIRONMENT DIVISION.
CONFIGURATION SECTION.
SOURCE-COMPUTER.  IBM-370.
OBJECT-COMPUTER.  IBM-370.
INPUT-OUTPUT SECTION.
FILE-CONTROL.
    SELECT TRANSACTION
    ASSIGN TO UT-S-TRANS.
```

2. *Subroutine Library.* A directory provides the names, descriptions, and access procedures for subroutines that have already been written and tested. These subroutines may be standard across industries such as certain statistical routines, or they may be applicable to particular applications within the company, such as order-entry processing. When needed as part of a new program, they are simply called from the subroutine library by their name, such as CALL ORDER-ENTRY.

3. *Copy Routines.* Many lines of code in COBOL's ENVIRONMENT DIVISION and DATA DIVISION are used over and over again. A copy routine enables large sections of this code to be copied from a library into the new program. These routines are written once but copied many times.

4. *Decision Table Processors.* Much of the code in the PROCEDURE DI-

VISION of COBOL is in IF-THEN form. If the decision table prepared by the systems analyst as part of specifications is correct, the source code generated by the decision table processor will also be correct.

5. *Editors.*   Text editors permit programmers to make a variety of changes, deletions, and additions easily. Syntax-directed editors list syntax errors during the editing process.

6. *Workstation Network.*   Programmers can do their work online and in real time at workstations connected to other workstations with print servers, file servers, and other facilities such as programming aids we just covered and various debugging facilities. Moreover, such a network speeds up communications in the programming team.

Debugging, Testing, and Documentation Aids

A number of aids exist to help programmers test program logic, detect bugs, and document results. These aids are discussed as follows:

1. *Traces.*   Traces show the status of memory locations at different stages throughout a program's execution, identify invalid instructions or data that caused the interrupt, and attempt to correct the invalid instruction or data that caused the interrupt so the program can continue processing.

2. *Automatic Flowcharters.*   A flowcharter package accepts COBOL programs, as well as other languages, and provides a conventional flowchart. This flowchart can be used as documentation of the program or as an aid in reviewing it.

3. *Cross-referencers.*   Cross-reference listings usually are part of automatic flowcharter packages. Listed are each data name, procedure name, file name, and the names of procedures referencing these elements. In addition, a cross-reference sequential listing, called a procedure skeleton, gives each procedure name in the PROCEDURE DIVISION, together with all procedures referenced by that procedure and all procedures referring to that procedure.

4. *Test Data Generators.*   This package automatically produces test files to drive a program through all its branches.

5. *Performance Monitors.*   This system keeps track of those parts of a program in which it spends most of its execution time.

6. *Program Librarian.*   A program librarian such as PANVALET is designed for storage, security, and documentation of all application programs and the job control language (JCL). A large information system can usually store all its application programs on a hard disk under control of the librarian package. This program librarian provides a directory listing of names of all application programs along with authorized users; program status such as production, test, active, or inactive; and a complete audit trail of program changes. When management no longer wants a program in the library, its status is changed from enable to disable. This change flags a program for deletion. Only authorized personnel have access to change a program or delete it from the library.

20.6 PROGRAMMING ORGANIZATION STRUCTURES

Today's software is more complex and powerful than ever before and represents around 80 percent of total large information systems' costs. Therefore, its development demands more organization and management than ever before.

Some authorities say that worldwide costs of software development and maintenance runs over $150 billion per year, and the gap continues to widen between demand for qualified software personnel and supply. The Department of Defense states this demand is growing at three times the rate of supply.

A single company cannot do much about supply and demand of programmers, but it can do something about its own reliance on programming needs and programming productivity by applying information system techniques discussed and illustrated throughout this book. These techniques include the systems development methodology, prototyping, fourth-generation languages (4GLs), data base management systems and easy-to-use query languages, various modeling diagrams, computer-aided software engineering (CASE) packages, expert systems, off-the-shelf packages, structured programming, and various programming aids.

Unfortunately, the use of these techniques will not eliminate programming needs entirely or reduce management's responsibility for sufficient and careful consideration of how the programming effort is organized. Programming organization will indeed affect programming productivity and the quality of the system implemented. The following sections examine three types of organization structures for programmers. Each has its strengths and weaknesses.

SHAPING UP THE PROGRAMMING FUNCTION

In his 1986 book, *Nations at Risk,* Ed Yourdon describes the American programming culture as an "overpaid, sloppy, error-prone, labor-intensive, ragtag band of anarchists."

He says, "Americans refer to mistakes in their software as 'bugs.' Referring to a bug implies that it's an independent life form that somehow crawled into your computer all by itself, and it's not your fault. The Japanese refer to the same things as 'spoilage,' which has connotations of personal guilt and all sorts of things that we don't have as American programmers."

Excerpted from John Desmond, "The Friendly Master," *Software Magazine,* February 1988, pp. 38–43.

Traditional Programming Organization Structures

Chapter 1 presented key organizational factors that play a role in dictating the kind of information system developed and deployed in organizations. The same analysis may also help us determine the way in which programmers are organized to perform their tasks better.

In many traditional organizations, programmers are simply members of a programming group or department and are assigned work as it becomes available. If new programming tasks are relatively small and the organization has many application programs to maintain, programmers organized along divisional or functional lines may be sufficient.

A project-based team structure is often employed when a prototyping approach to systems development is used, and is especially compatible in matrix organizations. Often, the project team is composed of members from the user group and information systems area. This kind of programming team organization generally works well in systems development with a high degree of uncertainty.

If a programming team approach is used, programming team sizes should be relatively small, between two and eight members. Larger teams tend to spend most of their time communicating rather than programming. Moreoover, the use of large teams makes it difficult to partition programming into modules because such modularization often results in poor cohesion and complex coupling. With smaller teams, modularization is easier and structured programming standards can be imposed and monitored.

Adaptive Programming Teams

Adaptive programming teams are composed of 5 to 10 programmers. These teams are informal although a titular team leader may emerge, or some form of leadership may rotate among its members. Work to be carried out is discussed by the team as a whole and the tasks are allocated to each member according to ability and experience. More complex tasks are carried out by senior team members. Simpler, lower-level tasks are assigned to junior members.

Team members are responsible for examining and evaluating one another's work. This relationship is supposed to foster a feeling of joint responsibility for the quality of the program, because programs are regarded as team property rather than personal property. This way, no one's programming ego is threatened. That is why this approach to programming is often called "egoless" programming. This free flow of information and democrary increases team spirit with a resulting increase in productivity. If this is indeed the case, then an adaptive team is especially suited for programming tasks where a high level of uncertainty exists.

On the other hand, if an adaptive or egoless team is comprised mostly of incompetent members, the results will be unsatisfactory. No definite authority exists to direct work and remove incompetents from the team. The team will flounder, suck up money, and eventually fail. Even adaptive teams with moderately experienced and competent members restrict innovative and highly efficient programming because the team culture enforces uniformity of behavior and punishes any deviations from the norm.

Chief Programmer Team

In 1971, IBM completed a project for The New York Times that required around 83,000 lines of source code. The system was completed on time after less than 24 months and 11 programmer-years of work. Only 21 errors were found during testing and 25 more during the system's first year of operation. The programming organization structure used has come to be known as the chief programmer team, a special form of project-based teams.

Chief Programmer Team Definition

The chief programmer of the team manages all technical aspects of the project, including preparation of the program design and supervision of coding, testing, integrating modules, and documentation.

The chief programmer is supported by a lead assistant, who acts as the main backup person on the project. The lead assistant also communicates with everyone else on the team and acts as a "sounding board" for the chief programmer's ideas. Depending on the size of the project, these two people are supported by some or all of the following personnel:

1. *Support Programmers.* These programmers are needed for large projects that cannot be handled by the chief programmer and backup programmer alone. These support programmers generally code lower-level modules.
2. *Librarian.* This person maintains the program production library, indexes files of compilations and tests, and keeps source code and object code libraries up to date.
3. *Administrator.* The administrator handles all nontechnical support details, such as budgets, personnel matters, and space allocation. The administrator also interacts with the rest of the organization's bureaucracy.
4. *Editor.* Even though the chief programmer creates the systems documentation, the editor is responsible for editing and critiquing the documentation, for searching out references about it, and for overseeing all phases of documentation reproduction and distribution. In smaller projects, the editor may also perform librarian duties.
5. *Toolsmith.* The toolsmith is a programmer who writes special programs to interface with the operating system software. It is common for a toolsmith to be on several chief programmer teams.
6. *Tester.* The tester makes up test data for individual programs and systems testing. The tester should be independent from the programming function.
7. *Language Specialist.* The language specialist understands all the nuances of a language and acts as a consultant for several chief programmers. The language specialist may also write small programs that demand a high level of expertise in the programming language.
8. *Program Clerk.* The program clerk keeps track of all technical records for the programming team. The program clerk also provides whatever secretarial duties are needed by the programming team.

Structured Program Walkthrough

The structured program walkthrough is a significant procedure of the chief programmer team. It is essentially a review method regularly used to examine the programming and determine adherence to specifications and standards.

Specifically, the walkthrough's purpose is to find omissions, errors, bad logic, and otherwise faulty program construction. In addition to producing correct code of sound quality, another walkthrough benefit is that programs become more readable because programmers know their programs will be reviewed by others, some of whom may be from other teams or user groups.

Because of the hierarchical nature of structured programming, the walkthrough team is able to concentrate on higher levels of design during early reviews. Subsequent iterations provide increasing amounts of detail for review. Usually, several members of the walkthrough team are from other areas to increase the objectivity of the review.

A moderator controls the meeting; the programmers describe their work; the reviewers comment; and a recorder documents all errors, discrepancies, and inconsistencies uncovered during the walkthrough. Documentation produced by the walkthrough team contains an action list to correct errors and provide general recommendations.

The walkthrough team is responsible for identifying problems; the programmers who wrote the code are responsible for correcting them. Subsequent walkthroughs ensure that proper corrections are made.

Chief Programmer Team Analysis

The chief programmer team approach is often compared to a surgical team in which the ultimate responsibility rests on the chief surgeon who is supported by a skilled, specialized staff, such as a backup surgeon and other observing surgeons, anaesthetist, chief nurse, nurses, and other technicians.

The chief programmer team indeed represents a clear alternative to the other programming organization structures. Many project-based organizations, for example, are often staffed by a potpourri of inexperienced personnel. Moreover, much of programming work is clerical, involving storage and maintenance of large amounts of data. Often these data are lost or misfiled.

In other programming organizations such as the adaptive team, an inordinate amount of communications is required just to perform a small amount of productive work. In a chief programmer team, all communications are coordinated and funneled through one or two individuals.

A number of authorities suggest that a chief programmer team is approximately twice as productive as other teams. Therefore, chief programmer teams are more likely to meet tight deadlines than other, more decentralized teams.

In organizations designed along divisional or functional lines, it may be difficult, if not impossible, however, to fit the chief programmer team in such organizations. Departmental boundaries and cultural norms simply may not allow it. If a chief programmer team is introduced, psychological problems may develop because the chief programmer takes credit for the team's success. Clearly, other members of the team may be resentful of the chief's status.

20.7 PROGRAM TESTING

Regardless of whether software is developed in-house or acquired from a vendor, program testing provides a documented basis for ensuring that the program will perform as required. Program testing is the final task and last chance to make sure that the program meets users' requirements.

Testing, however, can never demonstrate that a program is correct. Testing only shows the presence of errors; it cannot prove their absence. It is always possible that undetected errors exist even after the most comprehensive and rigorous testing is performed.

If extensive testing does not guarantee a total absence of errors, how long does one test and what testing methods should be employed? The answers depend on the particular program application. If it's a program that controls the space shuttle, 80 to 90 percent of the total systems development time is devoted to testing. Alternatively, in some low-level internal business reporting applications, program testing may represent only a fractional percentage of the total SDM time.

MIS-APPLICATIONS

A programming team had been working on the New Jersey Division of Motor Vehicle's new computer system for more than a year, using Ideal, a 4GL from Applied Data Research.

Fourth generation languages, untried for big production jobs, can produce programs that can overtax computer resources. The New Jersey Motor Vehicle's system was to have more than 1,000 terminals generating tens of thousands of transactions per day. The system crashed as if it had run into a wall.

The more difficult question is, how could such a mistake have been made? According to outside experts, testing before and during development should have determined the tool's inadequacy for the job. That the mistake was not discovered—or, if discovered, not corrected—until the system crashed on takeoff represents a management rather than a technical failure.

Log-on sometimes took an hour. Response times lagged up to three minutes. Nightly batch updates took days.

Why was the old, working system turned off before the new one was turned on? Parallel operation would have allowed for failure of the new system without wreaking havoc.

Excerpted from David Kull, "Anatomy of a 4GL Disaster," *Computer Decisions*, February 11, 1986, p. 58–65.

Error Types

Before we get into testing processes and procedures, let's analyze the types of errors that occur in programs. To defeat this "enemy," it helps to know what the enemy is and what is its nature. Then a mighty battle must be waged to detect and destroy it before it destroys us.

Three major categories of program errors or bugs exist. Syntactic errors are caused by not being in compliance with the underlying rules of grammar governing what is acceptable or unacceptable program language construction.

Semantic errors result in faulty logic. These errors are more difficult to detect than syntactic errors. Some semantic errors will cause the program to fail during execution, while others will generate attractive, but inaccurate, reports.

Algorithmic errors prevent a set of seemingly correct statements from yielding valid results. For example, a utility company used a formula for computing electric bills that appeared correct and produced "correct" bills, but because the wrong numerator in the formula was used, the utility company was actually undercharging its customers. Most algorithmic, like semantic, errors are extremely difficult to detect because the results "look" correct. In other instances, the program may actually produce correct results under all but the most unusual conditions.

Other authorities classify program errors as domain and computation errors. A program is said to exhibit a domain error when incorrect output is generated because a wrong path through a program is executed. A computation error occurs when the correct path is taken, but the output is incorrect because of faults in computation along that path.

A PROGRAM-MING BLOWUP Our star programmer had entered the wrong set of instructions into the bank's computer. Since Monday night, roughly 500,000 MasterCard and VISA cards had been wrongly invalidated. Several thousand had already been confiscated by automatic teller machines. By six o'clock Monday evening, every local television station had run stories on the credit-card snafu. Having half a million customers out there with potentially invalid cards was clearly a worst-case scenario.

Excerpted from Warren Rodgers, "My Terrible Vacation," *Inc.,* February 1988, pp. 116–17.

SOFTWARE BUGS CAN BE DEADLY A computerized therapeutic radiation machine has been blamed in incidents that have led to the deaths of two patients and serious injuries to several others. The deadly medical mystery posed by the machine was finally traced to a software bug.

Excerpted from Ed Joyce. "Software Bugs: A Matter of Life and Liability," *Datamation,* May 15, 1987, pp. 88–92.

Testing Levels

As we already know, structured programming requires modular construction. The testing process, therefore, follows these five stages.

1. *Function Testing.* The functions and procedures that make up a module are tested to ensure their correct operation.
2. *Module Testing.* The functions are combined to form a module. This module is tested to ensure that its performance meets specifications.
3. *Integration Testing.* Sometimes called subsystem or string testing, a set of modules are integrated. As these modules interact, the testing focus is on module interfaces because it is assumed that the modules themselves are correct.
4. *Total Program Testing.* Sometimes called systems testing, this level of testing combines all the subsystems into a total program package. At this stage, the testing process concentrates more on detecting design errors and determining how well users' requirements are met.
5. *Acceptance Testing.* Up to this stage, all testing has been conducted by systems development personnel. The focus of acceptance testing is on how well the program operates with real live data in the operating environment, its compliance with design specifications, and its ability to meet users' requirements. Typically, acceptance testing is performed by users or users' representatives. If the program passes this test, it is accepted by users and is converted to full operation.

Testing Approaches

Several approaches to testing can be used effectively. These include big-bang, incremental, top-down, and bottom-up. In all approaches, use of an independent testing team is recommended. The program to be tested is represented in Figure 20.3.

Big-Bang Testing

This testing approach combines all the modules and subjects the total program to testing. This approach is generally not recommended because of the difficulty

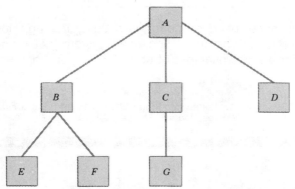

Figure 20.3 Structure of program to be tested.

encountered in developing test cases that exercise thoroughly all aspects of the program. Moreover, when errors are detected, it is difficult to localize them.

Unfortunately, if programs are written spaghetti style, unlike the modular structure in Figure 20.3, then big-bang testing is generally the only testing approach available. Because of multiple interparagraph GOTOs, the total program cannot be broken down into more manageable modules.

Incremental Testing

Incremental testing starts with a single module subjected to appropriate test cases. Once the testing of this module provides satisfactory results, a second module is introduced and more test cases are applied. The process continues until all modules are eventually integrated into a complete program.

It is assumed that if errors occur when a new module is introduced, these errors are caused by this new module. Therefore, the source of errors is localized and detection and correction of errors are easier.

Stubs and Drivers for Top-Down and Bottom-Up Testing

To perform top-down and bottom-up testing, the tester must develop additional software to provide stub and driver modules. For the test module that invokes and transmits data, stub modules must be written to model this relationship. For the test module that is invoked by a higher module and receives data from it, a driver module must be written. These relationships are illustrated in Figure 20.4.

Stubs and drivers are used to link program modules to enable them to run in an environment that approximates the real one. If an error is detected at any point during testing, it is fairly easy to locate the cause of the error and correct it.

Top-Down Testing

Earlier when we were discussing testing levels, we started with functional testing, then module testing, then integration testing, then total program testing, and,

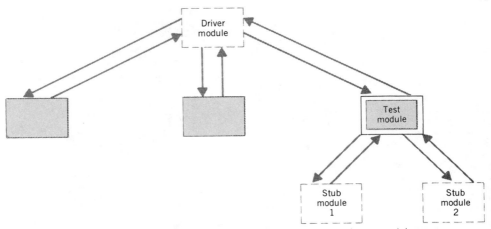

Figure 20.4 The role of driver and stub modules in testing a module.

finally, acceptance testing. Top-down testing involves starting at the integration testing level with lower-level modules represented by stubs. (See, for example, Figure 20.5.)

Boss module A is tested first. It requires stubs corresponding to modules B, C, and D, as shown in Figure 20.5. Then, modules B, C, and D are tested using module A and stubs for modules E, F, and G. Finally, modules E, F, and G are put together, and the program is tested as an integrated package.

A proper test of the invoking (or calling) module requires the stub to check the input parameters and return reasonable values for the output parameters. The stubs must simulate closely lower levels of the program for top-down testing to be effective.

Bottom-Up Testing

With bottom-up testing, the lowest-level modules are tested first, requiring driver modules. Next, modules are tested that connect to these low-level modules, and testing continues until the boss module is included. Referring to Figure 20.6, modules E, F, G, and D are tested first. Drivers required are B-driver for modules E and F, C-driver for module G, and A-driver for module D. Then modules E, F, G, D, C, and B are integrated and are tested with A-driver. Then, all modules are integrated and tested.

Trade-offs Between Top-Down and Bottom-Up Testing

One of the major trade-offs between top-down and bottom-up testing is the cost of preparing stubs and drivers. Generally, drivers and bottom-up testing are easier to develop and less costly; stubs and top-down testing are more difficult to develop and more costly. The advantages of bottom-up testing are the disadvantages of top-down testing, and vice versa.

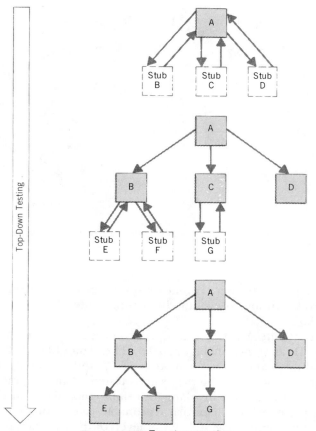

Figure 20.5 Top-down testing.

Top-down testing follows the path of top-down programming and there-fore can be performed in conjunction with program development. Essentially, coding and testing become a single function in which a module is tested as soon as it's coded.

Top-down testing detects design errors (not program errors) committed by the systems analyst early in the programming process, thus saving a lot of wasted effort in redesigning the system and rewriting code later on. Furthermore, to develop a working, although limited, program early on, provides a strong psychological boost to all involved in systems development.

On the other hand, if the systems application is complex, it is difficult, if not impossible, to write stub modules that adequately simulate the application. Another disadvantage of top-down testing is the inability, in many cases, to generate realistic output.

Bottom-up testing involves testing modules at lower levels in the structured hierarchy, and then working up the hierarchy of modules until the final boss

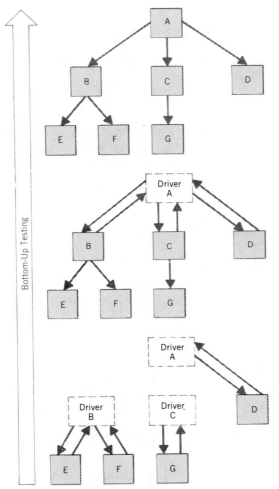

Figure 20.6 Bottom-up testing.

module is tested. Drivers provide lower-level modules with appropriate input. Generally, test cases are easier to develop.

A major disadvantage of bottom-up testing is that no working program is demonstrated until the last module is tested. Therefore, if systems design errors exist, they won't be detected until the last module is tested, and it is likely that the entire program will have to be rewritten and retested.

In summary, the following guidelines indicate when each testing approach should be used. If the boss and upper-level modules are complex and critical to the program's success, then top-down testing is recommended. On the other hand, if lower-level modules are more critical, then bottom-up testing should be used.

Creating Test Cases

Test cases should closely simulate the real data that the program is intended to process. Furthermore, an array of test cases should be created to exercise the program fully. Thorough testing includes application of test cases that contain multiple valid and invalid inputs.

Test Case Matrix

The test case matrix contains four sections: (1) test objective, (2) expected results, (3) test case, and (4) actual results. The test cases should be formalized, logged, and documented in a test case matrix similar to the one illustrated in Figure 20.7.

Test Objective	Expected Results			Test Case Design	Actual Results
	Reject	Display Error Message	Automatically Compute Correct Amount		
To determine if program computes check digit and rejects transposed account number	X	X		Input transposed account numbers	Rejected and displayed error message
To determine if department numbers are checked for validity	X	X		Input invalid department numbers	Rejected and displayed error message
To verify accuracy of overtime pay computations			X	Pay an hourly employee for 15 hours overtime	Overtime pay was computed at 1.5 times regular rate
To determine if program processes a credit memo accurately with missing general ledger code		X	X	Input a credit memo with all data except general ledger code	Credit memo was processed accurately and missing code error message was displayed

Figure 20.7 A test case matrix.

Black Box Test Cases

Black box test cases are created without any, or limited, knowledge of the program under test. Test cases are generated by reviewing external specifications and user requirements and concentrating on error-prone situations. Therefore, black box test cases are more appropriate at the integration, total program, and acceptance testing levels and are normally not used at the module level. Indeed, black box test cases are especially applicable for acceptance testing because the testers are users or users' representatives who generally do not have a detailed understanding and perspective of how the program should perform to meet users' requirements.

Some design specifications are fairly straightforward and can be precisely measured. For example, assume that a design specification states that a particular measurement will range from 0 to 100. This range results in three black box test classes: (1) valid values in the range of 0 to 100; (2) invalid values, which are less than 0; and (3) invalid values, which are greater than 100. A black box test case would include $X = 0$, $X = 100$, $X = -1$, and $X = 101$.

Other black box test cases are based on specifications not so easily measured as the preceding example. In such situations, intuition and semantic experience is necessary to create viable black box test cases.

White Box Test Cases

The white box (also called glass box) approach uses the program code and structure to create test cases. Whereas black box test cases test functional aspects and systems design specifications, white box test cases test directly the coding and structural aspects of the program. White box test cases are, therefore, especially appropriate for module tests.

VIRUSES ARE SPREADING   A new Macintosh software virus is damaging files and modifying normal programs that come into contact with it.

The easiest way to spot the virus is by looking at the icons that represent the Note Pad File and Scrapbook File in the Macintosh System Folder, officials said. These icons normally resemble small Macintoshes; but when infected, the icons become a rectangle with a bent corner.

The virus transmits itself from Mac to Mac by invading a standard executable application file on a contaminated computer. When this contaminated application is copied to a "sterile" Macintosh and executed, the virus attacks the new system by making changes to the contents of the System Folder. Once the system files on the target Macintosh have been infected, the virus will begin to attack applications.

Excerpted from Scott Mace, "New Virus Damaging Mac Data, Group Says," *InfoWorld*, April 11, 1988, p. 29.

A white box test case is designed to achieve the desired coverage of statements, paths, branches, conditions, and decisions incorporated in the module code. For example, a complete set of test cases to test thoroughly, if $A < 20$ and $B = 10$, is $(A = 19, B = 10)$, $(A = 20, B = 10)$, $(A = 19, B = 9)$, $(A = 19, B = 11)$, $(A = 20, B = 9)$, and $(A = 20, B = 11)$.

Seeding Errors to Test Reliability of Test Cases
The seeding errors testing technique purposely introduces artificial errors into the program or changes the functionality of the program. The purpose of this technique is to test the effectiveness and reliability of test cases used to test the program. If the test cases do not detect the error seeds or program modifications, the test cases are eliminated and new ones are devised.

The error seeding method assumes the reliability of a program is related to the number of errors removed from it. Someone other than the one creating test cases inserts a known number and type of artificial errors in the program before testing begins. When both real and seeded errors are detected, the number of remaining real errors is approximated by:

$$\frac{\text{Remaining Number of Real Errors}}{\text{Remaining Number of Seeded Errors}} = \frac{\text{Number of Real Errors Detected}}{\text{Number of Seeded Errors Detected}}$$

The proportion of errors not detected helps to determine the quality of test cases and the general testing process, which, in turn, estimates program reliability.

20.8 INPUT, OUTPUT, DATA BASE, AND CONTROLS TESTING

The technology platform including all software has been tested. While performing these tests, many features of input, output, data base, and controls were also tested. In this section, however, we focus on tests specifically applicable for these building blocks.

Input Testing

Input testing involves determining if paper and electronic forms and coding structures meet design guidelines and specifications. Users are also tested to determine if they are completing forms properly. Presumably, they were taught how to fill out forms during training. Testing at this stage is to determine if they were properly trained.

Many organizations hire people whose only function is to enter data. It is important that these people receive adequate training in data entry. For example, by testing the performance of order-entry personnel, additional on-the-job training can be given to correct inadequacies.

If input is handled by a POS device, a simple random sample of products is selected and passed by the reader to determine correctness of price and description. If certain products do not contain a bar code, then a keyboard must be available to enter the data manually. If input entered from a keyboard is displayed on a CRT, proper layout on the screen is important. Any screens that are cluttered and contain unnecessary data should be identified and corrected.

Output Testing

A great portion of output testing is a by-product of testing other building blocks. For example, while input and data base are tested, the resulting output is reviewed for accuracy and usability.

A substantive test of output involves nothing more than generating a report, giving it to the user, and seeing if it meets his or her information needs. In general, a good test to determine if the output format is understandable is to show the output to a person who is not involved in the system. If the person can "explain" the report, then the format is likely to be understandable by appropriate users.

Technical tests include checking for proper headings, edited amounts (e.g., leading zero suppression, debit/credit notation, dollar signs), correct page number sequence, clear end-of-report indicators, and correct dates (e.g., date the report was prepared and the current date).

Data Base Testing

Substantive tests to determine if contents of the data base meets users' requirements are, to a large extent, performed when output is tested. Additional tests, however, can be made to make sure that the data base meets all demands placed on it. These tests include creating a new record before the first record on a master file, creating a new record after the last record, creating a record for a nonexistent division or department, trying to read from or write to a file with the wrong header label, attempting to process past an end-of-file indicator, and trying to create and enter a record that is incomplete.

Files should be checked for completeness. Predetermined control totals should be compared with the totals produced from the new files. For instance, predetermined totals might be checked against the number of records in a file or the total amount of a specific amount field, such as AMOUNT-OWED in an accounts receivable master file. File description and layouts should be compared with the ENVIRONMENT and DATA DIVISION in COBOL programs for agreement.

In a query-intensive environment, tests of SQL joins are critical. Two-table, three-table, and, in some instances, four-table joins are common. All these joins should be tested with data that reflect live transactions.

The quality of the optimizer is the single most important component of an SQL-based DBMS. Therefore, it should be tested to ascertain its ability to handle joins efficiently. Test cases should be devised to test the optimizer's sensitivity to join conditions in the WHERE clause, such as:

```
SELECT  NAME
FROM    EMPLOYEE
WHERE   EMPLOYEE.EMP-NO = DEPARTMENT.EMP-NO
```

Then test by transposing the WHERE condition as follows:

```
DEPARTMENT.EMP-NO = EMPLOYEE.EMP-NO
```

The results may be different from the first query because optimizers can sometimes be tricked into using the wrong table indexes.

High-quality optimizers use statistics that are stored in the systems catalog to help ascertain the best index to use. In some situations, the optimizer may even build a temporary index if the optimizer determines performance can be improved.

Queries with AND or OR Boolean conditions are common but difficult to optimize, especially the OR operation. Both conditions should be tested.

A DBMS must ensure data integrity. Testing of multiuser updating in a LAN is crucial. Testing of the transaction manager indicates the type of logging and recovery options available and the number of users who can be handled concurrently. A high level of data consistency and concurrency are desirable. (If necessary, review concurrency controls in Chapter 14.)

Controls Testing

The purpose of controls testing is to ensure that they are in place and are working as intended. This is called compliance testing. The three phases involved in compliance testing are (1) to study and observe controls, (2) to conduct the actual tests of compliance, and (3) to evaluate how effectively the controls meet these compliance tests. As always, by testing other building blocks, some tests of controls will be already done. For example, when testing program procedures, programming controls are also tested.

Test transactions help to ensure processing controls, such as limit and reasonableness checks, arithmetic proof, and identification are in place and working correctly. These tests also help to cross-test other building blocks. For example, some of the test transactions prepared by clerks and terminal operators for special processing not only test the program and its ability to detect errors, but also check the way transactions are prepared and entered.

Some of the controls that would normally be tested by a series of test transactions are as follows:

- Check to see if control totals are prepared and reported back to the control group. For example, if 100 test records are processed, the number of transactions processed should read 100.
- Try to process a sensitive transaction without proper authorization (e.g., change of customer's credit limit) and see if the system rejects it.
- Make numeric, alphabetic, and special character checks. For example, if all the characters in a customer number are supposed to be numeric, input an alphabetic character in this field. A properly working check will detect this mistake before processing is performed.
- Input a field with a negative sign and see if it is handled as a negative value.

Security Control Questionnaire
(Partial)

	Answer	
	Yes	No
1. Are sign-in/sign-out registers maintained for visitors?	————	————
2. Are controls adequate over the removal of materials from the data processing area? Are sensitive reports shredded?	————	————
3. Does the system make use of		
a. Guards?	————	————
b. Cards?	————	————
c. Badges?	————	————
d. Closed-circuit television?	————	————
e. Limited entry points?	————	————
f. Central monitoring?	————	————
g. Detection devices?	————	————
h. Alarms?	————	————
i. Intercoms?	————	————
j. Mantrap doors?	————	————
k. Fire emergency exit-only doors?	————	————
4. Is the system backed up with power, air conditioning, and redundant equipment?	————	————
5. Are air conditioners adequate for peak thermal loads?	————	————
6. Are terminals located in secure areas to prevent access to the terminals by unauthorized users?	————	————
7. Do terminals include locking devices to prevent unauthorized use?	————	————
8. Are there hardware erase or sanitizing features? That is, are memory and peripherals cleared of residue between jobs?	————	————
9. Is the computer area housed in a fire-resistant, noncombustible structure?	————	————
10. Do all the materials used in construction of the computer area (e.g., walls, doors, ceilings) have at least one-hour fire rating?	————	————

Figure 20.8 Excerpt from a security control questionnaire.

In some systems, without proper control, the negative sign is converted to a positive sign. Divide an amount by zero.

- Perform validity checks on key data fields. For example, input an invalid code or try to process one department number as another department number.
- Make limit and reasonableness checks. If no employee can work more than 60 hours per week, process a time card with more than 60 hours worked.
- Check for proper transaction sequence. Where transactions are supposed to be in sequence, shuffle the order of several test transactions so that they are out of sequence.
- Include an account number with a predetermined self-checking digit and see if it is processed by the computer system properly.
- Use units of measure (e.g., feet for pounds) different from those allowed.
- Input several fields with incomplete or missing data.
- Insert characters in fields that cause an overflow condition.
- Try to read from or write to a wrong file.

The study of controls includes a review of documentation found in the systems development reports. Observation and walkthroughs are required for an on-site study of controls. The questionnaire is always a key tool used to study controls. An excerpt from a security control questionnaire is shown in Figure 20.8.

Although questionnaires provide effective means of gathering evidence on controls, more must be done. Often, respondents give automatic answers that will put them in a good light. For this reason, the tester must conduct compliance tests to determine whether or not answers to the questionnaires are true.

Testers may be able to satisfy themselves that a number of controls are working merely by observation. For example, they can observe a fire-suppression system and inspection tags. Testers may even "try out" particular control techniques to see if they work (e.g., various access controls). In other cases, the only way to tell that particular controls work is to set up a test situation and see what happens. For example, a "disaster simulation" may be run on a surprise basis. To run disaster simulations, the tester seals certain master files and tells the computer center manager the system is "down." This simulated situation requires data processing personnel to bring the system to a current status by using cycled and backup files, other backup facilities, and contingency procedures. If they fail, reasons for failure are ascertained and swift corrective action is taken. Also, with executive approval, the tester "pulls the power switch" to the computer center to test recovery procedures. Sometimes, professional penetrators are hired to attempt to obtain access to the computer center and data base. Unexpected fire drills are performed to see if standard operating procedures are followed.

20.9 SYSTEMS CONVERSION

The conversion process puts the system "on the air." As we analyze this systems conversion process, we can identify different approaches to accomplishing the conversion, the special considerations for the data base, and the importance of planning the conversion.

Approaches to Systems Conversions

Four basic approaches toward accomplishing the conversion of a new system are (1) direct, (2) parallel, (3) modular, and (4) phase-in. Figure 20.9 is a graphic representation of these four approaches.

1. *Direct Conversion.* A direct conversion is the implementation of the new system and the immediate discontinuance of the old system, sometimes called the "cold turkey" approach. This conversion approach is meaningful when (1) the system is not replacing any other system, (2) the old system is judged absolutely without value, (3) the new system is either very small or simple, and (4) the design of the new system is drastically different from that of the old system and comparisons between systems would be meaningless. The primary advantage to this approach is that it is relatively inexpensive; the primary disadvantage is that it involves a high risk of failure. When direct conversion is to be used, the systems testing activity discussed in the previous section takes on even greater importance.

   If the building blocks have been thoroughly tested with simulated test data and cases, and they have passed all tests, the risk of direct conversion is low. The system has already updated files, written payroll checks and vouchers, checked procedures, investigated the completeness and accuracy of the data base, checked the viability of controls, and determined the appropriateness of the output.

   A modification to cold turkey cutover is a trial conversion, which is like a dress rehearsal. Every employee/user does his or her scheduled part. Instead of going into actual production with the new system, files are copied and jobs are run. The output, the updated files, and other components are studied in detail to make sure everything is working correctly. After a successful dress rehearsal, the next cutover is real.

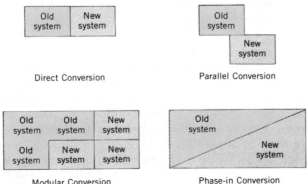

Figure 20.9 A graphic representation of the basic approaches to systems conversion.

2. *Parallel Conversion.*   Parallel conversion is an approach wherein both the old and the new system operate simultaneously for some period of time. It is the opposite of direct conversion. In a parallel conversion mode the outputs from each system are compared and differences reconciled. The advantage to this approach is that it provides a high degree of protection to the organization from a failure in the new system. The obvious disadvantages to this approach are the costs associated with duplicating facilities and personnel to maintain the dual systems. But because of the many difficulties experienced by organizations in the past when a new system was implemented, this approach to conversion has gained widespread popularity. When the conversion process of a system includes parallel operations, the analyst should plan for periodic reviews with operating personnel and users concerning the performance of the new system and designate a reasonable date for its acceptance and discontinuance of the old system.

Because of faulty training and testing activities, conversion projects are often burdened with additional tasks of training, testing, rewriting procedures and documentation, changing files, attempting to retrofit controls, and making major computer configuration adjustments. If this is the case, then parallel conversion is really the only sensible approach to use. Some would contend that parallel conversion is a form of testing. We do not argue with this contention. Other situations may exist, however, when different production methods, decision rules, accounting procedures, and inventory control models are to be used in the new system. In these situations, parallel conversion makes little sense and, obviously, will not work. In this case, and in all cases, we recommend stringent training and testing procedures before the conversion process begins.

If parallel conversion is used, a few points should be kept in mind. First, a target date should be set to indicate when parallel operation will cease and the system will operate on its own. If possible, the target date should be set at the end of the longest processing cycle (e.g., at the end of the fiscal period and after year-end closings). Second, if a discrepancy occurs between the old and new system, it should be verified that the inputs to both systems were the same. If the inputs are the same, the new program should be reviewed to make sure it is processing the transactions properly. In some instances, the old system may be the one that is not processing correctly.

3. *Modular Conversion.*   Modular conversion, sometimes termed the "pilot approach," refers to the implementation of a system into the organization on a piecemeal basis. For example, an order-entry system could be installed in one sales region and, if proved successful, installed in a second sales region, and so on. As another example, an inventory system might be converted with only a selected product grouping or with all products in one location of a multiple-location organization. The advantages to this approach are as follows: (1) the risk of a system's failure is localized, (2) the problems identified in the system can be corrected before further implementation is attempted, and (3) other operating personnel can be trained in a "live" environment before the system is implemented at their location.

One disadvantage to this approach is that the conversion period for the organization can be extremely lengthy. More important, this approach is not feasible for every system or organization.

4. *Phase-in Conversion.* The phase-in approach is similar to the modular approach; it differs, however, in that the system itself is segmented and not the organization. For example, the new data collection activities are implemented and an interface mechanism with the old system is developed. This interface allows the old system to operate with the new input data. Later, the new data base access, storage, and retrieval activities are implemented. Once again, an interface mechanism with the old system is developed. Another segment of the new system is installed until the entire system is implemented. Each time a new segment is added, an interface with the old system must be developed. The advantages to this approach are that the rate of change in a given organization can be minimized, and data processing resources can be acquired gradually over an extended period of time. The disadvantages to this approach include the costs incurred to develop temporary interfaces with old systems, limited applicability, and a demoralizing atmosphere in the organization of "never completing a system."

UNION PACIFIC PHASES IN ITS CSC   Union Pacific phased in its Customer Service Center (CSC) over an 18-month period during which the railroad consolidated its 40 regional customer service centers and trained about 500 people to operate the national center.

But UP planners are already looking at the potential for major improvements in operations control and service that could result in implementation of an Advanced Train Center System (ATCS). ATCS is now being tested.

"Keeping Shippers into EDI," *Railway Age*, March 1988, pp. 50–51.

Data Base Considerations During Systems Conversion

The success of systems conversion depends to a great degree on how well the systems analyst prepares for the creation and conversion of the data files required for the new system. This preparation is of particular importance in an organization where the information system has a high degree of integration through its data base. In some large organizations in which an integrated information system exists, the analyst may work closely with the data base administrator to prepare for data base creation and conversion. For our purposes, however, we will assume that the systems analyst must make all the preparations for the systems conversion. Additionally, to simplify the explanation of the many complexities of data base conversion, we will cast the data base in terms of file units.

By creating a file, we mean that data are collected and organized in some recognizable format on a given storage medium. By converting a file, we mean that an existing file must be modified in at least one of three ways: (1) in the format of the file, (2) in the content of the file, or (3) in the storage medium where the file is located. It is quite likely in a systems conversion that some files can experience all three aspects of conversion simultaneously.

When creating a file that is to be processed on the computer, it is sometimes necessary to provide special start-up software that defines and labels a specific physical or logical storage location for the file. This process is referred to as creating a "dummy" file. Once the "dummy" file is created, the new system will process and store the designated data in this file.

When converting a file that must be processed on the computer, the special start-up software, which may be part of a DBMS, contains logic that permits existing data to be input in the old format or on the old medium, and output in the new format or on the new medium. With regard to the aspect of converting the contents of a file, the special start-up software may simply initialize (e.g., set to zero) the new fields in the file so that these fields can be updated correctly when the system begins processing transactions.

Often, during the conversion of files, it is necessary to construct elaborate control procedures to ensure the integrity of the data available for use after the conversion. Using the following classification of files, note the kind of control procedures used during conversion:

1. *Master Files.*   Master files are the key files in the data base, and usually at least one master file is to be created or converted in every systems conversion. When an existing master file must be converted, the analyst should arrange for a series of hash and control totals to be matched between all the fields in the old file and all the same fields in the converted file. Special file backup procedures should be implemented for each separate processing step. This precaution is to prevent having to unnecessarily restart the conversion, from the beginning, in the event an error is discovered in the conversion logic at a later date. Timing considerations, particularly in online systems, are extremely important. If the converted file is not to be implemented immediately after conversion, special provisions must be made to track any update activity occurring between the time of conversion and the time of implementation.

2. *Transaction Files.*   Transaction files are usually created by the processing of an individual subsystem within the information system and can, consequently, be checked thoroughly during systems testing. The transaction files that are generated in areas of the information system other than the new subsystem, however, may have to be converted if the master files they update change in format or medium.

3. *Index Files.*   Index files contain the keys or addresses that link various master files. Therefore, new index files must be created whenever their related master files have undergone a conversion.

4. *Table Files.*   Table files can also be created and converted during the systems conversion. The same considerations required of master files are applicable here.

5. *Summary Files.*   Summary files are created during the processing of the new system in a manner similar to transaction files. Summary files created in other areas of the information system, however, do not usually have to be converted when a new subsystem is implemented.

6. *Archival Files.*   Archival files are another category of files similar to master files. The considerations that apply to master files during the systems conversion are applicable to archival files with two exceptions: the timing considerations are not as severe with archival files as they are with master files, even in an online processing mode; and the volume of data records in archival files is usually far greater than that contained in master files.

7. *Backup Files.*   The purpose of backup files is to provide security for the information system in the event of a processing error or a disaster in the data center. Therefore, when a file is converted or created, a backup file must be created. The backup procedures for the converted file more than likely will be the same as the procedures that existed for the original file. The one exception to this might be when a change in file medium took place. For example, a card file that was previously backed up by another card file, when converted to magnetic disk or tape would probably be backed up on disk or tape also.

IMPLEMENTATION FOLLOW-UP

The systems analyst's participation, along with other implementation team members, does not necessarily end when the new system is implemented. Several of the more significant tasks performed immediately after systems implementation are discussed in the following sections.

Checking Input, Processing, and Output

At first, the analyst should check regularly that input, processing, and output schedules are being met. After an operating routine is established, these checks can become less regular and can be directed only toward any trouble spots identified.

The activities of input preparation personnel (e.g., key entry personnel, order-entry clerks) should be reviewed periodically. A high probability exists that some manual procedures will need additional clarification. A programming bug might be identified that requires immediate resolution. On occasion, certain procedures, manual or computer, might be identified as being somewhat inefficient, and a minor change or fine-tuning will eliminate a bottleneck situation in the systems operations.

Perhaps the most important follow-up activity the analyst performs is to verify that the systems controls are functioning properly. During the learning period, the analyst can assist the operations of the system either by providing a quick method for reconciling errors or by recommending to appropriate supervisors where additional control support is required.

Freezing Improvement Requests

One problem the analyst will have during the follow-up period is distinguishing between improvements and additional "niceties" suggested by various users and identifying actual systems problems. Suggestions for improvements to the system are welcomed and encouraged; however, these suggestions are compiled, evaluated, and then, if appropriate, developed after only implementation is complete. In this way, all users are given an opportunity to be heard, and further improvements to the system can be effectively implemented in total, as they relate to specific subsystems (or modules) of the new system. Without this distinction, the implementation activity of the system will continue indefinitely.

Purging Extraneous and Old Material from the New System

Another activity the analyst might perform during follow-up is to remove all outdated and start-up procedures, programs, and forms that are part of the old system or conversion effort. This action eliminates the possibility of someone inadvertently referring to (or using) the wrong procedure, program, or form.

Acceptance Meeting

An acceptance meeting should be held, attended by the systems analyst, systems operating management, and user personnel. At this time an official termination of the developmental project is given and a final systems "sign-off" is obtained. The systems analyst then becomes available for a new assignment or to design and implement some of the system improvement requests and suggestions that were frozen earlier.

THE NSU TIGERS EVENT CENTER
Preparing the Final Implementation Report

FINAL IMPLEMENTATION REPORT

February 15, 19x0

To: All Department Heads, Supervisors, and Digit Representatives
From: Sally Forth, Chief Systems Analyst
Subject: Scheduling of Events and Ticketing System (SEATS)
Copies: John Ball, Event Center Director and Tyronne Topps, CISO

Overall Implementation Plan
The following is a PERT diagram of the overall implementation plan for SEATS:

Implementation Activities

Order Technology
NSU officials signed the contract with Digit. Then, the purchasing department prepared and released the purchase order to Digit. Delivery dates for the technology platform were established to coincide with site preparation.

Review Specifications
A programmer from Digit reviewed specifications for input, models, output, and the data base, to prepare the necessary program code for ticketing, event recording and resources planning, accounting, and data base maintenance models, as described in the Final Detailed Systems Design Report.

Site Preparation and Installation
The goal of site preparation is to ensure quick and easy installation of the technology platform.

The equipment will be burned in by Digit at their plant to simulate four weeks of continuous operation. During this time, the departments have been informed to prepare the site for the equipment. The environment must be clean and antistatic mats are to be used. Sufficient room is to be provided for shelving, stands, tables, and disk and tape storage trays and cabinets.

Representatives from Digit will be at the event center to coordinate the installation of cabling. They will provide recommendations on improving human factors, such as acoustics, privacy panels, printer enclosures, and ergonomically designed furniture and workstations.

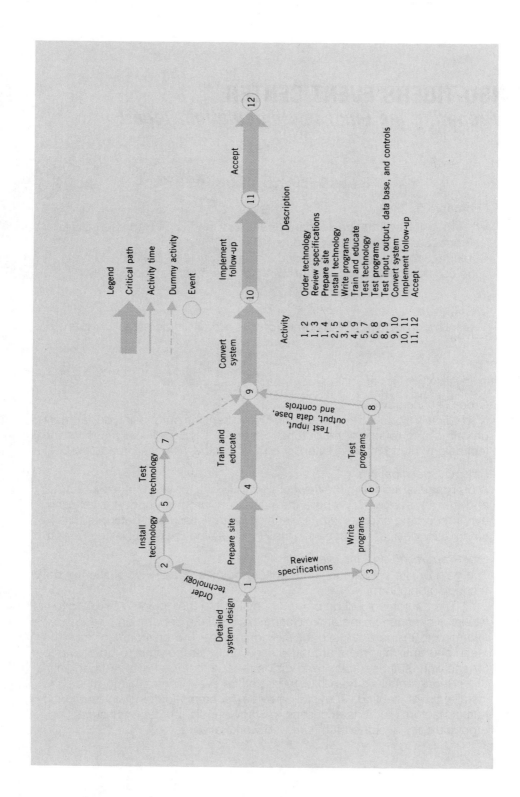

Legend

Critical path

Activity time

Dummy activity

Event

Activity	Description
1, 2	Order technology
1, 3	Review specifications
1, 4	Prepare site
2, 5	Install technology
3, 6	Write programs
4, 9	Train and educate
5, 7	Test technology
6, 8	Test programs
8, 9	Test input, output, data base, and controls
9, 10	Convert system
10, 11	Implement follow-up
11, 12	Accept

Detailed system design

Order technology

Install technology

Test technology

Test input, output, data base, and controls

Prepare site

Train and educate

Review specifications

Write programs

Test programs

Convert system

Implement follow-up

Accept

Test Technology

Digit plans to install hardware monitors on the CPU and disk drives for three weeks to monitor their operation. A software monitor will be installed permanently to monitor the usage of the software. Code modifications will be performed to increase efficiency. Digit will provide utilities such as data set organizers to improve throughput by reducing wasted file storage on disk. They will also provide schedulers to help meet timing demands and balance job mix.

Write Programs

Comparing the detailed programming specifications against the turnkey system provided by Digit revealed the need for additional programming. The following is a description and a listing of the programs written for the models presented in narrative form in the Final Detailed Systems Design Report.

1. Ticketing Model

Menu option 1.11 allows the user to input seating assignments. When a ticket is sold and paid for, the input screen records information about the patron, the amount paid, the purchase date, and the seats assigned. The "available" relation is updated and the "issued" attribute is updated to read "Y" for yes, which means the ticket or seat has been issued. The ticket is then printed.

In this module, the relation called "events" is opened. The system looks up the event number for the event the user has selected. The event number is stored in a temporary memory variable called "number" for further use by the model.

```
OPEN THE events RELATION
   LOOKUP THE event_number WHERE the RECORD NUMBER =
   select STORE event_number TO number
```

In this module, the relation called "assigned" is opened. The input screen is displayed and the patron's ticket order is input and stored in the "assigned" relation. The event number is stored in the "assigned" relation using the data stored in the temporary memory variable called "number."

```
OPEN THE assigned RELATION

DISPLAY THE INPUT SCREEN
    INPUT log_number
    INPUT patron
    INPUT phone
    INPUT reservation_date
    INPUT number_of_reservations
    INPUT amount_paid
    INPUT amount_due
    INPUT purchase_date
    INPUT seat_assigned_1
    INPUT seat_assigned_2
    INPUT seat_assigned_3
    INPUT seat_assigned_4
    INPUT seat_assigned_5
    INPUT seat_assigned_6
    INPUT seat_assigned_7
    INPUT seat_assigned_8
    INPUT seat_assigned_9
    INPUT seat_assigned_10
    INPUT seat_assigned_11
    INPUT seat_assigned_12
    INPUT seat_assigned_13
    INPUT seat_assigned_14
    INPUT seat_assigned_15
    INPUT seat_assigned_16
    INPUT seat_assigned_17
    INPUT seat_assigned_18
    INPUT seat_assigned_19
    INPUT seat_assigned_20

REPLACE event_number WITH number
```

In this module, the routine is repeated 20 times to check if the user has entered a seat assignment or ticket number in 1 of 20 input areas provided in the input screen. If a seat assignment or ticket number has been entered, the system looks up the ticket number in the "available" relation and stores a "Y" for yes in the "issued" data attribute to indicate that the ticket or seat has been issued. The model then prints the ticket.

```
DO A BIG LOOP UNTIL loop > 20
    IF seat_assigned_1  NOT BLANK AND loop = 1
    THEN PERFORM START
    IF seat_assigned_2  NOT BLANK AND loop = 2
    THEN PERFORM START
    IF seat_assigned_3  NOT BLANK AND loop = 3
    THEN PERFORM START
    IF seat_assigned_4  NOT BLANK AND loop = 4
    THEN PERFORM START
    IF seat_assigned_5  NOT BLANK AND loop = 5
    THEN PERFORM START
    IF seat_assigned_6  NOT BLANK AND loop = 6
    THEN PERFORM START
    IF seat_assigned_7  NOT BLANK AND loop = 7
    THEN PERFORM START
    IF seat_assigned_8  NOT BLANK AND loop = 8
    THEN PERFORM START
    IF seat_assigned_9  NOT BLANK AND loop = 9
    THEN PERFORM START
    IF seat_assigned_10 NOT BLANK AND loop = 10
    THEN PERFORM START
    IF seat_assigned_11 NOT BLANK AND loop = 11
    THEN PERFORM START
    IF seat_assigned_12 NOT BLANK AND loop = 12
    THEN PERFORM START
    IF seat_assigned_13 NOT BLANK AND loop = 13
    THEN PERFORM START
    IF seat_assigned_14 NOT BLANK AND loop = 14
    THEN PERFORM START
    IF seat_assigned_15 NOT BLANK AND loop = 15
    THEN PERFORM START
    IF seat_assigned_16 NOT BLANK AND loop = 16
    THEN PERFORM START
    IF seat_assigned_17 NOT BLANK AND loop = 17
    THEN PERFORM START
    IF seat_assigned_18 NOT BLANK AND loop = 18
    THEN PERFORM START
    IF seat_assigned_19 NOT BLANK AND loop = 19
    THEN PERFORM START
    IF seat_assigned_20 NOT BLANK AND loop = 20
    THEN PERFORM START

    START
        OPEN THE available RELATION
        REPLACE issued Y/N IN available WITH "Y"
```

```
    FOR event_number = number AND date =
    reservation_date
    PRINT THE TICKET
    STORE loop + 1 TO loop
END OF THE BIG LOOP
```

2. Event Recording Model

Menu option 2.12 allows the user to add, change, or delete an event. If the user chooses to add an event, then the system must sequentially assign a new event number to the event and store the number in the data base. The following module assigns a new event number and inputs a new event.

```
OPEN THE events RELATION
    LOOKUP THE LAST event_number
    STORE 1 + event_number TO new_number
ADD A BLANK TO THE events RELATION
REPLACE event_number WITH new_number
DISPLAY THE INPUT SCREEN
    INPUT event_name
    INPUT first_date
    INPUT second_date
    INPUT third_date
    INPUT fourth_date
    INPUT fifth_date
    INPUT sixth_date
    INPUT seventh_date
    INPUT eighth_date
    INPUT ninth_date
    INPUT tenth_date
    INPUT contact_name
    INPUT contact_title
    INPUT contact_address
    INPUT seating_code
    INPUT financial_code
    INPUT reservation_minimum
```

3. Resources Planning Model

Menu option 2.22 allows the user to add, change, or delete facility requirements for an event. When a request for a resource is made, the availability is checked against all other requests on the same date. The user is notified if the resource is unavailable.

```
In this module, the "committed" relation is opened.
The add, change, or delete facilities requirements
screen 2.22 is displayed.
```

```
OPEN THE committed RELATION

DISPLAY THE INPUT SCREEN
    INPUT date
    INPUT event_number
    INPUT group_number

STORE group_number TO group
STORE date TO check_date
STORE 0 TO committed_count
```

> In this module, the number of inventory items within a group are counted in the committed relation for the date and group requested by the user.

```
DO A SMALL LOOP UNTIL THE END OF THE committed
RELATION
    IF group_number = group AND date =
    check_date
    THEN STORE 1 + committed_count TO committed_
    count
    END OF THE IF
END OF THE SMALL LOOP

STORE 0 TO resources_count
```

> In this module, the number of inventory items within a group are counted in the resources relation for the group requested by the user.

```
OPEN THE resources RELATION

DO A SMALL LOOP UNTIL THE END OF resources RELATION
    IF group_number = group
    THEN STORE 1 + resources_count TO resources_count
    END OF THE IF

MOVE TO THE NEXT RECORD IN THE resources RELATION
END OF THE SMALL LOOP
```

In this module, the number of inventory items counted for the group and date in the "committed" relation are compared to the number of inventory items counted for the group in the "resources" relation. If not enough facility inventory items are available to meet commitments, the user is prompted with a message indicating an inability to commit the facility resource. If the request can be met, the system finds the next available inventory number in the "resources" relation and stores the inventory number to a temporary memory variable called "number" for further use in the model.

```
IF committed_count IS EQUAL TO OR GREATER THAN
resources_count THEN DISPLAY THE MESSAGE
    "All facility inventory resources are currently
    committed on the date MM/DD/YY"
ELSE
    MOVE committed_count + 1 RECORDS INTO resources
    STORE inventory_number TO number
END OF THE IF
```

In this module, the available inventory item found in the "resources" relation and stored in the temporary memory variable called "number" is recorded in the "committed" relation.

```
OPEN THE committed RELATION
    REPLACE inventory_number WITH number
```

4. Accounting Model (Payables)

Menu option 3.4 is used to print accounts payable checks to vendors.

In this module, the "payables" relation is opened. The user is prompted for the vendor number of the vendor to be printed. The temporary memory variables debit_total and credit_total are initialized to 0 for further use in the model.

```
OPEN THE payables RELATION

DISPLAY THE INPUT SCREEN
    INPUT vendor_number_input

STORE 0 TO debit_total
STORE 0 TO credit_total
```

> In this module, the debit and credit entries are totaled.

```
DO A SMALL LOOP UNTIL THE END OF THE payables
RELATION
    IF debit/credit = "C" AND vendor_number =
    vendor_number_input
    THEN STORE amount + credit_total TO
    credit_total
    END OF THE IF

    IF debit/credit = "D" AND vendor_number =
    vendor_number_input
    THEN STORE amount + debit_total TO
    debit_total
    END OF THE IF
MOVE TO THE NEXT RECORD IN THE payables RELATION
END OF THE SMALL LOOP

STORE credit_total - debit_total TO grand_total
```

> In this module, the vendor checks are printed using additional information contained in the "vendor" relation.

```
OPEN THE vendors RELATION

PRINT THE CHECK USING vendor_name, vendor_address,
grand_total

REPLACE balance IN vendor WITH 0
```

5. Data Base Maintenance Model

Menu option 4.4 is used to copy all the ticket numbers available for sale for an event into the "available" relation. A seating code is assigned when a new event is booked. The seating codes are used in the model to load the tickets "available" relation from files containing master seating layouts.

```
In this module, the user is prompted for the event num-
ber, which triggers the loading of tickets into the
"available" relation.
```

```
DISPLAY THE INPUT SCREEN
   INPUT event_number_input
```

```
In this module, the "events" relation is opened. Based
on the user's input for the event number, the record
that contains information on the requested event is
read.
```

```
OPEN THE events RELATION
   READ RECORD WHERE event_number
   = event_number_input
```

```
This module performs a loop 10 times to load tickets
into the "available" relation for the 10 pos-
sible dates an event can be booked.
```

```
STORE 1 TO loop
DO A BIG LOOP UNTIL loop > 10
   IF date_1  IS NOT BLANK AND loop = 1
   PERFORM START
   IF date_2  IS NOT BLANK AND loop = 2
   PERFORM START
   IF date_3  IS NOT BLANK AND loop = 3
   PERFORM START
   IF date_4  IS NOT BLANK AND loop = 4
   PERFORM START
```

```
    IF date_5  IS NOT BLANK AND loop = 5
    PERFORM START
    IF date_6  IS NOT BLANK AND loop = 6
    PERFORM START
    IF date_7  IS NOT BLANK AND loop = 7
    PERFORM START
    IF date_8  IS NOT BLANK AND loop = 8
    PERFORM START
    IF date_9  IS NOT BLANK AND loop = 9
    PERFORM START
    IF date_10 IS NOT BLANK AND loop = 10
    PERFORM

START
    IF loop = 1  THEN STORE date_1  TO load_date
    IF loop = 2  THEN STORE date_2  TO load_date
    IF loop = 3  THEN STORE date_3  TO load_date
    IF loop = 4  THEN STORE date_4  TO load_date
    IF loop = 5  THEN STORE date_5  TO load_date
    IF loop = 6  THEN STORE date_6  TO load_date
    IF loop = 7  THEN STORE date_7  TO load_date
    IF loop = 8  THEN STORE date_8  TO load_date
    IF loop = 9  THEN STORE date_9  TO load_date
    IF loop = 10 THEN STORE date_10 TO load_date

STORE event_number  TO number
STORE ticket_scheme TO scheme

IF seating_code = 1 OPEN THE configure1 RELATION
IF seating_code = 2 OPEN THE configure2 RELATION
IF seating_code = 3 OPEN THE configure3 RELATION
IF seating_code = 4 OPEN THE configure4 RELATION
IF seating_code = 5 OPEN THE configure5 RELATION
IF seating_code = 6 OPEN THE configure6 RELATION

DO A SMALL LOOP UNTIL ALL RECORDS ARE COPIED

    ADD A BLANK RECORD TO THE available RELATION
    COPY ticket_number IN configure TO available
    REPLACE data IN available WITH load_date
    REPLACE event_number IN available WITH number
    REPLACE issued(Y/N) IN available WITH "N"
    ADVANCE ONE RECORD IN configure

    END OF THE SMALL LOOP

STORE loop + 1 to loop

END OF THE BIG LOOP
```

Test Programs

Tommy Tune performed a structured walkthrough of all the foregoing program modules written by Digit. After the modules were tested and integrated with Digit's core software packages, both valid and invalid test transactions were run to test the total software system. No errors were found, and Tommy Tune certified the software system 100 percent reliable.

Programming changes to the core system in the future will be performed by Digit as specified in the contract between the event center and Digit. The event center is allowed to produce custom reports and develop programs that read from the data base. Tommy Tune will receive specialized training in SQL to aid users in preparing ad hoc reports.

Training and Educating

Based on an assessment of the tasks required to operate the new system, it is deemed unnecessary to hire new employees.

Digit provides one week of on-site training before the hardware is installed. The company provides seminars and group instruction during this week. Digit remains on-site two weeks after the hardware is installed to provide on-the-job training to operators and users. Interactive video programs on CD-ROM are also provided for personnel who wish to review training material. Digit also provides a toll-free hot line to answer any questions.

Training is conducted by three representatives from Digit with assistance from Sally Forth and Tommy Tune. Training is customized for top management, supervisors, operating personnel, and direct users. Personnel are advised to make available the time necessary to attend appropriate sessions based on the following training schedule:

1. Top Management Overview Seminars
   Attendees:
      John Ball, Executive Director
      Tyronne Topps, Chief Information Systems Officer

   Seminar Session 1 (Monday 8:00–12:00)
   a. Technology Platform Review
   b. SEATS Design Overview
   c. SEATS Data Base

   Seminar Session 2 (Wednesday 8:00–12:00)
   a. Administrative and Procedural Controls
   b. Maintenance
   c. Reports

2. Supervisors Group Instruction
   Attendees:
      Ned Travis, Accounting Manager
      Donna McDermott, Activities Manager
      John Fairchild, Facilities Manager

Group Instruction Session 1 (Monday 1:00–5:00)
a. SEATS Design Overview
b. .Menus and Screens Descriptions
c. Logical Relationship of SEATS Data Base

Group Instruction Session 2 (Tuesday 1:00–5:00)
a. Events Module Specifics
b. Accounting Module Specifics
c. Ticketing Module Specifics

Group Instruction Session 3 (Wednesday 1:00–5:00)
a. Procedural Controls
b. Administrative Controls
c. File Maintenance

3. Operating Personnel Procedural Training
   Attendees:
   Susie Ticketaker, Box Office Manager
   Trixy Stub, Ticketing Manager
   Nancy Treadwell, Principal Accounting Clerk
   Patty Noble, Publicity Director
   Sam Springer, Events Coordinator

   Events Module Procedural Training Session 1
   (Tuesday 8:00–12:00)
   a. Date Scheduling
   b. Advertising and Marketing Requirements
   c. Staffing Requirements
   d. Reports

   Ticketing Module Procedural Training Session 2
   (Thursday 8:00–12:00)
   a. Seating Assignments and Ticket Sales
   b. Ticketing Pricing Structure Setup
   c. Financial Inquiry
   d. Ticket Sales Inquiry
   e. Reports

   Accounting Module Procedural Training Session 3
   (Friday 8:00–12:00)
   a. Accounts Receivable
   b. Accounts Payable
   c. General Journal
   d. Reporting

4. Direct Users On-the-Job and Tutorial Training
   Attendees:
   Mollie Murchison, Ticket Seller
   Ronand Coleman, Ticket Seller
   Terrence Wilson, Assistant to the Publicity Director

Shelly Norton, Assistant to the Events Coordinator

On-the-Job Training Session 1 (Thursday 1:00–5:00)
a. Terminals
b. Printers
c. Documentation
d. Online Help Screens
e. Source Data
f. Problem Resolution

On-the-Job Training Session 2 (Friday 1:00–5:00)
a. Event Menus and Screens
b. Ticketing Menus and Screens
c. Accounting Menus and Screens

Input Testing

One week prior to delivery of hardware, the departments will be instructed on how to fill out the forms. Users will be tested to determine if they are completing the forms correctly. Accuracy and speed of data entry personnel will be evaluated. The efficiency of screen input layouts will be evaluated. Any screens that are cluttered or contain unnecessary data will be identified and corrected.

Output Testing

Reports and inquiry screens will be tested for accuracy based on live data that are entered during the training sessions. All reports will be issued to the final users, and each user will be required to fill out a questionnaire to see if the reports meet his or her information needs. The questionnaire will address the following issues:

1. Are headings accurate and understandable?
2. Are editing characteristics of report fields correct?
3. Are debit/credit and dollar sign notations correct?
4. Are page numbers in correct sequence?
5. Are end-of-report indicators understandable?
6. Are reports issued with the correct date?
7. Are reports understandable and accurate?
8. Comments?

Data Base Testing

After live data are entered, data files are tested for completeness by comparing batch control totals to totals produced from the data base. Other data base tests are performed by Digit during development.

Controls Testing

Controls testing emphasizes the way transactions are prepared and entered. Specific items to be tested are as follows:

1. Are new events being booked with proper authorization?

2. Are customer accounts being created with proper authorization?
3. Are ticket transactions being performed in proper sequence?
4. Is the use of passwords being controlled?
5. Are control totals being prepared and reported back to the control group?

Controls built into the system by Digit to be tested are:

1. Numeric, alphabetic, and special character checks
2. Validity checks on key data fields
3. Limit and reasonableness checks

Systems Conversion

The systems conversion process is performed in parallel with the manual system currently in place for six months in all areas except ticketing, which will be converted directly on MM/DD/YY. Parallel conversion in accounting, events, and resources is necessary to reconcile differences that may occur. Parallel conversion of ticketing is not practical. The new system is converted directly and must perform on its own.

All current data are converted directly and reconciled during the training sessions in cooperation with Digit. A rehearsal for direct conversion of the ticketing operations is to be performed on Sunday, February XX, 19X0. The ticket office is normally closed on Sunday and will remain closed during the rehearsal. If the rehearsal is performed successfully, then the SEATS ticketing system will be used on Monday, February XX, 19X0.

Implementation Follow-up and Acceptance Meeting

Implementation Follow-up

A user representative assigned by John Ball will perform implementation follow-up. Sally and Tommy are available to answer questions. The representative will be responsible to review and report on a monthly basis how SEATS is operatng.

The review covers the following areas:

1. Input, processing, and output schedules
2. Activities of input preparation personnel
3. Backup procedures
4. Computer operator procedures
5. Report utilization
6. Hardware maintenance

The user representative report will contain:

1. Areas that need improvement.
2. Recommended methods for reconciling errors.
3. Recommended areas where additional control is required.

4. Areas where old material will be eliminated from the system.

5. Requested upgrades to the system.

Acceptance Meeting

An acceptance meeting will be held on MM/DD/YY to discuss the recently completed training sessions and to determine if the event center is ready to perform parallel conversion. The meeting will be attended by systems analysts, systems operating personnel, and users. If a consensus is reached that the system installed is ready for use, then the systems analysts will be released from working on the development of SEATS to perform work on The Facilities Management and Seating Layout System, a follow-up to SEATS. After systems conversion, SEATS will become the responsibility of John Ball and his staff.

SUMMARY

Systems implementation is the last phase of systems development. When it is over, primary responsibility for the system shifts from the systems analyst to end users and operations personnel.

Part of the deliverable for this phase, the Final Implementation Report, contains a detailed implementation plan prepared before implementation work begins. For large systems, this plan must set out the tasks and activities to be performed and coordinated by the implementation team.

An important step in systems implementation is the additional testing of the technology that was selected during the evaluation phase. Tools and techniques to perform tests on the selected technology include burn-in and site preparation, job accounting system, hardware and software monitors, performance utilities, and ergonomics.

If a new system is to be implemented successfully, everyone who is affected by it must be made aware of his or her system responsibilities and what the system provides them. Approaches to educating and training personnel include seminars and group instruction, procedural training, tutorial training, simulation, on-the-job training, and the use of an information center. Providing adequate education and training, both initially and on a continuing basis, is absolutely essential if the new system is to achieve its objectives.

Programming is a process performed by programmers to write instructions (code) that are executed by computers. Because of the magnitude of the programming effort, any gain in productivity or enhancement in coding practices can result in significant economies in the system being implemented. Programming practices such as the elimination of unstructured code and the application of structured programming techniques can make programs more understandable and maintainable. Using programming, debugging, testing, and documentation aids can also increase the productivity of programmers. Moreover, large gains in productivity have been attained when the programming effort has been organized around the chief programmer team concept.

Program testing is the last chance to ensure that the programs meet users' requirements. It parallels the approach of modular program development, in that stages of function testing, module testing, integration testing, total program testing, and acceptance testing are followed. Whether a big-bang, incremental, top-down, or bottom-up approach to the testing is adopted, the use of an independent testing team is recommended.

Systems conversion takes place after the input, output, data base, and controls building blocks are tested. Conversion to the new system can follow a direct or parallel approach, and incorporate aspects of the modular and phase-in approaches. Special consideration should be given the data base during the conversion process.

Once the system is implemented, the systems analyst should check regularly that input, processing, and output schedules are being met. As a final activity, the systems analyst should review the old system and conversion documentation and purge all outdated and start-up procedures, programs, and forms.

IMPORTANT TERMS

acceptance meeting

acceptance test

adaptive programming team

administrator

algorithmic error

archival file

automatic flowcharter

backup file

big-bang test

black box test case

bottom-up test

chief programmer team

code optimizers

completeness test

compliance test

computation error

copy routine

cross-reference

data set reorganizers

decision table processor

direct conversion

domain error

driver module

editor

egoless programming

ergonomics

Final Implementation Report

function test

group instruction

hardware monitor

implementation plan

incremental test

index file

information center

integration test

job accounting system

language specialist

lead assistant

librarian

master file

modular conversion

module test

on-the-job (OTJ) training
operating personnel
paging
parallel conversion
performance monitor
phase-in conversion
procedural training
program clerk
program library
program restructuring
program testing
program walkthrough
programming
schedulers
seeding errors
semantic error
seminars
shorthand aid
simulation
site preparation
software monitor
structured programming

stub module
subroutine library
substantive test
summary file
support programmer
syntactic error
syntax editor
table file
technical test
test data generator
tester
text editor
toolsmith
top-down test
total program test
trace
transaction file
tutorial training
unstructured program code
virtual storage code reorganizers
white box test case
workstation network

Assignment

REVIEW QUESTIONS

20.1 What are the two major parts of the Final Implementation Report? When are they prepared?

20.2 Define burn-in tests.

20.3 What does a job accounting system such as IBM's system management facility show?

20.4 List the components that are commonly measured by a software monitor.

20.5 Define four types of performance utilities.

20.6 Describe two broad categories of people who must receive training in the system being implemented; six approaches to educating and training these people.

20.7 Define the term "programming." In restructuring code, what kind of statements are eliminated? What are some of the software tools used in program restructuring?

20.8 Define what is meant by the structure theorem. What three program functions does it allow?

20.9 Programming aids reduce the time and effort of writing code. Describe six programming aids.

20.10 Aids exist to help programmers test program logic, detect bugs, and document results. Describe six of these aids.

20.11 Why is the adaptive programming team approach often referred to as "egoless programming?"

20.12 List the people who make up a chief programmer team, and describe the duties of each person.

20.13 What is a structured program walkthrough? What is its purpose? Who attends the walkthrough and what is the role of each person?

20.14 Define the three major categories of program errors.

20.15 If structured programming requires modular construction, what five stages of program testing might be observed?

20.16 Identify the differences in the big-bang, incremental, top-down, and bottom-up approaches to program testing.

20.17 What are "black box" test cases? "white box" test cases?

20.18 In controls testing, compliance testing is performed. Define compliance testing and identify its three phases.

20.19 List and describe four approaches to systems conversion.

20.20 The success of systems conversion depends to a great degree on how well the systems analyst prepares for the creation and conversion of the data files required for the new system. For each of the seven major classifications of files, list the control procedures used during conversion.

20.21 Describe four important activities or events that comprise systems implementation follow-up.

QUESTIONS FOR DISCUSSION

20.22 List some techniques that a programmer can use to find errors during a program walkthrough (examples include: rounding of numbers, and limits on accuracy).

20.23 How does the documentation of the systems analyst relate to computer programming?

20.24 Explain how the systems team may have to coordinate with purchasing or contracting personnel.

20.25 Make a list of some of the courses you believe would be necessary to train personnel when a new system is installed. Write a short description of each course.

20.26 How would you begin systems testing if the computer was not delivered for six months?

20.27 How does the approach to systems design presented in this book facilitate training and conversion activities?

20.28 At some stage, a newly implemented system is defined to be "operational" and responsibility for it usually shifts to a maintenance programming group. How can we determine at what point the system is operational?

20.29 Why is it unwise to make a major change in the organization (e.g., a departmental restructuring) concomitantly with the implementation of a new information system?

20.30 Conversion may involve change in one or several of the following areas:

1. People.   3. Data.   5. Operations.
2. Facilities.   4. Procedures.

Explain this concept.

20.31 The following chart depicts the estimated percentage of reasons for failures in data processing systems. Discuss.

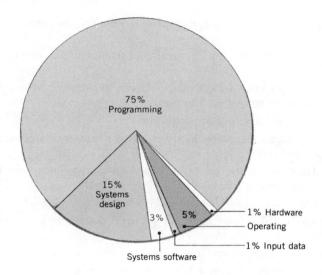

EXERCISES AND PROBLEMS

20.32 Write three or four paragraphs discussing the role of the programmer in the systems implementation phase.

20.33 Advance planning for testing activities is built into the project at points where commitments of personnel and resources must be made in advance because of the critical nature of given activities. Before any testing begins, specific procedures or plans should be developed. Construct an activity network chart for systems testing.

20.34 Analyze the following situations. Which approach to systems conversion would you recommend for each? Note that you may elect to use more than a single conversion approach for each situation. Explain fully your recommendations.

1. Implementing a check deposit system utilizing OLRT (online real-time) devices into a bank with 40 area branches.

2. Implementing an inventory control system for 50,000 items at three warehouses.

3. Implementing a centralized order-entry system servicing 40 sales offices.

4. Implementing a sales statistics system to be accessed by CRT devices.

5. Implementing a lottery system (where one had not existed before), with 250 ticket offices and remote batch entry.

6. Implementing a computer-based accounts receivable system, where a manual system existed previously.

7. Implementing an integrated system that includes order entry, inventory control, accounts receivable, sales statistics, and product forecasting, into a multiple-plant organization with sales of more than $100,000,000.

20.35 The modular concept of programming essentially means subdividing the logic of the program into logical parts, which are usually called modules. To separate effectively the program into logic modules, the programmer must understand the parts that make up the program. For example, a banking system must produce account statements; it also might keep records and deduct amounts from checking accounts for federal and state government, savings plan, credit payments, and insurance programs and provide for bank accounting functions. Construct an example of modular programming using a banking system.

20.36 Construct an example of a user training checklist.

20.37 The manual accounts receivable system of Calico Pet Supply is being converted to a computer-based system. The present manual accounts receivable system has the following characteristics: (1) each customer with a nonzero accounts receivable balance has a folder containing a copy of all unpaid invoices and credit notes issued; (2) when a payment and accompanying remittance is received from a customer, the remittance is matched to an unpaid invoice and both documents are placed in a "current closed" file, which, in turn, is purged every six months; (3) a "permanent closed" file, composed of purged "current closed" file documents, is maintained for a period of seven years; and (4) at month's end, the balance of each customer's account is classified according to the age of the balance outstanding. This is done by a clerk tallying and dating folder amounts.

The frequency of access to the three files varies considerably. The "folder" file is accessed frequently. The "current closed" file is accessed periodically, normally at the request of the credit manager or a customer. The "permanent closed" file is accessed infrequently.

The new system to be implemented will contain three files: (1) a customer master file, containing information pertinent to each customer; (2) an open item file, corresponding to the "folder" file of the manual system; and (3) a closed item file, assembling a combined "current closed" and "permanent closed" file.

Assume you were given the responsibility of converting the old system to the new system. Please answer the following questions:

1. Would you suggest a direct or a parallel conversion approach? Why?
2. Is a phase-in conversion approach appropriate? Why?
3. What special clerical procedures would need to be established to validate the correctness of the new system's operation against the old system?
4. What special initialization and validation programming is required for the data base conversion?

20.38 An employee time card contains the following data:

Field	Length	Comment
Employee number	10	(1) First character must be alphabetic. (2) Next nine digits are his or her social security number.
Department	2	(1) Must be numeric. (2) Must match valid department table.
Shift	1	(1) Must be numeric. (2) Day = 0; Afternoon = 1; Midnight = 2.
Start time	4	(1) Must be numeric. (2) First two digits must be between 00 and 23. (3) Last two digits must be between 00 and 59.
Stop time	4	(1) Must be numeric. (2) First two digits must be between 00 and 23. (3) Last two digits must be between 00 and 59.

This card is punched daily and submitted for computer processing. Only time cards with valid data, based on an edit subroutine, are accepted for further processing.

Required: Prepare a set of decision tables that describes the subroutine for editing the time cards. Also, format the time card error report and provide examples of several types of errors.

BIBLIOGRAPHY

BABICK, WAYNE A. *Software Configuration Management.* Reading, Mass.: Addison-Wesley, 1986.

CANNING, RICHARD C. "Strategies for Introducing New Systems." *EDP Analyzer,* July 1985.

CHARETTE, ROBERT N. *Software Engineering Environments.* New York: Intertext, 1986.

DESMOND, JOHN. "The Friendly Master." *Software Magazine,* February 1988.

HARRISON, WARREN, and BAHRAM ADRANGI. "Programming Language and Software Development Costs." *Journal of Management Information Systems,* Winter 1986–1987.

JONES, CAPERS. *Programming Productivity.* New York: McGraw-Hill, 1986.

JOYCE, ED. "Software Bugs: A Matter of Life and Liability." *Datamation,* May 15, 1987.

"Keeping Shippers into EDI." *Railway Age,* March 1988.

KROENKE, DAVID M., and KATHLEEN A. DOLAN. *Business Computer Systems,* 3rd ed. Santa Cruz, Calif.: Mitchell, 1987.

KULL, DAVID. "Anatomy of a 4GL Disaster." *Computer Decisions,* February 11, 1986.

MACE, SCOTT. "New Virus Damaging Mac Data, Group Says." *InfoWorld,* April 11, 1988.

MACRO, ALLEN, and JOHN BUXTON. *The Craft of Software Engineering.* Reading, Mass.: Addison-Wesley, 1987.

PARIKH, GIRISH. *Handbook of Software Maintenance.* New York: John Wiley, 1986.

PRICE, STAN. *Managing Computer Projects.* New York: John Wiley, 1986.

RODGERS, WARREN. "My Terrible Vacation." *Inc.,* February 1988.

SIMPSON, W. DWAIN. *New Techniques in Software Project Managment.* New York: John Wiley, 1987.

SWARTZ, STEVE. "Former Mortgage Security Head Blames First Boston's Controls for Expected Loss." *The Wall Street Journal,* February 29, 1988.

21

INFORMATION SYSTEMS MANAGEMENT

21.1 INTRODUCTION

The PC revolution of the early 1980s has caused plenty of fallout, both good and bad. To build on the positive fallout and develop strategic information systems, an information systems (IS) leader is needed, such as a chief information officer (CIO).

Many believe that a new IS focus has spawned the end-user era. End users and their needs and requirements are the reason and justification for the information system's existence.

The IS revolution continues on many fronts. The CIO will, consequently, have to deal with the hot issues and bring peace between warring factions. Examples are information centers versus management information systems/data processing (MIS/DP), mainframes versus personal computers (PCs), and centralization versus decentralization.

Specifically the objectives of this chapter are:

1. To report on the information systems upheaval.
2. To discuss the role of the chief information officer.
3. To consider the era of the end user.
4. To describe the controversy milieu in which IS management and professionals must work.

21.2 INFORMATION SYSTEMS UPHEAVAL

For managers who work in the IS function, this is the "worst of times and the best of times." For bureaucratic-minded managers, technology and user needs have passed them by. For entrepreneurially-minded managers, however, opportunities abound for building information systems, the likes of which have not been seen before.

The Shot Heard Round the World

Frustrated by long development cycles, application backlogs measured in years, and bureaucratic barriers, some intrepid user years ago smuggled an Apple II into his office, convinced that this 8-bit machine would give him the information that he couldn't get from MIS/DP. At this point, the PC revolution was on and soon spread like wildfire yet to be extinguished.

Today, in many organizations, former high priests of MIS/DP (a narrower concept than information systems or simply IS) have lost some of their control over the IS function because of the PC anarchy. PCs, the major weapons in the information systems revolution, are being used effectively in some instances and misused in others. Many sit idle collecting dust. Worse than this, "information systems," supported by PC platforms, are fragmented and in great need of leadership and of a coordinating force.

Indeed, there are no winners in the war between MIS/DP czars and PC revolutionists. MIS/DP cannot continue as insular bureaucracies, and PC users cannot continue independently. If such a standoff continues, not only will both groups of combatants lose, but the companies that employ them will also lose.

Ushering in a New Era

To be sure, emergence of end-user computing has significantly altered the role of MIS/DP in organizations. With mainframe power on end users' desks, and improved connectivity between network nodes, the entire relationship between MIS/DP and end users must be rethought. The old, red tape–ladened methods of "serving" end users won't work. A new era must be characterized by close interaction and cooperation among management, end users, vendors, and new IS professionals.

Many companies are seeking ways to make peace and join the forces for a new synergy. Enlightened MIS/DP professionals now understand the needs of end users, and end users understand more about information technology. Despite occasional misapplications and underutilization, the microcomputer revolution has produced do-it-yourself, computer-literate users with a positive attitude toward information technology, something an entrepreneurial-minded, strategic-oriented information systems leader can build on.

21.3 LOOKING FOR A LEADER: IS THE CHIEF INFORMATION OFFICER THE ANSWER?

Information systems need visionary, entrepreneurial (infopreneurial?) leadership as an alternative to both bureaucratized MIS/DP empires and microcomputer mobocracies. Many authorities suggest a chief information officer.

To some, the CIO represents information system's rise in status as a strategic weapon and valuable corporate resource. To others, CIO is nothing more than title inflation.

In any event, a large number of companies are looking for people who can build information systems congruent with and supportive of business strategy. Such people are members of management's inner circle and often have direct access to the board of directors.

DuWayne Peterson, Merrill Lynch's IS mastermind, has responsibilities that may go even beyond those of a CIO's. Peterson's salary is nearly $1.5 million. He has a budget of over $1 billion and manages over 15,000 IS professionals. Moreover, he has direct access to and full support from the board of directors.

A sampling of other titles used besides CIO to reflect this strategic position include vice-president of information services, information czar, vice-president of information systems, vice-president of information management, executive director of MIS, and director of corporate systems. According to John Diebold and Associates, over one-third of the nation's major companies have a CIO in function, if not in title.

The Mission

With this new strategic-level title, such as CIO, owners and executives expect new kinds of information systems. Such systems will help companies increase profitability and productivity, differentiate products and services, improve management, and satisfy all users' requirements.

To accomplish their missions, CIOs must be business strategists with sufficient background in information technology to build information systems that leverage business strategy. CIOs are not only strategists, but orchestrators and architects who are skilled in personal communications and who are comfortable with executives and directors. Some CIOs call themselves corporate integrators.

Frequently, the CIO must cross traditional departmental and political boundaries and become involved in the affairs of manufacturing, marketing, logistics, and finance. Therefore, the CIO must understand these different functions and employ a great deal of diplomacy and know-how to communicate with both line personnel and executives. Moreover, the CIO must continually inform management and other users about the technology that affects their areas. At

---

SEARS SEEKS SYNERGY BY CREATING CIO POSITION

Sears, Roebuck and Company created a CIO position several years ago. This is a senior vice-president post that reports directly to the chairman and chief executive officer (CEO).

The CIO's responsibilities include Sears communication network and information systems for the business groups: Merchandising, Dean Witter, Allstate Insurance Company, and Coldwell Banker Real Estate Group. The CIO's mission is to generate synergies, find overlaps, and establish backup among Sears business units, which are highly decentralized. Sears also expects the CIO post to continue to enhance Sears' ability to use information technology as a strategic management tool.

the same time, the CIO must aid in strategic information systems planning and help users identify needs and priorities of their departments. In no way can the CIO ever be perceived by users and the corporate culture as an intruder.

If a company wishes to decentralize management and information systems, the CIO must exploit the advantages of decentralization yet maintain a cohesive, coordinated information system to support the corporate agenda. If, on the other hand, a company has a centralized management philosophy, the CIO must leverage the advantages of centralization while meeting the requirements of end users, especially those who are remote from corporate headquarters. Above all, the CIO must understand the business, bring disciplines and people together, and build information systems that are within budget.

PILLSBURY'S DOUGH RISES FROM STRATEGIC INFORMATION SYSTEMS

John Hammitt, vice-president of information management at Pillsbury, states that his company competes with many other organizations for a "share of the stomach." The goal of Pillsbury is to double its share of the "stomach market" within five years. Hammitt's primary responsibility is to identify strategic opportunities and present a number of ways in which information technology can leverage these opportunities and help accelerate Pillsbury's growth goal.

The CIO Strategy and Focus

The CIO does not create new products or services, but envisions how other areas of the company can use information technology in innovative ways, and encourages them to do so. The CIO also views the information system itself as a strategic opportunity rather than simply as a support resource. The CIO's information systems development is based on a cohesive strategy stemming from sound and thorough strategic information systems planning (SISP).

Figure 21.1 depicts the CIO's focus for information system opportunities. Strategic opportunities occupy most of the CIO's time. At this level, executive information systems (EIS), decision support systems (DSS), and corporate war rooms are developed. Ways to collect and disseminate strategic intelligence are installed. Moreover, the information system becomes a tool to support new ways of doing business such as implementation of electronic data interchange (EDI).

Tactical opportunities include those things that can be accomplished within a fiscal period. Examples include monitoring systems that provide variance reporting, programmed decision making, automatic notification, and expert systems. Channel systems are built for major suppliers and customers. Filtering algorithms provide tailor-made reports for different levels of users.

At the foundation level, the CIO's agenda is to leverage technology and procedures to the fullest to increase effectiveness and efficiency and drive costs down. Use of structured programming, programming aids, fourth-generation

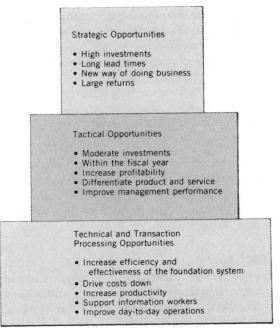

Figure 21.1 CIO focus for information system opportunities.

MARKETING THE USE OF INFORMATION SYSTEMS

Anthony Dandolo, MIS director of Fininvest Servizi, the information system division of Italian conglomerate Fininvest, Milan, confirms, "There is a definite lean toward marketing and hiring marketing people so we can approach the rest of the company with our services. We are active rather than reactive. We look for every opportunity to show the company the strategic use of information systems."

"At first," Dandolo recalls, "we tried to impose change, but then ended up directing change instead. The corporate culture has to adapt. Part of the continuing education here is to show that each job is part of the organic whole of the company, not an isolated unit."

"The idea of entrepreneurship very much applies in this IS department," says Hans van Mierop, corporate IS manager of Dutch wholesale and packing conglomerate Buhrmann Tetterode outside Amsterdam. "We are doing a selling job internally, selling IS as a tool of management and as a business function."

Excerpts from James Etheridge, Janette Martin, Robert Poe, and Paul Tate, "From DP Dept. to IS Inc.," *Datamation*, November 1, 1987, pp. 56-3 to 56-8.

languages (4GLs), data base management systems with easy-to-use query languages, a well-defined systems development methodology, prototyping, and computer-aided software engineering (CASE) systems represent some of the methods used by the CIO's staff to provide a solid foundation for the tactical- and strategic-level systems opportunities. Other efficiency-producing technology includes point-of-sale (POS) devices, facsimile, electronic mail, and word processing.

21.4 THE END-USER ERA

Many IS professionals state that we are in the era of the end user, the ultimate information systems "customer." In the final analysis, the success of information systems and the fulfillment of this new period in information systems history, depends on how well IS professionals, led by CIOs (or some other title), meet end users' needs and requirements.

The End-User Manifesto

The information system must provide the platform and environment that recognizes and handles a spectrum of applications and meets the diversity of all users, inside and outside the organization, at all levels, whether they are novice, occasional knowledgeable, frequent light, or frequent power users. Essentially, this entire book is directed toward how information systems can be built to serve end users.

End Users on Center Stage

The end user is the focal point of information systems as spotlighted in Figure 21.2. The building blocks, as we know, provide the information system's infra-

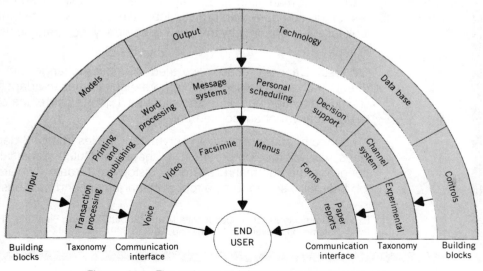

Figure 21.2 The end user on information system's center stage.

structure. The taxonomy includes all the functions, processes, and operations that serve all the end users' basic requirements. The system processes accounting transactions and handles a number of office procedures, such as publishing, word processing, and message systems. End users can also use the system for personal management and scheduling. Decision support and executive information is provided by applying scenario analysis, expert systems, heuristics, and other models. Channel systems provide direct linkage to stakeholders. The experimental component allows the testing of prototypes for possible implementation. It permits IS professionals and end users to test ideas in a practical low-cost, low-risk manner before committing to full-scale development. This component, therefore, provides a large window of opportunity for infopreneuring and keeps the entrepreneurial ball rolling.

The communication interface is how and where end users interact with the system. The user/system interface design force dominates at this point. Different media and formats are used to accommodate end users' cognitive styles and communication choices, thus building a strong, useful, and friendly user/system interface.

21.5 THE CONTROVERSY MILIEU

Lulls may occur from time to time, but various facets of the information systems revolution will never really end. The main goal of the CIO position, or equivalent post, is to turn this ongoing revolution into a constructive force. It's simply a matter of the CIO rising above the conflict, putting the fallout to good use, and managing change. Some major battles that are being waged hot and heavy today and ones that CIOs must deal with are discussed in the following sections.

Information Centers Versus MIS/DP

Originally, PCs were shunned by MIS/DP as toys. As we already know, however, more and more end users began to acquire their own PCs and bypass MIS/DP. But when the PC revolution began to flounder and get out of control, many companies established information centers at first to drive and nurture end users, then later to oversee and coordinate end-user activity. In fact, many of the information centers were established by MIS/DP.

The Changing Mission and Focus of Information Centers

Early on, end-user computing was the focus of information centers. The mission of information centers was to train and support end users. Moreover, they were to help end users deal with the onslaught of information technology and exploit its benefits.

Information centers have come a long way from their earlier mission and focus. Why? Because end users have come a long way. Moreover, information centers developed close ties with users. In fact, some information centers are running into some of the very same problems that besieged MIS/DP and prompted the establishment of information centers in the first place, such as rising end-user demands and expectations, application backlogs, and inadequate staff and resources.

Training has led to consulting, consulting has led to systems analyst work, and systems analyst work has led to programming and systems implementation. Information centers have become experts in finding, acquiring, and implementing software and hardware to meet the requirements of users in marketing, logistics, production, and accounting. They provide special services, hot lines, newsletters, various end-user classes, libraries, and data downloads from the mainframe.

While MIS/DP has stayed with the mainframe, some information centers are helping end users install minicomputers and arranging for multiuser local area networks (LANs). They are even taking direct responsibility for systems design and implementation.

Indeed, new mission statements at a number of information centers indicate a more autonomous role in the organization, not a support tool for MIS/DP. These information centers have enjoyed great successes in working with end users and bringing information technology to "new systems customers," who otherwise would not have become users.

The Tug-of-War

Most information centers are under the aegis of MIS/DP. Generally, the relationship between information centers and MIS/DP is described as a "partnership" or "association." The relationship, no matter what form it takes, is often strained with political and turf skirmishes. Moreover, self-promotion by information centers to influential users and people who control the purse strings has rankled MIS/DP personnel.

Information center personnel are antagonistic toward MIS/DP because they feel they are doing all the front-line work. On the other side, MIS/DP personnel believe the information center dilutes their power and influence. This situation results in a tug-of-war over resource control and influence. Information centers, in such circumstances, seek independence and autonomy. MIS/DP, which

---

THE CASE OF THE JEALOUS MIS/DP DEPARTMENT

In New York, a MIS/DP manager closed the information center he created. It was a classic case of jealousy in which the teacher resents the pupil's success then lashes out.

Some MIS/DP personnel felt they were betrayed when the information center bypassed them to take more responsibilities. This sudden independent attitude bred resentment and counteraction.

David Phillips, a system consultant, says that such a case indicates some of the conflicts that simmer between many MIS/DP and information center affiliations. Mr. Phillips claims, "It's all very subtle and under the surface, but these struggles exist."

originally gave up control of PCs with relief and contempt, has realized its mistake.

The CIO knows that one world of end-user computing and another world of MIS/DP is dysfunctional. Therefore, the CIO must step into this breach and integrate the two funtions into a smooth working relationship. Clearly, they both have important roles to play in developing successful information systems.

Big Iron Versus Little Iron

Historically, a mainframe was big in size, cost, and processing power and required a special site for its installation. Today, mainframes are much smaller, prices have fallen sharply, and some have less processing power than some desktop computers.

The Mainframe Mystique

Historically, MIS/DP used the mainframe to perform all computing for the organization. The corporate culture viewed the mainframe or data center as where serious computing and transaction processing took place, such as accounting, electronic funds transfer, credit validation, inventory control, reservations, and financial reporting—high-volume, big-production jobs.

The mainframe was, and in many organizations still is, the command-and-control center of the corporation. The mainframe approach to processing is, however, more a paradigm or concept than a big box with integrated circuitry. It, for a number of people, still represents information systems orthodoxy.

The Diminished Meaning of Size and Titles

What is big and what is little are becoming blurred. Supercomputing workstations provide 64-bit reduced instruction set computing (RISC)–based parallel processing at around 100 million instructions per second (MIPS) with three-dimensional graphics. In some instances, their random access memories (RAMs) and MIPS exceed those of some mainframes.

These new desktop workstations can support computation-intensive, mission-critical applications, such as desktop publishing, lab analysis, robotics, simulation, and computer-aided design. They provide 100 to 200 Mbytes of main memory and over 3 Gbytes of peripheral online storage with a total "footprint" about the size of a three-drawer file cabinet. But at the same time, mainframe-driven machines are also getting smaller, faster, more powerful, and cheaper.

Diseconomies of Scale

The cost of processing on workstations is only about 10 percent of the cost of processing the same instructions and data on minicomputers, and with supercomputing workstations, the cost is even less. Processing the same load on minicomputers costs about 20 to 30 percent of what it costs on a mainframe. Clearly, such economies provide a strong incentive for distributing the computing work load over several machines and away from the host mainframe.

One million 32-bit instructions per second on a traditional mainframe costs over $100,000. A nearly comparable MIPS processing on a microcomputer runs around $1,000. This 100-to-1 price differential for equal MIPS performance will significantly impact the demand for and survivability of traditional mainframe-based systems.

STRIVING FOR ESPRIT DE CORPS   "I hope MIS doesn't retreat back into its large mainframe systems," says Kay Fletcher, technical specialist at Los Alamos National Laboratory. "For everything to work, MIS and information centers have to work together."

Charles Marques, vice-president of a financial firm in New York, says, "Until now, MIS has spoken only one language, that of the mainframe. But now, they'll have to be bilingual and also speak to end users."

Condensed from Stan Kolodziej, "Control Up for Grabs, Power Tug-of-War Between MIS, ICs," *Computerworld*, October 7, 1987, pp. 17–19.

Proper Application is the Key

Too much attention is probably paid, however, to computer size and titles, such as mainframes, midrange or departmental, minicomputers, workstations, and microcomputers. They are just tools used to provide various hardware platforms for different systems designs. The box drives the software and data, the software models the application, the systems work develops the application, and the application is developed to meet users' requirements.

As far as the boxes are concerned, the goal of good systems design is to make optimum use of all resources and assign the right application to the appropriate level of processor power. For an analogy, common carriers use ships and trains to carry large, heavy loads of freight over long distances with relatively long delivery times. The same common carriers will use trucks and airplanes of different sizes and capacities to deliver smaller, individual loads with short delivery times. All these freight-carrying resources are integrated by common carriers for one basic goal: to get freight to customers when and where they want it at the least cost. The same applies to designers of information systems and their application of computers.

As PCs become more powerful, more and more mainframe and minicomputer applications will migrate to PCs. Upward and downward program and data migration, porting mainframe applications to desktop computers, and PC-level development of mainframe programs (e.g., COBOL) are the trends. Moreover, computing platforms of equivalent size can be established in a mainframe or by connecting multiple PCs together in a LAN, just so long as the PCs don't have to apply all their collective power at one time to the same part of an application.

It is inappropriate to view a PC-based LAN as a substitute for a mainframe. Generally, the mainframe is made to handle big production jobs, whereas a PC-based LAN is applicable for resource sharing and processing a number of small, interactive tasks.

The Connectivity Issue

Connectivity is a concept that has been debated for a long time, but has not been totally implemented yet. It is one of those concepts that many strive for but few may ever fully achieve. But enough connectivity will be achieved to make stand-alone mainframes, minis, or micros a thing of the past, except in small shops and for very specific, mission-critical applications.

For the information system to serve the entire organization, the boxes must be linked together to form an information system that appears to end users as a single resource and natural extension of their workstations. Connectivity, however, goes beyond mere micro-mini-mainframe linkage. It requires cooperative processing and logical interconnection of information systems building blocks. Any user has the ability to access information and interact with other users in a peer-to-peer relationship throughout the organization. Connectivity assumes full networking capabilities that enable users to navigate easily through the system, to use a portfolio of resources and services, and to extract data from any source on a need-to-know basis.

Clearly, the corporate culture and top management must support logical and systems connectivity. Physical connectivity support comes from architectural and telecommunication standards (review Chapter 10), such as open systems

---

PUTTING IT ALL TOGETHER

Dupont is focusing on SNA and DECnet, its two strategic networks as a way to improve its connectivity and incorporating electronic data interchange (EDI) capabilities to reach outside the company to customers and suppliers.

"What we need now are improved interconnections between different hardware platforms and better information management tools," says John H. Taylor, Dupont's scientific computer division manager.

On the desktop, Taylor sees a new generation of high-performance workstations redefining the way Dupont views computing. "It used to be we had what we called four types of computing in the company: business data processing, technical and scientific, process automation, and electronic office," he says. "Now, those distinctions are becoming fuzzy, partly because of the spread of low-cost, high-performance workstations throughout the company." According to Taylor, the sharing of information is now the name of the game at DuPont.

Condensed from Jeff Moad, "Dupont Seeks Global Communications Reach," *Datamation*, January 15, 1988, p. 72.

interconnect (OSI), transmission control protocol/internet protocol (TCP/IP), integrated services digital network (ISDN), DEC's DECnet, IBM's systems network architecture (SNA), and IBM's inclusion of peer-to-peer protocols.

Also, X.25, the international standard for packet switching, is a dominant transmission mode for WANs. The major method for transaction connectivity between companies is electronic data interchange.

Gateways and bridges continue to serve as the glue between the network seams. Because no single vendor, including AT&T, DEC, or IBM, can deliver a full complement of systems applications and total connectivity, vendors should work together to achieve interconnection and interoperability between products for seamless connectivity. Until they do, gateways, bridges, and other interfacing schemes will be necessary to link disparate products.

What is the value of connectivity to information systems and the company it serves? First, without networks and viable protocols, we cannot have connectivity. Next, without connectivity, we cannot achieve integration. Without integration, we cannot enjoy unimpeded communications and the free flow of information. As long as companies need a good flow of information to operate effectively and efficiently, there will be a need for connectivity.

Centralization Versus Decentralization

The pendulum keeps swinging from centralization to decentralization and back again, or to some hybrid thereof such as three-tier systems. This shifting back

---

THE BEST LAID PLANS OF MICE AND MEN EVEN IN SYSTEMS SOMETIMES GO AWRY

Kendall, a Boston-based hospital supplies manufacturer, decided that decentralization was the road to success. But the MIS department was heading in the opposite direction. The then-MIS director, a centralist, believed strongly in mainframe-oriented, top-down control.

The MIS staff knew that this strategy was "flying in the face of reality in terms of where the company was going," says Ronald Cipolla, current corporate director of MIS. But the department could not persuade its boss that other options, such as departmental processors running manufacturing resource planning could be implemented at one-fifth the cost.

Upper management started to question the MIS direction as well. "Are we doing the right thing?" was a frequently heard question, but no one insisted on an answer, Cipolla says.

After Cipolla took over, the centralist MIS strategy was brought to an abrupt halt. The out-of-pocket cost of stopping the centralized strategy and starting a decentralized one cost nearly $6 million in terms of hardware, software, and labor, plus the uncalculated cost in man-hours for new planning and retraining.

Abridged from Glenn Rifkin and Mitch Betts, "Strategic Systems Plans Gone Awry," *Computerworld*, March 14, 1988, pp. 1, 104–105.

and forth is evidence of companies trying to gain an optimum balance between central control and coordination while at the same time providing distributed functionality, processing resources, and connectivity to end users.

The amount of distribution skew to one end or the other of the centralization/decentralization spectrum probably has more to do with management's philosophy and the corporate culture than it does with information technology. It is also evidence of companies trying to implement a cohesive strategic information systems plan that mirrors the organization's business goals, management, and operating dynamics.

Most information systems professionals will agree that it is technologically feasible to centralize or decentralize to any extent one can imagine. The key to successful implementation of either approach, or a hybrid, is, however, proper alignment of the information system with the particular company it serves. (If necessary, review Chapter 5, especially Figure 5.6, to see how organization and culture factors influence the degree of information systems centralization or decentralization.)

Another interesting facet of the centralization/decentralization controversy is how systems can be centralized within decentralization. For example, a large, nationwide retailer, such as J. C. Penney, has a number of large data processing units distributed throughout the country and connected by satellites and terrestrial telecommunications. But each data processing unit within each region functions as a centralized facility for that particular region.

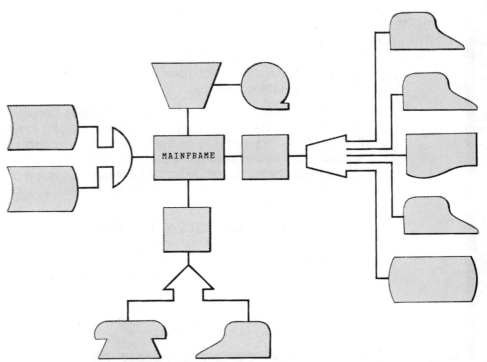

Figure 21.3 Centralized systems schema.

Alternatively, a system may be decentralized within centralization. A large bank and its information system may be highly centralized, but certain branches and other support facilities are served with distributed systems within their local operations.

Centralization Advocacy

Figure 21.3 portrays a centralized schema, which typically is represented by a star network topology. Most of the major processing power is concentrated in a mainframe host at a central site such as the home office. Most of the corporate data base is also kept at the central site. This arrangement provides a high comfort level for some people who want the data kept in a central, highly controlled site.

Most applications, especially big jobs requiring long run times, are performed by the central processor. Most of the information systems professionals, such as systems analysts, programmers, telecommunications personnel, and data base administrators, are at the central site.

With a mainframe-terminal platform, if users are not using their terminals, the mainframe continues processing, turning to applications waiting in the job queue. Therefore, a centralized system provides a good opportunity for efficient capacity utilization.

TWO FOR RECENTRALI-ZATION Security Pacific Corp. in Los Angeles and Merrill Lynch in New York are as different as chalk and cheese—but they agree on one thing: IS budgets everywhere have been out of control for years, largely because corporations have been investing in information technology on the basis of intuition or blind faith. Moreover, these companies have had no idea what return, if any, they have been getting on their money.

Both of these companies lost control of ambitious decentralization programs and are now reverting to centralized structures under the control of powerful IS executives. The trend to recentralization is surfacing elsewhere in the financial services sector as IBM's customers attempt to integrate their data structures and acquire competitors. These companies are learning the benefits of centralized purchasing and telecommunications, in addition to the new IS management techniques.

These techniques—collectively known as the management-by-results (MBR) program—don't just pay lip service to the notion that the customer is king, but put the idea into practice in such a way that wild swings in the IS budget and wrenching cycles of MIS centralization and decentralization will become a thing of the past.

Abridged from Ralph Emmett Carlyle, "Leading IS Shops Shifting to a Centralized Structure," *Datamation*, November 15, 1987, pp. 17–19.

Decentralization Advocacy

Advocates for decentralized systems, demonstrated in Figure 21.4, declare that mainframe, centralized systems are an endangered and doomed species. They believe most information systems will be microprocessor-dominated, connected by protocol-compatible, peer-to-peer networks based on bus, loop, ring, or mesh network topologies. Decentralization proponents have taken their cue from politicians who promise "power to the people" and a "chicken in every pot," which can be paraphrased as "power to the end user" and a "workstation on every desk."

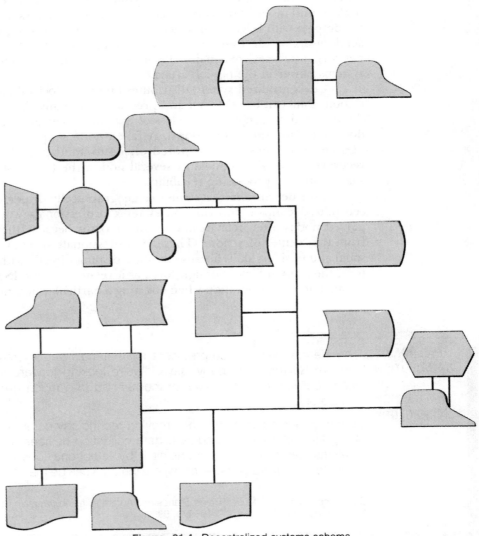

Figure 21.4 Decentralized systems schema.

Decentralization advocates state that the processing power of all workstations in a network is much greater than a mainframe. This is generally true, but for big jobs requiring long run times, a central mainframe-based system is typically more efficient. All the power under the skin of a workstation is available to a single user. Therefore, many MIPS are unavailable for full use by the company. In many end-user applications, the workstation or PC capacity far exceeds the user's ability to feed either machine a constant stream of relevant data and worthwhile applications.

In some systems, network managers and parallel processing schemes are used to concentrating the power of distributed systems for batch processing of big file-oriented applications. Instead of waiting for the jobs to be completed, users continue with their local tasks while the large batch job is processed in a background mode. This kind of parallel processing allows decentralized systems to compete with large, centralized mainframes by releasing the stranglehold of single users on all those underutilized MIPS. In fact, robust and standardized network interfaces are a major ally of decentralized systems to match centralized systems power in the big-job arena.

A decentralized system distributes building blocks throughout the organization. Data can be retrieved and processed from any site, regardless of where the transactions originate. The loss of data or processing capabilities at one site does not bring the system down. A failed node simply switches its backed-up files and programs that are stored offsite to another node to process until it recovers. Even with the loss of several nodes, the total system maintains high availability and processing reliability.

Some decentralized systems are geographically dispersed but have strong centralized control. Information systems professionals working in these dispersed nodes often fear dead-end career paths because they are far removed from the "center of action." These IS professionals also have to learn new personal and business skills because they are dealing directly with end users. Therefore, the human factors design force as it relates to these IS professionals must be taken into consideration when effecting a particular decentralization strategy.

RAILROAD'S DISTRIBUTION OF INFORMATION TECHNOLOGY

John Tierney, senior vice-president for materials and systems at Burlington Northern Railroad Company, says, "We're looking forward to pushing technology out into the operations of the railroad to a much greater extent than ever before."

Currently, Burlington Northern is moving technology out into the field by supplying its workers with hand-held data collection devices. Workers in remote locations gather data and transmit it by telephone to either their personal computer or mainframe receivers where the data can be manipulated as needed.

Condensed from Rose Mula, "Trains, Planes and Automobiles: Automation Boom Drives Need for MIS," *Computerworld*, March 7, 1988, p. 99.

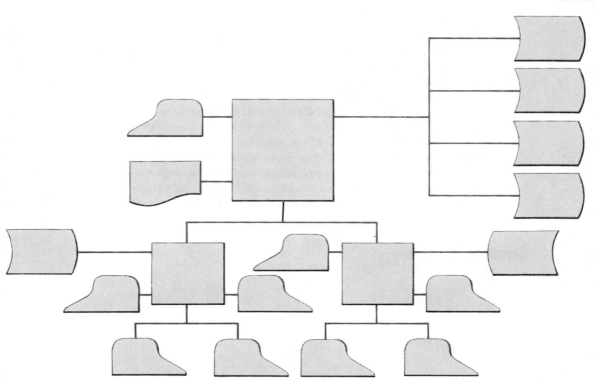

Figure 21.5 Three-tier systems schema.

Three-Tier Advocacy

In a three-tier information system, depicted in Figure 21.5, the mainframe is used as a data base machine and a network manager. Midrange or minicomputers function as departmental machines. Microcomputers and workstations serve individuals or small groups of end users. This three-tier strategy is based on a hierarchical network topology with full connectivity from mainframe to workstation. Similar to decentralized systems, the processing load is distributed across tiers.

SUMMARY

Managers of the information systems function in organizations face many challenges today. They must react to a loss in their control over computing that came with more end users doing private processing on their PCs. The fact that mainframe power now sits on the desks of end users and connectivity between network nodes is improving has given cause to rethink the entire relationship between traditional MIS/DP and end users. Top management is seeking ways to make peace and join these forces for a new synergy. They are looking for a chief information officer who can provide the leadership to build information systems that are congruent with and supportive of their business strategy. Moreover, they expect the CIO to take advantage of tactical opportunities afforded by variance reporting, expert systems, and channel systems, and to leverage technology and procedures to the fullest at the foundation level to increase effectiveness and efficiency and drive costs down.

Most experts agree that we are in a period where the end user is king—at center stage of the information systems theater. What they do not agree on, however, are the specifics of how the mission and focus of the information center should be set up to meet the needs of end users best. They also disagree on the relative proportion of mainframe versus PC processing that should be done to make optimum use of all resources within the organization and to assign the right application to the appropriate level of processor power, the value of connectivity of the information systems, and the best balance between central control of the IS resource and functional distribution of the IS resource to end users.

IMPORTANT TERMS

bridge	connectivity
centralization	decentralization
channel systems	end user
chief information officer (CIO)	gateway
	information center

Assignment

REVIEW QUESTIONS

21.1 For what type of managers is the IS function going through a period described as the "worst of times and the best of times?"

21.2 What titles other than chief information officer might be found for such positions in organizations?

21.3 List the types of information sytems a CIO might focus on at the strategic, tactical, and technical level.

21.4 What was the reasoning behind organizations establishing information centers in the first place? How have these information centers evolved?

21.5 What is the nature of the antagonism between information center personnel and MIS/EDP people?

21.6 What is at the heart of the connectivity issue?

21.7 Why will the pendulum between centralization and decentralization of the IS resource continue to swing in one direction and then in the other direction?

21.8 List the arguments given by advocates of a centralized IS resource arrangement; a decentralized systems arrangement.

21.9 What comprises each of the tiers of a three-tier information system?

QUESTIONS FOR DISCUSSION

21.10 Discuss why you believe that all processing hasn't shifted from mainframe to workstation given the dramatic economies associated with workstation processing.

21.11 Why won't all computing needs in the future be met by faster, more powerful PCs?

21.12 Prepare a list of the responsibilities of information centers. Discuss how you believe each of these responsibilities is changing.

21.13 List the advantages of instituting a position called manager of end-user services. This individual would be responsible for the functions of corporate modeling, DSS, and the information center. The manager of end-user services would report directly to the CIO.

21.14 Discuss the pros and cons of making the PC purchase decision within corporations largely the responsibility of end users.

BIBLIOGRAPHY

BHALLA, SUSHIL K. *The Effective Management of Technology.* Reading, Mass.: Addison-Wesley, 1987.

CARLYLE, RALPH EMMETT. "Leading IS Shops Shifting to a Centralized Structure." *Datamation,* November 15, 1987.

ETHERIDGE, JAMES, JANETTE MARTIN, ROBERT POE, and PAUL TATE. "From DP Dept. to IS Inc." *Datamation,* November 1, 1987.

GREMILLION, LEE, and PHILIP PYBURN. *Computers and Informations Systems in Business.* New York: McGraw-Hill, 1988.

HENDERSON, JOHN C., and MICHAEL E. TREACY. "Managing End-user Computing for Competitive Advantage." *Sloan Management Review,* Winter 1986.

KEEN, JEFFREY S. *Managing Systems Development,* 2nd ed. New York: John Wiley, 1987.

KELLER, THOMAS, and ERNEST N. SAVAGE. *Administrative Information Systems.* Boston, Mass.: Kent, 1987.

KOLODZIEJ, STAN. "Control Up for Grabs, Power Tug-of-War Between MIS, ICs." *Computerworld,* October 7, 1987.

MOAD, JEFF. "Dupont Seeks Global Communications Reach." *Datamation,* January 15, 1988.

MULA, ROSE. "Trains, Planes and Automobiles: Automation Boom Drives Need for MIS." *Computerworld,* March 7, 1988.

PYBURN, PHILIP J. "Managing Personal Computer Use: The Role of Corporate Management Information System." *Journal of Management Information Systems,* Winter 1986–1987.

RIFKIN, GLENN, and MITCH BETTS. "Strategic Systems Plans Gone Awry." *Computerworld,* March 14, 1988.

SYNNOTT, WILLIAM R. *The Information Weapon.* New York: John Wiley, 1987.

WATSON, HUGH J., and HOUSTON H. CARR. "Organizing for DSS Support: The End-User Services Alternative." *Journal of Management Information Systems,* Summer 1987.

INDEX

Printed and bound in Singapore by
Chong Moh Offset Printing Pte. Ltd.